**Front Cover Photo Credits:** (outer ring): ©Roman Voloshyn/Shutterstock, (inner ring): ©Javier Martin/Shutterstock, (c) ©Carrie Garcia/Houghton Mifflin Harcourt, (c overlay): ©Eyewire/Getty Images, (bc overlay): ©elenamiv/Shutterstock

**Back Cover Photo Credits:** (Units 1-6): ©Paul Bradbury/Caiaimage/Getty Images; ©Eclipse Images/iStock/Getty Images Plus/Getty Images; ©Krzysztof Wiktor/Adobe Stock; ©Tonktiti/Shutterstock; ©Tayfun Cokun/Anadolu Agency/Getty Images; ©Anthony J Hall/iStock/Getty Images Plus/Getty Images

Printed in the U.S.A.

ISBN 978-1-328-47481-0

4 5 6 7 8 9 10    0928    27 26 25 24 23 22 21 20 19

4500762001      B C D E F G

HMH | into Literature™

**GRADE 10**

Program Consultants:
Kylene Beers
Martha Hougen
Elena Izquierdo
Carol Jago
Erik Palmer
Robert E. Probst

### Kylene Beers

Nationally known lecturer and author on reading and literacy; coauthor with Robert Probst of *Disrupting Thinking, Notice & Note: Strategies for Close Reading,* and *Reading Nonfiction;* former president of the National Council of Teachers of English. Dr. Beers is the author of *When Kids Can't Read: What Teachers Can Do* and coeditor of *Adolescent Literacy: Turning Promise into Practice,* as well as articles in the *Journal of Adolescent and Adult Literacy.* Former editor of *Voices from the Middle,* she is the 2001 recipient of NCTE's Richard W. Halle Award, given for outstanding contributions to middle school literacy. She recently served as Senior Reading Researcher at the Comer School Development Program at Yale University as well as Senior Reading Advisor to Secondary Schools for the Reading and Writing Project at Teachers College.

### Martha Hougen

National consultant, presenter, researcher, and author. Areas of expertise include differentiating instruction for students with learning difficulties, including those with learning disabilities and dyslexia; and teacher and leader preparation improvement. Dr. Hougen has taught at the middle school through graduate levels. In addition to peer-reviewed articles, curricular documents, and presentations, Dr. Hougen has published two college textbooks: *The Fundamentals of Literacy Assessment and Instruction Pre-K–6* (2012) and *The Fundamentals of Literacy Assessment and Instruction 6–12* (2014). Dr. Hougen has supported Educator Preparation Program reforms while working at the Meadows Center for Preventing Educational Risk at The University of Texas at Austin and at the CEEDAR Center, University of Florida.

### Elena Izquierdo

Nationally recognized teacher educator and advocate for English language learners. Dr. Izquierdo is a linguist by training, with a Ph.D. in Applied Linguistics and Bilingual Education from Georgetown University. She has served on various state and national boards working to close the achievement gaps for bilingual students and English language learners. Dr. Izquierdo is a member of the Hispanic Leadership Council, which supports Hispanic students and educators at both the state and federal levels. She served as Vice President on the Executive Board of the National Association of Bilingual Education and as Publications and Professional Development Chair.

## Carol Jago

Teacher of English with 32 years of experience at Santa Monica High School in California; author and nationally known lecturer; former president of the National Council of Teachers of English. Ms. Jago currently serves as Associate Director of the California Reading and Literature Project at UCLA. With expertise in standards assessment and secondary education, Ms. Jago is the author of numerous books on education, including *With Rigor for All* and *Papers, Papers, Papers,* and is active with the California Association of Teachers of English, editing its scholarly journal *California English* since 1996. Ms. Jago also served on the planning committee for the 2009 NAEP Reading Framework and the 2011 NAEP Writing Framework.

## Erik Palmer

Veteran teacher and education consultant based in Denver, Colorado. Author of *Well Spoken: Teaching Speaking to All Students* and *Digitally Speaking: How to Improve Student Presentations.* His areas of focus include improving oral communication, promoting technology in classroom presentations, and updating instruction through the use of digital tools. He holds a bachelor's degree from Oberlin College and a master's degree in curriculum and instruction from the University of Colorado.

## Robert E. Probst

Nationally respected authority on the teaching of literature; Professor Emeritus of English Education at Georgia State University. Dr. Probst's publications include numerous articles in *English Journal* and *Voices from the Middle,* as well as professional texts including (as coeditor) *Adolescent Literacy: Turning Promise into Practice* and (as coauthor with Kylene Beers) *Disrupting Thinking, Notice & Note: Strategies for Close Reading,* and *Reading Nonfiction.* He regularly speaks at national and international conventions including those of the International Literacy Association, the National Council of Teachers of English, the Association of Supervisors and Curriculum Developers, and the National Association of Secondary School Principals. He has served NCTE in various leadership roles, including the Conference on English Leadership Board of Directors, the Commission on Reading, and column editor of the NCTE journal *Voices from the Middle.* He is also the 2004 recipient of the CEL Exemplary Leader Award.

# UNIT 1

## OURSELVES AND OTHERS

PAGE 1

? **ESSENTIAL QUESTION:**

How do we engage with others while staying true to ourselves?

## ANALYZE & APPLY

NOTICE & NOTE
READING MODEL

**SHORT STORY**
**What, of This Goldfish, Would You Wish?** ........................................... 4
by Etgar Keret

**MEMOIR**                                    **MENTOR TEXT**
**By Any Other Name** ....................................... 18
by Santha Rama Rau

**POEM**
**Without Title** ........................................... 32
by Diane Glancy

## COLLABORATE & COMPARE

COMPARE
ARGUMENTS

**COURT OPINION**
*from* **Texas v. Johnson Majority Opinion** ........................................... 40
by William J. Brennan

**EDITORIAL**
**American Flag Stands for Tolerance** ............................................. 50
by Ronald J. Allen

**INDEPENDENT READING** ................................. 62
These selections can be accessed through the digital edition.

 **MEMOIR**
*from* **The Pleasure of Reading**
by Kamila Shamsie

 **POEM**
**Magic Island**
by Cathy Song

 **SHORT STORY**
**The Wife's Story**
by Ursula K. Le Guin

 **ARGUMENT**
**America: The Multinational Society**
by Ishmael Reed

## Suggested Novel Connection

 **NOVEL**
**Frankenstein**
by Mary Shelley

Unit **1** **Task**
• Write a Personal Essay ....................................... 64

**Reflect on the Unit** ....................................... 71

## Key Learning Objectives
- Analyze literary devices
- Analyze author's purpose
- Make inferences
- Evaluate evidence
- Evaluate an argument
- Analyze rhetoric

 **Visit the Interactive Student Edition for:**
- Unit and Selection Videos
- Media Selections
- Selection Audio Recordings
- Enhanced Digital Instruction

# UNIT (2)

# HOW WE SEE THINGS

PAGE 72

**?** ***ESSENTIAL QUESTION:***

How does our point of view shape what we think we know?

## ANALYZE & APPLY

NOTICE & NOTE
READING MODEL

SCIENCE ESSAY
**Coming to Our Senses** ..................................... 76
by Neil deGrasse Tyson

SHORT STORY                                    MENTOR TEXT
**The Night Face Up** ........................................ 90
by Julio Cortázar

POEM
**Mirror** .................................................... 106
by Sylvia Plath

## COLLABORATE & COMPARE

INFOGRAPHIC
**The World as 100 People** ................................. 114
by Jack Hagley

COMPARE DETAILS

POEM
**A Contribution to Statistics** .............................. 120
by Wisława Szymborska

**INDEPENDENT READING** ................................ 130

These selections can be accessed through the digital edition.

 POEM
**Before I got my eye put out**
by Emily Dickinson

 ESSAY
**What Our Telescopes Couldn't See**
by Pippa Goldschmidt

 INFORMATIONAL TEXT
*from* **Big Bang: The Origin of the Universe**
by Simon Singh

 SHORT STORY
**By the Waters of Babylon**
by Stephen Vincent Benét

## Suggested Novel Connection

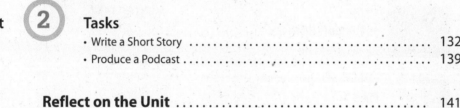 NOVEL
**Brave New World**
by Aldous Huxley

**Unit 2 Tasks**
- Write a Short Story .......................................... 132
- Produce a Podcast ........................................... 139

**Reflect on the Unit** ....................................... 141

### Key Learning Objectives
- Analyze development of ideas
- Analyze tone
- Analyze plot structure
- Analyze speaker
- Analyze figurative language
- Interpret graphics
- Analyze poetic structure
- Compare details

 **Visit the Interactive Student Edition for:**

- Unit and Selection Videos
- Media Selections
- Selection Audio Recordings
- Enhanced Digital Instruction

# UNIT (3)
# THE NATURAL WORLD
PAGE 142

**?** **ESSENTIAL QUESTION:**

What effect do we have on nature, and how does nature affect us?

## ANALYZE & APPLY

NOTICE & NOTE
READING MODEL

**SHORT STORY**
**My Life as a Bat** ......................................... 146
by Margaret Atwood

**ESSAY**                                    **MENTOR TEXT**
**Joyas Voladoras** ........................................ 158
by Brian Doyle

**PUBLIC SERVICE ADVERTISEMENT**
**Find Your Park** ......................................... 170
by National Park Service

## COLLABORATE & COMPARE

COMPARE THEMES

**SHORT STORY**
**The Seventh Man** ....................................... 174
by Haruki Murakami

**POEM**
**Carry** ................................................... 196
by Linda Hogan

**INDEPENDENT READING** ................................ 206

These selections can be accessed through the digital edition.

ARGUMENT
*from* **Hope for Animals and Their World**
by Jane Goodall

ESSAY
**Sea Stars**
by Barbara Hurd

POEM
**Starfish**
by Lorna Dee Cervantes

SHORT STORY
**Wolves**
by José Luis Zárate

**Suggested Novel Connection**

NOVEL
**Life of Pi**
by Yann Martel

**Unit 3 Tasks**
• Write an Explanatory Essay .................................... 208
• Deliver a Multimedia Presentation ........................... 215

**Reflect on the Unit** ...................................... 217

## Key Learning Objectives

- Analyze structure in fiction and nonfiction
- Analyze language and style
- Analyze media techniques
- Analyze purpose
- Analyze symbol and theme
- Analyze plot
- Analyze free verse

**Visit the Interactive Student Edition for:**

- Unit and Selection Videos
- Media Selections
- Selection Audio Recordings
- Enhanced Digital Instruction

# UNIT (4)
# HARD-WON LIBERTY
PAGE 218

**?** ***ESSENTIAL QUESTION:***

What do we need in order to feel free?

## ANALYZE & APPLY

NOTICE & NOTE
READING MODEL

ARGUMENT
**Letter from Birmingham Jail** .............................. 222
by Martin Luther King Jr.

POEM
**Elsewhere** ................................................ 248
by Derek Walcott

MEMOIR
**The Hawk Can Soar** ....................................... 256
by Randi Davenport

SHORT STORY
**The Briefcase** ............................................ 268
by Rebecca Makkai

## COLLABORATE & COMPARE

COMPARE ACCOUNTS

ARGUMENT              MENTOR TEXT
***from* Letter to Viceroy, Lord Irwin** ....................... 284
by Mohandas K. Gandhi

DOCUMENTARY FILM
***from* Gandhi: The Rise to Fame** .......................... 296
by BBC

© Houghton Mifflin Harcourt Publishing Company • Image Credits (t to b): ©Tonkiriti/Shutterstock • ©CSU Archives/

**INDEPENDENT READING** .................................. 304

These selections can be accessed through the digital edition.

**SPEECH**
*from* **Speech at the March on Washington**
by Josephine Baker

**SHORT STORY**
**The Book of the Dead**
by Edwidge Danticat

**POEM**
**Cloudy Day**
by Jimmy Santiago Baca

**HISTORY WRITING**
*from* **Crispus Attucks**
by Kareem Abdul-Jabbar

### Suggested Nonfiction Connection

**NONFICTION**
**Why We Can't Wait**
by Martin Luther King Jr.

**Unit 4 Tasks**

• Write an Argument ......................................... 306
• Deliver an Argument ....................................... 313

**Reflect on the Unit** ....................................... 315

## Key Learning Objectives

- Analyze argument
- Analyze rhetorical devices
- Analyze poetic structure
- Analyze diction and syntax
- Analyze character and theme
- Analyze media techniques

 **Visit the Interactive Student Edition for:**

- Unit and Selection Videos
- Media Selections
- Selection Audio Recordings
- Enhanced Digital Instruction

# UNIT (5)

# RESPONSES TO CHANGE

PAGE 316

**? ESSENTIAL QUESTION:**

How do changes around us reveal who we are?

## ANALYZE & APPLY

NOTICE & NOTE
READING MODEL

**ESSAY**
*from* **Total Eclipse** ........................................... 320
by Annie Dillard

**SCIENCE WRITING**    **MENTOR TEXT**
*from* **The Fever: How Malaria Has Ruled Humankind for 500,000 Years** ........................................ 332
by Sonia Shah

**SHORT STORY**
**A Sound of Thunder** ........................................ 344
by Ray Bradbury

**POEM**
**5 P.M., Tuesday, August 23, 2005** ........................... 364
by Patricia Smith

## COLLABORATE & COMPARE

COMPARE THEMES
ACROSS GENRES

**DOCUMENTARY FILM**
*from* **Rivers and Tides** ..................................... 372
by Thomas Riedelsheimer

**POEM**
**Sonnets to Orpheus, Part Two, XII** ......................... 376
by Rainer Maria Rilke

## INDEADENT READING ................................ 382

These selections can be accessed through the digital edition.

**SHORT STORY**

**The Norwegian Rat**
by Naguib Mahfouz

**MEMOIR**

**After the Storm**
by Orhan Pamuk

**SCIENCE WRITING**

*from* **Simplexity**
by Jeffrey Kluger

**NOVELLA**

*from* **The Metamorphosis**
by Franz Kafka

## Suggested Novel Connection

**NOVEL**

**A Separate Peace**
by John Knowles

Unit **5** **Task**
• Write a Research Report ...................................... 384

**Reflect on the Unit** ........................................ 391

---

## Key Learning Objectives

- Analyze literary nonfiction
- Analyze style
- Analyze text structure
- Analyze purpose and audience
- Analyze plot and setting
- Analyze word choice
- Analyze media techniques
- Analyze purpose and theme

 **Visit the Interactive Student Edition for:**

- Unit and Selection Videos
- Media Selections
- Selection Audio Recordings
- Enhanced Digital Instruction

# UNIT ⑥
# ABSOLUTE POWER
PAGE 392

***ESSENTIAL QUESTION:***

What are the sources of true power?

## ANALYZE & APPLY

**Shakespearean Drama** . . . . . . . . . . . . . . . . . . . . . . . . . . . . . . . . . . . 396

NOTICE & NOTE
READING MODEL

DRAMA
**The Tragedy of Macbeth** . . . . . . . . . . . . . . . . . . . . . . . . . . . 398
by William Shakespeare

FILM CLIP
***from* Macbeth** . . . . . . . . . . . . . . . . . . . . . . . . . . . . . . . . . . . . 484
by Rupert Goold

SHORT STORY
**The Macbeth Murder Mystery** . . . . . . . . . . . . . . . . . . . . . . 488
by James Thurber

## COLLABORATE & COMPARE

COMPARE ACROSS
GENRES

GRAPHIC NOVEL
***from* Manga Shakespeare: Macbeth** . . . . . . . . . . . . . . . . . . . . . 500
by Robert Deas and Richard Appignanesi

BOOK REVIEW                    MENTOR TEXT
**Shakespeare and Samurai
(and Robot Ninjas?)** . . . . . . . . . . . . . . . . . . . . . . . . . . . . . . . . . . 518
by Caitlin Perry

**INDEPENDENT READING** ................................... 526

These selections can be accessed through the digital edition.

**HISTORY WRITING**
*from* **Holinshed's Chronicles**
by Raphael Holinshed

**ARGUMENT**
**Why Read Shakespeare?**
by Michael Mack

**POEM**
**Ozymandias**
by Percy Bysshe Shelley

**DRAMA**
**Julius Caesar, Act III, Scene 2**
by William Shakespeare

**Suggested Novel Connection**

**NOVEL**
**Animal Farm**
by George Orwell

Unit **6** **Task**
• Write a Literary Analysis ...................................... 528

**Reflect on the Unit** ....................................... 535

## Key Learning Objectives

- Analyze drama
- Analyze character and theme
- Analyze media representations
- Analyze satire
- Analyze visual elements
- Analyze evidence

 **Visit the Interactive Student Edition for:**

- Unit and Selection Videos
- Media Selections
- Selection Audio Recordings
- Enhanced Digital Instruction

# SELECTIONS BY GENRE

## FICTION

### GRAPHIC NOVEL

**from Manga Shakespeare: Macbeth**
Robert Deas and Richard Appignanesi . . . . 500

### NOVELLA

**from The Metamorphosis**
Franz Kafka . . . . . . . . . . . . . . . . . . . . . . Online

### SHORT STORY

**The Book of the Dead**
Edwidge Danticat . . . . . . . . . . . . . . . . . Online

**The Briefcase** Rebecca Makkai . . . . . . . 268

**By the Waters of Babylon**
Stephen Vincent Benét . . . . . . . . . . . . . Online

**The Macbeth Murder Mystery**
James Thurber . . . . . . . . . . . . . . . . . . . . 488

**My Life as a Bat**
Margaret Atwood . . . . . . . . . . . . . . . . . . 146

**The Night Face Up**
Julio Cortázar . . . . . . . . . . . . . . . . . . . . . 90

**The Norwegian Rat**
Naguib Mahfouz . . . . . . . . . . . . . . . . . . Online

**The Seventh Man**
Haruki Murakami . . . . . . . . . . . . . . . . . . 174

**A Sound of Thunder**
Ray Bradbury . . . . . . . . . . . . . . . . . . . . . 344

**The Wife's Story**
Ursula K. Le Guin . . . . . . . . . . . . . . . . . . Online

**What, of This Goldfish, Would You
Wish?** Etgar Keret . . . . . . . . . . . . . . . . . 4

**Wolves**
José Luis Zárate . . . . . . . . . . . . . . . . . . Online

## NONFICTION

### ARGUMENT

**American Flag Stands for Tolerance**
Ronald J. Allen . . . . . . . . . . . . . . . . . . . . 50

**America: The Multinational Society**
Ishmael Reed . . . . . . . . . . . . . . . . . . . . . Online

**from Hope for Animals and Their
World** Jane Goodall . . . . . . . . . . . . . . . Online

**Letter from Birmingham Jail**
Martin Luther King Jr. . . . . . . . . . . . . . . . 222

**from Letter to Viceroy, Lord Irwin**
Mohandas K. Gandhi . . . . . . . . . . . . . . . 284

**from Speech at the March on Washington**
Josephine Baker SPEECH . . . . . . . . . . . . . Online

**from Texas v. Johnson Majority
Opinion** William J. Brennan . . . . . . . . . . 40

**Why Read Shakespeare?**
Michael Mack SPEECH . . . . . . . . . . . . . . Online

### AUTOBIOGRAPHY/MEMOIR

**After the Storm**
Orhan Pamuk . . . . . . . . . . . . . . . . . . . . . Online

**By Any Other Name**
Santha Rama Rau . . . . . . . . . . . . . . . . . . 18

**The Hawk Can Soar**
Randi Davenport . . . . . . . . . . . . . . . . . . 256

**from The Pleasure of Reading**
Kamila Shamsie . . . . . . . . . . . . . . . . . . Online

## INFORMATIONAL TEXT

*from* **Big Bang** Simon Singh............ Online

**Coming to Our Senses** Neil deGrasse Tyson SCIENCE ESSAY .................... 76

*from* **The Fever** Sonia Shah SCIENCE WRITING ..................... 332

*from* **Simplexity** Jeffrey Kluger ...... Online

*from* **Crispus Attucks** Kareem Abdul-Jabbar HISTORY WRITING ......... Online

*from* **Holinshed's Chronicles** Raphael Holinshed HISTORY WRITING ..... Online

### LITERARY ANALYSIS

**Shakespeare and Samurai (and Robot Ninjas?)** Caitlin Perry BOOK REVIEW ....................... 518

### LITERARY NONFICTION

**Joyas Voladoras** Brian Doyle ........ 158

**Sea Stars** Barbara Hurd ............. Online

*from* **Total Eclipse** Annie Dillard ...... 320

**What Our Telescopes Couldn't See** Pippa Goldschmidt .................. Online

## POETRY

**Before I got my eye put out** Emily Dickinson .................... Online

**Carry** Linda Hogan ................. 196

**Cloudy Day** Jimmy Santiago Baca ..... Online

**A Contribution to Statistics** Wisława Szymborska ................. 120

**Elsewhere** Derek Walcott ........... 248

**5 P.M., Tuesday, August 23, 2005** Patricia Smith ...................... 364

**Magic Island** Cathy Song ........... Online

**Mirror** Sylvia Plath ................. 106

**Ozymandias** Percy Bysshe Shelley .... Online

**Sonnets to Orpheus, Part Two, XII** Rainer Maria Rilke .................. 376

**Starfish** Lorna Dee Cervantes ....... Online

**Without Title** Diane Glancy ......... 32

## DRAMA

**Julius Caesar, Act III, Scene 2** William Shakespeare ................. Online

**The Tragedy of Macbeth** William Shakespeare .................. 398

## MEDIA STUDY

**Find Your Park** National Park Service PUBLIC SERVICE ADVERTISEMENT .......... 170

*from* **Gandhi: The Rise To Fame** BBC DOCUMENTARY FILM ................... 296

*from* **Macbeth** Rupert Goold FILM ......................... 484

*from* **Rivers and Tides** Thomas Riedelsheimer DOCUMENTARY FILM ................... 372

**The World as 100 People** Jack Hagley INFOGRAPHIC ........................ 114

# HMH
# *Into Literature* Dashboard

## *Easy to use and personalized for your learning.*

Monitor your progress in the course.

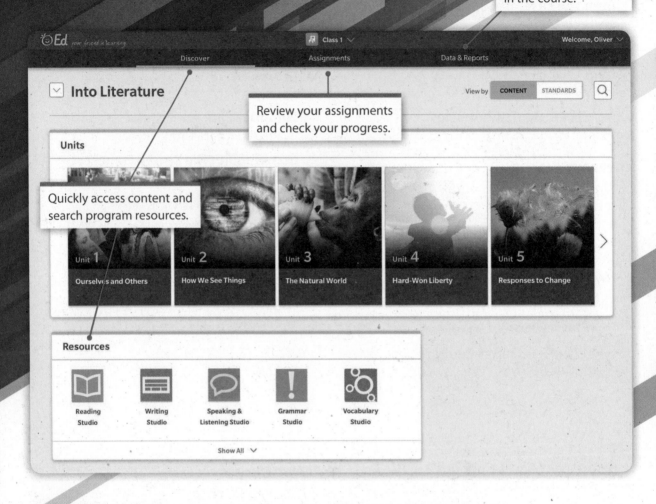

**Ed** *your friend is learning*

Class 1 ∨

Welcome, Oliver ∨

Discover     Assignments     Data & Reports

### Into Literature

View by   CONTENT   STANDARDS

Review your assignments and check your progress.

**Units**

Quickly access content and search program resources.

Unit 1
Ourselves and Others

Unit 2
How We See Things

Unit 3
The Natural World

Unit 4
Hard-Won Liberty

Unit 5
Responses to Change

**Resources**

Reading Studio

Writing Studio

Speaking & Listening Studio

Grammar Studio

Vocabulary Studio

Show All ∨

Online
**Ed**
*your friend is learning*

# Explore Online to Experience the Power of HMH *Into Literature*

## All in One Place

Readings and assignments are supported by a variety of resources to bring literature to life and give you the tools you need to succeed.

## Supporting 21st-Century Skills

Whether you're working alone or collaborating with others, it takes effort to analyze the complex texts and competing ideas that bombard us in this fast-paced world. What will help you succeed? Staying engaged and organized. The digital tools in this program will help you take charge of your learning.

COMING TO OUR SENSES
Science Essay by Neil deGrasse Tyson

BACKGROUND
Most people experience fear

## Ignite Your Investigation

You learn best when you're engaged. The **Stream to Start** videos at the beginning of every unit are designed to spark your interest before you read. Get curious and start reading!

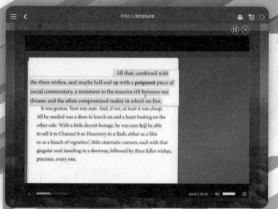

## Learn How to Close Read

Close reading effectively is all about examining the details. See how it's done by watching the **Close Read Screencasts** in your eBook. Hear modeled conversations on targeted passages.

## Personalized Annotations

**My Notes** encourages you to take notes as you read and allows you to mark the text in your own customized way. You can easily access annotations to review later as you prepare for exams.

## Interactive Graphic Organizers

Graphic organizers help you process, summarize, and keep track of your learning and prepare for end-of-unit writing tasks. **Word Networks** help you learn academic vocabulary, and **Response Logs** help you explore and deepen your understanding of the **Essential Question** in each unit.

## No Wi-Fi? No problem!

With HMH *Into Literature,* you always have access: download when you're online and access what you need when you're offline. Work offline and then upload when you're back online.

**Communicate** "Raise a Hand" to ask or answer questions without having to be in the same room as your teacher.

**Collaborate** Collaborate with your teacher via chat and work with a classmate to improve your writing.

# HMH
# *Into Literature*
# STUDIOS

All the help you need to be successful in your literature class is one click away with the Studios. These digital-only lessons are here to tap into the skills that you already use and help you sharpen those skills for the future.

WRITING STUDIO

## Ways to Organize Reasons and Evidence

Every argument must include reasons and evidence to support a claim. There are several effective ways you can organize that support. Check out some of those ways here.

Read the following techniques that will help you achieve cohesion, or coherence, in your writing.

### Order of Importance

Least to most important

Claim: Homewood must switch from a volunteer fire department to a full-time fire department.

- Reason 1: The town is growing and getting more calls during they day when volunteers are at their full-time jobs
- Reason 2: Full-time firefighters can train daily instead of once a month, giving them more time to improve firefighting skills.

# Easy-to-find resources, organized in five separate STUDIOS. On demand and on ED!

**Look for links in each lesson to take you to the appropriate Studio.**

## READING STUDIO

Go beyond the book with the Reading Studio. With over 100 full-length downloadable titles to choose from, find the right story to continue your journey.

## WRITING STUDIO

Being able to write clearly and effectively is a skill that will help you throughout life. The Writing Studio will help you become an expert communicator—in print or online.

## SPEAKING & LISTENING STUDIO

Communication is more than just writing. The Speaking & Listening Studio will help you become an effective speaker and a focused listener.

## GRAMMAR STUDIO

Go beyond traditional worksheets with the Grammar Studio. These engaging, interactive lessons will sharpen your grammar skills.

## VOCABULARY STUDIO

Learn the skills you need to expand your vocabulary. The interactive lessons in the Vocabulary Studio will grow your vocabulary to improve your reading.

# THE PERSPICACIOUS READER (And **yes**, you want to be one)

YOUR TEACHER AGREES!

## Dr. Kylene Beers and Dr. Robert E. Probst

### From Dr. Beers:

When Dr. Probst said he wanted to call this essay "The Perspicacious Reader," I had to ask him what that word meant. Did we want kids in high school to be perspicacious? Is that a good thing? Dr. Probst—who knows more words than anyone I know—said, "Of course it is good to be a perspicacious reader," and then he made me look it up. Yes, he's one of those folks who believes looking up words you don't know is good for you. So, off I went, to look it up . . .

I discovered that if you were to be a perspicacious reader, it would be a very good thing. It would mean that you were able to think deeply about what you are reading and make smart inferences. It would mean that you notice a lot as you are reading. And since we wrote a book for teachers titled **Notice and Note**, we like the idea that being a perspicacious reader means you would notice a lot as you read!

Notice & Note
STRATEGIES for CLOSE READING
KYLENE BEERS & ROBERT E. PROBST

## From **Both** of Us

We both think reading is one of the most important skills you will ever learn. We know that every day you read. Take a moment and think of all you read each day. Here is our combined list.

Text messages
Emails
Tweets
FB posts
Newspaper/magazine articles
How-to info for texting/using our technology
Novels we choose to read for fun
Articles for work — some we have to read and some we choose to read
Bills we get that have to be paid
Food magazines (Who do you think reads these?)
Books about teaching
Articles about technology (And who do you think reads these?)
Crossword puzzles

## And then there are some things we occasionally read:

Party/wedding invitations
Birth announcements
Jokes or cartoons
Job applications
Report cards
School test results
Income tax information
Reports from doctors
Sympathy cards when someone has died
Information about world events

No matter what you read, we want you to read well. We want you to know what to do when you get confused because we all get confused from time to time as we read. We want you to know what to do when you come to a word you might not know (such as *perspicacious*). We want you to be able to figure out the author's theme if you are reading fiction or the author's purpose and main idea if you are reading nonfiction. We don't want you to have to wait around for someone else to tell you what the text means, which would make you dependent on that person.

We suspect, now that you're in high school, the last thing you want is to depend on others all the time. So, we want you to read smart, read critically, read closely, and always read wondering just what else there is you need to know.

## But Sometimes I **Hate** to Read

We don't doubt that. You've got a lot going on in your life. Friends. Sports. Music. Jobs, maybe. Homework. Worrying about who likes whom and who is invited to what and if your grades are good and how things are going at home and who you'll sit with at lunch, stand with in the hall, go to the party with — even if you'll get invited to the party. First, it will all work out. How do we know? We've been your age. It will all work out.

What's important—along with the many other things that are important in your life right now—is to remember that you want to end up getting smarter about a lot of things each year, and the best way—yes THE BEST WAY—to do that is to make sure you become a better reader each year. So, sometimes this year your teacher may ask you to read a text that makes you say, "Really? Seriously?" We want you to dig in deep and do it because we promise there's a reason, and the reason is about making sure you, the young adult you're becoming, are prepared to deal with all the texts that get thrown your way.

Because here's what most people won't tell you: not all the texts will be honest. Right. That online ad about the used car might not mention everything you need to know. The social media post about your favorite presidential candidate just might be fake news. That Instagram photo showing everyone looking so perfect, so very happy? Chances are it was posed, shot, reshot, put through several filters, and touched up. The newspaper story about why your school district should or shouldn't build a new school might only offer one perspective. You—not a teacher, not a parent, not your best buddy—you have an obligation to yourself and to the community you live in to always ask yourself if you are reading closely enough to know when you should agree and when you shouldn't. So, we want you to always read with these three questions in mind:

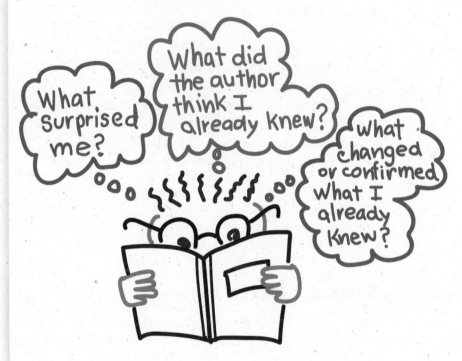

If you'll do that, then we know you'll be on your way to becoming a smarter reader.

## AND (Of course there is an AND) . . .

. . . we also want you to learn to read being aware of something we call

## signposts.

A signpost is simply a cue an author gives you as you read that can help you figure out the theme (if reading fiction) or author's purpose (if reading nonfiction). In the same way that drivers pay attention (we hope!) to signs as they drive, we want you paying attention to signposts as you read.

# So I'm Supposed to Read Just to Look for Signposts?

No, of course not! No one should ever set out to read an article, a chapter in a book, an online essay, a play, or a novel just to hunt for signposts. That would be like taking a drive to your favorite destination just so you can count the stop signs you see on your way there. **No!** You drive to that favorite place to see it and to enjoy the scenery along the way. But if you don't notice the stop signs or one-way signs or curve ahead signs while driving there, you might not ever get there. The signs help you make the journey safely, but noticing the signs isn't the point of the journey.

**No!**

The same is true of reading. You read to enjoy the journey, to learn some things along the way, and to get to the end of the text with new insights and understandings. Understanding those insights means also noticing the signposts so that you are better able to understand what the author has in mind.

## The End!

# IN CONCLUSION

This is a signpost showing that we are about to wrap this up!

We are always reading. We may not always be reading books, poems, articles, newspapers, webpages, or texts of any kind, but we are always reading. We read the weather, the teacher's mood, the expression on our friend's face, the demeanor of a group of strangers we encounter on the street, the unusual silence—or noise—in the hallway. We observe and listen, we try to make sense of what we have noticed, and then we act accordingly. We can't get through the day without reading.

And the essence of all of this reading—of both texts and the world around us—is simply paying attention. If we don't see the storm on the horizon, if we don't see the expression on our friend's face, if we don't see the teacher's devious grin, then we won't be able to react intelligently. Noticing is the first step.

So it is with the reading of texts. If you aren't paying attention, if you aren't noticing, then you may as well not be staring at the page at all. If you look out the window and don't notice the storm clouds forming, then you'll be drenched in the afternoon. Looking out the window without seeing what is there—noticing—does you little good.

And then you must do more. You must take note of what you have noticed. If you do notice the clouds but fail to ask yourself what they might mean, fail to recognize that they forewarn you of the approaching storm, you'll still get soaked. Noticing alone isn't enough; you have to take note of it and ask what it means.

Again, so it is with reading. If you notice what the character has said, what the author has emphasized or ignored, what the setting is like, and you don't bother asking what all that you have noticed tells you, then you may as well not have noticed it in the first place. Looking out the window and noticing the clouds—without thinking about what they mean—does you little good.

## NOW WHAT?

Finally, after noticing and noting, you must do something. You must ask yourself, "So what? Now what do I need to do (or think, or feel, or say)?" If you don't reach that third step, the first two have been little more than an exercise.

Again, so it is with reading texts. If you notice what the text offers, think about it, and simply lay it aside without considering how you might change your own thinking or your own actions, then you will have missed an opportunity to grow and change. The effort of reading will have been wasted. If you notice the clouds forming, take note of that and realize that it warns you of the approaching storm, and still walk out the door without your raincoat or your umbrella, you will *still* get drenched. Reading—of the sky or of the book —should enable us to deal with life more effectively.

That's because the pages of a book allow you to explore places you've never been, meet people and characters who are far different from you, and discover through all this that reading— more than anything else— is what gives you the opportunity to reflect and in that reflection perhaps change something about yourself. Reading is a changemaker. We hope this is your year for growing and changing as a reader. We hope this is the year when, as you read, you learn to notice and note.

# NOTICE & NOTE SIGNPOSTS

| Signpost | Definition | Anchor Question(s) |
|---|---|---|
| **FICTION** | | |
| **Contrasts and Contradictions** | A sharp contrast between what we would expect and what we observe the character doing; behavior that contradicts previous behavior or well-established patterns | Why would the character act (feel) this way? |
| **Aha Moment** | A character's realization of something that shifts his actions or understanding of himself, others, or the world around him | How might this change things? |
| **Tough Questions** | Questions a character raises that reveal his or her inner struggles | What does this question make me wonder about? |
| **Words of the Wiser** | The advice or insight about life that a wiser character, who is usually older, offers to the main character | What is the life lesson, and how might this affect the character? |
| **Again and Again** | Events, images, or particular words that recur over a portion of the story | Why might the author bring this up again and again? |
| **Memory Moment** | A recollection by a character that interrupts the forward progress of the story | Why might this memory be important? |
| **NONFICTION** | | |
| **Contrasts and Contradictions** | A sharp contrast between what we would expect and what we observe happening. A difference between two or more elements in the text. | What is the difference, and why does it matter? |
| **Extreme or Absolute Language** | Language that leaves no doubt about a situation or an event, allows no compromise, or seems to exaggerate or overstate a case. | Why did the author use this language? |
| **Numbers and Stats** | Specific quantities or comparisons to depict the amount, size, or scale. Or, the writer is vague and imprecise about numbers when we would expect more precision. | Why did the author use these numbers or amounts? |
| **Quoted Words** | Opinions or conclusions of someone who is an expert on the subject, or someone who might be a participant in or a witness to an event. Or, the author might cite other people to provide support for a point. | Why was this person quoted or cited, and what did this add? |
| **Word Gaps** | Vocabulary that is unfamiliar to the reader— for example, a word with multiple meanings, a rare or technical word, a discipline-specific word, or one with a far-removed antecedent. | Do I know this word from someplace else? Does it seem like technical talk for this topic? Can I find clues in the sentence to help me understand the word? |

# READING AND WRITING ACROSS GENRES

by Carol Jago

Reading is a first-class ticket around the world. Not only can you explore other lands and cultures, but you can also travel to the past and future. That journey is sometimes a wild ride. Other books can feel like comfort food, enveloping you in an imaginative landscape full of friends and good times. Making time for reading is making time for life.

## Genre

One of the first things readers do when we pick up something to read is notice its genre. You might not think of it exactly in those terms, but consider how you approach a word problem in math class compared to how you read a science fiction story. Readers go to different kinds of text for different purposes. When you need to know how to do or make something, you want a reliable, trusted source of information. When you're in the mood to spend some time in a world of fantasy, you happily suspend your normal disbelief in dragons.

In every unit of *Into Literature,* you'll find a diverse mix of genres all connected by a common theme, allowing you to explore a topic from many different angles.

GENRE:
INFORMATIONAL TEXT

GENRE:
SHORT STORY

GENRE:
LITERARY NONFICTION

GENRE:
POETRY

## Writer's Craft

Learning how writers use genre to inform, to explain, to entertain, or to surprise readers will help you better understand—as well as enjoy—your reading. Imitating how professional writers employ the tools of their craft—descriptive language, repetition, sensory images, sentence structure, and a variety of other features—will give you many ideas for making your own writing more lively.

*Into Literature* provides you with the tools you need to understand the elements of all the critical genres and advice on how to learn from professional texts to improve your own writing in those genres.

**GENRE ELEMENTS: SHORT STORY**
- is a work of short fiction that centers on a single idea and can be read in one sitting
- usually includes one main conflict that involves the characters and keeps moving
- includes the basic ele of fiction—plot, chara setting, and theme
- may be based on real and historical events

**GENRE ELEMENTS: INFORMATIONAL TEXT**
- provides factual information
- includes evidence to support ideas
- contains text features
- includes many forms, such as news articles and essays

**GENRE ELEMENTS: LITERARY NONFICTION**
- shares factual information, ideas, or experiences
- develops a key insight about the topic that goes beyond the facts
- uses literary tech as figurative lang narration
- reflects a person involvement in t

**GENRE ELEMENTS: POETRY**
- may use figurative language, including personification
- often includes imagery that appeals to the five senses
- expresses a theme, or a "big idea" message about life

## Reading with Independence

Finding a good book can sometimes be a challenge. Like every other reader, you have probably experienced "book desert" when nothing you pick up seems to have what you are looking for (not that it's easy to explain exactly what you are looking for, but whatever it is, "this" isn't it). If you find yourself in this kind of reading funk, bored by everything you pick up, give yourself permission to range more widely, exploring graphic novels, contemporary biographies, books of poetry, historical fiction. And remember that long doesn't necessarily mean boring. My favorite kind of book is one that I never want to end.

Take control over your own reading with *Into Literature's* Reader's Choice selections and the HMH Digital Library. And don't forget: your teacher, librarian, and friends can offer you many more suggestions.

**Frankenstein**
Or, The Modern Prometheus
Mary Shelley

**The Turn of the Screw**
Henry James

**SHORT STORY**
**The Wife's Story**
Ursula K. Le Guin

*Is the narrator's husband, who has begun acting strangely, really one of the group, or has he become something else?*

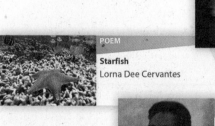

**POEM**
**Starfish**
Lorna Dee Cervantes

*This poem explores the human fascination with starfish: their life cycle, beauty, and ocean habitat.*

**HISTORY**
**Crispus Attucks**
Kareem Abdul-Jabbar

*Learn the story of Crispus Attucks, an African American remembered as the first American to die in the Revolutionary War.*

# OURSELVES AND OTHERS

**? ESSENTIAL QUESTION:**

How do we engage with others while staying true to ourselves?

> **We, as human beings, must be willing to accept people who are different from ourselves.**
>
> Barbara Jordan

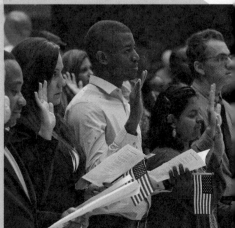

## ACADEMIC VOCABULARY

Academic Vocabulary words are words you use when you discuss and write about texts. In this unit you will practice and learn five words.

☑ **discriminate**    ☐ **diverse**    ☐ **inhibit**    ☐ **intervene**    ☐ **rational**

Study the Word Network to learn more about the word **discriminate**.

**SYNONYMS**
differentiate, distinguish

**DEFINITION**
to note clear differences; to separate into categories

**ANTONYMS**
confuse, equate

**discriminate**
(dĭ-skrĭm´ə-nāt)
*v.*

**CLARIFYING EXAMPLE**
To discriminate between male and female cockatoos, check the color of their eyes.

**WORD ROOT OR ORIGIN**
Comes from the Latin word *discrimināre*, meaning "distinction"

**RELATED WORDS**
discrimination, discriminatory

**Write and Discuss** Discuss the completed Word Network with a partner, making sure to talk through all of the boxes until you both understand the word, its synonyms, antonyms, and related forms. Then, fill out Word Networks for the remaining four words. Use a dictionary or online resource to help you complete the activity.

*Go online to access the Word Networks.*

## RESPOND TO THE ESSENTIAL QUESTION

In this unit, you will explore how people interact with others who agree or disagree with their ideas, yet stay true to themselves. As you read, you will revisit the **Essential Question** and gather your ideas about it in the **Response Log** that appears on page R1. At the end of the unit, you will have the opportunity to write a **personal essay** in which you will reflect on a significant event in your life. Filling out the Response Log will help you prepare for this writing task.

*You can also go online to access the Response Log.*

For more information on these and other signposts to Notice & Note, visit the **Reading Studio**.

## WHAT, OF THIS GOLDFISH, WOULD YOU WISH?

You are about to read the short story "What, of This Goldfish, Would You Wish?" You will notice and note signposts that will give you clues about the story's characters and themes. Here are three key signposts to look for as you read this story and other works of fiction.

Some **Tough Questions** are easy to spot. Others are signaled by phrases that express doubt or confusion:

"How could I…?"

"What could I possibly do…?"

"I can't imagine how I could cope with…"

"But what if…?"

"Never had I been so confused about…"

**Tough Questions** Would you rather be stuck at a party where you don't know anyone or stuck in a car with a relative who never stops talking? The "Would You Rather . . .?" game requires you to choose between two equally bad or good options. The way you respond can be funny, but it can also reveal something about your personality or what matters to you.

Likewise, when an author confronts a character with a tough question, the answer usually reveals something important. Paying attention to a **Tough Question** and its answer can:

- tell you something deeply personal about the character
- reveal a character's internal conflict or motivation
- provide insight into the story's message about life

The paragraph below illustrates a student's annotation within "What, of This Goldfish, Would You Wish?" and a response to a Notice and Note signpost.

**Anchor Question**

When you notice this signpost, ask: What does this question make me wonder about?

1    Yonatan had a brilliant idea for a documentary. He'd knock on doors. Just him. No camera crew, no nonsense. Just Yonatan, on his own, a small camera in hand, asking, "If you found a talking goldfish that granted you three wishes, what would you wish for?"

| | |
|---|---|
| What's the tough question? | If you had three wishes, what would you wish for? |
| What does the question make you wonder about? | What's the catch? Can the fish be trusted? Can I wish for more wishes? |

**Memory Moment** Have you ever noticed a landmark that triggers a long-ago memory? A memory can change the way you experience something in the present. When an author pauses to revisit a character's memory, it also has a strong effect. Paying attention to a **Memory Moment** can:

- explain or provide insight into the current situation
- show what motivates or drives a character's actions
- hint at the theme or a lesson of the story

Here is how a student might mark a Memory Moment in this story:

When you read and encounter a phrase like these, pause to see if it's a Memory Moment signpost:

"I remembered when . . ."

"That reminded me of . . ."

"Grandma used to tell a story about . . ."

"A local legend said that . . ."

> 8  Sergei Goralick doesn't much like strangers banging on his door. Especially when those strangers are asking him questions. In Russia, when Sergei was young, it happened plenty. The KGB felt right at home knocking on his door. His father had been a Zionist, which was pretty much an invitation for them to drop by any old time.

**Anchor Question**
When you notice this signpost, ask: Why might this memory be important?

| | |
|---|---|
| What memory is introduced? | When Sergei was young, the KGB, or secret police, often showed up knocking on the door to question his father. |
| Why do you think this memory is important to the story? | Yonatan is knocking on Sergei's door. Is something bad about to happen? |

**Words of the Wiser** In movies, an older character often offers sage advice to the main character. In any story, a wise character's advice may provide an insight about life or help the main character with a problem or decision.

In this example, a student marked some Words of the Wiser from the story:

> 20  "Nonsense," the fish says. "He was only here to make a little something for TV."
> 21  "But he said . . ."
> 22  "He said," says the fish, interrupting, "exactly what he was doing. But you didn't get it. Honestly, your Hebrew, it's terrible."

**Anchor Question**
When you notice this signpost, ask: What is the life lesson, and how might it affect the character?

| | |
|---|---|
| What insight does the wiser character provide? | Sergei misunderstood what Yonatan wanted to do. |
| How might this affect the character? | Sergei will understand that he made a mistake and might make a different choice. |

# WHAT, OF THIS GOLDFISH, WOULD YOU WISH?

Short Story by **Etgar Keret**
translated by Nathan Englander

**? ESSENTIAL QUESTION:**

How do we engage with others while staying true to ourselves?

## QUICK START

If you were granted three wishes, what would you wish for? Would you use your wishes right away or save them? Discuss your answers with a partner.

## ANALYZE ARCHETYPES

A character who grants three wishes sounds familiar, right? That's because it's an **archetype**—a character or situation that shows up in many works from different cultures.

Brainstorm examples of archetypal characters from stories, movies, or shows.

| ARCHETYPE | EXAMPLE CHARACTER / WORK |
| --- | --- |
| The Hero | |
| The Mentor | |
| The Villain | |
| The Sidekick | |

## ANALYZE LITERARY DEVICES

A **literary device** is a technique used to convey meaning or create interest.

- When a writer uses **irony**, the opposite of what is expected happens. For example, a character getting a speeding ticket the day he earns an A+ in Driver's Education would be ironic.

- **Sarcasm** is the taunting use of praise to mean its opposite. For example, *"I heard zombies only eat brains, so you should be fine."*

- A **motif** is an image or idea that occurs many times in a work of literature. This repetition may create a particular tone, reveal the meaning of a symbol, or point toward a theme, or message, of the story.

As you read the story, note examples of irony, sarcasm, and motif.

| DEVICE | WHAT HAPPENS? |
| --- | --- |
| Irony | |
| Sarcasm | |
| Motif | |

GENRE ELEMENTS:
SHORT STORY

- includes the basic elements of fiction—setting, characters, plot, conflict, resolution, and theme

- centers on one particular moment or event in life

- can be read in one sitting

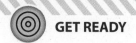

## CRITICAL VOCABULARY

| poignant | wizened | beleaguered | fluent |
|----------|---------|-------------|--------|

**Practice and Apply** Complete the sentences to see how many Critical Vocabulary words you already know.

1. Before visiting Mexico, I want to be _____ in Spanish so I can easily speak to the people I meet.

2. Gabriella felt _____ by the demands of school and her job.

3. My eyes welled with tears as the _____ music ended the movie.

4. The older apples turned _____ and rotten.

## LANGUAGE CONVENTIONS

**Tone** An author's word choices and sentence structures express a particular tone, or attitude, toward characters and events. The tone may also reflect the personality of one or more characters.

An **informal tone** resembles how you might speak to friends. It may include short or incomplete sentences and slang, as in this example from the story:

> **Until one day some kid with a ring in his ear . . . comes knocking. Hard like that—rapping at his door. Just the way Sergei doesn't like.**

A **formal tone** includes proper grammar and complex sentences. This is the tone you would use for formal writing, such as a business letter. For example:

> **Until one day, a young man knocked on his door, hard. It was the kind of knock that Sergei did not like.**

### ANNOTATION MODEL

**NOTICE & NOTE**

As you read, notice and note signposts, including **Tough Questions, Memory Moments,** and **Words of the Wiser.** Here is an example of how one reader marked the opening paragraphs of the text.

It was ⟨genius,⟩ Yoni was sure. And, if not, at least it was ⟨cheap.⟩ All he needed was a door to knock on and a heart beating on the other side. With a little decent footage, he was sure he'd be able to sell it to Channel 8 or Discovery in a flash, either as a film or a bunch of vignettes, little <u>cinematic</u> corners, . . . <u>precious</u>, every one.

Even better, maybe he'd <u>cash out</u>, <u>package</u> it with a <u>slogan</u> and sell it to a bank or cellular phone company. Maybe <u>tag</u> it with something like, "Different dreams, different wishes, one bank." Or "The bank that makes dreams come true."

*The contrast between "genius" and "cheap" is ironic.*

*He wants to make something artistic.*

*Here, though, he thinks it's "even better" to be commercial, and he sounds sarcastic.*

## BACKGROUND

*The Jewish people were expelled from their homeland in the first century CE. In the late 1800s, Jews from Europe, Asia, Africa, and the Americas began returning to the region; World War II and the Holocaust drastically increased this immigration. Israel became an independent nation in 1948, but tensions with its Arab neighbors and its Arab citizens have led to conflict. With the collapse of the Soviet Union in 1991, many Russian Jews were able to move to Israel and make their own mark on the nation's culture. In this story, Israeli writer **Etgar Keret** (b. 1967) explores the hopes and dreams of people in this diverse society.*

# WHAT, OF THIS GOLDFISH, WOULD YOU WISH?

**Short Story by Etgar Keret**
**translated by Nathan Englander**

## SETTING A PURPOSE

*After reading the title, what questions do you have about the topic of this story? As you read, add questions you have about the text. After reading, reread or discuss with a partner to clear up any remaining questions you have.*

1  Yonatan had a brilliant idea for a documentary. He'd knock on doors. Just him. No camera crew, no nonsense. Just Yonatan, on his own, a small camera in hand, asking, "If you found a talking goldfish that granted you three wishes, what would you wish for?"

2  Folks would give their answers, and Yoni would edit them down and make clips of the more surprising responses. Before every set of answers, you'd see the person standing stock-still in the entrance to his house. Onto this shot he'd superimpose[1] the subject's name, family situation, monthly income, and maybe even the party he'd voted for in the last election. All that, combined with the three wishes, and maybe he'd end up with a **poignant** piece of social commentary, a testament to the massive

**Notice & Note**

You can use the side margins to notice and note signposts in the text.

**poignant**
(poin´yənt) *adj.* emotionally moving or stimulating.

---

[1] **superimpose:** place one thing on top of another so that both remain visible.

rift between our dreams and the often compromised reality in which we live.

3   It was genius, Yoni was sure. And, if not, at least it was cheap. All he needed was a door to knock on and a heart beating on the other side. With a little decent footage, he was sure he'd be able to sell it to Channel 8 or Discovery in a flash, either as a film or as a bunch of vignettes,[2] little cinematic corners, each with that singular soul standing in a doorway, followed by three killer wishes, precious, every one.

4   Even better, maybe he'd cash out, package it with a slogan and sell it to a bank or cellular phone company. Maybe tag it with something like "Different dreams, different wishes, one bank." Or "The bank that makes dreams come true."

5   No prep, no plotting, natural as can be, Yoni grabbed his camera and went out knocking on doors. In the first neighborhood he went to, the kindly folk that took part generally requested the foreseeable things: health, money, bigger apartments, either to shave off a couple of years or a couple of pounds. But there were also powerful moments. One drawn, **wizened** old lady asked simply for a child. A Holocaust survivor with a number on his arm asked very slowly, in a quiet voice—as if he'd been waiting for Yoni to come, as if it wasn't an exercise at all—he'd been wondering (if this fish didn't mind), would it be possible for all the Nazis left living in the world to be held accountable for their crimes? A cocky, broadshouldered lady-killer put out his cigarette and, as if the camera wasn't there, wished he were a girl. "Just for a night," he added, holding a single finger right up to the lens.

6   And these were wishes from just one short block in one small, sleepy suburb of Tel Aviv. Yonatan could hardly imagine what people were dreaming of in the development towns and the collectives[3] along the northern border, in the West Bank settlements and Arab villages, the immigrant absorption centers full of broken trailers and tired people left to broil out in the desert sun.

7   Yonatan knew that if the project was going to have any weight, he'd have to get to everyone, to the unemployed, to the ultrareligious, to the Arabs and Ethiopians and American expats.[4] He began to plan a shooting schedule for the coming days: Jaffa, Dimona, Ashdod, Sderot, Taibe, Talpiot. Maybe Hebron, even. If he could sneak past the wall, Hebron would be great. Maybe somewhere in that city some **beleaguered** Arab man would stand in his doorway and, looking through Yonatan and his camera, looking out into nothingness, just pause for a minute, nod his head, and wish for peace—that would be something to see.

---

[2] **vignettes:** small scenes or images.

[3] **collectives:** here, communal settlements.

[4] **expats:** expatriates, people living in a foreign country.

**ANALYZE LITERARY DEVICES**

**Annotate:** Mark references to doors and doorways up to this point in the story.

**Analyze:** What might a door or doorway symbolize? Why do you think the author uses this motif?

**wizened**
(wĭz´ənd) *adj.* shrunken and wrinkled.

**beleaguered**
(bĭ-lē´gərd) *adj.* troubled with many problems.

8    Sergei Goralick doesn't much like strangers banging on his door. Especially when those strangers are asking him questions. In Russia, when Sergei was young, it happened plenty. The KGB felt right at home knocking on his door. His father had been a Zionist,[5] which was pretty much an invitation for them to drop by any old time.

9    When Sergei got to Israel and then moved to Jaffa, his family couldn't wrap their heads around it. They'd ask him, What are you looking to find in a place like that? There's no one there but addicts and Arabs and pensioners.[6] But what is most excellent about addicts and Arabs and pensioners is that they don't come around knocking on Sergei's door. That way Sergei can get his sleep, and get up when it's still dark. He can take his little boat out into the sea and fish until he's done fishing. By himself. In silence. The way it should be. The way it was.

---

[5] **Zionist:** supporter of a separate state for Jewish people.
[6] **pensioners:** people living on modest retirement payments.

**LANGUAGE CONVENTIONS**

**Annotate:** Mark unusual or informal word choices and sentence structures in paragraphs 10 and 11.

**Analyze:** How do these choices develop Sergei's character?

10   Until one day some kid with a ring in his ear . . . comes knocking. Hard like that—rapping at his door. Just the way Sergei doesn't like. And he says, this kid, that he has some questions he wants to put on the TV.

11   Sergei tells the boy, tells him in what he thinks is a straightforward manner, that he doesn't want it. Not interested. Sergei gives the camera a shove, to help make it clear. But the earring boy is stubborn. He says all kinds of things, fast things. And it's hard for Sergei to follow; his Hebrew isn't so good.

12   The boy slows down, tells Sergei he has a strong face, a nice face, and that he simply has to have him for this movie picture. Sergei can also slow down, he can also make clear. He tells the kid to shove off. But the kid is slippery, and somehow between saying no and pushing the door closed, Sergei finds that the kid is in his house. He's already making his movie, running his camera without any permission, and from behind the camera he's still telling Sergei about his face, that it's full of feeling, that it's tender. Suddenly the kid spots Sergei's goldfish flitting around in its big glass jar in his kitchen.

13   The kid with the earring starts screaming, "Goldfish, goldfish," he's so excited. And this, this really pressures Sergei, who tells the kid, it's nothing, just a regular goldfish, stop filming it. Just a goldfish, Sergei tells him, just something he found flapping around in the net, a deep-sea goldfish. But the boy isn't listening. He's still filming and getting closer and saying something about talking and fish and a magic wish.

14   Sergei doesn't like this, doesn't like that the boy is almost at it, already reaching for the jar. In this instant Sergei understands the boy didn't come for television, what he came for, specifically, is to snatch Sergei's fish, to steal it away. Before the mind of Sergei Goralick really understands what it is his body has done, he seems to have taken the burner off the stove and hit the boy in the head. The boy falls. The camera falls with him. The camera breaks open on the floor, along with the boy's skull. There's a lot of blood coming out of the head, and Sergei really doesn't know what to do.

15    That is, he knows exactly what to do, but it really would complicate things. Because if he takes this kid to the hospital, people are going to ask what happened, and it would take things in a direction Sergei doesn't want to go.

16    "No reason to take him to the hospital anyway," says the goldfish, in Russian. "That one's already dead."

17    "He can't be dead," Sergei says, with a moan. "I barely touched him. It's only a burner. Only a little thing." Sergei holds it up to the fish, taps it against his own skull to prove it. "It's not even that hard."

18    "Maybe not," says the fish. "But, apparently, it's harder than that kid's head."

19    "He wanted to take you from me," Sergei says, almost crying.

20    "Nonsense," the fish says. "He was only here to make a little something for TV."

21    "But he said . . . "

22    "He said," says the fish, interrupting, "exactly what he was doing. But you didn't get it. Honestly, your Hebrew, it's terrible."

23    "Yours is better?" Sergei says. "Yours is so great?"

24    "Yes. Mine's supergreat," the goldfish says, sounding impatient. "I'm a magic fish. I'm **fluent** in everything." All the while the puddle of blood from the earring kid's head is getting bigger and bigger and Sergei is on his toes, up against the kitchen wall, desperate not to step in it, not to get blood on his feet.

25    "You do have one wish left," the fish reminds Sergei. He says it easy like that, as if Sergei doesn't know—as if either of them ever loses count.

26    "No," Sergei says. He's shaking his head from side to side. "I can't," he says. "I've been saving it. Saving it for something."

27    "For what?" the fish says.

28    But Sergei won't answer.

29    That first wish, Sergei used up when they discovered a cancer in his sister. A lung cancer, the kind you don't get better from. The fish undid it in an instant—the words barely out of Sergei's mouth. The second wish Sergei used up five years ago, on Sveta's boy. The kid was still small then, barely three, but the doctors already knew something in her son's head wasn't right. He was going to grow big but not in the brain. Three was about as smart as he'd get. Sveta cried to Sergei in bed all night. Sergei walked home along the beach when the sun came up, and he called to the fish, asked the goldfish to fix it as soon as he'd crossed through the door. He never told Sveta. And a few months later she left him for some cop, a Moroccan with a shiny Honda. In his heart, Sergei kept telling himself it wasn't for Sveta that he'd done it, that he'd wished his wish purely for the boy. In his mind, he was less sure, and all kinds of thoughts about other things he could have done with that wish continued to gnaw at him, half driving him mad. The third wish, Sergei hadn't yet wished for.

30    "I can restore him," says the goldfish. "I can bring him back to life."

31    "No one's asking," Sergei says.

32    "I can bring him back to the moment before," the goldfish says. "To before he knocks on your door. I can put him back to right there. I can do it. All you need to do is ask."

33    "To wish my wish," Sergei says. "My last."

34    The fish swishes his fish tail back and forth in the water, the way he does, Sergei knows, when he's truly excited. The goldfish can already taste freedom. Sergei can see it on him.

35    After the last wish, Sergei won't have a choice. He'll have to let the goldfish go. His magic goldfish. His friend.

36    "Fixable," Sergei says. "I'll just mop up the blood. A good sponge and it'll be like it never was."

37    That tail just goes back and forth, the fish's head steady.

**TOUGH QUESTIONS**

**Notice & Note:** In paragraphs 38–40, mark an example of a tough question.

**Make Connections:** Think about Sergei's two earlier wishes. Do you think he considers them wasted wishes?

38    Sergei takes a deep breath. He steps out into the middle of the kitchen, out into the puddle. "When I'm fishing, while it's dark and the world's asleep," he says, half to himself and half to the fish, "I'll tie the kid to a rock and dump him in the sea. Not a chance, not in a million years, will anyone ever find him."

39    "You killed him, Sergei," the goldfish says. "You murdered someone—but you're not a murderer." The goldfish stops swishing his tail. "If, on this, you won't waste a wish, then tell me, Sergei, what is it good for?"

40    It was in Bethlehem, actually, that Yonatan found his Arab, a handsome man who used his first wish for peace. His name was Munir; he was fat with a big white mustache. Superphotogenic.[7] It was moving, the way he said it. Perfect, the way in which Munir wished his wish. Yoni knew even as he was filming that this guy would be his promo for sure.

41    Either him or that Russian. The one with the faded tattoos that Yoni had met in Jaffa. The one that looked straight into the camera and said, if he ever found a talking goldfish he wouldn't ask of it a single thing. He'd just stick it on a shelf in a big glass jar and talk to him all day, it didn't matter about what. Maybe sports, maybe politics, whatever a goldfish was interested in chatting about.

42    Anything, the Russian said, not to be alone.

---

[7] **superphotogenic:** looking extremely good in photos or on film.

## CHECK YOUR UNDERSTANDING

Answer these questions before moving on to the **Analyze the Text** section on the following page.

**1** Why does Yonatan come to Sergei's door?

**A** He has gone to the wrong apartment by accident.

**B** He is with the KGB and has tracked Sergei from Russia.

**C** He wants to interview Sergei for a documentary film.

**D** He has come to thank Sergei for his kindness.

**2** What misunderstanding causes the story's main problem?

**F** The fish lies to Sergei about why Yonatan is there.

**G** Sergei thinks that Yonatan wants to take the goldfish.

**H** Sergei and Yonatan understand nothing of each other's language.

**J** Yonatan feels threatened by Sergei, who means him no harm.

**3** Sergei does not want to use his last wish because —

**A** the fish is his only friend

**B** Yonatan was a genuine threat

**C** he plans to use it to get rich

**D** he is saving it for a true emergency

## ANALYZE THE TEXT

Support your responses with evidence from the text.   📓 NOTEBOOK

1. **Analyze** Consider how Sergei reacts when Yoni comes to his door. Does his response seem reasonable? How does Sergei's cultural experience help explain his reaction?

2. **Infer** When you **infer**, you use details in a text to draw a conclusion about something that the author does not state directly. What can you infer about Sergei's character based on the way he used his first two wishes?

3. **Draw Conclusions** How does the motif of wishing apply to each of the story's major characters: Yoni, Sergei, and the goldfish? What is similar and different about their wishes?

4. **Evaluate** The last section of the story is a flash forward. Readers must infer what happens in the time between Sergei's conversation with the fish and Yoni's final report on his video. Is this structure effective, or would it have been better to know the details about Sergei's decision? Explain.

5. **Notice & Note** Reread what the goldfish tells Sergei in paragraph 22. What lesson is this archetypal wise character trying to convey? How does this lesson reveal a theme of the story?

## RESEARCH

**RESEARCH TIP**
To begin your research, type the key words "rule of three and traditional tales" into your web browser. Take notes from each story so you can use the details to synthesize, or come to a new understanding, of the information.

This story provides a modern twist on two features of many folk tales: talking animals and the rule of three. Work with a small group to research traditional tales that include one or both of these elements. Then, synthesize the story ideas your group has gathered to make a comparison between these stories and Etgar Keret's story. In what ways are the talking animals similar and different? What kinds of events, characters, or details appear in groups of three?

|  | KERET'S STORY | OTHER STORIES |
|---|---|---|
| **Talking Animals** |  |  |
| **Rule of Three** |  |  |

**Extend** Write a summary of your group's conclusions about Keret's story in comparison with the traditional tales you researched.

## CREATE AND PRESENT

**Write a Fable** Write a fable to teach a lesson about life, using an archetypal character.

❏ Begin with details that introduce the archetypical character(s) and establish the conflict. Include dialogue and details that make the tale colorful and entertaining.

❏ Then, describe events that build the conflict toward a turning point. That buildup may mean that the same basic sequence of events plays out a second time. The repetition builds tension.

❏ Resolve the conflict and draw your fable to a logical conclusion.

**Present a Fable** Adapt your fable for presentation to your classmates.

❏ Practice reading the fable, adjusting your pace and expression to emphasize the content. For example, change your voice when different characters are speaking.

❏ Consider memorizing key parts of your fable so you can recite them without reading from a script. This frees you to make eye contact with listeners. It's fine to paraphrase parts that are mostly narration.

❏ Use visuals and gestures to bring your story to life for your audience.

Go to the **Writing Studio** for more on writing a narrative.

Go to the **Speaking and Listening Studio** for more on giving a presentation.

## RESPOND TO THE ESSENTIAL QUESTION

 **?** How do we engage with others while staying true to ourselves?

**Gather Information** Review your annotations and notes on "What, of This Goldfish, Would You Wish?" Then, add relevant information to your Response Log. As you determine which information to include, think about:

UNIT 1
RESPONSE LOG

**?** Essential Question:
How do we engage with others while staying true to ourselves?

| | |
|---|---|
| What, of This Goldfish, Would You Wish? | |
| By Any Other Name | |
| Without Title | |
| from Texas v. Johnson Majority Opinion | |
| American Flag Stands for Tolerance | |

• what makes people happy
• how people who have been hurt by others tend to respond
• internal conflict created by that response

At the end of the unit, you will use your notes to help you write a personal essay.

**ACADEMIC VOCABULARY**

As you write and discuss what you learned from the short story, be sure to use the Academic Vocabulary words. Check off each of the words that you use.

❏ **discriminate**

❏ **diverse**

❏ **inhibit**

❏ **intervene**

❏ **rational**

**WORD BANK**
poignant
wizened
beleaguered
fluent

## CRITICAL VOCABULARY

**Practice and Apply** Answer these questions to demonstrate your understanding of each Critical Vocabulary word.

1. You have just read a **poignant** blog post. Will you still be thinking about it tomorrow, or will you forget it immediately? Explain.

2. The flowers you received last week appear **wizened**. What will you do with them? Why?

3. Maria feels **beleaguered** on the first day of school. Does her facial expression show that she is confident or that she is overwhelmed? Why?

4. Doug is **fluent** in French. Does he need to pack a French dictionary when he travels to France? Explain.

## VOCABULARY STRATEGY:
### Context Clues

For more on using context clues, visit the **Vocabulary Studio**.

If you come across an unfamiliar word while reading, you can use **context clues**, or information within a sentence or in the surrounding text, to figure out the word's meaning. For example, the word *fluent* appears in the context of a conversation about Sergei's poor understanding of the Hebrew language. The goldfish says, "Mine's supergreat . . . I'm fluent in everything." The contrast between Sergei's poor Hebrew and the fish's fluent Hebrew helps you guess that *fluent* means "able to express oneself clearly and easily."

**Practice and Apply** Find the following words in the story: *testament* (paragraph 2), *foreseeable* (paragraph 5), *accountable* (paragraph 5), *promo* (paragraph 40). Working with a partner, complete the chart, using context clues to determine each word's meaning as it is used in the story.

| TERM | PART OF SPEECH | CONTEXT CLUES | MY DEFINITION |
|---|---|---|---|
| testament | | | |
| foreseeable | | | |
| accountable | | | |
| promo | | | |

## LANGUAGE CONVENTIONS:
### Tone

An author might use word choice and sentence structure to express a particular **tone**, or attitude, toward characters and events. The tone may also reflect the personality of one or more characters. Etgar Keret uses techniques such as slang and incomplete sentences to create an informal tone. Read this passage from the story:

> **Yonatan had a brilliant idea for a documentary. He'd knock on doors. Just him. No camera crew, no nonsense. Just Yonatan, on his own, a small camera in hand, asking, "If you found a talking goldfish that granted you three wishes, what would you wish for?"**

The author could have used more formal language, such as this:

> **Yonatan had a brilliantly simple idea for a documentary. He would do all the filming himself, without a camera crew. Knocking on people's doors with a small hand-held camera, he would inquire of each person, "If you found a talking goldfish that granted you three wishes, what would you wish for?"**

The informal language that Etgar Keret chose sets a tone that is better suited to Yoni's youthful enthusiasm and his spirit of adventure.

Here are some other examples of language from the story and how they contribute to the informal tone.

| EXAMPLE FROM TEXT | HOW IT AFFECTS TONE |
|---|---|
| **three killer wishes** | *Killer* is slang for "excellent." Slang is the language of casual, everyday speech. |
| **When Sergei got to Israel and then moved to Jaffa, his family couldn't wrap their heads around it.** | The expression *wrap their heads around* (meaning "understand") is an idiom that people use in conversation but not in formal writing or speech. |
| **But the earring boy is stubborn.** | Calling Yoni "the earring boy" reflects Sergei's private thoughts. The humor in this mild insult fits the informal tone of the story. |

**Practice and Apply** Write two versions of a paragraph describing an experience you have had. Choose words, phrases, and sentence structures that create a formal tone in the first version and an informal tone in the second. Identify which version best fits the event your writing describes.

# BY ANY OTHER NAME

Memoir by **Santha Rama Rau**

**?** **ESSENTIAL QUESTION:**

How do we engage with others while staying true to ourselves?

## QUICK START

The title of this piece comes from Shakespeare's *Romeo and Juliet*. Because their families are enemies, Juliet wishes that Romeo had a different surname. "What's in a name?" Juliet asks. "That which we call a rose / By any other name would smell as sweet."

How important is a person's name? How would you react if someone took your name away and assigned you a new one? Turn to a partner and share your thoughts.

## ANALYZE HISTORICAL CONTEXT

At the time of this account (around 1928), India was a colony of Great Britain. Educated Indians were expected to learn English in addition to their native languages. (Many languages are spoken in India.) The headmistress, or principal, of Santha Rama Rau's school was British, as were most of the students, who were the children of British civil servants sent to India as colonial rulers. Great Britain ruled the Indian subcontinent from 1858 to 1947.

To analyze the point of view that Santha Rama Rau brings to her experiences at school, identify details of history and culture that help to define India in the 1920s. Then, make inferences about Rama Rau's perspective on these details.

| TEXT EXCERPT | INFERENCE |
|---|---|
| Up to then, my mother had refused to send Premila to school in the British-run establishments of that time . . . | Rama Rau notices her parents have mixed feelings about the British. |
| I had never really grasped the system of competitive games. . . . it was not for years that I really learned the spirit of the thing. | Rama Rau finds the competitive atmosphere of the British school different from the caring atmosphere at home. |

## ANALYZE AUTHOR'S PURPOSE

An **author's purpose** is the reason the author writes a particular piece, whether to inform, persuade, or entertain the audience. As you read this piece, analyze Rama Rau's authorial choices. What historical and cultural details does she share with readers? Based on her choices, what can you infer about her purpose for writing?

- As you read, mark details about history and culture. The details may relate to food, dress, customs, language, class, or ways of interacting. They may also relate to the people Rama Rau comes into contact with.

- Think about why Rama Rau shares these details. What do the details reveal about her purpose for writing?

### GENRE ELEMENTS: MEMOIR

- a true story told as a memory, usually in the past tense
- the author is the narrator, who uses a first-person point of view
- does not retell the author's entire life
- a selected memory or memories reflect a message or lesson

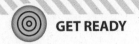
## CRITICAL VOCABULARY

| **precarious** | **insular** | **sedately** | **tepid** |
|---|---|---|---|

To see how many Critical Vocabulary words you already know, use them to complete the sentences.

1. My former best friend greeted me with a(n) _____ half-hug.

2. The painter balanced atop a very old and _____ three-story ladder.

3. No longer an over-excited pup, our Max responds _____ to the sight of another dog.

4. She found the experience of living in a tiny cabin miles from the nearest neighbor _____.

## LANGUAGE CONVENTIONS

**Appropriate Verb Tense**  In this lesson, you will learn about how the author of a memoir uses verb tense to orient the reader. The author describes a central episode in her life but also alludes to events that came before it. She also describes her present-day feelings about the events.

Notice how one writer uses the past perfect tense to indicate an action completed before something else happened:

**I had talked to Tara on the phone three times before we met in person.**

As you read "By Any Other Name," note the author's use of verb tenses to make the order of events clear.

---

ANNOTATION MODEL                                    **NOTICE & NOTE**

As you read, note passages that interest you and any questions or observations you have. In the model, you can see one reader's notes about the opening of "By Any Other Name."

> At the Anglo-Indian day school in Zorinabad to which my sister and I were sent when she was eight and I was five and a half, they changed our names. On the first day of school, a hot, windless morning of a north Indian September, we stood in the headmistress's study, and she said, "Now you're the *new* girls. What are your names?"

*author and her sister were very young*

*changing names is dramatic detail*

*"headmistress" shows that the school was run on a British model*

## BACKGROUND

**Santha Rama Rau** *(1923–2009) was born into one of India's most influential families but spent most of her life in other lands. After living for some time in England, Rama Rau returned to India, making a conscious effort to reorient herself to her homeland and her extended family. She recorded her impressions in her first book,* Home to India *(1944). Rama Rau published numerous travel books, several novels, and an autobiography.*

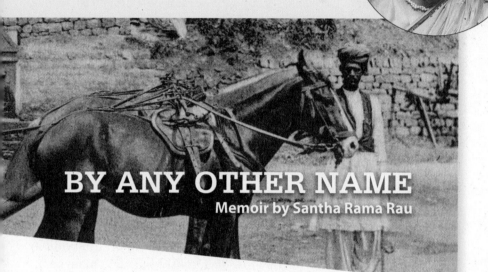

# BY ANY OTHER NAME
### Memoir by Santha Rama Rau

## SETTING A PURPOSE

*As you read, think about how the author's experiences remind you of your own experiences or other experiences you have heard or read about.*

1    At the Anglo-Indian[1] day school in Zorinabad to which my sister and I were sent when she was eight and I was five and a half, they changed our names. On the first day of school, a hot, windless morning of a north Indian September, we stood in the headmistress's study, and she said, "Now you're the *new* girls. What are your names?"

2    My sister answered for us. "I am Premila, and she"—nodding in my direction—"is Santha."

3    The headmistress had been in India, I suppose, fifteen years or so, but she still smiled her helpless inability to cope with Indian names. Her rimless half-glasses glittered, and the **precarious** bun on the top of her head trembled as she shook her head. "Oh, my dears, those are much too hard for me. Suppose

**precarious**
(prĭ-kâr´ē-əs) *adj.* dangerously insecure.

---
[1] **Anglo-Indian:** English and Indian; also refers to the British colonists living in India.

we give you pretty English names. Wouldn't that be more jolly? Let's see, now—Pamela for you, I think." She shrugged in a baffled way at my sister. "That's as close as I can get. And for *you*," she said to me, "how about Cynthia? Isn't that nice?"

4   My sister was always less easily intimidated than I was, and while she kept a stubborn silence, I said "Thank you," in a very tiny voice.

5   We had been sent to that school because my father, among his responsibilities as an officer of the civil service, had a tour of duty to perform in the villages around that steamy little provincial town, where he had his headquarters at that time. He used to make his shorter inspection tours on horseback, and a week before, in the stale heat of a typically postmonsoon[2] day, we had waved goodbye to him and a little procession—an assistant, a secretary, two bearers, and the man to look after the bedding rolls and luggage. They rode away through our large garden, still bright green from the rains, and we turned back into the twilight of the house and the sound of fans whispering in every room.

6   Up to then, my mother had refused to send Premila to school in the British-run establishments of that time, because, she used to say, "You can bury a dog's tail for seven years and it still comes out curly, and you can take a Britisher away from his home for a lifetime and he still remains **insular**." The examinations and degrees from entirely Indian schools were not, in those days, considered valid. In my case, the question had never come up and probably never would have come up if Mother's extraordinary good health had not broken down. For the first time in my life, she was not able to continue the lessons she had been giving us every morning. So our Hindi[3] books were put away, the stories of the Lord Krishna[4] as a little boy were left in midair, and we were sent to the Anglo-Indian school.

7 That first day at school is still, when I think of it, a remarkable one. At that age, if one's name is changed, one develops a curious form of dual personality. I remember having a certain detached and disbelieving concern in the actions of "Cynthia," but certainly no responsibility. Accordingly, I followed the thin, erect back of the headmistress down the veranda to my classroom, feeling, at most, a passing interest in what was going to happen to me in this strange, new atmosphere of School.

8   The building was Indian in design, with wide verandas opening onto a central courtyard, but Indian verandas are usually whitewashed, with stone floors. These, in the tradition of British

**insular**
(in´sə-lər) *adj.* narrow-minded or detached from others.

**ANALYZE HISTORICAL CONTEXT**

**Annotate:** In paragraph 6, mark the author's reasons for avoiding British schools.

**Analyze:** Why are the girls sent to the school despite these reasons?

---

[2] **postmonsoon:** after the monsoon, or seasonal heavy rains.
[3] **Hindi:** official language of India.
[4] **Lord Krishna:** in the Hindu religion, human form taken by the god Vishnu. Many Hindu stories recount episodes in the life of Krishna.

schools, were painted dark brown and had matting on the floors. It gave a feeling of extra intensity to the heat.

9    I suppose there were about a dozen Indian children in the school—which contained perhaps forty children in all—and four of them were in my class. They were all sitting at the back of the room, and I went to join them. I sat next to a small, solemn girl, who didn't smile at me. She had long, glossy black braids and wore a cotton dress, but she still kept on her Indian jewelry—a gold chain around her neck, thin gold bracelets, and tiny ruby studs in her ears. Like most Indian children, she had a rim of black kohl[5] around her eyes. The cotton dress should have looked strange, but all I could think of was that I should ask my mother if I couldn't wear a dress to school, too, instead of my Indian clothes.

10    I can't remember too much about the proceedings in class that day, except for the beginning. The teacher pointed to me and asked me to stand up. "Now, dear, tell the class your name."

11    I said nothing.

12    "Come along," she said, frowning slightly. "What's your name, dear?"

13    "I don't know," I said, finally.

14    The English children in the front of the class—there were about eight or ten of them—giggled and twisted around in their chairs to look at me. I sat down quickly and opened my eyes very wide, hoping in that way to dry them off. The little girl with the braids put out her hand and very lightly touched my arm. She still didn't smile.

15    Most of that morning I was rather bored. I looked briefly at the children's drawings pinned to the wall, and then concentrated on a lizard clinging to the ledge of the high, barred window behind the teacher's head. Occasionally it would shoot out its long yellow tongue for a fly, and then it would rest, with its eyes closed and its belly palpitating, as though it were swallowing several times quickly. The lessons were mostly concerned with reading and writing and simple numbers—things that my mother had already taught me—and I paid very little attention. The teacher wrote on the easel-blackboard words like "bat" and "cat," which seemed babyish to me; only "apple" was new and incomprehensible.

16    When it was time for the lunch recess, I followed the girl with braids out onto the veranda. There the children from the other classes were assembled. I saw Premila at once and ran over to her, as she had charge of our lunchbox. The children were all opening packages and sitting down to eat sandwiches. Premila and I were the only ones who had Indian food—thin wheat chapatis,[6] some vegetable curry, and a bottle of buttermilk. Premila thrust half of it into my hand and

ANALYZE AUTHOR'S PURPOSE

**Annotate:** Underline the author's responses in paragraphs 10–14.

**Analyze:** Why is the author unable to answer this basic question?

---

[5] **kohl:** dark powder used as eye makeup.
[6] **chapatis:** thin, flat bread.

whispered fiercely that I should go and sit with my class, because that was what the others seemed to be doing.

17    The enormous black eyes of the little Indian girl from my class looked at my food longingly, so I offered her some. But she only shook her head and plowed her way solemnly through her sandwiches.

18    I was very sleepy after lunch, because at home we always took a siesta. It was usually a pleasant time of day, with the bedroom darkened against the harsh afternoon sun, the drifting off into sleep with the sound of Mother's voice reading a story in one's mind, and, finally, the shrill, fussy voice of the ayah[7] waking one for tea.

19    At school, we rested for a short time on low, folding cots on the veranda, and then we were expected to play games. During the hot part of the afternoon we played indoors, and after the shadows had begun to lengthen and the slight breeze of the evening had come up, we moved outside to the wide courtyard.

20    I had never really grasped the system of competitive games. At home, whenever we played tag or guessing games, I was always allowed to "win"—"because," Mother used to tell Premila, "she is the youngest, and we have to allow for that." I had often heard her say it, and it seemed quite reasonable to me, but the result was that I had no clear idea of what "winning" meant.

21    When we played twos-and-threes[8] that afternoon at school, in accordance with my training I let one of the small English boys catch me but was naturally rather puzzled when the other children did not return the courtesy. I ran about for what seemed like hours without ever catching anyone, until it was time for school to close. Much later I learned that my attitude was called "not being a good sport," and I stopped allowing myself to be caught, but it was not for years that I really learned the spirit of the thing.

22    When I saw our car come up to the school gate, I broke away from my classmates and rushed toward it yelling, "Ayah! Ayah!" It seemed like an eternity since I had seen her that morning—a wizened, affectionate figure in her white cotton sari,[9] giving me dozens of urgent and useless instructions on how to be a good girl at school. Premila followed more **sedately**, and she told me on the way home never to do that again in front of the other children.

23  When we got home, we went straight to Mother's high, white room to have tea with her, and I immediately climbed onto the bed and bounced gently up and down on the springs. Mother asked how we had liked our first day in school. I was so pleased to be home and to

**Notice & Note:** What details does Santha remember about home in paragraph 18?

**Infer:** Why does the author mention this difference between what she usually does and what happens at school?

**LANGUAGE CONVENTIONS**

**Annotate:** Mark the verbs in the second sentence of paragraph 22.

**Interpret:** Which actions take place during the time of the story the author tells? Which actions took place before that time?

**sedately**
(sĭ-dāt´ lē) *adv.* in a calm and dignified manner.

---

[7] **ayah:** Anglo-Indian for nanny or maid.

[8] **twos-and-threes:** game similar to tag.

[9] **sari:** long piece of cloth wrapped around the body. a long skirt; the other crosses the chest and shoulder.

The pupils of the Jaora School, Indore, India. 3rd August 1928

have left that peculiar Cynthia behind that I had nothing whatever to say about school, except to ask what "apple" meant. But Premila told Mother about the classes, and added that in her class they had weekly tests to see if they had learned their lessons well.

24    I asked, "What's a test?"

25    Premila said, "You're too small to have them. You won't have them in your class for donkey's years." She had learned the expression that day and was using it for the first time. We all laughed enormously at her wit. She also told Mother, in an aside, that we should take sandwiches to school the next day. Not, she said, that she minded. But they would be simpler for me to handle.

26    That whole lovely evening I didn't think about school at all. I sprinted barefoot across the lawns with my favorite playmate, the cook's son, to the stream at the end of the garden. We quarreled in our usual way, waded in the **tepid** water under the lime trees, and waited for the night to bring out the smell of the jasmine. I listened with fascination to his stories of ghosts and demons, until I was too frightened to cross the garden alone in the semidarkness. The ayah found me, shouted at the cook's son, scolded me, hurried me in to supper—it was an entirely usual, wonderful evening.

**tepid**
(tep′id) *adj.* neither hot nor cold; lukewarm.

27    It was a week later, the day of Premila's first test, that our lives changed rather abruptly. I was sitting at the back of my class, in my usual inattentive way, only half listening to the teacher. I had started a rather guarded friendship with the girl with the braids, whose name turned out to be Nalini (Nancy in school). The three other Indian children were already fast friends. Even at that age, it was apparent to all of us that friendship with the English or Anglo-Indian children was out of the question. Occasionally, during the class, my new friend and I would draw pictures and show them to each other secretly.

**ANALYZE HISTORICAL CONTEXT**
**Annotate:** Mark what was apparent to the Indian children in paragraph 27.

**Infer:** Why might such young children consider this a fact?

28     The door opened sharply and Premila marched in. At first, the teacher smiled at her in a kindly and encouraging way and said, "Now, you're little Cynthia's sister?"

29     Premila didn't even look at her. She stood with her feet planted firmly apart and her shoulders rigid and addressed herself directly to me. "Get up," she said. "We're going home."

30     I didn't know what had happened, but I was aware that it was a crisis of some sort. I rose obediently and started to walk toward my sister.

31     "Bring your pencils and your notebook," she said.

32     I went back for them, and together we left the room. The teacher started to say something just as Premila closed the door, but we didn't wait to hear what it was.

33     In complete silence we left the school grounds and started to walk home. Then I asked Premila what the matter was. All she would say was, "We're going home for good."

34     It was a very tiring walk for a child of five and a half, and I dragged along behind Premila with my pencils growing sticky in my hand. I can still remember looking at the dusty hedges and the tangles of thorns in the ditches by the side of the road, smelling the faint fragrance from the eucalyptus trees, and wondering whether we would ever reach home. Occasionally a horse-drawn tonga[10] passed us, and the women, in their pink or green silks, stared at Premila and me trudging along on the side of the road. A few coolies[11] and a line of women carrying baskets of vegetables on their heads smiled at us. But it was nearing the hottest time of day, and the road was almost deserted. I walked more and more slowly, and shouted to Premila, from time to time, "Wait for me!" with increasing peevishness. She spoke to me only once, and that was to tell me to carry my notebook on my head, because of the sun.

35     When we got to our house, the ayah was just taking a tray of lunch into Mother's room. She immediately started a long, worried questioning about what are you children doing back here at this hour of the day.

36     Mother looked very startled and very concerned and asked Premila what had happened.

37     Premila said, "We had our test today, and She made me and the other Indians sit at the back of the room, with a desk between each one."

38     Mother said, "Why was that, darling?""

39     She said it was because Indians cheat," Premila added. "So I don't think we should go back to that school."

---

[10] **tonga:** a two-wheeled carriage.
[11] **coolies:** a term referring to unskilled laborers.

40    Mother looked very distant and was silent a long time. At last she said, "Of course not, darling." She sounded displeased.

41    We all shared the curry she was having for lunch, and afterward I was sent off to the beautifully familiar bedroom for my siesta. I could hear Mother and Premila talking through the open door.

42    Mother said, "Do you suppose she understood all that?"

43    Premila said, "I shouldn't think so. She's a baby."

44    Mother said, "Well, I hope it won't bother her."

45    Of course, they were both wrong. I understood it perfectly, and I remember it all very clearly. But I put it happily away, because it had all happened to a girl called Cynthia, and I never was really particularly interested in her.

**ANALYZE AUTHOR'S PURPOSE**

**Annotate:** Mark what the author's mother and sister were wrong about in paragraph 45.

**Analyze:** Why did the author make a distinction between herself and "Cynthia" as a child?

## CHECK YOUR UNDERSTANDING

Answer these questions before moving on to the **Analyze the Text** section on the following page.

1 What conflict do Santha and Premila experience when they meet the headmistress?

   **A** She disapproves of their Indian clothing and food.

   **B** She changes their names to make them easier for her to pronounce.

   **C** They want to take a siesta but are not allowed to.

   **D** She does not want them to interact with the English children.

2 Which of these does Santha learn at school?

   **F** How to spell simple English words like "bat" and "cat."

   **G** How her name is pronounced properly in English.

   **H** That English children play more competitively than she does.

   **J** That a midday siesta is unnecessary for older children.

3 Why does Premila take Santha out of school in the middle of the day?

   **A** Premila's teacher says that Indians cheat.

   **B** Premila is nervous about her afternoon test.

   **C** The girls' father is on his way home from a business trip.

   **D** Santha isn't paying attention in her classes.

## ANALYZE THE TEXT

Support your responses with evidence from the text. 📓 NOTEBOOK

1. **Interpret** What do the headmistress's gestures and expressions tell you about her motivation for changing the girls' names?

2. **Cite Evidence** Name two ways in which the Indian girls who have been at the school for a while imitate the English girls. How do these examples reflect the historical context of the memoir?

3. **Infer** Based on the last paragraph, explain how Santha views the conflict with the headmistress. How does this view fit the author's purpose for writing this memoir?

4. **Analyze** Many ideas are passed from generation to generation. How might Premila's teacher have passed on a prejudice to her students? What values did Santha's mother pass on to her children? Based on your responses, what do you think is the story's theme or insight about life?

5. **Notice & Note** What does the text suggest about how the experience of childhood is remembered? Cite Memory Moments from the text in your answer.

## RESEARCH

**RESEARCH TIP**
The best search terms are very specific, but it's hard to be specific when you're not sure what you're looking for. If you search online, you might start with something like "effects of name change." As you find a story or stories you want to pursue, continue refining your search terms.

How do you think Santha Rama Rau would answer Juliet's question, "What's in a name?" How important do you think a person's name is to his or her sense of identity? Find out more about a situation in which someone's name has been changed, either by their choice or someone else's.

| RESEARCH QUESTIONS | WHAT YOU LEARNED |
|---|---|
| Whose name was changed? | |
| Whose idea was it to change the name? | |
| Why was the name changed? | |
| How did the name change affect the person or others around him or her? | |

**Connect** Reread the last paragraph of the story. Recall why the school's headmistress renamed Santha "Cynthia." How did Santha use "Cynthia" to get through a difficult experience? Discuss with a partner or small group.

## CREATE AND DISCUSS

**Write a Poem**  Write a free-verse poem about your own name—and your relationship with it.

- ❏ Free verse includes unrhymed lines of varying length. There is no fixed metrical pattern.
- ❏ Include the name your teachers call you, other names people refer to you by, and where they came from.
- ❏ What do all of these names mean to you? How do you feel about having them? Address these questions in your poem.

**Discuss with a Small Group**  Have a discussion about why names matter.

- ❏ Include evidence from your research task.
- ❏ Include insight you gained from the process of writing your free-verse poem.
- ❏ What common patterns and themes do you notice in the information shared by members of your group?

 Go to the **Speaking and Listening Studio** for more on participating in collaborative discussions.

## RESPOND TO THE ESSENTIAL QUESTION

**?**  How do we engage with others while staying true to ourselves?

**Gather Information**  Review your annotations and notes on "By Any Other Name." Then, add relevant information to your Response Log. As you determine which information to include, think about:

- where names come from and what they say to others about us
- why people have different names at different points in their lives
- what a shift from one name to another can mean to a person and the people around him or her

At the end of the unit, use your notes to help you write a personal essay.

**ACADEMIC VOCABULARY**

As you write and discuss what you learned from the memoir, be sure to use the Academic Vocabulary words. Check off each of the words that you use.

- ❏ **discriminate**
- ❏ **diverse**
- ❏ **inhibit**
- ❏ **intervene**
- ❏ **rational**

**WORD BANK**
insular
precarious
sedately
tepid

## CRITICAL VOCABULARY

**Practice and Apply** Mark the letter of the best answer to each question. Then, explain your response.

1. Which statement represents an **insular** attitude?
   a. No place is as great as my home town.
   b. The world is full of interesting places.

   _____

2. Which of these could be described as **precarious**?
   a. a house painter who forgot to bring brushes and dropcloths
   b. a house painter standing on one foot on a wobbly ladder

   _____

3. Which of the following might happen **sedately**?
   a. a canoe trip on a rocky river
   b. a canoe trip on a quiet lake

   _____

4. Which of the following is likely to be **tepid**?
   a. juice that was left out all night
   b. a freshly-poured cup of coffee

   _____

## VOCABULARY STRATEGY:
### Foreign Words Used in English

 Go to the **Vocabulary Studio** for more on foreign words used in English.

English speakers use many words from other languages. "By Any Other Name" includes *veranda*, which comes from the Hindi language, and *siesta*, which comes from Spanish.

**Practice and Apply** Use context clues and a dictionary, if needed, to write the meaning of the boldfaced term in your own words.

1. Tobias is in a rare good mood, so please don't upset the **status quo**.

   _____

2. When our 20-point lead began to shrink with minutes to play, I had an odd **déjà vu** about last season and losing the national championship.

   _____

3. It may sound old-school today, but there was a time when punk music was aggressively **avant-garde**.

   _____

4. The cruel military dictator was overthrown in a violent **coup d'état**.

   _____

## LANGUAGE CONVENTIONS:
## Appropriate Verb Tense

Use verb tense accurately to indicate when actions or events take place. The author of a memoir uses appropriate verb tense to orient the reader about actions and events in the present day, the past, and the distant past. Different tenses are appropriate, depending on the time and time order in which events happened.

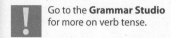

Go to the **Grammar Studio** for more on verb tense.

In "By Any Other Name," Santha Rama Rau uses different tenses to indicate when events happened. Here are examples from the memoir:

- The past tense reflects the time when the main event occurred.

  **My sister answered for us.**

- The past perfect shares events that happened before the main action.

  **The headmistress had been in India, I suppose, fifteen years or so . . .**

- The present tense allows the author to reflect now on what happened during the event.

  **That first day at school is still, when I think of it, a remarkable one.**

**Practice and Apply**  Think of an exciting or striking experience you had. Write a few sentences using appropriate verb tenses to describe the experience, events that came before it, and your current perspective on it. When you are finished, share your sentences with a partner. Ask your partner to make a time line of events that matches your use of verb tenses.

# WITHOUT TITLE

Poem by **Diane Glancy**

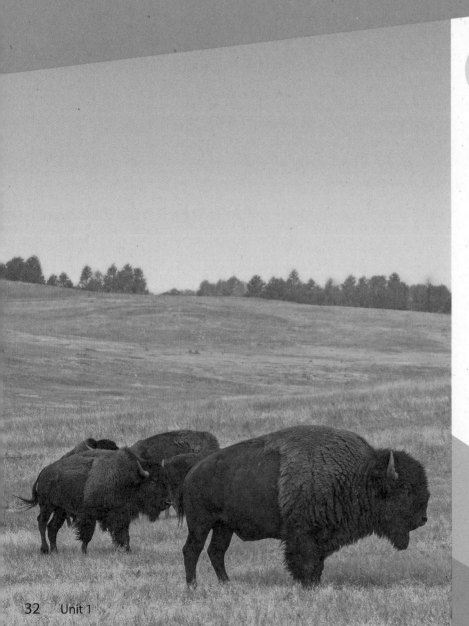

**?** ***ESSENTIAL QUESTION:***

How do we engage with others while staying true to ourselves?

## QUICK START

Imagine being suddenly uprooted from your current life and moving to a new place with different customs and a different way of life. What aspects of your current life would you miss? How would this change affect how you think about who you are? Write a brief journal entry exploring your ideas.

## ANALYZE SETTING

The setting of a work of literature encompasses much more than simply the time and place where the action occurs. In the poem you will read, the interplay between two historical and cultural settings is crucial to the theme:

- The poem's present is in the late 20th century, in a modern American city.

- The poem's past is in the father's previous Native American culture.

The way the characters think of and react to these settings drives the choices that they make in their lives.

As you read "Without Title," use this chart to record references to the historical and cultural settings. In particular, note how the speaker seems to feel about each of these settings. One example is shown for you.

**GENRE ELEMENTS: LYRIC POETRY**

- expresses the speaker's thoughts and feelings

- implies, rather than states, the speaker's emotion

- written in free verse without regular meter

- uses the rhythm of natural speech to create its musical quality

| DETAIL (LINE NUMBER) | SETTING IT BELONGS TO | SPEAKER'S TONE |
|---|---|---|
| buffalo (line 1) | Native American past | sympathetic |
| | | |
| | | |
| | | |

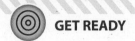

## MAKE INFERENCES ABOUT THEME

Most often, poets do not state the theme, or message, of a work. Instead, making inferences that lead to the theme is part of the experience of reading the poem. This reader involvement adds impact in a way that merely stating a message could never accomplish.

As you read "Without Title," keep in mind the historical and cultural settings that are central to the poem's theme. The information you record in your setting chart will help you infer what the poet hopes to communicate about the lives of Native Americans. To infer the theme, you will consider the details and the speaker's tone in light of your own experiences and knowledge.

In addition to historical and cultural details, here are some other keys to inferring the theme of a poem:

- **Title:** Some poems have no title or a title that merely tells the subject. But for many poems, the title (and subtitles, such as this poem has) contributes to the overall meaning of the poem.

- **Repetition:** Poets use words sparingly, so if a word, image, or idea is repeated, it's for an important purpose.

- **Changes and shifts:** Changes in people or places, as well as shifts in tone or structure, can signal central ideas in a poem.

---

### ANNOTATION MODEL

**NOTICE & NOTE**

As you read "Without Title," make inferences about the poem's theme. Here is how a reader might annotate the beginning of the poem.

> It's hard you kn<u>ow</u> without the buffalo,
> the shaman, the arrow,
> but my father went out each day to hunt
> as th<u>ough</u> he had them.

The speaker shows admiration for her father, who has lost his way of life.

A repeated "o" sound is like a chant, as if echoes of the past remain.

## BACKGROUND

*After World War II, the United States government's Urban Relocation Program promised Native Americans better jobs if they moved to cities and tried to join mainstream American society.* **Diane Glancy** *(b. 1941), a writer of Cherokee descent, has explored issues such as the difficulty of assimilation in her many novels, poems, and plays as well as in nonfiction works. Glancy's work has been awarded numerous literary prizes over a career spanning three decades.*

# WITHOUT TITLE

## for my Father who lived without ceremony

**Poem by Diane Glancy**

## SETTING A PURPOSE

*As you read, think about ways in which the life of the speaker's father is different from the traditional life of his people.*

It's hard you know without the buffalo,
the shaman,[1] the arrow,
but my father went out each day to hunt
as though he had them.
5 He worked in the stockyards.
All his life he brought us meat.
No one marked his first kill,
no one sang his buffalo song.

**Notice & Note**

You can use the side margins to notice and note signposts in the text.

**ANALYZE SETTING**

**Annotate:** Mark details in lines 1–4 that reveal the historical and cultural background of the speaker's father.

**Analyze:** Why does the speaker begin by sharing details that no longer apply to her father's life?

---

[1] **shaman:** a person who interacts with the spiritual world.

Without a vision[2] he had migrated to the city
10 and went to work in the packing house.
When he brought home his horns and hides
my mother said
get rid of them.
I remember the animal tracks of his car
15 backing out the drive in snow and mud,
the aerial[3] on his old car waving
like a bow string.
I remember the silence of his lost power,
the red buffalo painted on his chest.
20 Oh, I couldn't see it
but it was there, and in the night I heard
his buffalo grunts like a snore.

_____

[2] **vision:** a guiding experience that often comes in a dream or a trance.
[3] **aerial:** a thin, metal antenna.

**MAKE INFERENCES ABOUT THEME**

**Annotate:** Mark details in lines 18–22 that make connections between the father's past and present.

**Infer:** What theme do these connections point toward?

## CHECK YOUR UNDERSTANDING

Answer these questions before moving on to the **Analyze the Text** section on the following page.

1 The father in the poem —

   **A** has adjusted well to life in the city

   **B** agrees with his wife's wish to keep the house tidy

   **C** holds on to thoughts of his past every day

   **D** makes it clear that his current life is better than his old one

2 The speaker's repeated references to <u>buffalo</u> —

   **F** make use of multiple meanings in a humorous way

   **G** reflect a stereotype about Native American culture

   **H** establish a clear structure for the poem

   **J** point out the importance of the father's memories

3 Throughout the poem, the speaker makes connections between —

   **A** the father's past culture and present experiences

   **B** the competing views of her mother and father

   **C** positive and negative aspects of life in the city

   **D** the lives of her generation and those of her father's generation

## ANALYZE THE TEXT

Support your responses with evidence from the text.  📓 NOTEBOOK

1. **Identify**  What details does the speaker use to contrast life in her father's original culture and life in the city? What tone is used to describe these two settings?

2. **Infer**  What can you infer about the speaker's feelings toward her father? Why doesn't she try to intervene in the conflict between her parents? Cite evidence from the text to support your answer.

3. **Analyze**  What theme about tradition and community does this poem convey? Draft an objective summary and then cite key details that help develop the theme over the course of the poem.

4. **Interpret**  What do the poem's title and subtitle mean? How do these ideas relate to the theme of the poem?

5. **Evaluate**  Does the speaker think her father has remained true to himself? Would the father agree? Support your response with evidence from the poem.

## RESEARCH

**RESEARCH TIP**
Look for sources from a Native American perspective, such as a particular group's history website. Comparing information from sources developed from multiple perspectives can give you a more complete picture of the change your research explores.

Work with a partner to learn more about changes in the lives of Native Americans. Gather information from at least three sources, evaluating the credibility and accuracy of the information using the criteria below.

| TITLE OF SOURCE: | |
|---|---|
| Who created it? | |
| What viewpoints and/ or biases are expressed? | |
| What does the source convey about the culture? | |

**Extend**  Discuss or write about a connection you can make between your source information and the situation described in "Without Title."

## CREATE AND DISCUSS

**Write a Narrative** The speaker of "Without Title" gives a clear picture of her family's day-to-day life. Using details from the poem, your research, and your imagination, write a short narrative that depicts one typical day for the family in the poem.

❏ Decide who will narrate: the speaker, one of the speaker's parents, or a third-person narrator outside the family.

❏ Describe the events of one day through your chosen narrator's voice, incorporating details from the poem.

❏ Make sure your narrative builds to a logical conclusion that reflects what the characters experience in the poem.

**Present a Narrative** Read your completed narrative aloud, clearly and expressively.

❏ Consider the personality of your narrator, and use conventions of language the way this person would. For example, how would the register of an outside narrator differ from that of the father?

❏ Speak using appropriate volume, pauses for effect, and meaningful gestures to enhance your ideas.

❏ Request feedback from listeners on your delivery and ideas.

 For help with brainstorming ideas for your narrative, visit the **Writing Studio**.

For help with delivering an oral presentation, visit the **Speaking and Listening Studio**.

## RESPOND TO THE ESSENTIAL QUESTION

 How do we engage with others while staying true to ourselves?

**Gather Information** Review your annotations and notes on "Without Title." Then, add relevant information to your Response Log. As you determine which information to include, think about:

• how the father feels about who he is in the poem's two settings
• how the speaker views the father
• the causes and results of compromises people make

At the end of the unit, use your notes to help you write a personal essay.

**ACADEMIC VOCABULARY**
As you write and discuss what you learned from the poem, be sure to use the Academic Vocabulary words. Check off each of the words that you use.

❏ **discriminate**
❏ **diverse**
❏ **inhibit**
❏ **intervene**
❏ **rational**

COURT OPINION

# *from* TEXAS *v.* JOHNSON MAJORITY OPINION

by **William J. Brennan**
pages 43–45

## COMPARE ARGUMENTS

As you read, identify the argument made in each selection. Compare the author's purpose and intended audience for each selection. After you review both selections, you will complete an independent project.

 **ESSENTIAL QUESTION:**

How do we engage with others while staying true to ourselves?

EDITORIAL

# AMERICAN FLAG STANDS FOR TOLERANCE

by **Ronald J. Allen**
pages 53–55

# *from* **Texas** *v.* **Johnson Majority Opinion**

## QUICK START

You have rights that allow you to enjoy your life and to fulfill your potential. But at what point do your wants interfere with someone else's? List two examples of times when your rights could clash with those of another person. Be ready to share one example with the class.

## MONITOR COMPREHENSION

Legal documents tend to be complex because the authors use specialized terms that most people do not recognize. Plan to use your background knowledge and reread sections of the text to aid your comprehension. The strategies below will also help you monitor your comprehension.

- **Annotation:** Mark the text with your notes and questions. Underline important ideas. Mark unfamiliar words to look up after your first read. Write notes in the margin as you think about the author's meaning.

- **Notetaking:** Take notes about important ideas. Outlining the text or writing down keywords can help you track your thoughts as you read.

- **Freewriting:** Explore your understanding of the author's meaning by writing down everything that comes to your mind, without stopping, for a certain period of time, such as 2 minutes.

As you read the excerpt from *Texas* v. *Johnson Majority Opinion*, mark the text and keep your own notes.

## EVALUATE EVIDENCE

A well-written opinion makes a claim that is supported with evidence. The evidence helps readers to understand how the author came to his or her conclusions. Evidence includes data, anecdotes, and expert opinions. The authors of legal documents usually cite **precedents,** or past legal opinions, as evidence for their opinion. Use an organizer like the one below to record Brennan's claims and to track the evidence he uses to support them.

| CLAIM | EVIDENCE |
|---|---|
| The flag's special role in society is not in danger. | If the flag's status were in danger, nobody would be offended by the idea of flag burning. |
| | |
| | |
| | |

**GENRE ELEMENTS: COURT OPINION**

- expresses the opinion of the majority—the group of judges who have decided the case
- clearly states the judges' verdict at the beginning
- cites court cases from the past as evidence
- acknowledges and addresses counterarguments

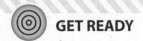

## CRITICAL VOCABULARY

To preview the Critical Vocabulary words, match the words to their definitions.

| | |
|---|---|
| 1. compulsion | a. the act of verifying or endorsing again |
| 2. implicit | b. the ability to return to a normal state after a change or an injury |
| 3. reaffirmation | c. understood but not expressed |
| 4. resilience | d. forced obligation |

## LANGUAGE CONVENTIONS

**Commas** Watching for commas can help you understand a lengthy sentence by dividing it into meaningful parts. Writers use commas to set off a dependent clause or a phrase in a sentence, as in this example from the text:

**The problem is whether, <u>under our Constitution,</u> compulsion as here employed is a permissible means for its achievement.**

As you read the court decision, watch for phrases and dependent clauses set off with commas. Take in each chunk of meaning on its own, and then put them back together to fully grasp Justice Brennan's points.

## ANNOTATION MODEL

**NOTICE & NOTE**

Here is how you might annotate the beginning of from *Texas* v. *Johnson Majority Opinion* to monitor your comprehension.

We <u>decline</u>, therefore, to create for the flag an <u>exception</u> to the ⊙joust⊙ of principles protected by the ⊙First Amendment.⊙ . . .

decline = refuse
exception = a change in rules

"joust" = competition, so principles or rights may compete with each other.

First Amendment covers several freedoms, including free speech.

My version: The rights in the First Amendment conflict, but that doesn't mean that symbols like the flag aren't covered by it.

## BACKGROUND

*At the 1984 Republican National Convention, people protested the policies of then-President Ronald Reagan. One of the protesters, Gregory Lee Johnson, set an American flag on fire. He was punished with a fine and a jail term for breaking a state law banning flag desecration. He appealed, and the case was sent to the Supreme Court to decide whether flag burning is a form of expression protected by the Constitution. The Court delivered its ruling in 1989.*
**William J. Brennan** *(1906–1997), who served on the Supreme Court from 1956 to 1990, wrote the majority opinion in the case. His staunch defense of First Amendment rights influenced many significant Court decisions.*

# *from*
# TEXAS *v.* JOHNSON
# MAJORITY OPINION
### Court Opinion by William J. Brennan

## PREPARE TO COMPARE

*As you read, make notes about the evidence that Brennan uses to support his opinion, and think about his audience and purpose for writing. Use your background knowledge and reread to monitor your comprehension.*

1   We decline, therefore, to create for the flag an exception to the joust[1] of principles protected by the First Amendment . . . [2]

2     To say that the government has an interest in encouraging proper treatment of the flag, however, is not to say that it may criminally punish a person for burning a flag as a means of political protest.

> National unity as an end which officials may foster by persuasion and example is not in question. The problem is whether, under our Constitution, **compulsion** as here employed is a permissible means for its achievement.
>
> *[Barnette, 319 U.S. at 640.]*

---

[1] **joust**: competition.
[2] **First Amendment**: the part of the Bill of Rights added to the U.S. Constitution that deals with freedom of speech, among other freedoms.

**compulsion**
(kəm-pŭl´shən) *n.* forced obligation.

**MONITOR COMPREHENSION**
**Annotate:** Mark the words that Brennan cites from another legal document.

**Interpret** Reread the citation. Paraphrase its meaning.

Justice William J. Brennan

**EVALUATE EVIDENCE**

**Annotate:** Mark the claim Brennan makes about the consequences of the decision.

**Interpret:** How does Brennan use a court case from the past (*Abrams* v. *United States*) to support this claim?

**implicit**
(ĭm-plĭs´ĭt) *adj.* understood, but not expressed.

**reaffirmation**
(rē´ăf-ər-mā´shən) n. the act of verifying or endorsing again.

3   We are fortified in today's conclusion by our conviction that forbidding criminal punishment for conduct such as Johnson's will not endanger the special role played by our flag or the feelings it inspires. To paraphrase Justice Holmes, we submit that nobody can suppose that this one gesture of an unknown man will change our Nation's attitude towards its flag [*Abrams* v. *United States*]. Indeed, Texas' argument that the burning of an American flag "is an act having a high likelihood to cause a breach of the peace," and its statute's **implicit** assumption that physical mistreatment of the flag will lead to "serious offense," tend to confirm that the flag's special role is not in danger; if it were, no one would riot or take offense because a flag had been burned.

4   We are tempted to say, in fact, that the flag's deservedly cherished place in our community will be strengthened, not weakened, by our holding today. Our decision is a **reaffirmation** of the principles of freedom and inclusiveness that the flag best reflects, and of the

conviction that our toleration of criticism such as Johnson's is a sign and source of our strength. Indeed, one of the proudest images of our flag, the one immortalized in our own national anthem, is of the bombardment it survived at Fort McHenry.[3] It is the Nation's **resilience**, not its rigidity, that Texas sees reflected in the flag—and it is that resilience that we reassert today.

5      The way to preserve the flag's special role is not to punish those who feel differently about these matters. It is to persuade them that they are wrong.

---

[3] **Fort McHenry**: War of 1812 battle site in Baltimore. In 1814, poet Francis Scott Key, being held prisoner on a ship nearby, was elated to see the American flag flying there and wrote the poem that became "The Star-Spangled Banner." to celebrate this American victory over the British.

## NOTICE & NOTE

**LANGUAGE CONVENTIONS**
**Annotate:** Underline the two phrases set off by commas in the first sentence of paragraph 4.

**Respond:** Reread the sentence without these phrases. What do they add to Brennan's meaning?

**resilience**
(rĭ-zĭl´yəns) *n.* ability to return to a normal state after a change or an injury.

## CHECK YOUR UNDERSTANDING

Answer these questions before moving on to the **Analyze the Text** section on the following page.

**1** What did the Supreme Court decide should happen to people who burn the flag?

**A** They should be punished for violating the First Amendment.

**B** Their punishment should be determined by state laws, not by the Supreme Court.

**C** Their punishment depends on which of the conflicting rights in the First Amendment is more important.

**D** They should not be punished because their actions are protected under the First Amendment.

**2** What is the purpose of the italicized words such as *Barnette* in the text?

**F** They identify the authors of Brennan's research sources.

**G** They identify important court decisions related to this decision.

**H** They are the names of previously charged flag burners.

**J** They list officials who disagree about whether flag burning is legal.

**3** Which of these describes Brennan's opinion of the American flag?

**A** It plays a special role in American society.

**B** Strong laws should protect it from disrespect.

**C** The government does not have reason to protect it.

**D** It is of no worth.

**RESPOND**

## ANALYZE THE TEXT

Support your responses with evidence from the text. 📓 NOTEBOOK

1. **Connect** What earlier points of law does Justice Brennan use to support the Supreme Court's opinion in this case? How does the information from previous cases support his claims?

2. **Compare** In its argument to make flag burning a criminal offense, what consequences did Texas predict might happen? How did the Supreme Court interpret the significance of these possible events?

3. **Cite Evidence** How does Justice Brennan support the idea that "the flag's deservedly cherished place in our community will be strengthened, not weakened" by the ruling?

4. **Analyze** How is the image of the flag flying over Fort McHenry related to the central idea of the court opinion?

5. **Infer** Justice Brennan repeatedly uses the word *resilience* to refer to the United States. What does the repetition of this word suggest about his view of the Constitution?

## RESEARCH

**RESEARCH TIP**
Many First Amendment cases have been controversial, and some online sources portray a biased, or one-sided, view. To find unbiased summaries of court decisions, look for text on educational (*.edu*) sites or official Supreme Court sites.

Read the text of the First Amendment on the next page. The U.S. courts have interpreted the language of the amendment many times through the nation's history. Conduct research to find examples of cases in which people challenged court rulings on the basis of the First Amendment. Use an organizer like the one below to summarize your findings by recording which rights in those cases are specifically covered under the First Amendment and which rights are not covered. Share what you learn with a partner.

| RIGHTS COVERED BY FIRST AMENDMENT | RIGHTS NOT COVERED BY FIRST AMENDMENT |
|---|---|
|  |  |

**Extend** With your partner, discuss your opinion whether First Amendment rights have been violated in these scenarios:

❏ A business refuses to allow posting of political flyers.

❏ Someone has been arrested for criticizing a politician's decisions.

❏ A student has been disciplined for insulting another student.

## CREATE AND PRESENT

**Write a Comparison** The Supreme Court determines whether actions are constitutional. In *Texas* v. *Johnson*, the Court's ruling centered around the First Amendment. Compare ideas in Brennan's court opinion and this amendment.

> **First Amendment** *Congress shall make no law respecting an establishment of religion, or prohibiting the free exercise thereof; or abridging the freedom of speech, or of the press; or the right of the people peaceably to assemble, and to petition the Government for a redress of grievances.*

❏ Identify concepts that are discussed in both the Supreme Court's majority opinion and the First Amendment. How does each document address the concepts?

❏ In a paragraph, compare and contrast the two documents. Support your points with examples from both texts.

**Create a Multimedia Presentation** You will present to the class what you have learned about the First Amendment.

❏ Review your annotations and notes about the selection from *Texas* v. *Johnson Majority Opinion*, the text of the First Amendment, and your research findings about the amendment. Summarize the rights that it covers and does not cover.

❏ Choose examples to support your summary. Cite cases that dealt with the First Amendment. Save images that illustrate the cases.

❏ Using the information you have gathered, put together a short presentation that will last under five minutes. Summarize your ideas, and then present images and descriptions of exemplary court cases.

For more on using textual evidence in a comparison, visit the **Writing Studio**.

 For more on using media in a presentation, visit the **Speaking and Listening Studio**.

## RESPOND TO THE ESSENTIAL QUESTION

**?** How do we engage with others while staying true to ourselves?

**Gather Information** Review your annotations and notes on the selection from *Texas* v. *Johnson Majority Decision* and highlight those that help answer the Essential Question. Then, add relevant details to your Response Log.

At the end of the unit, use your notes to write a personal essay.

**ACADEMIC VOCABULARY**
As you write and discuss what you learned from the speech, be sure to use the Academic Vocabulary words. Check off each of the words that you use.

❏ **discriminate**

❏ **diverse**

❏ **inhibit**

❏ **intervene**

❏ **rational**

**WORD BANK**

compulsion

reaffirmation

resilience

implicit

## CRITICAL VOCABULARY

**Practice and Apply**  Choose which Critical Vocabulary word is most closely associated with the situation in each sentence.

**1.** Citizens of a town ravaged by hurricanes work together to rebuild each other's homes.

_____

**2.** Abby asks to borrow the car, but her father raises an eyebrow and looks at her pile of homework.

_____

**3.** Our grandparents renewed their wedding vows on their 45th anniversary.

_____

**4.** Anthony wants to go hang out with friends, but has to babysit his little brother instead.

_____

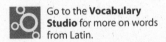 Go to the **Vocabulary Studio** for more on words from Latin.

## VOCABULARY STRATEGY:
## Words from Latin

The Critical Vocabulary words *compulsion, reaffirmation,* and *resilience* have Latin roots. Knowing the meaning of a root helps you define the various words derived from it. This chart defines several Latin roots and shows English words that derive from them.

| LATIN ROOT AND ITS MEANING | RELATED WORDS |
|---|---|
| *firmus* means "strong" | reaffirmation, firmament |
| *resilire* means "to leap back" | resilience |
| *pulsus* means "to drive, to force" | compulsion, compel |

**Practice and Apply**  Use a separate page to explore these roots. For each row of the chart, identify one new word that belongs to the word family. (You may use a dictionary if needed.) For each word you choose, follow these steps:

**1.** Write a definition that incorporates the meaning of the Latin root.

**2.** Identify the part of speech.

**3.** Use the word in a sentence that reflects its meaning.

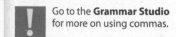

## LANGUAGE CONVENTIONS:
## Commas to Set Off Phrases and Clauses

A **clause** is a group of words that contains a subject and a verb. There are two types of clauses: the **independent clause**, which can stand alone as a sentence, and the **dependent clause**, which cannot stand alone as a sentence. Dependent clauses act as modifiers that add meaning to independent clauses. Dependent clauses often begin with subordinating conjunctions: *as if, as, since, than, that, though, until, whenever, where, while, who,* and *why.*

**Phrases** include prepositional phrases, such as *across the room* and *on the kitchen counter.*

Separate independent clauses in a compound sentence with a comma and a coordinating conjunction, or use a semicolon if there is no conjunction.

> **Brennan respects the flag, but he defends Johnson's right to burn it.**
> **Brennan respects the flag; he defends Johnson's right to burn it.**

In general, if a clause or phrase appears at the beginning of a sentence, or if it appears in the middle of the sentence, it should be set off with commas. Clauses and phrases at the ends of sentences usually are not set off with commas. Look at the following examples:

> **The judges ruled in favor of Johnson because of the First Amendment.**
> **Because of the First Amendment, the judges ruled in favor of Johnson.**
> **The judges, because of the First Amendment, ruled in favor of Johnson.**

**Practice and Apply**  Write a one-paragraph summary of the court case *Texas v. Johnson* and the Supreme Court's decision. Use prepositional phrases and dependent clauses. (Hint: Use the words *as if, as, since, than, that, though, until, whenever, where, while, who,* and *why* to start dependent clauses.) Vary the placement of phrases and clauses within your sentences. Trade your summary with a partner, and check each other's use of commas.

> **!**  Go to the **Grammar Studio** for more on using commas.

EDITORIAL

# AMERICAN FLAG STANDS FOR TOLERANCE

by **Ronald J. Allen**
pages 53–55

## COMPARE ARGUMENTS

Now that you have read the court opinion from *Texas* v. *Johnson Majority Opinion*, you will read a newspaper editorial—a type of argument—that was written in response to the *Texas* v. *Johnson* decision. Compare Allen's argument with the court's opinion. Also consider how the purpose and audience for the texts differ. After you review both selections, you will complete an independent project.

**?** **ESSENTIAL QUESTION:**

How do we engage with others while staying true to ourselves?

COURT OPINION

# *from* TEXAS *v.* JOHNSON MAJORITY OPINION

by **William J. Brennan**
pages 43–45

# American Flag Stands for Tolerance

## QUICK START

What is the appropriate way to react if people have opinions that you find hateful or disrespectful? How can you respond in a way that keeps the disagreement from turning into a fight? Discuss this dilemma in a small group.

## EVALUATE AN ARGUMENT

Editorials present an author's **argument** about a contested issue. A well-crafted argument contains the following elements:

| ELEMENT OF ARGUMENT | DESCRIPTION |
|---|---|
| Claim | A statement of the overall opinion |
| Reasons and Evidence | Data, anecdotes, facts, and other examples that support the claim |
| Counterclaims and Counterarguments | Acknowledgment of reasons an opponent might disagree and arguments against those reasons |
| Concessions and Rebuttals | Concession: agreement that a counterargument is valid; rebuttal: argument against the counterclaim |
| Conclusion | Usually a call to action for the reader |

As you read "American Flag Stands for Tolerance," evaluate how Allen includes the above elements of an argument.

## ANALYZE RHETORIC

Persuasive authors often use **rhetoric**, or specific words and language structures that make a message memorable. They also use **appeals** to a reader's emotions, sense of logic, and sense of justice (beliefs about what is right and wrong). Common rhetorical devices include the following:

- **Parallelism:** a form of repetition in which a grammatical pattern is repeated to create rhythm, link ideas, or evoke emotions
- **Antithesis:** placing two ideas side-by-side to show contrast between them
- **Shifts:** changes in mood, attitude, or point, often signaled by words such as *but, however,* and *although*
- **Logical Fallacy:** an error in reasoning that undermines an argument or renders it invalid

As you read, identify how Allen uses rhetoric to make his points memorable.

### GENRE ELEMENTS: ARGUMENT

- states the author's stance on an issue
- supports the opinion with relevant evidence
- addresses potential counterclaims
- ends with a call to action

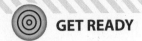 

## CRITICAL VOCABULARY

To preview the Critical Vocabulary words, match each word to its definition.

| | |
|---|---|
| 1. icon | a. symbol of deeply held values |
| 2. sanctity | b. traditionally accepted codes and customs |
| 3. dogma | c. sacredness or ultimate importance |

## LANGUAGE CONVENTIONS

**Dashes** A **dash** is a punctuation mark that sets a phrase or clause off from other parts of a sentence. Dashes can often take the place of commas, parentheses, or colons and allow a writer freedom to vary the flow of a text. Look at these examples of dashes used in place of other punctuation marks.

Instead of a colon:

**Thus, we do have one official dogma—each American may think and express anything he wants.**

Instead of parentheses:

**The American flag—which is one of our most important symbols—is the subject.**

Instead of commas:

**We wonder—soon after the court case has been decided—what to do next.**

As you read "American Flag Stands for Tolerance," notice how the author uses dashes to set off ideas.

## ANNOTATION MODEL

**NOTICE & NOTE**

Here is how you might annotate to help you identify how Allen uses an appeal to emotion—the reader's patriotism—as a rhetorical device.

The American flag is a cherished symbol of our national aspirations. It is the closest object to a national icon, rivaled only by the Constitution and the Declaration of Independence. Given the widespread and deeply felt reverence for this symbol of what we perceive to be the best of our civilization, what is the harm in insisting upon a modicum of respect for it?

*Allen appeals to readers' patriotism with words like "cherished symbol" and "reverence."*

*Mentioning the Declaration of Independence and the Constitution connects with other things Americans value.*

## BACKGROUND

*In the court case* Texas v. Johnson, *the Supreme Court decided, with a vote of 5 justices against 4, that burning the flag was an action protected by the First Amendment to the Constitution. The close vote among the judges reflected the opinion of people around the country. Controversy erupted at the ruling, with people still arguing on all sides. We can read newspaper reports, including editorials, from the time to understand the public sentiment. Law professor* **Ronald J. Allen** *published this editorial in the* Chicago Tribune *on June 30, 1989, in response to the* Texas v. Johnson *decision and the uproar that it caused.*

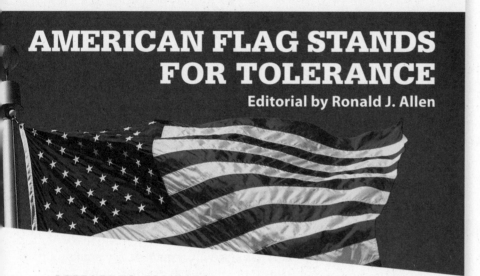

# AMERICAN FLAG STANDS FOR TOLERANCE

### Editorial by Ronald J. Allen

## PREPARE TO COMPARE

*As you read, consider your own opinion of the issue. How might your ideas defend or challenge those Allen presents? Mark ideas you agree or disagree with as you read, noting your thoughts on the page.*

1   In a controversial decision, the Supreme Court, by the closest possible margin of a 5-to-4 vote, held that a person has a right to express disagreement with governmental policies by burning the American flag. In a decision at least as controversial, the leadership of the People's Republic of China decided that citizens who peacefully express disagreement with government policies may be slaughtered.[1] On the surface, these two events may seem to bear little relationship to one another, but deep and fundamental lessons can be drawn from their comparison.

2   The American flag is a cherished symbol of our national aspirations. It is the closest object to a national **icon**, rivaled only by the Constitution and the Declaration of Independence. Given the widespread and deeply felt reverence for this symbol of what we perceive to be the best of our civilization, what is the harm

### Notice & Note

You can use the side margins to notice and note signposts in the text.

### ANALYZE RHETORIC
**Annotate:** Mark two ideas in paragraph 1 that the author places together in order to contrast them.

**Analyze:** What is the effect of the author's use of antithesis here?

**icon**
(ī′kăn) *n.* symbol of deeply held values

---

[1] **People's Republic of China . . . slaughtered:** In June 1989, government tanks fired on citizens who had gathered in Beijing's Tiananmen Square to demand democratic reforms. Hundreds were killed.

EVALUATE AN ARGUMENT

**Annotate:** Mark the claim Allen makes in paragraph 3.

**Analyze:** How does Allen support this claim?

**sanctity**
(săngk´tĭ-tē) *n.* sacredness or ultimate importance.

**WORD GAPS**

**Notice & Note:** Mark a word in paragraph 4 that might interfere with your understanding.

**Interpret:** How can you determine what this word means?

**dogma**
(dôg´mə) *n.* principles or beliefs that an authority insists are true.

in insisting upon a modicum[2] of respect for it? After all, no one can seriously equate a prohibition on flag burning with the imposition of governmental orthodoxy[3] in political speech. Any messages that burning the flag might convey easily can be communicated in other ways. Those are powerful points, deserving the greatest respect. If not rebutted,[4] they compel the conclusion that the Supreme Court was wrong in its decision.

3    The Supreme Court was not wrong. Indeed, a decision contrary to the one reached would have been a definitive step away from our national aspirations. A commitment to the intertwined freedoms of conscience and expression is at the core of those aspirations. What most distinguishes our civilization from both its predecessors and its contemporary competitors is a belief in the **sanctity** of the human conscience. Each individual is to have the freedom to develop by his or her own lights, and not by the command of officialdom. That requires not just the right to be let alone, but also the right to communicate with, to learn from and test views in conversations.

4    It is, thus, no surprise that the First Amendment is where it is in the Bill of Rights, for it is first in importance. A concomitant[5] of the commitment to freedom of conscience, in a sense its mirror image, is that no one has better access to truth than anyone else. Official **dogma** is not better (perhaps no worse) than the beliefs of private citizens.

5    The dissenters[6] in the flag-burning case and their supporters might at this juncture note an irony in my argument. My point is that freedom of conscience and expression is at the core of our self-conception and that commitment to it requires the rejection of official dogma. But how is that admittedly dogmatic belief different from any other dogma, such as the one inferring that freedom of expression stops at the border of the flag?

6    The crucial distinction is that the commitment to freedom of conscience and expression states the simplest and least self-contradictory principle that seems to capture our aspirations. Any other principle is hopelessly at odds with our commitment to freedom of conscience. The controversy surrounding the flag-burning case makes the case well.

7    The controversy will rage precisely because burning the flag is such a powerful form of communication. Were it not, who would care? Thus were we to embrace a prohibition on such communication, we would be saying that the First Amendment protects expression only when no one is offended. That would mean that this aspect of the First Amendment would be of virtually no consequence. It would protect a person only when no protection was needed. Thus, we do have one official dogma—each American may

---

[2] **modicum:** small amount offered as a symbol or gesture.
[3] **orthodoxy:** traditionally accepted codes and customs.
[4] **rebutted:** opposed using reasons and evidence.
[5] **concomitant:** one that occurs or exists concurrently with another.
[6] **dissenters:** those who disagree or refuse to accept.

think and express anything he wants. The exception is expression that involves the risk of injury to others and the destruction of someone else's property. Neither was present in this case.

8   At the core of what the flag symbolizes, then, is tolerance. More than anything else, the flag stands for free expression of ideas, no matter how distasteful. The ultimate irony would have been to punish views expressed by burning the flag that stands for the right to those expressions.

9   . . . Perhaps, though, there is another way to look at it—to acknowledge that not even such a fundamental value as the commitment to freedom of conscience should be free from controversy. With controversy comes debate, enlightenment and renewed commitment. Perhaps, then, we are in the court's debt for not treating the flag-burning case like the simple case it is. Let the controversy rage. After all, it is in robust debate that we are most true to ourselves.

**LANGUAGE CONVENTIONS**
**Annotate:** Mark the dash in paragraph 9.

**Analyze:** How does the dash link two ideas in this sentence?

## CHECK YOUR UNDERSTANDING

Answer these questions before moving on to the **Analyze the Text** section on the following page.

1  What is Allen's stance on people who burn the American flag?

   **A** No one should be offended when they burn it.

   **B** They are making an empty gesture and should be ignored.

   **C** They should be punished by the government.

   **D** Their offensive act is protected by the First Amendment.

2  Allen believes that, above all, the flag symbolizes tolerance and —

   **F** love

   **G** patriotism

   **H** free expression

   **J** law and order

3  What does Allen see as a bright point in the controversy?

   **A** The debate it inspires

   **B** The attention it gives the flag

   **C** The increasing support for the military

   **D** The growing tide of people willing to protest

## ANALYZE THE TEXTS

Support your responses with evidence from the text. NOTEBOOK

1. **Infer** What words or phrases in paragraph 2 convey Allen's feelings about the flag? Does understanding his attitude make you feel that his argument is stronger or weaker? Why?

2. **Analyze** In his editorial, Allen talks about the "sanctity of the human conscience" and the "enlightenment" that comes from debate. Explain how the connotations of these words convey his tone.

3. **Analyze** Allen presents a counterargument involving respect for the flag at the beginning of the editorial. How does this contribute to the structure of his argument? How does he address the counterargument?

4. **Evaluate** A **logical fallacy** is an error in reasoning. Suppose Allen had included this sentence in his editorial: *Anyone who wants to throw flag burners in jail is obviously not a supporter of the Constitution.* In what way is this statement a fallacy? How would this sentence have affected Allen's argument?

5. **Notice & Note** Allen discriminates, or distinguishes, between what people *should* do and what they *should be allowed* to do. How does he reconcile this apparent contradiction in his argument?

## RESEARCH

**RESEARCH TIP**
It can be tempting to call a source biased if you disagree with its content. Likewise, it can be easy not to notice bias if you *agree* with a source's bias. To determine whether bias exists, ask yourself how a reader with different views from yours would view the text. Also, check a variety of credible sources.

Find four online sources that provide opinions or information on the topic of flag burning. Since anyone can post information on the Internet, it's important to analyze sources for **credibility**, or the quality of being trustworthy. For each source you find, ask yourself if it comes from an established organization and if the author's background gives him or her the expertise to address the topic accurately and responsibly. Look for signs of **bias**, or unfairly choosing one side over another, and possible **omissions**, or information purposely left out. Using a chart like the one below, keep track of your sources and describe their credibility.

| URL / SOURCE | OPINION OR MAIN IDEA | NOTES ON CREDIBILITY |
|---|---|---|
|  |  |  |
|  |  |  |
|  |  |  |
|  |  |  |

**Connect** Share an example of a credible online source with your partner. Explain what factors led you to believe that the author or authors are credible.

## CREATE AND PRESENT

**Write a Letter to the Editor** Editors of newspapers and magazines receive letters from the public expressing their reactions to the content of the publications. Some of these letters to the editor are published in future issues. Write a letter to a newspaper editor. In your letter, respond to "American Flag Stands for Tolerance."

Go to the **Writing Studio** for more on using a formal style in your letter.

- ❏ Use a business letter format and formal language that addresses an adult.
- ❏ At the beginning of your letter, state your opinion clearly.
- ❏ Cite evidence from the editorial to support your opinion.

**Debate the Issue** People are strongly divided on whether burning the flag should be protected as a form of free speech. You have read multiple opinions about the topic. Use your knowledge to form an opinion, and debate the issue.

Go to the **Speaking and Listening Studio** for more on listening and responding constructively.

- ❏ Write your opinion as a statement. Draw evidence from the sources you have read to support your opinion. List your pieces of evidence as bullet points for quick reference.
- ❏ Form debate teams. One side should argue "Burning the flag should be protected as free speech under the First Amendment." The other side should oppose this argument. If all the students in your class agree, choose a group to take the opposite side and find evidence to support it.
- ❏ Establish the rules of debate. Decide on the order in which people will speak. Assign roles, such as a moderator and panel members. When debating, listen attentively to others, and take notes if you think of something you want to say in response. Use a respectful tone, even when disagreeing with others. After the debate, reevaluate your opinion.

## RESPOND TO THE ESSENTIAL QUESTION

 How do we engage with others while staying true to ourselves?

**Gather Information** Review your annotations and notes on "American Flag Stands for Tolerance" and highlight those that help answer the Essential Question. Then, add relevant details to your Response Log.

At the end of the unit, use your notes to write a personal essay.

### ACADEMIC VOCABULARY

As you write and discuss what you learned from the argument, be sure to use the Academic Vocabulary words. Check off each of the words that you use.

- ❏ **discriminate**
- ❏ **diverse**
- ❏ **inhibit**
- ❏ **intervene**
- ❏ **rational**

Go to the **Vocabulary Studio** to learn more about connotations.

## CRITICAL VOCABULARY

**Practice and Apply** Answer each question by incorporating the meaning of the Critical Vocabulary word.

**WORD BANK**
icon
dogma
sanctity

1. Which do you consider more of an **icon,** a statue of a past national leader or a very popular musician?

_____

2. Which do you think better exemplifies **sanctity,** a mayor being sworn into office or a solemn religious service?

_____

3. Who is more attached to **dogma,** a politician who votes against everything or a parent who refuses to change your curfew?

_____

## VOCABULARY STRATEGY:
### Connotations

A **connotation** is a feeling or value associated with a word. These associations are different from the word's dictionary definition. For example, *cheap* and *inexpensive* have the same meaning, but people tend to have a more negative view of something described as *cheap* than something described as *inexpensive*. Persuasive writers often use connotations to their advantage. **Loaded language** is an effort to appeal to emotions and convince others to share an opinion. Look at the following example:

**The American flag is a <u>cherished</u> symbol of our national aspirations. (paragraph 2)**

The neutral term *well-liked* has a meaning similar to that of the word *cherished*, but Allen's language would not appeal to readers' emotions in the same way if he called the flag a "well-liked symbol." The positive connotation of the word *cherished* communicates just how loved the American flag is.

**Practice and Apply** Find these words in the editorial: *reverence* (paragraph 2), *crucial* (paragraph 6), *rage* (paragraph 7). Working with a partner, discuss how the connotations of the words affect the author's meaning.

1. Look up each word and its synonyms.

2. Try using one of the synonyms in place of the word. How does it affect the meaning of the sentence?

3. Discuss and write down the purpose of the author's word choices. Base your answers on the words' connotations.

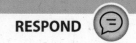
## LANGUAGE CONVENTIONS:
### Dashes

Like several other forms of punctuation, dashes cause readers to pause. Dashes and pairs of dashes are used to set off or emphasize ideas in place of commas, parentheses, or colons.

Here are two common uses of dashes.

Go to the **Grammar Studio** for more on dashes.

| PURPOSE | EXAMPLE |
|---|---|
| to set off a definition or explanation | The First Amendment—which addresses the right to free speech, among other things—was cited in the case. |
| to emphasize a word, a series of words, a phrase, or a clause | This flag—the banner of *all* Americans—matters. |

**Practice and Apply** Find two sentences in your letter to the editor that you can make more effective with the use of dashes. Rewrite your sentences and share them with a partner. Work together to discuss how the dashes affect the way the sentences are read.

*from* **TEXAS *v.* JOHNSON MAJORITY OPINION**
Court Opinion
by William J. Brennan

**AMERICAN FLAG STANDS FOR TOLERANCE**
Argument by Ronald J. Allen

# Collaborate & Compare

## COMPARE ARGUMENTS

While reading you may have noted that, in his editorial, Allen agrees with the Supreme Court's majority decision. In this way, the main opinions that are expressed in the texts overlap. The two authors have different purposes for writing their texts, however, and they consider different audiences when putting together their thoughts.

In a small group, reread both texts to identify clues that indicate who the intended audience is and why each author is writing. Keep track of these clues as shown below. Use your completed chart to draft a statement about the purpose and audience your group identified for each piece based on the clues.

| TEXT | CLUES ABOUT PURPOSE | CLUES ABOUT AUDIENCE |
|---|---|---|
| from *Texas v. Johnson Majority Opinion* | **We decline, therefore, . . .** | *[Barnette, 319 U.S. at 640.]* |
| "American Flag Stands for Tolerance" | | |

## ANALYZE THE TEXTS

Discuss these questions in your group.

1. **Compare** What ideas are expressed in both the court opinion and the argument? Which selection's argument do you find more convincing? Why?

2. **Evaluate** Does one author seem more credible than the other? Why?

3. **Connect** Arguments about the First Amendment are ongoing. Name a recent event that caused a debate about people's rights. How do you think the authors of these texts would respond to the debate?

4. **Analyze** Compare the tone of the two selections. What makes one selection more serious and thoughtful and the other more emotional?

## RESEARCH AND DISCUSS

Debates, such as those about flag burning, tend to involve heated emotions. People feel passionate about their opinions, and they can take dissenting opinions personally. **De-escalation** refers to strategies that prevent conflicts from getting out of control.

You may have de-escalated a fight between friends by talking to them calmly and pointing out that their positions are both legitimate. In debates about politics, de-escalation keeps everyone respectful and makes it possible to find solutions.

Research de-escalation techniques, and instruct others on what to do when they encounter an offensive opponent.

1. **Research Techniques** Research what experts do to de-escalate heated conflicts. Take notes on recommended strategies that you think might be effective.

**RESEARCH TIP**
To find strong sources, begin with an Internet search using a keyword such as "de-escalate" and check for sources from reputable sites.

2. **Create a Procedure** Using your notes, write a step-by-step plan for what someone should do when encountering someone who is engaging in a legal, but offensive, activity or expression.

3. **Give Instructions** Role-play a scenario in which you step in to help two people who are involved in a tense, rapidly escalating situation. Give them instructions on how to shift to a calm and respectful conversation. Then, trade roles and follow instructions given by another student. Finally, reflect on your role and the process you used.

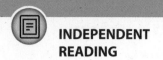
How do we engage with others while staying true to ourselves?

# Reader's Choice

**Setting a Purpose**   Select one or more of these options from your eBook to continue your exploration of the Essential Question.

- Read the descriptions to see which text grabs your interest.
- Think about which genres you enjoy reading.

## Notice & Note

In this unit, you practiced noticing and noting these signposts: **Tough Questions, Memory Moment,** and **Words of the Wiser.** As you read independently, these signposts and others will aid your understanding. Below are the key questions to ask when you read literature and nonfiction.

| Reading Literature: Stories, Poems, and Plays | | |
|---|---|---|
| **Signpost** | **Anchor Question** | **Lesson** |
| **Contrasts and Contradictions** | Why did the character act that way? | p. 145 |
| **Aha Moment** | How might this change things? | p. 394 |
| **Tough Questions** | What does this make me wonder about? | p. 2 |
| **Words of the Wiser** | What's the lesson for the character? | p. 3 |
| **Again and Again** | Why might the author keep bringing this up? | p. 145 |
| **Memory Moment** | Why is this memory important? | p. 3 |

| Reading Nonfiction: Essays, Articles, and Arguments | | |
|---|---|---|
| **Signpost** | **Anchor Question(s)** | **Lesson** |
| **Big Questions** | What surprised me?<br>What did the author think I already knew?<br>What challenged, changed, or confirmed what I already knew? | p. 220<br>p. 319<br>p. 74 |
| **Contrasts and Contradictions** | What is the difference, and why does it matter? | p. 318 |
| **Extreme or Absolute Language** | Why did the author use this language? | p. 221 |
| **Numbers and Stats** | Why did the author use these numbers or amounts? | p. 75 |
| **Quoted Words** | Why was this person quoted or cited, and what did this add? | p. 221 |
| **Word Gaps** | Do I know this word from someplace else?<br>Does it seem like technical talk for this topic?<br>Do clues in the sentence help me understand the word? | p. 75 |

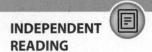
You can preview these texts in Unit 1 of your eBook.

Then, check off the text or texts that you select to read on your own.

**MEMOIR**

**from *The Pleasure of Reading***
Kamila Shamsie

*A writer from Pakistan reflects on how books helped her feel connected to the world when she was growing up.*

**POEM**

**Magic Island**
Cathy Song

*This poem explores how recent immigrants embrace a new culture without forgetting their past.*

**SHORT STORY**

**The Wife's Story**
Ursula K. Le Guin

*Is the narrator's husband, who has begun acting strangely, really one of the group, or has he become something else?*

**ARGUMENT**

**America: The Multinational Society**
Ishmael Reed

*What does it really mean to be American? A poet and novelist considers his own experiences.*

**Collaborate and Share** Discuss with a partner what you learned from at least one of your independent readings.

- Give a brief synopsis or summary of the text.
- Describe any signposts that you noticed in the text and explain what they revealed to you.
- Describe what you most enjoyed or found most challenging about the text. Give specific examples.
- Decide whether you would recommend the text to others. Why or why not?

 Go to the **Reading Studio** for more resources on **Notice & Note.**

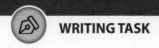

# Write a Personal Essay

Go to the **Writing Studio** for help writing a narrative such as a personal essay.

This unit focuses on how we relate to people who are different from us. For this writing task, you will write a personal essay about engaging with others despite differences. A personal essay is a work of nonfiction in which an author reflects on the significance of an experience. For an example of a well-written personal essay you can use as a mentor text, review the essay "By Any Other Name."

As you write your essay, you will want to look at the notes you made in your Response Log after reading the texts in this unit.

## Writing Prompt

**Read** the information in the box below.

*This is the topic or context for your essay.*

> Engaging with those who are different from you can be difficult, but it can also create a new understanding of who you are.

**Think** carefully about the following question.

*This is the Essential Question for the unit. How would you answer this question, based on the texts in this unit?*

> How do we engage with others while staying true to ourselves?

*Think about events in your own experience that relate to this topic.*

**Write** a personal essay that explores a time when you had to decide how to interact with others.

*Review these points as you write and again when you finish. Make any needed changes or edits.*

Be sure to—

☐ write an introduction that will grab the reader's interest

☐ describe a single, meaningful experience in vivid detail

☐ use appropriate verb tenses to orient the reader in time

☐ conclude with the insight you gained from the experience

# 1 Plan

The event you will choose to write about could be anything, such as a time you stood up for what you believed, or a moment when you quietly realized something about yourself. The event doesn't have to be big, but the way you reacted should lead to self-discovery.

Begin brainstorming ideas using the chart below. For each event you list, note its significance and the kinds of readers who would get the most out of your story. Your purpose for writing will be to reflect on your experience and share it with this audience to help them learn an important lesson.

| PERSONAL ESSAY BRAINSTORMING CHART | | |
|---|---|---|
| **Experience or Event** | **What I Learned from It** | **Who Would Be Interested?** |
| | | |
| | | |
| | | |

Go to **Writing as a Process** for help with planning and drafting.

## Notice & Note

### From Reading to Writing

As you plan your personal essay, apply what you've learned about signposts in your own writing. Think about how you can incorporate a **Memory Moment** into your essay.

Go to the **Reading Studio** for more resources on **Notice & Note**.

Use the notes from your Response Log as you plan your essay.

**Background Reading** Review the notes you have taken in your Response Log after reading the texts in this unit. The relationships explored in those texts may give you ideas about what experience you want to share in your essay.

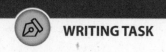 Go to **Writing as a Process: Task, Purpose, and Audience** for help choosing details that appeal to your audience.

**Develop Details** To help you choose the most promising idea from your brainstorming chart, consider your readers. While reading some memoirs can be as exciting as watching someone look at themselves in the mirror, *your* personal essay will be much more interesting. How? Because you'll plan vivid details and think about your audience every step of the way. You'll also take care to orient your reader about when, where, and why the event happened. Use the chart below to map out your ideas.

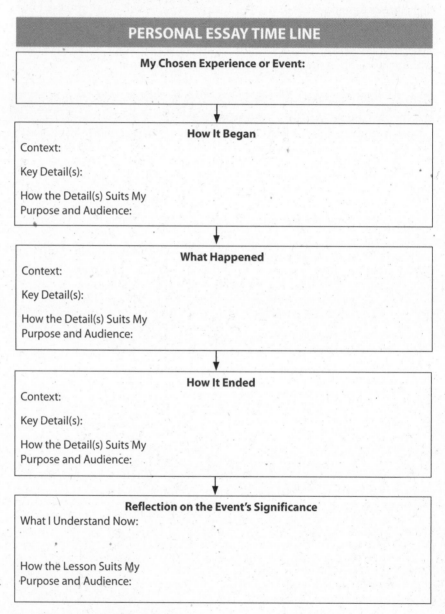

**PERSONAL ESSAY TIME LINE**

**My Chosen Experience or Event:**

**How It Began**

Context:

Key Detail(s):

How the Detail(s) Suits My Purpose and Audience:

**What Happened**

Context:

Key Detail(s):

How the Detail(s) Suits My Purpose and Audience:

**How It Ended**

Context:

Key Detail(s):

How the Detail(s) Suits My Purpose and Audience:

**Reflection on the Event's Significance**

What I Understand Now:

How the Lesson Suits My Purpose and Audience:

## ② **Develop a Draft**

 You might prefer to draft your essay online to make it easier to access from multiple locations.

Now, you're ready to begin drafting your personal essay. Refer to your time line as well as any notes you took as you read the texts in the unit to help guide you as you write. Use word-processing software or an online writing app to make it easier to reword ideas or move sentences around later when you are ready to revise your first draft.

## Use the Mentor Text

▶ *Genre Characteristics*

Although a personal essay often describes an event, it does not simply tell a story. The writer describes his or her feelings at the time, as well as thoughts and insights that came later. Note the way the writer reflects on the changing of her name in "By Any Other Name."

> That first day at school is still, when I think of it, a remarkable one. At that age, if one's name is changed, one develops a curious form of dual personality. I remember having a certain detached and disbelieving concern in the actions of "Cynthia," but certainly no responsibility.

*The author comments on an event she has described, choosing vivid words like "remarkable" and "disbelieving" to tell what she thinks about it now and how it made her feel at the time.*

**Apply What You've Learned** As you describe your life experience, comment on its meaning for you in order to help the reader understand your reactions.

▶ *Author's Craft*

An author may describe a sequence of events in time order, also known as chronological order. This is an easy way to help readers understand how the ideas are connected. Look at how the author uses time clues like *during* and *after* in the following example to make the order of events clear.

> At school, we rested for a short time on low, folding cots on the veranda, and then we were expected to play games. During the hot part of the afternoon we played indoors, and after the shadows had begun to lengthen and the slight breeze of the evening had come up, we moved outside to the wide courtyard.

*The author also uses the time clues "for a short time" and "then" to indicate the order of events.*

**Apply What You've Learned** The order of events in your essay should be clear. Use words and phrases that help the reader follow what is happening.

## ③ Revise

Go to **Writing as a Process** for help with revising and editing your essay.

**On Your Own** Once you've captured, sequenced, and elaborated your ideas in a draft, you need to reread what you've written with a fresh eye. Especially since you're writing about your own experience, it may be difficult to read your draft objectively. Try reading it as though you know nothing about the people and events involved. The chart below notes specific elements of a personal essay that might need extra attention.

| REVISION GUIDE | | |
|---|---|---|
| **Ask Yourself** | **Tips** | **Revision Techniques** |
| **1. Does the introduction grab the reader's attention?** | **Highlight** an attention-getting detail or intriguing dialogue in the first paragraph. | **Add** a vivid detail or dialogue from the event to get readers right into the experience. |
| **2. Is a single event told in a clear sequence?** | **Underline** words and phrases that provide time and sequence clues. | **Add** words and phrases that make the sequence of events clear. |
| **3. Are relationships among people and events clear?** | **Circle** names of people, places or events. **Highlight** where each is defined or explained. | **Add** explanations about people, places, or events that make their connection to your experience clear. |
| **4. Do vivid details bring the event to life?** | **Underline** sensory language and specific details about the experience and its setting. | **Add** descriptive, sensory details about the place and the people. |
| **5. Does the essay reveal why the experience was significant?** | **Underline** comments, thoughts, and feelings in your conclusion. | **Add** statements and reflections that explain the event's significance. |

**ACADEMIC VOCABULARY**
As you conduct your peer review, try to use these words.

❑ **discriminate**

❑ **diverse**

❑ **inhibit**

❑ **intervene**

❑ **rational**

**With a Partner** After you have worked through the Revision Guide on your own, exchange papers with a partner. Evaluate each other's drafts in a peer review, first noting parts of the essay that you think work well. Then, share a few ideas about how your partner could better engage readers and accomplish his or her purpose in writing. Be sure to provide reasons and specific suggestions.

## 4 Edit

Once you have addressed the organization, development, and flow of ideas in your essay, you can look to improve the finer points of your draft. Edit for the proper use of standard English conventions and make sure to correct any misspellings or grammatical errors.

### Language Conventions

**Appropriate Verb Tenses** In "By Any Other Name," the author began in the present and told an event from the past that included flashbacks to prior events. Because a memoir or personal essay may not follow a strict chronological order, it's important to indicate the time using appropriate verb tenses:

- **Present tense verbs** indicate that an action is taking place now. You will probably use this tense when stating the insight of your essay and when commenting on your central event.

- **Past tense verbs** indicate that an action happened in the past. You will use this tense to narrate your central event.

- **Past perfect tense verbs** indicate that an action was completed before an action in the past. You will use this tense to set the context for your central event, telling what happened *before* that event.

> ! For more about verb tenses, visit the **Grammar Studio.**

The chart contains examples of verb tenses from "By Any Other Name."

| Verb Tense | Example from "By Any Other Name" |
|---|---|
| Present | I <u>remember</u> it all very clearly. |
| Past | Mother <u>looked</u> very distant and <u>was</u> silent a long time. |
| Past Perfect | Up to then, my mother <u>had refused</u> to send Premila to school . . . |

## 5 Publish

Finalize your essay, and choose the best way to share it with your audience. Consider these options:

- If your audience is your classmates, present your essay as a speech to the class, or post it as a blog on a classroom or school website.

- If your audience is one person, send your essay as a letter.

- If you wrote for members of a certain community—for example, younger children or people who enjoy the same activities or face the same challenges as you—ask permission to post your essay to a website or share it in person where appropriate.

Use the scoring guide to evaluate your essay.

## WRITING TASK SCORING GUIDE: PERSONAL ESSAY

| | Organization/Progression | Development of Ideas | Use of Language and Conventions |
|---|---|---|---|
| **4** | • The organization is effective and appropriate to the purpose.<br>• The essay thoroughly addresses the ideas in the writing prompt.<br>• Transitions or sequence words clearly show the relationship among ideas and events. | • The introduction catches the reader's attention with a vivid detail or quotation.<br>• The essay centers on a single, clearly narrated life experience.<br>• The writer makes appropriate and clarifying comments on the narration.<br>• The conclusion expresses the significance and impact of the narrated event with insight. | • Language and word choice are vivid, purposeful, and precise.<br>• Verb tenses consistently orient the reader in time.<br>• Spelling, capitalization, and punctuation are correct.<br>• Grammar and usage are correct. |
| **3** | • The organization is for the most part effective and appropriate to the purpose.<br>• The essay adequately responds to the writing prompt.<br>• A few more transitions or sequence words are needed to show relationships among ideas or events. | • The introduction gets right into the event or experience.<br>• The essay mostly focuses on one clearly narrated life experience.<br>• The writer comments on the narration at times.<br>• The conclusion clearly states the significance of the narrated event. | • Language is for the most part specific and clear.<br>• Verb tenses are mostly correct and consistent.<br>• Some spelling, capitalization, or punctuation mistakes are present but do not affect meaning.<br>• Some minor grammar or usage errors occur. |
| **2** | • The organization is generally chronological but sometimes unclear.<br>• The writing prompt is evident but only partially addressed in the essay.<br>• Few transitions or sequence words indicate relationships among ideas or events. | • The introduction tells what the essay will discuss but does not grab attention.<br>• The essay shares a vaguely narrated life experience and may go off on tangents.<br>• The writer's comments on the narration are absent or repetitive.<br>• The conclusion hints at or makes a vague statement about the meaning of the narrated event. | • Language is somewhat vague and unclear.<br>• Some errors in verb tense cause reader confusion.<br>• Several errors in spelling, capitalization, or punctuation are present.<br>• Several errors in grammar or usage appear. |
| **1** | • The organization is not appropriate to the purpose.<br>• The essay fails to address key points in the writing prompt.<br>• No transitions are used, making the sequence of events difficult to understand. | • The introduction is missing or confusing.<br>• The essay may share multiple, unrelated experiences or fail to share an experience.<br>• No commentary or analysis of events is included.<br>• The conclusion is missing or merely summarizes an event. | • Language is imprecise, incorrect, or inappropriate.<br>• Verb tenses fail to orient the reader in time.<br>• Many errors in spelling, capitalization, or punctuation are present.<br>• Many errors in grammar or usage cause confusion. |

# Reflect on the Unit

In writing your personal essay, you incorporated ideas and techniques you learned from the reading you have done in this unit. Now is a good time to reflect on what you have learned.

## Reflect on the Essential Question

- How do we engage with others while staying true to ourselves? How has your answer to this question changed since you started this unit?

- What are some examples from the texts you've read that show how people interact with others without compromising themselves?

## Reflect on Your Reading

- Which selections were the most interesting or surprising to you?

- From which selection did you learn the most about engaging with others?

## Reflect on the Writing Task

- What difficulties did you encounter while working on your personal essay? How might you avoid them next time?

- What part of the essay was easiest to write? What part was the hardest? Why?

- What improvements or additions did you make to your essay as you were revising?

**UNIT 1 SELECTIONS**

- "What, of This Goldfish, Would You Wish?"

- "By Any Other Name"

- "Without Title"

- from *Texas* v. *Johnson Majority Opinion*

- "American Flag Stands for Tolerance"

# HOW WE SEE THINGS

**?** *ESSENTIAL QUESTION:*

How does our point of view shape what we think we know?

"The question is not what you look at, but what you see."

Henry David Thoreau

## ACADEMIC VOCABULARY

Academic Vocabulary words are words you use when you discuss and write about texts. In this unit you will practice and learn five words.

☑ **differentiate** ❑ **incorporate** ❑ **mode** ❑ **orient** ❑ **perspective**

Study the Word Network to learn more about the word **differentiate**.

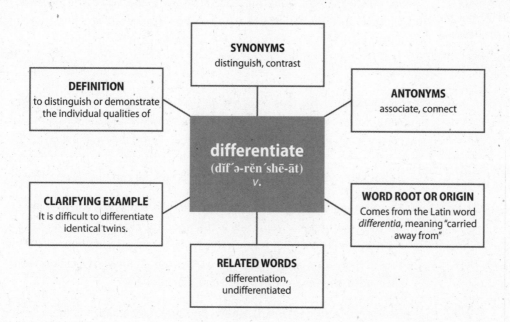

**SYNONYMS**
distinguish, contrast

**DEFINITION**
to distinguish or demonstrate the individual qualities of

**ANTONYMS**
associate, connect

**differentiate**
(dĭf´ə-rĕn´shē-āt)
v.

**CLARIFYING EXAMPLE**
It is difficult to differentiate identical twins.

**WORD ROOT OR ORIGIN**
Comes from the Latin word *differentia*, meaning "carried away from"

**RELATED WORDS**
differentiation, undifferentiated

**Write and Discuss** Discuss the completed Word Network with a partner, making sure to talk through all of the boxes until you both understand the word, its synonyms, antonyms, and related forms. Then, fill out Word Networks for the remaining four words. Use a dictionary or online resource to help you complete the activity.

 *Go online to access the Word Networks.*

## RESPOND TO THE ESSENTIAL QUESTION

In this unit, you will explore how individual perspective shapes our beliefs. As you read, you will revisit the **Essential Question** and gather your ideas about it in the **Response Log** that appears on page R2. At the end of the unit, you will have the opportunity to write a **short story** about how things are not as they first appear. Filling out the Response Log will help you prepare for this writing task.

 *You can also go online to access the Response Log.*

**UNIT 2
RESPONSE LOG**

Use this Response Log to record your ideas about how each of the texts in Unit 2 relates to or comments on the Essential Question.

**? Essential Question:**
How does our point of view shape what we think we know?

| | |
|---|---|
| Coming to Our Senses | |
| The Night Face Up | |
| Mirror | |
| The World as 100 People | |
| A Contribution to Statistics | |

R2 Student Resources

## COMING TO OUR SENSES

For more information on these and other signposts to Notice & Note, visit the **Reading Studio**.

You are about to read the science essay "Coming to Our Senses." In it, you will notice and note signposts that will give you clues about the ideas and information in the essay. Here are a question to ask and two signposts to look for as you read this science essay and other works of nonfiction.

Break down the parts of this **Big Question** as you read by asking yourself these smaller questions:

Does this fit what I already know about the topic?

How does this add to what I already knew?

Why doesn't this information match what I thought I knew?

**Big Questions**  Any time someone gives you information—in a speech or a nature show for example—you'll make some mental connections between what you already know and these new ideas. Without even thinking about it, you categorize these connections as things you already know, things that extend what you already know, and things that are completely new to you.

These categories apply to information you read, too. When you read about the world around you, your view of the world should change—even if it is in a very small way. By making connections to your own life, you will be able to read more carefully and attentively. Ask yourself this Big Question: *What challenged, changed, or confirmed what I already knew?*

Here is how a student might use this Big Question to mark and more deeply understand the author's ideas while reading "Coming to Our Senses":

> 2       When thought of as an ensemble of experimental tools, our senses enjoy an astonishing acuity and range of sensitivity. Our ears can register the thunderous launch of the space shuttle, yet they can also hear a mosquito buzzing a foot away from our head. Our sense of touch allows us to feel the magnitude of a bowling ball dropped on our big toe, just as we can tell when a one-milligram bug crawls along our arm.

| | |
|---|---|
| Which parts confirmed something you already knew or had experienced? | I've had some of these experiences with sound and touch. |
| How do these examples challenge what you thought about the acuity of human senses? | The details about bugs are striking because they're so specific. I never realized how fine-tuned our senses are. |

**Numbers and Stats** Think about the difference between a football team winning 24–21 and winning 49–0. What do you learn by looking at the score? What does the score indicate about the matchup?

As you read, look for meaning in numbers and statistics, including those spelled out as words. Not every number is important; you have to decide which numbers develop an idea and which merely provide context.

Here is how a student might mark Numbers and Stats in the essay:

> 3 . . . For example, if you increase the energy of a sound's volume by <u>a factor of 10</u>, your ears will judge this change to be rather small. Increase it by <u>a factor of 2</u> and you will barely notice. . . .

When you read and encounter phrases like these, pause to see if it's a **Numbers and Stats** signpost:

"The percentage of voters in their 20s rose by…"

"More than fifty million stars…"

"The runner improved her time by three minutes …"

**Anchor Question**
When you notice this signpost, ask: Why did the author use these numbers or amounts?

| What numbers or statistics are important or surprising? | Numbers related to increasing volume are surprising. |
|---|---|
| Why did the author include these numbers? | They illustrate ways that our senses are not very sensitive at all. |

**Word Gaps** Imagine that you're in a garden and notice a striped caterpillar. The gardener excitedly tells you that it's a monarch larva in its fifth instar, almost ready to shed its exoskeleton to pupate and metamorphose inside its chrysalis. If you don't know much about butterflies, this might sound like another language.

That's how reading is sometimes, when you come across multiple words you don't know. Don't give up. Instead, look for clues that help you decode them.

In this example, a student marked her own Word Gaps in the essay:

> 3 . . . The <u>stellar magnitude scale</u> of brightness, the well-known <u>acoustic decibel scale</u>, and the <u>seismic scale</u> for earthquake severity are each <u>logarithmic</u>, in part because of our <u>biological propensity</u> to see, hear, and feel the world that way. . . .

**Anchor Questions**
When you notice words that don't seem to make sense, ask yourself:

• Do I know this word from someplace else?

• Can I find clues in the sentence to help me understand the word?

• Does this seem like technical talk for experts on this topic?

| What words confuse me? Why? | All of these scientific terms are new to me. |
|---|---|
| What clues help me understand the words and the passage? | The footnotes give definitions and the text provides clues like "brightness" and "earthquake severity." |

# COMING TO OUR SENSES

Science Essay by **Neil deGrasse Tyson**

How does our point of view shape what we think we know?

## QUICK START

Some people use sensory deprivation to reduce stress. Would temporarily being deprived of information from your eyes, ears, and other senses be torture, or would it help you relax and focus? Share your ideas with a partner.

## ANALYZE DEVELOPMENT OF IDEAS

The central idea of a nonfiction text is developed through the use of a thesis, evidence, examples, and a conclusion. Analyzing the evidence and examples and how they work together can help you determine the thesis of an essay.

| PARTS OF AN ESSAY | EXAMPLE FROM TEXT |
|---|---|
| A **thesis** is the main idea the writer wants to make about a topic. It may be stated or inferred. | **Does there exist a way of knowing that transcends our biological interfaces with the environment?** |
| Strong **evidence** supports the idea. Each piece of evidence builds upon the next to develop the argument. | **In nearly every case, the job of scientific apparatus is to transcend the breadth and depth of our senses.** |
| **Examples** make the ideas interesting and relevant to the reader. They tell *who, what, when, where, why,* and *how*. | **If we were born with magnetic detectors, the compass would never have been invented because we wouldn't ever need one.** |
| A **conclusion** explains and summarizes the main idea developed by all of the evidence and examples. | **Discovering new ways of knowing has always heralded new windows on the universe . . . [We are] always coming to our senses.** |

## ANALYZE TONE

The author of this essay, Neil deGrasse Tyson, communicates his ideas with irony and sarcasm. Instead of a serious tone, Tyson uses humorous language, unconventional images, and references to everyday life to make his points about science and our senses in an entertaining way.

| EXAMPLES FROM TEXT | TYPE OF IRONY |
|---|---|
| **And here's a news headline none of us has seen, "Psychic Wins the Lottery."** | sarcastic reference to everyday life |
| **Without hardware to help our analysis, and without a particular urge to lick the stuff, all we can report back to the starship is, "Captain, it's a blob."** | unconventional image |
| **"If a tree falls in the forest and nobody is around to hear it, does it make a sound?" My best answer is, "How do you know it fell?" But that just gets people angry.** | humorous language |

### GENRE ELEMENTS: SCIENCE ESSAY

- the author introduces a key idea, often a surprising one

- uses analogies to move from familiar concepts to complex ideas

- may use scientific terminology or refer to established theories

- generally sticks to facts, not the author's opinions

## CRITICAL VOCABULARY

**acuity**    **stimuli**    **propensity**    **transcend**

To see how many Critical Vocabulary words you already know, use them to complete the sentences.

1. Working hard in school will help you to _____ many obstacles.

2. A hawk has remarkable visual _____ to help it see prey from afar.

3. The advanced theater students showed a strong _____ for acting.

4. We can detect even faint _____ , such as a bug landing on our arm.

## LANGUAGE CONVENTIONS

**Parallel Structure**  In this lesson, you will learn about **parallel structure,** the repetition of a pattern of words or phrases in a text. This technique helps writers organize and emphasize ideas.

Here is an example from the article:

**Our ears can register the thunderous launch of the space shuttle. . . . And our eyes can register the bright sandy terrain on a sunny beach. . . .**

The parallel constructions make a clear connection between the abilities of two different senses. As you read "Coming to Our Senses," note the author's use of parallel structure.

## ANNOTATION MODEL

**NOTICE & NOTE**

As you read, ask **Big Questions** and notice and note signposts, including **Numbers and Stats** and **Word Gaps**. Here is an example of how one reader responded to the opening paragraphs of "Coming to Our Senses":

Among our five senses, sight is the most special to us. Our eyes allow us to register information not only from across the room but also from across the universe. Without vision, the science of astronomy would never have been born and our capacity to measure our place in the universe would have been hopelessly stunted. Think of bats. Whatever bat secrets get passed from one generation to the next, you can bet that none of them is based on the appearance of the night sky.

*I never thought about it this way, but of course this makes sense.*

*Why does he say this? Can bats not see at all, or is vision just not important to them?*

## BACKGROUND

**Neil deGrasse Tyson** *(b. 1958) is an American astrophysicist and director of the Hayden Planetarium at the American Museum of Natural History. But he is best known for helping to explain science to the public through his many books and television appearances. Tyson is the author of* The Pluto Files: The Rise and Fall of America's Favorite Planet *and* Death by Black Hole and Other Cosmic Quandaries. *He also hosted the TV series* Cosmos: A Spacetime Odyssey *and the PBS miniseries* Origins *and* NOVA ScienceNOW.

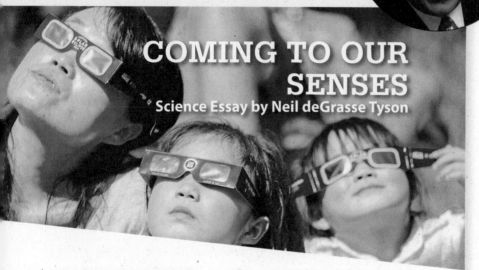

# COMING TO OUR SENSES

### Science Essay by Neil deGrasse Tyson

## SETTING A PURPOSE

*As you read, pay attention to the details the author provides about humans' five senses. Evaluate these details to help you determine the key ideas in the essay.*

> *Equipped with his five senses, man explores the universe around him and calls the adventure science.*
>
> —Edwin P. Hubble (1889–1953),
> *The Nature of Science*

1    Among our five senses, sight is the most special to us. Our eyes allow us to register information not only from across the room but also from across the universe. Without vision, the science of astronomy would never have been born and our capacity to measure our place in the universe would have been hopelessly stunted. Think of bats. Whatever bat secrets get passed from one generation to the next, you can bet that none of them is based on the appearance of the night sky.

2    When thought of as an ensemble of experimental tools, our senses enjoy an astonishing **acuity** and range of sensitivity. Our ears can register the thunderous launch of the space shuttle, yet they can also hear a mosquito buzzing a foot away from our head. Our

**ANALYZE TONE**

**Annotate:** Mark the humorous image about bats that the author presents.

**Infer:** Why might the author begin a serious scientific essay with a humorous image?

**acuity**
(ə-kyōō ′ĭ-tē) *n.* critical perceptiveness; awareness.

**NUMBERS AND STATS**

**Notice & Note:** Mark the measurements that appear in this paragraph.

**Analyze:** How do these measurements help the author illustrate the sensitivity of human senses?

**stimuli**
(stĭm´yə-lī) *n.* things that cause a response or reaction.

**propensity**
(prə-pĕn´sĭ-tē) *n.* a tendency to behave in a certain way.

**transcend**
(trăn-sĕnd´) *v.* to go beyond or rise above.

**ANALYZE DEVELOPMENT OF IDEAS**

**Annotate:** Mark the important questions that tell the thesis, or main idea.

**Predict:** How do you think the author will develop this thesis?

sense of touch allows us to feel the magnitude of a bowling ball dropped on our big toe, just as we can tell when a one-milligram bug crawls along our arm. Some people enjoy munching on habañero peppers while sensitive tongues can identify the presence of food flavors to the level of parts per million. And our eyes can register the bright sandy terrain on a sunny beach, yet these same eyes have no trouble spotting a lone match, freshly lit, hundreds of feet across a darkened auditorium.

3   But before we get carried away in praise of ourselves, note that what we gain in breadth we lose in precision: we register the world's **stimuli** in logarithmic[1] rather than linear increments. For example, if you increase the energy of a sound's volume by a factor of 10, your ears will judge this change to be rather small. Increase it by a factor of 2 and you will barely notice. The same holds for our capacity to measure light. If you have ever viewed a total solar eclipse you may have noticed that the Sun's disk must be at least 90 percent covered by the Moon before anybody comments that the sky has darkened. The stellar magnitude scale of brightness, the well-known acoustic decibel scale, and the seismic scale for earthquake severity[2] are each logarithmic, in part because of our biological **propensity** to see, hear, and feel the world that way.

4   What, if anything, lies beyond our senses? Does there exist a way of knowing that **transcends** our biological interfaces with the environment?

5   Consider that the human machine, while good at decoding the basics of our immediate environment—like when it's day or night or when a creature is about to eat us—has very little talent for decoding how the rest of nature works without the tools of science. If we want to know what's out there then we require detectors other than the ones we are born with. In nearly every case, the job of scientific apparatus is to transcend the breadth and depth of our senses.

6   Some people boast of having a sixth sense, where they profess to know or see things that others cannot. Fortune-tellers, mind readers, and mystics are at the top of the list of those who lay claim to mysterious powers. In doing so, they instill widespread fascination in others, especially book publishers and television producers. The questionable field of parapsychology[3] is founded on the expectation that at least some people actually harbor such talents. To me, the biggest mystery of them all is why so many fortune-telling psychics

---

[1] **logarithmic:** capable of being raised by repeated multiplication of itself; exponential.

[2] **stellar magnitude scale . . . acoustic decibel scale . . . seismic scale:** systems of measurement for the brightness of starlight, the loudness of sounds, and the intensity of earthquakes.

[3] **parapsychology:** the study of unexplainable or supernatural mental phenomena.

choose to work the phones on TV hotlines instead of becoming insanely wealthy trading futures contracts on Wall Street.[4] And here's a news headline none of us has seen, "Psychic Wins the Lottery."

7      Quite independent of this mystery, the persistent failures of controlled, double-blind experiments to support the claims of parapsychology suggest that what's going on is nonsense rather than sixth sense.

8      On the other hand, modern science wields dozens of senses. And scientists do not claim these to be the expression of special powers, just special hardware. In the end, of course, the hardware converts the information gleaned from these extra senses into simple tables, charts, diagrams, or images that our inborn senses can interpret. In the original *Star Trek* sci-fi series, the crew that beamed down from their starship to the uncharted planet always brought with them a tricorder—a handheld device that could analyze anything they encountered, living or inanimate, for its basic properties. As the tricorder was waved over the object in question, it made an audible spacey sound that was interpreted by the user.

9      Suppose a glowing blob of some unknown substance were parked right in front of us. Without some diagnostic tool like a tricorder to help, we would be clueless to the blob's chemical or nuclear composition. Nor could we know whether it has an electromagnetic

---

[4] **trading futures contracts on Wall Street:** a form of speculative investment in which someone agrees to pay a fixed price for an item at a future date. The success of the investment is measured by the difference between the agreed-upon price and the actual market price on that future date.

field, or whether it emits strongly in gamma rays, x-rays, ultraviolet, microwaves, or radio waves. Nor could we determine the blob's cellular or crystalline structure. If the blob were far out in space, appearing as an unresolved point of light in the sky, our five senses would offer us no insight to its distance, velocity through space, or its rate of rotation. We further would have no capacity to see the spectrum of colors that compose its emitted light, nor could we know whether the light is polarized.

10    Without hardware to help our analysis, and without a particular urge to lick the stuff, all we can report back to the starship is, "Captain, it's a blob." Apologies to Edwin P. Hubble, the quote that opens this chapter, while poignant and poetic, should have instead been:

> Equipped with our five senses, along with
> telescopes and microscopes and mass
> spectrometers and seismographs and
> magnetometers and particle accelerators
> and detectors across the electromagnetic
> spectrum, we explore the universe around
> us and call the adventure science.

**ANALYZE DEVELOPMENT OF IDEAS**

**Annotate:** Reread this quotation and the one that opens the science essay. Mark two things the two versions have in common. Underline a difference you see in the second quotation.

**Compare:** How are these quotations alike? How are they different?

**LANGUAGE CONVENTIONS**

**Annotate:** Mark the repeated phrase you see at the beginnings of sentences in paragraph 11.

**Respond:** How does repeating this structure help clarify Tyson's point?

11    Think of how much richer the world would appear to us and how much earlier the nature of the universe would have been discovered if we were born with high-precision, tunable eyeballs. Dial up the radio-wave part of the spectrum and the daytime sky becomes as dark as night. Dotting that sky would be bright and famous sources of radio waves, such as the center of the Milky Way, located behind some of the principal stars of the constellation Sagittarius. Tune into microwaves and the entire cosmos glows with a remnant from the early universe, a wall of light set forth 380,000 years after the big bang. Tune into x-rays and you immediately spot the locations of black holes, with matter spiraling into them. Tune into gamma rays and see titanic explosions scattered throughout the universe at a rate of about one per day. Watch the effect of the explosion on the surrounding material as it heats up and glows in other bands of light.

12    If we were born with magnetic detectors, the compass would never have been invented because we wouldn't ever need one. Just tune into Earth's magnetic field lines and the direction of magnetic north looms like Oz[5] beyond the horizon. If we had spectrum analyzers within our retinas, we would not have to wonder what we were breathing. We could just look at the register and know whether the air contained sufficient oxygen to sustain human life. And we would have learned thousands of years ago that the stars and nebulae in the Milky Way galaxy contain the same chemical elements found here on Earth.

---

[5] **Oz:** the magical city and destination for characters in L. Frank Baum's *The Wonderful Wizard of Oz*.

13     And if we were born with big eyes and built-in Doppler motion detectors, we would have seen immediately, even as grunting troglodytes,[6] that the entire universe is expanding—with distant galaxies all receding from us.

14     If our eyes had the resolution of high-performance microscopes, nobody would have ever blamed the plague and other sicknesses on divine wrath. The bacteria and viruses that made us sick would be in plain view as they crawled on our food or as they slid through open wounds in our skin. With simple experiments, we could easily tell which of these bugs were bad and which were good. And of course postoperative infection problems would have been identified and solved hundreds of years earlier.

15     If we could detect high-energy particles, we would spot radioactive substances from great distances. No Geiger counters necessary. We could even watch radon gas seep through the basement floor of homes and not have to pay somebody to tell us about it.

16  The honing of our senses from birth through childhood allows us, as adults, to pass judgment on events and phenomena in our lives, declaring whether they "make sense." Problem is, hardly any scientific discoveries of the past century flowed from the direct application of our five senses. They flowed instead from the direct application of sense-transcendent mathematics and hardware. This simple fact is entirely responsible for why, to the average person, relativity, particle physics, and 10-dimensional string theory make no sense. Include

**BIG QUESTIONS**

**Notice & Note:** Mark ideas in paragraphs 14 and 15 that challenge what you know about the dangers around us.

**Draw Conclusions:** Which improvements to our senses would benefit humanity the most? Why?

---

[6] **troglodyte:** a primitive creature or a cave dweller.

in the list black holes, wormholes, and the big bang. Actually, these ideas don't make much sense to scientists either, or at least not until we have explored the universe for a long time, with all the senses that are technologically available. What emerges, eventually, is a newer and higher level of "common sense" that enables a scientist to think creatively and to pass judgment in the unfamiliar underworld of the atom or in the mind-bending domain of higher-dimensional space. The twentieth-century German physicist Max Planck made a similar observation about the discovery of quantum mechanics:

> *Modern Physics impresses us particularly with the truth of the old doctrine which teaches that there are realities existing apart from our sense-perceptions, and that there are problems and conflicts where these realities are of greater value for us than the richest treasures of the world of experience.*
> (1931, p. 107)

17    Our five senses even interfere with sensible answers to stupid metaphysical questions like, "If a tree falls in the forest and nobody is around to hear it, does it make a sound?" My best answer is, "How do you know it fell?" But that just gets people angry. So I offer a senseless analogy, "Q: If you can't smell the carbon monoxide, then how do you know it's there? A: You drop dead." In modern times, if the sole measure of what's out there flows from your five senses then a precarious life awaits you.

18    Discovering new ways of knowing has always heralded new windows on the universe that tap into our growing list of nonbiological senses. Whenever this happens, a new level of majesty and complexity in the universe reveals itself to us, as though we were technologically evolving into supersentient beings, always coming to our senses.

**ANALYZE DEVELOPMENT OF IDEAS**

**Annotate:** Mark the words, phrases, and sentences that help you understand the author's conclusion.

**Paraphrase:** What is the author's conclusion? Explain it in your own words.

## CHECK YOUR UNDERSTANDING

Answer these questions before moving on to the **Analyze the Text** section on the following page.

**1** The author shares ideas in a tone that is —

   **A** serious and dry

   **B** informative yet humorous

   **C** lighthearted and imprecise

   **D** enthusiastic yet ill-informed

**2** The information about scientific instruments is used to —

   **F** describe various ways scientists gather information

   **G** provide a detailed overview of the latest technology

   **H** compare science fiction with actual developments

   **J** illustrate how our five senses are superior to artificial means

**3** Which idea is supported by the essay?

   **A** Science is sometimes wrong and has to revise statements.

   **B** Popular culture makes many valid observations about science.

   **C** Scientists are the most important people in our society.

   **D** We can always expand our awareness of the world around us.

## ANALYZE THE TEXT

Support your responses with evidence from the text.  NOTEBOOK

1. **Identify**  What is the thesis that the author develops throughout this essay? What evidence and examples support that thesis?

2. **Summarize**  What are some of the limitations of our five senses? Give a few examples from the text.

3. **Compare**  The author compares parapsychology and science. Why does Tyson compare these two methods of learning about the world? What differences does he find?

4. **Evaluate**  The author uses an ironic, sarcastic tone throughout the essay. Was his tone effective in helping him make his point? Why or why not?

5. **Notice & Note**  Give one example of how this essay challenged your understanding of science and of your five senses. Support your ideas with text evidence.

## RESEARCH

**RESEARCH TIP**

You can ask a question in a search engine, such as "How can you measure global temperature changes?" Look for key words on each page that you find, and then search for any specific instruments that are mentioned. Remember to use reliable websites, such as those maintained by a university or research agency.

Scientists use many instruments to find out about the world around them. Choose a scientific topic, such as hurricanes, cancer, nanotechnology, rainforests, or another topic. Then find out more about one of the instruments scientists use to study that topic. Draw a sketch in the chart of the instrument and record 2–3 facts about what the scientific instrument does.

| TOPIC | SCIENTIFIC INSTRUMENT | PICTURE | FACTS |
|---|---|---|---|
| | | | |

**Connect**  Share your work with a small group. Explain how the instrument you researched has helped scientists widen their understanding of the world. Discuss other ways this scientific instrument could be used.

## CREATE AND PRESENT

**Write an Explanation**  Choose one of the concepts or ideas Neil deGrasse Tyson mentions in this science essay. Write 1–2 paragraphs about this topic. Some possible topics may include carbon monoxide, black holes, bacteria and viruses, X-rays, a solar eclipse, or our senses.

❏ Introduce the topic and state your main idea.

❏ Provide some facts that tell more about the topic. You may choose to do some quick independent research about the topic. Also include details from "Coming to Our Senses."

❏ Share your own thoughts about this topic. What surprised or interested you? Were your ideas confirmed or challenged?

**Give a Presentation**  Share your paragraph and research with a partner. Discuss how we use scientific instruments to study each partner's topic.

❏ Listen to what your partner wrote and ask thoughtful questions to clarify facts or ideas.

❏ Share your research. Make at least one change or addition to your writing based on your partner's feedback.

❏ Check that you included a clear main idea.

❏ Join with another group and present your revised paragraphs. Listen respectfully to others. When it is your turn to speak, make eye contact with your audience and speak with a slow, steady pace.

For more on evaluating research sources, visit the **Writing Studio**.

For help with speaking in a discussion, visit the **Speaking and Listening Studio**.

## RESPOND TO THE ESSENTIAL QUESTION

 How does our point of view shape what we think we know?

**Gather Information**  Review your annotations and notes on "Coming to Our Senses." Then, add relevant details to your Response Log. As you determine which information to include, think about:

- how we use our senses to understand the world
- how scientific instruments help us learn
- why we should be open to learning more about our world

At the end of the unit, use your notes to help you write a short story.

### ACADEMIC VOCABULARY

As you write and discuss what you learned from the article, be sure to use the Academic Vocabulary words. Check off each of the words that you use.

❏ **differentiate**

❏ **incorporate**

❏ **mode**

❏ **orient**

❏ **perspective**

**WORD BANK**
acuity
stimuli
propensity
transcend

## CRITICAL VOCABULARY

**Practice and Apply** Demonstrate an understanding of each Critical Vocabulary word by responding to each question and explaining your answer. Use a dictionary or the definitions in the text to help you understand the meanings of the words.

**1.** If you possess high visual **acuity**, would you need glasses? Explain.

_____

**2.** Which of these **stimuli** would be more likely to make you respond quickly: a ringing cell phone or the smell of cookies baking?

_____

**3.** If you have a **propensity** for organization, is your room messy or tidy?

_____

**4.** If a singer's songs **transcend** musical genres, would you be able to easily classify the songs as country or rock?

_____

## VOCABULARY STRATEGY:
### Reference Sources

Go to the **Vocabulary Studio** for more on reference sources.

The author of the essay incorporates pop culture, historical, and scientific references into the text. For example, Tyson mentions a *total solar eclipse*, which is a scientific phenomenon that people rarely get to observe. Some readers may not be familiar with this event.

To determine the meaning of an unknown word, name, or reference, consult general and specialized reference materials, both print and digital. These may include college-level or bilingual dictionaries, encyclopedias, and online search engines that can lead you to specialized online resources that will help you identify more obscure references.

**Practice and Apply** Use print or digital resource materials to define or explain each reference from the essay.

**1.** Edwin P. Hubble

_____

**2.** double-blind experiment

_____

**3.** the *Star Trek* sci-fi series

_____

**4.** Geiger counters

_____

## LANGUAGE CONVENTIONS:
### Parallel Structure

**Parallel structure** is a technique in which authors repeat words or phrases within the same sentence or paragraph. Using parallel structure helps authors organize and clarify their thoughts, and it helps emphasize important ideas. Parallel structure can make writing more interesting, lyrical, and rhythmic.

In "Coming to Our Senses," Neil deGrasse Tyson uses parallel structure in different ways.

• To draw connections between seemingly different concepts:

> **Our eyes allow us to register information <u>not only from across the room but also from across the universe.</u>**

Here, the author uses parallel structure within a sentence to compare and draw connections between two very different distances: across a room and across the universe.

• To add rhythm and continuity throughout the essay:

> **<u>If we were born with</u> magnetic detectors, . . .**

> **And <u>if we were born with</u> big eyes and built-in Doppler motion detectors, . . .**

Here, the author starts two different paragraphs with similar phrasing. This carries his ideas throughout different paragraphs and emphasizes the conditional nature of his argument.

**Practice and Apply**  Do you believe it is important for humans to continue to explore space? Write one or two paragraphs that express your position on this issue, supporting your thinking with evidence and examples. Use parallel structure both within a sentence and between sentences by starting or ending two sentences in similar ways. When you are finished, share your sentences with a partner. Ask your partner to mark the examples of parallel structure.

# THE NIGHT FACE UP

Short Story by **Julio Cortázar**
translated by Paul Blackburn

**?** *ESSENTIAL QUESTION:*

How does our point of view shape what we think we know?

## QUICK START

The idea of dreams versus reality plays a central role in the story you are about to read. Think of three words that describe how you feel when you wake from a vivid dream. Share and discuss your words with a partner.

## MAKE INFERENCES

**Inferences** are logical guesses based on clues in the text and on your prior knowledge. "The Night Face Up" includes events in two very different settings. As you read, you can use story details to make inferences about the cultural environments and historical periods in the story. This will help you to develop a clear picture of the two worlds in which the protagonist finds himself. Record your inferences and the clues that helped you make them as shown.

| EVIDENCE/CLUES FROM THE TEXT | → | INFERENCE |
|---|---|---|
| **Setting 1:** But they kept him for a good while in a room with that hospital smell, filling out a form, getting his clothes off, and dressing him in a stiff, grayish smock. They moved his arm carefully, it didn't hurt him. The nurses were constantly making wisecracks, and if it hadn't been for the stomach contractions he would have felt fine, almost happy. | → | The man is hurt and in a hospital, but he feels like he is in good hands. The people taking care of him are happy and competent. |
| **Setting 2:** He had to press forward, to stay out of the bogs and get to the heart of the forest. Groping uncertainly through the dark, stooping every other moment to touch the packed earth of the trail, he took a few steps. | → | The man is in a dark, swampy forest. He is frightened and uncertain and is being chased. |

## ANALYZE PLOT STRUCTURE

When two plots share equal time and importance in a story, they are called **parallel plots**. A story with this structure moves back and forth between the plots. In "The Night Face Up," the author uses parallel plots that develop alongside each other and share a main character. As you read this story, use the questions below to analyze the parallel plots.

- How does the parallel plot structure create **tension**, or a sense of anxious anticipation?

- What is the **tone** of each plot? Are the tones similar or different?

- What is the **pace**, or speed, of each plot? Does the action of each plot move at the same or different paces?

- How does the author **bridge**, or connect, the two plots so that the story flows smoothly from one plot line to the other?

### GENRE ELEMENTS: SHORT STORY

- includes the four basic elements of fiction—setting, characters, plot, and theme

- may use a nonlinear or disrupted plot structure, such as parallel plots

- can be read in one sitting

## CRITICAL VOCABULARY

To preview the vocabulary words, choose the best answer to each question.

1. Which of the following might give you a feeling of **solace**?
   a. a difficult homework assignment
   b. a home-cooked meal

2. Which of the following describes something a **lucid** person might do?
   a. hallucinate
   b. follow directions

3. Which of the following is a **beneficent** act?
   a. donating supplies to a shelter
   b. throwing away a recyclable bottle

4. Which person has the authority to **consecrate** something?
   a. a religious leader
   b. a healthcare professional

5. Which of the following describes something that is **translucent**?
   a. frosted glass
   b. a cement wall

## LANGUAGE CONVENTIONS

A **complex sentence** has an independent clause and one or more dependent clauses. An independent clause can stand alone as a sentence; a dependent, or subordinate, clause cannot. Complex sentences like the one below from the story show the relationship between ideas or events:

**When he saw that the woman standing on the corner had rushed into the crosswalk while he still had the green light**, it was already somewhat too late for a simple solution.

In the example text, the dependent clause is underlined twice and the independent clause is underlined once. This complex sentence reflects the character's thought process.

Cortázar also uses sentence fragments and run-on sentences to reflect the character's thoughts. As you read, look for complex sentences, run-ons, and fragments and consider the effect these have on style and flow.

## ANNOTATION MODEL

**NOTICE & NOTE**

As you read, notice how the story moves between the two parallel plots and make notes about the tone, pace, and tension in each. In the model, you can see one reader's response to the first transition between plots in "The Night Face Up."

A woman's hands were arranging his head, he felt that they were moving him from one <u>stretcher</u> to another. The <u>man in white</u> came over to him again, <u>smiling</u>, something gleamed in his right hand. He patted <u>his cheek</u> and made a sign to someone stationed behind.

It was unusual as a dream because it was full of smells, and he never dreamt smells. First a <u>marshy smell</u>, there to the left of the <u>trail</u> the <u>swamps</u> began already, the <u>quaking bogs from which no one ever returned</u>.

> He is in a hospital. People are taking care of him. The tone is reassuring.
>
> He is dreaming of being in a jungle. The tone has an anxious edge.

## BACKGROUND

**Julio Cortázar** *(1914–1984) was an Argentine teacher, novelist, and short-story writer. A vocal opponent of the Argentinian government, Cortázar fled to Paris in 1951, where he remained until his death. He is best known for deftly weaving fantasy, hallucinations, and dreams into his fiction, as he does in this story. The Aztec sacrifice alluded to in this work was an important part of Aztec religious life. Human victims were usually prisoners of war or slaves; their sacrifice was thought to appease the gods and to make the gods stronger.*

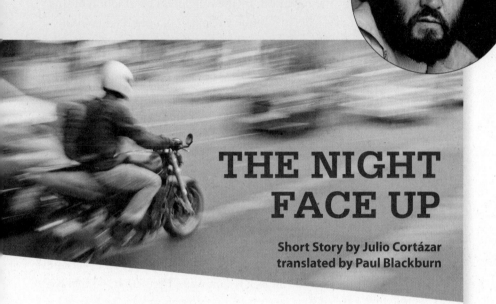

# THE NIGHT FACE UP

**Short Story by Julio Cortázar**
**translated by Paul Blackburn**

## SETTING A PURPOSE

*As you read, pay attention to the details that help you develop a mental image of the story's two cultural and historical settings.*

*And at certain periods they went out to hunt enemies; they called it the war of the blossom.\**

**Notice & Note**

You can use the side margins to notice and note signposts in the text.

1    Halfway down the long hotel vestibule,[1] he thought that probably he was going to be late, and hurried on into the street to get out his motorcycle from the corner where the next-door superintendent let him keep it. On the jewelry store at the corner he read that it was ten to nine; he had time to spare. The sun filtered through the tall downtown buildings, and he—because for himself, for just going along thinking, he did not have a name—he swung onto the machine, savoring the idea of the ride. The motor whirred between his legs, and a cool wind whipped his pantslegs.

---

\* The war of the blossom was the name the Aztecs gave to a ritual war in which they took prisoners for sacrifice. It is metaphysics to say that the gods see men as flowers, to be so uprooted, trampled, cut down. –Ed. [Cortázar's note]

[1] **vestibule:** a hall or entryway next to a building's exterior door.

**solace**
(sŏl´ĭs) *n.* source of relief and comfort.

**lucid**
(lōō´sĭd) *adj.* thinking rationally and clearly.

2    He let the ministries[2] zip past (the pink, the white), and a series of stores on the main street, their windows flashing. Now he was beginning the most pleasant part of the run, the real ride: a long street bordered with trees, very little traffic, with spacious villas whose gardens rambled all the way down to the sidewalks, which were barely indicated by low hedges. A bit inattentive perhaps, but tooling along on the right side of the street, he allowed himself to be carried away by the freshness, by the weightless contraction of this hardly begun day. This involuntary relaxation, possibly, kept him from preventing the accident. When he saw that the woman standing on the corner had rushed into the crosswalk while he still had the green light, it was already somewhat too late for a simple solution. He braked hard with foot and hand, wrenching himself to the left; he heard the woman scream, and at the collision his vision went. It was like falling asleep all at once.

3    He came to abruptly. Four or five young men were getting him out from under the cycle. He felt the taste of salt and blood, one knee hurt, and when they hoisted him up he yelped, he couldn't bear the pressure on his right arm. Voices which did not seem to belong to the faces hanging above him encouraged him cheerfully with jokes and assurances. His single **solace** was to hear someone else confirm that the lights indeed had been in his favor. He asked about the woman, trying to keep down the nausea which was edging up into his throat. While they carried him face up to a nearby pharmacy, he learned that the cause of the accident had gotten only a few scrapes on the legs, "Nah, you barely got her at all, but when ya hit, the impact made the machine jump and flop on its side . . ." Opinions, recollections of other smashups, take it easy, work him in shoulders first, there, that's fine, and someone in a dust coat giving him a swallow of something soothing in the shadowy interior of the small local pharmacy.

4    Within five minutes the police ambulance arrived, and they lifted him onto a cushioned stretcher. It was a relief for him to be able to lie out flat. Completely **lucid**, but realizing that he was suffering the effects of a terrible shock, he gave his information to the officer riding in the ambulance with him. The arm almost didn't hurt; blood dripped down from a cut over the eyebrow all over his face. He licked his lips once or twice to drink it. He felt pretty good, it had been an accident, tough luck; stay quiet a few weeks, nothing worse. The guard said that the motorcycle didn't seem badly racked up, "Why should it," he replied. "It all landed on top of me." They both laughed, and when they got to the hospital, the guard shook his hand and wished him luck. Now the nausea was coming back little by little; meanwhile they were pushing him on a wheeled stretcher toward a pavilion further back, rolling along under trees full of birds, he shut

---

[2] **ministries:** government offices.

his eyes and wished he were asleep or chloroformed.[3] But they kept him for a good while in a room with that hospital smell, filling out a form, getting his clothes off, and dressing him in a stiff, grayish smock. They moved his arm carefully, it didn't hurt him. The nurses were constantly making wisecracks, and if it hadn't been for the stomach contractions he would have felt fine, almost happy.

5    They got him over to X-ray, and twenty minutes later, with the still-damp negative lying on his chest like a black tombstone, they pushed him into surgery. Someone tall and thin in white came over and began to look at the X-rays. A woman's hands were arranging his head, he felt that they were moving him from one stretcher to another. The man in white came over to him again, smiling, something gleamed in his right hand. He patted his cheek and made a sign to someone stationed behind.

6    It was unusual as a dream because it was full of smells, and he never dreamt smells. First a marshy smell, there to the left of the trail the swamps began already, the quaking bogs from which no one ever returned. But the reek lifted, and instead there came a dark, fresh composite fragrance, like the night under which he moved, in flight from the Aztecs. And it was all so natural, he had to run from the Aztecs who had set out on their manhunt, and his sole chance was to find a place to hide in the deepest part of the forest, taking care not to lose the narrow trail which only they, the Motecas, knew.

7    What tormented him the most was the odor, as though, notwithstanding the absolute acceptance of the dream, there was something which resisted that which was not habitual, which until that point had not participated in the game. "It smells of war," he

---

[3] **chloroformed:** made unconscious by inhaling an anesthetic.

**ANALYZE PLOT STRUCTURE**

**Annotate:** Mark three details in paragraph 6 that help establish the setting and tone of the second parallel plot.

**Analyze:** How is the tone of the second plot different from the tone of the first plot? Cite text evidence in your answer.

**AGAIN AND AGAIN**

**Notice & Note:** Mark the sensory details in this paragraph that appear again and again.

**Predict:** How do these details change the mood and tone of this plot? What do you predict will happen next?

**ANALYZE PLOT STRUCTURE**

**Annotate:** Mark where the setting changes from the jungle to the hospital.

**Analyze:** How does the author bridge, or connect, the two plots so that the story flows smoothly from one plot line to the other?

thought, his hand going instinctively to the stone knife which was tucked at an angle into his girdle of woven wool. An unexpected sound made him crouch suddenly stock-still and shaking. To be afraid was nothing strange, there was plenty of fear in his dreams. He waited, covered by the branches of a shrub and the starless night. Far off, probably on the other side of the big lake, they'd be lighting the bivouac[4] fires; that part of the sky had a reddish glare. The sound was not repeated. It had been like a broken limb. Maybe an animal that, like himself, was escaping from the smell of war. He stood erect slowly, sniffing the air. Not a sound could be heard, but the fear was still following, as was the smell, that cloying incense of the war of the blossom. He had to press forward, to stay out of the bogs and get to the heart of the forest. Groping uncertainly through the dark, stooping every other moment to touch the packed earth of the trail, he took a few steps. He would have liked to have broken into a run, but the gurgling fens[5] lapped on either side of him. On the path and in darkness, he took his bearings. Then he caught a horrible blast of that foul smell he was most afraid of, and leaped forward desperately.

8    "You're going to fall off the bed," said the patient next to him. "Stop bouncing around, old buddy."

9    He opened his eyes and it was afternoon, the sun already low in the oversized windows of the long ward. While trying to smile at his neighbor, he detached himself almost physically from the final scene of the nightmare. His arm, in a plaster cast, hung suspended from an apparatus with weights and pulleys. He felt thirsty, as though he'd been running for miles, but they didn't want to give him much water, barely enough to moisten his lips and make a mouthful. The fever was winning slowly and he would have been able to sleep again, but he was enjoying the pleasure of keeping awake, eyes half-closed, listening to the other patients' conversation, answering a question from time to time. He saw a little white pushcart come up beside the bed, a blond nurse rubbed the front of his thigh with alcohol and stuck him with a fat needle connected to a tube which ran up to a bottle filled with a milky, opalescent liquid. A young intern arrived with some metal and leather apparatus which he adjusted to fit onto the good arm to check something or other. Night fell, and the fever went along dragging him down softly to a state in which things seemed embossed as through opera glasses,[6] they were real and soft and, at the same time, vaguely distasteful; like sitting in a boring movie and thinking that, well, still, it'd be worse out in the street, and staying.

10    A cup of a marvelous golden broth came, smelling of leeks, celery, and parsley. A small hunk of bread, more precious than a

---

[4] **bivouac:** a temporary camp.
[5] **fens:** wet, swampy land.
[6] **opera glasses:** small binoculars.

whole banquet, found itself crumbling little by little. His arm hardly hurt him at all, and only in the eyebrow where they'd taken stitches a quick, hot pain sizzled occasionally. When the big windows across the way turned to smudges of dark blue, he thought it would not be difficult for him to sleep. Still on his back so a little uncomfortable, running his tongue out over his hot, too-dry lips, he tasted the broth still, and with a sigh of bliss, he let himself drift off.

11      First there was a confusion, as of one drawing all his sensations, for that moment blunted or muddled, into himself. He realized that he was running in pitch darkness, although, above, the sky criss-crossed with treetops was less black than the rest. "The trail," he thought, "I've gotten off the trail." His feet sank into a bed of leaves and mud, and then he couldn't take a step that the branches of shrubs did not whiplash against his ribs and legs. Out of breath, knowing despite the darkness and silence that he was surrounded, he crouched down to listen. Maybe the trail was very near, with the first daylight he would be able to see it again. Nothing now could help him to find it. The hand that had unconsciously gripped the haft of the dagger climbed like a fen scorpion up to his neck where the protecting amulet[7] hung. Barely moving his lips, he mumbled the supplication of the corn which brings about the **beneficent** moons, and the prayer to Her Very Highness, to the distributor of all Motecan possessions. At the same time he felt his ankles sinking deeper into the mud, and the waiting in the darkness of the obscure grove of live oak grew intolerable to him. The war of the blossom had started at the beginning of the moon and had been going on for three days and three nights now. If he managed to hide in the depths of the forest, getting off the trail further up past the marsh country, perhaps the warriors wouldn't follow his track. He thought of the many prisoners they'd already taken. But the number didn't count, only the **consecrated** period. The hunt would continue until the priests gave the sign to return. Everything had its number and its limit, and it was within the sacred period, and he on the other side from the hunters.

12      He heard the cries and leaped up, knife in hand. As if the sky were aflame on the horizon, he saw torches moving among the branches, very near him. The smell of war was unbearable, and when the first enemy jumped him, leaped at his throat, he felt an almost-pleasure in sinking the stone blade flat to the haft into his chest. The lights were already around him, the happy cries. He managed to cut the air once or twice, then a rope snared him from behind.

13      "It's the fever," the man in the next bed said. "The same thing happened to me when they operated on my duodenum.[8] Take some water, you'll see, you'll sleep all right."

---

[7] **amulet:** a charm or necklace believed to have protective powers.
[8] **duodenum** (doo-ə-dē´nəm): part of the small intestine.

---

## LANGUAGE CONVENTIONS

**Annotate:** Place brackets around the second-to-last sentence in paragraph 10. Underline the independent clause within this sentence. Then circle the dependent, or subordinate clause.

**Analyze:** How are the ideas in the independent and subordinate clauses related in this sentence?

**beneficent** (bə-nĕf´ĭ-sənt) *adj.* beneficial; producing good.

**consecrate** (kŏn´sĭ-krāt) *v.* to make or define as sacred.

ANALYZE PLOT
STRUCTURE

**Annotate:** Mark the physical
actions that the main character
takes in paragraph 14.

**Evaluate:** Based on these
details, how would you describe
the pace, or speed, of the plot
that takes place in the hospital?
Cite evidence from the text in
your answer.

14      Laid next to the night from which he came back, the tepid
shadow of the ward seemed delicious to him. A violet lamp kept
watch high on the far wall like a guardian eye. You could hear
coughing, deep breathing, once in a while a conversation in whispers.
Everything was pleasant and secure, without the chase, no . . . But he
didn't want to go on thinking about the nightmare. There were lots
of things to amuse himself with. He began to look at the cast on his
arm, and the pulleys that held it so comfortably in the air. They'd left
a bottle of mineral water on the night table beside him. He put the
neck of the bottle to his mouth and drank it like a precious liqueur.
He could now make out the different shapes in the ward, the thirty
beds, the closets with glass doors. He guessed that his fever was
down, his face felt cool. The cut over the eyebrow barely hurt at all,
like a recollection. He saw himself leaving the hotel again, wheeling
out the cycle. Who'd have thought that it would end like this? He
tried to fix the moment of the accident exactly, and it got him very
angry to notice that there was a void there, an emptiness he could not
manage to fill. Between the impact and the moment that they picked
him up off the pavement, the passing out or what went on, there was
nothing he could see. And at the same time he had the feeling that
this void, this nothingness, had lasted an eternity. No, not even time,
more as if, in this void, he had passed across something, or had run
back immense distances. The shock, the brutal dashing against the
pavement. Anyway, he had felt an immense relief in coming out of
the black pit while the people were lifting him off the ground. With
pain in the broken arm, blood from the split eyebrow, contusion on
the knee; with all that, a relief in returning to daylight, to the day, and
to feel sustained and attended. That was weird. Someday he'd ask the
doctor at the office about that. Now sleep began to take over again, to
pull him slowly down. The pillow was so soft, and the coolness of the
mineral water in his fevered throat. The violet light of the lamp up
there was beginning to get dimmer and dimmer.

15      As he was sleeping on his back, the position in which he came
to did not surprise him, but on the other hand the damp smell,
the smell of oozing rock, blocked his throat and forced him to
understand. Open the eyes and look in all directions, hopeless. He
was surrounded by an absolute darkness. Tried to get up and felt
ropes pinning his wrists and ankles. He was staked to the ground on
a floor of dank, icy stone slabs. The cold bit into his naked back, his
legs. Dully, he tried to touch the amulet with his chin and found they
had stripped him of it. Now he was lost, no prayer could save him
from the final . . . From afar off, as though filtering through the rock
of the dungeon, he heard the great kettledrums of the feast. They
had carried him to the temple, he was in the underground cells of
Teocalli[9] itself, awaiting his turn.

---

[9] **Teocalli** (tē´ə-kăl´ē):  an ancient Mexican terraced pyramid and temple.

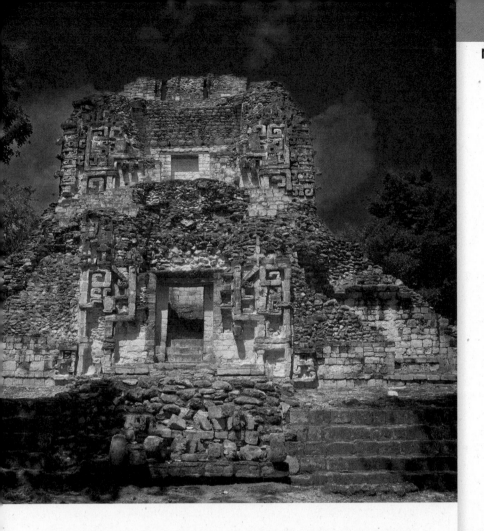

16    He heard a yell, a hoarse yell that rocked off the walls. Another yell, ending in a moan. It was he who was screaming in the darkness, he was screaming because he was alive, his whole body with that cry fended off what was coming, the inevitable end. He thought of his friends filling up the other dungeons, and of those already walking up the stairs of the sacrifice. He uttered another choked cry, he could barely open his mouth, his jaws were twisted back as if with a rope and a stick, and once in a while they would open slowly with an endless exertion, as if they were made of rubber. The creaking of the wooden latches jolted him like a whip. Rent, writhing, he fought to rid himself of the cords sinking into his flesh. His right arm, the strongest, strained until the pain became unbearable and he had to give up. He watched the double door open, and the smell of the torches reached him before the light did. Barely girdled by the ceremonial loincloths, the priests' acolytes[10] moved in his direction, looking at him with contempt. Lights reflected off the sweaty torsos and off the black hair dressed with feathers. The cords went slack, and in their place the grappling of hot hands, hard as bronze; he felt himself lifted, still face up, and jerked along by the four acolytes who carried him down the passageway. The torchbearers went ahead, indistinctly lighting up the corridor with its dripping walls and a ceiling so low that the acolytes had to duck their heads. Now they

---

[10] **acolytes:** people who assist in religious services.

## MAKE INFERENCES

**Annotate:** In paragraph 16, mark three historical and cultural details that help develop the setting of the Aztec plot.

**Infer:** Based on the details you marked, how would you describe the historical period and the culture of the Aztecs? Cite evidence in your answer.

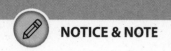

were taking him out, taking him out, it was the end. Face up, under a mile of living rock which, for a succession of moments, was lit up by a glimmer of torchlight. When the stars came out up there instead of the roof and the great terraced steps rose before him, on fire with cries and dances, it would be the end. The passage was never going to end, but now it was beginning to end, he would see suddenly the open sky full of stars, but not yet, they trundled him along endlessly in the reddish shadow, hauling him roughly along and he did not want that, but how to stop it if they had torn off the amulet, his real heart, the life-center.

17    In a single jump he came out into the hospital night, to the high, gentle, bare ceiling, to the soft shadow wrapping him round. He thought he must have cried out, but his neighbors were peacefully snoring. The water in the bottle on the night table was somewhat bubbly, a **translucent** shape against the dark azure shadow of the windows. He panted, looking for some relief for his lungs, oblivion for those images still glued to his eyelids. Each time he shut his eyes he saw them take shape instantly, and he sat up, completely wrung out, but savoring at the same time the surety that now he was awake, that the night nurse would answer if he rang, that soon it would be daybreak, with the good, deep sleep he usually had at that hour, no images, no nothing . . . It was difficult to keep his eyes open, the drowsiness was more powerful than he. He made one last effort, he sketched a gesture toward the bottle of water with his good hand and did not manage to reach it, his fingers closed again on a black emptiness, and the passageway went on endlessly, rock after rock, with momentary ruddy flares, and face up he choked out a dull moan because the roof was about to end, it rose, was opening like a mouth of shadow, and the acolytes straightened up, and from on high a waning moon fell on a face whose eyes wanted not to see it, were closing and opening desperately, trying to pass to the other side, to find again the bare, protecting ceiling of the ward. And every time they opened, it was night and the moon, while they climbed the great terraced steps, his head hanging down backward now, and up at the top were the bonfires, red columns of perfumed smoke, and suddenly he saw the red stone, shiny with the blood dripping off it, and the spinning arcs cut by the feet of the victim whom they pulled off to throw him rolling down the north steps. With a last hope he shut his lids tightly, moaning to wake up. For a second he thought he had gotten there, because once more he was immobile in the bed, except that his head was hanging down off it, swinging. But he smelled death, and when he opened his eyes he saw the blood-soaked figure of the executioner-priest coming toward him with the stone knife in his hand. He managed to close his eyelids again, although

**translucent**
(trăns-lōō´sənt) *adj.* semi-transparent; indistinct.

**AHA MOMENT**

**Notice & Note:** What does the main character suddenly realize in the second half of paragraph 17? Mark at least two clues in the text.

**Infer:** What does this realization suggest about the man's fate?

he knew now he was not going to wake up, that he was awake, that the marvelous dream had been the other, absurd as all dreams are—a dream in which he was going through the strange avenues of an astonishing city, with green and red lights that burned without fire or smoke, on an enormous metal insect that whirred away between his legs. In the infinite lie of the dream, they had also picked him off the ground, someone had approached him also with a knife in his hand, approached him who was lying face up, face up with his eyes closed between the bonfires on the steps.

## CHECK YOUR UNDERSTANDING

Answer these questions before moving on to the **Analyze the Text** section on the following page.

1 The story's parallel plots concern —

   A a modern hospital and an Aztec ritual

   B a pedestrian and a motorcyclist

   C the two sides of an ancient war

   D a busy city and a beautiful jungle

2 Which of the following is a similarity the two plots share?

   F A sense of fear and concern hangs over all of the events.

   G The protagonist is lying on his back while others control his fate.

   H Despite his difficulties, the protagonist is optimistic about his future.

   J It is entirely the protagonist's fault that he is in a dire situation.

3 What seems to be true of the protagonist at the end of the story?

   A He will make a full recovery from his motorcycle accident.

   B He lives in Aztec times and is going to be sacrificed.

   C He will continue to suffer from nightmares as a result of the accident.

   D He is living simultaneously in two different realities.

## ANALYZE THE TEXT

Support your responses with evidence from the text.  📓 NOTEBOOK

1. **Analyze** Cortázar begins the narrative with the plot concerning the motorcycle accident rather than the one about the manhunt. Why is this choice an effective way to structure the story?

2. **Evaluate** The author structures the story so that the parallel plots mirror each other. For example, the author describes a scene in which the protagonist is x-rayed, taken to surgery, and approached by a doctor. Where in the second plot does the author echo this scene? What is the effect of this mode of narration?

3. **Compare** In both plots, the author frequently refers to smells. Explain how the descriptions of smells differ in each plot. How do these differences affect the tone of each plot?

4. **Infer** The protagonist is never named, but his reality and his ongoing dream make up the parallel plots of the story. How does the reader's perception of the protagonist change throughout the story? Cite text evidence to support your ideas.

5. **Notice & Note** Identify two moments in "The Night Face Up" when the main character has a realization. What do these Aha Moments suggest about the man's changing state of mind and his lucidity?

## RESEARCH

**RESEARCH TIP**
Be sure to document the sources you use in order to give proper credit to the people who created them and to avoid plagiarism. Depending on the type of source you use, the elements of a source citation may include the title, the author's name, the publisher's name and location, date of publication or creation, URL, and page numbers.

Ancient Aztec culture was highly developed. It included sophisticated cities, complex religious beliefs, and advances in math, science, and the arts. With a partner, conduct research to learn more about ancient Aztec culture. Record what you learn in the chart.

| ASPECT OF AZTEC CULTURE | DETAILS |
|---|---|
| architecture | |
| education | |
| arts | |
| economy | |

**Extend** Conduct additional research on Aztec culture to learn about games and leisure activities. Are any of the games and activities that you discovered still enjoyed today?

## CREATE AND DISCUSS

**Write an Analysis** Write a one-page analysis of the story's **theme**, or central message about human nature or the human experience. Include information about how this theme is conveyed through the different story elements. Review your notes and annotations in the text before you begin.

❏ Introduce your analysis by revealing the theme.

❏ In the body of your analysis, describe how the theme is conveyed through the characters, plot, imagery, tone, and setting. Include specific details from the text to support your ideas.

❏ In your conclusion, remind readers of the theme and leave them with something to think about.

**Discuss Opinions** With a small group, discuss the ending of "The Night Face Up." Is the Aztec setting "real," or could it just be a dream?

❏ As a group, review the story, paying particular attention to the places where the story shifts from one plot to another and to the final paragraph.

❏ Then discuss whether the Aztec setting is real or a dream, using story details for support. As you discuss, listen closely to one another and ask questions to help clarify ideas.

❏ Finally, end the discussion by listing the opinion of each member in your group.

Go to the **Writing Studio** for help in using textual evidence in your analysis.

Go to the **Speaking and Listening Studio** for help with having a group discussion.

## RESPOND TO THE ESSENTIAL QUESTION

 How does our point of view shape what we think we know?

**Gather Information** Review your annotations and notes on "The Night Face Up." Then, add relevant information to your Response Log. As you determine which information to include, think about:

- the protagonist's attitude about life when he is in the hospital setting
- how this point of view changes during the manhunt
- how your point of view shapes your ideas about what is real and what is a dream in the story

At the end of the unit, use your notes to help you write a short story.

UNIT 2
RESPONSE LOG

### ACADEMIC VOCABULARY

As you write and discuss what you learned about "The Night Face Up," be sure to use the Academic Vocabulary words. Check off each of the words that you use.

❏ **differentiate**

❏ **incorporate**

❏ **mode**

❏ **orient**

❏ **perspective**

**WORD BANK**
solace
lucid
beneficent
consecrate
translucent

Go to the **Vocabulary Studio** for more on connotation and denotation.

## CRITICAL VOCABULARY

**Practice and Apply** Answer each question in a complete sentence that demonstrates your understanding of the meaning of each Critical Vocabulary word.

1. Have you ever visited a place or seen an item that was **consecrated**? Explain.

2. When have you sought **solace**? Why?

3. How can you tell someone is not completely **lucid**? Explain.

4. When did you behave in a **beneficent** manner? Explain.

5. Where might a **translucent** material be used in your home? Why?

## VOCABULARY STRATEGY:
### Denotation and Connotation

A word's literal meaning or definition is called its **denotation**. A word may also have an implied meaning, an association that evokes a particular emotion. This is the word's **connotation**. The emotions that words evoke range from positive to neutral to negative. Consider the meaning of the word *solace* in this sentence:

**After a hard day, Bella went for a healing hike in the desert, where she found solace in the beautiful atmosphere and peaceful sounds.**

The denotation of the word *solace* is "a source of relief and comfort." Finding solace in something connotes a positive feeling of relief and happiness.

**Practice and Apply** Find these three words in "The Night Face Up." Look up the words, and then decide on their connotations based on what you find in a dictionary or in the text. Work in a group to discuss denotation and connotation. Record the words and your group's ideas in the chart.

| WORD | DENOTATION | CONNOTATION |
|------|-----------|-------------|
| **reek** (paragraph 6) | | |
| **fragrance** (paragraph 6) | | |
| **odor** (paragraph 7) | | |

## LANGUAGE CONVENTIONS:
### Complex Sentences

A **complex sentence** contains one independent, or main, clause and one or more subordinate, or dependent, clauses. The subordinate clause(s) expresses ideas that are less important than, but related to, the main idea. Here is an example from the story:

subordinate clause

**While they carried him face up to a nearby pharmacy,** **he learned that the** **cause of the accident had gotten only a few scrapes on the legs**.

(paragraph 3)                                             independent clause

Julio Cortázar uses complex sentences in "The Night Face Up" for a variety of purposes and effects:

- To convey the narrator's frantic, worried situation:

   > **If he managed to hide in the depths of the forest, getting off the trail further up past the marsh country, perhaps the warriors wouldn't follow his track.** (paragraph 11)

- To show how events are related in time and to create suspense:

   > **When the stars came out up there instead of the roof and the great terraced steps rose before him, on fire with cries and dances, it would be the end.** (paragraph 16)

Good writers may also deliberately use incorrect sentence structures to achieve certain effects:

- A **sentence fragment** is a part of a sentence that is punctuated as if it were a complete sentence. Sentence fragments are often used in stories to make dialogue sound authentic.
- There are two kinds of **run-on sentences**. In the first, two or more sentences are run together without any punctuation marks to separate them. In the second, the writer uses a comma instead of a period between sentences. This second type of run-on is called a **comma splice**. Run-on sentences, used sparingly, can create a sense of frantic urgency, an effect Cortázar achieves in this story.

**Practice and Apply** Take a closer look at a piece of your own writing, such as the writing you did in response to "The Night Face Up." Revise it by combining shorter sentences to create three complex sentences. Check for and correct any fragments or run-on sentences in your work.

> Go to the **Grammar Studio** for more on using complex sentences.

# MIRROR

Poem by **Sylvia Plath**

**?** **ESSENTIAL QUESTION:**

How does our point of view shape what we think we know?

## QUICK START

Is a mirror's reflection of you an accurate depiction of who you are? When you stand in front of a mirror, what parts of you does the mirror reflect? What parts does it miss? Record your thoughts below. Then, share them with a partner.

| WHAT THE MIRROR REFLECTS | WHAT THE MIRROR CANNOT SEE |
| --- | --- |
|  |  |

## ANALYZE SPEAKER

In poetry, the **speaker** is the voice that "talks" to the reader. The speaker is not always the same as the poet, even in a poem that uses *I* and *me*. A poet chooses a particular speaker to convey a message and to elicit the reader's emotions. The speaker may be a child, an adult, an animal, or an object. The speaker could be a baby, a dog, or the wind.

When you read a poem, identify the speaker and the subject. Use the poem's words and images to help you get a sense of who the speaker is. Ask the following questions:

- What is the speaker paying attention to in the poem?

- What thoughts and feelings does the speaker express?

- What is the speaker's tone, or attitude, toward the subject?

As you read "Mirror," use this chart to record your inferences about the speaker and the details that led you to make these inferences.

| INFERENCES ABOUT THE SPEAKER | DETAILS FROM THE POEM |
| --- | --- |
|  |  |
|  |  |

**GENRE ELEMENTS: LYRIC POETRY**

- expresses the speaker's thoughts and feelings

- implies, rather than states, the speaker's emotion

- written in free verse without regular meter

- uses the rhythm of natural speech to create its musical quality

## ANALYZE FIGURATIVE LANGUAGE

**Figurative language** communicates ideas beyond the literal meaning of the words. Figurative language uses ordinary words in unusual ways and forces a reader to look at familiar things in a new way. Similes, metaphors, and personification are three figures of speech that poets use to create meaning.

A **simile** is a stated comparison between two things that are actually unlike, but that have something in common. A simile contains the words *like* or *as*.

> The snow settled on the roof *like* a comforting blanket.

A **metaphor** is a figure of speech that makes a comparison between two unlike things that have something in common. It does not contain the words *like* or *as*.

> The flowers *are* a carpet of color.

**Personification** is a figure of speech in which human qualities are attributed to an animal, object, or idea. In some poems, poets use personification by making the speaker the voice of the animal, object, or idea.

> The tree *stretched its arms* to the sky.

---

**ANNOTATION MODEL**                    **NOTICE & NOTE**

As you read, watch for figurative language. Analyze how it adds meaning to the poem's message. This model shows one reader's notes about lines from "Mirror."

I am silver and exact. I have no preconceptions.

Whatever I see I swallow immediately

Just as it is, unmisted by love or dislike.

> The verb "swallow" makes me think the mirror wants to devour what it sees, which is a little disturbing. Or maybe the mirror means that it doesn't judge what it sees.

## BACKGROUND

**Sylvia Plath** *(1932–1963) was born in Boston and won literary awards as a teen for her stories and poems. She attended Cambridge University in London as a Fulbright Scholar. There, she met and married poet Ted Hughes. Plath's intensely personal and complex poems explore the painful dilemmas of her own life as poet, wife, mother, and daughter. A critic called her final poems a "triumph for poetry at the moment that they are a defeat for their author." After her premature death, her reputation continued to grow, and in 1982, her* Collected Poems *received the Pulitzer Prize.*

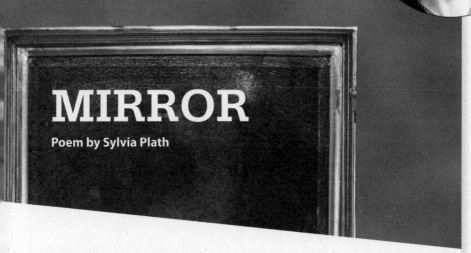

# MIRROR

Poem by Sylvia Plath

## SETTING A PURPOSE

As you read, consider how you react to what you see when you look in the mirror and compare this to the reaction of the woman in the poem.

I am silver and exact. I have no preconceptions.[1]
Whatever I see I swallow immediately
Just as it is, unmisted by love or dislike.
I am not cruel, only truthful –
5 The eye of a little god, four-cornered.
Most of the time I meditate on the opposite wall.
It is pink, with speckles. I have looked at it so long
I think it is a part of my heart. But it flickers.
Faces and darkness separate us over and over.

---

[1] **preconception:** an opinion in advance, a bias.

## Notice & Note

You can use the side margins to notice and note signposts in the text.

---

## ANALYZE SPEAKER

**Annotate:** Mark the words that help you identify and understand the speaker.

**Infer:** Why does the speaker claim "I am not cruel, only truthful?" Do you agree with the speaker? Why or why not?

## ANALYZE FIGURATIVE LANGUAGE

**Annotate:** What does the mirror compare itself to in the second stanza? Mark the words and phrases that help you understand this comparison.

**Analyze:** How would you describe the mirror's attitude toward the woman?

10 Now I am a lake. A woman bends over me,
   Searching my reaches for what she really is.
   Then she turns to those liars, the candles or the moon.
   I see her back, and reflect it faithfully.
   She rewards me with tears and an agitation of hands.
15 I am important to her. She comes and goes.
   Each morning it is her face that replaces the darkness.
   In me she has drowned a young girl, and in me an old woman
   Rises toward her day after day, like a terrible fish.

## CHECK YOUR UNDERSTANDING

Answer these questions before moving on to the **Analyze the Text** section on the following page.

1 The first stanza suggests that the mirror —

   **A** schemes to make the woman unhappy

   **B** welcomes the faces that interrupt its meditation

   **C** lacks any emotion, even a beating heart

   **D** is critical, passing judgment on all it sees

2 In the second stanza, the candles and the moon are called <u>liars</u> because they —

   **F** come and go instead of being constantly present

   **G** alter the woman's perception of reality

   **H** seem to be harsh and judgmental

   **J** are at war with the mirror

3 What does the <u>terrible fish</u> in line 18 represent?

   **A** The mirror's anger toward the woman

   **B** Society's overemphasis on appearances

   **C** The reality of growing old

   **D** The sadness of the young girl

## ANALYZE THE TEXT

Support your responses with evidence from the text. 📓 NOTEBOOK

1. **Infer** Reread the first stanza. What is your impression of the speaker? What does the phrase "The eye of a little god" suggest about the mirror's personality?

2. **Analyze** Reread lines 6–9. How does the mirror feel about its daily meditation? What does the line "But it flickers" mean? How does this make the wall different from the mirror's heart?

3. **Draw Conclusions** Reread line 13. If the candles and the moon are "liars," why does the woman turn to them? How does this metaphor reveal the mirror's perspective?

4. **Analyze** In the second stanza, why is the woman agitated that the lake (mirror) reflects her "faithfully"? How does the woman's reaction support the idea that she is conflicted?

5. **Synthesize** What is the theme, or message, of this poem? Explain your answer using evidence from the poem as support.

## RESEARCH

**RESEARCH TIP**
When citing a poem, put quotation marks around the poem's title. The book in which the poem is located should be in italics if typed or underlined if handwritten. Remember to include the date of publication and the publisher's name. For a poem found online, include the URL.

Collaborate with a partner and choose 2–3 other poems by Sylvia Plath. Then, create a poetry poster to present them. Your poster should include the following:

- the full text of each poem, typed or written neatly and pasted on the poster

- lines from the poems that contain examples of metaphor, simile, or personification

- a brief explanation of why you chose each poem

| TITLE OF POEM | EXAMPLE LINE(S) | TYPE OF FIGURATIVE LANGUAGE |
|---|---|---|
|  |  |  |
|  |  |  |
|  |  |  |

**Extend** Explain what each example of figurative language helps readers to understand.

## CREATE AND DISCUSS

**Write a Poem** The poem "Mirror" is unusual because the speaker is an object—the mirror. Write a similar poem with a different speaker, such as the woman, the wall, the candles, or the moon. Or, you might write from the perspective of an outside narrator who knows the thoughts and feelings of both the mirror and the woman—like an omniscient narrator in fiction.

❏ Choose the speaker of your "Mirror" poem.

❏ Jot down notes about how the speaker feels and what the speaker notices. Your poem could be humorous or serious.

❏ Use similes, metaphors, or personification to convey the speaker's attitude.

**Discuss** The speaker in "Mirror" says that the woman is searching for "what she really is." In a small group, discuss whether mirrors show people the most accurate versions of themselves. Use details from the poem and personal experience to support your ideas.

❏ Read the poem aloud in your group. Share and discuss ideas that you and other group members wrote down in the Quick Start.

❏ Discuss societal values concerning appearance and the kinds of judgments and distorted thinking this might lead to.

❏ Consider how looking in the mirror can have positive and negative consequences.

❏ Discuss ways in which people can embrace their identities and achieve confidence in a society that is so focused on appearance.

Go to the **Speaking and Listening Studio** for more on participating in a discussion.

## RESPOND TO THE ESSENTIAL QUESTION

 How does our point of view shape what we think we know?

**Gather Information** Review your annotations and notes on "Mirror." Then, add relevant ideas to your Response Log. As you decide which ideas to include, think about:

- the difference between our physical appearance and our inner self
- the acceptance of our personal identity
- the difference between our own desires and the demands of society

At the end of the unit, use your notes to help you write a short story.

**ACADEMIC VOCABULARY**

As you write and discuss what you learned from the poem, be sure to use the Academic Vocabulary words. Check off each of the words that you use.

❏ **differentiate**

❏ **incorporate**

❏ **mode**

❏ **orient**

❏ **perspective**

INFOGRAPHIC

# THE WORLD AS 100 PEOPLE

by **Jack Hagley**

pages 117–119

## COMPARE DETAILS

As you read, notice how the ideas in both texts relate to the world around you, as well as how they help you understand ideas through mathematics. Then, look for ways that the ideas in the two texts relate to each other. After you read both selections, you will collaborate with a small group on a final project.

**?** ***ESSENTIAL QUESTION:***

How does our point of view shape what we think we know?

POEM

# A CONTRIBUTION TO STATISTICS

by **Wisława Szymborska**

pages 123–125

# The World as 100 People

## QUICK START

You can be classified in a wide range of groups: teenagers, Americans, athletes, people who live in suburbs, etc. With a group, brainstorm all the ways that you can statistically classify the world population.

| | |
|---|---|
| Demographic | *by age* |
| Geographic | *by country* |
| Personal | *by hobbies* |

## INTERPRET GRAPHICS

Graphics can sometimes communicate information more clearly than words. Texts often include one of more of the following types of graphics:

| TYPE OF GRAPHIC | WHAT IT DOES |
|---|---|
| Tables | Large amounts of data organized in a logical order that makes it easier for a reader to see and understand the data |
| Graphs | Two-dimensional representations of data that help the reader understand the relationships among the data |
| Photographs and Drawings | Visual illustrations of a topic discussed in a text that can show details that are difficult to explain in words |
| Diagrams | Illustrations that show the relationship of parts in an object or the steps in a process |
| Infographics | Combinations of charts, text, and images to create a visual that communicates statistical information |

**GENRE ELEMENTS: INFOGRAPHIC**

- provides numerical information
- uses a visual representation
- combines elements of charts, text, and images

## ANALYZE MOTIVES

Even though graphics present objective data, the creators of graphics make choices about how to present this data. Designers may choose to include or exclude certain types of data based on the point they hope to make and the overall purpose of the graphic.

For example, the creator of the infographic "The World as 100 People" chose to include data about age, religion, and literacy but did not include data about car ownership or types of employment.

When examining "The World as 100 People," think about why the designer chose to include each category and how doing so serves the purpose of the graphic.

## ANNOTATION MODEL

**NOTICE & NOTE**

Here is how a student might annotate to analyze the motives of the infographic's creator.

87 have safe water    13 do not

The infographic tells me that, out of every 100 people, 87 people have safe drinking water and 13 people do not.

That means 13 out of every 100 people have to spend time and energy getting safe water to drink—time and energy they can't use to work or to gather food.

This data matters because access to clean drinking water is necessary for life.

## BACKGROUND

*Representing statistical information in terms of a small group of people is popular in advertising ("Three out of five dentists recommend . . .") because it makes a point easy to understand. This infographic both shares information and makes some persuasive points. The Artist's Statement by designer* **Jack Hagley** *provides context for choices he made, including why he chose this particular shape for the infographic.*

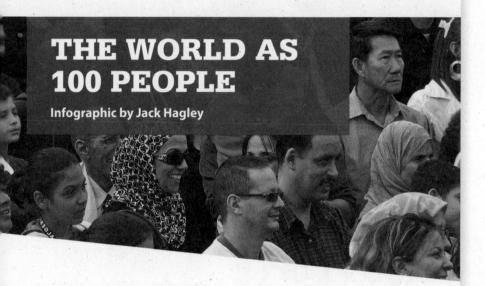

# THE WORLD AS 100 PEOPLE

**Infographic by Jack Hagley**

## PREPARE TO COMPARE

*As you read the statement and infographic that follow, think about how the data relates to the world around you. What parts of the data confirm your expectations? What data surprises you? Why?*

## ARTIST'S STATEMENT

When I was a boy in the '90s, my mother had a printout of a chain e-mail pinned to the wall in our kitchen. It was called "The World as 100 People," and it was just a simple list. I never forgot it because it was a simple but clever idea – a child could understand it without knowing the concept of percentages. One day, I didn't have any other work to do and I was sitting in my studio. The idea and the method came to me very quickly. I knew that I wanted to make it round, like the world. I wanted to use colors that might remind people of flags. I made the first draft in the morning and it was on the Internet by the afternoon.

**Notice & Note**

You can use the side margins to notice and note signposts in the text.

**ANALYZE MOTIVES**

**Annotate:** Mark the text that describes the author's inspiration for creating the infographic.

**Analyze:** Why might this type of infographic appeal to a child? What information does it make easier to understand?

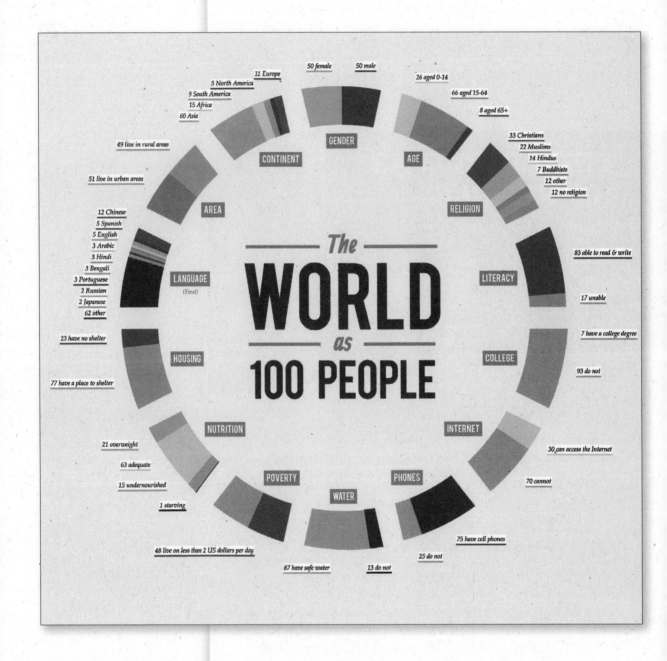

The World as 100 People

**GENDER**
50 female
50 male

**AGE**
26 aged 0-14
66 aged 15-64
8 aged 65+

**RELIGION**
33 Christians
22 Muslims
14 Hindus
7 Buddhists
12 other
12 no religion

**LITERACY**
83 able to read & write
17 unable

**COLLEGE**
7 have a college degree
93 do not

**INTERNET**
30 can access the Internet
70 cannot

**PHONES**
75 have cell phones
25 do not

**WATER**
87 have safe water
13 do not

**POVERTY**
48 live on less than 2 US dollars per day

**NUTRITION**
21 overweight
63 adequate
15 undernourished
1 starving

**HOUSING**
23 have no shelter
77 have a place to shelter

**LANGUAGE** (First)
12 Chinese
5 Spanish
5 English
3 Arabic
3 Hindi
3 Bengali
3 Portuguese
2 Russian
2 Japanese
62 other

**AREA**
49 live in rural areas
51 live in urban areas

**CONTINENT**
11 Europe
5 North America
9 South America
15 Africa
60 Asia

## CHECK YOUR UNDERSTANDING

Answer these questions before moving on to the next selection.

1  Which of the following is true of this infographic?

   **A** It represents everything we need to know about people.

   **B** Its design shows that it is inaccurate and biased.

   **C** It includes only people who live in the United States.

   **D** It provides a quick view of some key population facts.

2  The categories in the infographic are —

   **F** topics that people often argue about

   **G** characteristics for which factual information is available

   **H** based on emotions more than on hard data

   **J** arranged in order of their importance in people's lives

3  The concept of showing the world's population as 100 people —

   **A** makes it easy to understand challenges most people in the world face

   **B** reveals the difficulty that many children and adults have with math

   **C** distorts and oversimplifies the world's population

   **D** shows how the people in all of the categories overlap with each other

POEM

# A CONTRIBUTION TO STATISTICS

by **Wisława Szymborska**

pages 123–125

## COMPARE DETAILS

Now that you have examined the infographic "The World as 100 People," read "A Contribution to Statistics" and explore how this poem expresses similar ideas. As you read, think about how the author uses literary devices and poetic structure to analyze people and their experiences. After you are finished, you will collaborate with a small group on a final project that involves an analysis of both texts.

**?** *ESSENTIAL QUESTION:*

How does our point of view shape what we think we know?

INFOGRAPHIC

## THE WORLD AS 100 PEOPLE

by **Jack Hagley**

pages 117–119

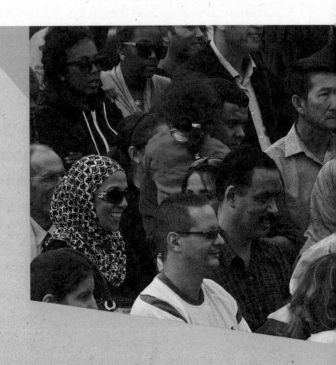

# A Contribution to Statistics

## QUICK START

During any given day, each human being experiences a range of emotions from jubilation to sadness and from doubt to confidence. Think about a day in which you experienced numerous emotions. Discuss your experience with your group.

## ANALYZE LITERARY DEVICES

**Literary devices** are techniques writers use to communicate their ideas to readers. The use of literary devices often enhances a writer's work and leads readers to a deeper understanding of the writer's message. Here are three devices used in the poem:

**Idioms** are phrases or expressions whose meaning is different from their literal meaning. The figurative meaning of an idiom usually develops over time and is often specific to a particular culture or language.

| IDIOM IN POEM | FIGURATIVE MEANING |
|---|---|
| **glad to lend a hand** | happy to help another person do something |

**Parallelism** repeats a grammatical construction to show a connection between ideas.

| PARALLELISM IN POEM | HOW IT LINKS IDEAS |
|---|---|
| **Those who always know better —fifty-two,**<br><br>**doubting every step —nearly all the rest,** | The poem repeatedly uses the structure of presenting a human characteristic followed by a long dash and a statistical estimate of it. |

**Shifts** occur when the writer's tone or focus changes. Shifts help keep a reader interested in a text and can enhance the clarity of a writer's presentation.

| SHIFT IN POEM | EFFECT ON TONE |
|---|---|
| **glad to lend a hand if it doesn't take too long —as high as forty-nine,** | The first line seems very positive, but the second line shifts to show that convenience may be more important than kindness for some people. |

## GENRE ELEMENTS: POETRY

- uses figurative language and literary devices
- expresses a theme, or a message about life
- is arranged in lines and stanzas

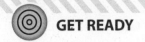
## ANALYZE STRUCTURE

Poems are often divided into stanzas, with an extra line space separating lines. A **stanza** functions in a way similar to a paragraph in a story or essay, forming a meaningful section of the work. A very long stanza may provide context or detail, while a very short stanza will usually make an important point.

In "A Contribution to Statistics," Szymborska uses the stanzas to communicate her theme. In each stanza, the poem presents a human characteristic followed by a statistic. The predictable structure of the stanzas links the poet's ideas and heightens their impact.

As you read, note the topic or characteristic that each stanza explores as shown below. Considering all of the stanza topics together can help you understand the poem's theme, or message about human nature.

## ANNOTATION MODEL

**NOTICE & NOTE**

Make annotations to help you analyze the structure of a poem. In this model, you can see one reader's notes about the beginning of "A Contribution to Statistics."

Out of a hundred people ⟵ ——————— The poet is creating each stanza in relation to 100 people.

Those who always know better
—fifty-two,

The first topic is overconfidence. This sets up a contrast with the next topic, which is insecurity.

doubting every step
—nearly all the rest,

## BACKGROUND

**Wisława Szymborska** *(1923–2012) was a poet and essayist. Szymborska lived in Poland her entire life and had to continue her education in underground classes during World War II. The poet often employed literary devices to write about philosophy, obsessions, war, and sometimes quirky subjects. Some of her poetry appeared in songs and pop culture and was translated into many languages. She won the 1996 Nobel Prize in Literature and was still working on new poetry at the time of her death at age 88.*

# A CONTRIBUTION TO STATISTICS

**Poem by Wisława Szymborska**
**translated by Stanislaw Barańczak and Clare Cavanagh**

## PREPARE TO COMPARE

*This poem uses the same approach to analyzing people as the infographic does. Watch for similarities and differences between the details Szymborska and Hagley choose as you read.*

**Notice & Note**

You can use the side margins to notice and note signposts in the text.

**ANALYZE STRUCTURE**
**Annotate:** Mark the first three stanzas in the poem. What pattern do they establish?

**Paraphrase:** Restate lines 1–5 in your own words. Remember to maintain the order and meaning of the original text.

Out of a hundred people

Those who always know better
—fifty-two,

doubting every step
5    —nearly all the rest,

glad to lend a hand
if it doesn't take too long
—as high as forty-nine,

always good,
10    because they can't be otherwise
—four, well maybe five,

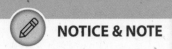
able to admire without envy
—eighteen,

15  suffering illusions
induced by fleeting youth
—sixty, give or take a few,

not to be taken lightly
—forty and four,

20  living in constant fear
of someone or something
—seventy-seven,

capable of happiness
—twenty-something tops,

harmless singly,
25  savage in crowds
—half at least,

cruel
when forced by circumstances
—better not to know
30  even ballpark figures,

**ANALYZE LITERARY DEVICES**

**Annotate:** Mark the word *ballpark* in line 30.

**Evaluate:** A number "in the ballpark" is approximate, not precise. How does this idiom affect the tone of this stanza?

wise after the fact
—just a couple more
than wise before it,

taking only things from life
35  —thirty
(I wish I were wrong),

hunched in pain,
no flashlight in the dark
—eighty-three
40  sooner or later,

**ANALYZE LITERARY DEVICES**

**Annotate:** Mark a word that is repeated in lines 41–45.

**Analyze:** How does the author use repetition and parallelism to show a contrast here?

righteous
—thirty-five, which is a lot,

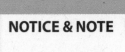
righteous
and understanding
45 —three,

worthy of compassion
—ninety-nine,

mortal
—a hundred out of a hundred.
50 Thus far this figure still remains unchanged.

CONTRASTS AND
CONTRADICTIONS

**Notice & Note:** Mark the
contrast that appears at the
end of this poem.

**Interpret:** Why might you
find the ending surprising or
jarring?

## CHECK YOUR UNDERSTANDING

Answer these questions before moving on to the **Analyze the Text** section on
the following page.

1 The statistics in the poem —

   A indicate the poet's assessments of human nature

   B are based on scientific surveys of how people act

   C help the reader predict how people react in particular circumstances

   D show that the poet has a negative view of human behavior

2 The poem's structure —

   F emphasizes the rhythm and rhyme of the statistics the poet chose

   G is predictable to allow the reader to focus on the poet's message
   about humanity

   H arranges the statistics in numerical order to show what characteristics
   are less and more important

   J moves from humorous examples to increasingly serious ones

3 What is the meaning of the final stanza of the poem?

   A The negatives of life outweigh the positives of life.

   B Each person should try to live the best life he or she can.

   C There is no way to avoid the ups and downs of life.

   D Every person dies regardless of how they live their life.

## ANALYZE THE TEXTS

Support your responses with evidence from the text. 🗐 NOTEBOOK

1. **Draw Conclusions** How does the use of an infographic help you to better understand the data presented in "The World as 100 People"?

2. **Make Inferences** Why do you think the creator of the infographic "The World as 100 People" placed the data about continent, gender, and age at the top of the graphic?

3. **Analyze** Based on the numbers used in the poem, what is the poet's opinion of humanity? Use text evidence in your answer.

4. **Evaluate** How effective do you find the predictable, parallel structure of this poem in communicating a message about human nature? Support your response with examples from the poem.

5. **Notice & Note** How does the poet's use of specific numbers relate to the title and ultimate message of the poem? Use text evidence in your answer.

## RESEARCH

**RESEARCH TIP**
It's best to begin a research project by creating a research question. Before you begin researching, decide exactly what you are looking for. If you cannot find the information you need, be willing to alter your research question.

Choose one statistical category from the infographic to explore further. Determine if your research matches Hagley's infographic or if the conditions have changed in the years since he created the graphic. Be sure to credit the source of the information you use.

| CATEGORY | RECENT DATA | SOURCE |
|---|---|---|
|  |  |  |
|  |  |  |
|  |  |  |
|  |  |  |

**Extend** Create a color-coded map that shows how your chosen statistic plays out in various countries or on different continents.

## CREATE AND DISCUSS

**Write a Letter** Choose one statistical category from Szymborska's poem, and write a friendly letter to a real or imagined person who fits into that category.

- ❏ Review the format of a friendly letter.
- ❏ Identify the audience of the letter.
- ❏ Provide advice to or request advice from your reader about a topic related to the category you chose.

**Give Instructions** In pairs, ask a partner a question related to a problem Szymborska identifies in her poem. For example, "What can I do to be able to admire someone without feeling envious of them?"

- ❏ Provide step-by-step instructions to your partner for solving the problem they ask about.
- ❏ Then, switch roles and ask a question of your partner. Listen to your partner carefully and take notes about what was said.

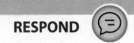 Go to the **Writing Studio** for more on writing for a specific audience and purpose.

Go to the **Speaking and Listening Studio** for more on giving and following instructions.

## RESPOND TO THE ESSENTIAL QUESTION

 How does our point of view shape what we think we know?

**Gather Information** Review your annotations and notes on "The World as 100 People" and "A Contribution to Statistics." Then, add relevant details to your Response Log. As you determine which information to include, think about

- what the statistics in the poem and infographic reveal about the human condition
- which statistics or ideas surprised you
- which statistics you would like to learn more about

At the end of the unit, you will use your notes to write a short story.

**ACADEMIC VOCABULARY**

As you write and discuss what you learned about "The World as 100 People" and "A Contribution to Statistics," be sure to use the Academic Vocabulary words. Check off each of the words that you use.

- ❏ **differentiate**
- ❏ **incorporate**
- ❏ **mode**
- ❏ **orient**
- ❏ **perspective**

# Collaborate & Compare

## COMPARE DETAILS

The infographic and the poem are based on the same idea but emphasize different details. In a small group, complete the charts to track the details and their effect on the message of the infographic and the poem.

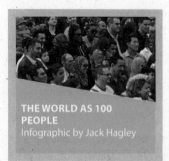

**THE WORLD AS 100 PEOPLE**
Infographic by Jack Hagley

**"The World as 100 People"**

| DETAIL FROM TEXT | MESSAGE |
|---|---|
| Literacy | Almost a fifth of people cannot read or write. |
| Housing | |
| Internet | |
| Poverty | |

**A CONTRIBUTION TO STATISTICS**
Poem by Wislawa Szymborska

**"A Contribution to Statistics"**

| DETAIL FROM TEXT | MESSAGE |
|---|---|
| able to admire without envy —eighteen, | Most people feel envy. |
| not to be taken lightly —forty and four, | |
| capable of happiness —twenty-something tops, | |
| worthy of compassion —ninety-nine, | |

## ANALYZE THE TEXTS

Discuss these questions in your group.

1. **Compare** What are the similarities between the infographic and poem?

2. **Contrast** What are the differences between the two?

3. **Evaluate** How are the purposes of the texts similar? Different?

4. **Synthesize** What have you learned about the world's population from these two texts?

## RESEARCH AND PRESENT

Now, your group can continue exploring the ideas in these texts by researching more statistics and using them to create a multimedia presentation. Follow these steps:

1. **Develop a Question** In your group, brainstorm what the members of your group would like to learn more about. Decide what statistics you could find about the area of interest your group selects. Select a statistic that is not included on the infographic "The World as 100 People."

2. **Gather Information** Try a variety of methods for locating valid, relevant sources of statistical information. You might search in a library database or conduct an online search. If you do not find sources that answer your original question, modify your research question to a related topic and try again. Document each source using an approved citation format.

3. **Synthesize Ideas** Draw a conclusion about your question using information from two or more sources. You can use a chart to record the information you find.

| My Question: | |
|---|---|
| **Source 1:** | **Source 2:** |
| **Source 1 Information:** | **Source 2 Information:** |
| My Answer: | |

4. **Present to the Class** Your group will present what you have learned in a brief multimedia presentation. You will share your original question, the information you gathered, and an answer in the form of a statistic with elaboration. Present images and graphics to support your ideas. Be sure to compare the idea you present with the details in the infographic and the poem. Which of the two works does your topic best fit?

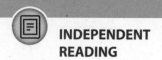

**INDEPENDENT READING**

**? ESSENTIAL QUESTION:**

How does our point of view shape what we think we know?

# Reader's Choice

**Setting a Purpose** Select one or more of these options from your eBook to continue your exploration of the Essential Question.

- Read the descriptions to see which text grabs your interest.
- Think about which genres you enjoy reading.

## Notice & Note

In this unit, you practiced asking a **Big Question** and noticing and noting two signposts: **Numbers and Stats** and **Word Gaps**. As you read independently, these signposts and others will aid your understanding. Below are the anchor questions to ask when you read literature and nonfiction.

| Reading Literature: Stories, Poems, and Plays | | |
|---|---|---|
| **Signpost** | **Anchor Question** | **Lesson** |
| **Contrasts and Contradictions** | Why did the character act that way? | p. 145 |
| **Aha Moment** | How might this change things? | p. 394 |
| **Tough Questions** | What does this make me wonder about? | p. 2 |
| **Words of the Wiser** | What's the lesson for the character? | p. 3 |
| **Again and Again** | Why might the author keep bringing this up? | p. 145 |
| **Memory Moment** | Why is this memory important? | p. 3 |

| Reading Nonfiction: Essays, Articles, and Arguments | | |
|---|---|---|
| **Signpost** | **Anchor Question(s)** | **Lesson** |
| **Big Questions** | What surprised me? <br> What did the author think I already knew? <br> What challenged, changed, or confirmed what I already knew? | p. 220 <br> p. 319 <br> p. 74 |
| **Contrasts and Contradictions** | What is the difference, and why does it matter? | p. 318 |
| **Extreme or Absolute Language** | Why did the author use this language? | p. 221 |
| **Numbers and Stats** | Why did the author use these numbers or amounts? | p. 75 |
| **Quoted Words** | Why was this person quoted or cited, and what did this add? | p. 221 |
| **Word Gaps** | Do I know this word from someplace else? <br> Does it seem like technical talk for this topic? <br> Do clues in the sentence help me understand the word? | p. 75 |

You can preview these texts in Unit 2 of your eBook.

Then, check off the text or texts that you select to read on your own.

**POEM**

**Before I got my eye put out**
Emily Dickinson

*Read what one of our most famous poets has to say about how we see things.*

**ESSAY**

**What Our Telescopes Couldn't See**
Pippa Goldschmidt

*When we look to the skies, what do we miss seeing here on Earth?*

**INFORMATIONAL TEXT**

from *Big Bang: The Origin of the Universe*
Simon Singh

*Find out how an ancient genius measured how far it is around the Earth, using only a stick and a well.*

**SHORT STORY**

**By the Waters of Babylon**
Stephen Vincent Benét

*A young narrator sets off on his own to try to understand a post-apocalyptic world he has only heard rumors of.*

**Collaborate and Share**   Discuss with a partner what you learned from at least one of your independent readings.

Go to the **Reading Studio** for more resources on **Notice & Note.**

- Give a brief synopsis or summary of the text.

- Describe any signposts that you noticed in the text, and explain what they revealed to you.

- Describe what you most enjoyed or found most challenging about the text. Give specific examples.

- Decide whether you would recommend the text to others. Why or why not?

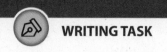 

# Write a Short Story

Go to the **Writing Studio** for help writing a narrative, such as a short story.

This unit focuses on the sometimes surprising differences between how we see things and how they really are. Look back at the texts from this unit, and think about the ways in which things are not as they may first appear in these texts. Use those surprising insights as the basis of a suspenseful or surprising narrative of your own. For an example of a short story you can use as a mentor text, review the story "The Night Face Up."

As you write your story, you will want to look at the notes you made in your Response Log after reading the texts in this unit.

## Writing Prompt

**Read** the information in the box below.

*This is the starting point or premise for your story.*

> We often see what we expect to see, based on what we already have experienced.

**Think** carefully about the following question.

*This is the Essential Question for the unit. How would you answer this question, based on the texts in this unit?*

> How does our point of view shape what we think we know?

**Write** a short story in which things are revealed to be different from how they first appeared.

*Pay attention to the words that describe exactly what you are supposed to write.*

Be sure to—

*Review these points as you write and again when you finish. Make any needed changes or edits.*

- ❏ begin by introducing a setting, a narrator, a main character, and a distinct point of view
- ❏ have an engaging plot with a central conflict
- ❏ use a variety of narrative techniques to develop characters, plot, theme, and suspense or surprise
- ❏ include sensory language and descriptive details
- ❏ end with a logical and satisfying resolution to the conflict

# 1 Plan

Before you begin to write a short story, you need to have an idea. Begin by brainstorming, discussing, and journaling about experiences, events, or conflicts you know about that involved an element of suspense or surprise. Then, freewrite about any of these ideas. Use your imagination to create fictional characters, setting, plot, conflict, and theme related to this experience or event. Remember that even though this is a fictional account, you may use ideas from real life to help you get started. Use the chart below to plan your story.

| SHORT STORY PLANNING CHART |
|---|
| **Topic, Experience, or Event:**  |

| **Characters:** | **Setting:** |
|---|---|
| | |
| **Conflict:** | **Resolution:** |
| | |

| **Theme or Message:** |
|---|
| |

### Notice & Note
### From Reading to Writing

As you plan your short story, apply what you've learned about signposts to your own writing. Think about how you can incorporate an **Aha Moment** into your short story.

Go to the **Reading Studio** for more resources on **Notice & Note**.

Use the notes from your Response Log as you plan your story.

**Background Reading** Review the notes you have taken in your Response Log after reading the texts in this unit. These texts provide background reading that will help you think about what you want to say in your story.

Go to **Writing Narratives: Narrative Structure** for help organizing your ideas.

**Organize Your Ideas**  Combine the techniques you identified in the texts with your own ideas. Consider these points:

- How does the story begin? What can you do to grab the attention of your readers right from the start?

- How does the plot develop? How does the sequence of events lead to a climax—a turning point or moment of greatest intensity and excitement? Pay attention to how you develop the element of surprise or suspense.

- How is the conflict resolved? Is there a moment of sudden insight? How does the story end?

- Who will tell what happens—a character in the story or a narrator observing and reporting events? Whose thoughts will readers understand?

- What details will bring your setting and characters to life for readers?

You might prefer to draft your story online.

## ② Develop a Draft

Once you have completed your planning activities, you will be ready to begin drafting your short story. Refer to your graphic organizers and/or the outline you have created, as well as any notes you took as you studied the texts in the unit. These will provide a kind of map for you to follow as you write. Finish a first draft and then read it over before you decide to make changes or move sentences around.

## Use the Mentor Text

> ### Author's Craft
> Sensory and descriptive details can be very effective in evoking a setting. Note the way the author uses an appeal to the sense of smell when introducing the Aztec setting in "The Night Face Up."

**THE NIGHT FACE UP**

---

It was unusual as a dream because it was full of smells, and he never dreamt smells. First a marshy smell, there to the left of the trail the swamps began already, the quaking bogs from which no one ever returned. But the reek lifted, and instead there came a dark, fresh composite fragrance, like the night under which he moved, in flight from the Aztecs.

*The author brings the scene to life for readers by describing the smells using precise, vivid language.*

---

**Apply What You've Learned**  Be creative in your use of sensory and descriptive details when you describe your setting.

> ### Genre Characteristics
> In a story that creates suspense by playing with the reader's sense of reality, the author may drop clues, possibly false, that lead the reader to lean toward one conclusion or another. Notice how Cortázar does this as his protagonist lies in the hospital.

---

He tried to fix the moment of the accident exactly, and it got him very angry to notice that there was a void there, an emptiness he could not manage to fill. Between the impact and the moment that they picked him up off the pavement, the passing out or what went on, there was nothing he could see. And at the same time he had the feeling that this void, this nothingness, had lasted an eternity.

*Does this mean that the other reality is true, or is this just a description of a temporary loss of memory?*

---

**Apply What You've Learned**  Making the reader wonder what's going on can create suspense and mystery.

**WRITING TASK**

Go to **Writing Narratives: The Language of Narrative** for help making your story more engaging.

## 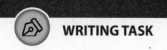 ③ Revise

**On Your Own**  The best fiction writers know that a draft is only a beginning. In fact, some of the most important and creative work is done in the revision process, including bringing realism and color to a story by introducing vivid descriptions, sensory details, suspenseful elements, and effective narrative techniques. Use the Revision Guide below to help you make your writing stronger.

| REVISION GUIDE | | |
|---|---|---|
| **Ask Yourself** | **Tips** | **Revision Techniques** |
| 1. Does the narrative begin in an engaging way and introduce characters, setting, conflict, and point of view? | **Underline** the engaging opening and **mark** clues about the characters, setting, conflict, or point of view. | **Revise** your introduction to begin with action or dialogue, and **add** details about characters, setting, conflict, or narrator. |
| 2. Do narrative techniques and precise language bring the story and characters to life? | **Underline** dialogue, sensory details, and vivid verbs. | **Add** dialogue, sensory details, and vivid verbs where they are lacking. |
| 3. Does the central conflict develop in a logical and engaging way? | **Mark** points at which the conflict advances the plot. **Underline** phrases or sentences that build suspense. | **Revise** passages that do not advance the plot. **Add** phrases or sentences that build suspense. |
| 4. Is surprise used effectively to bring the conflict to its peak? | **Mark** surprising passages. | **Add** a surprising event or narration that links the surprise to the central conflict. |
| 5. Does the conclusion resolve the conflict in a logical way? | **Underline** the explanation of how the conflict is resolved. | **Add** dialogue or narration that logically resolves the conflict. |

**ACADEMIC VOCABULARY**

As you conduct your peer review, try to use these words.

❏ **differentiate**

❏ **incorporate**

❏ **mode**

❏ **orient**

❏ **perspective**

**With a Partner**  After you revise based on the points above, exchange stories with a partner. Evaluate each other's drafts in a peer review. Point out parts of the story that work well, and ask questions about any confusing or unrealistic events or characters. Provide concrete suggestions for improving the draft as appropriate.

# 4 Edit

No matter how good your story is, readers will not fully appreciate it if they are confused by misspellings or other problems with language conventions. Edit for proper use of standard English conventions and make sure to correct any misspellings and usage or grammatical errors.

## Language Conventions

**Use Complex Sentences**  A complex sentence includes an independent clause and one or more dependent clauses.

Go to the **Grammar Studio** for help with complex sentences.

- An **independent clause** has a subject and a verb and can stand alone. If two independent clauses are joined only by a comma, they form a **comma splice.** When no punctuation joins them but they are in the same sentence, they form a **run-on sentence.**

- A **dependent clause** has a subject and a verb and cannot stand alone. It can act as an adverb or an adjective, modifying another part of the sentence. If it is not attached to an independent clause, it is a **sentence fragment.**

Here are examples of complex sentences from "The Night Face Up":

| Type of Dependent Clause | Examples from Text |
|---|---|
| Adverb Clause | **When the big windows across the way turned to smudges of dark blue, he thought it would not be difficult for him to sleep.** |
| Adjective Clause | **A young intern arrived with some metal and leather apparatus which he adjusted to fit onto the good arm to check something or other.** |

# 5 Publish

Finalize your story and choose a way to share it with your audience. Consider these options:

- Read your story aloud to the class.
- Produce your story as a podcast to be posted on a classroom or school website.

Use the scoring guide to evaluate your short story.

| WRITING TASK SCORING GUIDE: SHORT STORY | | |
|---|---|---|
| **Organization/Progression** | **Development of Ideas** | **Use of Language and Conventions** |
| **4** • The sequence of events is effective, clear, and logical.<br>• Virtually all events serve the plot and/or the character development.<br>• The pace and organization keep the reader curious about what will happen next. | • The beginning of the story catches the reader's attention and establishes the conflict.<br>• The conflict of the story is developed and resolved in a logical and interesting way.<br>• The theme emerges from the plot events and character development.<br>• The story is told from a distinct point of view that advances the theme or tone. | • Language and word choice is precise and descriptive.<br>• Complex sentences are used effectively to build tension.<br>• Text is free from unintended sentence fragments, run-on sentences, and comma splices.<br>• Spelling, capitalization, and punctuation are correct.<br>• Grammar and usage are correct. |
| **3** • The sequence of events is, for the most part, effective, clear, and logical.<br>• Most events serve the plot and/or the character development.<br>• The pace and organization sometimes make the reader curious about what will happen next. | • The beginning of the story catches the reader's attention fairly well and establishes the conflict.<br>• The conflict of the story is developed and resolved fairly well.<br>• For the most part, the theme emerges from the plot events and character development.<br>• The story's point of view is clear and consistent. | • Language is for the most part specific and descriptive.<br>• Complex sentences are used.<br>• There are some unintended sentence fragments, run-on sentences, and comma splices.<br>• There are some spelling, capitalization, and punctuation mistakes.<br>• Some grammar and usage errors occur. |
| **2** • The sequence of events is sometimes confusing.<br>• Only some events serve the plot and/or the character development.<br>• The pace and organization rarely make the reader curious about what will happen next. | • The beginning of the story does not catch the reader's attention well and the establishment of the conflict is vague.<br>• The conflict of the story needs to be better developed and resolved.<br>• The theme does not emerge from the plot events and character development well, but it does exist.<br>• The point of view is vague but generally sticks with either the first or third person. | • Language is somewhat vague and lacking in detail.<br>• There are unintended sentence fragments, run-on sentences, and comma splices.<br>• Conventions including spelling, capitalization, punctuation, grammar, and usage, are often incorrect but do not make reading difficult. |
| **1** • The sequence of events is mostly unclear.<br>• Events do not serve the plot and/or the character development.<br>• The pace and organization do not make the reader curious about what will happen next. | • The beginning of the story does not catch the reader's attention and the conflict is missing.<br>• The conflict of the story is not developed or resolved.<br>• The theme does not emerge from the plot events and character development.<br>• The point of view is inconsistent and confusing. | • Language is inappropriate for the text.<br>• There are many unintended sentence fragments, run-on sentences, and comma splices.<br>• Many spelling, capitalization, and punctuation errors are present.<br>• Grammatical and usage errors interfere with the writer's meaning. |

# Produce a Podcast

You will now adapt your short story into a podcast that your classmates can listen to. You also will listen to their podcasts, ask questions to better understand what they are trying to accomplish, and help them improve their work.

Go to the **Speaking and Listening Studio** for a lesson on using media in a presentation.

## ① Adapt Your Story as a Podcast

Review your short story and use the chart below to guide you as you adapt your story for a podcast, including the creation of a script, music, or other sound effects.

| PODCAST PLANNING CHART | | |
|---|---|---|
| **Beginning** | How will you revise the story's beginning to capture listener's attention? Is there a way to effectively use sound effects or music? | |
| **Voices** | Will you read the story by yourself? Could you use classmates to read certain characters' dialogue? | |
| **Transitions** | Are there parts of your story that should be simplified? Can you use audio signals to help identify changes in time or place? | |
| **Sound** | Should you use music in your podcast? Are there sound effects that will help you create a mood of suspense or surprise? | |

As you work to improve your own podcast and those of your classmates, follow these rules of constructive criticism:

- ❏ be objective about the podcaster's purpose
- ❏ begin feedback with the strong points of the work
- ❏ provide honest but respectful criticism that includes concrete suggestions for improvement

## ② Practice with a Partner or Group

When your script is ready and you've decided whether to include music and/or sound effects, practice before you record your podcast.

### Practice Effective Verbal Techniques

- ❏ **Enunciation**  Be sure not to swallow the ends of letters or words. Pronounce each letter, such as a final *g* in *going* or *beginning*.
- ❏ **Voice Modulation and Pitch**  Adjust your voice and pitch to display appropriate emotion and emphasis for the content.
- ❏ **Speaking Rate**  Adjust your rate of speaking to the emotion or mood of the content to ensure the listeners' interest.
- ❏ **Microphone Skills**  Practice speaking into a microphone to ensure appropriate volume and to avoid distracting feedback from the microphone, such as pops or hisses.

### Create Your Podcast

- ❏ **Recording Location**  If your school doesn't have a music practice room or a studio, record in a space with as little background noise as possible.
- ❏ **Recording**  If you make a mistake while recording, just continue. If you can edit, pause and go back to the beginning of a paragraph so that you can incorporate your correction more smoothly.
- ❏ **Editing**  If your school has audio editing software, or if you can download an open source app, tighten up the transitions between segments of your recorded podcast.
- ❏ **Music**  Find appropriate free music from a site such as archive.org or the Library of Congress music collection. Always check copyright restrictions before using someone else's music.

### Provide and Consider Advice for Improvement

**As an audience,** listen closely. Take notes about ways that podcasters can improve their presentations and more effectively present their stories.

**As a podcaster,** pay attention to feedback and consider ways to improve your podcast to make it more effective. Remember to ask for suggestions about your music and sound effects, if you chose to use them.

## ③ Post Your Podcast

Use the advice you received during practice to make final changes to your podcast. Then, make it available to your classmates on your school's website. Reflect on listeners' comments to improve future podcasts.

# Reflect on the Unit

When you were writing your short story, you were inspired by your thoughts about the reading you have done in this unit. Now is a good time to reflect on what you have learned.

## Reflect on the Essential Question

- How does our point of view shape what we think we know? How has your answer to this question changed since you first considered it when you started this unit?

- What are some examples from the texts you've read that show how our point of view shapes what we think of as reality?

## Reflect on Your Reading

- Which selections were the most interesting or surprising to you?

- From which selection did you learn the most about the differences between what is real and what we think is real?

## Reflect on the Writing Task

- What difficulties did you encounter while working on your short story? How might you avoid these challenges the next time?

- What part of the short story was the easiest to write? What was the most difficult to write? Why?

- What improvements did you make to your story as you were revising?

# THE NATURAL WORLD

**?** *ESSENTIAL QUESTION:*

What effect do we have on nature, and how does nature affect us?

" Wildness reminds us what it means to be human, what we are connected to rather than what we are separate from. "

Terry Tempest Williams

## ACADEMIC VOCABULARY

Academic Vocabulary words are words you use when you discuss and write about texts. In this unit you will practice and learn five words.

☑ advocate ☐ discrete ☐ domain ☐ evoke ☐ enhance

Study the Word Network to learn more about the word **advocate**.

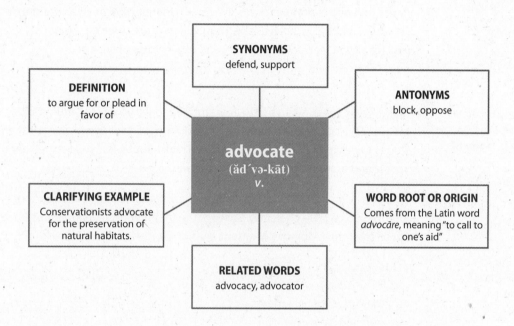

**SYNONYMS**
defend, support

**DEFINITION**
to argue for or plead in favor of

**ANTONYMS**
block, oppose

**advocate**
(ăd´və-kāt)
*v.*

**CLARIFYING EXAMPLE**
Conservationists advocate for the preservation of natural habitats.

**WORD ROOT OR ORIGIN**
Comes from the Latin word *advocāre*, meaning "to call to one's aid"

**RELATED WORDS**
advocacy, advocator

**Write and Discuss** Discuss the completed Word Network with a partner, making sure to talk through all of the boxes until you both understand the word, its synonyms, antonyms, and related forms. Then, fill out Word Networks for the remaining four words. Use a dictionary or online resource to help you complete the activity.

*Go online to access the Word Networks.*

## RESPOND TO THE ESSENTIAL QUESTION

In this unit, you will read various genres that explore how we affect nature and how it affects us. As you read, you will revisit the **Essential Question** and gather your ideas about it in the **Response Log** that appears on page R3. At the end of the unit, you will have the opportunity to write an **explanatory essay** about an interaction between humans and nature. Filling out the Response Log will help you prepare for this writing task.

*You can also go online to access the Response Log.*

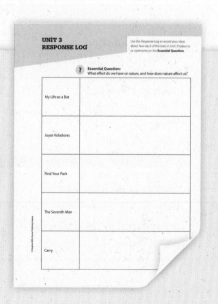

UNIT 3
RESPONSE LOG

Use this Response Log to record your ideas about how each of the texts in Unit 3 relates to or comments on the Essential Question.

**? Essential Question:**
What effect do we have on nature, and how does nature affect us?

My Life as a Bat

Joyas Voladoras

Find Your Park

The Seventh Man

Carry

# Notice & Note

For more information on these and other signposts to Notice & Note, visit the **Reading Studio**.

## MY LIFE AS A BAT

You are about to read the short story "My Life as a Bat." As you read, you will notice and note signposts that will help you identify and analyze the story's structure and the author's use of language. Here are three key signposts to look for as you read this short story and other works of fiction.

When you read and encounter a phrase like these, pause to see if it's a **Memory Moment** signpost:

"I remembered when . . ."

"that reminded me of . . ."

"I always thought of the time when . . ."

"Something like this had happened before . . ."

"We used to . . ."

**Memory Moment** Has a friend ever stopped to tell you a story from his or her past? Was it a funny story? The story of an important event? Friends share stories to get to know each other better. Think about what you learned about your friend from the story he or she told you.

When an author includes a memory or a flashback, it can reveal important information about a character. Some of the things you can learn about a character from a **Memory Moment** are:

- strengths and weaknesses
- fears and desires
- opinions and perspectives
- motivations and obstacles

Read this part of "My Life as a Bat" to see how a student might annotate a Memory Moment:

**Anchor Question**
When you notice this signpost, ask: Why might this memory be important to the character?

> 6   I have recurring nightmares.
> 7       In one of them, I am clinging to the ceiling of a summer cottage while a red-faced man in white shorts and a white V-necked T-shirt jumps up and down, hitting at me with a tennis racket. There are cedar rafters up here, and sticky flypapers attached with tacks, dangling like toxic seaweeds. I look down at the man's face, foreshortened and sweating, the eyes bulging and blue, the mouth emitting furious noise. . . .

| What memory is introduced? | a nightmare of being attacked by an angry man inside a house |
|---|---|
| What does the memory reveal about the narrator's opinions? | The narrator sees humans as ugly and irrational and a threat to her safety. |

**Contrasts and Contradictions**  Have you ever heard the saying "cruel to be kind?" The idea of this contradiction is that it is kinder to be brutally honest with a person in order to help him or her in the long term.

**Contrasts and Contradictions** can also highlight important elements in a story. They can establish a character's world view, create tension in the story's mood, or signal plot developments. They may help to better define an idea or experience by setting it up against what it is not. Taking note of contradictions and contrasts can help you more fully understand a story.

Here is how a student might annotate a contrast in "My Life As a Bat":

> 5 . . . When they kill, they kill <u>without mercy, but without hate</u>. . . .

**Anchor Question**
When you notice this signpost, ask: What point is the author making with this contrast?

| What ideas are contrasted? | mercy and hate |
| --- | --- |
| Why is this an important distinction to the narrator? | The contrast shows bats as neither good nor evil. |

**Again and Again**  Imagine that a friend keeps mentioning a big basketball game coming up next week. You already know about the game, so why keep talking about it? Clearly, it's important to your friend. Maybe she's worried about it.

Authors repeat words, phrases, and imagery to make a point. Repetition can reveal important information about the characters or setting. **Again and Again** signposts may foreshadow future events or develop a story's theme.

In this example, a student underlined repeated elements:

> 3    Consider also: previous lives have entered the world of commerce. Money can be made from them. *You were* Cleopatra, *you were* a Flemish duke, *you were* a Druid priestess, and money changes hands. If the stock market exists, so must previous lives.

Pause to see if it's an **Again and Again** signpost when you see repetition of:

words

phrases

colors

images

descriptions

**Anchor Question**
When you notice this signpost, ask: Why might the author bring up this idea again and again?

| What phrase or idea is repeated? | You were |
| --- | --- |
| What does this repetition accomplish in the text? | It sounds like someone might be told they were all of these things or that someone goes around telling many people stories about previous lives. |

# MY LIFE AS A BAT

Short Story by **Margaret Atwood**

**?**

**ESSENTIAL QUESTION:**

What effect do we have on nature, and how does nature affect us?

## QUICK START

Imagine what life would be like if you were an animal. Quickwrite about what animal you would be. What would you be afraid of? What would humans seem like to you? Would you avoid them or live near them?

## ANALYZE STRUCTURE

Most stories follow a **structure** that includes these elements:

- **Exposition:** introduces characters, setting, and conflict.

- **Rising Action:** introduces complications and builds suspense.

- **Climax:** the most exciting part; makes the conflict's outcome clear.

- **Falling Action:** eases tension and shows main character's response.

- **Resolution:** reveals how events turn out; also called the denouement.

In this story, the author dispenses with traditional narrative structure. Instead, she arranges events, conflicts, and reflections using an informative essay format with numbered heads. Readers must piece together the narrative to determine the order and significance of events. When reading any story that uses an unusual narrative structure, consider the effect of the author's choices: How does the structure maintain reader interest and develop theme? How does it help you make, correct, and confirm predictions?

## ANALYZE LANGUAGE

An author's language can create vivid images, convey specific meanings, and set the mood or tone of the story. Figurative language and sensory descriptions are two ways that authors use language.

**Figurative language** makes imaginative comparisons between dissimilar things. **Similes** are comparisons that use the words *like* or *as*; **metaphors** are comparisons that are implied rather than stated.

**Sensory descriptions** rely on the senses to convey vivid images. An author will show how something looks, tastes, sounds, smells, or feels.

To analyze the language that Margaret Atwood uses in "My Life as a Bat," form a mental image of what the language describes. Then, ask yourself questions such as the ones in the following examples.

- **Simile**: "flypapers . . . dangling like toxic seaweeds." In what way are the items being compared similar? What feeling does the word *toxic* convey?

- **Metaphor**: "his breath, . . . the breath of the monster." Is the man really a monster? What does this comparison suggest about him or his likely actions? What is the narrator's **tone**, or attitude, toward him?

- **Sensory description**: "sound of water trickling through limestone . . . a glistening hush." What senses does this description rely on? How does the description enhance, or strengthen, the imagery of the story?

### GENRE ELEMENTS: SHORT STORY

- centers on the thoughts and actions of one or more characters

- includes a narrator who may or may not be a character

- contains one or more settings

- includes a series of events or actions that may be told in or out of order

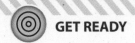
## CRITICAL VOCABULARY

| consensus | interlude | subtleties | incendiary | denizen |
|---|---|---|---|---|

To see how many Critical Vocabulary words you already know, use them to complete the sentences.

**1.** I am a(n) _____ of the town where I live.

**2.** When the whole class agrees, we have a(n) _____.

**3.** The graduation party invitation specified no _____ materials, such as fireworks.

**4.** Our coach gave us a brief _____ between running laps so we could get a drink of water.

**5.** The _____ of foreign languages take time to distinguish.

## LANGUAGE CONVENTIONS

**Colons**  Writers can use colons to introduce a list or a direct quotation. A colon may also set up an explanation of a preceding idea. A reader pauses at a colon to prepare for what comes after it. Here is an example from the story:

**There was also my dislike for headfuls of human hair, so like nets or the tendrils of poisonous jellyfish: I feared entanglements.**

A colon is set at the end of a word and is followed by a space. As you read, watch for ways that Atwood uses colons for effect.

---

**ANNOTATION MODEL**                                       **NOTICE & NOTE**

As you read, notice and note signposts, including **Memory Moment, Contrasts and Contradictions,** and **Again and Again**. Here is an example of how one reader responded to the structure and the author's use of language in the opening of "My Life as a Bat":

> **1. Reincarnation** ⟵
> In my previous life I was a bat.
>
>     If you find previous lives amusing or unlikely, you are not a serious person. Consider: a great many people believe in them, and if sanity is a general consensus about the content of reality,[who are you to disagree?]

*Sets up story structure*

*Surprising statement*

*Narrator is speaking directly to the reader.*

## BACKGROUND

**Margaret Atwood** (b. 1939) has published more than fifty works of fiction, poetry, and nonfiction. This Canadian author uses her keen intellect and sharp wit to explore ideas about nature, science, the search for identity, social criticism, and human rights. Her award-winning novels include The Handmaid's Tale, which was made into a movie and award-winning television series, Cat's Eye, Alias Grace, and Oryx and Crake.

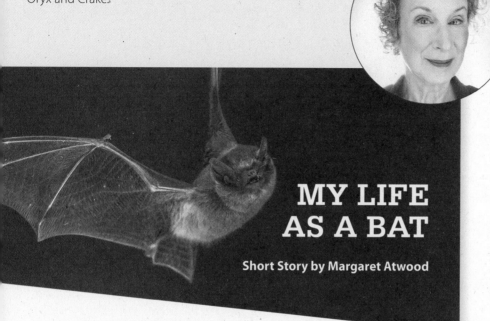

# MY LIFE AS A BAT

### Short Story by Margaret Atwood

## SETTING A PURPOSE

*As you read, make predictions about what each section of the story will be about and how it will contribute to the story's structure.*

## 1. Reincarnation

1   In my previous life I was a bat.

2       If you find previous lives amusing or unlikely, you are not a serious person. Consider: a great many people believe in them, and if sanity is a general **consensus** about the content of reality, who are you to disagree?

3       Consider also: previous lives have entered the world of commerce. Money can be made from them. *You were Cleopatra,*[1] *you were a Flemish duke, you were a Druid priestess,* and money changes hands. If the stock market exists, so must previous lives.

4       In the previous-life market, there is not such a great demand for Peruvian ditch-diggers as there is for Cleopatra; or for Indian latrine-cleaners, or for 1952 housewives living in California split-levels. Similarly, not many of us choose to remember our lives as vultures, spiders, or rodents, but some of us do. The fortunate

---

[1] **Cleopatra:** Queen of Egypt in the first century B.C.E.

### Notice & Note

You can use the side margins to notice and note signposts in the text.

**consensus**
(kən-sĕn´səs) *n.*
agreement.

**ANALYZE STRUCTURE**
**Annotate:** Mark two details in paragraphs 1–4 that help explain the section heading.

**Analyze:** What role does this section play in the structure of the story? Cite evidence in your answer.

**interlude**
(ĭn´tər-lōōd) *n.* a time of rest between two tasks.

**ANALYZE LANGUAGE**

**Annotate:** Mark two similes in paragraph 7.

**Analyze:** How do the comparisons that the author makes create tension?

**MEMORY MOMENT**

**Notice & Note:** Mark positive images and impressions in paragraph 9.

**Draw Conclusions:** How does the narrator feel about the memory of being a bat? Why is this passage a "nightmare"?

few. Conventional wisdom has it that reincarnation as an animal is a punishment for past sins, but perhaps it is a reward instead. At least a resting place. An **interlude** of grace.

5     Bats have a few things to put up with, but they do not inflict. When they kill, they kill without mercy, but without hate. They are immune from the curse of pity. They never gloat.

## 2. Nightmares

6     I have recurring nightmares.

7     In one of them, I am clinging to the ceiling of a summer cottage while a red-faced man in white shorts and a white V-necked T-shirt jumps up and down, hitting at me with a tennis racket. There are cedar rafters up here, and sticky flypapers attached with tacks, dangling like toxic seaweeds. I look down at the man's face, foreshortened and sweating, the eyes bulging and blue, the mouth emitting furious noise, rising up like a marine float, sinking again, rising as if on a swell of air.

8     The air itself is muggy, the sun is sinking; there will be a thunderstorm. A woman is shrieking, "My hair! My hair!" and someone else is calling, "Anthea! Bring the stepladder!" All I want is to get out through the hole in the screen, but that will take some concentration and it's hard in this din of voices, they interfere with my sonar.[2] There is a smell of dirty bathmats—it's his breath, the breath that comes out from every pore, the breath of the monster. I will be lucky to get out of this alive.

9     In another nightmare I am winging my way—flittering, I suppose you'd call it—through the clean-washed demilight before dawn. This is a desert. The yuccas are in bloom, and I have been gorging myself on their juices and pollen. I'm heading to my home, to my home cave,

---

[2] **sonar:** a system for identifying objects with reflected sound.

where it will be cool during the burnout of day and there will be the sound of water trickling through limestone, coating the rock with a glistening hush, with the moistness of new mushrooms, and the other bats will chirp and rustle and doze until night unfurls again and makes the hot sky tender for us.

10    But when I reach the entrance to the cave, it is sealed over. It's blocked in. Who can have done this?

11    I vibrate my wings, sniffing blind as a dazzled moth over the hard surface. In a short time the sun will rise like a balloon on fire and I will be blasted with its glare, shriveled to a few small bones.

12    Whoever said that light was life and darkness nothing?

13    For some of us, the mythologies are different.

## 3. Vampire Films

14    I became aware of the nature of my previous life gradually, not only through dreams but through scraps of memory, through hints, through odd moments of recognition.

15    There was my preference for the **subtleties** of dawn and dusk, as opposed to the vulgar blaring hour of high noon. There was my déjà vu experience in the Carlsbad Caverns—surely I had been there before, long before, before they put in the pastel spotlights and the cute names for stalactites and the underground restaurant where you can combine claustrophobia and indigestion and then take the elevator to get back out.

16    There was also my dislike for headfuls of human hair, so like nets or the tendrils of poisonous jellyfish: I feared entanglements. No real bat would ever suck the blood of necks. The neck is too near the hair. Even the vampire bat will target a hairless extremity—by choice a toe, resembling as it does the teat of a cow.

17    Vampire films have always seemed ludicrous to me, for this reason but also for the idiocy of their bats—huge rubbery bats, with red Christmas-light eyes and fangs like a sabertoothed tiger's, flown

CONTRASTS AND
CONTRADICTIONS

**Notice & Note:** Mark a statement in this section that expresses the opposite of conventional thinking.

**Compare:** How does this statement serve to contrast humans and bats?

**subtleties**
(sŭt´l-tēz) *n.* fine details or nuances.

### ANALYZE LANGUAGE
**Annotate:** In paragraph 15, mark a context clue for the meaning of the commonly used foreign phrase *déjà vu*.

**Analyze:** How does the use of the phrase *déjà vu* support the narrator's claim of a past life?

in on strings, their puppet wings flapped sluggishly like those of an overweight and degenerate bird. I screamed at these filmic moments, but not with fear; rather with outraged laughter, at the insult to bats.

18     O Dracula, unlikely hero! . . . Why was it given to you by whoever stole your soul to transform yourself into bat and wolf, and only those? Why not a vampire chipmunk, a duck, a gerbil? Why not a vampire turtle? Now that would be a plot.

## 4. The Bat as Deadly Weapon

19     During the Second World War they did experiments with bats. Thousands of bats were to be released over German cities, at the hour of noon. Each was to have a small **incendiary** device strapped onto it, with a timer. The bats would have headed for darkness, as is their habit. They would have crawled into holes in walls, or secreted themselves under the eaves of houses, relieved to have found safety. At a preordained moment they would have exploded, and the cities would have gone up in flames.

20     That was the plan. Death by flaming bat. The bats too would have died, of course. Acceptable megadeaths.

21     The cities went up in flames anyway, but not with the aid of bats. The atom bomb had been invented, and the fiery bat was no longer thought necessary.

22     If the bats had been used after all, would there have been a war memorial to them? It isn't likely.

23     If you ask a human being what makes his flesh creep more, a bat or a bomb, he will say the bat. It is difficult to experience loathing for something merely metal, however ominous. We save these sensations for those with skin and flesh: a skin, a flesh, unlike our own.

## 5. Beauty

24     Perhaps it isn't my life as a bat that was the interlude. Perhaps it is this life. Perhaps I have been sent into human form as if on a dangerous mission, to save and redeem my own folk. When I have gained a small success, or died in the attempt—for failure, in such a task and against such odds, is more likely—I will be born again, back into that other form, that other world where I truly belong.

25     More and more, I think of this event with longing. The quickness of heartbeat, the vivid plunge into the nectars of crepuscular flowers, hovering in the infrared of night; the dank lazy half-sleep of daytime, with bodies rounded and soft as furred plums clustering around me, the mothers licking the tiny amazed faces of the newborn; the swift love of what will come next, the anticipations of the tongue and of the infurled, corrugated and scrolled nose, nose like a dead leaf, nose like a radiator grille, nose of a **denizen** of Pluto.

26    And in the evening, the supersonic hymn of praise to our Creator, the Creator of bats, who appears to us in the form of a bat and who gave us all things: water and the liquid stone of caves, the woody refuge of attics, petals and fruit and juicy insects, and the beauty of slippery wings and sharp white canines and shining eyes.

27    What do we pray for? We pray for food as all do, and for health and for the increase of our kind; and for deliverance from evil, which cannot be explained by us, which is hair-headed and walks in the night with a single white unseeing eye, and stinks of half-digested meat, and has two legs.

28    Goddess of caves and grottoes: bless your children.

**ANALYZE STRUCTURE**

**Annotate:** Mark two details in the section "Beauty" that describe the future the narrator envisions.

**Analyze:** How does this section serve as a resolution for the story?

## CHECK YOUR UNDERSTANDING

Answer these questions before moving on to the **Analyze the Text** section on the following page.

**1** How does the author structure this story?

**A** As a stream-of-consciousness reflection on the narrator's thoughts

**B** As a collection of very short stories that are increasingly serious

**C** In chronological order showing a sequence of events in the narrator's life

**D** In sections that include brief scenes or facts to illustrate ideas

**2** References to popular culture and historical events serve to —

**F** use funny stories to keep the interest of readers who don't like bats

**G** show how the lives of bats and humans have always been intertwined

**H** illustrate why the narrator considers humans to be evil

**J** reveal that the narrator is wrong about how much humans value bats

**3** Which statement best reflects the narrator's attitude toward the relationship between bats and people?

**A** People fear bats, yet humans are the real monsters.

**B** People and bats should appreciate each other more.

**C** Bats have good reason to attack people like they do.

**D** Bats miss out on the day, yet people miss out on the night.

## ANALYZE THE TEXT

Support your responses with evidence from the text. 📓 NOTEBOOK

1. **Analyze**  Throughout the story, the author uses wry, humorous language in the form of exaggeration and irony. Give an example of humor from the text. How does the humor develop the character of the narrator?

2. **Interpret**  The narrator, as a bat, describes the sun rising "like a balloon on fire" (paragraph 11). What meaning is conveyed by this simile in the context of the nightmare?

3. **Compare**  What are some of the main contrasts the narrator makes between humans and bats? Cite specific statements as well as stories that imply the differences. What theme about people is developed through these contrasts?

4. **Evaluate**  How did the narrative structure and section headings help you make, correct, and confirm predictions about where the story would go? How do the structure and headings help develop a theme?

5. **Notice & Note**  Consider the way the narrator contrasts ideas about and images of bats in the sections "Vampire Films," "The Bat as Deadly Weapon," and "Beauty." Explain how comparison and contrast help to highlight an essential contradiction between people's perceptions of bats and bats in reality.

## RESEARCH

**RESEARCH TIP**
Paraphrase the information from a source to better track important information. Mark the text where you find descriptions about bats. Write the details in your own words to guide your research.

"My Life as a Bat" includes many details about bats that counteract misconceptions people hold about them. With a partner, choose one aspect of bats listed below, and conduct research to determine how accurately the story reflects the facts.

| ASPECTS OF BATS | STORY DETAILS | RESEARCH FINDINGS | POPULAR MISCONCEPTIONS |
|---|---|---|---|
| where they live | | | |
| how they behave | | | |
| what they eat | | | |
| what they look like | | | |

**Extend**  With a partner, review your research and determine how accurate the descriptions in the story were and whether popular misconceptions have any basis in fact. Discuss reasons for any differences, including faulty reasoning, bias, or conflicting information.

## CREATE AND PRESENT

**Write an Analysis**  Write a three-to four-paragraph essay in which you compare and contrast the facts that you found in your research and those that were included in the selection.

- ❏ Introduce the topic and discuss the selection's focus on bats and life as a bat.

- ❏ Then, discuss the accuracy of facts and descriptions that the story provides. Use evidence from your research to support or refute both details from the story and popular misconceptions about bats.

- ❏ In your final paragraph, state your conclusion about the overall accuracy of the facts included in "My Life as a Bat."

**Present Research**  Share your findings in a brief presentation about the accuracy of facts about bats in "My Life as a Bat."

- ❏ Review your analysis and choose a few facts or descriptions to illustrate your analysis. Create a three-factor Venn diagram to compare the story details and facts that you have chosen.

- ❏ Display the diagram and discuss the information you chose to include.

- ❏ Present your conclusion about the accuracy of the facts and descriptions about bats in "My Life as a Bat." Invite your audience to ask questions at the end of your presentation.

Visit the **Writing Studio** for more on writing informative texts.

Go to the **Speaking and Listening Studio** for help with giving a presentation.

TIP:  Here is an example of a three-factor Venn diagram. Commonalities should appear in overlapping areas.

## RESPOND TO THE ESSENTIAL QUESTION

 What effect do we have on nature, and how does nature affect us?

**Gather Information**  Review your annotations and notes on "My Life as a Bat." Then, add relevant information to your Response Log. As you determine which information to include, think about:

- the opinions and attitude of the narrator
- the language the author uses to build meaning
- the non-traditional structure of the story

At the end of the unit, use your notes to help you write an explanatory essay.

### ACADEMIC VOCABULARY

As you write and discuss what you learned from the short story, be sure to use the Academic Vocabulary words. Check off each of the words that you use.

- ❏ **advocate**
- ❏ **discrete**
- ❏ **domain**
- ❏ **evoke**
- ❏ **enhance**

**WORD BANK**
consensus
interlude
subtleties
incendiary
denizen

Go to the **Vocabulary Studio** for more on reference sources.

## CRITICAL VOCABULARY

**Practice and Apply**  Answer the questions to demonstrate your understanding of each Critical Vocabulary word.

1. What **consensus** do humans hold about bats?

2. What do bats usually do in the **interlude** between dawn and dusk?

3. What are some of the **subtleties** of life inside a bat colony?

4. Why might military strategists use **incendiary** weapons?

5. What environments can a bat be considered a **denizen** of?

## VOCABULARY STRATEGY:
### Reference Sources

If you come across an unfamiliar word while reading, look first for a footnote on the page. If one is not provided, you can use the context—the words and sentences around the unfamiliar word—to help you determine the meaning. If context is not helpful, turn to a reference source, such as a **glossary**, **dictionary**, or **thesaurus**. For advanced or foreign terms, you may need to consult a college-level or bilingual dictionary.

| GLOSSARY | DICTIONARY | THESAURUS |
|---|---|---|
| **Where it is found:** at the back of the book in which the word is used | **Where it is found:** library; Internet; print and digital versions | **Where it is found:** library; Internet; print and digital versions |
| **What it includes:** pronunciation; definition as it is used in the text | **What it includes:** part of speech; syllable division; pronunciation; definitions; synonyms; etymology | **What it includes:** synonyms; shades of meaning |

**Practice and Apply**  Use reference sources to find the specified information about each of the Critical Vocabulary words. Write your answers and explain which reference source you used and why.

1. Write three synonyms for **consensus**.

2. Write two different uses of the word **interlude**.

3. Write the pronunciation for **subtleties**.

4. Write the etymology, or origin, of the word **incendiary**.

5. Write the part of speech and syllable division for **denizen**.

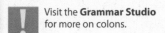

## LANGUAGE CONVENTIONS: Colons

A writer's use of punctuation helps clarify meaning for the reader by showing places of emphasis or change of tone. In "My Life as a Bat," Margaret Atwood uses colons not only for meaning but also to create an engaging style.

Colons are used to introduce lists, as in the following passage from the story:

**And in the evening, the supersonic hymn of praise to our Creator, the Creator of bats, who appears to us in the form of a bat and who gave us all things: water and the liquid stone of caves, the woody refuge of attics, petals and fruit and juicy insects, and the beauty of slippery wings and sharp white canines and shining eyes.**

Colons can also be used to introduce direct quotations, as in this example:

**Atwood suggests that humans could learn from animals' lives: "When they kill, they kill without mercy, but without hate. They are immune from the curse of pity. They never gloat."**

Colons can be used to provide examples or clarify and expand on the clause or clauses that precede it, such as:

**Consider: a great many people believe in them, and if sanity is a general consensus about the content of reality, who are you to disagree?**

Additionally, colons can be used to precede a direct address, such as:

**Goddess of caves and grottoes: bless your children.**

**Practice and Apply**  Look back at the presentation you created about bats. Revise your written presentation to include at least one colon. Then, discuss with a partner how the colon clarifies or enhances the meaning of your ideas.

Visit the **Grammar Studio** for more on colons.

# JOYAS VOLADORAS

Essay by **Brian Doyle**

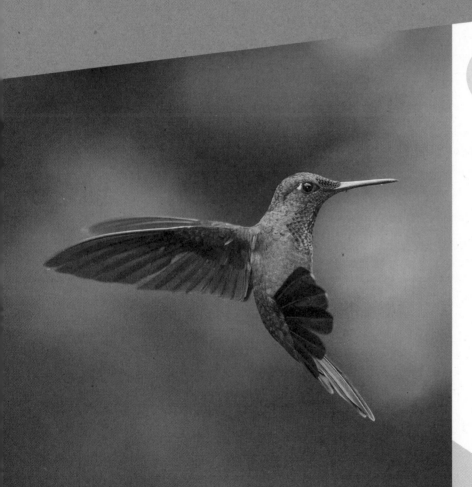

**?** **ESSENTIAL QUESTION:**

What effect do we have on nature, and how does nature affect us?

## QUICK START

Think about the human heart. Make a list of words that come to mind when you think about the heart. Share your list with a partner and discuss the kinds of words you chose, such as anatomical words or emotional words, and what the idea of the heart means to you.

## ANALYZE STYLE

Writers craft their work with a particular **style.** Two key elements of style are diction and syntax. **Diction** includes the author's word choices and register (language that sounds academic or casual, for example). **Syntax** involves the types of sentences and grammatical structures that a writer employs. Prose may be written in a straightforward and direct style, or a more lyrical style that evokes an emotional reaction in readers.

In this essay, Doyle intertwines scientific facts with figurative language and vivid descriptions to take readers on a philosophical journey that explores what the heart means to different animals. He varies his syntax from simple, factual sentences to long, winding sentences that build meaning and emotional impact. As you read, look closely at Doyle's style choices and note their effect.

**GENRE ELEMENTS: EXPLANATORY ESSAY**

- explores and explains a single topic
- may include the writer's own thoughts or experiences
- provides factual information supported with evidence
- invites the reader to consider an everyday topic in more depth

## ANALYZE STRUCTURE

Writers of informational essays choose logical structures to clearly convey key ideas. One or more **main ideas** are supported with **details** that explain or provide examples. Different sections of a text may have main ideas that relate to the central idea of the whole text. The **central idea,** or what the writer wants you to learn about the topic, may be directly stated or implied.

You can track main ideas and details as you read using a graphic organizer.

| TOPIC: | | |
|---|---|---|
| MAIN IDEA: | MAIN IDEA: | MAIN IDEA: |
| KEY DETAILS: | KEY DETAILS: | KEY DETAILS: |
| CENTRAL MESSAGE: | | |

Consider the way that the information is organized in the essay and how that organization helps the reader identify the central message.

## CRITICAL VOCABULARY

| taut | harrowed | felled |
|------|----------|--------|

Choose the synonym for each word to see how many of the Critical Vocabulary words you already know.

1. **taut**      **a.** uncomfortable      **b.** stretched

2. **harrowed**      **a.** remembered      **b.** pained

3. **felled**      **a.** struck down      **b.** traveled with

## LANGUAGE CONVENTIONS

**Parallelism** An author's sentence structure can affect a text's force and clarity. **Parallelism** is the use of similar grammatical constructions to express related ideas or ideas of equal importance. Writers create parallel sentences, clauses, or phrases using the same parts of speech in the same order, as in this example from the essay you will read:

**A hummingbird's heart beats ten times a second. A hummingbird's heart is the size of a pencil eraser. A hummingbird's heart is a lot of the hummingbird.**

This use of parallelism repeats the subject "A hummingbird's heart" followed by a verb phrase to link three facts about the subject. As you read, notice how Doyle uses parallelism to create meaning.

---

### ANNOTATION MODEL

**NOTICE & NOTE**

As you read, note the author's style along with the essay's structure. Mark word choices that stand out to you, especially those that carry strong emotional connotations. Mark also where the structure shifts from one main idea to another. In the model, you can see one reader's notes about "Joyas Voladoras":

Consider the hummingbird for a long moment. A hummingbird's heart beats ten times a second. A hummingbird's heart is the size of a pencil eraser. A hummingbird's heart is a lot of the hummingbird. [*Joyas voladoras*, flying jewels, the first white explorers in the Americas called them, and the white men had never seen such creatures, for hummingbirds came into the world only in the Americas, nowhere else in the universe, more than three hundred species of them whirring and zooming and nectaring in hummer time zones nine times removed from ours, their hearts hammering faster than we could clearly hear if we pressed our elephantine ears to their infinitesimal chests.]

*Short sentences with facts*

*Long, winding sentence with musical language and expressive words that show movement or imitate natural sounds*

## BACKGROUND

*We are often fascinated by extremes in nature: minute, complex organisms that function at a high level of efficiency, as well as enormous animals that make us feel insignificant by comparison. In this essay,* **Brian Doyle** *(1956–2017) explores the heart from both of these angles, as well as from an emotional one. Doyle wrote several books of essays, including* The Wet Engine, *a meditation on the heart.*

# JOYAS VOLADORAS

**Essay by Brian Doyle**

## SETTING A PURPOSE

*As you read, pay attention to the author's style and what the arrangement of the ideas in the text makes you think and feel.*

1  Consider the hummingbird for a long moment. A hummingbird's heart beats ten times a second. A hummingbird's heart is the size of a pencil eraser. A hummingbird's heart is a lot of the hummingbird. *Joyas voladoras*, flying jewels, the first white explorers in the Americas called them, and the white men had never seen such creatures, for hummingbirds came into the world only in the Americas, nowhere else in the universe, more than three hundred species of them whirring and zooming and nectaring in hummer time zones nine times removed from ours, their hearts hammering faster than we could clearly hear if we pressed our elephantine ears to their infinitesimal[1] chests.

2  Each one visits a thousand flowers a day. They can dive at sixty miles an hour. They can fly backward. They can fly more

---

[1] **infinitesimal:** so small it cannot be measured.

---

**Notice & Note**

You can use the side margins to notice and note signposts in the text.

**CONTRASTS AND CONTRADICTIONS**

**Notice & Note:** What words are synonyms for *big* and *small*? Mark the synonyms in the last sentence of paragraph 1.

**Analyze:** What contrast is presented here? What idea does the contrast help to define?

than five hundred miles without pausing to rest. But when they rest they come close to death: on frigid nights, or when they are starving, they retreat into torpor, their metabolic rate slowing to a fifteenth of their normal sleep rate, their hearts sludging nearly to a halt, barely beating, and if they are not soon warmed, if they do not soon find that which is sweet, their hearts grow cold, and they cease to be. Consider for a moment those hummingbirds who did not open their eyes again today, this very day, in the Americas: bearded helmetcrests and booted racket-tails, violet-tailed sylphs and violet-capped woodnymphs, crimson topazes and purple-crowned fairies, red-tailed comets and amethyst woodstars, rainbow-bearded thornbills and glittering-bellied emeralds, velvet-purple coronets and golden-bellied star-frontlets, fiery-tailed awlbills and Andean hillstars, spatuletails and pufflegs, each the most amazing thing you have never seen, each thunderous wild heart the size of an infant's fingernail, each mad heart silent, a brilliant music stilled.

3    Hummingbirds, like all flying birds but more so, have incredible enormous immense ferocious metabolisms.[2] To drive those metabolisms they have race car hearts that eat oxygen at an eye-popping rate. Their hearts are built of thinner, leaner fibers than ours. Their arteries are stiffer and more **taut.** They have more mitochondria in their heart muscles—anything to gulp more oxygen. Their hearts are stripped to the skin for the war against gravity and inertia, the mad search for food, the insane idea of flight. The price of their ambition is a life closer to death; they suffer more heart attacks and aneurysms[3] and ruptures than any other living creature. It's expensive to fly. You burn out. You fry the machine. You melt the engine. Every creature on earth has approximately two billion heartbeats to spend in a lifetime. You can spend them slowly, like a tortoise, and live to be two hundred years old, or you can spend them fast, like a hummingbird, and live to be two years old.

4    The biggest heart in the world is inside the blue whale. It weighs more than seven tons. It's as big as a room. It is a room, with four chambers. A child could walk around in it, head high, bending only to step through the valves. The valves are as big as the swinging doors in a saloon. This house of a heart drives a creature a hundred feet long. When this creature is born it is twenty feet long and weighs four tons. It is waaaaay bigger than your car. It drinks a hundred gallons of milk from its mama every day and gains two hundred pounds a day, and when it is seven or eight years old it endures an unimaginable puberty and then it essentially disappears from human ken,[4] for next to nothing is known of the mating habits, travel patterns, diet, social

[2] **metabolism:** the process of turning food into energy.
[3] **aneurysm:** a blood-filled sac in a blood vessel caused by disease or trauma.
[4] **ken:** understanding.

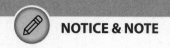
**LANGUAGE CONVENTIONS**

**Annotate:** Mark examples of parallelism in paragraph 5.

**Analyze:** How does the use of parallel structure link the ideas in this paragraph?

**harrowed**
(hăr´ōd) *adj.* greatly distressed.

**felled**
(fĕld) *v.* knocked down.

life, language, social structure, diseases, spirituality, wars, stories, despairs, and arts of the blue whale. There are perhaps ten thousand blue whales in the world, living in every ocean on earth, and of the largest mammal who ever lived we know nearly nothing. But we know this: the animals with the largest hearts in the world generally travel in pairs, and their penetrating moaning cries, their piercing yearning tongue, can be heard underwater for miles and miles.

5      Mammals and birds have hearts with four chambers. Reptiles and turtles have hearts with three chambers. Fish have hearts with two chambers. Insects and mollusks have hearts with one chamber. Worms have hearts with one chamber, although they may have as many as eleven single-chambered hearts. Unicellular bacteria have no hearts at all; but even they have fluid eternally in motion, washing from one side of the cell to the other, swirling and whirling. No living being is without interior liquid motion. We all churn inside.

6      So much held in a heart in a lifetime. So much held in a heart in a day, an hour, a moment. We are utterly open with no one, in the end—not mother and father, not wife or husband, not lover, not child, not friend. We open windows to each but we live alone in the house of the heart. Perhaps we must. Perhaps we could not bear to be so naked for fear of a constantly **harrowed** heart. When young we think there will come one person who will savor and sustain us always; when we are older we know this is the dream of a child, that all hearts finally are bruised and scarred, scored and torn, repaired by time and will, patched by force of character, yet fragile and rickety forevermore, no matter how ferocious the defense and how many bricks you bring to the wall. You can brick up your heart as stout and tight and hard and cold and impregnable[5] as you possibly can and down it comes in an instant, **felled** by a woman's second glance, a child's apple breath, the shatter of glass in the road, the words "I have something to tell you", a cat with a broken spine dragging itself into the forest to die, the brush of your mother's papery ancient hand in the thicket of your hair, the memory of your father's voice early in the morning echoing from the kitchen where he is making pancakes for his children.

---

[5] **impregnable:** impossible to get through or past.

## CHECK YOUR UNDERSTANDING

Answer these questions before moving on to the **Analyze the Text** section on the following page.

**1** Which sentence best describes the way ideas are presented in the essay?

   **A** Factual information is followed by intensely personal reflections.

   **B** The way that the brain controls the heart's function is explained.

   **C** Claims about mammal and bird hearts are presented and refuted.

   **D** Vivid pictures of life in the wild support the author's opinion.

**2** What ideas about the heart provide the overall structure of this essay?

   **F** How hummingbird hearts function and why they burn out so fast

   **G** How little is known about either blue whales or hummingbirds

   **H** Relative sizes of hearts and emotions attributed to the heart

   **J** Why the heart matters to animals and humans

**3** Why did the author most likely begin the essay by discussing hummingbirds?

   **A** Hummingbirds are more interesting than other animals.

   **B** Hummingbirds represent how fragile life can be.

   **C** Hummingbirds represent the adaptability of nature.

   **D** Hummingbirds are unique to the Americas.

## ANALYZE THE TEXT

Support your responses with evidence from the text. ▤ NOTEBOOK

1. **Analyze**  What is the central message of the essay? What main ideas and details lead to the central message? Cite text evidence.

2. **Interpret**  What does the writer mean by the phrase "we live alone in the house of the heart" in the last paragraph?

3. **Compare**  How does the writer's use of the word *heart* shift in the last paragraph of the essay? How does this affect the meaning of the earlier parts of the essay?

4. **Evaluate**  In paragraph 3, the author uses the phrase "incredible enormous immense ferocious metabolisms." What effect do the compounded adjectives have on his tone?

5. **Notice & Note**  The writer mentions time throughout the essay. What is significant about this repetition?

## RESEARCH

Think about the topic of the heart. What do you wonder about it? Pose a question and decide how you will go about answering it. Try multiple search methods and examine multiple sources as you research answers to your question. Notice how effective each source was in answering the question. Complete the following journal entries. Record the information you found and evaluate the effectiveness of each search method.

**RESEARCH TIP**

Take notes on the information you find in your sources. Record the author and book or article title of the source along with the notes that you take so you will be able to find the information again.

**My Question:** _____

**Source 1:** _____

**Notes:** _____

_____

**How effective was this method? Do I need to change my approach?** _____

**Source 2:** _____

**Notes:** _____

_____

**How effective was this method? Do I need to change my approach?** _____

_____

**My Answer:** _____

## CREATE AND PRESENT

**Write an Explanation** Write a one- to two-paragraph explanation in which you present the question that you posed about the heart, describe your research findings, and discuss the answer that you developed.

❏ Introduce the topic and the question that guided your research.

❏ Evaluate your research process and the sources that you used. Highlight the important information you learned from each of the sources.

❏ State the answer to the question you asked. Discuss how this knowledge adds to your understanding of the heart.

**Participate in a Panel Discussion** Use your research, along with the information in "Joyas Voladoras," to consider how the ideal heart would function.

❏ Gather your notes and write an opening statement that includes one way that the ideal heart would function.

❏ Follow rules for discussion by listening attentively while others talk, building on others' ideas, and considering everyone's ideas. Support your own ideas in the discussion with information from your research.

❏ Work toward a consensus on a list of features or functions of the ideal heart. Display a list of those features or functions as they are agreed upon.

Go to the **Writing Studio** for more on synthesizing research information.

Go to the **Speaking and Listening Studio** for help with participating in a discussion.

## RESPOND TO THE ESSENTIAL QUESTION

**?** What effect do we have on nature, and how does nature affect us?

**Gather Information** Review your annotations and notes on "Joyas Voladoras." Then, add relevant information to your Response Log. As you determine which information to include, think about:

• the central message of the essay
• the author's style, including his diction and syntax
• the purpose each paragraph plays in the structure of the essay

At the end of the unit, use your notes to help you write an explanatory essay.

**ACADEMIC VOCABULARY**
As you write and discuss what you learned from the explanatory essay, be sure to use the Academic Vocabulary words. Check off each of the words that you use.

❏ **advocate**
❏ **discrete**
❏ **domain**
❏ **evoke**
❏ **enhance**

**WORD BANK**
taut
harrowed
felled

 Go to the **Vocabulary Studio** for more on denotation and connotation.

## CRITICAL VOCABULARY

**Practice and Apply** Use the Critical Vocabulary words to answer each question. Discuss your responses with a partner.

1. In what ways might a tightrope walker be affected by how **taut** the line is?

2. What is an experience that might leave you feeling **harrowed**?

3. How can **felled** refer both to cutting down trees and to feeling strong emotions?

## VOCABULARY STRATEGY:
### Denotation and Connotation

The **denotation** of a word is the meaning found in a dictionary. The **connotation** of a word refers to the feelings or ideas associated with it. In writing "Joyas Voladoras," Brian Doyle chose words for both their denotations and their connotations. In this sentence, he describes the heart as *harrowed*: "Perhaps we could not bear to be so naked for fear of a constantly harrowed heart." The denotation of *harrowed* is "greatly distressed." But by choosing *harrowed*, Doyle suggests that the heart is not just distressed, but tormented to a great degree. This chart shows the connotations and denotations of the remaining Critical Vocabulary words:

| WORD | DENOTATION | CONNOTATION |
|------|-----------|-------------|
| taut | tense | stretched to breaking point |
| felled | knocked down | overpowered |

**Practice and Apply** Work with a partner to brainstorm at least two synonyms for these words from the essay. Note the connotation of each original word, and discuss how the connotation of each synonym changes the meaning of the original sentence.

1. frigid (paragraph 2)

_____

2. mad (paragraph 3)

_____

3. churn (paragraph 5)

_____

## LANGUAGE CONVENTIONS:
### Parallelism

A writer's use of parallelism helps reinforce meaning for readers by emphasizing connections among ideas. It is also used to enhance style by creating a rhythm. In "Joyas Voladoras," Brian Doyle uses parallelism in both ways.

Parallelism can be created using words:

> **. . . whirring and zooming and nectaring . . .**

Parallelism can be created using phrases:

> **. . . their penetrating moaning cries, their piercing yearning tongue . . .**

Parallelism can be used across sentences:

> **Mammals and birds have hearts with four chambers. Reptiles and turtles have hearts with three chambers. Fish have hearts with two chambers. Insects and mollusks have hearts with one chamber. . . .**

Often, a main idea or other piece of important information interrupts a series of parallel phrases or sentences. The stark shift between the regular pattern and the new construction helps to highlight that information or imagery as important.

> **. . . each the most amazing thing you have never seen, each thunderous wild heart the size of an infant's fingernail, each mad heart silent, a brilliant music stilled.**

**Practice and Apply**  Look back at the explanation you wrote about your research. Revise your written presentation to include at least one instance of parallelism. Then, read the section containing the parallelism aloud to a partner and discuss which ideas your parallelism has linked.

## MEDIA

# FIND YOUR PARK

Public Service Advertisement by
**The National Park Service**

**? ESSENTIAL QUESTION:**

What effect do we have on nature, and how does nature affect us?

## QUICK START

Have you ever visited a national park, state park, nature preserve, or living history museum? What surprised you? Discuss your experiences.

## ANALYZE MEDIA TECHNIQUES AND PURPOSES

A media message may be created for many **purposes**, or reasons: to entertain, to share information, to persuade. Underlying any of these purposes may be a specific motive. For example, the maker of a media message may have a social, commercial, or political goal in mind. Many messages are created with a combination of purposes and motives.

**GENRE ELEMENTS: PUBLIC SERVICE ADVERTISEMENT**

- addresses a wide, public audience
- provides information free of charge to raise awareness or change attitudes
- includes images and words with an emotional impact
- is multimodal: print, audio, or video

**Public Service Advertisements**, or **PSAs**, are messages created to give the public useful, helpful information rather than to sell something. They may appear in magazines, and on billboards, radio, and television. The main purpose of a PSA is to provide needed information, but a PSA may also make a persuasive appeal. Media techniques such as those listed can give you clues about the motives behind an audiovisual message.

### Sound Elements

| MUSIC AND SOUND EFFECTS | Sounds from nature and music can work to build a particular mood that affects the emotional response of the viewer. |
|---|---|
| VOICE-OVER NARRATION | Word choices can appeal to viewer emotions, but so can the speaker's vocal expression, emphasis, and pace. |

### Visual Elements

| IMAGES | Art, photos, animation, graphs, and video can work together to share information and create emotional appeal. |
|---|---|
| WORDS | Onscreen text in the form of titles, subtitles, captions, or visual guides to the narration can emphasize key ideas. |
| JUXTAPOSITION | Sequencing shots implies a connection between ideas or events, adding meaning in ways that enhance the message. |

## BACKGROUND

*The National Park Service was established to preserve meaningful places, moments in history, and monuments. The National Park Service is a bureau of the U.S. Department of the Interior, led by a director appointed by the president and voted in by the Senate. Over 20,000 people work for the National Park Service and over 300,000 people volunteer at the parks to preserve these national treasures and educate the public about them. More than 400 areas in the United States and its territories—including American Samoa, Guam, Puerto Rico, and the Virgin Islands—provide the public with history, archeology, and a celebration of wildlife and the natural world, to be protected for all time.*

## SETTING A PURPOSE

*Consider what you think of or feel when you hear the phrase* National Parks. *As you view and listen to the video, adjust your view of parks as needed based on the evidence presented in the PSA.* NOTEBOOK

To view the video, log in online and select **"FIND YOUR PARK"** from the unit menu.

As needed, pause the video to make notes about what impresses you or about ideas you might want to talk about later. Replay or rewind so that you can clarify anything you do not understand.

## ANALYZE MEDIA

Support your responses with evidence from the PSA.  📓 NOTEBOOK

1. **Cite Evidence**  The PSA sequences images and words in categories to build toward an overall impression of its subject. List examples of details from each category to map the structure of the message.

| NATURE→ | HISTORY / CULTURE→ | PEOPLE→ | ACTIVITIES→ | OVERALL IMPRESSION |
|---|---|---|---|---|
|  |  |  |  |  |

2. **Analyze**  Describe the interaction between the music and the onscreen text reading "PARK." How does this interaction help organize the PSA into the categories listed in the chart above?

3. **Evaluate**  How would you characterize the pace, or speed, of cuts between images? How does this pace serve the purpose of motivating viewers to go visit a National Park?

4. **Analyze**  What kinds of sentence lengths and structures are used in the voiceover? How do these types of sentences enhance the pacing and message of the PSA?

5. **Evaluate**  What is the overall effect of this PSA? Explain how it does or does not achieve its purpose through media techniques.

## RESEARCH

The National Park Service has 417 areas that provide a wide variety of experiences for the public. Research one National Park: What features does it have? Why should people visit? What audience might enjoy it most? Record what you learn about your chosen park in the chart, and then create a poster advertising it.

| NATIONAL PARK | | |
|---|---|---|
| **Features** | **Reasons to Visit** | **Target Audience** |
|  |  |  |

**Connect**  In the video, the narrator describes the experiences offered by the National Park Service as fun. With a small group, discuss how visitors can enjoy the park system and at the same time help to preserve it.

## CREATE AND PRESENT

**Write a Letter to the Editor** Write a letter to the editor advocating for a new National Park. Your proposed park may be a real place you have visited or a place you imagine. Your letter should be brief, about 100–200 words long.

❏ Use a business letter format and formal language for your letter.

❏ State your thesis clearly, and support it with facts and details.

❏ End your letter with a call to action.

**Give Instructions** Consider the PSA video and the poster you created for the Research task. Then, develop instructions that a younger student could follow for creating a compelling advertisement.

❏ Remember what you found compelling about the PSA video and what you used to make your own poster PSA compelling.

❏ Deliver the instructions to create a compelling PSA using clear and detailed steps in a logical sequence.

❏ Review the instructions with a partner and make suggestions about how your partner might improve his or her instructions. Listen closely and respectfully to all ideas.

For more on writing arguments, visit the **Writing Studio.**

For more on speaking constructively, visit the **Speaking and Listening Studio.**

## RESPOND TO THE ESSENTIAL QUESTION

**?** What effect do we have on nature, and how does nature affect us?

**Gather Information** Review your notes on "Find Your Park." Then, add relevant information to your Response Log. As you determine which information to include, think about:

• the reasons for creating a national park system
• what experiences the parks offer to the public
• how people can interact with nature by using the national parks

At the end of the unit, use your notes to write an explanatory essay.

### ACADEMIC VOCABULARY
As you write and discuss what you learned from the public service advertisement, be sure to use the Academic Vocabulary words. Check off each of the words that you use.

❏ **advocate**
❏ **discrete**
❏ **domain**
❏ **evoke**
❏ **enhance**

SHORT STORY

# THE SEVENTH MAN

by **Haruki Murakami**

pages 177–191

**COMPARE THEMES**

As you read, notice how authors working in two different genres address similar themes. What are the texts' messages about the world in general? How do the authors express those messages? After you read both selections, you will work on a final project about the texts' themes.

**?** **ESSENTIAL QUESTION:**

What effect do we have on nature, and how does nature affect us?

POEM

# CARRY

by **Linda Hogan**

pages 199–201

# The Seventh Man

## QUICK START

In the 1930s, President Franklin Roosevelt told the American people, "The only thing we have to fear is fear itself." What do you think Roosevelt meant by that? Do you agree? Why or why not? Share your thoughts with a partner.

## ANALYZE SYMBOL AND THEME

A **symbol** is a person, place, object, or activity that stands for something beyond itself. Our culture has established common symbols, such as doves (peace), red roses (love), and flags (countries). Writers can use these symbols to make connections among ideas without stating them explicitly.

In a text, recurring symbols make up a pattern called a **motif**. Symbols and motifs help develop a text's theme. The **theme** of a work is the underlying message about life or human nature that the writer wants to communicate.

As you read "The Seventh Man," look for symbols and motifs like the ones shown in the chart. Write what each might represent.

**GENRE ELEMENTS:
SHORT STORY**

- centers around characters, conflict, and plot development
- usually focuses on one or very few settings, moments in time, and characters
- can usually be read in one sitting

| SYMBOL OR MOTIF | WHAT IT MIGHT REPRESENT |
|---|---|
| wave/sea | |
| typhoon | |
| K.'s paintings | |

## ANALYZE PLOT

Stories are often told in chronological, or linear, order, meaning that the narrator tells plot events in the order in which the characters experience them. Within a linear plot, an author can depart from the main time line for effect. For example, a **flashback** interrupts the chronological flow of a story with an account of a prior event relevant to the present action of the story. "The Seventh Man" is structured as a **frame story,** in which a present-day narrator relates the main story, which happens in the past, and then returns to the present day. Mapping plot events sequentially in a graphic organizer will help you keep track of the actual order of events in a story.

As you read, think about how each plot event affects the plot as a whole.

## CRITICAL VOCABULARY

| | | | |
|---|---|---|---|
| frail | entranced | delirium | sociable |
| premonition | permeate | sentiment | reconciliation |

To see how many Critical Vocabulary words you already know, use them to complete the sentences.

1. The musty odor of my wet dog began to _____ my room.
2. The _____ old man had trouble walking up the stairs.
3. At the party, I pledged to be _____ and talk to others.
4. After the argument, we shook hands and had a _____.
5. She was in a _____, confused about where she was.
6. My dream was a _____ that my grandmother would visit.
7. The child was_____, transfixed by the cartoon.
8. The _____ in the heartfelt poem was touching.

## LANGUAGE CONVENTIONS

**Complex Sentences** To add interest, writers vary sentence structure. A **complex sentence** includes an independent clause and at least one dependent clause. An independent clause can stand alone as a sentence. A dependent clause has a subject and verb, but does not express a complete thought.

In this complex sentence from the story, the underlined dependent clause adds information to the independent clause.

"It happened one September afternoon <u>when I was ten years old</u>."

As you read the selection, notice how the author uses complex sentences to create variety and elaborate on ideas.

## ANNOTATION MODEL

**NOTICE & NOTE**

Here is how you might annotate to help you analyze symbols.

"A huge wave nearly swept me away," said the seventh man, almost whispering.

"It happened one September afternoon when I was ten years old."

The man was the last one to tell his story that night. The hands of the clock had moved past ten. The small group that huddled in a circle could hear the <u>wind tearing through the darkness outside</u>, heading west. <u>It shook the trees, set the windows to rattling, and moved past the house with one final whistle.</u>

*The wind might symbolize either real or emotional turmoil that people need to protect themselves from. It sets an ominous tone for the story the seventh man will tell.*

## BACKGROUND

*As a boy, **Haruki Murakami** (b. 1949) preferred reading American paperbacks to studying traditional Japanese literature. He went on to become a novelist and short-story writer known for his unique and whimsical works that break away from typical Japanese forms. Murakami combines mystery, comedy, and fantasy in his work while keeping his messages practical, profound, and believable.*

# THE SEVENTH MAN

**Short Story by Haruki Murakami**
**translated by Jay Rubin**

## PREPARE TO COMPARE

*As you read the author's vivid descriptions and figurative language, create mental images of the story's setting and events. You might find it useful to sketch the images that come up for you. As the story is set in the author's home country of Japan, call upon your prior knowledge of the country to help you picture the setting.*

**Notice & Note**

You can use the side margins to notice and note signposts in the text.

1   A huge wave nearly swept me away," said the seventh man, almost whispering.

2   "It happened one September afternoon when I was ten years old."

3   The man was the last one to tell his story that night. The hands of the clock had moved past ten. The small group that huddled in a circle could hear the wind tearing through the darkness outside, heading west. It shook the trees, set the windows to rattling, and moved past the house with one final whistle.

4   "It was the biggest wave I had ever seen in my life," he said. "A strange wave. An absolute giant."

5   He paused.

6    "It just barely missed me, but in my place it swallowed everything that mattered most to me and swept it off to another world. I took years to find it again to recover from the experience—precious years that can never be replaced."

7    The seventh man appeared to be in his mid-fifties. He was a thin man, tall, with a moustache, and next to his right eye he had a short but deep-looking scar that could have been made by the stab of a small blade. Stiff, bristly patches of white marked his short hair. His face had the look you see on people when they can't quite find the words they need. In his case, though, the expression seemed to have been there from long before, as though it were part of him. The man wore a simple blue shirt under a grey tweed coat, and every now and then he would bring his hand to his collar. None of those assembled there knew his name or what he did for a living.

8    He cleared his throat, and for a moment or two his words were lost in silence. The others waited for him to go on.

9    "In my case, it was a wave," he said. "There's no way for me to tell, of course, what it will be for each of you. But in my case it just happened to take the form of a gigantic wave. It presented itself to me all of a sudden one day, without warning. And it was devastating."

10    I grew up in a seaside town in the Province of S. It was such a small town, I doubt that any of you would recognize the name if I were to mention it. My father was the local doctor, and so I led a rather comfortable childhood. Ever since I could remember, my best friend was a boy I'll call K. His house was close to ours, and he was a grade behind me in school. We were like brothers, walking to and from school together, and always playing together when we got home. We never once fought during our long friendship. I did have a brother, six years older, but what with the age difference and differences in our personalities, we were never very close. My real brotherly affection went to my friend K.

11    K. was a **frail**, skinny little thing, with a pale complexion and a face almost pretty enough to be a girl's. He had some kind of speech impediment,[1] though, which might have made him seem retarded to anyone who didn't know him. And because he was so frail, I always played his protector, whether at school or at home. I was kind of big and athletic, and the other kids all looked up to me. But the main reason I enjoyed spending time with K. was that he was such a sweet, pure-hearted boy. He was not the least bit retarded, but because of his impediment, he didn't do too well at school. In most subjects, he could barely keep up. In art class, though, he was great. Just give him a pencil or paints and he would make pictures that were so full of life that even the teacher was amazed. He won prizes in one contest after another, and I'm sure he would have become a famous painter if he had continued with his art into adulthood. He liked to do seascapes. He'd go out to the shore for hours, painting. I would often sit beside

**ANALYZE PLOT**

**Annotate:** Mark details that indicate "The Seventh Man" is a frame story (a story within a story).

**Analyze:** Why do you think the author structures his tale this way?

**frail**
(frāl) *adj.* physically weak.

---

[1] **impediment** (ĭm-pĕd´ə-mənt): an obstacle.

him, watching the swift, precise movements of his brush, wondering how, in a few seconds, he could possibly create such lively shapes and colors where, until then, there had been only blank white paper. I realize now that it was a matter of pure talent.

12    One year, in September, a huge typhoon[2] hit our area. The radio said it was going to be the worst in ten years. The schools were closed, and all the shops in town lowered their shutters in preparation for the storm. Starting early in the morning, my father and brother went around the house nailing shut all the storm doors, while my mother spent the day in the kitchen cooking emergency provisions. We filled bottles and canteens with water, and packed our most important possessions in rucksacks for possible evacuation. To the adults, typhoons were an annoyance and a threat they had to face almost annually, but to the kids, removed as we were from such practical concerns, it was just a great big circus, a wonderful source of excitement.

13    Just after noon the color of the sky began to change all of a sudden. There was something strange and unreal about it. I stayed outside on the porch, watching the sky, until the wind began to howl and the rain began to beat against the house with a weird dry sound, like handfuls of sand. Then we closed the last storm door and gathered together in one room of the darkened house, listening to the radio. This particular storm did not have a great deal of rain, it said, but the winds were doing a lot of damage, blowing roofs off houses and capsizing[3] ships. Many people had been killed or injured by flying debris. Over and over again, they warned people against leaving their homes. Every once in a while, the house would creak and shudder as if a huge hand were shaking it, and sometimes there would be a great crash of some heavy-sounding object against a storm door. My father guessed that these were tiles blowing off the neighbors' houses. For lunch we ate the rice and omelettes my mother had cooked, waiting for the typhoon to blow past.

14    But the typhoon gave no sign of blowing past. The radio said it had lost momentum almost as soon as it came ashore at S. Province, and now it was moving north-east at the pace of a slow runner. The wind kept up its savage howling as it tried to uproot everything that stood on land.

15    Perhaps an hour had gone by with the wind at its worst like this when a hush fell over everything. All of a sudden it was so quiet, we could hear a bird crying in the distance. My father opened the storm door a crack and looked outside. The wind had stopped, and the rain had ceased to fall. Thick, grey clouds edged across the sky, and patches of blue showed here and there. The trees in the yard were still dripping their heavy burden of rainwater.

CONTRASTS AND CONTRADICTIONS

**Notice & Note:** In paragraphs 13–15, mark where the weather changes drastically.

**Analyze:** How does the contrast in the descriptions of the weather change the tone of the story?

---

[2] **typhoon** (tī-foon´): a tropical storm forming in the Pacific or Indian Ocean, consisting of violent winds and rain.

[3] **capsize** (kăp´sīz): flip upside-down in water.

16    "We're in the eye of the storm," my father told me. "It'll stay quiet like this for a while, maybe fifteen, twenty minutes, kind of like an intermission. Then the wind'll come back the way it was before."

17    I asked him if I could go outside. He said I could walk around a little if I didn't go far. "But I want you to come right back here at the first sign of wind."

18    I went out and started to explore. It was hard to believe that a wild storm had been blowing there until a few minutes before. I looked up at the sky. The storm's great "eye" seemed to be up there, fixing its cold stare on all of us below. No such "eye" existed, of course: we were just in that momentary quiet spot at the center of the pool of whirling air.

19    While the grown-ups checked for damage to the house, I went down to the beach. The road was littered with broken tree branches, some of them thick pine boughs that would have been too heavy for an adult to lift alone. There were shattered roof tiles everywhere, cars with cracked windshields, and even a doghouse that had tumbled into the middle of the street. A big hand might have swung down from the sky and flattened everything in its path.

20    K. saw me walking down the road and came outside.

21    "Where are you going?" he asked.

22    "Just down to look at the beach," I said.

23    Without a word, he came along with me. He had a little white dog that followed after us.

24    "The minute we get any wind, though, we're going straight back home," I said, and K. gave me a silent nod.

25    The shore was a 200-yard walk from my house. It was lined with a concrete breakwater—a big dyke that stood as high as I was tall in those days. We had to climb a short flight of steps to reach the water's edge. This was where we came to play almost every day, so there was no part of it we didn't know well. In the eye of the typhoon, though, it all looked different: the color of the sky and of the sea, the sound of the waves, the smell of the tide, the whole expanse of the shore. We sat atop the breakwater for a time, taking in the view without a word to each other. We were supposedly in the middle of a great typhoon, and yet the waves were strangely hushed. And the point where they washed against the beach was much farther away than usual, even at low tide. The white sand stretched out before us as far as we could see. The whole, huge space felt like a room without furniture, except for the band of flotsam[4] that lined the beach.

26    We stepped down to the other side of the breakwater and walked along the broad beach, examining the things that had come to rest there. Plastic toys, sandals, chunks of wood that had probably once been parts of furniture, pieces of clothing, unusual bottles, broken crates with foreign writing on them, and other, less recognizable

**ANALYZE PLOT**

**Annotate:** Mark details in paragraphs 25 and 26 that seem to foreshadow future plot events.

**Evaluate:** How does foreshadowing affect the tone of this part of the story?

---

[4] **flotsam** (flŏt´səm): pieces of floating debris.

items: it was like a big candy store. The storm must have carried
these things from very far away. Whenever something unusual
caught our attention, we would pick it up and look at it every which
way, and when we were done, K.'s dog would come over and give it a
good sniff.

27    We couldn't have been doing this more than five minutes when
I realized that the waves had come up right next to me. Without any
sound or other warning, the sea had suddenly stretched its long,
smooth tongue out to where I stood on the beach. I had never seen
anything like it before. Child though I was, I had grown up on the
shore and knew how frightening the ocean could be—the savagery
with which it could strike unannounced.

28    And so I had taken care to keep well back from the waterline. In
spite of that, the waves had slid up to within inches of where I stood.
And then, just as soundlessly, the water drew back—and stayed back.
The waves that had approached me were as unthreatening as waves
can be—a gentle washing of the sandy beach. But something ominous
about them—something like the touch of a reptile's skin—had sent
a chill down my spine. My fear was totally groundless—and totally
real. I knew instinctively that they were alive. They knew I was here
and they were planning to grab me. I felt as if some huge, man-
eating beast were lying somewhere on a grassy plain, dreaming of the
moment it would pounce and tear me to pieces with its sharp teeth. I
had to run away.

**ANALYZE SYMBOL AND THEME**

**Annotate:** Mark details that
suggest what the waves and
ocean symbolize in paragraphs
27 and 28.

**Analyze:** What message
about nature is the author
communicating through this
use of symbolism?

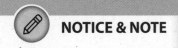
**LANGUAGE CONVENTIONS**

**Annotate:** Circle the independent clause and underline the dependent clauses in the third sentence of paragraph 30.

**Evaluate:** What is the effect of this complex sentence following two simple sentences?

29    "I'm getting out of here!" I yelled to K. He was maybe ten yards down the beach, squatting with his back to me, and looking at something. I was sure I had yelled loud enough, but my voice did not seem to have reached him. He might have been so absorbed in whatever it was he had found that my call made no impression on him. K. was like that. He would get involved with things to the point of forgetting everything else. Or possibly I had not yelled as loudly as I had thought. I do recall that my voice sounded strange to me, as though it belonged to someone else.

30    Then I heard a deep rumbling sound. It seemed to shake the earth. Actually, before I heard the rumble I heard another sound, a weird gurgling as though a lot of water was surging up through a hole in the ground. It continued for a while, then stopped, after which I heard the strange rumbling. Even that was not enough to make K. look up. He was still squatting, looking down at something at his feet, in deep concentration. He probably did not hear the rumbling. How he could have missed such an earth-shaking sound, I don't know. This may seem odd, but it might have been a sound that only I could hear—some special kind of sound. Not even K.'s dog seemed to notice it, and you know how sensitive dogs are to sound.

31    I told myself to run over to K., grab hold of him, and get out of there. It was the only thing to do. I *knew* that the wave was coming, and K. didn't know. As clearly as I knew what I ought to be doing, I found myself running the other way—running full speed toward the dyke, alone. What made me do this, I'm sure, was fear, a fear so overpowering it took my voice away and set my legs to running on their own. I ran stumbling along the soft sand beach to the breakwater, where I turned and shouted to K.

32    "Hurry, K.! Get out of there! The wave is coming!" This time my voice worked fine. The rumbling had stopped, I realized, and now, finally, K. heard my shouting and looked up. But it was too late. A wave like a huge snake with its head held high, poised to strike, was racing towards the shore. I had never seen anything like it in my life. It had to be as tall as a three-story building. Soundlessly (in my memory, at least, the image is soundless), it rose up behind K. to block out the sky. K. looked at me for a few seconds, uncomprehending. Then, as if sensing something, he turned towards the wave. He tried to run, but now there was no time to run. In the next instant, the wave had swallowed him.

33    The wave crashed on to the beach, shattering into a million leaping waves that flew through the air and plunged over the dyke where I stood. I was able to dodge its impact by ducking behind the breakwater. The spray wet my clothes, nothing more. I scrambled back up on to the wall and scanned the shore. By then the wave had turned and, with a wild cry, it was rushing back out to sea. It looked like part of a gigantic rug that had been yanked by someone at the other end of the earth. Nowhere on the shore could I find any trace of K., or of his dog. There was only the empty beach. The receding wave

had now pulled so much water out from the shore that it seemed to expose the entire ocean bottom. I stood along on the breakwater, frozen in place.

34    The silence came over everything again—a desperate silence, as though sound itself had been ripped from the earth. The wave had swallowed K. and disappeared into the far distance. I stood there, wondering what to do. Should I go down to the beach? K. might be down there somewhere, buried in the sand . . . But I decided not to leave the dyke. I knew from experience that big waves often came in twos and threes.

35    I'm not sure how much time went by—maybe ten or twenty seconds of eerie emptiness—when, just as I had guessed, the next wave came. Another gigantic roar shook the beach, and again, after the sound had faded, another huge wave raised its head to strike. It towered before me, blocking out the sky, like a deadly cliff. This time, though, I didn't run. I stood rooted to the sea wall, **entranced**, waiting for it to attack. What good would it do to run, I thought, now that K. had been taken? Or perhaps I simply froze, overcome with fear. I can't be sure what it was that kept me standing there.

36    The second wave was just as big as the first—maybe even bigger. From far above my head it began to fall, losing its shape, like a brick wall slowly crumbling. It was so huge that it no longer looked like a real wave. It was like something from another, far-off world, that just happened to assume the shape of a wave. I readied myself for the moment the darkness would take me. I didn't even close my eyes. I remember hearing my heart pound with incredible clarity.

37    The moment the wave came before me, however, it stopped. All at once it seemed to run out of energy, to lose its forward motion and simply hover there, in space, crumbling in stillness. And in its crest, inside its cruel, transparent tongue, what I saw was K.

38    Some of you may find this impossible to believe, and if so, I don't blame you. I myself have trouble accepting it even now. I can't explain what I saw any better than you can, but I know it was no illusion, no hallucination. I am telling you as honestly as I can what happened at that moment—what really happened. In the tip of the wave, as if enclosed in some kind of transparent capsule, floated K.'s body, reclining on its side. But that is not all. K. was looking straight at me, smiling. There, right in front of me, so close that I could have reached out and touched him, was my friend, my friend K. who, only moments before, had been swallowed by the wave. And he was smiling at me. Not with an ordinary smile—it was a big, wide-open grin that literally stretched from ear to ear. His cold, frozen eyes were locked on mine. He was no longer the K. I knew. And his right arm was stretched out in my direction, as if he were trying to grab my hand and pull me into that other world where he was now. A little closer, and his hand would have caught mine. But, having missed, K. then smiled at me one more time, his grin wider than ever.

39    I seem to have lost consciousness at that point. The next thing I knew, I was in bed in my father's clinic. As soon as I awoke the

**entranced**
(ĕn-trănsd´) *adj.* filled with wonder and delight.

▶ AGAIN AND AGAIN

**Notice & Note:** In paragraphs 36–38, mark ways in which the description of the second huge wave differs from previous descriptions of waves in the story.

**Synthesize:** How does this description of the second huge wave elaborate on the story's motif of waves?

nurse went to call my father, who came running. He took my pulse, studied my pupils, and put his hand on my forehead. I tried to move my arm, but couldn't lift it. I was burning with fever, and my mind was clouded. I had been wrestling with a high fever for some time, apparently. "You've been asleep for three days," my father said to me. A neighbor who had seen the whole thing had picked me up and carried me home. They had not been able to find K. I wanted to say something to my father. I had to say something to him. But my numb and swollen tongue could not form words. I felt as if some kind of creature had taken up residence in my mouth. My father asked me to tell him my name, but before I could remember what it was, I lost consciousness again, sinking into darkness.

40    Altogether, I stayed in bed for a week on a liquid diet. I vomited several times, and had bouts of **delirium**. My father told me afterwards that I was so bad that he had been afraid that I might suffer permanent neurological[5] damage from the shock and high fever. One way or another, though, I managed to recover—physically, at least. But my life would never be the same again.

41    They never found K.'s body. They never found his dog, either. Usually when someone drowned in that area, the body would wash up a few days later on the shore of a small inlet to the east. K.'s body never did. The big waves probably carried it far out to sea—too far for it to reach the shore. It must have sunk to the ocean bottom to be

**delirium**
(dĭ-lîr´ē-əm) *n.* a state of mental confusion.

---
[5] **neurological** (noor-ə-lŏj´ĭ-kəl): having to do with the body's nervous system.

eaten by the fish. The search went on for a very long time, thanks to the cooperation of the local fishermen, but eventually it petered out[6]. Without a body, there was never any funeral. Half crazed, K.'s parents would wander up and down the beach every day, or they would shut themselves up at home, chanting sutras[7].

42     As great a blow as this had been for them, though, K.'s parents never chided me for having taken their son down to the shore in the midst of a typhoon. They knew how I had always loved and protected K. as if he had been my own little brother. My parents, too, made a point of never mentioning the incident in my presence. But I knew the truth. I knew that I could have saved K. if I had tried. I probably could have run over and dragged him out of the reach of the wave. It would have been close, but as I went over the timing of the events in my memory, it always seemed to me that I could have made it. As I said before, though, overcome with fear, I abandoned him there and saved only myself. It pained me all the more that K.'s parents failed to blame me and that everyone else was so careful never to say anything to me about what had happened. It took me a long time to recover from the emotional shock. I stayed away from school for weeks. I hardly ate a thing, and spent each day in bed, staring at the ceiling.

43     K. was always there, lying in the wave tip, grinning at me, his hand outstretched, beckoning. I couldn't get that picture out of my mind. And when I managed to sleep, it was there in my dreams—

---

[6] **peter out:** gradually come to an end.
[7] **sutras** (sooˊtrəs): short Buddhist texts.

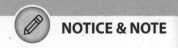
**ANALYZE SYMBOL AND THEME**

**Annotate:** In paragraph 44, mark phrases from the narrator's dream that seem to contain symbols.

**Interpret:** How would you interpret the symbolism in the narrator's dream?

except that, in my dreams, K. would hop out of his capsule in the wave and grab my wrist to drag me back inside with him.

44      And then there was another dream I had. I'm swimming in the ocean. It's a beautiful summer afternoon, and I'm doing an easy breaststroke far from shore. The sun is beating down on my back, and the water feels good. Then, all of a sudden, someone grabs my right leg. I feel an ice-cold grip on my ankle. It's strong, too strong to shake off. I'm being dragged down under the surface. I see K.'s face there. He has the same huge grin, split from ear to ear, his eyes locked on mine. I try to scream, but my voice will not come. I swallow water, and my lungs start to fill.

45      I wake up in the darkness, screaming, breathless, drenched in sweat.

46      At the end of the year I pleaded with my parents to let me move to another town. I couldn't go on living in sight of the beach where K. had been swept away, and my nightmares wouldn't stop. If I didn't get out of there, I'd go crazy. My parents understood and made arrangements for me to live elsewhere. I moved to Nagano Province in January to live with my father's family in a mountain village near Komoro. I finished elementary school in Nagano and stayed on through junior and senior high school there. I never went home, even for holidays. My parents came to visit me now and then.

47      I live in Nagano to this day. I graduated from a college of engineering in the City of Nagano and went to work for a precision toolmaker in the area. I still work for them. I live like anybody else. As you can see, there's nothing unusual about me. I'm not very **sociable**, but I have a few friends I go mountain climbing with. Once I got away from my hometown, I stopped having nightmares all the time. They remained a part of my life, though. They would come to me now and then, like debt collectors at the door. It happened when I was on the verge of forgetting. And it was always the same dream, down to the smallest detail. I would wake up screaming, my sheets soaked with sweat.

48      That is probably why I never married. I didn't want to wake someone sleeping next to me with my screams in the middle of the night. I've been in love with several women over the years, but I never spent a night with any of them. The terror was in my bones. It was something I could never share with another person.

49      I stayed away from my hometown for over forty years. I never went near that seashore—or any other. I was afraid that if I did, my dream might happen in reality. I had always enjoyed swimming, but after that day I never even went to swim in a pool. I wouldn't go near deep rivers or lakes. I avoided boats and wouldn't take a plane to go abroad. Despite all these precautions, I couldn't get rid of the image of myself drowning. Like K.'s cold hand, this dark **premonition** caught hold of my mind and refused to let go.

50      Then, last spring, I finally revisited the beach where K. had been taken by the wave.

**sociable**
(sō´shə-bəl) *adj.* able to enjoy the company of others.

**premonition**
(prĕm-ə-nĭsh´ən) *n.* an unproven feeling that something specific will happen.

51   My father had died of cancer the year before, and my brother had sold the old house. In going through the storage shed, he had found a cardboard carton crammed with childhood things of mine, which he sent to me in Nagano. Most of it was useless junk, but there was one bundle of pictures that K. had painted and given to me. My parents had probably put them away for me as a keepsake of K., but the pictures did nothing but reawaken the old terror. They made me feel as if K.'s spirit would spring back to life from them, and so I quickly returned them to their paper wrapping, intending to throw them away. I couldn't make myself do it, though. After several days of indecision, I opened the bundle again and forced myself to take a long, hard look at K.'s watercolors.

52   Most of them were landscapes, pictures of the familiar stretch of ocean and sand beach and pine woods and the town, and all done with that special clarity and coloration I knew so well from K.'s hand. They were still amazingly vivid despite the years, and had been executed with even greater skill than I recalled. As I leafed through the bundle, I found myself steeped in warm memories. The deep feelings of the boy K. were there in his pictures—the way his eyes were opened on the world. The things we did together, the places we went together began to come back to me with great intensity. And I realized that his eyes were my eyes, that I myself had looked upon the world back then with the same lively, unclouded vision as the boy who had walked by my side.

53   I made a habit after that of studying one of K.'s pictures at my desk each day when I got home from work. I could sit there for hours with one painting. In each I found another of those soft landscapes of childhood that I had shut out of my memory for so long. I had a sense, whenever I looked at one of K.'s works, that something was **permeating** my very flesh.

54   Perhaps a week had gone by like this when the thought suddenly struck me one evening: I might have been making a terrible mistake all those years. As he lay there in the tip of the wave, surely K. had not been looking at me with hatred or resentment; he had not been trying to take me away with him. And that terrible grin he had fixed me with: that, too, could have been an accident of angle or light and shadow, not a conscious act on K.'s part. He had probably already lost consciousness, or perhaps he had been giving me a gentle smile of eternal parting. The intense look of hatred I thought I saw on his face had been nothing but a reflection of the profound terror that had taken control of me for the moment.

55   The more I studied K.'s watercolor that evening, the greater the conviction with which I began to believe these new thoughts of mine. For no matter how long I continued to look at the picture, I could find nothing in it but a boy's gentle, innocent spirit.

## ANALYZE SYMBOL AND THEME

**Annotate:** Mark details in paragraphs 52 and 53 that show the narrator's emotional response to K.'s paintings.

**Analyze:** What might the paintings symbolize to the narrator?

**permeate**
(pûr´mē-āt) *v.* to spread through an area.

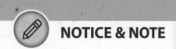
56     I went on sitting at my desk for a very long time. There was nothing else I could do. The sun went down, and the pale darkness of evening began to envelop the room. Then came the deep silence of night, which seemed to go on forever. At last, the scales tipped, and dark gave way to dawn. The new day's sun tinged the sky with pink.

57     It was then I knew I must go back.

58     I threw a few things in a bag, called the company to say I would not be in, and boarded a train for my old hometown.

59     I did not find the same quiet, little seaside town that I remembered. An industrial city had sprung up nearby during the rapid development of the Sixties, bringing great changes to the landscape. The one little gift shop by the station had grown into a mall, and the town's only movie theater had been turned into a supermarket. My house was no longer there. It had been demolished some months before, leaving only a scrape on the earth. The trees in the yard had all been cut down, and patches of weeds dotted the black stretch of ground. K.'s old house had disappeared as well, having been replaced by a concrete parking lot full of commuters' cars and vans. Not that I was overcome by **sentiment.** The town had ceased to be mine long before.

**sentiment**
(sĕn´tə-mənt) *n.* the emotion behind something.

60     I walked down to the shore and climbed the steps of the breakwater. On the other side, as always, the ocean stretched off into the distance, unobstructed, huge, the horizon a single straight line. The shoreline, too, looked the same as it had before: the long beach, the lapping waves, people strolling at the water's edge. The time was after four o'clock, and the soft sun of late afternoon embraced everything below as it began its long, almost meditative descent to the west. I lowered my bag to the sand and sat down next to it in silent appreciation of the gentle seascape. Looking at this scene, it was impossible to imagine that a great typhoon had once raged here, that a massive wave had swallowed my best friend in all the world. There was almost no one left now, surely, who remembered those terrible events. It began to seem as if the whole thing were an illusion that I had dreamed up in vivid detail.

61     And then I realized that the deep darkness inside me had vanished. Suddenly. As suddenly as it had come. I raised myself from the sand, and, without bothering to take off my shoes or roll up my cuffs, walked into the surf and let the waves lap at my ankles.

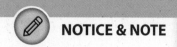

**reconciliation**
(rĕk-ən-sĭl-ē-ā´shən) *n.*
the act of coming to an
agreement.

62    Almost in **reconciliation**, it seemed, the same waves that had washed up on the beach when I was a boy were now fondly washing my feet, soaking black my shoes and pant cuffs. There would be one slow-moving wave, then a long pause, and then another wave would come and go. The people passing by gave me odd looks, but I didn't care.

63    I looked up at the sky. A few grey cotton chunks of cloud hung there, motionless. They seemed to be there for me, though I'm not sure why I felt that way. I remembered having looked up at the sky like this in search of the "eye" of the typhoon. And then, inside me, the axis[8] of time gave one great heave. Forty long years collapsed like a dilapidated house, mixing old time and new time together in a single swirling mass. All sounds faded, and the light around me shuddered. I lost my balance and fell into the waves. My heart throbbed at the back of my throat, and my arms and legs lost all sensation. I lay that way for a long time, face in the water, unable to stand. But I was not afraid. No, not at all. There was no longer anything for me to fear. Those days were gone.

64    I stopped having my terrible nightmares. I no longer wake up screaming in the middle of the night. And I am trying now to start life over again. No, I know it's probably too late to start again. I may not have much time left to live. But even if it comes too late, I am grateful that, in the end, I was able to attain a kind of salvation, to effect some sort of recovery. Yes, grateful: I could have come to the end of my life unsaved, still screaming in the dark, afraid.

65    The seventh man fell silent and turned his gaze upon each of the others. No one spoke or moved or even seemed to breathe. All were waiting for the rest of his story. Outside, the wind had fallen, and nothing stirred. The seventh man brought his hand to his collar once again, as if in search for words.

66    "They tell us that the only thing we have to fear is fear itself; but I don't believe that," he said. Then, a moment later, he added: "Oh, the fear is there, all right. It comes to us in many different forms, at different times, and overwhelms us. But the most frightening thing we can do at such times is to turn our backs on it, to close our eyes. For then we take the most precious thing inside us and surrender it to something else. In my case, that something was the wave."

**ANALYZE PLOT**

**Annotate:** Mark the shift back to the present day that occurs in paragraph 64.

**Interpret:** How does returning to the present add meaning to the man's story? Complete a plot diagram or time line of the story's events.

**ANALYZE SYMBOL AND THEME**

**Annotate:** Mark the details in paragraphs 64–66 that reveal what the narrator has learned from his experience.

**Synthesize:** Based on these and other details, what do you think is the theme of "The Seventh Man"?

---

[8] **axis** (ăk´sĭs): a line around which other things rotate.

## CHECK YOUR UNDERSTANDING

Answer these questions before moving on to the **Analyze the Text** section on the following page.

1 The story's narrator is haunted by —

   **A** his overwhelming fear of violent storms

   **B** his sorrow over the loss of his childhood home

   **C** his guilt over failing to save K. from the wave

   **D** his jealousy of his friend's artistic talent

2 What does the narrator do after the storm has passed?

   **F** He finds and promotes K.'s accomplished artwork.

   **G** He moves to another town and does not return for many years.

   **H** He walks the seawall attempting to find K. and his dog.

   **J** He runs back to the house to tell his family what has happened.

3 The narrator decides to go back to his hometown after he —

   **A** learns that his father is dying from cancer

   **B** finishes his engineering studies in another city

   **C** recognizes that his nightmares have kept him from getting married

   **D** receives a collection of K.'s paintings and looks at them

**RESPOND**

## ANALYZE THE TEXT

Support your responses with evidence from the text.  ☰ NOTEBOOK

1. **Evaluate**  Why is the frame story structure an effective way to tell this story? What effect would using a strictly chronological order of events have on the story?

2. **Interpret**  In paragraph 9, the narrator says, "In my case, it was a wave,"... "There's no way for me to tell, of course, what it will be for each of you...." What does he mean by this?

3. **Infer**  What might the huge wave symbolize? Support your response with evidence from the story and your own experience.

4. **Analyze**  In the last paragraph, the narrator says he disagrees with the saying that "the only thing we have to fear is fear itself." How does the author develop this message about fear?

5. **Notice & Note**  What advice does the narrator pass down to his listeners? How do these Words of the Wiser reflect the story's theme?

## RESEARCH

**RESEARCH TIP**
When looking online for the answer to a question, you can always type the question directly into the search engine. To save time, you can leave out the unimportant words from your question. For example, "major typhoons history" will give you almost the same results as searching for "What were the major typhoons throughout history?"

The narrator of the story experienced a typhoon as a child. Typhoons, cyclones, and hurricanes are all the same kind of storm; they are given different names depending on where on Earth they occur. Think of some questions about these storms that you would like to answer through online research. You might have questions about historically significant typhoons, the damage they can cause, how people prepare for them, or how people rebuild in the storm's aftermath.

Use multiple versions of the chart below to list your questions before you go online. Then, record the answers as you find them. Remember to keep track of your sources.

| Question: | |
| --- | --- |
| **Answer:** | **Source:** |

**Extend**  Choose a social media platform. Write a post telling the most interesting fact you learned about typhoons, and choose a picture that you could attach to your post. Share your post and a picture with a small group.

## CREATE AND DISCUSS

**Write a Vignette** A **vignette** is a short description, usually under one thousand words, that explores an idea or theme. Vignettes do not depend on short story elements such as plot events. Rather, they use words to create a snapshot of the unifying idea. Think about the theme you identified for "The Seventh Man." Write a vignette communicating your ideas about the theme. Use one or more symbols to talk about the theme.

❏ Think about how the theme relates to your experiences.

❏ What person, place, object, or activity from your own experience could stand as symbols of this theme?

❏ Use your ideas about theme and symbolism to write a vignette. Explore your thoughts or describe a scene in which you observe the symbol and ponder its importance. Share your vignette with a partner.

**Discuss with a Small Group** With some of your classmates, discuss the story's use of symbols and motifs, and work together to write a statement of theme that combines your perspectives.

 Go to the **Speaking and Listening Studio** for help with participating in a collaborative discussion.

❏ Come to the group discussion with notes about symbols and the development of theme in "The Seventh Man." Briefly explain your ideas when it's your turn. Listen actively and respond appropriately to other group members, and ask clarifying questions if you'd like more information about what they're thinking.

❏ There are several possibilities for the story's theme, and different group members might have picked up on different ones. See if you can find common ground to write a statement about the overall theme. The statement should include the theme and a few supporting examples.

❏ If your group can't come to a consensus, write separate statements and show how they are related.

## RESPOND TO THE ESSENTIAL QUESTION

**?** What effect do we have on nature, and how does nature affect us?

**Gather Information** Review your annotations and notes on "The Seventh Man" and highlight those that help answer the Essential Question. Then, add relevant details to your Response Log.

At the end of the unit, use your notes to write an explanatory essay.

**ACADEMIC VOCABULARY**
As you write and discuss what you learned from the story, be sure to use the Academic Vocabulary words. Check off each of the words that you use.

❏ **advocate**

❏ **discrete**

❏ **domain**

❏ **evoke**

❏ **enhance**

## RESPOND

**WORD BANK**

| | |
|---|---|
| frail | entranced |
| delirium | sociable |
| premonition | permeate |
| sentiment | reconciliation |

## CRITICAL VOCABULARY

**Practice and Apply**  Answer each question using the Critical Vocabulary word in a complete sentence.

1. How could you help a **frail** person at the grocery store?

2. What is one scene that has **entranced** you?

3. During what situations do you feel the most **sociable**?

4. What kind of **sentiment** is appropriate when signing a friend's yearbook?

5. How could you help two friends reach a **reconciliation**?

6. What signs would tell you that a person was experiencing **delirium**?

7. How might a **premonition** affect someone's plans?

8. How could you change a room to make light **permeate** it?

## VOCABULARY STRATEGY:
### Figurative Language

By now, you are familiar with many types of **figurative language**, including similes, metaphors, and personification. If you read too quickly or the comparison the writer is making with figurative language is subtle, you may miss its impact. To get the most from figurative language in a text:

• Pause when you notice a clue word such as *like* or *as* or when you see a reference to something that doesn't seem to fit.

• Note what two things or ideas are being compared.

• Identify what they have in common to understand the writer's point.

**Practice and Apply**  Working with a partner, locate the following examples of figurative language in the story. Then, follow the steps below:

> **. . . but to the kids, removed as we were from such practical concerns, it was just a great big circus . . .** (paragraph 12)

> **The whole, huge space felt like a room without furniture . . .** (paragraph 25)

> **And in its crest, inside its cruel, transparent tongue,** what I saw was K. (paragraph 37)

1. Is the figurative language an example of simile, metaphor, or personification? Form a mental image of the two things being compared. Determine what qualities of the two things are similar and different.

2. With your partner, discuss the effect of the figurative language. For example, does it help you visualize a scene or better understand the story's theme?

3. Find and discuss three other examples of figurative language in the story.

## LANGUAGE CONVENTIONS:
### Complex Sentences

A **clause** is a group of words with a subject and a verb. A **complex sentence** combines an **independent clause**, which can stand by itself as a sentence, with one or more **dependent clauses**, which cannot. Dependent clauses add meaning to independent clauses by acting as modifiers. Dependent clauses often begin with words or phrases called subordinating conjunctions such as: *as if, as, since, than, that, though, until, whenever, where, while, because, who,* and *why*. Subordinating conjunctions clarify the connection between clauses. A comma follows a dependent clause when it begins the sentence.

Look at the following examples of complex sentences from "The Seventh Man." The bold parts represent dependent clauses that add information to the independent clause:

> **Whenever something unusual caught our attention,** we would pick it up and look at it every which way . . .

> I did not find the same quiet, little seaside town **that I remembered.**

Reread paragraph 13 of "The Seventh Man." Notice how the author uses a variety of sentences. There are short, simple sentences such as "There was something strange and unreal about it." The sentence right after it—"I stayed outside on the porch . . ."—is a complex sentence with multiple clauses. Sentence variety enhances the rhythm of a story's language and adds interest for the reader.

**Practice and Apply**  Choose a paragraph from "The Seventh Man." How do the sentences vary? Are there simple, complex, and compound sentences within it? Try rewriting several of the sentences, keeping the meaning of the text but changing the sentences' complexity.

Go to the **Grammar Studio** for more on complex sentences.

POEM

# CARRY

by **Linda Hogan**

pages 199–201

## COMPARE THEMES

Now that you've read "The Seventh Man," read "Carry" and explore how this poem addresses a theme similar to that of the short story. As you read, ask yourself what ideas the author expresses about life or human nature and whether those ideas overlap with the ideas Haruki Murakami explores in "The Seventh Man." After you are finished, you will work on a final project that involves an analysis of both texts.

**?** **ESSENTIAL QUESTION:**

What effect do we have on nature, and how does nature affect us?

SHORT STORY

# THE SEVENTH MAN

by **Haruki Murakami**

pages 177–191

# Carry

## QUICK START

Whether you live in a city, a rural area, or the suburbs, you have many opportunities to observe the natural world. Moments when you consider the night sky, a body of water, or windblown leaves might trigger thoughts about your place in the world. Talk with a partner about a time when you observed an aspect of the natural world. Describe what you noticed and what you thought about.

## ANALYZE SYMBOL AND THEME

The **theme** of a work is the message about life that the writer wants to communicate. Because readers make inferences in order to determine a text's theme, a text may reveal different meanings to different readers. Your interpretation of theme will be valid if you base it closely on evidence from the text.

To determine a theme in "Carry," look for clues in the poem's images and descriptive details, and think about the writer's use of symbols. A **symbol** is a person, place, object, or activity that stands for something beyond itself.

As you read "Carry," pay attention to how the writer uses details to shape and refine particular themes. This chart can help guide your analysis:

| TEXT EVIDENCE TO CONSIDER | EXAMPLES | ANALYSIS AND QUESTIONS |
|---|---|---|
| metaphors and similes that create strong images | | |
| descriptive details that create a mood or feeling | | |
| personification that conveys feelings or emotions | | |
| title | | |

### GENRE ELEMENTS: POETRY

- uses figurative language, including personification
- includes poetic elements, such as rhythm and rhyme
- may or may not be structured in stanzas
- includes imagery that appeals to the senses
- expresses a theme, or message about life

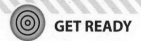
## ANALYZE FREE VERSE

"Carry" is written in a poetic style known as **free verse**. Free verse poetry is characterized by:

- rhythm that is similar to spoken language
- a flow that creates a particular tone
- unconventional structure which gives freedom to enhance meaning through word placement and varying line lengths

When reading a free verse poem, pause only when you would normally pause while speaking, such as when you reach a punctuation mark. Since poets writing free verse do not have to fit their words into a set structure, they are free to add to the poem's meaning through syntax—the arrangement of words and phrases—and different line lengths.

You may have read poems about nature written long ago and noticed that they fit into specific poem structures, such as sonnets. Though structured poetry was very prevalent in the 19th century and earlier, modern nature poetry is often in free verse form.

## ANNOTATION MODEL

**NOTICE & NOTE**

Here is how a student might annotate to analyze the elements of free verse in the poem's first lines:

> From water's broken mirror
> we pulled it,
> alive and shining,
> gasping the painful other element of air.
> It was not just fish.
> There was more.

The first four lines make up one sentence. I can read it as if I am speaking. Different parts of the sentence are on different lines to emphasize the different ideas—the setting, the speaker's action, a description, and what the fish is doing.

## BACKGROUND

**Linda Hogan** *(b. 1947) grew up in Oklahoma and Colorado. A member of the Chickasaw Nation, Hogan has received many awards and honors for her writing. She is a strong advocate for preserving endangered species, and her work reflects her deep interest in environmental issues, native cultures, and spirituality. Hogan says of her writing, "It takes perseverance. I will do it over and over again until I get it right." Her poetry collections include* The Book of Medicines *and* Rounding the Human Corners. *Her first novel,* Mean Spirit, *was a finalist for the Pulitzer Prize.*

# CARRY
### Poem by Linda Hogan

## PREPARE TO COMPARE

*Both "The Seventh Man" and "Carry" feature water as an irresistible natural force. As you read "Carry," think about how the poet's exploration of water and its strength echoes details from the short story. How do the speaker of the poem and the narrator of the story feel about water? How are their feelings similar?*

Notice & Note

You can use the side margins to notice and note signposts in the text.

From water's broken mirror
we pulled it,
alive and shining,
gasping the painful other element of air.
5 It was not just fish.
There was more.
It was hawk, once wild with
hunger, sharp talons
locked into the dying twist
10 and scale of fish,
its long bones
trailing like a ghost
behind fins
through the dark, cold water.

**ANALYZE FREE VERSE**

**Annotate:** Mark the places where you would pause while reading aloud lines 15–23.

**Analyze:** How does the poet structure the lines in a way that keeps it close to "sounding" like natural speech?

**ANALYZE SYMBOL AND THEME**

**Annotate:** Mark an example of personification in lines 26–32.

**Analyze:** How does this personification develop the water as a symbol?

15 It was beautiful, that water,
   like a silver coin stretched thin
   enough to feed us all,
   smooth as skin before anyone knew
   the undertow's¹ rough hands
20 lived inside it, working everything down
   to its absence,
   and water is never lonely,
   it holds so many.
   It says, come close, you who want to swallow me;
25 already I am part of you.
   Come near. I will shape myself around you
   so soft, so calm
   I will carry you
   down to a world you never knew or dreamed,
30 I will gather you
   into the hands of something stronger,
   older, deeper.

_____

¹ **undertow:** a strong current below the surface of water.

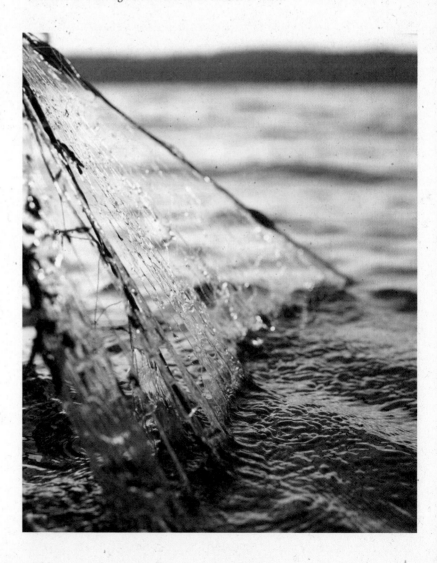

## CHECK YOUR UNDERSTANDING

Answer these questions before moving on to the **Analyze the Text** section on the following page.

**1** What does the speaker find?

   **A** A large fish swimming in the river

   **B** An undertow beneath the surface of the water

   **C** A friend who will provide solace

   **D** A hawk that has died catching its prey

**2** The voice that speaks from line 24 to the poem's end is that of —

   **F** the fish

   **G** the hawk

   **H** the water

   **J** the poet

**3** The speaker considers the water —

   **A** beautiful and peaceful

   **B** deceptive and powerful

   **C** rich and teeming with life

   **D** inspiring and mysterious

# RESPOND

## ANALYZE THE TEXT

Support your responses with evidence from the text. ☰ NOTEBOOK

1. **Summarize** Review what is stated explicitly in lines 1–14 and write a brief summary of what the speaker describes. How does the image created in these lines affect the **mood**, or emotion, of the poem?

2. **Analyze** In lines 1–14, the author uses sentences of different lengths. How do these varied sentence lengths affect your reading of the poem?

3. **Interpret** Explain what is meant by lines 22–23: "and water is never lonely, / it holds so many." Support your interpretation with evidence from other lines.

4. **Interpret** Review the descriptions of water in the poem. What does the water symbolize?

5. **Cite Evidence** What theme about our connection with nature does this poem convey? Support your theme statement with evidence from the poem.

## RESEARCH

**RESEARCH TIP**

To examine the credibility of a photo you find online, ask:

- Is it on a reputable website or on a site that anyone can post to?

- Is it credited to a photographer or photo agency?

- Does the photo appear to be altered digitally? Look for differences in focus and color, as well as awkward angles.

In this poem, Hogan describes a bizarre natural image. Sometimes strange things happen in nature, and photographs of unusual occurrences get spread around social media. Of course, it is important to study the picture for signs that it is may not actually represent reality. Photo-editing programs enable people to alter images drastically.

Look online for photographs of surprising occurrences in nature. For instance, you might think about unusual animal encounters or the strange effects of severe weather. Record your findings in a chart like the one below.

| SOURCE OF IMAGE (URL) | BRIEF DESCRIPTION OF IMAGE | WHAT MAKES THE PICTURE UNUSUAL? |
|---|---|---|
| | | |
| | | |
| | | |

**Extend** Choose one of the pictures you found and share it with a partner. Talk about why you find the picture striking. Examine each other's photos for signs that it might be altered, and help each other find new images if necessary.

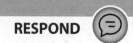

## CREATE AND DISCUSS

**Write a Free-Verse Poem** Write a free-verse poem about the photograph that you researched and shared with your partner.

❏ Write a description of the image. Assuming that your reader will not have access to the photograph, use sensory details in your description. Read through your description and decide how you would like to structure lines of poetry to communicate your ideas.

❏ In your poem, use figurative language such as metaphor, simile, and personification to help the reader connect to the photo.

❏ With a partner, practice reading your poem aloud. Explain the messages about nature that your poems contain.

**Discuss with a Small Group** In "Carry," descriptions of water are central to the poem's meaning. Discuss the choices the poet made in her use of water imagery.

❏ Form a small group of three or four students to analyze the descriptions of water throughout the poem.

❏ For each image of water in the poem, ask questions about what feelings or ideas the author wanted to convey. For example, why did the poet choose to use a "broken mirror" as an image?

❏ Consider how the images of water develop—from an inanimate object to a powerful living force—throughout the poem.

❏ The members of your group may have different ideas about the poem, but see if you can find common ground about your understanding of the poem. Set rules to ensure that everyone is able to contribute equally, if needed. Write a summary that includes the most important insights from the discussion.

 Go to the **Speaking and Listening Studio** for help with participating in a collaborative discussion.

## RESPOND TO THE ESSENTIAL QUESTION

 What effect do we have on nature, and how does nature affect us?

**Gather Information** Review your annotations and notes on "Carry" and highlight those that help answer the Essential Question. Then, add relevant details to your Response Log.

At the end of the unit, use your notes to write an explanatory essay.

**ACADEMIC VOCABULARY**

As you write and discuss what you learned from the poem, be sure to use the Academic Vocabulary words. Check off each of the words that you use.

❏ **advocate**

❏ **discrete**

❏ **domain**

❏ **evoke**

❏ **enhance**

# Collaborate & Compare

**THE SEVENTH MAN**
Short Story
by Haruki Murakami

**CARRY**
Poem by Linda Hogan

## COMPARE THEMES

Now that you have read "The Seventh Man" and "Carry," you can compare how the authors developed themes in their work. The short story and the poem explore a similar idea—the unstoppable power of water—even though the conclusions they draw about that idea are different. Analyzing how the authors built their themes will give you insight into each writer's craft.

Both authors rely on setting, events, the narrator's or speaker's thoughts, and word choice to develop the idea of water as a force that cannot be overcome. With a partner, review the texts. Use a chart like the one below to record your thoughts about the authors' use of narrative elements to develop a theme. Cite specific text evidence where you can. You will use the information from your chart to create a project about the themes in both texts.

|  | "THE SEVENTH MAN" | "CARRY" |
|---|---|---|
| **Setting** |  |  |
| **Key Events** |  |  |
| **Narrator's or Speaker's Thoughts** |  |  |
| **Use of Language** |  |  |

## ANALYZE THE TEXTS

Discuss these questions in your group.

1. **Compare**  What themes did you discover in both "The Seventh Man" and "Carry"? How do the authors' attitudes toward those themes differ?

2. **Evaluate**  Both authors use symbolism. Choose a symbol from each text and evaluate how the author uses it to enrich the text.

3. **Connect**  How did creating mental images help you understand both texts? Cite examples from each text when explaining.

4. **Compare**  Reread the biographies of Murakami and Hogan. How might their cultural backgrounds—Japanese and Native American, respectively—or geography have shaped their attitudes toward the topic of nature?

## CREATE AND SHARE

Now, you will create a project showing your understanding of how Murakami and Hogan both use the topic of water to express themes about our world. Imagine the "seventh man"—the narrator of the short story—and the speaker in the poem as characters. They are both looking at powerful bodies of water. What messages about the world would they like to pass along to an audience as they gaze at the water? Create a two-sided piece of artwork expressing their messages.

1. **Plan Your Artwork**  Create a two-sided piece of artwork using a medium you are comfortable with, such as drawing or creating a collage from images printed from a computer. Think about what each character would want to communicate about nature.

   **My Ideas:** _____

   _____

   _____

   _____

2. **Write Statements**  What "universal truths" about nature and humanity would each character want to share with an audience? Write a statement for each character, in his or her own voice, and add it to your artwork.

   **Statement 1:** _____

   _____

   _____

   _____

   **Statement 2:** _____

   _____

   _____

   _____

3. **Present**  Present your artwork to your group. Different group members may have different interpretations of the authors' themes. Consider how the topic of water—a major part of the natural world—allowed two writers working in different genres to express universal ideas about our world. Support your ideas with quotations from both texts as you present your artwork.

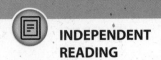
What effect do we have on nature, and how does nature affect us?

# Reader's Choice

**Setting a Purpose** Select one or more of these options from your eBook to continue your exploration of the Essential Question.

- Read the descriptions to see which text grabs your interest.
- Think about which genres you enjoy reading.

## Notice **&** Note

In this unit, you practiced noticing and noting three signposts: **Memory Moment, Contrasts and Contradictions,** and **Again and Again**. As you read independently, these signposts and others will aid your understanding. Below are the anchor questions to ask when you read literature and nonfiction.

| Reading Literature: Stories, Poems, and Plays | | |
|---|---|---|
| **Signpost** | **Anchor Question** | **Lesson** |
| **Contrasts and Contradictions** | Why did the character act that way? | p. 145 |
| **Aha Moment** | How might this change things? | p. 394 |
| **Tough Questions** | What does this make me wonder about? | p. 2 |
| **Words of the Wiser** | What's the lesson for the character? | p. 3 |
| **Again and Again** | Why might the author keep bringing this up? | p. 145 |
| **Memory Moment** | Why is this memory important? | p. 3 |

| Reading Nonfiction: Essays, Articles, and Arguments | | |
|---|---|---|
| **Signpost** | **Anchor Question(s)** | **Lesson** |
| **Big Questions** | What surprised me? <br> What did the author think I already knew? <br> What challenged, changed, or confirmed what I already knew? | p. 220 <br> p. 319 <br> p. 74 |
| **Contrasts and Contradictions** | What is the difference, and why does it matter? | p. 318 |
| **Extreme or Absolute Language** | Why did the author use this language? | p. 221 |
| **Numbers and Stats** | Why did the author use these numbers or amounts? | p. 75 |
| **Quoted Words** | Why was this person quoted or cited, and what did this add? | p. 221 |
| **Word Gaps** | Do I know this word from someplace else? <br> Does it seem like technical talk for this topic? <br> Do clues in the sentence help me understand the word? | p. 75 |

You can preview these texts in Unit 3 of your eBook.

Then, check off the text or texts that you select to read on your own.

**ARGUMENT**

from **Hope for Animals and Their World**
Jane Goodall

*The world's leading expert on chimpanzees explains why we should care about a little insect that has a big impact.*

**ESSAY**

**Sea Stars**
Barbara Hurd

*Consider the ability of the sea star to regenerate and the drama of its life from low to high tide, with truths that echo in human lives as well.*

**POEM**

**Starfish**
Lorna Dee Cervantes

*This poem explores the human fascination with starfish: their life cycle, beauty, and ocean habitat.*

**SHORT STORY**

**Wolves**
José Luis Zárate

*Nature both frightens us and draws us in, in this fantastic tale from Mexico.*

**Collaborate and Share**    Discuss with a partner what you learned from at least one of your independent readings.

- Give a brief synopsis or summary of the text.

- Describe any signposts that you noticed in the text and explain what they revealed to you.

- Describe what you most enjoyed or found most challenging about the text. Give specific examples.

- Decide whether you would recommend the text to others. Why or why not?

Go to the **Reading Studio** for more resources on **Notice & Note.**

# Write an Explanatory Essay

This unit focuses on our relationship with nature and wildness. For this writing task, you will write an explanatory essay focusing on one aspect of nature. In it, you will give a clear explanation of this aspect of nature and our relationship to it. For an example of a well-written explanatory essay you can use as a mentor text, review the essay "Joyas Voladoras."

As you write your essay, you will want to look at the notes you made in your Response Log after reading the texts in this unit.

## Writing Prompt

**Read** the information in the box below.

> *This is the topic or context for your essay.*

> Human beings are a part of nature and have a complex relationship with it.

**Think** carefully about the following question.

> *Mark the two most important words, phrases, or ideas in the prompts.*

> What effect do we have on nature, and how does nature affect us?

> *Now mark the word or words that identify the question you must answer in your essay.*

**Write** an explanatory essay about a specific aspect of nature and our relationship to it.

Be sure to—

> *Review these points as you write and again when you finish. Make any needed changes or edits.*

- ❏ maintain a narrow focus on your specific topic
- ❏ engage readers with an interesting observation, quotation, or detail
- ❏ organize central ideas in a logically structured body that clearly develops the thesis
- ❏ support ideas with evidence from research and experience
- ❏ emphasize ideas using precise and vivid word choices
- ❏ conclude by addressing the significance of the specific topic

# ① Plan

To decide what your explanatory essay will be about, begin with a general topic that interests you, and then do research to focus on one specific aspect of that topic. Also explore your own experiences with the specific topic to develop an idea about your relationship with it. You can then draft a thesis statement and identify a specific purpose for your writing and the audience that might get the most from your ideas. Use the chart below to help you plan.

| EXPLANATORY ESSAY PLANNING CHART | |
|---|---|
| **Focused Topic:** | |
| **Source 1:**<br><br>**Information:** | |
| **Source 2:**<br><br>**Information:** | |
| **Source 3:**<br><br>**Information:** | |
| **My Experience** | |
| **Thesis Statement:**<br><br>**Purpose for Writing:**<br><br>**Specific Audience:** | |

**Background Reading**  Review the notes you have taken in your Response Log after reading the texts in this unit. These texts provide background reading that will help you formulate the key ideas in your essay.

Go to **Writing Informative Texts: Developing a Topic** for help planning your essay.

## Notice & Note
### From Reading to Writing

As you plan your explanatory essay, apply what you've learned about signposts to your own writing. Think about how you can incorporate **Numbers and Stats** into your essay.

Go to the **Reading Studio** for more resources on Notice & Note.

Use the notes from your Response Log as you plan your essay.

Go to **Writing Informative Texts: Organizing Ideas** for more help.

**Organize Your Ideas** After you have researched your topic, organize your information in a way that's appropriate to your topic, purpose, and audience.

- To explain a process over time, choose chronological order.
- To tell what happens and the result, use cause-and-effect organization.
- You can present several key ideas in order of importance.
- You might even mix structures or incorporate a brief narrative passage that shows the effect your topic has had on you.

For any text structure, you will need to provide specific details, examples, and commentary to make your essay engaging and informative. Create an outline or use the chart below to organize your essay.

| EXPLANATORY ESSAY OUTLINE |
|---|
| **INTRODUCTION WITH THESIS:** |
| **BODY** |
| **Idea or Example 1:** <br><br> **Evidence:** <br><br><br> **Idea or Example 2:** <br><br> **Evidence:** <br><br><br> **Idea or Example 3:** <br><br> **Evidence:** |
| **CONCLUSION** |

## ② Develop a Draft

 You might prefer to draft your essay online.

As you write your draft, refer to your outline as well as any notes you took on the texts in the unit. Draft electronically to make it easier to make changes or move sentences around later when you are revising.

**JOYAS
VOLADORAS**

## Use the Mentor Text

### Author's Craft

An intriguing detail or an interesting quotation can be a good way to start an explanatory essay. It will catch your audience's attention and lead the way into the rest of the essay.

Consider the hummingbird for a long moment.
A hummingbird's heart beats ten times a second.
A hummingbird's heart is the size of a pencil eraser.
A hummingbird's heart is a lot of the hummingbird. . . .

*The writer begins with fascinating facts that make the reader want to know more.*

**Apply What You've Learned** Begin your essay in a way that makes people want to keep reading. An interesting fact about your topic is one good possibility.

### Genre Characteristics

An explanatory essay often has sections that use a narrative structure. This can be a highly effective way to provide information.

. . . When this creature is born it is twenty feet long and weighs four tons. It is waaaaay bigger than your car. It drinks a hundred gallons of milk from its mama every day and gains two hundred pounds a day, and when it is seven or eight years old it endures an unimaginable puberty and then it essentially disappears from human ken . . .

*The author tells about the blue whale as though it were a character in a story.*

**Apply What You've Learned** Use a narrative structure, when it's appropriate, to make your explanation clear and draw in your reader.

**Revise**

Go to **Writing Informative Texts: Precise Language and Vocabulary** for help revising your essay.

**On Your Own** A memorable explanatory essay is carefully crafted, in part through thoughtful revision, to achieve its purpose. Your revisions should make your explanation both clearer and more engaging. Use the chart below to focus on specific elements to make your writing stronger.

| REVISION GUIDE | | |
|---|---|---|
| **Ask Yourself** | **Tips** | **Revision Techniques** |
| 1. Does the introduction engage readers and state a clear thesis about a focused topic? | **Mark** an engaging idea in the introduction. **Underline** the thesis statement. | **Add** an attention-getting detail to the introduction and add a thesis statement |
| 2. Are ideas organized logically? | **Note** the central idea explored in each paragraph. | **Reorder** evidence to focus each paragraph on one idea. |
| 3. Is each key idea supported with evidence from research or experience? | **Number** each supporting fact, example, or quotation for a key idea. | **Add** facts, details, examples, or quotations to support ideas with only one or two pieces of support. |
| 4. Do precise and vivid word choices effectively communicate ideas about the specific topic? | **Mark** precise word choices in each section of the essay. | **Revise** vague word choices to make them more precise and descriptive. |
| 5. Does the conclusion effectively summarize ideas and address the importance of the topic? | **Underline** the restated thesis or summary of ideas in the conclusion. | **Add** a restatement of the thesis or summary of the essay's ideas. |

**ACADEMIC VOCABULARY**

As you conduct your peer review, try to use these words.

❑ advocate

❑ discrete

❑ domain

❑ evoke

❑ enhance

**With a Partner** After revising your draft, exchange papers with a partner for a peer review focused on evaluating how clear and engaging the writing is. Begin with the aspects you think work best in your partner's draft, and then note confusing passages and provide concrete suggestions for revision.

When receiving feedback from your partner, listen attentively and ask questions to make sure you fully understand the revision suggestions.

## ④ **Edit**

Once you have addressed the organization, development, and flow of ideas in your essay, you can look to improve the finer points of your draft. Edit for the proper use of standard English conventions and make sure to correct any misspellings and grammatical errors.

### Language Conventions

**Parallel Structure** Strategic use of **parallel structure**—using the same grammatical structure for two or more elements—can guide your readers to make meaningful links between your ideas and also make your writing flow more smoothly.

- **Within a sentence**, parallel construction involves repeated parts of speech or structures in two or more phrases or clauses.

- **Within a paragraph**, parallel construction may involve two or more sentences and is often used for emphasis.

Here are examples of parallel construction from "Joyas Voladoras":

| CONSTRUCTION | EXAMPLE FROM TEXT |
|---|---|
| Within a sentence | . . . more than three hundred species of them **whirring and zooming and nectaring** in hummer time zones . . . |
| Within a paragraph | . . . It's expensive to fly. **You burn out. You fry the machine. You melt the engine.** . . . |

## ⑤ **Publish**

Finalize your essay and choose a way to share it with your audience. Consider these options:

- Post your essay as a blog on a classroom or school website.

- Produce your essay as a multimedia presentation.

Use the scoring guide to evaluate your essay.

## WRITING TASK SCORING GUIDE: EXPLANATORY ESSAY

| | Organization/Progression | Development of Ideas | Use of Language and Conventions |
|---|---|---|---|
| **4** | • The organization is effective and appropriate to the purpose, and includes a purposeful narrative passage.<br>• All ideas are focused on a specific aspect of nature.<br>• Transitions clearly show the relationships among ideas. | • The introduction catches the reader's attention and clearly states a thought-provoking thesis.<br>• Key ideas are well developed with clear main ideas supported by specific and well-chosen facts, details, examples, and quotations.<br>• The conclusion effectively synthesizes ideas and expresses the importance of the topic. | • Word choice is purposeful and precise.<br>• Parallel structure is used correctly where appropriate.<br>• Spelling, capitalization, and punctuation are correct.<br>• Grammar and usage are correct. |
| **3** | • The organization is, for the most part, effective and appropriate to the purpose.<br>• Most ideas are focused on one aspect of nature.<br>• Transitions generally clarify the relationships among ideas. | • The introduction states the thesis but could be more engaging.<br>• Key ideas are adequately developed and supported with evidence.<br>• The conclusion synthesizes ideas and summarizes information. | • Word choices are generally clear.<br>• Parallel structure is used correctly in one or two instances.<br>• There are some spelling, capitalization, and punctuation mistakes.<br>• Some grammatical and usage errors occur but do not interfere with understanding. |
| **2** | • The organization is evident but is not always appropriate to the purpose.<br>• Extraneous ideas draw the focus away from the main topic at times.<br>• Relationships among ideas are sometimes unclear. | • The introduction is not engaging and the thesis statement does not express a clear point.<br>• Some ideas are supported with evidence.<br>• The conclusion may merely summarize key ideas or restate the thesis. | • Word choices are occasionally vague.<br>• An attempt is made to use parallel structure.<br>• Spelling, capitalization, and punctuation are often incorrect.<br>• Flawed grammar and usage sometimes make reading difficult. |
| **1** | • Organization is not evident or not appropriate to the purpose.<br>• Nature is addressed generally; a specific topic is not evident.<br>• Connections among ideas are missing, making the writer's ideas difficult to understand. | • The introduction and the thesis statement are missing or confusing.<br>• Development of ideas is minimal, with inappropriate, vague, or missing support.<br>• The conclusion is absent or fails to summarize ideas. | • Word choices are vague or inaccurate.<br>• Parallel construction is lacking.<br>• Many spelling, capitalization, and punctuation errors are present.<br>• Grammatical and usage errors make the writer's ideas unclear. |

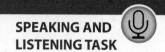
# Deliver a Multimedia Presentation

You will now adapt your explanatory essay into a multimedia presentation that you can deliver to your classmates. You also will watch and listen to their presentations, ask questions to better understand their ideas, and provide feedback.

Go to **Using Media in a Presentation** in the **Speaking and Listening Studio** to learn more.

## ❶ Adapt Your Essay as a Multimedia Presentation

Use the chart below to guide you as you adapt your essay into a script and gather media for your presentation. You may also choose to create a storyboard rather than a script.

| MULTIMEDIA PRESENTATION PLANNING CHART | |
|---|---|
| **Title and Introduction** | How will you revise your title and introduction to capture the listener's attention? Is there a more concise way to state your controlling idea or thesis? |
| **Purpose and Audience** | What text structure, vocabulary, language, and tone are appropriate for your intended purpose and audience? |
| **Effective Language and Organization** | Which parts of your essay should be simplified? Where can you link ideas with transitions such as *first*, *second*, and *finally*? |
| **Media** | What types of media best illustrate your written ideas? Are there sections of writing that can be removed and replaced with audio or video of the phenomenon you are explaining? |

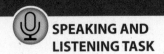
As you work to improve your presentations, follow these discussion rules:

- ❏ **listen closely to each other**
- ❏ **don't interrupt**
- ❏ **stay on topic**
- ❏ **ask only helpful, relevant questions**
- ❏ **provide only clear, thoughtful, and direct answers**

## ② Create Your Multimedia Presentation

When you've adapted your essay and decided on what kinds of visuals and sounds you want, use online search engines to help you find what you need. Use only elements for which you have permission or for which permission is not required. (Most sources allow use in educational settings.)

### Put the Media Together

If you use slideshow software, pay attention to these things:

- ❏ **Text** Keep any text you use to a minimum. Let your images speak for themselves; you can provide any needed commentary in your speech.
- ❏ **Images** Use images that are high enough resolution to be clear and easily seen.
- ❏ **Credits** You will need to give credit to your information sources. Create a slide for the end of your presentation that gives the sources for all the media you have used.

### Practice with a Partner or Group

Show your presentation to a partner or small group and ask for help in revising and improving it.

**As a listener,** take notes about ways that presenters can improve their content and media and more effectively enunciate, use purposeful gestures, and make eye contact. Paraphrase and summarize each presenter's key ideas and main points to confirm your understanding, and ask questions to clarify any confusing ideas.

**As a presenter,** listen closely to questions and feedback, and consider ways to revise your presentation to make it more effective. Remember to ask for suggestions about your visuals and audio to make your presentation clearer and more engaging.

## ③ Deliver Your Presentation

Use the advice you received during practice to make final changes to your presentation. If possible, practice incorporating your media before presenting to troubleshoot any technical problems. Then, deliver your presentation to your classmates.

# Reflect on the Unit

When you were writing your explanatory essay, you synthesized your ideas about the reading you have done in this unit. Now is a good time to reflect on what you have learned.

## Reflect on the Essential Question

- What effect do we have on nature, and how does nature affect us? How has your answer to this question changed since you first considered it when you started this unit?

- What are some examples from the texts you've read that show our relationship with nature?

## Reflect on Your Reading

- Which selections were the most interesting or surprising to you?

- From which selection did you learn the most about how nature affects us or how we affect nature?

## Reflect on the Writing Task

- What difficulties did you encounter while working on your explanatory essay? How might you avoid them next time?

- What part of the essay was the easiest and what part was the hardest to write? Why?

- What improvements did you make to your essay as you were revising?

**UNIT 3 SELECTIONS**
- "My Life as a Bat"
- "Joyas Voladoras"
- "Find Your Park"
- "The Seventh Man"
- "Carry"

# HARD-WON LIBERTY

What do we need in order to feel free?

" There is no easy walk to freedom anywhere. "

Jawaharlal Nehru

## ACADEMIC VOCABULARY

Academic Vocabulary words are words you use when you discuss and write about texts. In this unit you will practice and learn five words.

☑ **comprehensive**    ☐ **equivalent**    ☐ **incentive**    ☐ **innovate**    ☐ **subordinate**

Study the Word Network to learn more about the word **comprehensive**.

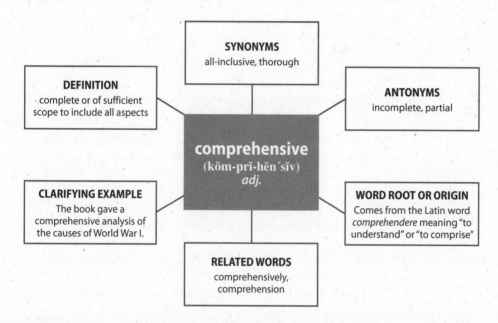

**SYNONYMS**
all-inclusive, thorough

**DEFINITION**
complete or of sufficient scope to include all aspects

**ANTONYMS**
incomplete, partial

**comprehensive**
(kŏm-prĭ-hĕn´sĭv)
adj.

**CLARIFYING EXAMPLE**
The book gave a comprehensive analysis of the causes of World War I.

**WORD ROOT OR ORIGIN**
Comes from the Latin word comprehendere meaning "to understand" or "to comprise"

**RELATED WORDS**
comprehensively, comprehension

**Write and Discuss** Discuss the completed Word Network with a partner, making sure to talk through all of the boxes until you both understand the word, its synonyms, antonyms, and related forms. Then, fill out Word Networks for the remaining four words. Use a dictionary or online resource to help you complete the activity.

 *Go online to access the Word Networks.*

## RESPOND TO THE ESSENTIAL QUESTION

In this unit, you will read various genres that explore what we need in order to feel free. As you read, you will revisit the **Essential Question** and gather your ideas about it in the **Response Log** that appears on page R4. At the end of the unit, you will have the opportunity to write an **argument** about what it means to be free. Filling out the Response Log will help you prepare for this writing task.

 *You can also go online to access the Response Log.*

**UNIT 4
RESPONSE LOG**

Use this Response Log to record your ideas about how each of the texts in Unit 4 relates to or comments on the Essential Question.

**? Essential Question:**
What do we need in order to feel free?

| Letter from Birmingham Jail | |
| Elsewhere | |
| The Hawk Can Soar | |
| The Briefcase | |
| from Letter to Viceroy, Lord Irwin | |
| from Gandhi: The Rise to Fame | |

R4    Student Resources

## LETTER FROM BIRMINGHAM JAIL

 For more information on these and other signposts to Notice & Note, visit the **Reading Studio.**

You are about to read the argument "Letter from Birmingham Jail." In it, you will notice and note signposts that provide clues about the argument's claims and evidence. Here are a key question and two signposts to look for as you read this argument and other nonfiction writing.

**Big Question** Have you ever watched a TV commercial or listened to a classmate's student council campaign speech and thought, *"REALLY?"* When you're presented with an idea that's hard to believe, determine whether the information makes you wonder about something new or is simply untrue.

A nonfiction writer may share fascinating, true information with you—or the writer may have a bias or purpose that affects how believable the information is. As you read, be prepared to ask yourself: *What surprised me?* Look for:

- New information ("I didn't know that!")
- Suspicious information ("Seriously? Is that really true?")
- Clarifying information ("Oh! Now I get it!")
- A different perspective ("I hadn't thought of it that way.")

Here is how a student might mark surprising elements in King's letter.

---

April 16, 1963
My Dear Fellow Clergymen:

1    While confined here in the Birmingham city jail, <u>I came across your recent statement calling my present activities "unwise and untimely."</u> Seldom do I pause to answer criticism of <u>my work and ideas.</u> If I sought to answer all the criticisms that cross my desk, my secretaries would have little time for anything other than such correspondence in the course of the day, and I would have no time for constructive work. But since I feel that you are men of genuine good will and that your criticisms are sincerely set forth, <u>I want to try to answer your statement</u> in what I hope will be <u>patient and reasonable terms.</u>

---

| What surprised you? | That Dr. King wrote to "fellow clergymen" who had criticized him. |
|---|---|
| Why did it surprise you? What other questions does it bring to mind? | I thought the letter was to the public or maybe political officials. What religious leaders criticized Dr. King, and what did they say? |

**Quoted Words** Backing up your ideas with documented evidence and expert opinions shows that you really know your topic. The same is true of professional writers and speakers. A strong argument is supported by:

- Personal Perspectives: the experience or views of an ordinary person
- Voices of Authority: an expert view, from someone with relevant credibility
- Documented Facts: verifiable information that supports an idea or claim

Here a student annotated part of King's letter that uses **Quoted Words:**

Any time you see quotation marks in an argument or informational text, pause to see whether they share important information or an expert opinion about the topic.

> 15    . . . One has not only a legal but a moral responsibility to obey just laws. Conversely, one has a moral responsibility to disobey unjust laws. I would agree with St. Augustine that "an unjust law is no law at all."

**Anchor Question**
When you notice this signpost, ask: Why is this person quoted, and what do the quoted words add?

| Who is quoted? | Saint Augustine |
|---|---|
| Why did the author include the quote? What did it add? | The words of a saint will resonate with an audience of clergy. It also shows that this is not a new or revolutionary idea. |

**Extreme or Absolute Language**  If a friend tells you that you *have* to play this new game because it has *the most intense plot line* and you'll be a *complete loser* if you don't, you should ask: Why all the extreme language?

In nonfiction, absolute words like *every, always, never,* or words that end in *-est* should also catch your attention. When you see extreme or absolute language, don't just accept it; determine why the author is using it.

In this example, a student marked **Extreme or Absolute Language:**

**Anchor Question**
When you notice this signpost, ask: Why would the author use this language? What does this reveal about the author's biases or purpose?

> 26    I have just received a letter from a white brother in Texas. He writes: "All Christians know that the colored people will receive equal rights eventually, but it is possible that you are in too great a religious hurry. . . . "

| What is extreme about this statement? | It doesn't acknowledge that some Christians don't "know" this and assumes that eventual equality will just happen. It also dismisses people's need for equality. |
|---|---|
| What does this language reveal about purpose, bias, or perspective? | It reflects the letter writer's perspective that things are going fine, which he may see because he isn't really affected by inequality. |

# LETTER FROM BIRMINGHAM JAIL

Argument by **Martin Luther King Jr.**

What do we need in order to feel free?

## QUICK START

Have you ever asked permission to do something new? Did you plan your case in advance? Did you anticipate and address possible reasons you might be told no? How did it go? Freewrite about your experience.

## ANALYZE ARGUMENT

A well-crafted argument includes these elements:

- A clear **claim** stating the writer's position on the issue or problem
- Relevant and appealing **reasons** and **evidence** that support the claim
- **Counterarguments** that anticipate and rebut, or refute, opposing views
- **Concession** acknowledging a valid point made by the opposition
- A convincing **conclusion,** often with a call to action

An effective argument will appeal to the interests of a specific audience and work toward a clear goal or purpose. Look for these features as you read.

## ANALYZE RHETORICAL DEVICES

**Rhetoric** is the art or study of using language effectively and persuasively. A **rhetorical device** is a technique writers use to enhance their arguments and communicate more effectively. King's letter uses these devices:

### GENRE ELEMENTS: ARGUMENT

- makes claims to persuade an audience
- includes evidence to support claims
- contains personalized appeals to connect with the audience
- includes rhetorical devices that strengthen the message
- acknowledges and disproves counterclaims through concession and rebuttal

| RHETORICAL DEVICE | HOW IT WORKS | EXAMPLE FROM TEXT |
|---|---|---|
| appeals | These include<br>*ethos*: establishes authority or credibility<br>*pathos*: speaks to emotions<br>*logos*: uses logic or reason | I have the honor of serving as president of the Southern Christian Leadership Conference. . . . |
| antithesis | Contrasting ideas are presented via parallel language. | Injustice anywhere is a threat to justice everywhere. . . . |
| parallelism | The use of similar grammatical constructions to express ideas that are related or equal in importance. | I . . . am here because I was invited here. I am here because I have organizational ties here. |
| shift | A change in mood or tone, often signaled by words like *but* or *however*. Here, King shifts the meaning of *extremist* from negative to positive. | Was not Jesus an extremist for love: . . . the question is not whether we will be extremists, but what kind of extremists we will be. . . . |

Point by point, King uses these and other techniques to show that each of the clergymen's criticisms is a **logical fallacy**, a statement based on an error in reasoning. As you read, keep in mind King's point and the techniques he uses to prove it.

## CRITICAL VOCABULARY

| cognizant | moratorium | retaliate | precipitate |
|---|---|---|---|
| complacency | manifest | mores | provocation |

Mark the letter of the best answer to each question. Then, explain your response to a partner using both words.

1. Which of the following would be used when talking about revenge?
   **a. manifest**     **b. retaliate**

2. Which of the following would be used when talking about values?
   **a. mores**     **b. moratorium**

3. Which of the following happens when someone incites or inflames a situation?
   **a. provocation**     **b. complacency**

4. Which of the following would be used when talking about being aware?
   **a. cognizant**     **b. precipitate**

## LANGUAGE CONVENTIONS

**Repetition** is a technique in which a word or phrase is repeated for emphasis or unity. **Parallelism** is the repetition of grammatical structures to express ideas that are related or equal in importance. This example is from the letter:

**... the white moderate, who is more devoted to "order" than to justice; who prefers a negative peace ... who constantly says ...**

Notice how King uses repetition and parallelism to strengthen his argument.

---

### ANNOTATION MODEL                    NOTICE & NOTE

Here is how a student marked the opening of "Letter from Birmingham Jail."

April 16, 1963

My Dear Fellow Clergymen:

While confined here in the Birmingham city jail, I came across your recent statement calling my present activities "unwise and untimely." Seldom do I pause to answer criticism of my work and ideas. If I sought to answer all the criticisms that cross my desk, my secretaries would have little time for anything other than such correspondence in the course of the day, and I would have no time for constructive work. But since I feel that you are men of genuine good will and that your criticisms are sincerely set forth, I want to try to answer your statement in what I hope will be patient and reasonable terms.

> King establishes audience and his own credibility—he's one of them.
>
> He explains why he's writing.
>
> He's not overly sensitive to criticism.
>
> He's polite and respectful.

## BACKGROUND

**Martin Luther King Jr.** (1929–1968) *led a nonviolent protest in 1963 against lunch counter segregation in Birmingham, Alabama. He was jailed along with many of his supporters. While in jail, King wrote this letter in response to the local clergy. As a Baptist minister and civil rights leader, King helped to organize the 1963 March on Washington, where he delivered his "I Have a Dream" speech. His leadership was crucial in passing the Civil Rights Act of 1964. That year, he received the Nobel Peace Prize. King was assassinated in 1968.*

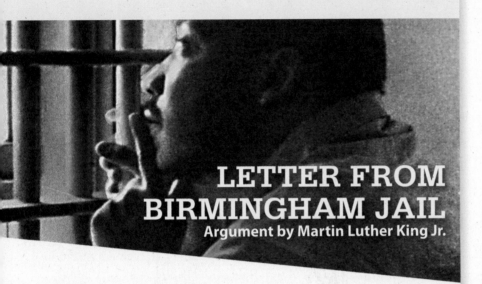

# LETTER FROM BIRMINGHAM JAIL
### Argument by Martin Luther King Jr.

## SETTING A PURPOSE

*As you read, monitor your understanding of King's lengthy and detailed argument by using a graphic organizer, note-taking, or annotations. Watch for and note key ideas he uses to make his case.*

April 16, 1963
My Dear Fellow Clergymen:

1   While confined here in the Birmingham city jail, I came across your recent statement calling my present activities "unwise and untimely." Seldom do I pause to answer criticism of my work and ideas. If I sought to answer all the criticisms that cross my desk, my secretaries would have little time for anything other than such correspondence in the course of the day, and I would have no time for constructive work. But since I feel that you are men of genuine good will and that your criticisms are sincerely set forth, I want to try to answer your statement in what I hope will be patient and reasonable terms.

2   I think I should indicate why I am here in Birmingham, since you have been influenced by the view which argues against "outsiders coming in." I have the honor of serving as president

### QUOTED WORDS

**Notice & Note:** Mark the direct quotation in paragraph 2. Who is being quoted?

**Interpret:** Why are these words central to King's argument?

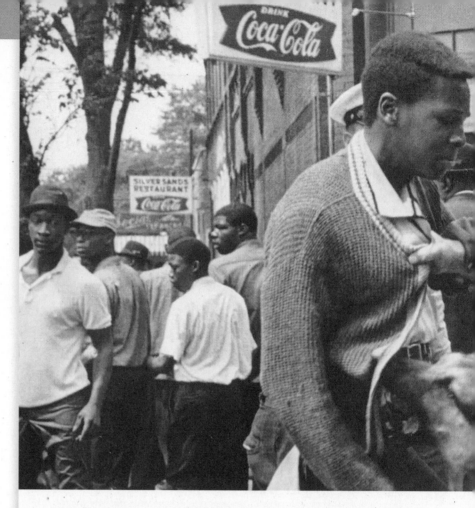

**Annotate:** Paragraph 3 is an extended **allusion**, an indirect reference to a famous person, place, event, or literary work. Mark the people, places, events, and/or literary works to which King alludes in this paragraph.

**Connect:** Why does King include religious allusions in his letter?

**cognizant**
(kŏg´nĭ-zənt) *adj.* aware or conscious of.

of the Southern Christian Leadership Conference, an organization operating in every southern state, with headquarters in Atlanta, Georgia. We have some eighty-five affiliated organizations across the South, and one of them is the Alabama Christian Movement for Human Rights. Frequently we share staff, educational and financial resources with our affiliates. Several months ago the affiliate here in Birmingham asked us to be on call to engage in a nonviolent direct-action program if such were deemed necessary. We readily consented, and when the hour came we lived up to our promise. So I, along with several members of my staff, am here because I was invited here. I am here because I have organizational ties here.

3      But more basically, I am in Birmingham because injustice is here. Just as the prophets of the eighth century B.C. left their villages and carried their "thus saith the Lord" far beyond the boundaries of their home towns, and just as the Apostle Paul left his village of Tarsus and carried the gospel of Jesus Christ to the far corners of the Greco-Roman world, so am I compelled to carry the gospel of freedom beyond my own home town. Like Paul, I must constantly respond to the Macedonian call for aid.[1]

4      Moreover, I am **cognizant** of the interrelatedness of all communities and states. I cannot sit idly by in Atlanta and not be concerned about what happens in Birmingham. Injustice anywhere is a threat to justice everywhere. We are caught in an inescapable

---

[1] **Macedonian call for aid:** according to the Bible (Acts 16), the apostle Paul received a vision calling him to preach in Macedonia, an area north of Greece.

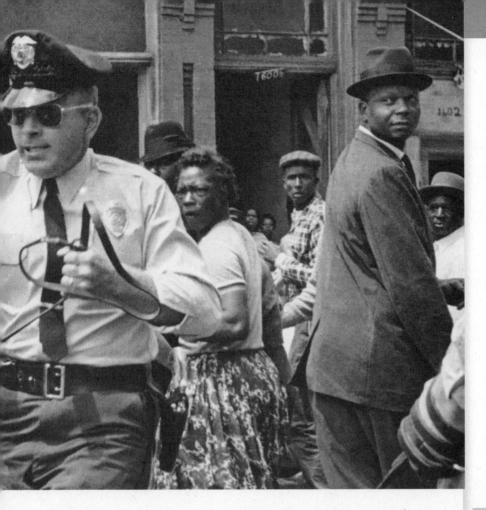

network of mutuality, tied in a single garment of destiny. Whatever affects one directly, affects all indirectly. Never again can we afford to live with the narrow, provincial "outside agitator" idea. Anyone who lives inside the United States can never be considered an outsider anywhere within its bounds.

5    You deplore the demonstrations taking place in Birmingham. But your statement, I am sorry to say, fails to express a similar concern for the conditions that brought about the demonstrations. I am sure that none of you would want to rest content with the superficial kind of social analysis that deals merely with effects and does not grapple with underlying causes. It is unfortunate that demonstrations are taking place in Birmingham, but it is even more unfortunate that the city's white power structure left the Negro community with no alternative.

6    In any nonviolent campaign there are four basic steps: collection of the facts to determine whether injustices exist; negotiation; self-purification; and direct action. We have gone through all these steps in Birmingham. There can be no gainsaying the fact that racial injustice engulfs this community. Birmingham is probably the most thoroughly segregated city in the United States. Its ugly record of brutality is widely known. Negroes have experienced grossly unjust treatment in the courts. There have been more unsolved bombings of Negro homes and churches in Birmingham than in any other city in the nation. These are the hard, brutal facts of the case. On the basis of these conditions, Negro leaders sought to negotiate with the city

**EXTREME OR ABSOLUTE LANGUAGE**

**Notice & Note:** Mark uses of the word *never* and other absolute language in paragraph 4.

**Connect:** How might King's choice of words make it difficult for his audience to disagree with him?

**ANALYZE ARGUMENT**

**Annotate:** Mark details in paragraphs 6–9 that list steps King and his associates have taken in Birmingham.

**Analyze:** How does going into such detail about these actions support King's argument?

**moratorium**

(môr-ə-tôr´ē-əm) *n.* a temporary suspension or agreed-upon delay.

fathers. But the latter consistently refused to engage in good-faith negotiation.

7    Then, last September, came the opportunity to talk with leaders of Birmingham's economic community. In the course of the negotiations, certain promises were made by the merchants—for example, to remove the stores' humiliating racial signs.[2] On the basis of these promises, the Reverend Fred Shuttlesworth and the leaders of the Alabama Christian Movement for Human Rights agreed to a **moratorium** on all demonstrations. As the weeks and months went by, we realized that we were the victims of a broken promise. A few signs, briefly removed, returned; the others remained.

8    As in so many past experiences, our hopes had been blasted, and the shadow of deep disappointment settled upon us. We had no

---

[2] **racial signs:** signs that marked segregated areas of buildings and other facilities.

alternative except to prepare for direct action, whereby we would present our very bodies as a means of laying our case before the conscience of the local and the national community. Mindful of the difficulties involved, we decided to undertake a process of self-purification. We began a series of workshops on nonviolence, and we repeatedly asked ourselves: "Are you able to accept blows without **retaliating**?" "Are you able to endure the ordeal of jail?" We decided to schedule our direct-action program for the Easter season, realizing that except for Christmas, this is the main shopping period of the year. Knowing that a strong economic withdrawal program³ would be the by-product of direct action, we felt that this would be the best time to bring pressure to bear on the merchants for the needed change.

9    Then it occurred to us that Birmingham's mayoralty election was coming up in March, and we speedily decided to postpone action until after election day. When we discovered that the Commissioner of Public Safety, Eugene "Bull" Connor, had piled up enough votes to be in the run-off, we decided again to postpone action until the day after the run-off so that the demonstrations could not be used to cloud the issues. Like many others, we waited to see Mr. Connor defeated, and to this end we endured postponement after postponement. Having aided in this community need, we felt that our direct-action program could be delayed no longer.

10    You may well ask: "Why direct action? Why sit-ins, marches and so forth? Isn't negotiation a better path?" You are quite right in calling for negotiation. Indeed, this is the very purpose of direct action. Nonviolent direct action seeks to create such a crisis and foster such a tension that a community which has constantly refused to negotiate is forced to confront the issue. It seeks so to dramatize the issue that it can no longer be ignored. My citing the creation of tension as part of the work of the nonviolent-resister may sound rather shocking. But I must confess that I am not afraid of the word "tension." I have earnestly opposed violent tension, but there is a type of constructive, nonviolent tension which is necessary for growth. Just as Socrates⁴ felt that it was necessary to create a tension in the mind so that individuals could rise from the bondage of myths and half-truths to the unfettered realm of creative analysis and objective appraisal, so must we see the need for nonviolent gadflies to create the kind of tension in society that will help men rise from the dark depths of prejudice and racism to the majestic heights of understanding and brotherhood.

**retaliate**
(rĭ-tăl´ē-āt) *v.* to respond in kind to having been acted upon, often with harmful intent.

**LANGUAGE CONVENTIONS**
**Annotate:** Mark the instances of the word *tension* in paragraph 10. How many times does King use the word?

**Evaluate:** How do the meaning and tone of *tension* change over the course of the paragraph? How does this repetition help King make a point?

---

³ **economic withdrawal program:** boycott.
⁴ **Socrates:** (c. 470–399 BCE) Greek philosopher and major influence in the development of Western thought.

11    The purpose of our direct-action program is to create a situation so crisis-packed that it will inevitably open the door to negotiation. I therefore concur with you in your call for negotiation. Too long has our beloved Southland been bogged down in a tragic effort to live in monologue rather than dialogue.

12    One of the basic points in your statement is that the action that I and my associates have taken in Birmingham is untimely. Some have asked: "Why didn't you give the new city administration time to act?" The only answer that I can give to this query is that the new Birmingham administration must be prodded about as much as the outgoing one, before it will act. . . . My friends, I must say to you that we have not made a single gain in civil rights without determined legal and nonviolent pressure. Lamentably, it is an historical fact that privileged groups seldom give up their privileges voluntarily. Individuals may see the moral light and voluntarily give up their unjust posture; but, as Reinhold Niebuhr[5] has reminded us, groups tend to be more immoral than individuals.

13    We know through painful experience that freedom is never voluntarily given by the oppressor; it must be demanded by the oppressed. Frankly, I have yet to engage in a direct-action campaign that was "well timed" in the view of those who have not suffered unduly from the disease of segregation. For years now I have heard the word "Wait!" It rings in the ear of every Negro with piercing familiarity. This "Wait" has almost always meant "Never." We must come to see, with one of our distinguished jurists, that "justice too long delayed is justice denied."

14    We have waited for more than 340 years for our constitutional and God-given rights. The nations of Asia and Africa are moving with jetlike speed toward gaining political independence, but we still creep at horse-and-buggy pace toward gaining a cup of coffee at a lunch counter. Perhaps it is easy for those who have never felt the stinging darts of segregation to say, "Wait." But when you have seen vicious mobs lynch your mothers and fathers at will and drown your sisters and brothers at whim; when you have seen hate-filled policemen curse, kick and even kill your black brothers and sisters; when you see the vast majority of your twenty million Negro brothers smothering in an airtight cage of poverty in the midst of an affluent society; when you suddenly find your tongue twisted and your speech stammering as you seek to explain to your six-year-old daughter why she can't go to the public amusement park that has just been advertised on television, and see tears welling up in her eyes when she is told that Funtown is closed to colored children, and see

**ANALYZE RHETORICAL DEVICES**

**Annotate:** To create **antithesis,** a writer contrasts ideas using parallel language. Mark the example of antithesis near the beginning of paragraph 14.

**Compare:** How do these contrasting ideas support King's argument?

---

[5] **Reinhold Niebuhr:** (1892–1971) American theologian whose writings address moral and social problems.

ominous clouds of inferiority beginning to form in her little mental sky, and see her beginning to distort her personality by developing an unconscious bitterness toward white people; when you have to concoct an answer for a five-year old son who is asking: "Daddy, why do white people treat colored people so mean?"; when you take a cross-country drive and find it necessary to sleep night after night in the uncomfortable corners of your automobile because no motel will accept you; when you are humiliated day in and day out by nagging signs reading "white" and "colored"; when your first name becomes "nigger," your middle name becomes "boy" (however old you are) and your last name becomes "John," and your wife and mother are never given the respected title "Mrs."; when you are harried by day and haunted by night by the fact that you are a Negro, living constantly at tiptoe stance, never quite knowing what to expect next, and are plagued with inner fears and outer resentments; when you are forever fighting a degenerating sense of "nobodiness"—then you will understand why we find it difficult to wait. There comes a time when the cup of endurance runs over, and men are no longer willing to be plunged into the abyss of despair. I hope, sirs, you can understand our legitimate and unavoidable impatience.

15    You express a great deal of anxiety over our willingness to break laws. This is certainly a legitimate concern. Since we so diligently urge people to obey the Supreme Court's decision of 1954 outlawing segregation in the public schools,[6] at first glance it may seem rather paradoxical for us consciously to break laws. One may well ask: "How can you advocate breaking some laws and obeying others?" The answer lies in the fact that there are two types of laws: just and unjust. I would be the first to advocate obeying just laws. One has not only a legal but a moral responsibility to obey just laws. Conversely, one has a moral responsibility to disobey unjust laws. I would agree with St. Augustine[7] that "an unjust law is no law at all."

16    Now, what is the difference between the two? How does one determine whether a law is just or unjust? A just law is a man-made code that squares with the moral law or the law of God. An unjust law is a code that is out of harmony with the moral law. To put it in the terms of St. Thomas Aquinas:[8] An unjust law is a human law that is not rooted in eternal law and natural law. Any law that uplifts human personality is just. Any law that degrades human personality is unjust. All segregation statutes are unjust because segregation distorts the soul and damages the personality. It gives the segregator a false sense of superiority and the segregated a false sense of inferiority.

**ANALYZE ARGUMENT**

**Annotate:** Mark the concession that King makes in paragraph 15.

**Connect:** How does this concession work to support King's argument?

---

[6] **Supreme Court . . . public schools:** The U.S. Supreme Court's decision in the case *Brown* v. *Board of Education of Topeka, Kansas.*

[7] **St. Augustine:** North African bishop (AD 354–430) regarded as a founder of Christianity.

[8] **St. Thomas Aquinas:** noted philosopher and theologian (1225–1274).

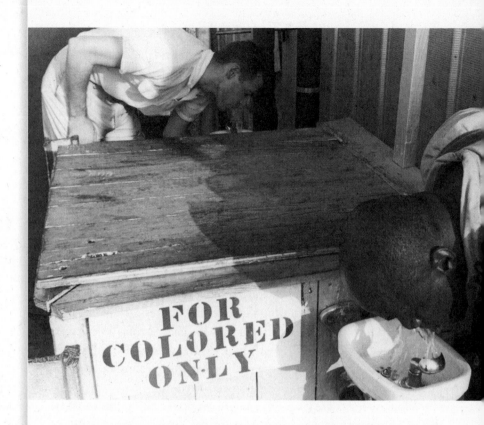

Segregation, to use the terminology of the Jewish philosopher Martin Buber,[9] substitutes an "I-it" relationship for an "I-thou" relationship and ends up relegating persons to the status of things. Hence segregation is not only politically, economically and sociologically unsound, it is morally wrong and sinful. Paul Tillich[10] has said that sin is separation. Is not segregation an existential expression of man's tragic separation, his awful estrangement, his terrible sinfulness? Thus it is that I can urge men to obey the 1954 decision of the Supreme Court, for it is morally right; and I can urge them to disobey segregation ordinances, for they are morally wrong.

17    Let us consider a more concrete example of just and unjust laws. An unjust law is a code that a numerical or power majority group compels a minority group to obey but does not make binding on itself. This is *difference* made legal. By the same token, a just law is a code that a majority compels a minority to follow and that it is willing to follow itself. This is *sameness* made legal.

18    Let me give another explanation. A law is unjust if it is inflicted on a minority that, as a result of being denied the right to vote, had no part in enacting or devising the law. Who can say that the legislature of Alabama which set up that state's segregation laws was democratically elected? Throughout Alabama all sorts

---

[9] **Martin Buber:** influential philosopher (1878–1965) with a great impact on Jewish and Christian theology.

[10] **Paul Tillich:** (1886–1965) influential German-American philosopher and Christian theologian.

of devious methods are used to prevent Negroes from becoming registered voters, and there are some counties in which, even though Negroes constitute a majority of the population, not a single Negro is registered. Can any law enacted under such circumstances be considered democratically structured?

19    Sometimes a law is just on its face and unjust in its application. For instance, I have been arrested on a charge of parading without a permit. Now, there is nothing wrong in having an ordinance which requires a permit for a parade. But such an ordinance becomes unjust when it is used to maintain segregation and to deny citizens the First-Amendment privilege of peaceful assembly and protest.

20    I hope you are able to see the distinction I am trying to point out. In no sense do I advocate evading or defying the law, as would the rabid segregationist. That would lead to anarchy. One who breaks an unjust law must do so openly, lovingly, and with a willingness to accept the penalty. I submit that an individual who breaks a law that conscience tells him is unjust, and who willingly accepts the penalty of imprisonment in order to arouse the conscience of the community over its injustice, is in reality expressing the highest respect for law.

21    Of course, there is nothing new about this kind of civil disobedience. It was evidenced sublimely in the refusal of Shadrach, Meshach and Abednego to obey the laws of Nebuchadnezzar,[11] on the ground that a higher moral law was at stake. It was practiced superbly by the early Christians, who were willing to face hungry lions and the excruciating pain of chopping blocks rather than submit to certain unjust laws of the Roman Empire. To a degree, academic freedom is a reality today because Socrates practiced civil disobedience. In our own nation, the Boston Tea Party[12] represented a massive act of civil disobedience.

22    We should never forget that everything Adolf Hitler did in Germany was "legal" and everything the Hungarian freedom fighters[13] did in Hungary was "illegal." It was "illegal" to aid and comfort a Jew in Hitler's Germany. Even so, I am sure that, had I lived in Germany at the time, I would have aided and comforted my Jewish brothers. If today I lived in a Communist country where certain principles dear to the Christian faith are suppressed, I would openly advocate disobeying that country's antireligious laws.

23    I must make two honest confessions to you, my Christian and Jewish brothers. First, I must confess that over the past few years I have been gravely disappointed with the white moderate. I have

---

[11] refusal . . . Nebuchadnezzar: Biblical account of three Hebrews condemned for refusing to worship an idol as required by the King of Babylon. The three were miraculously protected from the flames into which they were thrown.
[12] Boston Tea Party: a 1773 protest against the British Tea Act in which American colonists dumped 342 chests of tea into Boston Harbor.
[13] Hungarian freedom fighters: participants in the 1956 revolt against Hungary's Soviet-backed government.

**ANALYZE RHETORICAL DEVICES**

**Annotate:** Mark the allusions in paragraphs 21 and 22.

**Evaluate:** Are these allusions an effective way to support the idea of civil disobedience? Why or why not?

**BIG QUESTIONS**

**Notice & Note:** What surprising idea does King express in paragraph 23?

**Interpret:** Why might King's audience find this idea surprising? How might readers react to this statement?

almost reached the regrettable conclusion that the Negro's great stumbling block in his stride toward freedom is not the White Citizen's Counciler or the Ku Klux Klanner,[14] but the white moderate, who is more devoted to "order" than to justice; who prefers a negative peace which is the absence of tension to a positive peace which is the presence of justice; who constantly says: "I agree with you in the goal you seek, but I cannot agree with your methods of direct action"; who paternalistically believes he can set the timetable for another man's freedom; who lives by a mythical concept of time and who constantly advises the Negro to wait for a "more convenient season." Shallow understanding from people of good will is more frustrating than absolute misunderstanding from people of ill will. Lukewarm acceptance is much more bewildering than outright rejection.

24     I had hoped that the white moderate would understand that law and order exist for the purpose of establishing justice and that when they fail in this purpose they become the dangerously structured dams that block the flow of social progress. I had hoped that the white moderate would understand that the present tension in the South is a necessary phase of the transition from an obnoxious negative peace, in which the Negro passively accepted his unjust plight, to a substantive and positive peace, in which all men will respect the dignity and worth of human personality. Actually, we who engage in nonviolent direct action are not the creators of tension. We merely bring to the surface the hidden tension that is already alive. We bring it out in the open, where it can be seen and dealt with. Like a boil that can never be cured so long as it is covered up but must be opened with all its ugliness to the natural medicines of air and light, injustice must be exposed, with all the tension its exposure creates, to the light of human conscience and the air of national opinion before it can be cured.

25     In your statement you assert that our actions, even though peaceful, must be condemned because they **precipitate** violence. But is this a logical assertion? Isn't this like condemning a robbed man because his possession of money precipitated the evil act of robbery? Isn't this like condemning Socrates because his unswerving commitment to truth and his philosophical inquiries precipitated the act by the misguided populace in which they made him drink hemlock? Isn't this like condemning Jesus because his unique God-consciousness and never-ceasing devotion to God's will precipitated the evil act of crucifixion? We must come to see that, as the federal courts have consistently affirmed, it is wrong to urge an individual to cease his efforts to gain his basic constitutional rights because the quest may precipitate violence. Society must protect the robbed and punish the robber.

**precipitate**
(prĭ-sĭp′ĭ-tāt)  *v.* to cause something to happen rapidly or unexpectedly.

**ANALYZE RHETORICAL DEVICES**

**Annotate:** Mark the logical fallacy about peaceful protests that King introduces in paragraph 25.

**Evaluate:** What examples does King use to refute this fallacy?

---

[14]**White . . . Klanner:** members of white-supremacist groups.

26    I had also hoped that the white moderate would reject the myth concerning time in relation to the struggle for freedom. I have just received a letter from a white brother in Texas. He writes: "All Christians know that the colored people will receive equal rights eventually, but it is possible that you are in too great a religious hurry. It has taken Christianity almost two thousand years to accomplish what it has. The teachings of Christ take time to come to earth." Such an attitude stems from a tragic misconception of time, from the strangely irrational notion that there is something in the very flow of time that will inevitably cure all ills. Actually, time itself is neutral; it can be used either destructively or constructively. More and more I feel that the people of ill will have used time much more effectively than have the people of good will. We will have to repent in this generation not merely for the hateful words and actions of the bad people but for the appalling silence of the good people. Human progress never rolls in on wheels of inevitability; it comes through the tireless efforts of men willing to be coworkers with God, and without this hard work, time itself becomes an ally of the forces of social stagnation. We must use time creatively, in the knowledge that the time is always ripe to do right. Now is the time to make real the promise of democracy and transform our pending national elegy into a creative psalm[15] of brotherhood. Now is the time to lift our national policy from the quicksand of racial injustice to the solid rock of human dignity.

27    You speak of our activity in Birmingham as extreme. At first I was rather disappointed that fellow clergymen would see my nonviolent efforts as those of an extremist. I began thinking about the fact that I stand in the middle of two opposing forces in the Negro community. One is a force of **complacency**, made up in part of Negroes who, as a result of long years of oppression, are so drained of self-respect and a sense of "somebodiness" that they have adjusted to segregation; and in part of a few middleclass Negroes who, because of a degree of academic and economic security and because in some ways they profit by segregation, have become insensitive to the problems of the masses. The other force is one of bitterness and hatred, and it comes perilously close to advocating violence. It is expressed in the various black nationalist groups that are springing up across the nation, the largest and best known being Elijah Muhammad's Muslim movement.[16] Nourished by the Negro's frustration over the continued existence of racial discrimination, this movement is made up of people who have lost faith in America, who have absolutely

QUOTED WORDS

**Notice & Note:** Mark the quotation King provides in paragraph 26.

**Analyze:** How does King use his rebuttal of this quotation as a key part of his argument?

**complacency**
(kəm-plā´sən-sē) *n.* contented self-satisfaction.

---

[15] **elegy . . . psalm:** an elegy is a lament for the dead; a psalm is a song of praise.
[16] **black nationalist . . . Elijah Muhammad's Muslim movement:** groups that proposed economic and social independence for African American communities, including the Nation of Islam, founded in 1930 and led by Elijah Muhammad (1897–1975) from 1934 until his death.

repudiated Christianity, and who have concluded that the white man is an incorrigible "devil."

28     I have tried to stand between these two forces, saying that we need emulate neither the "do-nothingism" of the complacent nor the hatred and despair of the black nationalist. For there is the more excellent way of love and nonviolent protest. I am grateful to God that, through the influence of the Negro church, the way of nonviolence became an integral part of our struggle.

29     If this philosophy had not emerged, by now many streets of the South would, I am convinced, be flowing with blood. . . .

30     Oppressed people cannot remain oppressed forever. The yearning for freedom eventually **manifests** itself, and that is what has happened to the American Negro. Something within has reminded him of his birthright of freedom, and something without has reminded him that it can be gained. Consciously or unconsciously, he has been caught up by the *Zeitgeist*,[17] and with his black brothers of Africa and his brown and yellow brothers of Asia, South America and the Caribbean, the United States Negro is moving with a sense of great urgency toward the promised land of racial justice. If one recognizes this vital urge that has engulfed the Negro community, one should readily understand why public demonstrations are taking place. The Negro has many pent-up resentments and latent frustrations, and he must release them. So let him march; let him make prayer pilgrimages to the city hall; let him go on freedom rides—and try to understand why he must do so. If his repressed emotions are not released in nonviolent ways, they will seek expression through violence; this is not a threat but a fact of history. So I have not said to my people: "Get rid of your discontent." Rather, I have tried to say that this normal and healthy discontent can be channeled into the creative outlet of nonviolent direct action. And now this approach is being termed extremist.

31     But though I was initially disappointed at being categorized as an extremist, as I continued to think about the matter I gradually gained a measure of satisfaction from the label. Was not Jesus an extremist for love: "Love your enemies, bless them that curse you, do good to them that hate you, and pray for them which despitefully use you, and persecute you." Was not Amos[18] an extremist for justice: "Let justice roll down like waters and righteousness like an ever-flowing stream." Was not Paul an extremist for the Christian gospel: "I bear in my body the marks of the Lord Jesus." Was not Martin Luther[19] an extremist: "Here I stand; I cannot do otherwise, so help me God."

---

[17] *Zeitgeist* (tsīt´gīst): German for "the spirit of the time," referring to the attitudes and beliefs of most people living during a period.

[18] **Amos:** Hebrew prophet whose words are recorded in the Old Testament book bearing his name.

[19] **Martin Luther:** (1483-1546) German monk who launched the Protestant Reformation.

**manifest**
(măn´ə-fĕst) *v.* to show or reveal.

And John Bunyan:[20] "I will stay in jail to the end of my days before I make a butchery of my conscience." And Abraham Lincoln: "This nation cannot survive half slave and half free." And Thomas Jefferson: "We hold these truths to be self-evident, that all men are created equal . . ." So the question is not whether we will be extremists, but what kind of extremists we will be. Will we be extremists for hate or for love? Will we be extremists for the preservation of injustice or for the extension of justice? In that dramatic scene on Calvary's hill[21] three men were crucified. We must never forget that all three were crucified for the same crime—the crime of extremism. Two were extremists for immorality, and thus fell below their environment. The other, Jesus Christ, was an extremist for love, truth and goodness, and thereby rose above his environment. Perhaps the South, the nation and the world are in dire need of creative extremists.

32    I had hoped that the white moderate would see this need. Perhaps I was too optimistic; perhaps I expected too much. I suppose I should have realized that few members of the oppressor race can understand the deep groans and passionate yearnings of the

---

[20] **John Bunyan:** (1628-1688) English preacher and writer, author of *The Pilgrim's Progress*.

[21] **Calvary's hill:** the site of Jesus' crucifixion.

**ANALYZE ARGUMENT**

**Annotate:** Mark the disappointment that King uses to begin a new section of his argument in paragraph 33.

**Analyze:** How do the concessions King makes in paragraph 33 strengthen the point he makes in subsequent paragraphs?

oppressed race, and still fewer have the vision to see that injustice must be rooted out by strong, persistent and determined action. I am thankful, however, that some of our white brothers in the South have grasped the meaning of this social revolution and committed themselves to it. They are still all too few in quantity, but they are big in quality. Some—such as Ralph McGill, Lillian Smith, Harry Golden, James McBride Dabbs, Ann Braden and Sarah Patton Boyle—have written about our struggle in eloquent and prophetic terms. Others have marched with us down nameless streets of the South. They have languished in filthy, roach-infested jails, suffering the abuse and brutality of policemen who view them as "dirty nigger-lovers." Unlike so many of their moderate brothers and sisters, they have recognized the urgency of the moment and sensed the need for powerful "action" antidotes to combat the disease of segregation.

33    Let me take note of my other major disappointment. I have been so greatly disappointed with the white church and its leadership. Of course, there are some notable exceptions. I am not unmindful of the fact that each of you has taken some significant stands on this issue. I commend you, Reverend Stallings, for your Christian stand on this past Sunday, in welcoming Negroes to your worship service on a nonsegregated basis. I commend the Catholic leaders of this state for integrating Spring Hill College several years ago.

34    But despite these notable exceptions, I must honestly reiterate that I have been disappointed with the church. I do not say this as one of those negative critics who can always find something wrong with the church. I say this as a minister of the gospel, who loves the church; who was nurtured in its bosom; who has been sustained by its spiritual blessings and who will remain true to it as long as the cord of life shall lengthen.

35    When I was suddenly catapulted into the leadership of the bus protest in Montgomery, Alabama,[22] a few years ago, I felt we would be supported by the white church. I felt that the white ministers, priests and rabbis of the South would be among our strongest allies. Instead, some have been outright opponents, refusing to understand the freedom movement and misrepresenting its leaders; all too many others have been more cautious than courageous and have remained silent behind the anesthetizing security of stained glass windows.

36    In spite of my shattered dreams, I came to Birmingham with the hope that the white religious leadership of this community would see the justice of our cause and, with deep moral concern, would serve as the channel through which our just grievances could reach the power structure. I had hoped that each of you would understand. But again I have been disappointed.

---

[22]**bus protest in Montgomery, Alabama:** the 1955–1956 boycott that ended segregated seating in Montgomery's transportation system.

37    I have heard numerous southern religious leaders admonish their worshipers to comply with a desegregation decision because it is the law, but I have longed to hear white ministers declare: "Follow this decree because integration is morally right and because the Negro is your brother." In the midst of blatant injustices inflicted upon the Negro, I have watched white churchmen stand on the sideline and mouth pious irrelevancies and sanctimonious trivialities. In the midst of a mighty struggle to rid our nation of racial and economic injustice, I have heard many ministers say: "Those are social issues, with which the gospel has no real concern." And I have watched many churches commit themselves to a completely otherworldly religion which makes a strange, un-Biblical distinction between body and soul, between the sacred and the secular.

38    I have traveled the length and breadth of Alabama, Mississippi and all the other southern states. On sweltering summer days and crisp autumn mornings I have looked at the South's beautiful churches with their lofty spires pointing heavenward. I have beheld the impressive outlines of her massive religious-education buildings. Over and over I have found myself asking: "What kind of people worship here? Who is their God? Where were their voices when the lips of Governor Barnett dripped with words of interposition and nullification? Where were they when Governor Wallace[23] gave a clarion call for defiance and hatred? Where were their voices of support when bruised and weary Negro men and women decided to rise from the dark dungeons of complacency to the bright hills of creative protest?"

39    Yes, these questions are still in my mind. In deep disappointment I have wept over the laxity of the church. But be assured that my tears have been tears of love. There can be no deep disappointment where there is not deep love. Yes, I love the church. How could I do otherwise? I am in the rather unique position of being the son, the grandson and the great-grandson of preachers. Yes, I see the church as the body of Christ. But, oh! How we have blemished and scarred that body through social neglect and through fear of being nonconformists.

40    There was a time when the church was very powerful—in the time when the early Christians rejoiced at being deemed worthy to suffer for what they believed. In those days the church was not merely a thermometer that recorded the ideas and principles of popular opinion; it was a thermostat that transformed the **mores** of society. Whenever the early Christians entered a town, the people in power became disturbed and immediately sought to convict the Christians

**mores**
(môr´āz) *n.* established customs and conventions.

---

[23] **Gov. Barnett . . . Gov. Wallace:** Ross Barnett (1898–1987) and George Wallace (1919–1998), segregationist governors of Mississippi and Alabama, respectively, during the 1960s.

for being "disturbers of the peace" and "outside agitators." But the Christians pressed on, in the conviction that they were "a colony of heaven," called to obey God rather than man. Small in number, they were big in commitment. They were too God-intoxicated to be "astronomically intimidated." By their effort and example they brought an end to such ancient evils as infanticide and gladiatorial contests.[24]

41    Things are different now. So often the contemporary church is a weak, ineffectual voice with an uncertain sound. So often it is an archdefender of the status quo. Far from being disturbed by the presence of the church, the power structure of the average community is consoled by the church's silent—and often even vocal—sanction of things as they are.

42    But the judgment of God is upon the church as never before. If today's church does not recapture the sacrificial spirit of the early church, it will lose its authenticity, forfeit the loyalty of millions, and be dismissed as an irrelevant social club with no meaning for the twentieth century. Every day I meet young people whose disappointment with the church has turned into outright disgust.

43    Perhaps I have once again been too optimistic. Is organized religion too inextricably bound to the status quo to save our nation and the world? Perhaps I must turn my faith to the inner spiritual church, the church within the church, as the true *ekklesia*[25] and the hope of the world. But again I am thankful to God that some noble souls from the ranks of organized religion have broken loose from the paralyzing chains of conformity and joined us as active partners in the struggle for freedom. They have left their secure congregations and walked the streets of Albany, Georgia, with us. They have gone down the highways of the South on tortuous rides for freedom. Yes, they have gone to jail with us. Some have been dismissed from their churches, have lost the support of their bishops and fellow ministers. But they have acted in the faith that right defeated is stronger than evil triumphant. Their witness has been the spiritual salt that has preserved the true meaning of the gospel in these troubled times. They have carved a tunnel of hope through the dark mountain of disappointment.

44    I hope the church as a whole will meet the challenge of this decisive hour. But even if the church does not come to the aid of justice, I have no despair about the future. I have no fear about the outcome of our struggle in Birmingham, even if our motives are at present misunderstood. We will reach the goal of freedom in Birmingham and all over the nation, because the goal of America is freedom. Abused and scorned though we may be, our destiny is tied

[24]**ancient evils . . . contests:** despicable past practices of killing unwanted babies and of forcing men to fight to the death for sport.

[25]*ekklesia* (ĭ-klē´zē-ə): a Greek term meaning "an assembly of people for worship," often translated into English as "church."

up with America's destiny. Before the pilgrims landed at Plymouth, we were here. Before the pen of Jefferson etched the majestic words of the Declaration of Independence across the pages of history, we were here. For more than two centuries our forebears labored in this country without wages; they made cotton king; they built the homes of their masters while suffering gross injustice and shameful humiliation—and yet out of a bottomless vitality they continued to thrive and develop. If the inexpressible cruelties of slavery could not stop us, the opposition we now face will surely fail. We will win our freedom because the sacred heritage of our nation and the eternal will of God are embodied in our echoing demands.

45    Before closing I feel impelled to mention one other point in your statement that has troubled me profoundly. You warmly commended the Birmingham police force for keeping "order" and "preventing violence." I doubt that you would have so warmly commended the police force if you had seen its dogs sinking their teeth into unarmed, nonviolent Negroes. I doubt that you would so quickly commend the policemen if you were to observe their ugly and inhumane treatment of Negroes here in the city jail; if you were to watch them push and curse old Negro women and young Negro girls; if you were to see them slap and kick old Negro men and young boys; if you were to observe them, as they did on two occasions, refuse to give us food because we wanted to sing our grace together. I cannot join you in your praise of the Birmingham police department.

46    It is true that the police have exercised a degree of discipline in handling the demonstrators. In this sense they have conducted themselves rather "nonviolently" in public. But for what purpose? To preserve the evil system of segregation. Over the past few years I have consistently preached that nonviolence demands that the means we use must be as pure as the ends we seek. I have tried to make clear that it is wrong to use immoral means to attain moral ends. But now I must affirm that it is just as wrong, or perhaps even more so, to use moral means to preserve immoral ends. Perhaps Mr. Connor and his policemen have been rather nonviolent in public, as was Chief Pritchett in Albany, Georgia, but they have used the moral means of nonviolence to maintain the immoral end of racial injustice. As T. S. Eliot has said: "The last temptation is the greatest treason: To do the right deed for the wrong reason."

47    I wish you had commended the Negro sit-inners and demonstrators of Birmingham for their sublime courage, their willingness to suffer and their amazing discipline in the midst of great **provocation**. One day the South will recognize its real heroes. They will be the James Merediths,[26] with the noble sense of purpose that

---

[26] **James Merediths:** people like James Meredith, who endured violent opposition from whites to become the first African American to attend the University of Mississippi.

**ANALYZE ARGUMENT**

**Annotate:** Mark King's counterargument to the clergymen's praise for the police keeping "order" and "preventing violence."

**Analyze:** How does this counterargument strengthen King's argument?

**provocation**
(prŏv-ə-kā´shən) *n.* an action intended to elicit an angered response.

**QUOTED WORDS**

**Notice & Note:** Mark the quotation in paragraph 47 that uses humor and ungrammatical sentences.

**Respond:** What is the effect of King's choice to quote this woman?

enables them to face jeering and hostile mobs, and with the agonizing loneliness that characterizes the life of the pioneer. They will be old, oppressed, battered Negro women, symbolized in a seventy-two-year-old woman in Montgomery, Alabama, who rose up with a sense of dignity and with her people decided not to ride segregated buses, and who responded with ungrammatical profundity to one who inquired about her weariness: "My feets is tired, but my soul is at rest." They will be the young high school and college students, the young ministers of the gospel and a host of their elders, courageously and nonviolently sitting in at lunch counters and willingly going to jail for conscience' sake. One day the South will know that when these disinherited children of God sat down at lunch counters, they were in reality standing up for what is best in the American dream and for the most sacred values in our Judaeo-Christian heritage, thereby bringing our nation back to those great wells of democracy which were dug deep by the founding fathers in their formulation of the Constitution and the Declaration of Independence.

48    Never before have I written so long a letter. I'm afraid it is much too long to take your precious time. I can assure you that it would have been much shorter if I had been writing from a comfortable desk, but what else can one do when he is alone in a narrow jail cell other than write long letters, think long thoughts and pray long prayers?

49    If I have said anything in this letter that overstates the truth and indicates an unreasonable impatience, I beg you to forgive me. If I have said anything that understates the truth and indicates my having a patience that allows me to settle for anything less than brotherhood, I beg God to forgive me.

**ANALYZE ARGUMENT**

**Annotate:** Mark the long sentence in paragraph 50 that summarizes King's argument and message.

**Evaluate:** Do you think this conclusion enhances King's argument? Why or why not?

50    I hope this letter finds you strong in the faith. I also hope that circumstances will soon make it possible for me to meet each of you, not as an integrationist or a civil-rights leader but as a fellow clergyman and a Christian brother. Let us all hope that the dark clouds of racial prejudice will soon pass away and the deep fog of misunderstanding will be lifted from our fear-drenched communities, and in some not too distant tomorrow the radiant stars of love and brotherhood will shine over our great nation with all their scintillating beauty.

Yours for the cause of Peace and Brotherhood,

Martin Luther King, Jr.

## CHECK YOUR UNDERSTANDING

Answer these questions before moving on to the **Analyze the Text** section on the following page.

**1** King wrote this letter because —

   **A** doing so kept him occupied and helped to pass the time while in jail

   **B** he wanted to respond to criticism from a group of fellow clergymen

   **C** he needed to consider what he had done to wind up in jail

   **D** it helped him to organize his thoughts about his own motivations

**2** King mainly supports his ideas using —

   **F** acknowledgment of the many helpful good deeds of the police and public officials

   **G** emotional arguments centered on his own personal experience with discrimination

   **H** examples from the Bible and history that illustrate the fight against injustice

   **J** overstatement and exaggeration of the obstacles faced by African Americans

**3** King's argument makes clear that racial segregation is —

   **A** something that only happens in the South

   **B** solely the responsibility of its victims to change

   **C** a necessary evil that will eventually pass

   **D** an inhumane and immoral practice

**RESPOND**

## ANALYZE THE TEXT

Support your responses with evidence from the text.  📓 NOTEBOOK

1. **Analyze** How does King define just and unjust laws? To what opposing view is he providing a counterargument? Consider how defining certain laws as unjust provides an incentive for his readers to support his actions.

2. **Summarize** According to King, what are the four basic steps in a nonviolent campaign, and how did King's organization follow these steps in Birmingham?

3. **Draw Conclusions** King says that "This 'Wait' has almost always meant 'Never.'" To what does he refer, and how does he defend his position?

4. **Analyze** Discuss whether King uses valid reasoning when he states that "Injustice anywhere is a threat to justice everywhere." What evidence does he provide to support this idea? What appeal does he use?

5. **Notice & Note** Review the letter to identify all of the people King quotes. How would you categorize these people? What is the effect of King's quoting so many kinds of people on his overall argument?

## RESEARCH

**RESEARCH TIP**
Finding at least two different sources for each fact will help you verify that individual facts are accurate.

King refers to other leaders who were part of the Civil Rights movement. Choose one of them to research. Seek credible sources; avoid those with these flaws:

- **Bias:** overly favoring one side on a controversial topic
- **Omission:** leaving out information that doesn't support a particular bias
- **Misconceptions:** basing ideas on incorrect information
- **Faulty Reasoning:** drawing illogical conclusions from information

Record what you learn in a chart similar to this one.

| CIVIL RIGHTS FIGURE | ACCOMPLISHMENTS | INFORMATION SOURCES |
|---|---|---|
| | | |
| | | |
| | | |
| | | |
| | | |

**Extend** If you find conflicting information in your sources, visit multiple sources. Verification of an idea in multiple reliable resources should be considered valid.

## CREATE AND PRESENT

**Write a Friendly Letter** Write a one-page letter that shares with a friend what you have learned in your research and why it matters.

❏ Keep the tone friendly and casual.

❏ Treat this serious information with respect.

❏ Explain what you have learned in terms you and your friend can understand and relate to.

**Present Research** Give a brief, formal speech that shares what you learned about the Civil Rights leader you researched.

❏ Explain what you have learned, citing evidence from reliable sources.

❏ Connect your research to the information in Dr. King's letter.

❏ Include images or video of the person you researched if available.

Go to the **Writing Studio** for help with writing for a certain task, purpose, and audience.

Go to the **Speaking and Listening Studio** for help with giving a speech.

## RESPOND TO THE ESSENTIAL QUESTION

 What do we need in order to feel free?

**Gather Information** Review your annotations and notes on "Letter from Birmingham Jail." Then, add relevant information to your Response Log. As you determine which information to include, think about:

UNIT 4
RESPONSE LOG

- what some people sacrifice to preserve freedom for all
- why those in power must recognize that freedom cannot be delayed
- why power should not be preserved by oppressing others

At the end of the unit, use your notes to help you write an argument.

**ACADEMIC VOCABULARY**

As you write and discuss what you learned from the argument, be sure to use the Academic Vocabulary words. Check off each of the words that you use.

❏ **comprehensive**

❏ **equivalent**

❏ **incentive**

❏ **innovate**

❏ **subordinate**

## CRITICAL VOCABULARY

**Practice and Apply**   Answer each question in a complete sentence by thinking about the meaning of the Critical Vocabulary word.

**WORD BANK**
cognizant
moratorium
retaliate
precipitate
complacency
manifest
mores
provocation

1.  Which might cause someone to **retaliate**: Losing a point in a game because of a foul or getting a well-deserved award?

2.  Would a flood or potholes cause a **moratorium** on road construction?

3.  If I am **cognizant** of your plans, do I know about them or not?

4.  If a movie reflects a society's **mores**, does it show traditional or unconventional practices?

5.  If a motive for a crime begins to **manifest** itself, will it be easier or harder to prove the suspect's guilt?

6.  What might be a **provocation** for war, breaking a treaty or signing one?

7.  If you show **complacency**, how do you respond to demands?

8.  If my actions **precipitate** an accident, do I cause or prevent it?

## VOCABULARY STRATEGY:
### Context Clues

 Go to the **Vocabulary Studio** for more on using context clues.

A word's **context**, the words and sentences that surround it, often gives clues to its meaning. Context can also add shades of meaning to a word. Consider how context shapes the meaning of the word *tension* in King's letter:

| DEFINITION | CONTEXT CLUES |
| --- | --- |
| **tension**: a strained relationship | . . . Nonviolent direct action seeks to . . . foster such a **tension** that a community . . . is forced to confront the issue. . . . I have earnestly opposed violent **tension**, but there is a type of constructive, nonviolent **tension** which is necessary for growth. |

King's use of *tension* describes a force that can be positive. Think about how replacing it with *conflict* might change King's intended meaning.

**Practice and Apply**   Use context clues to define these words. Verify your definitions in a print or online dictionary. Discuss how King adds nuances to each word's meaning in the context of his letter.

1.  moderate (paragraph 23)

_____

2.  condemned/condemning (paragraph 25)

_____

3.  extremist (paragraph 31)

_____

## LANGUAGE CONVENTIONS:
### Repetition and Parallelism

**Repetition** is a technique in which a sound, word, or phrase is repeated for emphasis or unity. **Parallelism** is the use of similar grammatical forms to express ideas that are related or equal in importance. King skillfully uses repetition and parallelism to make his message resonate with his audience. Consider the following examples and their effects:

| EXAMPLES FROM TEXT | EFFECTS |
|---|---|
| **when you** have seen vicious mobs . . . **when you** have seen hate-filled policemen . . . **when you** see the vast majority of your twenty million Negro brothers smothering . . . **when you** suddenly find your tongue twisted . . . **when you** have to concoct an answer . . . **when you** take a cross-country drive . . . **when you** are humiliated . . . **when you** are harried by day and haunted by night . . . **when you** are forever fighting . . . —**then you** will understand why we find it difficult to wait. | Starting each subordinate clause with the words *when you* and then varying the parallellism at the end with the word *then* emphasizes and dramatizes King's point that African Americans have waited long enough for their constitutional and God-given rights. |
| To a degree, academic freedom is a reality today because Socrates practiced **civil disobedience**. In our own nation, the Boston Tea Party represented a massive act of **civil disobedience**.<br><br>We should never forget that everything Adolf Hitler did in Germany was "**legal**" and everything the Hungarian freedom fighters did in Hungary was "**illegal**." It was "**illegal**" to aid and comfort a Jew in Hitler's Germany. | Not only are the words *legal* and *illegal* repeated, they are contrasted as opposites to stress the unfairness of their application. King repeats *civil disobedience* to stress the distinction between what is legal or illegal. |
| **Was not** Jesus an extremist for love . . . **Was not** Amos an extremist for justice . . . **Was not** Paul an extremist for the Christian gospel . . . **Was not** Martin Luther an extremist . . . **And** John Bunyan . . . **And** Abraham Lincoln . . . **And** Thomas Jefferson . . . So the question is not whether **we will be extremists**, but what kind of **extremists we will be. Will we be extremists** for hate or for love? **Will we be extremists** for the preservation of injustice or for the extension of justice? | The repetition of the words *extremist* and *and* along with the parallelism created by the repeating phrase *was not* and the clause *we will be/will we be* link King's approach to that of other religious and historical figures. |

**Practice and Apply** Locate other examples of repetition and parallel structure in King's letter and consider their effects. Then, look back at the speech you wrote for this selection's Create and Present activity. Revise your speech to include an example of repetition and parallelism. Discuss with a partner the effects of your revisions.

# ELSEWHERE

Poem by **Derek Walcott**

**?** ***ESSENTIAL QUESTION:***

What do we need in order to feel free?

## QUICK START

What's going on right now, somewhere else in the world, that concerns you? Is there a war or a refugee crisis or a tyrannical leader committing atrocities against his own people? What is it like to live in a relatively peaceful, stable place knowing that these things are going on in another part of the world? Turn to a partner and share your thoughts.

## ANALYZE POETIC STRUCTURE

"Elsewhere" is written in four-line **stanzas,** or groups of lines, in **free verse,** which does not contain regular patterns of rhythm or rhyme. In free verse, the natural flow of lines often mimics the rhythm and flow of everyday speech.

Instead of exact rhymes, the poet may create interest with other structures, including slant rhyme and eye rhyme. End rhyme that is not exact but approximate is called **slant rhyme**, such as *seventh* and *heaven* or *crime* and *scream*. An **eye rhyme** appeals to the eye rather than to the ear. It pairs words with similar spellings but different sounds, such as *enough* and *although* or *mane* and *men*. Add your own examples to the chart below.

### GENRE ELEMENTS: POETRY

- explores an idea using figurative language and imagery
- might be arranged in lines and stanzas, which may have regular meter and rhyme
- may use devices such as repetition and symbolism to develop a theme
- the speaker may or may not be the poet's own voice

| RHYME TYPE | HOW IT WORKS | EXAMPLES | ALSO CALLED |
|---|---|---|---|
| **exact rhyme** | a pair of words end in similar or identical sounds | heat > complete<br>stab > taxicab<br>stranglehold > marigold<br>dish > squish | full rhyme<br>perfect rhyme |
| **slant rhyme** | a pair of words include the same vowel or consonant sound | care > dear<br>shape > keep<br>grudge > bridge<br>detach > unpack | half rhyme<br>imperfect rhyme<br>near rhyme<br>oblique rhyme<br>off rhyme |
| **eye rhyme** | a pair of words have similar spellings but are pronounced differently | love > move<br>through > tough<br>laughter > slaughter<br>enemies > flies | sight rhyme<br>visual rhyme |

## ANALYZE MOTIF

Within a work of literature, a **motif**, or repeated image, idea, or theme, can tie ideas together. For example, in his famous speech, Martin Luther King Jr. expresses hope for many different things, using the motif "I have a dream" to tie them all together. A motif is more concrete than a theme, though it can contribute to the development of both mood and theme within a work.

Complete the chart with the primary motif that occurs in each folk tale:

| | |
|---|---|
| **"The Three Little Pigs"** | |
| **"The Boy Who Cried Wolf"** | |
| **"Cinderella"** | |

The poem "Elsewhere" employs the motif of location. Although a location is never specified, the poem makes reference to a place using the words *somewhere, here, where,* or *elsewhere.* As you read, notice how this motif adds to the poem's meaning and tone.

---

ANNOTATION MODEL                           **NOTICE & NOTE**

As you read, look for the various types of rhyme and the use and effect of location-related words. This model shows one reader's notes about a stanza from "Elsewhere":

That <u>somewhere</u> there was an arrest.

<u>Somewhere</u> there was a small harvest

of bodies in the truck. Soldiers rest

<u>somewhere</u> by a road, or smoke in a forest.

All lines end with -*est* words. Use of "somewhere" 3x creates distant, disconnected mood.
Does the "where" matter? Are they the same or different?

## BACKGROUND

**Derek Walcott** *(1930–2017), a Caribbean poet and playwright, was raised on the tiny island of Saint Lucia. Of African, English, and Dutch descent, Walcott lost his father at a young age. Guided by his schoolteacher mother, Walcott published his first poem at age 14. About fifty years later, he won the Nobel Prize for Literature. Walcott's work explores the complex racial, cultural, and colonial history of the Caribbean. This poem is dedicated to English poet Stephen Spender, whose poetry examined themes of social injustice.*

# ELSEWHERE
### Poem by Derek Walcott

## SETTING A PURPOSE

*As you read, connect the impressions in this poem with real incidents of oppression that you have heard about around the world.*

(For Stephen Spender)

Somewhere a white horse gallops with its mane
plunging round a field whose sticks
are ringed with barbed wire, and men
break stones or bind straw into ricks.[1]

5  Somewhere women tire of the shawled sea's
weeping, for the fishermen's dories[2]
still go out. It is blue as peace.
Somewhere they're tired of torture stories.

---

[1] **ricks:** stacks of hay.
[2] **dories:** rowboats.

Notice & Note

You can use the side margins to notice and note signposts in the text.

---

**ANALYZE MOTIF**
**Annotate:** Mark the recurring use of *somewhere* in lines 1–20.

**Interpret:** What is the effect of the repetition? Where are these places and what do they have in common?

**ANALYZE POETIC STRUCTURE**

**Annotate:** Mark examples of eye rhyme in the third and fourth stanzas.

**Analyze:** How do these words that look like they should rhyme, but don't, affect your reading of the poem?

That somewhere there was an arrest.
10 Somewhere there was a small harvest
of bodies in the truck. Soldiers rest
somewhere by a road, or smoke in a forest.

Somewhere there is the conference rage
at an outrage. Somewhere a page
15 is torn out, and somehow the foliage
no longer looks like leaves but camouflage.

Somewhere there is a comrade,
a writer lying with his eyes wide open
on a mattress ticking,[3] who will not read
20 this, or write. How to make a pen?

**ANALYZE POETIC STRUCTURE**

**Annotate:** Mark the new location words used in the sixth stanza.

**Analyze:** What is the effect of this shift? Why do you think the writer included it?

And here we are free for a while, but
elsewhere, in one-third, or one-seventh
of this planet, a summary[4] rifle butt
breaks a skull into the idea of a heaven

25 where nothing is free, where blue air
is paper-frail, and whatever we write
will be stamped twice, a blue letter,
its throat slit by the paper knife of the state.

Through these black bars
30 hollowed faces stare. Fingers
grip the cross bars of these stanzas
and it is here, because somewhere else

---

[3] **ticking:** strong fabric, usually striped, used for mattress covers.
[4] **summary:** quickly done.

their stares fog into oblivion
thinly, like the faceless numbers
35 that bewilder you in your telephone
diary. Like last year's massacres.

The world is blameless. The darker crime
is to make a career of conscience,
to feel through our own nerves the silent scream
40 of winter branches, wonders read as signs.

## CHECK YOUR UNDERSTANDING

Answer these questions before moving on to the **Analyze the Text** section on the following page.

**1** The poem repeats the idea of "Somewhere" because —

  **A** the speaker has heard about these crimes but is unsure where they occurred

  **B** it would be unsafe for the writer to name the place where these events happened

  **C** the repetition is needed to show where each new sentence begins

  **D** these events are so pervasive that the location could be anywhere

**2** How does the poet describe the reactions of people not directly affected by the events described?

  **F** They understand that events in other places are not their problem.

  **G** They feel overwhelmed by how many people are affected.

  **H** They defeat oppression by writing letters and poems.

  **J** They know how lucky they are to be free.

**3** Which is an important idea emphasized throughout the poem?

  **A** Living overseas is dangerous.

  **B** People experience grief for lost loved ones.

  **C** Oppression and cruelty can happen anywhere.

  **D** Writers are an important voice for freedom.

**RESPOND**

## ANALYZE THE TEXT

Support your responses with evidence from the text. ⊟ NOTEBOOK

1. **Interpret** Reread lines 1–4. What might the horse represent in the poem? Where is the horse, and what is the significance of that location?

2. **Analyze** If the first 20 lines of the poem take place "somewhere," where do the remaining 20 take place? Explain.

3. **Draw Conclusions** Reread lines 29–36. What are "like the faceless numbers / that bewilder you in your telephone / diary"? What is being compared in these two stanzas?

4. **Analyze** What does the poet express about the world in the final stanza by using phrases such as "darker crime" and "a career of conscience"? Cite text evidence in your answer.

5. **Evaluate** What might be the social function of this poem with its "somewhere" motif? What does the writer want us to take away from the experience of reading the poem?

## RESEARCH

**RESEARCH TIP**
If you need help formatting your source citations, you can consult online sources such as the MLA Style Center (style.mla.org) or EasyBib (www.easybib.com).

Find an online news story that relates to an idea in the poem. Complete the chart below, and create a correctly formatted reference citation for your result. Your citation should include key information: the author (if known), the specific source title, the title of any larger source it comes from, the publisher and publication date. Here is how to format a citation of an online article.

author | title
United States Holocaust Memorial Museum. "Political Prisoners." | URL
source publication | Holocaust Encyclopedia. https://www.ushmm.org/wlc/en/article.
php?ModuleId=10007656. Accessed on January 24, 2019.
date accessed

| KEY IDEA FROM THE POEM: | SEARCH TERMS I MIGHT USE: |
|---|---|
|  |  |
| WEB LINK TO ARTICLE ||
|  ||
| MLA CITATION ||
|  ||

**Extend** Discuss what you learned with a partner, and come to a consensus about how effectively the poem addresses the problem of oppression in the world.

## CREATE AND DISCUSS

**Write an Analysis**  Write an analysis that argues the effectiveness of Walcott's poem. Might it stir readers to find out more about the problems that exist "elsewhere"? Why or why not? Cite evidence from the poem and your own experience.

- ❏ Review your notes and annotations from before, during, and after reading the poem.

- ❏ Reread the poem and take notes on your reaction to it. Note whether and how your reaction changed as a result of rereading the poem.

- ❏ Support your analysis with evidence from the poem and what you know from other sources.

**Discuss with a Group**  Meet with a small group to share your analysis and discuss the poem's impact.

- ❏ Provide specific lines as text evidence and paraphrase or summarize the evidence in support of your interpretation.

- ❏ Keep your comments brief and listen closely as others share theirs. Write down at least one relevant question or meaningful observation you might share in response to something someone else says.

- ❏ After everyone has participated, review similarities and differences in your analyses. What can you conclude as a group?

 Go to the **Writing Studio** for more on citing text evidence.

 Go to the **Speaking and Listening Studio** for more on participating in a discussion.

## RESPOND TO THE ESSENTIAL QUESTION

 **What do we need in order to feel free?**

**Gather Information**  Review your notes and annotations on "Elsewhere," then add relevant information to your Response Log. As you determine which information to include, think about:

- What does "freedom" look like?
- Who among us is really, truly free?
- What does it mean to *feel* free? Is it enough just to feel it, and what would that require?

At the end of the unit, use your notes to help you write an argument.

**ACADEMIC VOCABULARY**

As you write and discuss what you learned from the poem, be sure to use the Academic Vocabulary words. Check off each of the words that you use.

- ❏ **comprehensive**
- ❏ **equivalent**
- ❏ **incentive**
- ❏ **innovate**
- ❏ **subordinate**

# THE HAWK CAN SOAR

Memoir by **Randi Davenport**

**ESSENTIAL QUESTION:**

What do we need in order to feel free?

## QUICK START

Have you ever lost the ability to do something you normally could do because of an illness or injury? How did it make you feel? Discuss your experience with the class.

## ANALYZE DICTION AND SYNTAX

To understand how the author uses language to inform and shape the perception of readers, you need to analyze the author's diction and syntax. **Diction** refers to the author's choice of words. **Syntax** is the pattern and arrangement of words or other elements of sentence structure. The author's diction and syntax contribute to the mood, voice, and tone of the text. **Mood** is the atmosphere or feeling the writer creates for readers. **Voice** is the unique way of writing that allows a reader to sense the writer's personality. **Tone** is the author's attitude toward the subject or topic.

| EXAMPLE FROM TEXT | TECHNIQUE AND EFFECT |
|---|---|
| I'm also weak. Spastic. | **Syntax:** short sentence followed by a fragment: contributes to a matter-of-fact, casual voice; emphasizes the word *spastic* |
| *...transmitted in an autosomal dominant pattern,* the geneticist said. | **Diction:** formal, medical terminology creates a sterile, impersonal tone |

## ANALYZE TEXT STRUCTURE

**Text structure** is the way an author organizes a text to show connections between events and to develop ideas. The text structure of this memoir provides information about the author's disease in the context of narrative passages, which are not in chronological order.

Use the graphic organizer below to track events in the memoir that happen before and after the author's diagnosis.

**GENRE ELEMENTS: MEMOIR**

- self-written account that describes a significant experience in the author's life
- includes the author's feelings and attitude toward the experience
- includes purposeful stylistic choices to create voice, mood, and tone
- events may not be told in chronological order

| BEFORE DIAGNOSIS | DIAGNOSIS | PRESENT DAY |
|---|---|---|
| Event 1 | Event 3 | Event 5 |
| _____ | _____ | _____ |
| _____ | _____ | _____ |
| _____ | _____ | _____ |

Event 2 | Event 4

## CRITICAL VOCABULARY

To see how many Critical Vocabulary words you already know, mark the correct answer to each question.

1. Which of the following is **irrefutable**?
   a. A dollar bill is better than a dollar coin.
   b. A dollar bill is worth 100 cents.

2. Which of the following is an example of an **insidious** rumor?
   a. It spreads and ruins a person's reputation.
   b. It is ignored and believed to be false.

3. Which of the following might result in muscle **atrophy**?
   a. a person's broken leg in a cast for months
   b. a person lifting weights in the gym

4. Which of the following is an example of a **contemptuous** action?
   a. pointing and laughing at someone who fell
   b. comforting someone who is hurt

5. Which of the following is an example of an **occult** location?
   a. a covered bus stop on a busy sidewalk
   b. a mysterious grove hidden deep in a forest

## LANGUAGE CONVENTIONS

**Purposeful Fragments** In this lesson, you will learn about the intentional use of fragments in writing. While a fragment is usually an error, an author may choose to use fragments for effect, as in this example from the text:

**I tell myself that I'm working too hard. <u>Trying to do too much.</u>**

This fragment reflects the author's thought process. As you read, note other fragments that develop a conversational tone and emphasize key ideas.

### ANNOTATION MODEL                                    NOTICE & NOTE

As you read, note the author's use of diction and syntax to shape the reader's perception of her experience and mark descriptions that explain the author's unique experiences. Here are one reader's notes about "The Hawk Can Soar":

[I push the walker] in front of me, its front wheels larger than the wheels in back. [My right leg drags a little. My right foot drops.] <u>When I don't have the rollator in front of me—when I try to walk unaided</u>—I have to bring my right hand up to my waist to create my own version of balance. [<u>Elbow clamped to my side.</u> . . . ]

*descriptions of the author's challenges*

*Syntax reflects that the author is not in control, her elbow is.*

## BACKGROUND

Novelist and essayist **Randi Davenport** earned a MA in creative writing and a PhD in literature from Syracuse University. One of her award-winning books, The Boy Who Loved Tornadoes, is about her son's struggle with mental illness. In addition to writing, Davenport has also worked with state officials in North Carolina to change policies to provide more help for people with mental illnesses.

# THE HAWK CAN SOAR

Memoir by Randi Davenport

## SETTING A PURPOSE

In this memoir, the author describes an experience that may be unfamiliar to you. As you read, monitor your understanding, pausing to ask questions or rereading to clear up your understanding of what the author experiences.

1   I push the walker in front of me, its front wheels larger than the wheels in back. My right leg drags a little. My right foot drops. When I don't have the rollator[1] in front of me—when I try to walk unaided—I have to bring my right hand up to my waist to create my own version of balance. Elbow clamped to my side. Stiffness where most other people have swing.

2     I'm also weak. Spastic. I wear braces for balance and support. How many times has some bio-technician cradled my feet in his or her hands, stroking the wrapping in place from which a new brace will be cast? I cannot count, but I recall each time as if it were the same as the time before, the same as the time yet to come.

**Notice & Note**

You can use the side margins to notice and note signposts in the text.

**ANALYZE DICTION AND SYNTAX**

**Annotate:** Mark a repeated structure in paragraph 2.

**Analyze:** How does this repetition reflect what the author understands about her disease?

---

[1] **rollator:** a frame on wheels used to provide support and balance for walking.

3      My hands quake with tremors, as do my father's hands and as did his father's hands before him. But I'm the lucky one. I'm the one who gets the disease, a rare form of motor neuron disease, in its full expression. My father and grandfather didn't even know they had a disease — *transmitted in an autosomal dominant pattern,*[2] the geneticist said. They stopped being able to walk in their 70s and 80s and decided that this was caused by other things, perhaps by the nature of being old men, or a failure of the will to move, or the inconstant beating of their own blood.

4      It begins for me in my 30s. When I'm out running, my right foot goes out from under me, then comes back into position. It's nothing, I think. But over time, it happens more and more frequently. And other things come too, in silent waves: I stiffen like a tree trunk. I cannot easily rise from a chair. I cannot climb a flight of stairs. I cannot live my life without being overcome with profound fatigue, an exhaustion so deep and unmeasurable that I weep when I don't have the strength to make dinner.

5      I tell myself that I'm working too hard. Trying to do too much. That all single parents are beset by weariness without end. I stop running and walk instead. When I can no longer walk any distance,

**ANALYZE TEXT STRUCTURE**

**Annotate:** Mark words that indicate the passage of time in paragraph 4.

**Analyze:** How does the author's disease progress? Start your timeline with the first event.

---

[2] *autosomal dominant pattern:* a disease that requires only one copy of the gene to be inherited to transmit the disease.

I go to the gym. When I can no longer tolerate the gym, I go to the pool. But each new environment is a landscape of loss. What I could do and no longer can. What I can't do an **irrefutable** presence, as if lack has a shape and a weight.

6    A colleague at work points out my constant limp. I shrug. By this time, I have seen neurologists at Duke and Johns Hopkins. They're baffled. Something is wrong — on exam, my big toes point up, my reflexes jump, my muscles catch, my index finger shivers in a sign of a spinal lesion — but they can't say what. Only when I finally see a neuromuscular disease specialist at the big teaching hospital in Chapel Hill, N.C., do I find the doctor who knows what's gone wrong. In time, he delivers the news that I cannot be cured. I can only grow worse, my disability increasing in **insidious** increments that he will track by seeing me every three months.

7    Time passes. We watch, this doctor and I, as my disease moves through me. It's languid, quiet, but it moves. I grow weaker. I **atrophy** in discrete regions — my right foot and then my left and then my right hand — but I don't waste. I grow fat from immobility and then I grow thin again. I want to live as who I was, not as what this disease makes of me. This idea is a chimera[3] but it helps me to think that I am fighting. I am a fighter. I always have been, even when I cannot win. At other times in my life, I might have viewed this as a pathological neurosis akin to tilting at windmills. Now I think of it as a saving grace. These tales I tell myself. The way I plan to escape fate. All to keep myself going.

8    Eventually, however, I am disabled. Disabled. Like this word is the sum total of my existence. That dragging leg. That dropping foot. That unbearable fatigue. A woman with a rollator moving slowly through the world. These things signal my difference whenever I move. They are obvious. Unrestrained.

9    Soon, I leave my university career. I slowly begin to disappear from view. The things I have earned seem ever further away. This is the nature of this difference, I realize. The way disability stands in for everything you were or ever would have been. Even when you say it will not. Even when you refuse its existence. Disability is **contemptuous** of your refusal. It scoffs at your desperate concern. It pushes forward and it drags you after it.

10    I develop a serious side effect. A co-morbidity[4], my doctors call it. I nearly die. It doesn't matter that I said I would fight to stay upright. It doesn't matter that I have resisted the wheelchair. My body has other plans and it doesn't consult me. It is my own and yet it is blind to my dreams. My desires. Weirdly, I begin to understand that I am but a part of my body. My body is not a part of me.

---

[3] **chimera** (kī-mîr´ə): a mental illusion or fabrication.

[4] **co-morbidity** (kō-môr-bĭd´ ĭ-tē): an incidence of two diseases or disorders in the same person

**irrefutable**
(ĭ-rĕf´yə-tə-bəl) *adj.* impossible to disprove; unquestionable.

**insidious**
(ĭn-sĭd´ē-əs) *adj.* spreading harmfully in a subtle way.

**atrophy**
(ăt´rə-fē) *v.* to deteriorate due to disease, injury, or lack of use.

**ANALYZE DICTION AND SYNTAX**

**Annotate:** Mark the phrase "tilting at windmills" in paragraph 7.

**Interpret:** This phrase is an allusion to *Don Quixote*, in which a character who imagines he is a knight attempts to battle windmills. How does this reference fit the author's approach to her illness?

**contemptuous**
(kən-tĕmp´ch(ə)ŏŏ-əs) *adj.* scornful.

11     Thus subordinated, I live. And I keep on living.

12     This story should end with an epiphany, a moment when I discover that I can still soar. How we love this narrative in America! The ultimate act of bootstrapping[5]: refusing to give in to a body you cannot control and that medicine is helpless to cure.

13     And I nearly have such a moment. Leaning against my car in a gas station by the side of a highway, pumping gas, I see a man standing next to a pickup truck, an unremarkable sight save that he has a huge hawk on his arm. The hawk is unblinded, its hood draped over its neck like a collar, but it is lashed to the glove on the man's arm like a dog to a post. Unaccountably, it sees me and tilts its head and then tilts its head again.

14     What are you looking at? I think. As I so often think. But I wave to the man and call, "Beautiful bird."

15     He nods and says they've been out hunting.

16     It's a dreary morning, mist hanging in veils over the fields, a purplish tinge to the distant trees. I cannot imagine hunting in the rain with a bird aloft but then I do. The rivulets of water standing in the farm ditches. The fresh scent of the pines. The breeze lifting the sky and then lifting the sky again, each cloud turning. For just a moment, my heart lifts and, as if to answer me, the hawk rises and spreads its wings and then flaps back into place. Gives itself a shake as it strains against its bindings and then looks at me again, the expressionless light of its eyes seeming to say, What're you going to do?

17     Nothing, I say. I can do nothing.

18     I finish pumping my gas, and holding onto the side of my car for balance, I return the nozzle to its cradle, turn and climb back into the driver's seat and point my car south, toward home. A few minutes later, the man and the hawk are gone and nothing is left but the road ahead, **occult,** unknown, and yet so familiar by now that I feel every turn in my failing neurons. In my ever hopeful bones.

---

[5] **bootstrapping:** to develop using one's own work, without help from others.

## CHECK YOUR UNDERSTANDING

Answer these questions before moving on to the **Analyze the Text** section on the following page.

1  What has happened to the author?

   **A**  She has always had a disability, as did her father and grandfather.

   **B**  She learned she could have had a genetic disease but was lucky.

   **C**  She gradually loses motor skills due to an incurable disease.

   **D**  She is surprised to learn that she has a neurological disorder.

2  As the memoir concludes —

   **F**  the author has an epiphany

   **G**  a hawk soars above the long road

   **H**  the author drives toward home

   **J**  a hawk hunts for prey in a field

3  Which of these best describes the tone of the selection?

   **A**  Helpless but hopeful

   **B**  Joyful but nostalgic

   **C**  Angry but forgiving

   **D**  Fearful but brave

## ANALYZE THE TEXT

Support your responses with evidence from the text. ☰ NOTEBOOK

1. **Analyze**  The events of the memoir are not in chronological order. Use your timeline to help you describe the order of events. What is the effect of the way the author structures this text?

2. **Critique**  Reread paragraph 9. How does the author personify the idea of disability? How does this personification communicate her ongoing experience through a series of parallel sentences?

3. **Infer**  In paragraph 13, the author says, "And I nearly have such a moment." What moment did she nearly have, and why did it not come to pass?

4. **Cite Evidence**  In paragraph 18, the author describes the road using antonyms: "unknown, yet so familiar." Using evidence from the text, explain what is unknown and what is familiar to the author about her metaphorical road ahead.

5. **Evaluate**  What idea does the author repeat in paragraph 11? How might this very short paragraph serve as a statement of the memoir's theme, or message?

## RESEARCH

**RESEARCH TIP**
If you're not sure where to start your search, try searching for a list of degenerative diseases and then consider what interests you. For example, a baseball fan might choose to learn more about amyotrophic lateral sclerosis (ALS) and how it affected Lou Gehrig.

The author of "The Hawk Can Soar" suffers from a degenerative disease. Learn about another degenerative disease. Develop a plan for your research, such as determining general keywords and formulating a question to answer. Use a chart such as the one below to track how your plan and question change as you gather more information.

| Initial question: | Best information source: |
|---|---|
| | |
| Revised question: | Best information source: |
| | |
| What I learned: | How my plan changed: |
| | |

**Connect**  In paragraph 9, the author states, "I slowly begin to disappear from view." With a small group, discuss what people with the disability you researched do to keep from "disappearing," as well as what others can do to see the person.

## CREATE AND DISCUSS

**Design a Web Page** Use your research findings to create a web page about your research topic.

❏ Objectively introduce and develop your topic using concise sentences and a formal style.

❏ Use features such as boldfaced headings, sidebars, bulleted lists, and images to incorporate evidence and structure your information.

❏ Create your web page online or represent your page using a word processing program or a handwritten mock-up.

**Discuss with a Small Group** Have a discussion about how the memoir "The Hawk Can Soar" relates to the theme of Hard-Won Liberty. In what way is the author striving for freedom?

❏ Have group members prepare ideas and gather evidence from the memoir.

❏ Listen actively and respectfully to the members of your group. Ask questions for clarification if needed.

❏ Respond to questions appropriately.

 Go to the **Writing Studio** for more on publishing with technology.

 Go to the **Speaking and Listening Studio** for help with having a group discussion.

## RESPOND TO THE ESSENTIAL QUESTION

 What do we need in order to feel free?

**Gather Information** Review your annotations and notes on "The Hawk Can Soar." Then, add relevant information to your Response Log. As you determine which information to include, think about:

• what keeps people from feeling free
• why people fight against odds
• how changes and loss affect our sense of freedom

At the end of the unit, use your notes to help you write an argument.

### ACADEMIC VOCABULARY
As you write and discuss what you learned from the memoir, be sure to use the Academic Vocabulary words. Check off each of the words that you use.

❏ **comprehensive**
❏ **equivalent**
❏ **incentive**
❏ **innovate**
❏ **subordinate**

## CRITICAL VOCABULARY

WORD BANK
**irrefutable**
**insidious**
**atrophy**
**contemptuous**
**occult**

**Practice and Apply**  Answer each item using the Critical Vocabulary word in your response.

**1.** What is an **irrefutable** fact about life?

_____

**2.** What is a problem that you would consider **insidious**?

_____

**3.** What is a reason why a muscle might **atrophy**?

_____

**4.** Why might someone act **contemptuous**?

_____

**5.** What is **occult** about computer programming?

_____

## VOCABULARY STRATEGY:
### Allusions

An **allusion** is an indirect reference to a literary work or to a historical person, place, or event. In "The Hawk Can Soar," the author uses the allusion "tilting at windmills." When you encounter an expression such as this one that does not at first make sense, you can quickly research the allusion in a print or online dictionary to validate your understanding of its meaning.

**Practice and Apply**  Research these common allusions. Then, explain the meaning in your own words and describe the source.

**1.** Achilles' heel

_____

**2.** The handwriting is on the wall.

_____

**3.** It's Greek to me.

_____

**4.** met his/her Waterloo

_____

## LANGUAGE CONVENTIONS:
### Purposeful Fragments

Although it is grammatically incorrect, a writer may intentionally use a sentence fragment, or incomplete sentence, as a stylistic choice for effect. Fragments create a particular tone, breaking up the flow of writing. If not used appropriately, fragments can cause confusion, so they are not used in formal pieces of writing, such as a letter to a business.

In "The Hawk Can Soar," fragments are used in the following ways.

- To emphasize an idea

   **Disabled. Like this word is the sum total of my existence.**

- To develop tone

   **That dragging leg. That dropping foot. That unbearable fatigue.**

- To create a voice

   **In my ever hopeful bones.**

**Practice and Apply**  Read the following examples. Determine whether the fragment is a purposeful fragment or an incomplete thought. Explain your choices.

**1.** I want to live as I did before my injury. Before everything changed.

_____

_____

**2.** Sometimes life is unfair. Sometimes not.

_____

_____

**3.** She wears a brace on her leg. And on her back.

_____

_____

**4.** The hawk lifts its wings. Tries to fly, but can't.

_____

_____

**5.** The road ahead is a mystery. Winding and unfamiliar.

_____

_____

Go to the **Grammar Studio** for more on sentence fragments.

# THE BRIEFCASE

Short Story by **Rebecca Makkai**

***ESSENTIAL QUESTION:***

What do we need in order to feel free?

## QUICK START

Life events may cause us to question or even change who we are. Think of an experience in your life that changed you or your sense of yourself. Write one or two paragraphs about that time, describing how you changed.

## ANALYZE CHARACTER

**Characters** are the people who participate in the events in a story. Like real people, they display certain qualities and develop and change over time. You can understand characters through their thoughts, action, dialogue, and interactions with other characters. The setting also affects characterization in a story. Characters' **motivations**, or reasons for doing what they do, advance the plot of a story and reveal its theme.

In this story, only one character is fully developed. As you read, ask yourself about these key elements of character to analyze this unnamed main character.

| SETTING | Do the time, place, or cultural setting affect the character? |
|---|---|
| PHYSICAL DESCRIPTION | Do the physical descriptions of the character relate to his identity? |
| ACTIONS | What do his actions and reactions reveal about him? |
| MOTIVATIONS | What drives the character to make the choices he does? |
| THOUGHTS | What does he think about? What do his thoughts reveal about him? |
| INTERACTIONS | With whom does he interact? What does each interaction reveal about him? |
| CHANGES | How does he change throughout the story? |

## ANALYZE THEME

The **theme** is the central idea of a story. It is the moral, life lesson, or insight about life or human nature that the author wants to convey. Themes may be universal, such as "Money can't buy happiness" or "Love conquers all," or they may be more specific to the story. An author might state a theme directly, but most often readers must infer theme, relying on character development and unfolding events to make an educated guess about what message the author wants to convey.

To infer theme as you read, consider:
- the character's actions, thoughts, and motivations
- the character's interactions with others
- how the character changes over the course of the story
- unfolding events in the plot
- setting and its effect on the plot

### GENRE ELEMENTS: SHORT STORY

- uses the basic elements of setting, characters, plot, conflict, and theme
- focuses on one or two main characters and a single plot with minimal subplots
- can be read in its entirety in one sitting

## CRITICAL VOCABULARY

| | | |
|---|---|---|
| flail | inversion | equidistant |
| transpire | flagrantly | havoc |

To see how many Critical Vocabulary words you already know, use them to complete the sentences.

1. The tornado caused _____ in the neighborhoods where it touched down.

2. The two buildings are _____ from the street.

3. I have rarely seen rudeness displayed so _____.

4. He began to _____ his arms wildly to shoo the bee away.

5. The _____ of roles at my company means I am my former boss's new manager.

6. It was easy to predict what would _____ by the end of the movie.

## LANGUAGE CONVENTIONS

**Semicolons** In this lesson, you will learn about how writers use semicolons (;) to link closely related ideas in independent clauses. Here is an example from the story:

**Surely he could not teach at the university; surely he could not slip into the man's bed unnoticed.**

As you read "The Briefcase," note the author's use of semicolons and how they link ideas to create coherence.

## ANNOTATION MODEL

**NOTICE & NOTE**

As you read, note the main character's thoughts, actions, and interactions with others. Generate questions that will lead you to deepen your understanding. Here is one reader's response to the main character's initial appearance:

> He thought how strange that a <u>political prisoner</u>, marched through town in a line, chained to the man behind and chained to the man ahead, should take comfort in the fact that this had happened before. [He thought of other chains of men on other islands of the Earth, and he thought how since there have been men there have been prisoners.] [He thought of mankind as a line of miserable monkeys chained at the wrist, dragging each other back into the ground.]

*Who is the prisoner? What did he do?*

*takes comfort in universal suffering*

*seems resigned to his fate; hopeless*

## BACKGROUND

*The protagonist of "The Briefcase" is a political prisoner in an unnamed country, a man arrested for associating with the wrong people. Political prisoners are detained, imprisoned, and sometimes executed, without benefit of trial or jury, due to political associations or beliefs that conflict with those of the people in power. Such detentions happen all over the world under regimes that hold absolute power over the people and the press. In this story, author* **Rebecca Makkai** *(b. 1978) examines this issue through the lens of basic astronomy.*

# THE BRIEFCASE

**Short Story by Rebecca Makkai**

## SETTING A PURPOSE

*As you read, pay attention to details that reveal the protagonist's character. Write down questions you generate before you read, during your reading, and after you read. Your questions will lead you to a deeper understanding of the main character's motivations and will help you infer the theme.*

**Notice & Note**

You can use the side margins to notice and note signposts in the text.

1  He thought how strange that a political prisoner, marched through town in a line, chained to the man behind and chained to the man ahead, should take comfort in the fact that all this had happened before. He thought of other chains of men on other islands of the Earth, and he thought how since there have been men there have been prisoners. He thought of mankind as a line of miserable monkeys chained at the wrist, dragging each other back into the ground.

2  In the early morning of December first, the sun was finally warming them all, enough that they could walk faster. With his left hand, he adjusted the loop of steel that cuffed his right hand to the line of doomed men. His hand was starved, his wrist was thin, his body was cold: the cuff slipped off. In one beat of the heart he looked back to the man behind him and forward to the man limping ahead, and

### ANALYZE CHARACTER

**Annotate:** Mark words or phrases in paragraph 2 that describe the main character.

**Infer:** What can you tell about the main character based on these descriptions?

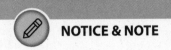

knew that neither saw his naked, red wrist; each saw only his own mother weeping in a kitchen, his own love on a bed in white sheets and sunlight.

3   He walked in step with them to the end of the block.

4   Before the war this man had been a chef, and his one crime was feeding the people who sat at his tables in small clouds of smoke and talked politics. He served them the wine that fueled their underground newspaper, their aborted revolution. And after the night his restaurant disappeared in fire, he had run and hidden and gone without food — he who had roasted ducks until the meat jumped from the bone, he who had evaporated three bottles of wine into one pot of cream soup, he who had peeled the skin from small pumpkins with a twist of his hand.

5   And here was his hand, twisted free of the chain, and here he was running and crawling, until he was through a doorway. It was a building of empty classrooms — part of the university he had never attended. He watched from the bottom corner of a second-story window as the young soldiers stopped the line, counted 199 men, shouted to each other, shouted at the men in the panicked voices of children who barely filled the shoulders of their uniforms. One soldier, a bigger one, a louder one, stopped a man walking by. A man in a suit, with a briefcase, a beard — some sort of professor. The soldiers stripped him of his coat, his shirt, his leather case, cuffed him to the chain. They marched again. And as soon as they were past — no, not that soon; many minutes later, when he had the stomach — the chef ran down to the street and collected the man's briefcase, coat and shirt.

6   In the alley, the chef sat against a wall and buttoned the professor's shirt over his own ribs. When he opened the briefcase, papers flew out, a thousand doves **flailing** against the walls of the alley. The chef ran after them all, stopped them with his feet and arms, herded them back into the case. Pages of numbers, of arrows and notes and hand-drawn star maps. Here were business cards: a professor of physics. Envelopes showed his name and address — information that might have been useful in some other lifetime, one where the chef could ring the bell of this man's house and explain to his wife about empty chains, empty wrists, empty classrooms. Here were graded papers, a fall syllabus, the typed draft of an exam. The question at the end, a good one: "Using modern astronomical data, construct, to the best of your ability, a proof that the sun actually revolves around the Earth."

7   The chef knew nothing of physics. He understood chemistry only insofar as it related to the baking time of bread at various elevations or the evaporation rate of alcohol. His knowledge of biology was limited to the deboning of chickens and the behavior

**ANALYZE THEME**

**Annotate:** Mark the major plot development that occurs in paragraph 5.

**Analyze:** Who is to blame for what happens to the professor? How does the chef respond to this injustice?

**flail**
(flāl)  *v.* to thrash or wave about wildly.

of *Saccharomyces cerevisiae*, common bread yeast. And what did he know at all of moving bodies and gravity? He knew this: he had moved from his line of men, creating a vacuum — one that had sucked the good professor in to fill the void.

8     The chef sat on his bed in the widow K—'s basement and felt, in the cool leather of the briefcase, a second vacuum: here was a vacated life. Here were salary receipts, travel records, train tickets, a small address book. And these belonged to a man whose name was not blackened like his own, a man whose life was not hunted. If he wanted to live through the next year, the chef would have to learn this life and fill it — and oddly, this felt not like a robbery but an apology, a way to put the world back in balance. The professor would not die, because he himself would become the professor, and he would live.

9     Surely he could not teach at the university; surely he could not slip into the man's bed unnoticed. But what was in this leather case, it seemed, had been left for him to use. These addresses of friends; this card of identification; this riddle about the **inversion** of the universe.

10 Five cities east, he now gave his name as the professor's, and grew out his beard so it would match the photograph on the card he now carried in his pocket. The two men did not, anymore, look entirely dissimilar. To the first name in the address book, the chef had written a typed letter: "Am in trouble and have fled the city. Tell my dear wife I am safe, but for her safety do not tell her where I am. If you are able to help a poor old man, send money to the following post box . . . I hope to remain your friend, Professor T—."

11     He had to write this about the wife; how could he ask these men for money if she held a funeral? And what of it, if she kept her happiness another few months, another year?

12     The next twenty-six letters were similar in nature, and money arrived now in brown envelopes and white ones. The bills came wrapped in notes — (Was his life in danger? Did he have his health?) — and with the money he paid another widow for another basement, and he bought weak cigarettes. He sat on café chairs and drew pictures of the universe, showed stars and planets looping each other in light. He felt, perhaps, that if he used the other papers in the

**inversion**
(ĭn-vûr´zhən) *n.*
reversal or upside-down placement.

**LANGUAGE CONVENTIONS**
**Annotate:** Mark the semicolon that links two independent clauses in paragraph 11.

**Analyze:** What is the effect of using a semicolon here instead of a period?

## ANALYZE THEME

**Annotate:** Mark the sentence in paragraph 13 that summarizes the chef's answer to the professor's question.

**Infer:** What does this answer reveal about how the chef's character is changing?

**equidistant**
(ē-kwĭ-dĭs´tənt) *adj.*
at equal distance from.

briefcase, he must also make use of the question. Or perhaps he felt that if he could answer it, he could put the universe back together. Or perhaps it was something to fill his empty days.

13    He wrote in his small notebook: "The light of my cigarette is a fire like the sun. From where I sit, all the universe is **equidistant** from my cigarette. Ergo,[1] my cigarette is the center of the universe. My cigarette is on Earth. Ergo, the Earth is the center of the universe. If all heavenly bodies move, they must therefore move in relation to the Earth, and in relation to my cigarette."

14    His hand ached. These words were the most he had written since school, which had ended for him at age sixteen. He had been a smart boy, even talented in languages and mathematics, but his mother knew these were no way to make a living. He was not blessed, like the professor, with years of scholarship and quiet offices and leather books. He was blessed instead with chicken stocks and herbs and sherry. Thirty years had passed since his last day of school, and his hand was accustomed now to wooden spoon, mandoline, peeling knife, rolling pin.

15    Today, his hands smelled of ink, when for thirty years they had smelled of leeks. They were the hands of the professor; ergo, he was now the professor.

16    He had written to friends A through L, and now he saved the rest and wrote instead to students. Here in the briefcase's outermost pocket were class rosters from the past two years; letters addressed to those young men care of the university were sure to reach them. The

_____
[1] **Ergo** (ûr´gō):  the Latin equivalent of "therefore."

amounts they sent were smaller, the notes that accompanied them more inquisitive. What exactly had **transpired**? Could they come to the city and meet him?

17    The post box, of course, was in a different city than the one where he stayed. He arrived at the post office just before closing, and came only once every two or three weeks. He always looked through the window first to check that the lobby was empty. If it was not, he would leave and come again another day. Surely one of these days, a friend of the professor would be waiting there for him. He prepared a story, that he was the honored professor's assistant, that he could not reveal the man's location but would certainly pass on your kindest regards, sir.

18    If the Earth moved, all it would take for a man to travel its distance would be a strong balloon. Rise twenty feet above, and wait for the Earth to turn under you; you would be home again in a day. But this was not true, and a man could not escape his spot on the Earth but to run along the surface. Ergo, the Earth was still. Ergo, the sun was the moving body of the two.

19    No, he did not believe it. He wanted only to know who this professor was, this man who would teach his students the laws of the universe, then ask them to prove as true what was false.

20    On the wall of the café: plate-sized canvas, delicate oils of an apple, half-peeled. Signed, below, by a girl he had known in school. The price was more than a month of groceries, and so he did not buy it, but for weeks he read his news under the apple and drank his coffee. Staining his fingers in cheap black ink were the signal fires of the world, the distress sirens, the dispatches from the trenches and hospitals and abattoirs[2] of the war; but here, on the wall, a sign from another world. He had known this girl as well as any other: had spoken with her every day, but had not made love to her; had gone to her home one winter holiday, but knew nothing of her life since then. And here, a clue, perfect and round and unfathomable. After all this time: apple.

21    After he finished the news, he worked at the proof and saw in the coil of green-edged skin some model of spiraling, of expansion. The stars were at one time part of the Earth, until the hand of God peeled them away, leaving us in the dark. They do not revolve around us: they escape in widening circles. The Milky Way is the edge of this peel.

22    Outside the café window, a beggar screeched his bow against a defeated violin. A different kind of case, open on the ground, this one

---

[2] **abattoirs** (ăb´ə-twärs): slaughterhouses.

**transpire**
(trăn-spīr´) *v.* to happen or occur.

**ANALYZE CHARACTER**
Annotate: Mark text in paragraph 17 that describes the chef's habits of approaching and entering the post office.

Infer: What do these habits reveal about the chef?

collecting the pennies of the more compassionate passers-by. The café owner shooed him away, and the chef sighed in guilty relief that he would not have to pass, on the way out, his double.

**ANALYZE CHARACTER**
**Annotate:** Mark text that explains why the chef is no longer reading current newspapers.

**Infer:** What does this change reveal about the chef's state of mind?

23 After eight months in the new city, the chef stopped buying his newspapers on the street by the café and began instead to read the year-old news the widow gave him for his fires. Here, fourteen months ago: Minister P—— of the Interior predicts war. One day he found that in a box near the widow's furnace were papers three, four, five years old. Pages were missing, edges eaten. He took his fragments of yellowed paper to the café and read the beginnings and ends of opinions and letters. He read reports from what used to be his country's borders.

24 When he had finished the last paper of the box, he began to read the widow's history books. The Americas, before Columbus; the oceans, before the British; the Romans, before their fall.

25 History was safer than the news, because there was no question of how it would end.

26 He took a lover in the city and told her he was a professor of physics. He showed her the stars in the sky and explained that they circled the Earth, along with the sun.

27 That's not true at all, she said. You tease because you think I'm just a silly girl.

28 No, he said and touched her neck, You are the only one who might understand. The universe has been folded inside out.

29 A full year had passed, and he paid the widow in coins. He wrote to friends M through Z. I have been in hiding for a year, he wrote. Tell my dear wife I have my health. May time and history forgive us all.

30 A year had passed, but so had many years passed for many men. And after all what was a year, if the Earth did not circle the sun?

31 The Earth does not circle the sun, he wrote. Ergo: The years do not pass. The Earth, being stationary, does not erase the past nor escape towards the future. Rather, the years pile on like blankets, existing at once. The year is 1848; the year is 1789; the year is 1956.

32 If the Earth hangs still in space, does it spin? If the Earth were to spin, the space I occupy I will therefore vacate in an instant. This city will leave its spot, and the city to the west will usurp its place. Ergo, this city is all cities at all times. This is Kabul; this is Dresden; this is Johannesburg.[3]

33 I run by standing still.

---

[3] **Kabul . . . Dresden . . . Johannesburg:** cities in Afghanistan, Germany, and South Africa, respectively.

34 At the post office, he collects his envelopes of money. He has learned from the notes of concerned colleagues and students and friends that the professor suffered from infections of the inner ear that often threw off his balance. He has learned of the professor's wife, A—, whose father died the year they married. He has learned that he has a young son. Rather, the professor has a son.

35     At each visit to the post office, he fears he will forget the combination. It is an old lock, and complicated: F1, clockwise to B3, back to A6, forward again to J3. He must shake the little latch before it opens. More than forgetting, perhaps what he fears is that he will be denied access — that the little box will one day recognize him behind his thick and convincing beard, will decide he has no right of entry.

36     One night, asleep with his head on his lover's leg, he dreams that a letter has arrived from the professor himself. *They freed me at the end of the march,* it says, *and I crawled my way home. My hands are bloody and my knees are worn through, and I want my briefcase back.*

37     In his dream, the chef takes the case and runs west. If the professor takes it back, there will be no name left for the chef, no place on the Earth. The moment his fingers leave the leather loop of the handle, he will fall off the planet.

38 He sits in a wooden chair on the lawn behind the widow's house. Inside, he hears her washing dishes. In exchange for the room, he cooks all her meals. It is March, and the cold makes the hairs rise from his arms, but the sun warms the arm beneath them. He thinks, the tragedy of a moving sun is that it leaves us each day. Hence the Aztec sacrifices, the ancient rites of the eclipse. If the sun so willingly leaves us, each morning it returns is a stay of execution, an undeserved gift.

39     Whereas: If it is we who turn, how can we so **flagrantly** leave behind that which has warmed us and given us light? If we are moving, then each turn is a turn away. Each revolution a revolt.

40 The money comes less often, and even old friends who used to write monthly now send only rare, apologetic notes, a few small bills. Things are more difficult now, their letters say. No one understood when he first ran away, but now it is clear: After they finished with the artists, the journalists, the fighters, they came for the professors. How wise he was, to leave when he did. Some letters come back unopened, with a black stamp.

41     Life is harder here, too. Half the shops are closed. His lover has left him. The little café is filled with soldiers. The beggar with the violin has disappeared, and the chef fears him dead.

**ANALYZE CHARACTER**
**Annotate:** Mark text in the description of the chef's dream that reveals what he fears most.

**Analyze:** What does this dream suggest about the chef's conflicted feelings about the professor?

**flagrantly**
(flā′grənt-lē) *adv.* in a blatantly or conspicuously offensive manner.

42     One afternoon, he enters the post office two minutes before closing. The lobby is empty but for the postman and his broom.

43     The mailbox is empty as well, and he turns to leave but hears the voice of the postman behind him. You are the good Professor T——, no? I have something for you in the back.

44     Yes, he says, I am the professor. And it feels as if this is true, and he will have no guilt over the professor's signature when the box is brought out. He is even wearing the professor's shirt, as loose again over his hungry ribs as it was the day he slipped it on in the alley.

45     From behind the counter, the postman brings no box, but a woman in a long gray dress, a white handkerchief in her fingers.

46     She moves towards him, looks at his hands and his shoes and his face. Forgive me for coming, she says, and the postman pulls the cover down over his window and vanishes. She says, No one would tell me anything, only that my husband had his health. And then a student gave me the number of the box and the name of the city.

47     He begins to say, You are the widow. But why would he say this? What proof is there that the professor is dead? Only that it must be; that it follows logically.

48     She says, I don't understand what has happened.

49     He begins to say, I am the good professor's assistant, madam — but then what next? She would ask questions he has no way to answer.

50     I don't understand, she says again.

51     All he can say is, This is his shirt. He holds out an arm so she can see the gaping sleeve.

52     She says, What have you done with him? She has a calm voice and wet, brown eyes. He feels he has seen her before, in the streets of the old city. Perhaps he served her a meal, a bottle of wine. Perhaps, in another lifetime, she was the center of his universe.

53     This is his beard, he says.

54     She begins to cry into the handkerchief. She says, Then he is dead. He sees now from the quiet of her voice that she must have known this long ago. She has come here only to confirm.

55     He feels the floor of the post office move beneath him, and he tries to turn his eyes from her, to ground his gaze in something solid: postbox, ceiling tile, window. He finds he cannot turn away. She is a force of gravity in her long gray dress.

56     No, he says. No, no, no, no, no, I am right here.

57     No, he does not believe it, but he knows that if he had time, he could prove it. And he must, because he is the only piece of the professor left alive. The woman does not see how she is murdering her husband, right here in the post office lobby. He whispers to her: Let me go home with you. I'll be a father to your son, and I'll warm your bed, and I'll keep you safe.

**ANALYZE CHARACTER**

**Annotate:** Mark the woman's actions and words in paragraphs 45–54.

**Analyze:** What do the chef's responses to these words and actions reveal about him?

**ANALYZE THEME**

**Annotate:** In paragraph 57, mark the text that reveals the chef's desperation.

**Infer:** What will happen to the chef if he loses the professor's identity?

58    He wraps his hands around her small, cold wrists, but she pulls loose. She might be the most beautiful woman he has ever seen.

59    As if from far away, he hears her call to the postmaster to send for the police.

60    His head is light, and he feels he might float away from the post office forever. It is an act of will not to fly off, but to hold tight to the Earth and wait. If the police aren't too busy to come, he feels confident he can prove to them that he is the professor. He has the papers, after all — and in the **havoc** of war, what else will they have the time to look for?

61    She is backing away from him on steady feet, and he feels it like a peeling off of skin.

62    If not the police, perhaps he'll convince a city judge. The witnesses who would denounce him are mostly gone or killed, and the others would fear to come before the law. If the city judge will not listen, he can prove it to the high court. One day he might convince the professor's own child. He feels certain that somewhere down the line, someone will believe him.

**havoc**
(hăv´ək)  *n.* destructive disorder or chaos.

## CHECK YOUR UNDERSTANDING

Answer these questions before moving on to the **Analyze the Text** section on the following page.

1  Why does the chef have the professor's briefcase?

   A  The professor dropped it when taken prisoner in the chef's place.

   B  He found it on the street and picked it up, hoping it might be helpful.

   C  He feels a responsibility to tell the professor's family what happened.

   D  It was left in the restaurant where the chef worked before his arrest.

2  What is the chef's strategy for survival?

   F  He conceals his location and asks the professor's friends for money.

   G  He plans to marry the professor's wife and help raise their son.

   H  He takes a job in a new restaurant where no one knows him.

   J  He has no strategy because he knows how hopeless his situation is.

3  At the end of the story —

   A  the chef finally understands the professor's question

   B  he has been evicted from his room because he has no more money

   C  his disguise has convinced the professor's son that he is his father

   D  the chef's secret has been discovered

**RESPOND**

## ANALYZE THE TEXT

Support your responses with evidence from the text.  📓 NOTEBOOK

1. **Cite Evidence**  What evidence does the author provide that the chef, even after a year in hiding, fears discovery?

2. **Summarize**  How does the chef justify the theft of the professor's briefcase and identity?

3. **Interpret**  In what way is the beggar outside the café the chef's "double"? Why does the chef not want to walk past him?

4. **Analyze**  Throughout the story, the author revisits the astronomy question. What is the connection between this question and the story's theme?

5. **Draw Conclusions**  Does the chef ever begin to believe his own lie? Cite evidence from the story to support your answer.

## RESEARCH

**RESEARCH TIP**
As you find information and begin to write it in the chart, be sure to document every source you use so that you can give proper credit. The main elements of a source citation are the author name, publisher name, publisher location (for books), date created or published, title, URL (for websites), and page number(s).

A political prisoner is imprisoned for his or her political beliefs or actions. With a partner, research political imprisonment around the world. Begin your research with an initial question. As you learn more, use your findings to generate, modify, and refine more questions to refocus your research plan. Use credible sources, such as objective news outlets or nonprofit websites (.org). Add your questions and research findings to the chart.

| QUESTIONS | FINDINGS |
|---|---|
| **Initial question:** | |
| **Modified question:** | |
| **Final question:** | |

**Extend**  Compare findings with others. How do the political prisoners' beliefs and actions compare? What comparisons can you make among the governments that imprisoned them? What conclusions can you draw about political prisoners?

## CREATE AND PRESENT

**Write a Letter** Assume the identity of the chef. Write a letter to the professor's son in which you attempt to convince him that you could serve as his father.

- ❏ Gather details from the story that support the chef's idea that he has become the professor.

- ❏ Write a brief letter to the son based on the details you have gathered from the text. Address the son, using a voice and logic suited to the chef's character.

- ❏ Make sure you use specificity and detail when you mention events and relationships of which the chef would be aware.

**Deliver a Summary** Summarize the story to classmates while maintaining meaning and logical order. Conclude with a prediction of what happens next to the chef.

- ❏ Review your notes about the chef's character and motivations. Outline the key events of the story, including the chef's actions and reactions.

- ❏ Based on what you know about the chef and the flow of the story, make a logical prediction about what happens to him after the story ends.

- ❏ If you have trouble expressing ideas about physics or political imprisonment, use strategies including synonyms, descriptions, or analogies as needed.

Go to the **Writing Studio** for more on persuasive techniques.

Go to the **Speaking and Listening Studio** for help with presentations.

## RESPOND TO THE ESSENTIAL QUESTION

**?** What do we need in order to feel free?

**Gather Information** Review your annotations and notes on "The Briefcase." Then add relevant information to your Response Log. As you determine which information to include, think about:

- the chef's actions and motivations
- what happened to the professor
- the setting's effects on character and plot
- themes in the story

At the end of the unit, use your notes to help you write an argument.

### ACADEMIC VOCABULARY

As you write about and discuss the short story, be sure to use the Academic Vocabulary words. Check off each of the words that you use.

- ❏ **comprehension**
- ❏ **equivalent**
- ❏ **incentive**
- ❏ **innovate**
- ❏ **subordinate**

**WORD BANK**
flail
inversion
equidistant
transpire
flagrantly
havoc

## CRITICAL VOCABULARY

**Practice and Apply** Answer each question to demonstrate your understanding of the Critical Vocabulary words. Then, explain your responses.

1. If the professor's arms were **flailing** when he was seized, did he resist arrest or comply meekly?

_____

2. When the chef reads the professor's test question, he interprets it as an **inversion**. Why?

_____

3. If the chef believes that all things in the universe are **equidistant** from him, is the sun farther from the chef than the moon?

_____

4. The professor's wife tracked down the chef to determine what had **transpired**. What did she hope to find out?

_____

5. The guards **flagrantly** disregarded the law in seizing the professor. How concerned were they about being caught making an unlawful arrest?

_____

6. The war created **havoc** in the chef's country. What might you assume everyday life was like for people?

_____

## VOCABULARY STRATEGY:
### Discipline-Specific Terms

Go to the **Vocabulary Studio** for more on discipline-specific terms.

The author of this story uses terms from cooking, physics, and history. Context clues, encyclopedias, or technical dictionaries can help you determine the meaning of an unfamiliar term specific to a particular field or discipline.

**Practice and Apply** Read these sentences from the story. Use context clues or other resources to write the meaning of each boldfaced term.

1. His knowledge of biology was limited to the deboning of chickens and the behavior of *Saccharomyces cerevisiae*, common bread yeast.

_____

2. Hence the **Aztec sacrifices**, the ancient rites of the eclipse. If the sun so willingly leaves us, each morning it returns is a stay of execution, an undeserved gift.

_____

3. Using modern **astronomical data**, construct, to the best of your ability, a proof that the sun actually revolves around Earth.

_____

## LANGUAGE CONVENTIONS:
## Semicolons

Writers use semicolons for three main purposes:

- to link two independent clauses, setting them off from each other without using a conjunction such as *and* or *but*
- to link an independent clause with another clause that begins with a conjunctive adverb (such as *therefore, meanwhile, also,* or *however*)
- to separate items in a list when the items already contain commas

Makkai uses semicolons to provide structure and organization in her writing, but she also uses them to influence meaning. Read this sentence from the story:

> **Surely he could not teach at the university; surely he could not slip into the man's bed unnoticed.**

The author could have separated the two independent clauses with a period, but placing them in the same sentence shows that the two thoughts are closely connected. By setting them off from each other in the same sentence without using a conjunction, Makkai lets the reader deduce how they are related. Now, read this sentence from the story:

> **They were the hands of the professor; ergo, he was now the professor.**

In this example, the semicolon links two thoughts, and a conjunctive adverb (*ergo*) shows that the second thought results from the first.

**Practice and Apply** Look back at the letter you wrote to the professor's son. Revise your letter to link two independent clauses with semicolons. Then, discuss with a partner how using semicolons helps clarify the meaning of your letter.

Go to the **Grammar Studio** for more on semicolons.

LETTER

# *from* LETTER TO VICEROY, LORD IRWIN

by **Mohandas K. Gandhi**
pages 287–291

## COMPARE ACCOUNTS

As you read the letter and view the documentary, notice how Gandhi presents his argument to Lord Irwin and how the film portrays the resulting nonviolent protest. How do these different formats affect your understanding of Gandhi's leadership in a movement to bring justice to the Indian people? After you review both selections, you will collaborate with a small group on a final project.

**?** **ESSENTIAL QUESTION:**

## What do we need in order to feel free?

DOCUMENTARY FILM

# *from* GANDHI: THE RISE TO FAME

by **BBC**
page 299

# *from* **Letter to Viceroy, Lord Irwin**

## QUICK START

Many countries throughout history have gained independence from rule by a foreign government. How does a fight for freedom get its start? With a group, discuss how one person might begin a movement for independence.

## ANALYZE ARGUMENT

A formal argument sets forth a specific and well supported claim. Gandhi's letter attempts to sway the British Viceroy to improve the living conditions of the Indian people. As you analyze his argument, consider these elements:

| ELEMENTS TO CONSIDER | CRITERIA FOR EVALUATION |
|---|---|
| **Claim:** the central point of an argument | Should be specific and reasonable |
| **Reasons:** the logical support for a claim | Must be **valid**—both accurate and relevant. Faulty reasoning, or logical fallacy, can weaken the argument. |
| **Evidence:** facts, details, examples, and anecdotes that elaborate on reasons | Must provide solid support. Irrelevant or insufficient evidence weakens a writer's argument. |
| **Counterarguments:** points that refute a counterclaim, or an argument against the central claim | Like a claim, must be supported by reasons and evidence |

**GENRE ELEMENTS: ARGUMENT**

- makes a claim that states the central point
- provides logical and accurate reasons for a claim
- includes evidence to support reasons
- includes counterarguments that address potential counterclaims

## ANALYZE RHETORIC

A writer uses **rhetoric** to effectively communicate ideas to an audience. A writer can construct a strong argument by establishing credibility and using an appropriate tone. The use of rhetoric can determine whether readers accept or reject an argument. Rhetoric includes these devices:

- **Appeals:** An appeal to logic, emotions, or the character of the speaker can strengthen the power of an argument.

- **Antithesis:** Opposing ideas linked in a sentence can provide a strong contrast, examine pros and cons, and make the argument more memorable.

- **Parallelism:** The repetition of words, phrases, and grammatical patterns can be used to emphasize points and provide a rhythm.

- **Shifts:** A shift in rhetoric is a change from one idea to another to prove a point. Shifts can be signaled by conjunctions such as *but* or *however*.

As you read, notice how Gandhi uses these devices to convince Lord Irwin.

## CRITICAL VOCABULARY

**unpalatable   unadulterated   humility   iniquitous   peremptory**

To preview the Critical Vocabulary words, fill in the blank with the word that best completes each sentence.

1. The milk had spoiled, so it was _____ to drink.

2. When she was honored, the activist showed _____ by saying that her contributions were merely simple acts.

3. The laws that keep many people from finding affordable housing are _____.

4. Learning to drive is _____ to actually getting your license.

5. I can drink safely from the stream because the water is _____.

## LANGUAGE CONVENTIONS

**Active and Passive Voice**  A sentence may express an idea in either the active or the passive voice. In **active voice,** the subject of the sentence performs the action. In **passive voice,** the subject is acted on rather than doing the action. Here is an example:

**Active Voice:** The protesters shouted demands as they marched down the street.
**Passive Voice:** Demands were shouted by the protesters as they marched down the street.

Most writing uses active voice. As you read Gandhi's letter, pay attention to where he strategically uses passive voice to achieve his persuasive goals.

## ANNOTATION MODEL

**NOTICE & NOTE**

Here is how a reader might annotate to identify a specific appeal that Gandhi uses:

> Before embarking on Civil Disobedience and taking the risk I have dreaded to take all these years, I would fain approach you and find a way out. My personal faith is absolutely clear. <u>I cannot intentionally hurt any thing that lives, much less fellow-human beings even though they may do the greatest wrong to me and mine.</u>

*The author tries to persuade the reader that he is credible by making an appeal to his own ethical character.*

## BACKGROUND

**Mohandas K. Gandhi** *(1869–1948), often called "Mahatma" ("Great Soul"), helped lead the Indian drive for independence from British rule. The Salt March protested living conditions endured by the Indian people, including a high tax on salt and a prohibition against producing it independently. Gandhi wrote this letter on March 2, 1930. The British colonial government refused Gandhi's demands. On April 6, Gandhi broke the law at the end of the Salt March by picking up handfuls of salt from the seashore. This action sparked a national campaign of nonviolent protest that led to independence from Britain in 1947.*

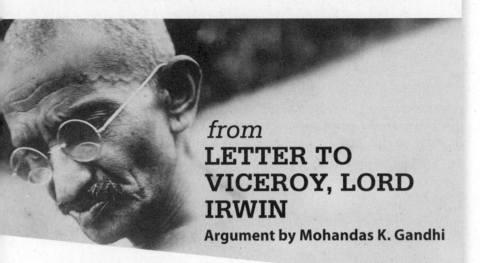

## *from* LETTER TO VICEROY, LORD IRWIN

### Argument by Mohandas K. Gandhi

## PREPARE TO COMPARE

*As you read, make notes about Gandhi's claim and the reasons and evidence he uses to support his argument. This will help you compare his letter with the information and statement made about the march in the video that follows.*

Dear Friend,

1    Before embarking on Civil Disobedience and taking the risk I have dreaded to take all these years, I would fain[1] approach you and find a way out. My personal faith is absolutely clear. I cannot intentionally hurt any thing that lives, much less fellow-human beings even though they may do the greatest wrong to me and mine. *Whilst therefore I hold the British rule to be a curse, I do not intend to harm a single Englishman or any legitimate interest he may have in India.*

2    I must not be misunderstood. Though I hold the British rule in India to be a curse, I do not therefore consider Englishmen in general to be worse than any other people on earth. I have the privilege of claiming many Englishmen as dearest friends. Indeed

---
[1] **fain:** with pleasure.

### Notice & Note

You can use the side margins to notice and note signposts in the text.

**ANALYZE ARGUMENT**
**Annotate:** Mark the counterclaim Gandhi anticipates in paragraph 2.

**Interpret:** What counterargument does Gandhi make to refute this counterclaim?

**unpalatable**
(ŭn-păl´ə-tə-bəl) *adj.*
unpleasant or unacceptable.

much that I have learnt of the evil of British rule is due to the writings of frank and courageous Englishmen who have not hesitated to tell the **unpalatable** truth about that rule.

3    And why do I regard the British rule as a curse?

4    It has impoverished the dumb millions by a system of progressive exploitation and by a ruinously expensive military and civil administration which the country can never afford.

5    It has reduced us politically to serfdom.[2] It has sapped the foundations of our culture, and, by the policy of disarmament,[3] it has degraded us spiritually. Lacking inward strength, we have been reduced by all but universal disarmament to a state bordering on cowardly helplessness.

**ANALYZE RHETORIC**

**Annotate:** Gandhi uses antithesis in paragraph 6 to explain his approach. Mark the two forces Gandhi states that his nonviolent force is opposing.

**Compare:** Are these two forces more alike or more different? How might nonviolence counter both of them?

6    . . . If India is to live as a nation, if the slow death by starvation of her people is to stop, some remedy must be found for immediate relief. The proposed conference is certainly not the remedy. It is not a matter of carrying conviction by argument. The matter resolves itself into one of matching forces. Conviction or no conviction Great Britain would defend her Indian commerce and interest by all the forces at her command. India must consequently evolve force enough to free herself from that embrace of death. It is common cause that, however disorganized and for the time being insignificant it may be, the party of violence is gaining ground and making itself felt. Its end is the same as mine. But I am convinced that it cannot bring the desired relief to the dumb millions. And the conviction is growing deeper and deeper in me that nothing but **unadulterated** non-violence can check the organized violence of the British Government. Many think that non-violence is not an active force. It is my purpose to set in motion that force as well against the organized violent force of the British rule as the unorganized violent force of the growing party of violence. To sit still would be to give rein to both the forces above mentioned. Having an unquestioning and immovable faith in the efficacy of non-violence as I know it, it would be sinful on my part to wait any longer. . . .

**unadulterated**
(ŭn-ə-dŭl´tə-rā-tĭd) *adj.*
pure and untainted.

7    I know that in embarking on non-violence, I shall be running what might fairly be termed a mad risk, but the victories of truth have never been won without risks, often of the gravest character. Conversion of a nation that has consciously or unconsciously preyed upon another far more numerous, far more ancient and no less cultured than itself is worth any amount of risk.

**AGAIN AND AGAIN**

**Notice & Note:** Mark the verb Gandhi repeats several times in paragraph 8.

**Infer:** What point does this repetition emphasize?

8    I have deliberately used the word conversion. For my ambition is no less than to convert the British people through non-violence and thus make them see the wrong they have done to India. I do not seek to harm your people. I want to serve them even as I want to serve my own. I believe that I have always served them. I served them up

---

[2] **serfdom:** the lowest class of a feudal system, which held people in bondage.
[3] **disarmament:** the reduction or elimination of weapons.

to 1919 blindly. But when my eyes were opened, and I conceived non-cooperation the object still was to serve them. I employed the same weapon that I have in all **humility** successfully used against the dearest members of my family. If I have equal love for your people with mine, it will not long remain hidden. It will be acknowledged by them even as the members of my family acknowledged it after they had tried me for several years. If the people join me as I expect they will, the sufferings they will undergo, unless the British nation sooner retraces its steps, will be enough to melt the stoniest hearts.

9   The plan through civil disobedience will be to combat such evils as I have sampled out.

10   If we want to sever the British connection it is because of such evils. When they are removed the path becomes easy. Then the way to friendly negotiation will be open. If the British commerce with India is purified of greed, you will have no difficulty in recognizing our independence. I respectfully invite you then to pave the way for an immediate removal of those evils and thus open a way for a real conference between equals, interested only in promoting the common good of mankind through voluntary fellowship and in arranging terms of mutual help and commerce suited to both. You have unnecessarily laid stress upon the communal problems that unhappily affect this land. Important though they undoubtedly are for the consideration of any scheme of government, they have little bearing on the greater problems which are above communities and which affect them all equally. *But if you cannot see your way to deal with these evils and my letter makes no appeal to your heart, on the 11th day of this month, I shall proceed with such co-workers of the*

**humility**
(hyōō-mĭl´ĭ-tē)  *n.*
modesty; lack of superiority over others.

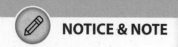

**NOTICE & NOTE**

**iniquitous**
(ĭ-nĭk′wĭ-təs) *adj.* wicked, evil.

**LANGUAGE CONVENTIONS**

**Annotate:** Mark the subject of the first sentence of paragraph 12.

**Respond:** How might the tone of this sentence change if the subject were "I"? What is the effect of Gandhi's wording in this key sentence?

**peremptory**
(pə-rĕmp′tə-rē) *adj.* imperative; required; not able to be denied.

*Ashram[4] as I can take to disregard the provisions of the Salt laws.* I regard this tax to be the most **iniquitous** of all from the poor man's standpoint. As the Independence Movement is essentially for the poorest in the land, the beginning will be made with this evil. The wonder is, that we have submitted to the cruel monopoly[5] for so long. It is, I know, open to you to frustrate my design by arresting me. I hope that there will be tens of thousands ready in a disciplined manner to take up the work after me, and in the act of disobeying the Salt Act to lay themselves open to the penalties of a law that should never have disfigured the Statute-book.

11      I have no desire to cause you unnecessary embarrassment or any at all so far as I can help. If you think that there is any substance in my letter, and if you will care to discuss matters with me, and if to that end you would like me to postpone publication of this letter, I shall gladly refrain on receipt of a telegram to that effect soon after this reaches you. You will however do me the favor not to deflect me from my course unless you can see your way to conform to the substance of this letter.

12      This letter is not in any way intended as a threat, but is a simple and sacred duty **peremptory** on a civil resister. Therefore I am having it specially delivered by a young English friend, who believes in the Indian cause and is a full believer in non-violence and whom Providence[6] seems to have sent to me as it were for the very purpose.

I remain,
Your Sincere friend,

*MKgandhi*

M.K. Gandhi

---

[4] **Ashram:** a secluded residence of a Hindu religious leader and followers.
[5] **monopoly:** the complete and exclusive control of a product or service.
[6] **Providence:** God or a supernatural power.

290   Unit 4

## CHECK YOUR UNDERSTANDING

Answer these questions before moving on to the **Analyze the Text** section on the following page.

1 Why did Gandhi want to meet with the Viceroy?

   **A** To discuss a proposed conference

   **B** To find a way out of his planned civil disobedience

   **C** To inform the Viceroy about the party of violence

   **D** To request help for his family

2 What evil did Gandhi describe as the main point of the letter?

   **F** The risks of civil disobedience

   **G** An expensive military

   **H** The Independence Movement

   **J** British rule of India

3 What did Gandhi say would happen if the letter had no effect?

   **A** He and his followers would disobey the Salt Act.

   **B** He would be arrested and put in prison.

   **C** He would ask his followers to protest violently.

   **D** He would no longer serve English people.

## ANALYZE THE TEXT

Support your responses with evidence from the text. 🗒 NOTEBOOK

1. **Analyze** Identify Gandhi's central claim in this letter. What key reasons does he provide to support this claim?

2. **Evaluate** Notice how Gandhi structures his argument. Why is this order of ideas effective?

3. **Draw Conclusions** Identify the places where Gandhi uses the words *curse* and *conversion*. Why are these word choices significant, and how do they affect his tone?

4. **Cite Evidence** How does Gandhi support his choice of the first action to take against the evils of British rule?

5. **Notice & Note** What contrasting ideas or rhetorical shift do you notice in the last two paragraphs of Gandhi's letter? What effect does this shift have on the tone of the letter?

## RESEARCH

**RESEARCH TIP**
Choose carefully as you look for primary sources. Use valid, reliable sources that relate to authentic historical events.

Explore another act or event of civil disobedience through a primary source such as a letter. A **primary source** contains original, firsthand information. It may be an eyewitness account, letter, diary, interview, speech, or autobiography. A **secondary source,** on the other hand, provides someone else's version of a primary source. It may be a news article, a documentary, a biography, or encyclopedia entry. Keep track of your sources in a chart like the one shown.

| EVENT | URL/ SOURCE | PARAPHRASED OR QUOTED INFORMATION |
| --- | --- | --- |
| | | |
| | | |

**Extend** Share what you learn with a small group. Be sure to identify your sources.

## CREATE AND DISCUSS

**Write an Analysis**  Overall, how would you evaluate the strength of Gandhi's argument?

❏ Write a one-paragraph analysis of his claims, reasons, evidence, and rhetoric, providing examples from the text of the letter.

❏ Then, discuss in a second paragraph why you think this argument failed to persuade the Viceroy to change the conditions imposed on the Indian people or even to respond to Gandhi.

**Share Information**  Now that you have read and analyzed "Letter to Viceroy, Lord Irwin" and researched another event of civil disobedience, meet with a partner to share what you have learned about civil disobedience. Delve deeper into the information by doing the following:

❏ Support the information you share using pictures or timelines.

❏ Take notes during your discussion.

❏ Ask and respond to questions as needed.

 Go to **Writing Arguments: Building Effective Support** in the **Writing Studio** help with your analysis.

Go to the **Speaking and Listening Studio** for help with collaborative discussions.

## RESPOND TO THE ESSENTIAL QUESTION

  What do we need in order to feel free?

**Gather Information**  Review your annotations and notes on Gandhi's letter and highlight those that help you answer the Essential Question. Then, add relevant details to your Response Log.

At the end of the unit, use your notes to write an argument.

**ACADEMIC VOCABULARY**

As you write and discuss what you learned from the argument in the letter, be sure to use the Academic Vocabulary words. Check off each of the words that you use.

❏ **comprehensive**

❏ **equivalent**

❏ **incentive**

❏ **innovate**

❏ **subordinate**

**RESPOND**

## WORD BANK
unpalatable

unadulterated

humility

iniquitous

peremptory

Go to the **Vocabulary Studio** for more on denotations and connotations.

## CRITICAL VOCABULARY

**Practice and Apply**  Mark which of the two situations best fits the word's meaning. Discuss with a partner why your choice is the best response.

1. **unpalatable**
   a. a sandwich covered with mold
   b. a sandwich too large to eat

2. **unadulterated**
   a. a sterile beaker of distilled water
   b. a precise mixture of water and iodine

3. **humility**
   a. a race winner pumping his fist in the air
   b. a race winner thanking his coach

4. **iniquitous**
   a. a hungry person stealing an apple
   b. a career criminal robbing people's homes

5. **peremptory**
   a. a passport carried by a traveler to China
   b. a map of Beijing bought by a tourist

## VOCABULARY STRATEGY:
### Denotations and Connotations

To persuade his audience, Gandhi uses words with strong **connotations**, or associated meanings and emotions. For example, he uses the Critical Vocabulary word *iniquitous*, which has a negative connotation of something that is not only wrong but also immoral. How would the meaning of the sentence change if the word *unjust* was used instead? *Unjust* has a **denotation**, or dictionary meaning, similar to that of *iniquitous*, but it carries a less immoral connotation.

**Practice and Apply**  Analyze the nuances presented by each pair of words with similar denotations. Note that the boldfaced words are from the letter. Use each word in a sentence, and then explain the connotation of each word.

1. feared/**dreaded** (paragraph 1)

_____

2. unpleasant/**unpalatable** (paragraph 2)

_____

3. silent/**dumb** (paragraph 4)

_____

4. weakened/**degraded** (paragraph 5)

_____

5. hunger/**starvation** (paragraph 6)

_____

6. wrong/**sinful** (paragraph 6)

_____

## LANGUAGE CONVENTIONS
### Active and Passive Voice

The subject of a sentence may either perform or receive the action expressed in a verb. In **active voice,** which is the more commonly used of the two voices, the subject of the sentence performs the action. In "Letter to Viceroy, Lord Irwin," Gandhi uses the active voice to express the action taken by the subject, British rule ("It"):

> **It has reduced us politically to serfdom.**

The active voice makes clear Gandhi's belief that British rule has actively taken away the rights of the Indian people.

Sometimes, a writer may choose passive voice, in which the subject receives the action. A form of *be* (*am, is, are, was, were*) and a past participle of the verb form passive voice. Here, the subject ("we") does not perform the action stated in the verb:

> **Lacking inward strength, we have been reduced . . . to a state bordering on cowardly helplessness.**

Gandhi's use of the passive voice emphasizes that the Indian people are being acted upon, rather than being able to take action themselves.

Notice that even though the main verb in these two sentences is the same, the voice is different because of the helping verbs used.

**Practice and Apply** Identify each sentence as active or passive voice. Then, rewrite each sentence using the other voice, and evaluate the effect of each version.

1. Great Britain would defend her Indian commerce and interest by all the forces at her command.

   _____

   _____

2. The same weapon was employed by me.

   _____

   _____

3. You are respectfully invited to pave the way for an immediate removal of those evils.

   _____

   _____

DOCUMENTARY FILM

*from*

# GANDHI: THE RISE TO FAME

by **BBC**

page 299

## COMPARE ACCOUNTS

Now that you've read "Letter to Viceroy, Lord Irwin," view an excerpt from the documentary film "Gandhi: The Rise to Fame." As you watch, think about how the clip relates to the concerns Gandhi stated in his letter as well as new information that you learn about him. After viewing, you will collaborate with a small group on a final project that involves an analysis of the text and the film.

 **ESSENTIAL QUESTION:**

What do we need in order to feel free?

LETTER

*from*

# LETTER TO VICEROY, LORD IRWIN

by **Mohandas K. Gandhi**

pages 287–291

# *from* **Gandhi: The Rise to Fame**

## QUICK START

A small action by one person can change history. We can learn about the action if at least one witness tells or shows others what happened. Why is it important for a witness to be reliable and accurate? How can technology be both a reliable and unreliable witness? Discuss with a partner.

## ANALYZE MOTIVES

Filmmakers create documentaries on a wide variety of subjects for different **motives**, or purposes. Here are a few examples:

| TYPE OF DOCUMENTARY | POSSIBLE SUBJECT | MAIN PURPOSE |
|---|---|---|
| music | a concert performance | to entertain |
| history | an event or person's life | to inform |
| social issue | a current problem | to persuade |
| nature or science | animal behavior | to inform |

Documentaries may have more than one purpose, depending on how the filmmakers' viewpoints and motives influence their choice of content and narration. This documentary centers on information about a historical figure. Viewers can examine the details provided for clues that reveal the filmmakers' motives, particularly those that show a positive or negative perspective on the subject.

Use the chart below to note a brief description of clues you see or hear in the film that help you determine the purpose and motive of the documentary.

| CLUE | POSITIVE OR NEGATIVE? | MOTIVE OR PURPOSE |
|---|---|---|
|  |  |  |
|  |  |  |
|  |  |  |
|  |  |  |

**GENRE ELEMENTS: DOCUMENTARY FILM**

- has an on-screen or voiceover narrator who provides context
- includes interviews with key people, experts, or eyewitnesses
- includes location shots of places discussed
- may use music and sound to enhance the message
- features archival film footage and/or photos of historical events

## ANALYZE MEDIA TECHNIQUES

Documentary filmmakers use techniques such as these to present their topics:

**Narration** is the commentary spoken by a narrator to explain, inform, and offer opinions to the audience from the filmmaker about the subject.

**Voiceover** is the narrator speaking while the film shows people, locations, or events.

**Interviews** may show the narrator speaking with and asking questions of people who are experts on the subject, or who were a part of, knew, or were influenced by a historical event or person.

**Juxtaposition** is the close placement of two images or scenes in order to compare and contrast or show a relationship. In a historical documentary, archival photos and film clips of people and places from the past may be juxtaposed with current photos and film of where events occurred.

**Music and sound** can be used to create drama, to appeal to emotions, and to enhance the realism of a place or the description of an event.

As you view the clip from *Gandhi: The Rise to Fame*, watch for uses of media techniques. Use the following chart to list these techniques and note your ideas about how they helped to inform or persuade you as the audience.

| MEDIA TECHNIQUE | EFFECT OF TECHNIQUE |
|---|---|
|  |  |
|  |  |
|  |  |
|  |  |
|  |  |

## BACKGROUND

*In 2009, the British Broadcasting Corporation (BBC) aired a three-part documentary series on the life and legacy of Mohandas Gandhi. In it, British-born journalist Mishal Husain retraces Gandhi's steps, interviews those who knew him personally, and provides context for historical footage and photos. Husain's heritage is Pakistani, but her grandfather served in the Indian army before partition, the division of the former British colony into the independent nations of India and Pakistan.*

## PREPARE TO COMPARE

*As you view the film, keep Gandhi's argument in mind. Write down any questions you generate during viewing.*

To view the video, log in online and select **"from GANDHI: THE RISE TO FAME"** from the unit menu.

As needed, pause the video to make notes about how the filmmaker and narrator tell about Gandhi and the Salt March. Replay or rewind so that you can clarify anything you do not understand.

**RESPOND**

## ANALYZE MEDIA

Support your responses with evidence from the video.  📓 NOTEBOOK

1. **Summarize**  At what point in history does the film clip begin? How does the narrator provide context?

2. **Interpret**  What is the effect of the filmmakers' use of past and present juxtapositions?

3. **Analyze**  There are no videos of the protest at the commercial salt works. To portray what happened, the video uses a combination of documentary techniques. What are these techniques? What effect do they have?

4. **Infer**  Why does the former companion of Gandhi tell the schoolchildren what Gandhi wrote to him in a book? How does this use of Gandhi's words enhance the documentary?

5. **Evaluate**  Why might this media piece have been created? What strategies were used in the video to advance its purpose? Complete the chart below.

| APPROACH | EXAMPLE | INTENT OR EFFECT |
|---|---|---|
| facts | | |
| opinions | | |
| scenes | | |
| interviews | | |

## RESEARCH

Find a brief online biography of Gandhi to provide context for the video clip. Note any information that conflicts with the video's view of Gandhi.

| VIDEO | ONLINE BIOGRAPHY |
|---|---|
| | |
| | |

**Extend**  How does the online biography complement the viewpoint expressed in the documentary?

**RESEARCH TIP**
It's always easier to begin a research project by creating a research plan. First, identify exactly what you want to learn. Then, create a step-by-step plan to guide your search.

## CREATE AND PRESENT

**Create a Multimodal Presentation** The news reports of Gandhi's Salt March and the protests at the salt works had a worldwide effect on perceptions of British rule in India. Write and create a brief multimodal presentation that illustrates how media coverage affects our perceptions of a particular event.

❏ Choose a specific event to feature in your presentation. Gather research on how the media covered this event. What was focused on in a limited time or space? How might this choice have affected audience perceptions of the event? How were these perceptions reflected in follow-up reports?

❏ Plan to use the most effective communication modes and technology, including written, oral, visual, and audio. You might do a podcast or photo essay. You could also include music, sound, recordings, and film clips.

❏ Outline your presentation and then write a narrative that describes the event and explains your perceptions of what happened.

**Present and Lead a Discussion** With a small group, lead a discussion of impressions and reactions to your presentation.

❏ Before you begin, list questions, such as the following: What was your perception of the event? How did the choice of media affect your perception? What might have been inadequately addressed by the choice of media? How would different coverage change your perceptions? Where do you see evidence of the viewpoint of a reporter or filmmaker?

❏ Restate or replay parts of your presentation to aid in the discussion. Make sure that everyone in the group has an opportunity to express ideas, opinions, and questions.

> Go to the **Speaking and Listening Studio** for help using media in a presentation.

## RESPOND TO THE ESSENTIAL QUESTION

**?** What do we need in order to feel free?

**Gather Information** Review your annotations and notes on the excerpt from *Gandhi: The Rise to Fame*. Think about Gandhi's methods and accomplishments. Then, add relevant details to your Response Log.

At the end of the unit, use your notes to write an argument.

**UNIT 4 RESPONSE LOG**

Use this Response Log to record your ideas about how each of the texts in Unit 4 relates to or comments on the **Essential Question**

**7 Essential Question:** What do we need in order to feel free?

| Letter from Birmingham Jail | |
| Elsewhere | |
| The Hawk Can Soar | |
| The Briefcase | |
| from Letter to Viceroy, Lord Irwin | |
| from Gandhi The Rise to Fame | |

R4 Student Resources

**ACADEMIC VOCABULARY**

As you write and discuss what you learned about Gandhi, be sure to use the Academic Vocabulary words. Check off each of the words that you use.

❏ **comprehensive**

❏ **equivalent**

❏ **incentive**

❏ **innovate**

❏ **subordinate**

*from* **LETTER TO
VICEROY, LORD IRWIN**
Letter by Mohandas K. Gandhi

*from* **GANDHI: THE
RISE TO FAME**
Documentary Film by BBC

# Collaborate & Compare

## COMPARE ACCOUNTS

When you compare two or more perspectives of the same material in different formats or genres, you **synthesize** the information, making connections and building on key ideas. Sometimes you can get a more thorough understanding of the topic by experiencing the material in different formats. This especially is true for historical topics when you can read, view, or hear both a primary source and a secondary source, such as a letter and a film about the topic.

In a small group, complete the Venn diagram to show some similarities and differences in the information, arguments, ideas, and points of view presented in the letter and the film. One example is completed for you.

Letter · Both · Film

Gandhi planning
Salt March

## ANALYZE THE ACCOUNTS

Discuss these questions in your group.

1. **Interpret** Describe the tone and word choice of the author and narrator, providing examples from the letter and film. What can you infer from those word choices about the purposes of each account?

2. **Evaluate** In the documentary, the history of Gandhi's rise to fame is documented in chronological order with the use of present-day narration and commentary interspersed with some supporting archival images. Why is this an effective way to organize a biography but not an argument, as was presented in the letter?

3. **Compare** What are some of the strengths and weaknesses of both the letter and the film?

4. **Synthesize** How do the film and letter work together to create a fuller picture of Gandhi than either could alone?

## COMPARE AND DEBATE

Now, your group can continue exploring the ideas in these different formats by participating in a debate to answer this question: Which format communicates Gandhi's ideas more effectively, the letter or the film?

Follow these steps:

Go to the **Speaking and Listening Studio** to find more information on tracing a speaker's argument.

1. **Form teams** of two to three students each with half defending the letter as more effective and half defending the film clip.

2. **Gather evidence** from both the letter and the film to support your team's position. Prepare a chart such as the following to help you gather evidence.

| Key Idea | How Best To Communicate Idea | Why This Medium is Effective | Why Other Medium is Less Effective |
|---|---|---|---|
|  |  |  |  |

3. **Follow the rules** of debating:
   - ❑ Appoint a **moderator** to present the topic and goals of the debate, keep track of the time, keep the debate moving, and introduce and thank the participants.
   - ❑ As a participant, anticipate possible **opposing claims**. Include evidence in your preparation to counter those claims.
   - ❑ Follow the **moderator's instructions** on whose turn it is to speak and how much time each speaker has.
   - ❑ Maintain a **respectful presentation** for the exchange of ideas.

4. **Write a brief evaluation** of which side presented a more compelling argument.

# Reader's Choice

**? ESSENTIAL
QUESTION:**

What do we
need in order to
feel free?

**Setting a Purpose**  Select one or more of these options from your eBook to
continue your exploration of the Essential Question.

- Read the descriptions to see which text grabs your interest.

- Think about which genres you enjoy reading.

## Notice & Note

In this unit, you practiced asking a **Big Question** and noticing and noting two
signposts: **Extreme or Absolute Language** and **Quoted Words.** As you read
independently, these signposts and others will aid your understanding. Below
are the anchor questions to ask when you read literature and nonfiction.

| Reading Literature: Stories, Poems, and Plays | | |
|---|---|---|
| **Signpost** | **Anchor Question** | **Lesson** |
| **Contrasts and Contradictions** | Why did the character act that way? | p. 145 |
| **Aha Moment** | How might this change things? | p. 394 |
| **Tough Questions** | What does this make me wonder about? | p. 2 |
| **Words of the Wiser** | What's the lesson for the character? | p. 3 |
| **Again and Again** | Why might the author keep bringing this up? | p. 145 |
| **Memory Moment** | Why is this memory important? | p. 3 |

| Reading Nonfiction: Essays, Articles, and Arguments | | |
|---|---|---|
| **Signpost** | **Anchor Question** | **Lesson** |
| **Big Questions** | What surprised me?<br>What did the author think I already knew?<br>What challenged, changed, or confirmed what I already knew? | p. 220<br>p. 319<br>p. 74 |
| **Contrasts and Contradictions** | What is the difference, and why does it matter? | p. 318 |
| **Extreme or Absolute Language** | Why did the author use this language? | p. 221 |
| **Numbers and Stats** | Why did the author use these numbers or amounts? | p. 75 |
| **Quoted Words** | Why was this person quoted or cited, and what did this add? | p. 221 |
| **Word Gaps** | Do I know this word from someplace else?<br>Does it seem like technical talk for this topic?<br>Do clues in the sentence help me understand the word? | p. 75 |

You can preview these texts in Unit 4 of your eBook.

Then, check off the text or texts that you select to read on your own.

**SPEECH**

*from* **Speech at the March on Washington**
Josephine Baker

*An international musical and political icon speaks about civil rights at the 1963 March on Washington.*

**SHORT STORY**

**The Book of the Dead**
Edwidge Danticat

*A young Haitian-American sculptor must come to terms with her father's troubled past.*

**POEM**

**Cloudy Day**
Jimmy Santiago Baca

*A poet explores his ability to survive and endure his time in prison.*

**HISTORY**

*from* **Crispus Attucks**
Kareem Abdul-Jabbar

*Learn the story of Crispus Attucks, an African American remembered as the first American to die in the Revolutionary War.*

**Collaborate and Share**    Discuss with a partner what you learned from at least one of your independent readings.

- Give a brief synopsis or summary of the text.
- Describe any signposts that you noticed in the text and explain what they revealed to you.
- Describe what you most enjoyed or found most challenging about the text. Give specific examples.
- Decide whether you would recommend the text to others. Why or why not?

Go to the **Reading Studio** for more resources on **Notice & Note.**

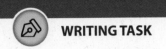 

# Write an Argument

Go to the **Writing Studio** for help writing an argument.

This unit explores the idea of freedom, what it means, and what people have done to become free. For this writing task, you will write an argument that reveals what freedom means to you. For an example of a well-written argumentative text you can use as a mentor text, review Gandhi's "Letter to Viceroy, Lord Irwin" or King's "Letter from Birmingham Jail."

As you write your argument, you will want to look at the notes you made in your Response Log after reading the texts in this unit.

## Writing Prompt

**Read** the information in the box below.

*This is the topic or context for your argument.*

> **Freedom means different things to different people.**

**Think** carefully about the following question.

*This is the Essential Question of the unit. Circle the most important words in the question.*

> **What do we need in order to feel free?**

**Write** an argument about what freedom means to you.

*Now mark the words that identify exactly what you are supposed to write.*

Be sure to—

❑ make a clear, specific claim

❑ develop the claim with valid reasons and relevant evidence

❑ anticipate and address counterclaims, or opposing arguments, by providing counterarguments

*Review these points as you write and again when you finish. Make any needed changes.*

❑ use transitions to link reasons and evidence to the claim

❑ maintain a formal tone through the use of standard English

❑ conclude by effectively summarizing the argument and leaving readers with a thought-provoking idea

# ① Plan

Writing an argument depends on good planning. Think about the selections you've read in this unit and the questions they raise about political, physical, and emotional freedom. Does the meaning of freedom vary from person to person and culture to culture, or is it more universal? Use the word web below to help you explore your thoughts and feelings about freedom. Include ideas from the unit texts.

You also need to think about what you hope to achieve in your argument and for whom you are writing—your purpose and your audience.

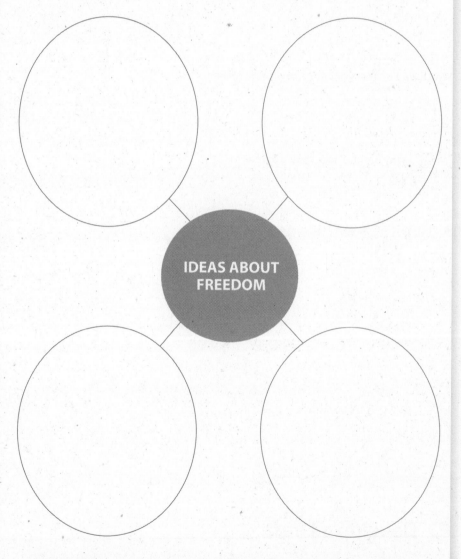

IDEAS ABOUT FREEDOM

**Background Reading** Review the notes you have taken in your Response Log after reading the texts in this unit. These texts provide background reading that will help you think about what you want to say in your argument.

Go to **Writing Arguments: What Is a Claim?** for help planning your argument.

## Notice & Note

### From Reading to Writing

As you plan your argument, apply what you've learned about signposts to your own writing. Think about how you can incorporate **Quoted Words** into your argument.

Go to the **Reading Studio** for more resources on Notice & Note.

Use the notes from your Response Log as you plan your argument.

Go to **Writing Arguments: Building Effective Support** for help developing and organizing your ideas.

**Organize Your Ideas**  Use the chart below to write an outline with a clear thesis statement. Your thesis should express the claim you want to support. Acknowledge a counterclaim, or opposing view, that you will address by providing a counterargument. Then, clearly organize your reasons and relevant evidence, progressing logically from one idea to the next. Conduct more research to find additional details and examples you need. Write a conclusion that follows logically from the information you've presented.

| ARGUMENT: THE NATURE OF FREEDOM |
| --- |
| **Thesis with Claim:** |
| **Why the audience might not agree (counterclaim):** |
| **Why the audience should agree:** |

| Reason 1 | Reason 2 | Reason 3 |
| --- | --- | --- |
| Evidence | Evidence | Evidence |

| Conclusion: |
| --- |

You might prefer to draft your essay online.

## ② Develop a Draft

Once you have completed your planning activities, you can begin drafting your argument. Use your outline or graphic organizer to keep your argument on track. Refer to any notes you took as you studied the texts in the collection so that you can use evidence from multiple texts. Use word processing software or an online writing app to make it easier to make changes or move sentences around later when you are ready to revise your first draft.

## Use the Mentor Text

### ▶ Genre Characteristics

In any argument, it's crucial to write a clear thesis statement with your claim. If your reader doesn't understand the core of your argument, the rest of what you write will not fully make sense, no matter how well you write it. Notice how Gandhi states his claim in the first paragraph of "Letter to Viceroy, Lord Irwin."

> *Whilst therefore I hold the British rule to be a curse, I do not intend to harm a single Englishman or any legitimate interest he may have in India.*

Gandhi makes a clear, strong statement by stating that British rule is a curse.

**Apply What You've Learned** State your claim clearly in the first paragraph of your argument.

### ▶ Author's Craft

When pressing home an argument, authors frequently use repetition to make their points more effectively. Gandhi uses the repetition of grammatical structure, or parallel structure, when he gives evidence for why he considers British rule over India a curse.

> It has impoverished the dumb millions by a system of progressive exploitation and by a ruinously expensive military and civil administration which the country can never afford.
>
> It has reduced us politically to serfdom. It has sapped the foundations of our culture, and, by the policy of disarmament, it has degraded us spiritually.

The repetition of the words "It has . . ." indicates three points he is making.

**Apply What You've Learned** When you present evidence for your claim, use words effectively as well as clearly.

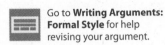

Go to **Writing Arguments: Formal Style** for help revising your argument.

## ③ Revise

**On Your Own** When you revise your draft, check for clear organization and the inclusion of all elements of your argument. As you revise, think about whether you have achieved your purpose for your intended audience. The Revision Guide will help you focus on specific elements to make your writing stronger.

| REVISION GUIDE | | |
|---|---|---|
| **Ask Yourself** | **Tips** | **Revision Techniques** |
| 1. Does the introduction state a clear claim? | **Underline** the claim. | **Add** a claim or **revise** the claim to make it clearer. |
| 2. Does the argument address one or more counterclaims? | **Mark** both the counterclaim and the response to it. | **Add** a counterclaim and counterargument that addresses the counterclaim. |
| 3. Are reasons and evidence presented in a logical, organized way? | **Mark** each important idea and the supporting reasons or evidence. | **Reorganize** ideas to make the structure more logical. |
| 4. Are appropriate and varied transitions used to link ideas? | **Note** transitions that move ideas smoothly from paragraph to paragraph. | **Add** transition words and phrases to provide continuity. |
| 5. Does the conclusion give the reader something to think about? | **Underline** the concluding insight offered to readers. | **Add** a final, thought-provoking statement about freedom. |
| 6. Is an appropriately formal tone used throughout the argument? | **Highlight** each academic word or phrase that contributes to a formal tone. | **Replace** informal word choices and sentence structures as needed. |

**ACADEMIC VOCABULARY**
As you conduct your peer review, try to use these words.

❏ comprehensive
❏ equivalent
❏ incentive
❏ innovate
❏ subordinate

**With a Partner** After you have worked through the Revision Guide on your own, exchange papers with a partner. Evaluate each other's drafts in a peer review, using the chart to guide you. Give your partner specific suggestions for improving clarity, organization, and the development of ideas.

When receiving feedback from your partner, listen attentively and ask questions to make sure you fully understand the revision suggestions.

##  Edit

After you have drafted and revised your argument, there is one final step before you're ready to publish. In the editing process, you will make sure that your writing meets the conventions of grammar, spelling, and word usage.

### Language Conventions

**Correct Writing Conventions**  One definition of a **convention** is a way of doing things that most people accept. In a sense, writing is all about conventions. We agree to spell words in a certain way, using certain patterns of letters to stand for the sounds we use. We also agree to use a period to show that we've finished a sentence and quotation marks to indicate that we are using someone else's words.

All of these conventions make text easier to read. Ignoring the conventions of grammar, spelling, punctuation, and capitalization can indicate either that you don't care about what you're communicating or that you did not spend enough time on your writing. Either way, you are signaling to the reader that they don't need to take your argument seriously.

Finally, while it may be tempting to set some words in all capital letters for emphasis when you are writing an argument, departing from this convention tells readers that they can't trust what you're saying. Reserve capital letters for proper nouns, initials, and the beginnings of sentences, and let your logical and well-crafted argument speak for itself.

> **!** Go to the **Grammar Studio** to learn more about conventions of capitalization, punctuation, and spelling.

## ⑤ Publish

When you choose a way to share your argument, consider who your audience is and what method of publication they would find understandable, clear, and convincing. Consider these options:

- Deliver your argument as an oral presentation.
- Use online software to prepare a slide show presentation.
- Present your argument as a letter to the editor. Submit it to your school or community newspaper or an online magazine.

**WRITING TASK**

Use the scoring guide to evaluate your argument.

| | Organization/Progression | Development of Ideas | Use of Language and Conventions |
|---|---|---|---|
| **WRITING TASK SCORING GUIDE: ARGUMENT** | | | |
| **4** | • The organization is effective and appropriate to the purpose.<br>• All ideas center on a specific claim.<br>• Transitions clearly show the relationships among ideas. | • The introduction catches the reader's attention and clearly states the claim.<br>• Reasons are compelling and supported by evidence including quotations and facts.<br>• A counterclaim is effectively presented and addressed.<br>• The conclusion synthesizes the ideas, effectively summarizes the argument, and provides a thought-provoking insight. | • Language and word choice is purposeful and precise.<br>• The style is appropriately formal.<br>• Spelling, capitalization, and punctuation are correct.<br>• Grammar and usage are correct. |
| **3** | • The organization is, for the most part, effective and appropriate to the purpose.<br>• Most ideas are focused on the claim.<br>• A few more transitions are needed to show the relationship among ideas. | • The introduction could be more engaging. The claim is stated.<br>• Appropriate reasons for the claim are supported by relevant evidence.<br>• A counterclaim is presented and addressed.<br>• The conclusion summarizes the argument effectively. | • Language is for the most part specific and clear.<br>• The style is generally formal.<br>• Minor spelling, capitalization, and punctuation mistakes do not interfere with the message.<br>• Some grammar and usage errors occur but do not cause confusion. |
| **2** | • The organization is evident but is not always appropriate to the purpose.<br>• Only some ideas are focused on the claim presented in the thesis.<br>• Relationships among ideas are sometimes unclear. | • The introduction is not engaging. A vague claim is stated.<br>• One or more reasons may be provided but lack sufficient evidence.<br>• A counterclaim may be hinted at or not adequately addressed.<br>• The conclusion merely restates the claim. | • Language is somewhat vague and unclear.<br>• The style is often informal.<br>• Spelling, capitalization, and punctuation are often incorrect.<br>• Several errors in grammar and usage appear. |
| **1** | • The organization is not apparent.<br>• Ideas are often tangential to a claim.<br>• No transitions are used, making the argument difficult to understand. | • The introduction is missing or fails to make a claim.<br>• Reasons are irrelevant or unsupported by evidence.<br>• A counterclaim is either absent or not addressed.<br>• The conclusion is missing. | • The style of language is inappropriate for the text.<br>• Many spelling, capitalization, and punctuation errors make reading difficult.<br>• Grammatical and usage errors cause significant confusion. |

# Deliver an Argument

You will now prepare to deliver your argument as an oral presentation to your classmates. You also will listen to your classmates' arguments, ask questions to better understand their ideas, and help them improve their presentations.

Go to **Giving a Presentation** in the **Speaking and Listening Studio** to learn more.

## 1 Adapt Your Argument for Presentation

Review your argument, and use the chart below to guide your presentation.

| DELIVERING AN ARGUMENT PLANNING CHART | | |
|---|---|---|
| **Title and Introductory Paragraph** | How can you revise your introduction to capture listeners' attention and make a powerful statement of your claim? | |
| **Audience** | What information will your audience already know about your claim? What counterclaims might they make? How will you address those counterclaims? | |
| **Effective Language and Organization** | Which parts of your argument should be simplified? Where can you add transitions to clarify relationships among ideas? How can you make your conclusion stronger? | |
| **Delivery** | What words or ideas might you emphasize with your voice or gestures to make your argument more convincing? | |

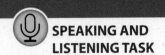

As you work to improve your own delivery and that of your classmates, follow these discussion rules:

❏ listen attentively

❏ be respectful and considerate of other students' feelings

❏ stay focused on one student's work at a time

❏ raise questions and counterarguments that might not have occurred to the author

❏ be clear and specific in your suggestions for improvement

## ② Practice with a Partner or Group

When you have adapted your argument, practice with a partner or group to improve your delivery.

### Practice Effective Verbal Techniques

❏ **Enunciation.** Consider replacing words that you stumble over if you can find effective alternatives. Rearrange sentences that are not as understandable in speech as in writing.

❏ **Voice Modulation and Pitch** Use your voice to express enthusiasm, emphasis, or emotion.

❏ **Speaking Rate** Adjust your speaking rate to the points in your argument. Pause briefly at points you want your audience to ponder or consider carefully.

❏ **Volume** Adjust your volume to the size of the room and the distance of the audience.

### Practice Effective Nonverbal Techniques

❏ **Eye Contact** Try to make eye contact with everyone in your audience at least once.

❏ **Facial Expression** Use facial expressions as well as your words and your voice to show your audience your feelings about various points of your argument.

❏ **Gestures** Don't force gestures, but add them if they improve meaning and interest.

### Provide and Consider Advice for Improvement

**As a listener,** pay close attention to how effectively each speaker expresses and supports a point of view. Take notes about ways that presenters can improve their deliveries and more effectively use verbal and nonverbal techniques. Paraphrase and summarize each presenter's key ideas and main points to confirm your understanding, and ask questions to clarify any confusing ideas.

**As a presenter,** listen closely to questions and consider ways to revise your delivery to make sure your points are clear and logically sequenced. Remember to ask for suggestions about how you might make your delivery more interesting.

## ③ Deliver Your Argument

Use the advice you received during practice to make final changes to your argument delivery. Then, using effective verbal and nonverbal techniques, present your argument to your classmates.

# Reflect on the Unit

In this writing task, you wrote about your idea of the meaning of freedom in the light of ideas and insights from the readings in this unit. Now is a good time to reflect on what you have learned.

## Reflect on the Essential Question

- What do we need in order to feel free? How has your answer to this question changed since you first considered it when you started this unit?

- What are some examples from the texts you've read that show what freedom means to people?

## Reflect on Your Reading

- Which selections were the most interesting or surprising to you?

- From which selection did you learn the most about the nature of freedom?

## Reflect on the Writing Task

- What difficulties did you encounter while working on your argument? How might you avoid them next time?

- What part of the argument was the easiest and what part was the hardest to write? Why?

- What improvements did you make to your argument as you were revising?

**UNIT 4 SELECTIONS**
- "Letter from Birmingham Jail"
- "Elsewhere"
- "The Hawk Can Soar"
- "The Briefcase"
- *from* "Letter to Viceroy, Lord Irwin"
- from *Gandhi: The Rise to Fame*

# RESPONSES TO CHANGE

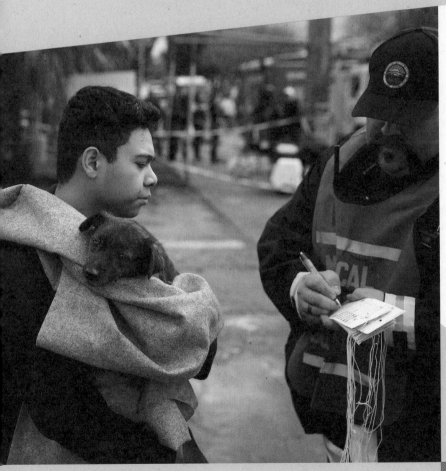

? **ESSENTIAL QUESTION:**

How do changes around us reveal who we are?

"When the wind of change blows, some build walls while others build windmills."

Chinese Proverb

## ACADEMIC VOCABULARY

Academic Vocabulary words are words you use when you discuss and write about texts. In this unit you will practice and learn five words.

☑ **abstract**    ❑ **evolve**    ❑ **explicit**    ❑ **facilitate**    ❑ **infer**

Study the Word Network to learn more about the word **abstract.**

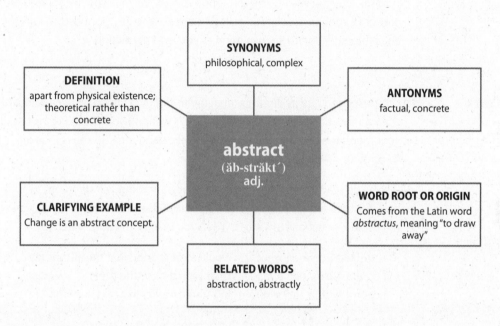

**SYNONYMS**
philosophical, complex

**DEFINITION**
apart from physical existence; theoretical rather than concrete

**ANTONYMS**
factual, concrete

**abstract**
(ăb-străkt´)
adj.

**CLARIFYING EXAMPLE**
Change is an abstract concept.

**WORD ROOT OR ORIGIN**
Comes from the Latin word *abstractus*, meaning "to draw away"

**RELATED WORDS**
abstraction, abstractly

**Write and Discuss** Discuss the completed Word Network with a partner, making sure to talk through all of the boxes until you both understand the word, its synonyms, antonyms, and related forms. Then, fill out Word Networks for the remaining four words. Use a dictionary or online resource to help you complete the activity.

*Go online to access the Word Networks.*

## RESPOND TO THE ESSENTIAL QUESTION

In this unit, you will explore how changes reveal who people really are. As you read, you will revisit the **Essential Question** and gather your ideas about it in the **Response Log** that appears on page R5. At the end of the unit, you will have the opportunity to write a **research report** about how people reveal who they are through their responses to changes around them. Filling out the Response Log will help you prepare for this writing task.

*You can also go online to access the Response Log.*

**UNIT 5
RESPONSE LOG**

Use this Response Log to record your ideas about how each of the texts in Unit 5 relates to or comments on the **Essential Question.**

**? Essential Question:**
How do changes around us reveal who we are?

| | |
|---|---|
| *from* Total Eclipse | |
| *from* The Fever | |
| A Sound of Thunder | |
| 5 P.M., Tuesday, August 23, 2005 | |
| *from* Rivers and Tides | |
| Sonnets to Orpheus, Part Two, XII | |

# Notice & Note

## *from* TOTAL ECLIPSE

You are about to read an excerpt from the literary nonfiction essay "Total Eclipse." In it you will encounter signposts that will give you insight into the author's experience of a total eclipse. Here are two key signposts to look for and a big question to keep in mind as you read nonfiction.

For more information on these and other signposts to Notice & Note, visit the **Reading Studio**.

When you see phrases like these, pause to see if it's a **Contrasts and Contradictions** signpost:

"On the other hand, . . ."

"However, . . ."

"Instead, . . ."

"You might be surprised to learn . . ."

**Contrasts and Contradictions** Imagine trying to catch up with a friend after a big game, when everyone in the crowd is wearing your team's color. Luckily, your friend is wearing her lucky psychedelic bandanna, so she stands out in the crowd.

When you read, sometimes the most important thing will stand out as well. Authors set up **Contrasts and Contradictions** to make sure you'll pay attention when it matters most. When you read nonfiction, watch for:

- a contrast between what you would expect and what the author says
- a contrast between two ideas or approaches to the topic
- a contradiction about something stated earlier in a text

Here is how a student marked this signpost in "Total Eclipse":

**Anchor Question**
When you notice this signpost, ask: What is the difference, and why does it matter?

> 1 . . . Usually it is a bit of a trick to keep your knowledge from blinding you. But during an eclipse it is easy. What you see is much more convincing than any wild-eyed theory you may know.

| What two ideas does the author contrast? | How we usually think about things and how that way of thinking changes during an eclipse. |
|---|---|
| What is the effect of this contrast? | It emphasizes how the experience of viewing a total eclipse is completely different from what you would expect. |

**Extreme or Absolute Language**  Remember in elementary school, when an exclamation like "I love that shirt!" was met with a sarcastic "Then why don't you marry it?" Extreme language should be met with that kind of skepticism.

Nonfiction authors share information or real experiences. So when an author seems to exaggerate, it gets your attention. **Extreme or Absolute Language** may emphasize what matters to the author or reveal a bias about the topic.

Here is how a student marked Extreme or Absolute Language in the essay:

> 2    You may read that the moon has something to do with eclipses. I have <u>never</u> seen the moon yet. <u>You do not see the moon</u>. So near the sun, it is as <u>completely invisible</u> as the stars are by day….

When you encounter words and phrases like these, pause to see if it's an **Extreme or Absolute Language** signpost:

"Everyone knows that . . ."

*never* or *always*

words ending in *-est*

"We must all agree . . ."

**Anchor Question**
When you notice this signpost, ask: Why did the author use this language?

| What does the author describe with extreme or absolute language? | She describes the moon as completely invisible, even though it is the reason for the eclipse. |
|---|---|
| What effect does extreme or absolute language have on your understanding? | It makes it clear that even though I would expect to see the moon during an eclipse, there is no way that I would. |

**Big Questions**  Maybe you've had the experience of a friend telling you a story that involves people you don't know. If your friend assumes you know these people, the story might make no sense at all to you.

You might have the same experience reading nonfiction. An author may not be able to provide *all* of the background knowledge you might need to understand the topic in one essay. Instead, he or she must decide what information it's safe to assume that you already know. When you read nonfiction, ask yourself: *What did the author think I already knew?*

Here is how a student might annotate with this **Big Question** in mind:

> 1    What you see in an eclipse is <u>entirely different from what you know</u>. It is especially <u>different for those of us whose grasp of astronomy is so frail</u> that, given a flashlight, a grapefruit, two oranges, and 15 years, we still could not figure out which way to set the clocks for daylight saving time. . . .

| What does the author think I already know? | She thinks I might know some basic astronomy but not much. |
|---|---|
| How does this fit with what I actually know, and how does this affect my reading? | Her example is funny because it shows no understanding at all; I know more than that, but this introduction makes the scientific information friendly. |

# *from* TOTAL ECLIPSE

Essay by **Annie Dillard**

**?** *ESSENTIAL QUESTION:*

How do changes around us reveal who we are?

## QUICK START

Events of nature can often leave us questioning reality. How might a powerful storm or some rare phenomenon such as hail leave you disoriented? Discuss your reaction with the class.

## ANALYZE LITERARY NONFICTION

**Literary nonfiction** shares factual information, ideas, or experiences using literary techniques, such as figurative language and narration. The author of literary fiction has a specific purpose, audience, and message in mind. Literary nonfiction can include essays like Annie Dillard's as well as autobiographies, biographies, and speeches. How can you tell the difference between literary nonfiction and other informational texts?

- Look for artistic descriptions that go beyond simple explanation.

- Take notice of how the author interprets what he or she is explaining or describing. Watch for evidence presented in a lyrical or poetic manner.

- Be aware of how the author becomes involved with the topic or the subject of their reporting. Often the author will describe his or her reactions to events.

## ANALYZE STYLE

**Style** is the particular way literature is written to produce a desired effect. Style is not just *what* is said but *how* it is said. Here are some of the key elements that contribute to an author's style:

| ELEMENT | EXAMPLE FROM TEXT | EFFECT |
|---|---|---|
| word choice | **Only the thin river held a trickle of sun.** | expresses how unsubstantial this usually strong force of nature is |
| tone | **What you see is much more convincing than any wild-eyed theory you may know.** | friendly and informal; seems to be chatting directly with the reader |
| sentence structure | **It gets narrower and narrower, as the waning moon does, and, like the ordinary moon, it travels alone in the simple sky.** | long and meandering sentence mirrors the slow process of the moon across the sun's face and creates a pensive mood |

As you read, pay attention to how Annie Dillard uses style to recreate the effect of experiencing the eclipse.

**GENRE ELEMENTS: LITERARY NONFICTION**

- shares factual information, ideas, or experiences
- develops a key insight about the topic that goes beyond the facts
- uses literary techniques such as figurative language and narration
- reflects a personal involvement in the topic

## CRITICAL VOCABULARY

| wane | saturate | hue | recede |
|------|----------|-----|--------|

To see how many Critical Vocabulary words you already know, use them to complete the sentences.

1. As the falling tide began to _____ , we gathered shells left behind.

2. Water began to _____ the furniture as the flood waters rose.

3. The moon will _____ each month until it temporarily disappears from view.

4. The artist mixed paints until she had the perfect _____ for the sky.

## LANGUAGE CONVENTIONS

**Sentence Variety** Mixing sentence lengths and patterns can engage readers and develop a particular mood or tone. Read this example from the essay:

**What you see in an eclipse is entirely different from what you know. It is especially different for those of us whose grasp of astronomy is so frail that, given a flashlight, a grapefruit, two oranges, and 15 years, we still could not figure out which way to set the clocks for daylight saving time.**

The long, winding second sentence sounds almost like Dillard is thinking aloud about a confusing science demonstration from the past. As you read, notice how she varies sentence lengths to grab your attention and express her ideas.

## ANNOTATION MODEL

**NOTICE & NOTE**

As you read, notice and note the author's use of style and elements of literary nonfiction. In this model, you can see how one reader marked the text.

Stuck up into that unworldly sky was the cone of Mount Adams, and the alpenglow was upon it. The alpenglow is that red light of sunset which holds out on snowy mountaintops long after the valleys and tablelands are dimmed. "Look at Mount Adams," I said, and that was the last sane moment I remember.

    I turned back to the sun. It was going. The sun was going, and the world was wrong. The grasses were wrong; they were platinum. Their every detail of stem, head, and blade shone lightless and artificially distinct as an art photographer's platinum print.

> *Details about the setting create a strange mood*
>
> *Preview of what is to come*
>
> *Repetition of the word "wrong" emphasizes the strangeness of the experience.*

## BACKGROUND

*In a solar eclipse, the moon passes between Earth and the sun. While solar eclipses are not rare, totality (seeing the sun completely covered) can be viewed only from a narrow band on Earth.* **Annie Dillard** *(b. 1945) won the Pulitzer Prize for the book* Pilgrim at Tinker Creek, *which details her extended stay at a cabin while pondering life's big questions. "Total Eclipse," Dillard's first-hand account of a total solar eclipse she witnessed in Washington State in 1979, comes from her essay collection* Teaching a Stone to Talk.

*from*
# TOTAL ECLIPSE
### Essay by Annie Dillard

## SETTING A PURPOSE

*As you read, use Annie Dillard's vivid descriptions and figurative language to develop a mental image of what the experience of viewing a total eclipse would be like.*

1    What you see in an eclipse is entirely different from what you know. It is especially different for those of us whose grasp of astronomy is so frail that, given a flashlight, a grapefruit, two oranges, and 15 years, we still could not figure out which way to set the clocks for daylight saving time. Usually it is a bit of a trick to keep your knowledge from blinding you. But during an eclipse it is easy. What you see is much more convincing than any wild-eyed theory you may know.

2    You may read that the moon has something to do with eclipses. I have never seen the moon yet. You do not see the moon. So near the sun, it is as completely invisible as the stars are by day. What you see before your eyes is the sun going through phases. It gets narrower and narrower, as the **waning** moon does, and, like the ordinary moon, it travels alone in the simple sky. The sky is of course background. It does not appear to eat the

### Notice & Note

You can use the side margins to notice and note signposts as you read.

### EXTREME OR ABSOLUTE LANGUAGE

**Notice & Note:** Mark examples of extreme or absolute language in paragraph 1.

**Analyze:** How do these word choices prepare the reader to learn about the experience of viewing an eclipse?

**wane**
(wān) *v.*
to gradually decrease in size or intensity.

sun; it is far behind the sun. The sun simply shaves away; gradually, you see less sun and more sky.

3    The sky's blue was deepening, but there was no darkness. The sun was a wide crescent, like a segment of tangerine. The wind freshened and blew steadily over the hill. The eastern hill across the highway grew dusky and sharp. The towns and orchards in the valley to the south were dissolving into the blue light. Only the thin river held a trickle of sun.

4    Now the sky to the west deepened to indigo, a color never seen. A dark sky usually loses color. This was a **saturated**, deep indigo, up in the air. Stuck up into that unworldly sky was the cone of Mount Adams,[1] and the alpenglow was upon it. The alpenglow is that red light of sunset which holds out on snowy mountaintops long after the valleys and tablelands are dimmed. "Look at Mount Adams," I said, and that was the last sane moment I remember.

5    I turned back to the sun. It was going. The sun was going, and the world was wrong. The grasses were wrong; they were platinum. Their every detail of stem, head, and blade shone lightless and artificially distinct as an art photographer's platinum print. This color has never been seen on Earth. The **hues** were metallic; their finish was matte. The hillside was a 19th-century tinted photograph from which the tints had

---

[1] **Mount Adams:** a volcano in the Cascades mountain range in southern Washington State.

**saturate**
(săch´ə-rāt) *v.*
to soak with liquid to the point where nothing more can be absorbed.

**hue**
(hyōō) *n.*
a color, shade, or tint.

faded. All the people you see in the photograph, distinct and detailed as their faces look, are now dead. The sky was navy blue. My hands were silver. All the distant hills' grasses were finespun metal which the wind laid down. I was watching a faded color print of a movie filmed in the Middle Ages; I was standing in it, by some mistake. I was standing in a movie of hillside grasses filmed in the Middle Ages. I missed my own century, the people I knew, and the real light of day.

6      I looked at Gary. He was in the film. Everything was lost. He was a platinum print, a dead artist's version of life. I saw on his skull the darkness of night mixed with the colors of day. My mind was going out; my eyes were **receding** the way galaxies recede to the rim of space. Gary was light-years away, gesturing inside a circle of darkness, down the wrong end of a telescope. He smiled as if he saw me; the stringy crinkles around his eyes moved. The sight of him, familiar and wrong, was something I was remembering from centuries hence, from the other side of death: Yes, that is the way he used to look, when we were living. When it was our generation's turn to be alive. I could not hear him; the wind was too loud. Behind him the sun was going. We had all started down a chute of time. At first it was pleasant; now there was no stopping it. Gary was chuting away across space, moving and talking and catching my eye, chuting down the long corridor of separation. The skin on his face moved like thin bronze plating that would peel.

### ANALYZE LITERARY NONFICTION

**Annotate:** Mark imaginative comparisons that appear in paragraph 5.

**Analyze:** Why does the author choose this style to describe what she sees?

**recede**
(rĭ-sēd´) v.
to move back or away from something.

### CONTRASTS AND CONTRADICTIONS

**Notice & Note:** Underline what Gary is doing in paragraph 6, and circle how the author perceives him.

**Infer:** Why is there such a strong contrast between how Gary is acting and how Dillard sees him?

**Mount Adams, Cascade Range, Washington**

7  The grass at our feet was wild barley. It was the wild einkorn wheat which grew on the hilly flanks of the Zagros Mountains, above the Euphrates valley, above the valley of the river we called River. We harvested the grass with stone sickles, I remember. We found the grasses on the hillsides; we built our shelter beside them and cut them down. That is how he used to look then, that one, moving and living and catching my eye, with the sky so dark behind him, and the wind blowing. God save our life.

8  From all the hills came screams. A piece of sky beside the crescent sun was detaching. It was a loosened circle of evening sky, suddenly lighted from the back. It was an abrupt black body out of nowhere; it was a flat disk; it was almost over the sun. That is when there were screams. At once this disk of sky slid over the sun like a lid. The sky snapped over the sun like a lens cover. The hatch in the brain slammed. Abruptly it was dark night, on the land and in the sky. In the night sky was a tiny ring of light. The hole where the sun belongs is very small. A thin ring of light marked its place. There was no sound. The eyes dried, the arteries drained, the lungs hushed. There was no world. We were the world's dead people rotating and orbiting

around and around, embedded in the planet's crust, while the Earth rolled down. Our minds were light-years distant, forgetful of almost everything. Only an extraordinary act of will could recall to us our former, living selves and our contexts in matter and time. We had, it seems, loved the planet and loved our lives, but could no longer remember the way of them. We got the light wrong. In the sky was something that should not be there. In the black sky was a ring of light. It was a thin ring, an old, thin silver wedding band, an old, worn ring. It was an old wedding band in the sky, or a morsel of bone. There were stars. It was all over.

**ANALYZE STYLE**

**Annotate:** Mark repeated words and ideas in the last four sentences of paragraph 8.

**Analyze:** How does this repetition emphasize what Dillard sees and how she thinks about it?

## CHECK YOUR UNDERSTANDING

Answer these questions before moving on to the **Analyze the Text** section on the following page.

**1** In this excerpt, Dillard's central focus is —

   **A** the moment when a solar eclipse reaches totality

   **B** a time when she experienced a bizarre hallucination

   **C** learning that she and her husband perceived the world differently

   **D** how the wisdom of other times in history applies today

**2** Dillard's writing style in the essay serves to —

   **F** objectively teach readers key facts about eclipses

   **G** reflect her disoriented state of mind during the experience

   **H** amuse readers with her humor about her limited understanding

   **J** persuade readers that nothing is more amazing than an eclipse

**3** What was the main effect of experiencing the eclipse?

   **A** Dillard lost her memory of events before the eclipse.

   **B** People became physically separated from each other.

   **C** No one was able to speak or hear during totality.

   **D** The appearances of everyday things changed dramatically.

**RESPOND**

## ANALYZE THE TEXT

Support your responses with evidence from the text.  NOTEBOOK

1. **Interpret** What historical allusions does the author make? How do these allusions contribute to the tone of the essay?

2. **Compare** To what other things does the author compare what she sees during the eclipse? What message or main idea do these images reflect?

3. **Summarize** What actually happens during the total eclipse?

4. **Critique** Did you think that the author's word choices and tone helped the reader appreciate a total eclipse? Cite examples from the essay.

5. **Notice & Note** How does contrast and contradiction serve as a better way of describing a true event than merely relating what was observed?

## RESEARCH

**RESEARCH TIP**
Documenting your sources gives credit for the information cited. Research the person or organization that is providing the information. Are there complaints about their accuracy or doubts cast by other professional news sources? If so, search for more reliable sources of information.

Many witnesses have written their own accounts of solar eclipses. Research eyewitness accounts of the 2017 total solar eclipse that was visible in much of the United States. Summarize what you learn during your research, and document the sources using a standard method of citation.

| | |
|---|---|
| **Source 1 Citation:** | |
| **Summary:** | |
| **Source 2 Citation:** | |
| **Summary:** | |

**Extend** With a small group, evaluate how typical Dillard's experience is for people who experience an eclipse.

## WRITE AND SHARE

**Write a Comparison** Write a two-paragraph comparison between Annie Dillard's description and the 2017 eyewitness eclipse account you researched.

- ❏ Introduce the topic and explain the sources of these two accounts, emphasizing that Dillard's account is literary nonfiction while the researched account is likely informational nonfiction.

- ❏ Include similarities and differences between these accounts, using appropriate register and vocabulary—in particular, accurate scientific and academic terms.

- ❏ Support your ideas with quotations and paraphrases.

**Share Your Opinion** Have a discussion and share your opinion.

- ❏ Explain why eclipses still capture human imagination, even though we can now predict them and understand them better.

- ❏ Use appropriate tone and voice, expressing your ideas in a reasonable and academic way that still sounds like you.

- ❏ Be respectful of other peoples' and eras' knowledge and belief systems, recognizing that you might have different knowledge and beliefs.

- ❏ Support ideas with details from both texts.

 Go to the **Writing Studio** for help with quoting and paraphrasing sources.

Go to the **Speaking and Listening Studio** for help with sharing your opinion during a group discussion.

## RESPOND TO THE ESSENTIAL QUESTION

 How do changes around us reveal who we are?

**Gather Information** Review your annotations and notes on *from* Total Eclipse. Then, add relevant information to your Response Log. As you determine which information to include, think about:

- why people long ago became upset when the sun disappeared during a total eclipse
- why people thought a total eclipse was a sign
- what effect an eclipse has after it passes

At the end of the unit, use your notes to help you write a research report.

**ACADEMIC VOCABULARY**

As you write and discuss what you learned from the literary nonfiction essay, be sure to use the Academic Vocabulary words. Check off each of the words that you use.

- ❏ **abstract**
- ❏ **evolve**
- ❏ **explicit**
- ❏ **facilitate**
- ❏ **infer**

**WORD BANK**
wane
saturate
hue
recede

## CRITICAL VOCABULARY

**Practice and Apply**  Answer each question, incorporating the meaning of the Critical Vocabulary word in your response.

**1.** If daylight began to **wane**, would it be morning or evening?

_____

**2.** How would you react if rain started to **saturate** your backpack?

_____

**3.** How would you describe any **hue** of a rainbow?

_____

**4.** What might a farmer do when flood waters **recede**?

_____

## VOCABULARY STRATEGY:
### Figurative Meanings

**Figurative language** develops an idea through an imaginative comparison. In some cases, a word with a concrete meaning is used to describe an abstract idea or process. For example, the Critical Vocabulary word *recede* in paragraph 6 is not used literally. When Dillard says her "eyes were receding the way galaxies recede to the rim of space," her eyes aren't actually going anywhere; she is sharing her reaction to describe vividly how distant and strange Gary looks.

**Practice and Apply**  Explain the meaning of the figurative language in each example from the selection.

**1. The sun simply shaves away; gradually, you see less sun and more sky.**

_____

**2. The towns and orchards in the valley to the south were dissolving into the blue light.**

_____

**3. We had all started down a chute of time.**

_____

**4. The skin on his face moved like thin bronze plating that would peel.**

_____

## LANGUAGE CONVENTIONS:
### Sentence Variety

Writers vary sentences as an element of style. If every sentence were the same length or pattern, readers might lose interest. A change in **syntax,** or sentence structure, can signal an important idea or a change in mood. Dillard mixes short and simple sentences with long, stream-of-consciousness sentences in the excerpt from "Total Eclipse." Here are some examples from the essay:

Go to the **Grammar Studio** for more on sentence variety.

- Simple: Subject and Predicate
  > **Everything was lost.**

- Compound: Two Independent Clauses Combined with a Conjunction
  > **The sky's blue was deepening, but there was no darkness.**

- Compound: Two Independent Clauses Combined with Semicolon
  > **He smiled as if he saw me; the stringy crinkles around his eyes moved.**

- Complex: One Independent Clause with One Dependent Clause
  > **In the sky was something that should not be there.**

**Practice and Apply** Write your own sentences of varying lengths and patterns using examples found in the essay as models. Your sentences can be about your own experiences with strange situations like an eclipse. When you have finished, compare your sentences with a partner.

# from
# THE FEVER
## HOW MALARIA HAS RULED HUMANKIND FOR 500,000 YEARS

Science Writing by **Sonia Shah**

**?** **ESSENTIAL QUESTION:**

How do changes around us reveal who we are?

Color enhanced Transmission Electron Micrograph (TEM) showing malaria (*Plasmodium cathemerium*) infecting blood.

## QUICK START

You're about to learn about a microscopic change that altered the course of human history. What is a small change that you can think of that has had far-reaching effects? Discuss your ideas with a partner.

## ANALYZE TEXT STRUCTURE

The structure of a text refers to the purposeful arrangement of ideas and information to achieve a particular goal. With a clear structure, the author can clearly communicate facts in an informational text. Here are some structural elements an author may use:

- **Thesis:** The thesis is the central idea for an entire text that is expressed in one or two sentences.

- **Evidence:** The information that supports a thesis may include facts, quotations, examples, statistics, or narration of personal experiences.

- **Conclusion:** A conclusion is a statement of belief based on evidence, experience, and reasoning. A valid conclusion logically follows from facts or statements. A **deductive** conclusion follows from a generalization or premise. An **inductive** conclusion may be a broad generalization that comes from specific facts and examples.

- **Organizational Structures or Patterns:** The most common organizational text patterns are cause-and-effect, chronological, comparison-and-contrast, classification, deductive (general to specific) or inductive (specific to general) reasoning, order of importance, problem-solution, sequential, and spatial (physical relationships).

As you read the excerpt, note the text structures the author uses, including cause-and-effect and narration. Identifying text structures will help you understand the author's purpose and audience, as well as the topic.

## ANALYZE PURPOSE AND AUDIENCE

An author's main **purpose** for writing informational text may be to inform, but authors may also write nonfiction text to:

- express thoughts or feelings
- explain
- persuade
- entertain

The **audience** likely determines the author's purpose. An author has in mind particular readers and will construct the text to appeal to those readers. For example, an author may explain technical research to an audience of fellow experts. Another author may narrate the story of a significant event for readers who are interested in history and especially in a specific time period.

Readers can determine the purpose and audience by paying attention to the topic and the language the author uses.

### GENRE ELEMENTS: INFORMATIONAL TEXT

- provides factual information and cites sources as needed
- includes evidence to support ideas
- is organized in a clear structure
- includes many forms, such as news articles and essays

## CRITICAL VOCABULARY

**virulence**   **malevolence**   **anomalous**   **intrinsic**   **vestige**

To see how many Critical Vocabulary words you already know, use them to complete the sentences.

1. The tornado left only a(n) _____ of the house that had once been there.

2. _____ was clear in the movie villain's angry expression.

3. Desert plants have a(n) _____ ability to survive in hot, dry conditions.

4. The flu spread with such _____ that many people were soon sick.

5. The snowstorm was a(n) _____ event for late spring.

## LANGUAGE CONVENTIONS

**Subject-Verb Agreement**  One or more phrases may come between a subject and verb. An intervening phrase does not change the number (singular or plural) that the verb should take. A singular verb must agree with a singular subject, and a plural verb must agree with a plural subject. Here is an example:

**An anthropologist examines in painstaking detail the condition of ancient human bones and identifies diseases the people had.**

The subject of this sentence is "an anthropologist." The main verb "examines" agrees with the singular subject. The singular verb "identifies" also agrees with the subject and not with the plural "bones" in the intervening phrase.

---

**ANNOTATION MODEL**                               **NOTICE & NOTE**

As you read, note language and details that help you determine the author's purpose and intended audience. Here is how one reader marked the text:

In Europe, when those pathogens first emerged, they were probably reckless killers, taking millions of lives. The survivors learned how to withstand the diseases' ravages, though, and in time both measles and smallpox settled into being unremarkable childhood illnesses, felling scores only when encountering virgin populations, such as those in the New World of the fifteenth century.

*Author shares basic information that an expert in science or history would already know; purpose is to help curious non-experts understand the topic.*

## BACKGROUND

*The only disease that has been eradicated worldwide by vaccine is smallpox. With routine immunizations and monitoring of breakouts, it is possible that one day the disease of measles may be eliminated worldwide, too. Malaria, a disease traced to the* Plasmodium *parasite in Africa thousands of years ago, still kills millions of people, especially young children. Malaria is a leading cause of death and disease in developing countries. In this book excerpt, investigative journalist* **Sonia Shah** *(b. 1969) explores the causes, treatments, and effects of malaria. Shah's writing on wide-ranging topics, including science, politics, and human rights, has won numerous awards.*

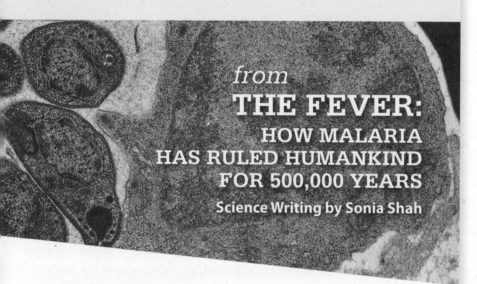

*from*
# THE FEVER:
## HOW MALARIA HAS RULED HUMANKIND FOR 500,000 YEARS
### Science Writing by Sonia Shah

## SETTING A PURPOSE

*As you read, pay attention to details that help you draw a conclusion about how* Plasmodium *developed into the form it takes today. Also, note the sources the author cites for those details.*

1   Most pathogens mellow as they age. It's enlightened self-interest, as the theory goes. Diminishing **virulence** is a superior strategy for survival. It doesn't make much sense for a pathogen to rapidly destroy its victim—a dead body just means it's time to move on. Take measles and smallpox, for example. In Europe, when those pathogens first emerged, they were probably reckless killers, taking millions of lives. The survivors learned how to withstand the diseases' ravages, though, and in time both measles and smallpox settled into being unremarkable childhood illnesses, felling scores only when encountering virgin populations, such as those in the New World of the fifteenth century.[1]

2   Which begs the question as to malaria's tenacity and continuing **malevolence**. Malaria has been plaguing humans in Africa for some five hundred thousand years, with the first

---
[1] Roy Porter, *The Greatest Benefit to Mankind* (New York: W. W. Norton, 1997), 25.

## Notice & Note

You can use the side margin to notice and note signposts as you read.

**virulence**
(vîr´yə-ləns) *n.* the quality of aggressively causing disease.

## ANALYZE TEXT STRUCTURE

**Annotate:** Mark details about how measles and smallpox changed over time.

**Interpret:** Why does the author begin by explaining the progression of diseases other than malaria?

**malevolence**
(mə-lĕv´ə-ləns) *n.* the quality of having a harmful influence.

Feeding female *Anopheles merus* mosquito; a member of the *A. gambiae* species complex, *A. merus* is a known vector for the parasitic disease malaria.

encounters between human, mosquito, and malaria parasite probably occurring around the time our ancestors discovered fire. Malaria existed in Africa before then, too, feeding on the birds, chimps, and monkeys that lived in the canopy.[2] We've had plenty of time—our entire evolutionary history, in fact—to adapt to malaria, and it to us. Or, at least, to devise tools and strategies to blunt its appetite. And yet, despite the millennia-long battles between us, malaria still manages to infect at least three hundred million of us—that is one out of twenty-one human beings on the planet—and kills nearly one million, year after year. As an extinguisher of human lives, write the malariologists Richard Carter and Kamini Mendis, malaria historically and to this day "has few rivals."[3] It remains essentially wild and untamed, despite its great antiquity.

3    And experts such as Terrie Taylor have spent lifetimes trying to figure out why.

**BIG QUESTIONS**

**Notice & Note:** Mark details in paragraph 4 that reveal what the author thinks you already know.

**Infer:** How does the author's language reveal the audience she is speaking to?

4    One simple reason for malaria's ferocity is that the protozoan creature that causes the disease is, by definition, a cheater at the game of life. It is a parasite, a creature that can eke out its livelihood only by depleting others of theirs. The rest of us all do our obscure little part in the drama of life, weaving ourselves deeper into local ecology and strengthening its fabric, the bees pollinating the flowers, predators culling the herds of their weakest members. Parasites don't help anyone. They're degenerates.

5    Take the parasitic barnacle, *Sacculina carcini*. It is born with a head, mouth, segmented body, and legs, just like any respectable barnacle. But then, because it is a parasite, it stops developing into

[2] Andrew Spielman and Michael D'Antonio, *Mosquito: A Natural History of Our Most Persistent and Deadly Foe* (New York: Hyperion, 2001), 44-45.

[3] Richard Carter and Kamini Mendis, "Evolutionary and Historical Aspects of the Burden of Malaria," *Clinical Microbiology Reviews* 15, no. 4 (October 2002): 570.

an independent creature. It burrows into the shells of the crabs off of which it will spend its life feeding. There it loses its segments, its legs, its tail, and even its mouth, devolving into a pulsing plantlike form, little more than a blob with tendrils sucking food from the forlorn crab's body.[4] It's the very definition of repellent. In 1883, Scottish lecturer Henry Drummond called parasitism "one of the gravest crimes of nature" and a "breach of the law of Evolution." Who can blame him?[5]

6     And yet parasites such as *Plasmodium* are not **anomalous** on this earth. According to science writer Carl Zimmer, one third of all described species practice the parasitic lifestyle.[6] To be fair, for *Plasmodium*, parasitism arose as an accommodation to newfound opportunities, not because of any **intrinsic** quality or irreversible mechanism within it. *Plasmodium* did not start out life hardwired to steal. This killer first emerged on the planet as a plantlike creature, most likely some kind of aquatic algae. We know this because 10 percent of the proteins in modern-day *Plasmodium* parasites contain **vestiges** of the machinery of photosynthesis.[7]

---

[4] Carl Zimmer, *Parasite Rex: Inside the Bizarre World of Nature's Most Dangerous Creatures* (New York: Touchstone, 2000), 17.

[5] Ibid., 17-18.

[6] David J. Marcogliese and Judith Price, "The Paradox of Parasites," *Global Bio-diversity* 3 (1997): 7-15.

[7] "Herbicide Hope for Malaria," BBC News, January 31, 2003.

**anomalous**
(ə-nŏm′ə-ləs) *adj.* unusual; different from the norm.

**intrinsic**
(ĭn-trĭn′zĭk, -sĭk) *adj.* of or relating to the essential nature of a thing.

**vestige**
(vĕs′tĭj) *n.* a visible trace of something that once existed.

Color enhanced scanning electron micrograph of *Plasmodium gallinaceum* invading mosquito midgut.

**ANALYZE PURPOSE AND AUDIENCE**

**Annotate:** Mark the superscript numbers in paragraph 7 and key details related to these numbers.

**Interpret:** What is the author's purpose for including this information?

**LANGUAGE CONVENTIONS**

**Annotate:** Mark phrases in paragraph 8 that come between the subject and verb.

**Evaluate:** How do you know there is agreement between the subject and verb?

7    *Plasmodium's* ancestors probably rubbed shoulders with the eggs and larvae of mosquitoes, similarly floating on sun-dappled waters.[8] When the mosquitoes took wing, malaria's ancestors likely went quietly along with them.[9] It must have happened, then and again, that when a mosquito pierced a bird or chimp or some other blood-filled creature, malaria's algae ancestors fell into the wound. Most probably died. But through the blind ticking clock of evolution, one day some subset of the interlopers found themselves thriving in those crimson seas, and a vampiric parasite was born.

8    Such are the ironies of surviving on this protean planet. A creature at the very bottom of the zoological scale, a humble being beneficently converting sunlight into living tissue (and thereby providing the basis for the planet's entire food chain), turns into one of the most ruthlessly successful parasites ever known, commanding two separate spheres of the living world, human and entomological.[10]

9    Henry Drummond would have been appalled.

---

[8] Graeme O'Neill, "Pathways to Destruction," *The Bulletin*, February 12, 2003.

[9] Carter and Mendis, "Evolutionary and Historical Aspects of the Burden of Malaria," 564-94.

[10] Lewis W. Hackett, *Malaria in Europe: An Ecological Study* (London: Oxford University Press, 1937), 201.

Colored scanning electron micrograph of the stomach wall of a mosquito *Anopholes stephansii* infected with malarial parasites *Plasmodium sp.*

## CHECK YOUR UNDERSTANDING

Answer these questions before moving on to the **Analyze the Text** section on the following page.

1 What is different about the pathogen that causes malaria, compared with other pathogens?

   **A** It is not as well understood by researchers.

   **B** It is the only disease carried by mosquitoes.

   **C** It has not become less deadly over the centuries.

   **D** It never traveled from its home continent to other places.

2 The author discusses barnacles in this passage because —

   **F** they are parasites, just like *Plasmodium*

   **G** they develop to adulthood in the same way as *Plasmodium*

   **H** their existence shows how common repellent creatures are in nature

   **J** their way of life is the exact opposite of *Plasmodium's*

3 How did the malaria pathogen develop?

   **A** Like measles and smallpox, it began in Europe and spread to the New World.

   **B** It first existed in chimps and monkeys living in trees in Africa.

   **C** It originated in barnacles as part of their parasitic burrowing.

   **D** An ancient, algae-like aquatic creature was taken up by mosquitoes.

## ANALYZE THE TEXT

Support your responses with evidence from the text.  📓 NOTEBOOK

1. **Infer**  What was the author's purpose for writing this informational text? How do you know?

2. **Cite Evidence**  The author writes that malaria is "essentially wild and untamed." Cite evidence from the text that supports her claim.

3. **Evaluate**  Review paragraph 5. How does the author's description of a parasitic barnacle help readers to understand how malaria operates?

4. **Identify Patterns**  Describe the organizational pattern the author uses to explain the process of how *Plasmodium* developed.

5. **Notice & Note**  How does the extreme language in the final sentence of the excerpt sum up the author's point?

## RESEARCH

Investigate recommended methods of preventing the spread of a specific disease. The method might be steps in a process or specific procedures to follow at home or in a public space. To develop ideas, you can read recent news articles or discuss options in a small group. Keep track of your sources and key information in the chart.

| DISEASE | TIPS FOR PREVENTION | SOURCES |
|---------|---------------------|---------|
|         |                     |         |
|         |                     |         |
|         |                     |         |

**Extend**  To extend your research, look for information that tells how experts discovered these methods for preventing specific diseases. Discuss what you find with a small group.

## CREATE AND EVALUATE

**Write a Procedural Brochure** Share the information you have gathered from your research by writing a procedural brochure or a public service announcement. A brochure is a folded booklet of one or more pages. A public service announcement can be written or spoken to alert people to an issue, such as a health or safety topic.

- ❏ Consider your audience. You will be informing professionals in a particular field or place, or adults who need clear and specific information on a topic.

- ❏ Use headings and lists to make your information easily accessible.

- ❏ Organize your information succinctly. Introduce your purpose and main idea, list and describe a procedure or recommendations in a logical order, and conclude with a summary statement.

**Follow and Give Instructions** In the excerpt, Sonia Shah describes a complex process that occurs in nature. Work with a small group to focus on a complex process that occurs at school.

- ❏ As a group, identify a process.

- ❏ Choose specific tasks within your group, such as documenting steps, gathering supplies, and testing the process.

- ❏ Take turns giving and following the instructions you develop.

- ❏ Write a paragraph reflecting on and evaluating the role you had in the process.

Go to the **Writing Studio** for more on writing informative texts.

Go to the **Speaking and Listening Studio** for help with having a group discussion.

## RESPOND TO THE ESSENTIAL QUESTION

**?** How do changes around us reveal who we are?

**Gather Information** Review your annotations and notes on the excerpt from *The Fever*. Then, add relevant information to your Response Log. As you determine which information to include, think about:

UNIT 5
RESPONSE LOG

- how malaria has affected the human species
- how scientists have dedicated themselves to figuring out how to conquer malaria
- how a plant can turn into a killer

At the end of the unit, use your notes to help you write a research report.

**ACADEMIC VOCABULARY**

As you write and discuss what you learned from the science writing, be sure to use the Academic Vocabulary words. Check off each of the words that you use.

- ❏ **abstract**
- ❏ **evolve**
- ❏ **explicit**
- ❏ **facilitate**
- ❏ **infer**

## CRITICAL VOCABULARY

**Practice and Apply**  Complete each sentence, incorporating the meaning of the Critical Vocabulary word in your response.

**1.** This year's flu strain demonstrated its **virulence** when . . .

_____

**2.** Some players joked that **malevolence** was behind the coach's instruction to . . .

_____

**3.** Because the results of the experiment were **anomalous**, . . .

_____

**4.** Something **intrinsic** to my personality is . . .

_____

**5.** We tried to leave no **vestige** of our presence on the hiking trail, but . . .

_____

## VOCABULARY STRATEGY:
### Affixes

Go to the **Vocabulary Studio** for more on affixes.

**Affixes** include prefixes and suffixes. Affixes are common in terms used in scientific writing. Knowing the meaning of affixes helps to understand technical or discipline-based vocabulary. The word *malevolence* contains the Latin prefix *mal-*, which means "bad." Here are other examples:

| AFFIX | MEANING | EXAMPLE |
|-------|---------|---------|
| *para-* | Greek prefix meaning "feeding beside, disordered, abnormal" | *parasite* |
| *-ic* | Latin suffix meaning "characteristic of" | *aquatic* |
| *-al* | Latin suffix meaning "pertaining to" | *entomological* |

**Practice and Apply**  Follow these steps for each example word in the chart.

**1.** Define the word using the meaning of the affix.

**2.** Use a print or online resource, such as a technical dictionary or a glossary, to clarify or validate the definition.

**3.** Use the word in a sentence that accurately reflects its meaning.

## LANGUAGE CONVENTIONS:
### Subject-Verb Agreement

The excerpt from *The Fever* contains several complex and compound sentences, some of which include phrases or clauses that intervene between the subject and the verb. Here is an example from the text:

> And yet, despite the millennia-long battles between us, malaria still manages to infect at least three hundred million of us—that is one out of twenty-one human beings on the planet—and kills nearly one million, year after year.

The subject of the sentence is *malaria*. The compound verbs *manages* and *kills* agree with the singular subject. Notice that the verb *kills* appears after the intervening clause *that is one out of twenty-one human beings on the planet*. This clause does not change the number the verb should take. The verb *kills* agrees with the singular subject *malaria* and not with the plural *human beings* in the intervening clause.

**Practice and Apply** Underline the subject and circle the verbs in each of the following sentences. Look for intervening phrases or clauses. Then, write and revise the sentences in which the subject and the verb do not agree.

**1.** Over time, survivors learn how to withstand the ravages of disease and passes along some immunity to the next generation.

_____

_____

**2.** A parasite ekes out a livelihood and at the same time depletes others of their lives.

_____

_____

**3.** We weave ourselves deeper into local ecology and strengthen its fabric.

_____

_____

**4.** A killer emerges on the planet as a plantlike creature, most likely some kind of aquatic algae, and then evolve into a parasite.

_____

_____

Go to the **Grammar Studio** for more on subject-verb agreement.

# A SOUND OF THUNDER

Short Story by **Ray Bradbury**

**?** **ESSENTIAL QUESTION:**

How do changes around us reveal who we are?

## QUICK START

If you could travel to any place in time—past or future—where would you go? What would you want to do or see there? Turn and talk about your ideas with a partner.

## ANALYZE PLOT AND SETTING

Every story has a **setting**—a time and place for its action. For science fiction writers, the setting may be in any place in the past, present, or future. "A Sound of Thunder" takes place in two distinct settings—the far distant future and the prehistoric past.

In some stories, the setting is just a backdrop to the **plot**, or sequence of events. In "A Sound of Thunder," the action centers on characters who travel through time, and the setting directly affects the way the plot unfolds.

As you read, note how the setting causes events to happen, or causes them to happen in a certain way, at different stages of the plot. Use a chart like this:

| EXPOSITION / RISING ACTION | CLIMAX | FALLING ACTION / RESOLUTION |
|---|---|---|
| | | |

### GENRE ELEMENTS: SCIENCE FICTION

- usually set in the future or in a different reality
- presents an imagined view of the past or future
- based on scientific facts and theories
- comments in some way on present-day society

## MAKE INFERENCES

When you make an **inference** while reading, you make a logical guess based on information in a text and your own knowledge, including what you know about genre conventions, or characteristics of a particular type of story. Use your understanding of science fiction characteristics to help you make predictions and draw conclusions about characters, settings, and events in "A Sound of Thunder." Use a chart like this one to record them:

| TEXT DETAILS / SCIENCE FICTION CONVENTIONS | MY PREDICTIONS AND CONCLUSIONS |
|---|---|
| | |
| | |
| | |

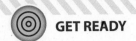 

## CRITICAL VOCABULARY

| expendable | subtle | paradox | undulate | subliminal |

To see how many Critical Vocabulary words you already know, answer the following questions.

1. What word means to move in a smooth, wave-like motion?

2. What word means something that exists below the level of consciousness?

3. What word means that something is unnecessary?

4. What word means a statement that combines ideas that are opposites?

5. What word means something that is hard to detect?

## LANGUAGE CONVENTIONS

**Transitions** Authors use transitions, or connecting words, to show readers how the details in a paragraph are related. Some common transitions show relationships of comparison and contrast. Other transitions, like the one in this line of dialogue from the story, point out a cause-and-effect relationship.

cause
↓

**"Not knowing it, we might kill an important animal, a small bird, a roach, a flower even, thus destroying an important link in a growing species."**

↑　　　　　　　↑
transition　　　effect

The transition word *thus* introduces an effect of killing even a small plant or animal. Other transition words that signal cause-and-effect relationships include *because*, *consequently*, *as a result*, and *therefore*. As you read "A Sound of Thunder," watch Bradbury's use of transitions to show cause and effect.

## ANNOTATION MODEL

**NOTICE & NOTE**

As you read, use story details and your knowledge of science fiction conventions to make inferences about the setting and plot. Here is how one reader made inferences about setting and plot in "A Sound of Thunder":

# TIME SAFARI, INC.

Safaris to any year in the past.

You name the animal.

We take you there.

You shoot it.

Time travel is technology of the future—story is probably set in the future.

What kind of animals would you travel to the past to hunt?

## BACKGROUND

*Although **Ray Bradbury** (1920–2012) is best known as a science fiction writer for* Fahrenheit 451, *he was never comfortable with that label. Bradbury also wrote imaginative short stories, novels, poems, plays, and nonfiction. At age 12, he wrote his own sequel to a popular novel because he couldn't wait for the next book to be published. In high school, he bought a ten-dollar typewriter and wrote for the school newspaper. At 19, he sold newspapers until he could support himself—about three years later—on his writing alone. Bradbury once remarked that having total recall of every book he's ever read helped his writing.*

# A SOUND OF THUNDER

**Short Story by Ray Bradbury**

## SETTING A PURPOSE

*As you read, imagine yourself in the main character's role. Consider how you might react in the situations this character faces and what actions you might take.*

**Notice & Note**

You can use the side margins to notice and note signposts in the text.

1   The sign on the wall seemed to quaver under a film of sliding warm water. Eckels felt his eyelids blink over his stare, and the sign burned in this momentary darkness:

> # TIME SAFARI, INC.
> Safaris to any year in the past.
> You name the animal.
> We take you there.
> You shoot it.

**ANALYZE PLOT AND SETTING**

**Annotate:** In paragraph 4, mark the consequences for disobeying instructions.

**Infer:** Why do you think the consequences are so severe? Make a prediction about what Eckels will do later in the story based on the official's warning.

2    A warm phlegm gathered in Eckels's throat; he swallowed and pushed it down. The muscles around his mouth formed a smile as he put his hand slowly out upon the air, and in that hand waved a check for ten thousand dollars to the man behind the desk.

3    "Does this safari guarantee I come back alive?"

4    "We guarantee nothing," said the official, "except the dinosaurs." He turned. "This is Mr. Travis, your Safari Guide in the Past. He'll tell you what and where to shoot. If he says no shooting, no shooting. If you disobey instructions, there's stiff penalty of another ten thousand dollars, plus possible government action, on your return."

5    Eckels glanced across the vast office at a mass and tangle, a snaking and humming of wires and steel boxes, at an aurora[1] that flickered now orange, now silver, now blue. There was a sound like a gigantic bonfire burning all of Time, all the years and all the parchment calendars, all the hours piled high and set aflame.

6    A touch of the hand and this burning would, on the instant, beautifully reverse itself. Eckels remembered the wording in the advertisements to the letter. Out of chars and ashes, out of dust and coals, like golden salamanders, the old years, the green years, might leap; roses sweeten the air, white hair turn Irish-black, wrinkles vanish; all, everything fly back to seed, flee death, rush down to their beginnings, suns rise in western skies and set in glorious easts, moons eat themselves opposite to the custom, all and everything cupping one in another like Chinese boxes,[2] rabbits into hats, all and everything returning to the fresh death, the seed death, the green death, to the time before the beginning. A touch of a hand might do it, the merest touch of a hand.

7    "Unbelievable." Eckels breathed, the light of the Machine on his thin face. "A real Time Machine." He shook his head. "Makes you think. If the election had gone badly yesterday, I might be here now running away from the results. Thank God Keith won. He'll make a fine President of the United States."

8    "Yes," said the man behind the desk. "We're lucky. If Deutscher had gotten in, we'd have the worst kind of dictatorship. There's an anti-everything man for you, a militarist, anti-Christ, anti-human, anti-intellectual. People called us up, you know, joking but not joking. Said if Deutscher became President they wanted to go live in 1492. Of course it's not our business to conduct Escapes, but to form Safaris. Anyway, Keith's President now. All you got to worry about is—"

9    "Shooting my dinosaur," Eckels finished it for him.

10    "A *Tyrannosaurus rex*. The Tyrant Lizard, the most incredible monster in history. Sign this release. Anything happens to you, we're not responsible. Those dinosaurs are hungry."

11    Eckels flushed angrily. "Trying to scare me!"

---

[1] **aurora:** a colorful display of light that appears at night in the skies near the North and South Poles.

[2] **Chinese boxes:** a set of decorated boxes in which each fits into the next-larger one.

12    "Frankly, yes. We don't want anyone going who'll panic at the first shot. Six Safari leaders were killed last year, and a dozen hunters. We're here to give you the severest thrill a *real* hunter ever asked for. Traveling you back sixty million years to bag the biggest game in all of Time. Your personal check's still there. Tear it up."

13    Mr. Eckels looked at the check. His fingers twitched.

14    "Good luck," said the man behind the desk. "Mr. Travis, he's all yours."

15    They moved silently across the room, taking their guns with them, toward the Machine, toward the silver metal and the roaring light.

16    First a day and then a night and then a day and then a night, then it was day-night-day-night-day. A week, a month, a year, a decade! A.D. 2055. A.D. 2019, 1999! 1957! Gone! The Machine roared.

17    They put on their oxygen helmets and tested the intercoms.

18    Eckels swayed on the padded seat, his face pale, his jaw stiff. He felt the trembling in his arms, and he looked down and found his hands tight on the new rifle. There were four other men in the Machine. Travis, the Safari Leader; his assistant, Lesperance; and two other hunters, Billings and Kramer. They sat looking at each other, and the years blazed around them.

19    "Can these guns get a dinosaur cold?" Eckels felt his mouth saying.

20    "If you hit them right," said Travis on the helmet radio. "Some dinosaurs have two brains, one in the head, another far down the spinal column. We stay away from those. That's stretching luck. Put your first two shots into the eyes, if you can, blind them, and go back into the brain."

21    The Machine howled. Time was a film run backward. Suns fled and ten million moons fled after them. "Think," said Eckels. "Every hunter that ever lived would envy us today. This makes Africa seem like Illinois."

**MAKE INFERENCES**

**Annotate:** Mark the names of the historic and classical figures that Travis alludes to in paragraph 25.

**Infer:** What ideas do you associate with these well-known figures? Why do you think Travis mentions them at this particular moment?

22    The Machine slowed; its scream fell to a murmur. The Machine stopped.

23    The sun stopped in the sky.

24    The fog that had enveloped the Machine blew away and they were in an old time, a very old time indeed, three hunters and two Safari Heads with their blue metal guns across their knees.

25    "Christ isn't born yet," said Travis. "Moses has not gone to the mountain to talk with God. The Pyramids are still in the earth, waiting to be cut out and put up. *Remember* that. Alexander, Caesar, Napoleon, Hitler—none of them exists."

26    The men nodded.

27    "That"—Mr. Travis pointed—"is the jungle of sixty million two thousand and fifty-five years before President Keith."

28    He indicated a metal path that struck off into green wilderness, over steaming swamp, among giant ferns and palms.

29    "And that," he said, "is the Path, laid by Time Safari for your use. It floats six inches above the earth. Doesn't touch so much as one grass blade, flower, or tree. It's an anti-gravity metal. Its purpose is to keep you from touching this world of the Past in any way. Stay on the Path. Don't go off it. I repeat. *Don't go off*. For *any* reason! If you fall off, there's a penalty. And don't shoot any animal we don't okay."

30    "Why?" asked Eckels.

31    They sat in the ancient wilderness. Far birds' cries blew on a wind, and the smell of tar and an old salt sea, moist grasses, and flowers the color of blood.

32    "We don't want to change the Future. We don't belong here in the Past. The government doesn't *like* us here. We have to pay big graft[3] to keep our franchise. A Time Machine is finicky business. Not knowing it, we might kill an important animal, a small bird, a roach, a flower even, thus destroying an important link in a growing species."

33    "That's not clear," said Eckels.

34    "All right," Travis continued, "say we accidentally kill one mouse here. That means all the future families of this one particular mouse are destroyed, right?"

35    "Right."

36    "And all the families of the families of the families of that one mouse! With a stamp of your foot, you annihilate first one, then a dozen, then a thousand, a million, a *billion* possible mice!"

37    "So they're dead," said Eckels. "So what?"

38    "So what?" Travis snorted quietly. "Well, what about the foxes that'll need those mice to survive? For want of ten mice, a fox dies. For want of ten foxes, a lion starves. For want of a lion, all manner of insects, vultures, infinite billions of life forms are thrown into chaos and destruction. Eventually it all boils down to this: Fifty-nine million years later, a cave man, one of a dozen in the *entire world*,

**LANGUAGE CONVENTIONS**

**Annotate:** In paragraph 38, number the steps in the cause-and-effect sequence chain, and mark the transition words that connect the steps.

**Analyze:** What point is Travis trying to impress on the travelers? How do transitions emphasize this point?

---

[3] **graft:** bribes.

goes hunting wild boar or saber-toothed tiger for food. But you, friend, have *stepped* on all the tigers in that region. By stepping on *one* single mouse. So the cave man starves. And the cave man, please note, is not just *any* **expendable** man, no! He is an *entire future nation*. From his loins would have sprung ten sons. From *their* loins one hundred sons, and thus onward to a civilization. Destroy this one man, and you destroy a race, a people, an entire history of life. It is comparable to slaying some of Adam's grandchildren. The stomp of your foot, on one mouse, could start an earthquake, the effects of which could shake our earth and destinies down through Time, to their very foundations. With the death of that one cave man, a billion others yet unborn are throttled in the womb. Perhaps Rome never rises on its seven hills. Perhaps Europe is forever a dark forest, and only Asia waxes healthy and teeming. Step on a mouse and you crush the Pyramids. Step on a mouse and you leave your print, like a Grand Canyon, across Eternity. Queen Elizabeth might never be born, Washington might not cross the Delaware, there might never be a United States at all. So be careful. Stay on the Path. *Never* step off!"

39    "I see," said Eckels. "Then it wouldn't pay for us even to touch the *grass*?"

40    "Correct. Crushing certain plants could add up infinitesimally. A little error here would multiply in sixty million years, all out of proportion. Of course maybe our theory is wrong. Maybe Time *can't* be changed by us. Or maybe it can be changed only in little **subtle** ways. A dead mouse here makes an insect imbalance there, a population disproportion later, a bad harvest further on, a depression, mass starvation, and, finally, a change in *social* temperament in far-flung countries. Something much more subtle, like that. Perhaps only a soft breath, a whisper, a hair, pollen on the air, such a slight, slight change that unless you looked close you wouldn't see it. Who knows? Who really can say he knows? We don't know. We're guessing. But until we do know for certain whether our messing around in Time *can* make a big roar or a little rustle in history, we're being careful. This Machine, this Path, your clothing and bodies, were sterilized, as you know, before the journey. We wear these oxygen helmets so we can't introduce our bacteria into an ancient atmosphere."

41    "How to we know which animals to shoot?"

42    "They're marked with red paint," said Travis. "Today, before our journey, we sent Lesperance here back with the Machine. He came to this particular era and followed certain animals."

43    "Studying them?"

44    "Right," said Lesperance. "I track them through their entire existence, noting which of them lives longest. Very few. How many times they mate. Not often. Life's short. When I find one that's going to die when a tree falls on him, or one that drowns in a tar pit, I note the exact hour, minute, and second. I shoot a paint bomb. It leaves

**expendable**
(ĭk-spĕn´də-bəl) *adj.* worth sacrificing to gain an objective.

**subtle**
(sŭt´l) *adj.* so slight as to be difficult to detect or describe.

a red patch on his side. We can't miss it. Then I correlate our arrival in the Past so that we meet the Monster not more than two minutes before he would have died anyway. This way, we kill only animals with no future, that are never going to mate again. You see how *careful* we are?"

45    "But if you came back this morning in Time," said Eckels eagerly, "you must've bumped into *us,* our Safari! How did it turn out? Was it successful? Did all of us get through—alive?"

46    Travis and Lesperance gave each other a look.

47    "That'd be a **paradox**," said the latter. "Time doesn't permit that sort of mess—a man meeting himself. When such occasions threaten, Time steps aside. Like an airplane hitting an air pocket. You felt the Machine jump just before we stopped? That was us passing ourselves on the way back to the Future. We saw nothing. There's no way of telling *if* this expedition was a success, *if we* got our monster, or whether all of us—meaning *you,* Mr. Eckels—got out alive."

48    Eckels smiled palely.

49    "Cut that," said Travis sharply. "Everyone on his feet!"

50    They were ready to leave the Machine.

51    The jungle was high and the jungle was broad and the jungle was the entire world forever and forever. Sounds like music and sounds like flying tents filled the sky, and those were pterodactyls soaring with cavernous gray wings, gigantic bats of delirium and night fever. Eckels, balanced on the narrow Path, aimed his rifle playfully.

52    "Stop that!" said Travis. "Don't even aim for fun, blast you! If your guns should go off—"

53    Eckels flushed. "Where's our *Tyrannosaurus*?"

54    Lesperance checked his wristwatch. "Up ahead. We'll bisect his trail in sixty seconds. Look for the red paint! Don't shoot till we give the word. Stay on the Path. *Stay on the Path!*"

55    They moved forward in the wind of morning.

56    "Strange," murmured Eckels. "Up ahead, sixty million years, Election Day over. Keith made President. Everyone celebrating. And here we are, a million years lost, and they don't exist. The things we worried about for months, a lifetime, not even born or thought of yet."

57    "Safety catches off, everyone!" ordered Travis. "You, first shot, Eckels. Second, Billings. Third, Kramer."

58    "I've hunted tiger, wild boar, buffalo, elephant, but now, this is *it*," said Eckels. "I'm shaking like a kid."

59    "Ah," said Travis.

60    Everyone stopped.

61    Travis raised his hand. "Ahead," he whispered. "In the mist. There he is. There's His Royal Majesty now."

62    The jungle was wide and full of twitterings, rustlings, murmurs, and sighs.

**paradox**
(păr´ə-dŏks) *n.* something that has or seems to have contradictory qualities.

**MAKE INFERENCES**

**Annotate:** Mark Travis's words in paragraph 52.

**Infer:** Finish Travis's sentence at the end of the paragraph.

63    Suddenly it all ceased, as if someone had shut a door.

64    Silence.

65    A sound of thunder.

66    Out of the mist, one hundred yards away, came *Tyrannosaurus rex*.

67    "It," whispered Eckels. "It . . ."

68    "Sh!"

69    It came on great oiled, resilient, striding legs. It towered thirty feet above half of the trees, a great evil god, folding its delicate watchmaker's claws close to its oily reptilian chest. Each lower leg was a piston, a thousand pounds of white bone, sunk in thick ropes of muscle, sheathed over in a gleam of pebbled skin like the mail[4] of a terrible warrior. Each thigh was a ton of meat, ivory, and steel mesh. And from the great breathing cage of the upper body those two delicate arms dangled out front, arms with hands which might pick up and examine men like toys, while the snake neck coiled. And the head itself, a ton of sculptured stone, lifted easily upon the sky. Its mouth gaped, exposing a fence of teeth like daggers. Its eyes rolled, ostrich eggs, empty of all expression save hunger. It closed its mouth in a death grin. It ran, its pelvic bones crushing aside trees and bushes, its taloned feet clawing damp earth, leaving prints six inches

---

[4] **mail:** flexible metal armor.

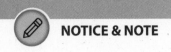

**AHA MOMENT**

**Notice & Note:** Mark what Eckels suddenly realizes in paragraph 72.

**Predict:** Do you think Eckels is right? What science fiction characteristics can help you correct or confirm this prediction?

**undulate**
(ŭn´jə-lāt) *v.* to move in waves.

deep wherever it settled its weight. It ran with a gliding ballet step, far too poised and balanced for its ten tons. It moved into a sunlit arena warily, its beautifully reptilian hands feeling the air.

70   "Why, why," Eckels twitched his mouth. "It could reach up and grab the moon."

71   "Sh!" Travis jerked angrily. "He hasn't seen us yet."

72   "It can't be killed." Eckels pronounced this verdict quietly, as if there could be no argument. He had weighed the evidence and this was his considered opinion. The rifle in his hands seemed a cap gun. "We were fools to come. This is impossible."

73   "Shut up!" hissed Travis.

74   "Nightmare."

75   "Turn around," commanded Travis. "Walk quietly to the Machine. We'll remit one half your fee."

76   "I didn't realize it would be this *big*," said Eckels. "I miscalculated, that's all. And now I want out."

77   "It *sees* us!"

78   "There's the red paint on its chest!"

79   The Tyrant Lizard raised itself. Its armored flesh glittered like a thousand green coins. The coins, crusted with slime, steamed. In the slime, tiny insects wriggled, so that the entire body seemed to twitch and **undulate** even while the monster itself did not move. It exhaled. The stink of raw flesh blew down the wilderness.

80   "Get me out of here," said Eckels. "It was never like this before. I was always sure I'd come through alive. I had good guides, good safaris, and safety. This time, I figured wrong. I've met my match and admit it. This is too much for me to get hold of."

81   "Don't run," said Lesperance. "Turn around. Hide in the Machine."

82   "Yes." Eckels seemed to be numb. He looked at his feet as if trying to make them move. He gave a grunt of helplessness.

83   "Eckels!"

84   He took a few steps, blinking, shuffling.

85   "Not *that* way!"

86   The Monster, at the first motion, lunged forward with a terrible scream. It covered one hundred yards in six seconds. The rifles jerked up and blazed fire. A windstorm from the beast's mouth engulfed them in the stench of slime and old blood. The Monster roared, teeth glittering with sun.

87   Eckels, not looking back, walked blindly to the edge of the Path, his gun limp in his arms, stepped off the Path, and walked, not knowing it, in the jungle. His feet sank into green moss. His legs moved him, and he felt alone and remote from the events behind.

88   The rifles cracked again. Their sound was lost in shriek and lizard thunder. The great level of the reptile's tail swung up, lashed sideways. Trees exploded in clouds of leaf and branch. The Monster

twitched its jeweler's hands down to fondle at the men, to twist them in half, to crush them like berries, to cram them into its teeth and its screaming throat. Its boulder-stone eyes leveled with the men. They saw themselves mirrored. They fired at the metallic eyelids and the blazing black iris.

89    Like a stone idol, like a mountain avalanche, *Tyrannosaurus* fell. Thundering, it clutched trees, pulled them with it. It wrenched and tore the metal Path. The men flung themselves back and away. The body hit, ten tons of cold flesh and stone. The guns fired. The Monster lashed its armored tail, twitched its snake jaws, and lay still. A fount of blood spurted from its throat. Somewhere inside, a sac of fluids burst. Sickening gushes drenched the hunters. They stood, red and glistening.

90    The thunder faded.

91    The jungle was silent. After the avalanche, a green peace. After the nightmare, morning.

92    Billings and Kramer sat on the pathway and threw up. Travis and Lesperance stood with smoking rifles, cursing steadily.

93    In the Time Machine, on his face, Eckels lay shivering. He had found his way back to the Path, climbed into the Machine.

94    Travis came walking, glanced at Eckels, took cotton gauze from a metal box, and returned to the others, who were sitting on the Path.

95    "Clean up."

96    They wiped the blood from their helmets. They began to curse too. The Monster lay, a hill of solid flesh. Within, you could hear the sighs and murmurs as the furthest chambers of it died, the organs malfunctioning, liquids running a final instant from pocket to sac to spleen, everything shutting off, closing up forever. It was like standing by a wrecked locomotive or a steam shovel at quitting time, all valves being released or levered tight. Bones cracked; the tonnage of its own

flesh, off balance, dead weight, snapped the delicate forearms, caught underneath. The meat settled, quivering.

97      Another cracking sound. Overhead, a gigantic tree branch broke from its heavy mooring, fell. It crashed upon the dead beast with finality.

98      "There." Lesperance checked his watch. "Right on time. That's the giant tree that was scheduled to fall and kill this animal originally." He glanced at the two hunters. "You want the trophy picture?"

99      "What?"

100      "We can't take a trophy back to the Future. The body has to stay right here where it would have died originally, so the insects, birds, and bacteria can get at it, as they were intended to. Everything in balance. The body stays. But we *can* take a picture of you standing near it."

101      The two men tried to think, but gave up, shaking their heads.

102      They let themselves be led along the metal Path. They sank wearily into the Machine cushions. They gazed back at the ruined Monster, the stagnating mound, where already strange reptilian birds and golden insects were busy at the steaming armor.

103      A sound on the floor of the Time Machine stiffened them. Eckels sat there, shivering.

104      "I'm sorry," he said at last.

105      "Get up!" cried Travis.

106      Eckels got up.

107      "Go out on that Path alone," said Travis. He had his rifle pointed. "You're not coming back in the Machine. We're leaving you here!"

108      Lesperance seized Travis's arm. "Wait—"

109      "Stay out of this!" Travis shook his hand away. "This fool nearly killed us. But it isn't *that* so much, no. It's his *shoes*! Look at them! He ran off the Path. That *ruins* us! We'll forfeit! Thousands of dollars of insurance! We guarantee no one leaves the Path. He left it. Oh, the fool! I'll have to report to the government. They might revoke our license to travel. Who knows *what* he's done to Time, to History!"

110      "Take it easy, all he did was kick up some dirt."

111      "How do we *know*?" cried Travis. "We don't know anything! It's all a mystery! Get out of here, Eckels!"

112      Eckels fumbled his shirt. "I'll pay anything. A hundred thousand dollars!"

113      Travis glared at Eckels's checkbook and spat. "Go out there. The Monster's next to the Path. Stick your arms up to your elbows in his mouth. Then you can come back with us."

114      "That's unreasonable!"

115      "The Monster's dead, you idiot. The bullets! The bullets! They can't be left behind. They don't belong in the Past; they might change anything. Here's my knife. Dig them out!"

ANALYZE PLOT AND SETTING

Annotate: In paragraph 109, mark Travis's explanation of why he is angry.

Analyze: How does the setting influence events in this part of the story?

116    The jungle was alive again, full of the old tremorings and bird cries. Eckels turned slowly to regard the primeval⁵ garbage dump, that hill of nightmares and terror. After a long time, like a sleepwalker he shuffled out along the Path.

117    He returned, shuddering, five minutes later, his arms soaked and red to the elbows. He held out his hands. Each held a number of steel bullets. Then he fell. He lay where he fell, not moving.

118    "You didn't have to make him do that," said Lesperance.

119    "Didn't I? It's too early to tell." Travis nudged the still body. "He'll live. Next time he won't go hunting game like this. Okay." He jerked his thumb wearily at Lesperance. "Switch on. Let's go home."

120    1492. 1776. 1812.

121    They cleaned their hands and faces. They changed their caking shirts and pants. Eckels was up and around again, not speaking. Travis glared at him for a full ten minutes.

122    "Don't look at me," cried Eckels. "I haven't done anything."

123    "Who can tell?"

124    "Just ran off the Path, that's all, a little mud on my shoes—what do you want me to do—get down and pray?"

125    "We might need it. I'm warning you, Eckels, I might kill you yet. I've got my gun ready."

126    "I'm innocent. I've done nothing!"

127    1999. 2000. 2055.

128    The Machine stopped.

129    "Get out," said Travis.

130    The room was there as they had left it. But not the same as they had left it. The same man sat behind the same desk. But the same man did not quite sit behind the same desk.

131    Travis looked around swiftly. "Everything okay here?" he snapped.

132    "Fine. Welcome home!"

133    Travis did not relax. He seemed to be looking at the very atoms of the air itself, at the way the sun poured through the one high window.

134    "Okay, Eckels, get out. Don't ever come back."

135    Eckels could not move.

136    "You heard me," said Travis. "What're you *staring* at?"

137    Eckels stood smelling of the air, and there was a thing to the air, a chemical taint so subtle, so slight, that only a faint cry of his **subliminal** senses warned him it was there. The colors, white, gray, blue, orange, in the wall, in the furniture, in the sky beyond the window, were . . . were . . . And there was a *feel*. His flesh twitched. His hands twitched. He stood drinking the oddness with the pores of his body. Somewhere, someone must have been screaming one of those whistles that only a dog can hear. His body screamed silence

**subliminal**
(sŭb-lĭm´ə-nəl) *adj.* below the level of awareness.

---

⁵ **primeval:** primitive; of the earliest times.

in return. Beyond this room, beyond this wall, beyond this man who was not quite the same man seated at this desk that was not quite the same desk . . . lay an entire world of streets and people. What sort of world it was now, there was no telling. He could feel them moving there, beyond the walls, almost, like so many chess pieces blown in a dry wind. . . .

138    But the immediate thing was the sign painted on the office wall, the same sign he had read earlier today on first entering.

139    Somehow, the sign had changed:

**ANALYZE PLOT AND SETTING**

**Annotate:** In paragraphs 138–145, mark the things that are different from the way they were before the trip.

**Interpret:** What do the differences reveal about how the country has changed?

# TYME SEFARI INC.
Sefaris tu any yeer en the past.
Yu naim the animall.
Wee taek yu thair.
Yu shoot itt.

140    Eckels felt himself fall into a chair. He fumbled crazily at the thick slime on his boots. He held up a clod of dirt, trembling, "No, it *can't* be. Not a *little* thing like that. No!"

141    Embedded in the mud, glistening green and gold and black, was a butterfly, very beautiful and very dead.

142    "Not a little thing like *that*! Not a butterfly!" cried Eckels.

143    It fell to the floor, an exquisite thing, a small thing that could upset balances and knock down a line of small dominoes and then big dominoes and then gigantic dominoes, all down the years across Time. Eckels's mind whirled. It *couldn't* change things. Killing one butterfly couldn't be *that* important! Could it?

144    His face was cold. His mouth trembled, asking: "Who—who won the presidential election yesterday?"

145    The man behind the desk laughed. "You joking? You know very well. Deutscher, of course! Who else? Not that fool weakling Keith. We got an iron man now, a man with guts!" The official stopped. "What's wrong?"

146    Eckels moaned. He dropped to his knees. He scrabbled at the golden butterfly with shaking fingers. "Can't we," he pleaded to the world, to himself, to the officials, to the Machine, "can't we take it *back*, can't we *make* it alive again? Can't we start over? Can't we—"

147    He did not move. Eyes shut, he waited, shivering. He heard Travis breathe loud in the room; he heard Travis shift his rifle, click the safety catch, and raise the weapon.

148    There was a sound of thunder.

## CHECK YOUR UNDERSTANDING

Answer these questions before moving on to the **Analyze the Text** section on the following page.

**1** What kind of business does Time Safari, Inc. operate?

  **A** They sell watches with bands made from exotic animal skins.

  **B** They offer trips back in time to hunt extinct animals.

  **C** They make virtual-reality, time-travel games.

  **D** They research and report on environmental issues.

**2** Why are the travelers warned to be careful not to step off the Path?

  **F** The safari company wants to be sure travelers are safe.

  **G** Once a person steps off the Path, they can never get back on.

  **H** Changing anything in the past could drastically alter the future.

  **J** The Path offers the best vantage point for shooting dinosaurs.

**3** What does Eckels do that has such far-reaching consequences?

  **A** He attempts to kill a large dinosaur.

  **B** He chooses to go on a dangerous safari.

  **C** He leaves his boot in the past.

  **D** He accidentally kills a butterfly.

## ANALYZE THE TEXT

Support your responses with evidence from the text. ⬚ NOTEBOOK

1. **Draw Conclusions** The story begins and ends in the future. What is significant about these two scenes? What do you think the author wanted you to notice or think about in them? Cite textual evidence to support your conclusions.

2. **Analyze** How did the two settings influence the way story events unfolded? Cite evidence from the text to support your analysis.

3. **Infer** What motivates Travis to shoot Eckels at the end of the story? Support your response with evidence from the text.

4. **Synthesize** What theme or message does this story convey? In what ways is setting important to the theme? Cite evidence from the text to support your response.

5. **Notice & Note** Think about the Tough Questions Eckels asks at the end of the story. What theme might these questions support?

## RESEARCH

**RESEARCH TIP**

A source that seems factual at first may turn out to be based on opinion or personal interpretation. Make sure the sources you use are authored by a recognized authority on your subject from a respected university or institution. Also, ask yourself whether the author seems to have a bias.

The scientific concept called the "butterfly effect" states that a single small change can alter the future in momentous ways. Explore this concept by conducting research to answer the questions in the chart below.

| QUESTION | ANSWER |
|---|---|
| Who was Edward Lorenz? | |
| How did the butterfly effect get this name? | |
| What is chaos theory? | |
| How is the butterfly effect connected to chaos theory? | |

**Connect** How does "A Sound of Thunder" reflect the butterfly effect and chaos theory? Based on your research, which scientific elements in "A Sound of Thunder" now seem realistic? Discuss your ideas in a small group.

## CREATE AND PRESENT

**Write a Story** Write your own story about characters who travel through time. What technological advances will allow your characters to time travel?

- ❏ Decide on your main and supporting characters and develop two settings for your story: the characters' present setting and the past or future setting to which they travel.

- ❏ Determine the problems characters will encounter and whether these problems will be solved. Use a timeline to help you figure out what will happen in the beginning, middle, and end of your story.

- ❏ Consider telling the story in the first-person, using the main character as your narrator. Develop a strong and engaging voice, using dialogue to reveal reactions.

**Deliver a Sales Pitch** Imagine that you have a time travel company. Deliver a sales pitch to convince listeners that the adventures they will have if they take a trip with your company are worth the high price you charge.

- ❏ Create a company name and slogan. Then choose the adventures you will offer, for example witnessing important historical events or shopping for fashions of the future.

- ❏ Use persuasive language and details that will stimulate interest in the adventures you offer.

- ❏ Incorporate visuals or other media to enhance your presentation.

- ❏ Deliver your pitch with an engaging and persuasive tone, adequate volume, and effective pauses. Rehearse before delivering it to the class.

Go to the **Writing Studio** for more on writing a short story.

Go to the **Speaking and Listening Studio** for help with delivering a speech.

## RESPOND TO THE ESSENTIAL QUESTION

 How do changes around us reveal who we are?

**Gather Information** Review your annotations and notes on "A Sound of Thunder." Then add relevant information to your Response Log. As you determine which information to include, think about:

- the kinds of changes people experience
- how behavior in times of crisis reveals character
- what kinds of situations require courage or strength

At the end of the unit, use your notes to help you write a research report.

**ACADEMIC VOCABULARY**
As you write and discuss what you learned about "A Sound of Thunder," be sure to use the Academic Vocabulary words. Check off each of the words that you use.

- ❏ **abstract**
- ❏ **evolve**
- ❏ **explicit**
- ❏ **facilitate**
- ❏ **infer**

Go to the **Vocabulary Studio** for more on synonyms and antonyms.

## CRITICAL VOCABULARY

**Practice and Apply**   Answer each question, incorporating the meaning of the Critical Vocabulary word in your explanation.

1. Which would you consider more **expendable**, interacting through social media or interacting in person?

2. Which is more **subtle**, a sigh or a shrug?

3. Which is a greater **paradox**: "Less is more" or "Love hurts"?

4. What would you feel if the pain from an injury were to **undulate**?

5. How might a **subliminal** idea affect your behavior?

## VOCABULARY STRATEGY:
### Synonyms and Antonyms

A **synonym** is a word with a meaning similar to that of another word. An **antonym** is a word with a meaning opposite of another word. A synonym for the Critical Vocabulary word *undulate* appears in the first paragraph of the story: *quaver*. Both words mean "to fluctuate." Other synonyms for *undulate* include *ripple* and *billow*.

Sometimes an unfamiliar word will have a synonym or an antonym in the context of a sentence or paragraph. Knowing the meaning of the word's synonym or antonym can help you figure out its meaning. You can find synonyms and antonyms in a thesaurus. In a dictionary, synonyms are often given as part of the definition of a word.

**Practice and Apply**   Search through the story to find all the synonyms and antonyms for the word *annihilate* in paragraph 36. Use a thesaurus to find other synonyms and antonyms. Record the words in the chart.

| SYNONYMS OF *ANNIHILATE* | ANTONYMS OF *ANNIHILATE* |
|---|---|
|  |  |

## LANGUAGE CONVENTIONS:
### Transitions

**Transitions** are words and phrases that connect ideas in writing, making the ideas easier to understand. Many ideas in "A Sound of Thunder" have a cause-and-effect relationship. Ray Bradbury uses well-placed transitions to guide readers through chains of causes and effects.

Note the underlined transitions in this passage of dialogue from the story. The repeated use of the transition "for want of" helps readers understand the momentous effects that could result from the death of a single mouse.

**"Well, what about the foxes that'll need those mice to survive? <u>For want of</u> ten mice, a fox dies. <u>For want of</u> ten foxes, a lion starves. <u>For want of</u> a lion, all manner of insects, vultures, infinite billions of life forms are thrown into chaos and destruction."**

In addition, the transitions allow Bradbury to briefly but clearly describe the long sequence of effects. Without transitions such as those listed in the chart below, the ideas in this section would be difficult to follow.

| TRANSITIONS THAT SHOW CAUSE-AND-EFFECT RELATIONSHIPS | | |
|---|---|---|
| accordingly | as a result | because |
| consequently | due to | eventually |
| for this reason | hence | if . . . then |
| in that case | owing to | since |
| so | therefore | thus |

**Practice and Apply** Revise your time travel story to add at least two transitional phrases that show cause-and-effect relationships. Discuss with a partner how each transition improves the meaning, flow, and cohesion of your writing.

# 5 P.M., TUESDAY, AUGUST 23, 2005

Poem by **Patricia Smith**

**?** *ESSENTIAL QUESTION:*

How do changes around us reveal who we are?

## QUICK START

The poem you are about to read relies on what the reader already knows about the potential violence of a hurricane, in particular Hurricane Katrina, which devastated New Orleans in August 2005. Think about the power of a hurricane. With a partner, discuss what you know or can imagine about the strength of hurricanes, and make a list of the potential damage these storms can cause. Consider the impact a hurricane would have in different geographic areas, such as cities, rural areas, and coastal towns.

| HURRICANE DAMAGE |
| --- |
| 1. |
| 2. |
| 3. |
| 4. |

## ANALYZE WORD CHOICE

Poetry packs a lot of meaning into a small space, so poets must choose and arrange their words carefully. Using **figurative language**, or words that communicate meaning beyond a literal interpretation, is one way that poets can add extra dimensions to their poems. Many types of figurative language create meaning through comparison:

| TYPES OF FIGURATIVE LANGUAGE |
| --- |
| A **metaphor** implies a comparison between two unlike things. The comparison draws attention to a key characteristic that both things share. |
| **Personification** gives human qualities to a nonhuman subject. Like a metaphor, personification makes a comparison between two things that are dissimilar in order to shed new light on one or both of them. |
| An **extended metaphor** is a comparison developed at length, often continuing across several stanzas or throughout an entire poem. |

Poets also choose words for their **connotative** meanings, or the feelings associated with them. By interpreting the figurative and connotative language in a poem, readers can infer the speaker's **tone**, or attitude, toward the subject, which often reveals the poet's meaning.

As you read this poem, look for comparisons. Note the two things being compared and the meaning or emotions that the comparisons evoke. Also notice the connotations of the words Smith uses.

**GENRE ELEMENTS:
LYRIC POETRY**

• attempts to recreate emotions and experiences

• uses figurative language and sensory details

• words and lines are arranged to add meaning

## CREATE MENTAL IMAGES

**Creating mental images** means using your imagination to form pictures in your mind. Through word choice, imagery, and figurative language, poets help readers visualize the ideas in the poems they write.

In the poem you are about to read, poet Patricia Smith uses personification to characterize a storm as a living person. In addition, she uses sensory description and vivid verbs to create a powerful impression of the storm's appearance and movement. For example, the following excerpt from the poem presents an image that readers can easily picture.

> A muted thread of gray light

As you read "5 P.M., Tuesday, August 23, 2005," creating mental images of the storm will help you understand Smith's characterization of it. You might use the side margin to note or sketch the pictures the poem creates in your mind. Ask yourself whether the images remind you of feelings or experiences that you have had.

## ANNOTATION MODEL

**NOTICE & NOTE**

As you read, note examples of figurative language, imagery, and word choices that stand out to you. Here are one reader's notes about the beginning of the poem:

> A muted <u>thread of gray light</u>, <u>hovering ocean</u>,
> <u>becomes throat</u>, pulls in <u>wriggle</u>, anemone, kelp,
> <u>widens</u> with the want of it.

I can picture a wispy cloud, dangling down to touch the ocean and then growing powerful, like a sea creature.

## BACKGROUND

*A hurricane develops in stages. At any point, the storm may either fall apart or become more organized and intense, progressing to the next stage. In the first stage, a tropical disturbance occurs, in which loosely-organized, heavy rain clouds develop. The storm system draws moisture from the warm, humid air on the ocean's surface. This warm air rises and cooler air moves down to replace it, creating a swirling pattern of winds, a tropical depression. If the winds reach 39 to 73 miles per hour, the depression becomes a tropical storm. At 74 miles per hour, the storm becomes a hurricane.*

# 5 P.M., TUESDAY, AUGUST 23, 2005

### Poem by Patricia Smith

*On August 23, 2005, a tropical depression formed off the southern coast of the United States. It developed over the next few days into Hurricane Katrina, one of the most powerful and devastating hurricanes to ever hit U.S. soil. Katrina's massive winds and torrential rainfall created a storm surge of more than 25 feet, breaching a crucial levee and plunging most of the city of New Orleans under water. The hurricane resulted in at least 1,800 deaths and left a lasting impact on the Gulf Coast and its inhabitants.*

**Patricia Smith** *(b. 1955) is an award-winning poet, performance artist, and four-time National Poetry Slam champion. She is known for using personas—first-person voices that range from gang members to monsters of Greek mythology—to expose uncomfortable truths about situations that most people don't want to face. Her work evokes such themes as self-destruction, betrayal, and vindictiveness, highlighting the spiritual and political impact of the subjects she explores. This poem appears in her book* Blood Dazzler, *a collection that traces the environmental and human costs of Hurricane Katrina. The book earned Smith a National Book Award nomination in 2008.*

**Notice & Note**

You can use the side margin to notice and note signposts in the text.

## SETTING A PURPOSE

*As you read, note words and phrases that reveal the speaker's character. Write down any questions you generate during reading.*

> *"Data from an Air Force reserve unit reconnaissance aircraft . . . along with observations from the Bahamas and nearby ships . . . indicate the broad low pressure area over the southeastern Bahamas has become organized enough to be classified as tropical depression twelve."*
> —NATIONAL HURRICANE CENTER

**CREATE MENTAL IMAGES**

**Annotate:** Mark examples of personification in lines 1–10.

**Analyze:** In what ways is the storm described as human? What images does this create in your mind?

1 A muted thread of gray light, hovering ocean,
becomes throat, pulls in wriggle, anemone, kelp,[1]
widens with the want of it. I become
a mouth, thrashing hair, an overdone eye. How dare
5 the water belittle my thirst, treat me as just
another
small
disturbance,

try to feed me
10 from the bottom of its hand?

I will require praise,
unbridled winds to define my body,
a crime behind my teeth
because

**ANALYZE WORD CHOICE**

**Annotate:** In lines 15–18, mark phrases that develop an extended metaphor.

**Interpret:** What is being compared in these lines? What effect does this comparison have in the poem?

15 every woman begins as weather,
sips slow thunder, knows her hips. Every woman
harbors a chaos, can
wait for it, straddling a fever.

For now,
20 I console myself with small furies,
those dips in my dawning system. I pull in
a bored breath. The brine[2] shivers.

---

[1] **anemone, kelp:** sea anemones are brightly colored, tentacled sea creatures; kelp is a kind of seaweed.
[2] **brine:** salt water or sea water.

## CHECK YOUR UNDERSTANDING

Answer these questions before moving on to the **Analyze the Text** section on the following page.

1 This poem mainly describes —

   **A** the anger of a woman as compared to a hurricane

   **B** the effect of a hurricane on the people and places it hits

   **C** the development of a hurricane compared to a woman

   **D** how fragile a developing storm can be

2 The introductory text from the National Hurricane Center serves to —

   **F** list the facts that the poem will address

   **G** set up the structure and focus of the poem

   **H** contrast with the poem's ideas about the storm

   **J** provide context for what the poem will describe

3 The last stanza in the poem suggests that —

   **A** the storm has not yet become a hurricane

   **B** the storm has blown over

   **C** the storm is just a dream

   **D** the storm has ended, leaving the ocean calm again

**RESPOND**

## ANALYZE THE TEXT

Support your responses with evidence from the poem. 　NOTEBOOK

1. **Draw Conclusions** What information does the quotation from the National Hurricane Center at the poem's beginning convey? Paraphrase it, maintaining a logical order. Why did Smith include this quotation?

2. **Cite Evidence** What nonhuman subject is personified in the poem? Identify specific words and phrases that give the subject human qualities.

3. **Analyze** Describe the speaker's tone in this poem. What words and phrases does the poet use to establish this tone?

4. **Interpret** What words and phrases from the poem helped you develop a mental image of a hurricane gaining strength? What mood did this mental image create?

5. **Infer** What ultimate **theme**, or deeper message about life, does the poet convey through the personification and imagery in the poem?

## RESEARCH

Patricia Smith uses figurative language and imagery to describe the development of a hurricane. How does her description compare to the stages in the development of a real hurricane? With a partner, conduct research to learn about these stages. Take notes about what you learn. Then, compare this information with the details in the poem. Which details about hurricanes are similar in both sources? Which details are different? Record your ideas in the Venn diagram.

**Details in the Poem**　　　　**Both**　　　　**Facts from Research**

**Extend** Read a newspaper article that was written about Hurricane Katrina as it happened. Compare the tone of the article to the tone of the poem. Note the words and phrases in the article that create the tone. Then discuss how reading the article helped you better understand the poem.

**RESEARCH TIP**

When you conduct research on natural disasters and weather-related phenomena, look for information from organizations dedicated to these topics, such as the National Oceanic and Atmospheric Administration (NOAA), National Weather Service, or Federal Emergency Management Agency (FEMA).

## CREATE AND PRESENT

**Write a Literary Analysis**  In the poem "5 P.M., Tuesday, August 23, 2005," Patricia Smith uses personification to describe the storm that will eventually become Hurricane Katrina. Write a paragraph to interpret the effect of the personification in the poem.

❏ Identify the storm's human qualities. Remember that personification can refer to emotions as well as physical characteristics.

❏ Describe what each example of personification means and what it tells you about the speaker's attitude or frame of mind.

❏ Write a topic sentence for your paragraph that states a theme or key idea conveyed through the personification. Support your interpretation with details from the poem.

**Give a Poetry Reading**  Patricia Smith is a National Poetry Slam Champion, and this poem, like most others, is meant to be spoken. Work with a small group to adapt the poem for a male voice and practice reading it aloud.

❏ Discuss which words and phrases in the poem stand out. How should those words be spoken? Ominously? Angrily?

❏ Think about how the poem could have instead personified the hurricane as male. Discuss what words and phrases could be substituted to adapt this poem for a male voice.

❏ Memorize, practice, and recite your adaptation, using your voice and body language, to contribute to a class poetry reading.

 Go to the **Writing Studio** for more on writing analytical text.

 Go to the **Speaking and Listening Studio** to learn more about presenting a recitation.

## RESPOND TO THE ESSENTIAL QUESTION

 How do changes around us reveal who we are?

**Gather Information**  Review your annotations and notes on "5 P.M., Tuesday, August 23, 2005." Then, add relevant information to your Response Log. As you determine which information to include, think about:

- how our need for respect can dictate our responses to others
- the way we hold on to grudges and feed our anger over time
- that storms are out of anyone's control but can bring out the best and worst in people

At the end of the unit, use your notes to help you write a research report.

| UNIT 5 RESPONSE LOG | Use the Response Log to record your ideas about how each of the texts in Unit 5 relates to or comments on the **Essential Question**. |
| --- | --- |
| **Essential Question:** How do changes around us reveal who we are? | |
| *from* Total Eclipse | |
| *from* The Fever | |
| A Sound of Thunder | |
| 5 P.M., Tuesday, August 23, 2005 | |
| *from* Rivers and Tides | |
| Sonnets to Orpheus, Part Two, XII | |

**ACADEMIC VOCABULARY**

As you write and discuss what you learned about "5 P.M., Tuesday, August 23, 2005," be sure to use the Academic Vocabulary words. Check off each of the words that you use.

❏ **abstract**

❏ **evolve**

❏ **explicit**

❏ **facilitate**

❏ **infer**

DOCUMENTARY FILM

*from*
# RIVERS AND TIDES

by **Thomas Riedelsheimer**
page 375

## COMPARE THEMES ACROSS GENRES

As you view and read, notice how the ideas in both the film and the text relate to your own experiences, as well as how they relate to the experiences of other people you know. Then, look for ways that the ideas in the two texts relate to each other. After you view and read both selections, you will collaborate with a small group on a final project.

**?** **ESSENTIAL QUESTION:**

How do changes around us reveal who we are?

POEM

# SONNETS TO ORPHEUS, PART TWO, XII

by **Rainer Maria Rilke**
page 376–377

## QUICK START

How do you relate to the natural world and changes that occur within it? What effect do the changes you notice have on you? With a group, discuss how human beings see themselves in the changes that occur in nature.

## ANALYZE MEDIA TECHNIQUES

Like a writer, a filmmaker works to develop ideas in a logical fashion. The **central idea** is the most important idea about a topic that a film conveys. Filmmakers use a combination of media elements, including storytelling and production elements, to express a central idea. Storytelling elements are nontechnical elements that filmmakers use to help convey the central idea.

| STORYTELLING ELEMENTS | WHAT THEY DO |
|---|---|
| **Setting:** the locations in which a film is shot | Settings can be an integral part of how a filmmaker conveys the central idea. |
| **Mood:** the atmosphere created by visual and sound elements | Mood helps support the central idea by reinforcing what the viewer is seeing. |
| **Sequence:** the order in which images are presented | A filmmaker presents images in a logical order. Sometimes this is a chronological order, but other times, the images or scenes are shown in an order that helps the viewer relate the ideas being shown. |

In addition to storytelling elements, filmmakers use production elements such as those listed below to help them convey the central idea.

| PRODUCTION ELEMENTS | EXAMPLES |
|---|---|
| **Visual elements** help the filmmaker convey connections among ideas. | • **camera shot:** a single, continuous view taken by a camera<br>• **camera angle:** the angle at which the camera is positioned during the recording of a shot or image |
| **Sound elements** may give additional information and set the mood for a scene. | • **music:** instrumental and vocal compositions<br>• **voice-over:** the voice of an unseen narrator<br>• **sound effects:** sounds other than speech and music that are used to make a scene seem more realistic |
| **Special effects** are manipulated video images that can heighten drama and create mood. | • **speed:** fast-or slow-motion sequences<br>• **lighting:** unusually bright or dim lighting and changes in lighting<br>• **time-lapse:** starting and stopping filming to connect images from one time period to the same images in another time period |

### GENRE ELEMENTS: DOCUMENTARY FILM

- presents a factual account of a specific topic
- focuses on a central idea about the topic
- incorporates visuals, sound, and special effects
- uses setting, mood, and sequence to convey the central idea

## ANALYZE PURPOSE AND THEME

As you view the clip from *Rivers and Tides*, think about the purpose of the images, sounds, and **juxtaposition**, or side-by-side placement of key elements in the film. If you were to summarize the clip for someone who had not seen it, what details would you emphasize? What theme is the director trying to communicate using these details? Use the chart below to track details in the clip and infer how they point toward a particular purpose.

| DETAIL IN THE CLIP | PURPOSE IT IMPLIES |
|---|---|
|  |  |
|  |  |
|  |  |

After viewing the clip from *Rivers and Tides,* you will read a poem that expresses a similar purpose and theme. You can add details from the poem to this chart to help you understand both works.

## BACKGROUND

**Andy Goldsworthy** *(b. 1956) is a British artist who creates sculptures from items found in nature. Unlike most sculptors, Goldsworthy creates work that he knows will be destroyed by nature relatively quickly. Goldsworthy has photographed many of his works and has held exhibits primarily featuring photographs of his sculptures. Director* **Thomas Riedelsheimer** *(b. 1963) is also a photographer and recently worked with Goldsworthy on the documentary* Leaning into the Wind.

## PREPARE TO COMPARE

*Pay attention to settings in the film clip and how they affect your perception of the artist's work. Note any questions you generate during viewing. This information will help you compare the film with the poem that follows it.*

To view the video, log in online and select **"from RIVERS AND TIDES"** from the unit menu.

As needed, pause the video to make notes about what impresses you or about ideas you might want to talk about later. Replay or rewind so that you can clarify anything you do not understand.

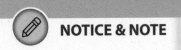
## BACKGROUND

**Rainer Maria Rilke** *(1875–1926) was born in Prague. At age 11, he was sent to military school, but his uncle made sure he was schooled in literature, his true passion. In 1901, Rilke married Clara Westhoff, who had studied with the sculptor Auguste Rodin. Rilke became Rodin's secretary. In Paris, Rilke's poetry evolved into verses that used simple vocabulary to describe everyday subjects. "Sonnets to Orpheus" reveals what poetry means to him and is considered one of his best works. His works were lauded by European artists of his time, and his unique style of lyrical poetry continues to place him among the masters of his craft.*

# SONNETS TO ORPHEUS, PART TWO, XII

**Poem by Rainer Maria Rilke**
**translated by Anita Barrows and Joanna Macy**

## Notice & Note

You can use the side margins to notice and note signposts in the text.

---

## ANALYZE PURPOSE AND THEME

**Annotate:** Mark the first sentence of the poem.

**Interpret:** How would you restate this theme in a way that applies to your own life?

## PREPARE TO COMPARE

*As you read the poem, keep the ideas about change that you gathered from the* Rivers and Tides *film clip in mind.*

Want the change. Be inspired by the flame
Where everything shines as it disappears.
The artist, when sketching, loves nothing so much
as the curve of the body as it turns away.

5 What locks itself in sameness has congealed[1].
Is it safer to be gray and numb?
What turns hard becomes rigid
and is easily shattered.

---

[1] **congealed:** solidified.

Pour yourself like a fountain.
10 Flow into the knowledge that what you are seeking
finishes often at the start, and, with ending, begins.

Every happiness is the child of a separation
it did not think it could survive. And Daphne, becoming a laurel,
dares you to become the wind.

**ANALYZE PURPOSE AND THEME**
**Annotate:** Mark the reference to Daphne, a figure from mythology who chose being turned into a laurel tree over being pursued by the god Apollo.

**Infer:** How does the allusion to mythology elaborate on the poem's theme?

## CHECK YOUR UNDERSTANDING

Answer these questions before moving on to the **Analyze the Text** section on the following page.

1  A major theme of the poem is that —

  **A** art and literature are important

  **B** change makes us feel alive

  **C** nature is full of surprises

  **D** we crave feeling safe and secure

2  How is "sameness" described in the poem?

  **F** As the only way to avoid a separation

  **G** As the way most people live

  **H** As both dull and fragile

  **J** As how all things must end

3  What images in the poem show positive change?

  **A** Fire burning, water flowing, and wind blowing

  **B** An artist, knowledge, and a tree

  **C** Things congealed, numb, and shattered

  **D** Disappearing, finishing, and separating

**RESPOND**

## ANALYZE THE TEXTS

Support your responses with evidence from the texts.　NOTEBOOK

1. **Analyze**  What special effect does the film use to help the viewer link the sculptures to the idea of time and changes over time?

2. **Compare**  What effect does the filmmaker's use of close-up shots of the artist's work and shots taken from farther away have on your understanding of the connections between the sculptures?

3. **Infer**  Think about the end of Goldsworthy's statement about what his work might represent. How do you think that statement might be finished, based on the film clip and your own experience?

4. **Summarize**  What central idea about change does Rilke's poem convey? Support your answer with evidence from the poem.

5. **Identify Patterns**  What do Rilke's images of elements like fire, light, water, and wind have in common? How do these images support the poem's theme?

## ANALYZE MEDIA

Analyze the way music, juxtapositions, time lapses, and interviews are used in the clip from *Rivers and Tides*. First, use the chart below to record your ideas about the effects each technique creates in the clip. Then consider how these techniques work together to develop an overall impression of Goldsworthy's work. Present your ideas about this in a paragraph, a poster, a podcast, or an oral presentation.

| MEDIA TECHNIQUE | EFFECT IN THE CLIP |
| --- | --- |
| music | |
| juxtaposition | |
| time lapse | |
| interview | |

**Extend**  What is the unifying theme that these impressions point to?

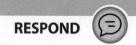

## CREATE AND DISCUSS

**Create a Reflection** What connections can you make between changes you see in nature or your community and the kinds of major life changes people experience? Share your ideas in a media presentation.

❏ Develop an idea to write about and present by journaling or discussing with a partner.

❏ Take photographs, make video recordings, or organize a collection of existing images of a meaningful change. (Be sure any images made by others are copyright-free or are allowed for classroom use.)

❏ Record an audio track to accompany your visuals that tells what change the visuals show and how that change is a good metaphor for a specific life change—moving, changing schools, growing up, etc.

**Share and Discuss Opinions** With a small group, discuss your opinions about the connections between changes in nature and changes in human beings. Does Andy Goldsworthy's art represent any changes in your life?

❏ Review the film clip with your group to identify the ideas about change and connections with nature that Goldsworthy makes.

❏ Then, discuss what the changes in nature reveal about human nature. As you discuss, listen closely and ask each other questions to help clarify ideas.

❏ Finally, end your discussion by listing the conclusions of each member of your group.

 Go to the **Speaking and Listening Studio** to learn more about having a group discussion.

## RESPOND TO THE ESSENTIAL QUESTION

 How do changes around us reveal who we are?

**Gather Information** Review your annotations on the clip from *Rivers and Tides* and "Sonnets to Orpheus, Part Two, XII." Pick an image or idea and connect it with an aspect of human nature. Think about the changes in the natural world as you respond. Then, add relevant details to your Response Log.

At the end of the unit, use your notes to write a research report.

**ACADEMIC VOCABULARY**

As you write and discuss what you learned about change through these works, be sure to use the Academic Vocabulary words. Check off each of the words that you use.

❏ **abstract**

❏ **evolve**

❏ **explicit**

❏ **facilitate**

❏ **infer**

# Collaborate & Compare

## COMPARE THEMES ACROSS GENRES

When you compare two or more texts with the same theme across genres,
you synthesize the information, making connections and expanding on
key ideas. You can get a more thorough understanding of the theme by
comparing texts from different genres—like a documentary film and a poem.
Remember that the **theme** of a text is the message about life expressed in
the work. A work does not have to be literature, or even use words at all, to
communicate a theme.

In a small group, complete the chart shown below. In the center column, write
themes expressed in the film clip and the poem. In the right column, note the
details in each work that imply its theme.

| TITLE OF WORK | STATEMENTS OF THEME | DETAILS THAT IMPLY THEME |
|---|---|---|
| from *Rivers and Tides* | | |
| "Sonnets to Orpheus, Part Two, XII" | | |

## ANALYZE THE TEXTS

Discuss these questions in your group.

1. **Connect** What similarities do you see between Andy Goldsworthy's
   ideas about using nature to make art and the ideas presented in the
   poem?

2. **Contrast** What differences are there between the art Goldsworthy
   makes and the ideas in the poem by Rilke?

3. **Infer** Why does Goldsworthy use only materials he finds in nature to
   make his art? What is his intention, based on what he says in the film?

4. **Synthesize** What have you learned from these sources together about
   how changes in nature affect humans?

## COMPARE AND PRESENT

Now, your group can continue exploring the key ideas and themes in these texts by collaborating on research to present an overview of the themes. Follow these steps:

1. **Identify Themes** In your group, compile direct statements of theme from both works that you wrote in your charts, and analyze their similarities and differences.

2. **Gather Information** Choose two key images from each work, and draft a statement expressing the theme or main idea of each image. You can use the framework below to synthesize what you learn.

| KEY IMAGES | KEY IDEAS / THEMES |
|---|---|
| Image 1 from film clip: | |
| Image 2 from film clip: | |
| Image 1 from poem: | |
| Image 2 from poem: | |

3. **Present an Overview** Create a presentation comparing the view of change in each work. Be sure to cite examples from both works to support the analysis.

 Go to the **Speaking and Listening Studio** for help with giving a presentation.

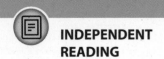
# Reader's Choice

**? ESSENTIAL QUESTION:**

How do changes around us reveal who we are?

**Setting a Purpose**   Select one or more of these options from your eBook to continue your exploration of the Essential Question.

- Read the descriptions to see which text grabs your interest.
- Think about which genres you enjoy reading.

## Notice & Note

In this unit, you practiced asking **Big Questions** and noticing and noting two signposts: **Contrasts and Contradictions** and **Extreme or Absolute Language.** As you read independently, these signposts and others will aid your understanding. Below are the anchor questions to ask when you read literature and nonfiction.

| Reading Literature: Stories, Poems, and Plays | | |
|---|---|---|
| **Signpost** | **Anchor Question(s)** | **Lesson** |
| **Contrasts and Contradictions** | Why did the character act that way? | p. 145 |
| **Aha Moment** | How might this change things? | p. 394 |
| **Tough Questions** | What does this make me wonder about? | p. 2 |
| **Words of the Wiser** | What's the lesson for the character? | p. 3 |
| **Again and Again** | Why might the author keep bringing this up? | p. 145 |
| **Memory Moment** | Why is this memory important? | p. 3 |

| Reading Nonfiction: Essays, Articles, and Arguments | | |
|---|---|---|
| **Signpost** | **Anchor Question(s)** | **Lesson** |
| **Big Questions** | What surprised me? | p. 220 |
| | What did the author think I already knew? | p. 319 |
| | What challenged, changed, or confirmed what I already knew? | p. 74 |
| **Contrasts and Contradictions** | What is the difference, and why does it matter? | p. 318 |
| **Extreme or Absolute Language** | Why did the author use this language? | p. 221 |
| **Numbers and Stats** | Why did the author use these numbers or amounts? | p. 75 |
| **Quoted Words** | Why was this person quoted or cited, and what did this add? | p. 221 |
| **Word Gaps** | Do I know this word from someplace else? | p. 75 |
| | Does it seem like technical talk for this topic? | |
| | Do clues in the sentence help me understand the word? | |

You can preview these texts in Unit 5 of your eBook.

Then, check off the text or texts that you select to read on your own.

**SHORT STORY**

**The Norwegian Rat**
Naguib Mahfouz

*Residents of an apartment building take action to protect themselves from an invasion of rats. But who are the real rats?*

**MEMOIR**

**After the Storm**
Orhan Pamuk

*A Nobel-winning Turkish writer finds meaning in the changes that occur during and after a violent storm.*

**SCIENCE WRITING**

*from* **Simplexity**
Jeffrey Kluger

*How do people react when they have to evacuate in an emergency? The answer is both simple and complicated.*

**NOVELLA**

*from* **The Metamorphosis**
Franz Kafka

*What would you do if you woke up and you weren't human anymore? Would you still be you?*

**Collaborate and Share**   With a partner, discuss what you learned from at least one of your independent readings.

- Give a brief synopsis or summary of the text.
- Describe any signposts that you noticed in the text, and explain what they revealed to you.
- Describe what you most enjoyed or found most challenging about the text. Give specific examples.
- Decide whether you would recommend the text to others. Why or why not?

Go to the **Reading Studio** for more resources on **Notice & Note.**

# Write a Research Report

Go to the **Writing Studio** for help writing a research report.

The texts in this unit present various perspectives on how we respond to changes around us and how those changes occur. Choose three texts from the unit. Identify a way in which humans respond to major changes, and conduct research about it. Synthesize your findings in a report that develops a clear thesis. For an example of a well-researched report you can use as a mentor text, review the excerpt from *The Fever*.

As you write your report, you will want to look at the notes you made in your Response Log after reading the texts in this unit.

## Writing Prompt

**Read** the information in the box below.

*This is the topic or context for your report.*

> Undergoing change may alter the way someone approaches the world, or it may magnify characteristics he or she already had.

**Think** carefully about the following question.

*This is the Essential Question for the unit. How would you answer this question, based on the texts in this unit?*

> How do changes around us reveal who we are?

*Think about how you will find a specific topic for your report.*

**Write** a research report about a specific way humans respond to changes in the world or in their own lives.

Be sure to—

*Review these points as you write and again when you finish. Make any needed changes.*

- ❑ research your topic and keep careful notes about your sources
- ❑ narrow your topic so that it addresses a specific research question
- ❑ clearly structure your ideas and subtopics, linking ideas with transitions
- ❑ smoothly integrate researched information and cite sources correctly
- ❑ use precise word choice and an appropriately formal tone and style
- ❑ end by summarizing your information or drawing a conclusion

# ① Plan

Begin to formulate a question you have about how humans respond to changes, either personal changes that affect their own lives or larger changes that affect their community or world. This question will guide your research.

Next, gather evidence about your question from credible print or online resources. Skim many sources to get an overview of the general topics they address and determine how credible they seem. Consider the author or organization that created the source, and look for signs of a bias. Reject sources that use faulty reasoning, including making hasty generalizations about human nature based on just a few examples. Once you find credible sources, note important details or quotations in the chart below or on index cards.

 Go to **Conducting Research: Starting Your Research** for help with identifying sources.

### Notice & Note

#### From Reading to Writing

As you plan your research report, apply what you've learned about signposts to your own writing. Think about how you can incorporate **Quoted Words** into your report.

 Go to the **Reading Studio** for more resources on **Notice & Note**.

| RESEARCH REPORT PLANNING CHART ||
|---|---|
| **Research Question:** ||
| **Source:** ||
| **Quotation or fact:** | **Page number or Date accessed:** |
| **Source:** ||
| **Quotation or fact:** | **Page number or Date accessed:** |
| **Source:** ||
| **Quotation or fact:** | **Page number or Date accessed:** |
| **Source:** ||
| **Quotation or fact:** | **Page number or Date accessed:** |
| **Source:** ||
| **Quotation or fact:** | **Page number or Date accessed:** |

Use the notes from your Response Log as you plan your report.

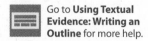
## WRITING TASK

Go to **Using Textual Evidence: Writing an Outline** for more help.

**Organize Your Ideas** After you have researched your topic, you need to organize your information. First, write a thesis statement that identifies your research question. Then, choose the textual and research evidence that most effectively supports your thesis. Decide what organizational pattern you will use for your report, and use this pattern to sort your textual evidence and research information into a logical order. You can use the chart below to make an outline of the points you will cover. You may find that you need to do additional research or omit some information you have gathered.

| RESEARCH REPORT OUTLINE |
| --- |
| Thesis Statement Identifying the Research Question: |
| Key Idea 1:<br>Supporting Points: |
| Key Idea 2:<br>Supporting Points: |
| Key Idea 3:<br>Supporting Points: |
| Conclusion That Answers the Research Question: |

You might prefer to draft your essay online.

## ❷ Develop a Draft

Use your notes and outline to guide your writing. Your introduction should grab readers' attention and clearly state your thesis. Cite sources for facts, quotations, and examples that elaborate on your ideas, and use introductory phrases to provide context for quotations. Any time you discuss a new text or a new key point, include transitions to help guide your readers.

## Use the Mentor Text

### Genre Characteristics

Using another person's words without credit is called plagiarism and is not acceptable. To avoid plagiarism, paraphrase information and give credit to the source by using footnotes or endnotes, or enclose exact words from the source in quotation marks. Here is an example of paraphrasing and citing a source from *The Fever*:

**Text:**
According to the science writer Carl Zimmer, one third of all described species practice the parasitic lifestyle.[4]

*The footnote gives credit to the source where the information was found.*

**Note:**
[4] Carl Zimmer, *Parasite Rex: Inside the Bizarre World of Nature's Most Dangerous Creatures* (New York: Touchstone, 2000), 17.

**Apply What You've Learned** Look carefully through your draft, adding either footnotes or endnotes (whichever your teacher prefers) to document the source of every quotation and every paraphrased fact that isn't common knowledge. The two most accepted methods of source documentation are those of the Modern Language Association (MLA) and the American Psychological Association (APA). For help formatting your citations, see page 389.

### Author's Craft

Even when you enclose the exact words from a source in quotation marks, the quoted text still needs to be placed in context for readers by using introductory words. Notice how the author of *The Fever* gives context to a quotation:

In 1883, Scottish lecturer Henry Drummond called parasitism "one of the gravest crimes of nature . . . "

*The introductory words explain who said these words and when.*

**Apply What You've Learned** When you include a quotation, provide some context in the same sentence. You may also give more information in a note inside parentheses.

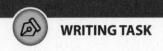

# WRITING TASK

## ③ Revise

Go to **Using Textual Evidence: Attribution** for help incorporating research material.

**On Your Own** Revise your draft to make sure it is clear, coherent, and engaging. Use the chart below as a guide. The Revision Guide will help focus on specific elements to make your writing stronger.

| REVISION GUIDE | | |
|---|---|---|
| **Ask Yourself** | **Tips** | **Revision Techniques** |
| 1. Does the introduction grab reader attention and state a clear thesis? | **Mark** the attention-getting opener. Underline the thesis statement or research question. | **Add** an interesting fact, example, or quotation that illustrates the topic. **Add** a thesis or **revise** to clarify it. |
| 2. Is the body of the report logically organized and linked with transitions? | **Note** the topic addressed in each part of the report. **Underline** transitions that link sections or show sequence. | **Rearrange** information as needed to provide a clearer organizational pattern. **Add** transitions that link ideas. |
| 3. Is each key idea in the report supported by text evidence? | **Mark** each piece of evidence for each section of the report. | **Add** supporting evidence from a variety of sources for any sections lacking evidence. |
| 4. Are quotations smoothly integrated into sentences that provide context? | **Underline** sentence parts that provide context for quotations from sources. | **Revise** sentences containing quotations to add context. |
| 5. Are sources correctly cited for quotations and facts that are not common knowledge? | **Mark** quotations and facts. **Mark** their citations in footnotes or endnotes. | **Add** correctly formatted footnotes or endnotes to cite the sources of facts or quotations as needed. |
| 6. Does the conclusion sum up ideas in an insightful way? | **Underline** the summary of ideas in the conclusion. | **Add** a summary or answer to the research question if needed. |

## ACADEMIC VOCABULARY

As you conduct your peer review, try to use these words.

- ❏ abstract
- ❏ evolve
- ❏ explicit
- ❏ facilitate
- ❏ infer

**With a Partner** After you have revised your report using the Revision Guide on your own, exchange papers with a partner. Evaluate each other's drafts in a peer review. Look to see whether quotations are smoothly integrated into sentences and that quotations and facts are correctly cited. Be sure you and your partner are using source materials correctly to avoid plagiarism.

In this type of academic writing, it's especially important to respond to what you have read using appropriate register and voice. **Register** refers to the level and context of the writing—a research report should sound like writing suitable for college. But it should also express the writer's **voice,** or unique style of self-expression. Consider reading your report aloud to get your partner's feedback on your register and voice.

##  Edit

Always give credit to both quoted and paraphrased sources in your research report. It's ethical, and it provides credibility so readers will take your writing seriously. Use footnotes or endnotes to tell the reader where your information came from. Footnotes appear at the bottom of the same page as the information they document; endnotes are grouped together at the end of the report. The notes are numbered in sequence.

> ! Go to **Quotation Marks** in the **Grammar Studio** to learn more.

### Crediting a Source

When you present information from a source, you may or may not name that source in the body of your text. However, you must credit the source in your notes. This chart shows a standard footnoting format for three types of sources.

| Print Article | Author First Name Last Name, "Article Title," *Magazine or Journal Title,* volume number, issue number (year): page number or numbers. |
| --- | --- |
| | David J. Marcogliese and Judith Price, "The Paradox of Parasites," *Global Biodiversity* 3 (1997): 7-15. |
| Book | Author First Name Last Name, *Book Title* (City of Publication: Publisher, year), page number or numbers. |
| | Roy Porter, *The Greatest Benefit to Mankind* (New York: W. W. Norton, 1997), 25. |
| Internet Site | Author First Name Last Name if available, "Title of Web Page," *Publishing Organization or Name of Website,* Publication Month Day, Year, URL (accessed Month Day, Year). |
| | Tom Phillips, "Brazilian explorers search 'medicine factory' to save lives and rainforest," *The Guardian,* April 27, 2009, http://www.theguardian.com/environment/2009/apr/27/amazon-rainforest-medicine (accessed January 27, 2019). |

## ⑤ Publish

Finalize your research report and choose a way to share it with your audience. Be sure that the report is up to college-level academic standards before you publish it. Consider these options:

- Print your research report and make it available to others.
- Post your research report on a class web page. Embed links to footnotes or endnotes in the citation numbers to help readers locate your sources faster.

Use the scoring guide to evaluate your report.

| | WRITING TASK SCORING GUIDE: RESEARCH REPORT | | |
|---|---|---|---|
| | **Organization/Progression** | **Development of Ideas** | **Use of Language and Conventions** |
| **4** | • The organization is effective and appropriate to the purpose.<br>• All ideas are focused on the topic specified in the prompt.<br>• Transitions clearly show the relationship among ideas. | • The introduction is compelling and informative; the thesis statement clearly identifies a research question.<br>• The topic is well developed with clear main ideas supported by specific and well-chosen facts, details, examples, and quotations.<br>• The conclusion effectively summarizes the answer to the research question and makes a thoughtful observation. | • The essay uses formal language, and word choice is purposeful and precise.<br>• Spelling, capitalization, and punctuation are correct.<br>• Grammar and usage are correct.<br>• Several credible research sources are cited using correctly formatted footnotes or endnotes. |
| **3** | • The organization is, for the most part, effective and appropriate to the purpose.<br>• Most ideas are focused on the topic specified in the prompt.<br>• Transitions usually connect ideas. | • The introduction is adequate; the thesis statement identifies a research question.<br>• The ideas are sufficiently developed and are supported by specific and appropriate facts, details, examples, and quotations.<br>• The concluding section summarizes the answer to the research question. | • Language is for the most part formal, specific, and clear.<br>• Some minor spelling, capitalization, and punctuation mistakes occur.<br>• Some grammatical and usage errors occur but do not interfere with understanding.<br>• Several credible research sources are cited using footnotes or endnotes with some formatting errors. |
| **2** | • The organization is evident but is not always appropriate to the purpose.<br>• Only some ideas are focused on the topic specified in the prompt.<br>• More transitions are needed to show the relationship among ideas. | • The introduction states a vague thesis but does not engage readers.<br>• The development of ideas is minimal. The writer uses facts, details, examples, or quotations that are inappropriate or ineffectively presented.<br>• The conclusion merely restates the thesis. | • Language is somewhat informal, vague, and unclear.<br>• Spelling, capitalization, and punctuation, as well as grammar and usage, are often incorrect and sometimes make the writer's ideas unclear.<br>• Only one or two research sources are cited, using incorrect format. |
| **1** | • The organization is absent or not appropriate to the purpose.<br>• Ideas are not focused on the topic specified in the prompt.<br>• No transitions are used, making the report difficult to understand. | • The introduction and the thesis statement are missing or confusing.<br>• The development of ideas is weak. Supporting facts, details, examples, or quotations are unreliable, vague, or missing.<br>• The conclusion is missing. | • Language is inappropriate for the text.<br>• Many spelling, capitalization, and punctuation errors are present.<br>• Frequent grammatical and usage errors cause confusion.<br>• Citations of research sources are missing. |

# Reflect on the Unit

When you were writing your research report, you gathered and expressed many of your thoughts about the reading you have done in this unit. Now is a good time to reflect on what you have learned.

## Reflect on the Essential Question

- How do changes around us reveal who we are? How has your answer to this question changed since you first considered it when you started this unit?

- What are some examples from the texts you've read that show how humans respond to changes around them?

## Reflect on Your Reading

- Which selections were the most interesting or surprising to you?

- From which selection did you learn the most about how humans respond to change?

## Reflect on the Writing Task

- What difficulties did you encounter while working on your research report? How might you avoid them next time?

- What part of the report was the easiest and what part was the hardest to write? Why?

- What improvements did you make to your report as you were revising?

**UNIT 5 SELECTIONS**
- from "Total Eclipse"
- from *The Fever*
- "A Sound of Thunder"
- "5 P.M., Tuesday, August 23, 2005"
- from *Rivers and Tides*
- "Sonnets to Orpheus, Part Two, XII"

# ABSOLUTE POWER

? **ESSENTIAL QUESTION:**

What are the sources of true power?

**"**
Be bloody, bold, and resolute.
Laugh to scorn
The power of man, . . . **"**

*Macbeth*, **Act IV, Scene 1**

## ACADEMIC VOCABULARY

Academic Vocabulary words are words you use when you discuss and write about texts. In this unit you will practice and learn five words.

- ☑ **comprise**
- ❑ **incidence**
- ❑ **predominant**
- ❑ **priority**
- ❑ **ultimate**

Study the Word Network to learn more about the word **comprise.**

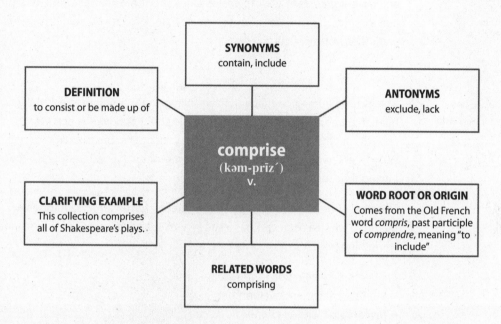

**SYNONYMS**
contain, include

**DEFINITION**
to consist or be made up of

**ANTONYMS**
exclude, lack

**comprise**
(kəm-prīz´)
v.

**CLARIFYING EXAMPLE**
This collection comprises all of Shakespeare's plays.

**WORD ROOT OR ORIGIN**
Comes from the Old French word *compris*, past participle of *comprendre*, meaning "to include"

**RELATED WORDS**
comprising

**Write and Discuss** Discuss the completed Word Network with a partner, making sure to talk through all of the boxes until you both understand the word, its synonyms, antonyms, and related forms. Then, fill out Word Networks for the remaining four words. Use a dictionary or online resource to help you complete the activity.

*Go online to access the Word Networks.*

## RESPOND TO THE ESSENTIAL QUESTION

In this unit, you will explore what true power means to different people. As you read, you will revisit the **Essential Question** and gather your ideas about it in the **Response Log** that appears on page R6. At the end of the unit, you will have the opportunity to write a **literary analysis** about different perspectives of true power. Filling out the Response Log will help you prepare for this writing task.

*You can also go online to access the Response Log.*

UNIT 6
RESPONSE LOG

Use this Response Log to record your ideas about how each of the texts in Unit 6 relates to or comments on the **Essential Question**.

**? Essential Question:**
What are the sources of true power?

| The Tragedy of Macbeth | |
| from Macbeth (film version) | |
| The Macbeth Murder Mystery | |
| from Manga Shakespeare: Macbeth | |
| Shakespeare and Samurai (and Robot Ninjas?) | |

R6   Student Resources

# Notice & Note

## THE TRAGEDY OF MACBETH

 For more information on these and other signposts to Notice & Note, visit the **Reading Studio**.

You are about to read the drama *The Tragedy of Macbeth*. In it, you will notice and note signposts that will give you clues about the drama's characters, plot, and themes. Here are three key signposts to look for as you read this drama and other works of fiction.

When you see a phrase like this, pause to see if it's an **Aha Moment:**

"All of a sudden . . ."

"for the first time . . ."

"and just like that . . ."

"I realized . . ."

**Aha Moment**  Imagine that you have an important problem to solve. You've been thinking about it from every possible angle, and no solution you consider seems right. One night you give your brain a break and go to bed early . . . and when you wake up the next morning, the perfect solution pops into your head!

This kind of breakthrough is an **Aha Moment**. These moments happen in literature when a character has a sudden realization or comes to understand something fully. Aha Moments tend to:

- signal a new direction in the plot
- indicate character development
- reveal some kind of change
- resolve a character's internal conflict

Here is how a student might mark an Aha Moment in the play:

**Anchor Question**
When you notice this signpost, ask: How might this change things?

> **Macbeth.**  If chance will have me king, why, <u>chance may crown me Without my stir.</u>

| | |
|---|---|
| What does the character realize? | He may not have to take any action to become king. |
| How might this moment change things? | He might decide to just enjoy his new title with the anticipation that it will lead to bigger things. |

**Again and Again** When you think of picture books, you probably think of repetition. Repetition of words, ideas, or images helps young readers understand the message. The same is true, but more subtle, in literary works. When a word, phrase, or image comes up **Again and Again,** it may suggest a theme, a symbol, or character motives.

Here is how a student noted repetition of an image:

> **Lady Macbeth.** The raven himself is hoarse
> That croaks the fatal entrance of Duncan
> Under my battlements. (Act I, Scene 5, lines 35–37)
>
> **Banquo.** This guest of summer,
> The temple-haunting martlet, does approve . . . (Act I, Scene 6, lines 3–4)

**Anchor Question**
When you notice this signpost, ask: Why might the author bring this up again and again?

| What image is repeated? | references to birds |
|---|---|
| Why does the author repeat this image? | These birds seem to represent human emotions. |

**Tough Questions** Classic literature is created when main characters face difficult choices. A character's decisions provide insight into internal conflicts, complex personalities, and often suggest themes. Look for moments of confusion, doubt, conflict, and anxiety as you read.

In this example, a student marked a **Tough Question** in the play:

> **Macbeth.** This supernatural soliciting
> Cannot be ill, cannot be good. If ill,
> Why hath it given me earnest of success
> Commencing in a truth? I am Thane of Cawdor.
> If good, why do I yield to that suggestion
> Whose horrid image doth unfix my hair
> And make my seated heart knock at my ribs
> Against the use of nature?

**Anchor Question**
When you notice this signpost, ask: What does this question make me wonder about?

| What tough question is the character facing? | Is the Witches' influence good or bad? |
|---|---|
| What does this make me wonder about? | whether Macbeth will make the right choice |

# SHAKESPEAREAN DRAMA

*One reason Shakespeare's works have endured for over 400 years is that his characters, whether from history or his imagination, transcend any particular time or place. Many of these characters are archetypes—familiar character types that appear over and over again in literature. The scheming characters and conspiracies at the heart of* The Tragedy of Macbeth *are as relevant today as they were in Shakespeare's time.*

## CHARACTERISTICS OF SHAKESPEAREAN TRAGEDY

A **tragedy** is a drama in which a series of actions leads to the downfall of the main character, called the tragic hero. The plot builds to a catastrophe, or a disastrous final outcome. A tragic hero —

- is of high social rank
- has a tragic flaw that leads to a downfall
- suffers ruin or death, but faces this downfall with courage and dignity

**Dramatic Conventions**  As you read, notice how Shakespeare builds suspense with these techniques:

- **Dramatic irony** results when the audience knows something that a character does not know.
- **Soliloquy** is a speech given by a character alone on stage, revealing private thoughts, feelings, and motivations.
- **Aside** is a character's remark, either to the audience or to another character, that no one else on stage is supposed to hear. Like a soliloquy, an aside reveals a character's secret thoughts.

## THE LANGUAGE OF SHAKESPEARE

Shakespearean language can be challenging because of its unfamiliar vocabulary and sentence structure, but it shouldn't stop you from getting caught up in the intriguing plot that drives *Macbeth*. Here are some keys to reading Shakespeare's language:

**Blank Verse**  Shakespeare's plays are **verse dramas**, in which most of the dialogue is written in the metrical patterns of poetry. Shakespeare wrote primarily in **blank verse,** or unrhymed lines of iambic pentameter. **Iambic pentameter** is a pattern of rhythm that has five unstressed syllables ( ˘ ), each followed by a stressed syllable ( ′ ). Read this line aloud, noticing how the rhythm mimics that of everyday speech:

> ˘ ′ ˘ ′ ˘ ′ ˘ ′ ˘ ′
> *So foul and fair a day I have not seen.*

Most of *Macbeth* is written in blank verse. In some places, however, Shakespeare broke the pattern to vary the rhythm, create dramatic tension, or distinguish low-ranking characters from those of higher rank.

**Rhetorical Devices**  In *Macbeth*, characters often attempt to persuade each other as they struggle to reach their goals. One key to persuasion is the use of rhetorical devices such as these:

| RHETORICAL DEVICE | EXAMPLE |
|---|---|
| **Repetition:** the use of words and phrases more than once to emphasize ideas | Thrice to thine, and thrice to mine And thrice again, to make up nine. <br> —Act I, Scene 3, lines 35–36 |
| **Parallelism:** the repetition of grammatical structures to express ideas that are related or of equal importance | When the hurly-burly's done, When the battle's lost and won. <br> —Act I, Scene 1, lines 3–4 |
| **Rhetorical Questions:** the use of questions that require no answer to make the speaker's rightness seem self-evident | Do you not hope your children shall be kings When those that gave the Thane of Cawdor to me Promised no less to them? <br> —Act I, Scene 3, lines 118–120 |
| **Antithesis:** the use of contrasting ideas within a sentence for effect | Fair is foul, and foul is fair, . . . <br> —Act I, Scene 1, line 10 |

## READING SHAKESPEAREAN DRAMA

Understanding Shakespearean drama can be challenging for modern readers. Use these strategies to help you appreciate and analyze *Macbeth*.

- Study the opening **cast of characters**, which in *Macbeth* will tell you the characters' ranks and how they are related to one another.
- Try to visualize the setting and action by using information in the **stage directions** and **dialogue**.
- Use the **side notes** to understand unfamiliar words and expressions.
- Remember that the end of a line does not necessarily mean the end of a thought. Look closely at each line's punctuation, and try to figure out the meaning of the complete sentence or phrase.
- Paraphrase passages to help you understand the characters' public personas as well as their private schemes. When you **paraphrase** a passage, you restate its key points in your own words.

# THE TRAGEDY OF MACBETH

Drama by **William Shakespeare**

What are the sources of true power?

Ray Fearon as Macbeth and Tara Fitzgerald as Lady Macbeth, directed by Iqban Khan, The Globe Theatre, London, England, 2016.

## QUICK START

Inspirational speakers, politicians, Internet bloggers, television commercials, print ads, and even ordinary people can all be persuasive. People may be tempted or even convinced to do something based on what they read or listen to, even when they doubt and question the information. With a partner, discuss unlikely examples of effective persuasion you have seen or heard.

## ANALYZE DRAMA

Use what you learned about the characteristics of Shakespearean tragedy to help you analyze drama, including understanding the characters and plot of *Macbeth*. Watch for ways in which the play's tragic hero, asides, soliloquies, and dramatic irony build suspense and develop a theme.

Use these aspects of drama to help you as you read:

| FEATURE | HOW IT HELPS |
|---|---|
| Cast of Characters | Provides a preview of "who's who" and their relationships with one another |
| Stage Directions | Tell where and when events occur, describe how actions are performed, and note emotions or how a character says a line of dialogue |
| Side Glosses | Provide definitions and explanations of unfamiliar terms and expressions |

If you still find a passage confusing, read it aloud with a partner and then paraphrase and discuss it.

## ANALYZE CHARACTER AND THEME

The **theme** is the insight about life or human nature that the writer wants to communicate. Theme is often developed through characterization, or the way a writer reveals the characters' personalities, and plot. In *The Tragedy of Macbeth*, Shakespeare explores themes related to ambition and power. These themes are supported by the actions, thoughts, and speech of the characters.

Shakespeare shaped the character of Macbeth into a complex and believable character who is driven by ambition. He develops his characters through a range of literary devices, such as:

- **character foils,** or characters who provide a striking contrast to another character. A foil can call attention to certain traits of the main character.
- **soliloquies** and **asides** that reveal a character's motivations and secrets
- **dialogue** that shows what others think about a character
- **responses** of characters to others
- **change** and growth of a character

### GENRE ELEMENTS: DRAMA

- is meant to be performed before an audience
- tells a story with a plot, characters, setting, conflict, and theme
- includes stage directions, speaker tags, and dialogue

## LANGUAGE CONVENTIONS

**Inverted Sentence Structure** In an **inverted sentence,** the usual word order is reversed, usually in one of these ways:

- all or part of the predicate comes before the subject

- a subject comes between a helping verb and a main verb

- a direct object precedes a verb

- a prepositional phrase comes before the noun or verb it modifies

Here is an example from Act 1, Scene 2, of *Macbeth*:

> **Duncan.** Dismayed not this our captains, Macbeth and Banquo?

In the example, the verb precedes the subject.

The sentence could be written in this way:

> Were our captains, Macbeth and Banquo, not dismayed by this?

To understand an inverted sentence, find the subject and verb so you can reorder the ideas.

## ANNOTATION MODEL

**NOTICE & NOTE**

As you read, notice the setting in italics and the stage directions that appear in brackets. Also pay attention to who is speaking by referring to the boldface speaker tags. Here is how one reader marked the play's beginning:

ACT I

**Scene 1** *An open place in Scotland.*

[*Thunder and lightning. Enter three* Witches.]

**First Witch.** When shall we three meet again?

In thunder, lightning, or in rain?

**Second Witch.** When the hurly-burly's done,

When the battle's lost and won.

**Third Witch.** That will be ere the set of sun.

**First Witch.** Where the place?

**Second Witch.**               Upon the heath.

**Third Witch.** There to meet with Macbeth.

The setting of this first scene is outside during a storm. The first characters we meet are three Witches, who are not named.

Prediction?

They plan to meet Macbeth.

**William Shakespeare** (1564–1616) was born in Stratford-upon-Avon to a fairly prosperous family. He attended the local grammar school, studying Latin and classical literature. At age 18, he married Anne Hathaway. They had a daughter and then twins, a boy and a girl.

Around 1590, Shakespeare moved to London. He worked as an actor and began a successful career as a playwright. As part of a company called the Lord Chamberlain's Men, he performed for Queen Elizabeth I and helped renovate the Globe Theater for its performances. Shakespeare's success enabled him to buy a family home in Stratford, where he returned in 1612. He continued to write until his death four years later at age 52.

# THE TRAGEDY OF
# MACBETH
### Drama by William Shakespeare

Shakespeare is recognized as the most influential writer in the English language. He mastered the sonnet form, making it his own with his highly original approach; he composed long narrative poems; and he left a dramatic legacy unsurpassed by any playwright before or since. Four centuries later, his plays continue to be performed on stage and made into films.

Shakespeare's plays are often grouped based on when they were written. In the early 1590s, he wrote history plays and comedies with plots derived from earlier stories. In the late 1590s, he wrote comedies, including A Midsummer Night's Dream, in which he skillfully interwove complex plots to convey his themes. As the century ended, Shakespeare began exploring darker views of human nature in his work. Between 1600 and 1607, he wrote his greatest tragedies, including Macbeth, Hamlet, and King Lear. His later comedies, such as The Tempest, are often called tragicomedies, as they are tinged with sadness.

After Shakespeare died, his plays were published in an edition known as the First Folio. In the introduction, playwright Ben Jonson wrote that Shakespeare "was not of an age, but for all time."

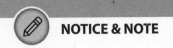

## BACKGROUND

*It is believed that Shakespeare wrote* Macbeth *largely to please King James I. The Scottish-born king claimed to be descended from an 11th-century historical figure named Banquo. In* Macbeth, *the Witches predict that Banquo will sire a long line of kings. James's interest in witchcraft—he wrote a book on the subject in 1597—may explain the prominence of the Witches in the play. The play also addressed James's fears of assassination; he had survived several attempts on his life.*

## SETTING A PURPOSE

*Before you begin reading, use the cast list to make a diagram on a separate piece of paper that shows characters and their relationships. Revisit your diagram at the beginning of each act of the play. Add brief notes about what you learn about the characters.*

**THE TIME:** The 11th century

**THE PLACE:** Scotland and England

## CHARACTERS

**Duncan,** King of Scotland
*His Sons*
  **Malcolm**
  **Donalbain**
*Noblemen of Scotland*
  **Macbeth**
  **Banquo**
  **Macduff**
  **Lennox**
  **Ross**
  **Menteith** (měn-tēth´)
  **Angus**
  **Caithness** (kāth´nĭs)
**Fleance** (flā´əns), son to Banquo
**Siward** (syōō´ərd), earl of Northumberland, general of the English forces
**Young Siward,** his son

**Seyton** (sā´tən), an officer attending on Macbeth
**Son,** to Macduff
**An English Doctor**
**A Scottish Doctor**
**A Porter**
**An Old Man**
**Three Murderers**
**Lady Macbeth**
**Lady Macduff**
**A Gentlewoman** attending on Lady Macbeth
**Hecate** (hěk´ĭt), goddess of witchcraft
**Three Witches**
**Apparitions**
**Lords, Officers, Soldiers, Messengers, and Attendants**

# ACT I

**Scene 1** *An open place in Scotland.*

[*Thunder and lightning. Enter three* Witches.]

**First Witch.** When shall we three meet again?
In thunder, lightning, or in rain?

**Second Witch.** When the hurly-burly's done,
When the battle's lost and won.

5 **Third Witch.** That will be ere the set of sun.

**First Witch.** Where the place?

**Second Witch.**                    Upon the heath.

**Third Witch.** There to meet with Macbeth.

**First Witch.** I come, Graymalkin.

**Second Witch.** Paddock calls.

**Third Witch.**                    Anon.

10 **All.** Fair is foul, and foul is fair,
Hover through the fog and filthy air.

[*They exit.*]

**3 hurly-burly:** turmoil; uproar.

**8–9 Graymalkin . . .
Paddock:** two demon helpers
in the form of a cat and a toad;
**Anon:** at once.

**Scene 2** *King Duncan's camp near the battlefield.*

[*Alarum within. Enter* King Duncan, Malcolm, Donalbain,
Lennox, *with* Attendants, *meeting a bleeding* Captain.]

**Duncan.** What bloody man is that? He can report,
As seemeth by his plight, of the revolt
The newest state.

**Malcolm.**          This is the sergeant
Who, like a good and hardy soldier, fought
5 'Gainst my captivity.—Hail, brave friend!
Say to the King the knowledge of the broil
As thou didst leave it.

**Captain.**          Doubtful it stood,
As two spent swimmers that do cling together
And choke their art. The merciless Macdonwald
10 (Worthy to be a rebel, for to that
The multiplying villainies of nature
Do swarm upon him) from the Western Isles
Of kerns and gallowglasses is supplied;

[Stage Direction] **Alarum
within:** the sound of a trumpet
offstage, a signal that soldiers
should arm themselves.

**5 'Gainst my captivity:** to save
me from capture.

**6 broil:** battle.

**9–13** Macdonwald's evils
(**multiplying villainies**) swarm
like insects around him. His
army consists of soldiers (**kerns
and gallowglasses**) from the
Hebrides (**Western Isles**).

**Annotate:** Mark words in the Captain's speech that reveal Macbeth's character traits.

**Predict:** What kind of person is Macbeth?

**19 valor's minion:** the favorite of valor, meaning the bravest of all.

**22 unseamed him . . . chops:** split him open from the navel to the jaw.

**25–28** As the rising sun is sometimes followed by storms, a new assault on Macbeth began.

**36 sooth:** the truth.
**37 double cracks:** a double load of ammunition.

**39–40** The officer claims he cannot decide whether (**except**) Macbeth and Banquo wanted to bathe in blood or make the battlefield as famous as Golgotha, the site of Christ's crucifixion.

**45 Thane:** a Scottish noble.

And Fortune, on his damnèd quarrel smiling,
15 Showed like a rebel's whore. But all's too weak;
For brave Macbeth (well he deserves that name),
Disdaining Fortune, with his brandished steel,
Which smoked with bloody execution,
Like valor's minion, carved out his passage
20 Till he faced the slave;
Which ne'er shook hands, nor bade farewell to him,
Till he unseamed him from the nave to th' chops,
And fixed his head upon our battlements.

**Duncan.** O valiant cousin, worthy gentleman!

25 **Captain.** As whence the sun 'gins his reflection
Shipwracking storms and direful thunders break,
So from that spring whence comfort seemed to come
Discomfort swells. Mark, King of Scotland, mark:
No sooner justice had, with valor armed,
30 Compelled these skipping kerns to trust their heels,
But the Norweyan lord, surveying vantage,
With furbished arms and new supplies of men,
Began a fresh assault.

**Duncan.** Dismayed not this our captains, Macbeth and Banquo?

35 **Captain.** Yes, as sparrows eagles, or the hare the lion.
If I say sooth, I must report they were
As cannons overcharged with double cracks,
So they doubly redoubled strokes upon the foe.
Except they meant to bathe in reeking wounds
40 Or memorize another Golgotha,
I cannot tell—
But I am faint. My gashes cry for help.

**Duncan.** So well thy words become thee as thy wounds:
They smack of honor both.—Go, get him surgeons.

[*The* Captain *is led off by* Attendants.]
[*Enter* Ross *and* Angus.]
45 Who comes here?

**Malcolm.**　　　　The worthy Thane of Ross.

**Lennox.** What a haste looks through his eyes!
So should he look that seems to speak things strange.

**Ross.** God save the King.

**Duncan.** Whence cam'st thou, worthy thane?

50 **Ross.** From Fife, great king,
Where the Norweyan banners flout the sky
And fan our people cold.

Norway himself, with terrible numbers,
Assisted by that most disloyal traitor,
55 The Thane of Cawdor, began a dismal conflict,
Till that Bellona's bridegroom, lapped in proof,
Confronted him with self-comparisons,
Point against point, rebellious arm 'gainst arm,
Curbing his lavish spirit. And to conclude,
60 The victory fell on us.

**Duncan.**                Great happiness!

**Ross.** That now Sweno,
The Norways' king, craves composition.
Nor would we deign him burial of his men
Till he disbursèd at Saint Colme's Inch
65 Ten thousand dollars to our general use.

**Duncan.** No more that Thane of Cawdor shall deceive
Our bosom interest. Go, pronounce his present death,
And with his former title greet Macbeth.

**Ross.** I'll see it done.

70 **Duncan.** What he hath lost, noble Macbeth hath won.

[*They exit.*]


**Scene 3** *A bleak place near the battlefield.*

[*Thunder. Enter the three* Witches.]

**First Witch.** Where hast thou been, sister?

**Second Witch.** Killing swine.

**Third Witch.** Sister, where thou?

**First Witch.** A sailor's wife had chestnuts in her lap
5 And munched and munched and munched. "Give me," quoth I.
"Aroint thee, witch," the rump-fed runnion cries.
Her husband's to Aleppo gone, master o' th' Tiger;
But in a sieve I'll thither sail
And, like a rat without a tail,
10 I'll do, I'll do, and I'll do.

**Second Witch.** I'll give thee a wind.

**First Witch.** Th' art kind.

**Third Witch.** And I another.

**First Witch.** I myself have all the other,
15 And the very ports they blow,
All the quarters that they know
I' th' shipman's card.

**49–59** Ross has arrived from Fife, where Norway's troops had invaded. There the king of Norway, with the Thane of Cawdor, met Macbeth (described as the husband of **Bellona**, the goddess of war). Macbeth, in heavy armor (**proof**), challenged the enemy.

**62 craves composition:** wants a treaty.

**63 deign:** allow.

**64 disbursèd at Saint Colme's Inch:** paid at Saint Colme's Inch, an island in the North Sea.

**66–67 deceive our bosom interest:** betray our friendship; **present death:** immediate execution.

**6 "Aroint thee, witch," . . . runnion cries:** "Go away, witch!" the fatbottomed (**rump-fed**), ugly creature (**runnion**) cries.

**7–8** The woman's husband, the master of a merchant ship (**th' *Tiger***), has sailed to Aleppo. The witch will pursue him. Witches were thought to sail on strainers (**sieve**).

**14–23** The witch controls the winds, covering all points of a compass (**shipman's card**). She will make the sailor sleepless, keeping his eyelids (**penthouse lid**) from closing. Thus, he will lead an accursed (**forbid**) life for weeks (**sev'nnights**), wasting away with fatigue.

**33 posters:** quick riders.

**36** Nine was considered a magical number by superstitious people.

**42–46 aught:** anything; **choppy:** chapped; **your beards:** Beards on women identified them as witches.

AGAIN AND AGAIN

**Notice & Note:** Mark the word the Witches repeat again and again in lines 48–69.

**Analyze:** What is persuasive about their repetition of this word?

**53 are you fantastical:** Are you (the Witches) imaginary?

I'll drain him dry as hay.
Sleep shall neither night nor day
20 Hang upon his penthouse lid.
He shall live a man forbid.
Weary sev'nnights, nine times nine,
Shall he dwindle, peak, and pine.
Though his bark cannot be lost,
25 Yet it shall be tempest-tossed.
Look what I have.

**Second Witch.** Show me, show me.

**First Witch.** Here I have a pilot's thumb,
Wracked as homeward he did come.

[*Drum within*]

30 **Third Witch.** A drum, a drum!
Macbeth doth come.

**All.** [*Dancing in a circle*] The Weïrd Sisters, hand in hand,
Posters of the sea and land,
Thus do go about, about,
35 Thrice to thine, and thrice to mine
And thrice again, to make up nine.
Peace, the charm's wound up.

[*Enter Macbeth and Banquo.*]

**Macbeth.** So foul and fair a day I have not seen.

**Banquo.** How far is 't called to Forres?—What are these,
40 So withered, and so wild in their attire,
That look not like th' inhabitants o' th' earth
And yet are on 't?—Live you? Or are you aught
That man may question? You seem to understand me
By each at once her choppy finger laying
45 Upon her skinny lips. You should be women,
And yet your beards forbid me to interpret
That you are so.

**Macbeth.** Speak, if you can. What are you?

**First Witch.** All hail, Macbeth! Hail to thee, Thane of Glamis!

**Second Witch.** All hail, Macbeth! Hail to thee, Thane of Cawdor!

50 **Third Witch.** All hail, Macbeth, that shalt be king hereafter!

**Banquo.** Good sir, why do you start and seem to fear
Things that do sound so fair? I' th' name of truth,
Are you fantastical, or that indeed
Which outwardly you show? My noble partner
55 You greet with present grace and great prediction
Of noble having and of royal hope,

Janet Whiteside, Ann Firbank, and Jane Thorne as the Witches and Simon Russell Beale as Macbeth, Almeida Theatre, London.

That he seems rapt withal. To me you speak not.
If you can look into the seeds of time
And say which grain will grow and which will not,
60 Speak, then, to me, who neither beg nor fear
Your favors nor your hate.

**First Witch.** Hail!

**Second Witch.** Hail!

**Third Witch.** Hail!

65 **First Witch.** Lesser than Macbeth and greater.

**Second Witch.** Not so happy, yet much happier.

**Third Witch.** Thou shalt get kings, though thou be none.
So all hail, Macbeth and Banquo!

**First Witch.** Banquo and Macbeth, all hail!

70 **Macbeth.** Stay, you imperfect speakers. Tell me more.
By Sinel's death I know I am Thane of Glamis.
But how of Cawdor? The Thane of Cawdor lives
A prosperous gentleman, and to be king
Stands not within the prospect of belief,
75 No more than to be Cawdor. Say from whence
You owe this strange intelligence or why
Upon this blasted heath you stop our way
With such prophetic greeting. Speak, I charge you.

[Witches *vanish*.]

**Banquo.** The earth hath bubbles, as the water has,
80 And these are of them. Whither are they vanished?

**Macbeth.** Into the air, and what seemed corporal melted,
As breath into the wind. Would they had stayed!

**54–57** The witches' prophecies of noble possessions (**having**)— the lands and wealth of Cawdor—and kingship (**royal hope**) have left Macbeth dazed (**rapt withal**).

**80 whither:** where.

**81 corporal:** physical; real.

The Tragedy of Macbeth, Act I, Scene 3   407

**84 insane root:** A number of plants were believed to cause insanity when eaten.

**92–93** King Duncan hesitates between awe (**wonders**) and gratitude (**praises**) and is, as a result, speechless.

**96–97** Although Macbeth left many dead (**strange images of death**), he obviously did not fear death himself.

**104 earnest:** partial payment.

**AHA MOMENT** ◀

**Notice & Note:** Mark the predictions that Banquo and Macbeth realize must be true in lines 107–120.

**Predict:** How might knowing these future events affect the choices these characters make?

**111–116** Whether the former thane of Cawdor allied (**combined**) with the king of Norway or supported the traitor Macdonwald (**did line the rebel**), he is guilty of treasons that deserve the death penalty (**treasons capital**), having aimed at the country's ruin (**wrack**).

**Banquo.** Were such things here as we do speak about?
Or have we eaten on the insane root
85 That takes the reason prisoner?

**Macbeth.** Your children shall be kings.

**Banquo.**                                         You shall be king.

**Macbeth.** And Thane of Cawdor too. Went it not so?

**Banquo.** To th' selfsame tune and words.—Who's here?

[*Enter* Ross *and* Angus.]

**Ross.** The King hath happily received, Macbeth,
90 The news of thy success, and, when he reads
Thy personal venture in the rebels' fight,
His wonders and his praises do contend
Which should be thine or his. Silenced with that,
In viewing o'er the rest o' th' selfsame day
95 He finds thee in the stout Norweyan ranks,
Nothing afeard of what thyself didst make,
Strange images of death. As thick as hail
Came post with post, and every one did bear
Thy praises in his kingdom's great defense,
100 And poured them down before him.

**Angus.**                                         We are sent
To give thee from our royal master thanks,
Only to herald thee into his sight,
Not pay thee.

**Ross.** And for an earnest of a greater honor,
105 He bade me, from him, call thee Thane of Cawdor,
In which addition, hail, most worthy thane,
For it is thine.

**Banquo.**              What, can the devil speak true?

**Macbeth.** The Thane of Cawdor lives. Why do you dress me
In borrowed robes?

**Angus.**                        Who was the Thane lives yet,
110 But under heavy judgment bears that life
Which he deserves to lose. Whether he was combined
With those of Norway, or did line the rebel
With hidden help and vantage, or that with both
He labored in his country's wrack, I know not;
115 But treasons capital, confessed and proved,
Have overthrown him.

**Macbeth** [*aside*].              Glamis and Thane of Cawdor!
The greatest is behind. [*To Ross and* Angus] Thanks for your pains.
[*Aside to* Banquo] Do you not hope your children shall be kings

When those that gave the Thane of Cawdor to me
120 Promised no less to them?

**Banquo.** That, trusted home,
Might yet enkindle you unto the crown,
Besides the Thane of Cawdor. But 'tis strange.
And oftentimes, to win us to our harm,
The instruments of darkness tell us truths,
125 Win us with honest trifles, to betray 's
In deepest consequence.—
Cousins, a word, I pray you. [*They step aside.*]

**Macbeth** [*aside*]. Two truths are told
As happy prologues to the swelling act
Of the imperial theme.—I thank you, gentlemen.
130 [*Aside*] This supernatural soliciting
Cannot be ill, cannot be good. If ill,
Why hath it given me earnest of success
Commencing in a truth? I am Thane of Cawdor.
If good, why do I yield to that suggestion
135 Whose horrid image doth unfix my hair
And make my seated heart knock at my ribs
Against the use of nature? Present fears
Are less than horrible imaginings.
My thought, whose murder yet is but fantastical,
140 Shakes so my single state of man
That function is smothered in surmise,
And nothing is but what is not.

**Banquo.** Look how our partner's rapt.

**Macbeth** [*aside*]. If chance will have me king, why, chance may
crown me
Without my stir.

**Banquo.** New honors come upon him,
145 Like our strange garments, cleave not to their mold
But with the aid of use.

**Macbeth** [*aside*]. Come what come may,
Time and the hour runs through the roughest day.

**Banquo.** Worthy Macbeth, we stay upon your leisure.

**Macbeth.** Give me your favor. My dull brain was wrought
150 With things forgotten. Kind gentlemen, your pains
Are registered where every day I turn
The leaf to read them. Let us toward the King.
[*Aside to* Banquo] Think upon what hath chanced, and
at more time,

**120 home:** fully; completely.
**121 enkindle you unto:** inflame your ambitions.
**123–126** Banquo warns that evil powers often offer little truths to tempt people. The witches may be lying about what matters most (**in deepest consequence**).

**144 my stir:** my doing anything.

**146–147 Come what . . . roughest day:** The future will arrive no matter what.
**148 stay:** wait.
**150–152 your pains . . . read them:** I will always remember your efforts. The metaphor refers to keeping a diary and reading it regularly.
**153–155** Macbeth wants to discuss the prophecies later, after he and Banquo have had time to think about them.

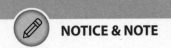
The interim having weighed it, let us speak
155 Our free hearts each to other.

**Banquo.**                              Very gladly.

**Macbeth.** Till then, enough.—Come, friends.

[*They exit.*]

**Scene 4** *A room in the king's palace at Forres.*

[*Flourish. Enter* King Duncan, Lennox, Malcolm, Donalbain,
*and* Attendants.]

**Duncan.** Is execution done on Cawdor? Are not
Those in commission yet returned?

**Malcolm.**                              My liege,
They are not yet come back. But I have spoke
With one that saw him die, who did report
5 That very frankly he confessed his treasons,
Implored your Highness' pardon, and set forth
A deep repentance. Nothing in his life
Became him like the leaving it. He died
As one that had been studied in his death
10 To throw away the dearest thing he owed
As 'twere a careless trifle.

**Duncan.**                              There's no art
To find the mind's construction in the face.
He was a gentleman on whom I built
An absolute trust.

[*Enter* Macbeth, Banquo, Ross, *and* Angus.]

                              O worthiest cousin,
15 The sin of my ingratitude even now
Was heavy on me. Thou art so far before
That swiftest wing of recompense is slow
To overtake thee. Would thou hadst less deserved,
That the proportion both of thanks and payment
20 Might have been mine! Only I have left to say,
More is thy due than more than all can pay.

**Macbeth.** The service and the loyalty I owe
In doing it pays itself. Your Highness' part
Is to receive our duties, and our duties
25 Are to your throne and state children and servants,
Which do but what they should by doing everything
Safe toward your love and honor.

**Duncan.**                              Welcome hither.
I have begun to plant thee and will labor
To make thee full of growing.—Noble Banquo,

---

2 **those in commission:** those who have the responsibility for Cawdor's execution.

6 **set forth:** showed.

8–11 **He died as . . . trifle:** He died as if he had rehearsed (**studied**) the moment. Though losing his life (**the dearest thing he owed**), he behaved with calm dignity.

14–21 The king feels that he cannot repay (**recompense**) Macbeth enough. Macbeth's qualities and accomplishments are of greater value than any thanks or payment Duncan can give.

**ANALYZE CHARACTER AND THEME**

**Annotate:** Mark ideas in lines 22–27 that reflect the duties of a king's subjects.

**Evaluate:** Do you agree that these duties are appropriate? Do you think Macbeth does? Explain.

28–29 The king plans to give more honors to Macbeth.

30 That hast no less deserved nor must be known
No less to have done so, let me enfold thee
And hold thee to my heart.

**Banquo.**                    There, if I grow,
The harvest is your own.

**Duncan.**                    My plenteous joys,
Wanton in fullness, seek to hide themselves
35 In drops of sorrow.—Sons, kinsmen, thanes,
And you whose places are the nearest, know
We will establish our estate upon
Our eldest, Malcolm, whom we name hereafter
The Prince of Cumberland; which honor must
40 Not unaccompanied invest him only,
But signs of nobleness, like stars, shall shine
On all deservers.—From hence to Inverness,
And bind us further to you.

**Macbeth.** The rest is labor which is not used for you.
45 I'll be myself the harbinger and make joyful
The hearing of my wife with your approach.
So humbly take my leave.

**Duncan.**                    My worthy Cawdor.

**Macbeth** [*aside*]. The Prince of Cumberland! That is a step
On which I must fall down or else o'erleap,
50 For in my way it lies. Stars, hide your fires;
Let not light see my black and deep desires.
The eye wink at the hand, yet let that be
Which the eye fears, when it is done, to see.

[*He exits.*]

**Duncan.** True, worthy Banquo. He is full so valiant,
55 And in his commendations I am fed:
It is a banquet to me.—Let's after him,
Whose care is gone before to bid us welcome.
It is a peerless kinsman.

[*Flourish. They exit.*]

**Scene 5** *Macbeth's castle at Inverness.*

[*Enter* Lady Macbeth, *alone, with a letter.*]

**Lady Macbeth.** [*Reading the letter*] "They met me in the day of
success, and I have learned by the perfect'st report they have more
in them than mortal knowledge. When I burned in desire to
question them further, they made themselves air, into which they
5 vanished. Whiles I stood rapt in the wonder of it came missives
from the King, who all-hailed me 'Thane of Cawdor,' by which

**33–35 My plenteous . . .
sorrow:** The king is crying tears
of joy.

**39 Prince of Cumberland:**
the title given to the heir to the
Scottish throne.

**42 Inverness:** site of Macbeth's
castle, where the king has just
invited himself, giving another
honor to Macbeth.

**45 harbinger:** a representative
sent before a royal party to
make proper arrangements for
its arrival.

**ANALYZE DRAMA**
**Annotate:** Mark stage
directions at the beginning of
Scene 5 that provide important
information.

**Interpret:** How has the scene
changed? Whose words are
being spoken by Lady Macbeth
in lines 1–11?

title, before, these Weïrd Sisters saluted me and referred me to
the coming on of time with 'Hail, king that shalt be.' This have I
thought good to deliver thee, my dearest partner of greatness, that
10 thou might'st not lose the dues of rejoicing by being ignorant of
what greatness is promised thee. Lay it to thy heart, and farewell."

Glamis thou art, and Cawdor, and shalt be
What thou art promised. Yet do I fear thy nature;
It is too full o' th' milk of human kindness
15 To catch the nearest way. Thou wouldst be great,
Art not without ambition, but without
The illness should attend it. What thou wouldst highly,
That wouldst thou holily; wouldst not play false
And yet wouldst wrongly win. Thou'd'st have, great Glamis,
20 That which cries "Thus thou must do," if thou have it,
And that which rather thou dost fear to do,
Than wishest should be undone. Hie thee hither,
That I may pour my spirits in thine ear
And chastise with the valor of my tongue
25 All that impedes thee from the golden round
Which fate and metaphysical aid doth seem
To have thee crowned withal.

[*Enter* Messenger.]

What is your tidings?

**Messenger.** The King comes here tonight.

**Lady Macbeth.**                                        Thou'rt mad to say it!
Is not thy master with him? who, were't so,
30 Would have informed for preparation.

**Messenger.** So please you, it is true. Our Thane is coming.
One of my fellows had the speed of him,
Who, almost dead for breath, had scarcely more
Than would make up his message.

**Lady Macbeth.**                                  Give him tending.
35 He brings great news.

[Messenger *exits.*]

The raven himself is hoarse
That croaks the fatal entrance of Duncan
Under my battlements. Come, you spirits
That tend on mortal thoughts, unsex me here,
And fill me from the crown to the toe top-full
40 Of direst cruelty. Make thick my blood.
Stop up th' access and passage to remorse,
That no compunctious visitings of nature
Shake my fell purpose, nor keep peace between

**13–18** Lady Macbeth fears her husband is too good (**too full o' th' milk of human kindness**) to seize the throne by murder (**the nearest way**). Lacking the necessary wickedness (**illness**), he wants to gain power virtuously (**holily**).

**32 had the speed of him:** rode faster than he.

**35 raven:** The harsh cry of the raven, a bird symbolizing evil and misfortune, was supposed to indicate an approaching death.

Th' effect and it. Come to my woman's breasts
45 And take my milk for gall, you murd'ring ministers,
Wherever in your sightless substances
You wait on nature's mischief. Come, thick night,
And pall thee in the dunnest smoke of hell,
That my keen knife see not the wound it makes,
50 Nor heaven peep through the blanket of the dark
To cry "Hold, hold!"

[*Enter* Macbeth.]

Great Glamis, worthy Cawdor,
Greater than both by the all-hail hereafter!
Thy letters have transported me beyond
This ignorant present, and I feel now
55 The future in the instant.

**Macbeth.**                    My dearest love,
Duncan comes here tonight.

**Lady Macbeth.**               And when goes hence?

**Macbeth.** Tomorrow, as he purposes.

**Lady Macbeth.**                    O, never
Shall sun that morrow see!
Your face, my thane, is as a book where men
60 May read strange matters. To beguile the time,
Look like the time. Bear welcome in your eye,
Your hand, your tongue. Look like th' innocent flower,
But be the serpent under 't. He that's coming
Must be provided for; and you shall put
65 This night's great business into my dispatch,
Which shall to all our nights and days to come
Give solely sovereign sway and masterdom.

**Macbeth.** We will speak further.

**Lady Macbeth.**               Only look up clear.
To alter favor ever is to fear.
70 Leave all the rest to me.

[*They exit.*]

**Scene 6** *In front of Macbeth's castle.*

[*Hautboys and Torches. Enter* King Duncan, Malcolm,
Donalbain, Banquo, Lennox, Macduff, Ross, Angus, *and*
Attendants.]

**Duncan.** This castle hath a pleasant seat. The air
Nimbly and sweetly recommends itself
Unto our gentle senses.

**37–51** Lady Macbeth calls on the spirits of evil to rid her of feminine weakness (**unsex me**) and to block out guilt. She wants no normal pangs of conscience (**compunctious visitings of nature**) to get in the way of her murderous plan. She asks that her mother's milk be turned to bile (**gall**) by the unseen evil forces (**murd'ring ministers, sightless substances**) that exist in nature. Furthermore, she asks that the night wrap (**pall**) itself in darkness as black as hell so that no one may see or stop the crime.

**60–63 To beguile ... under 't:** To fool (**beguile**) everyone, act as expected at such a time.

**65 my dispatch:** my management.

**67 give solely sovereign sway:** bring absolute royal power.

**69 To alter ... fear:** To change your expression (**favor**) is a sign of fear.

[Stage Direction] **hautboys:** oboes.

**ANALYZE DRAMA**
Annotate: Mark King Duncan's impression of Macbeth's castle.

Analyze: What makes this view ironic? What do you know that Duncan does not know?

**3–10** The martin (**martlet**) usually built its nest on a church (**temple**), where every projection (**jutty**), sculptured decoration (**frieze**), support (**buttress**), and convenient corner (**coign of vantage**) offered a good nesting site. Banquo sees the presence of the martin's hanging (**pendant**) nest, a breeding (**procreant**) place, as a sign of healthy air.

**16 single business:** weak service.

**20 we rest your hermits:** we can only repay you with prayers. The rich hired hermits to pray for the dead.

**21 coursed him at the heels:** followed closely.

**22 purveyor:** one who makes advance arrangements for a royal visit.

**25–28** Legally, Duncan owned everything in his kingdom. Lady Macbeth politely says that they hold his property in trust (**compt**), ready to return it (**make their audit**) whenever he wants.

[Stage Direction] **Sewer:** the steward, the servant in charge of arranging the banquet and tasting the king's food; **divers:** various.

**Banquo.**                    This guest of summer,
The temple-haunting martlet, does approve,
5 By his loved mansionry, that the heaven's breath
Smells wooingly here. No jutty, frieze,
Buttress, nor coign of vantage, but this bird
Hath made his pendant bed and procreant cradle.
Where they most breed and haunt, I have observed,
10 The air is delicate.

[*Enter* Lady Macbeth.]

**Duncan.**                    See, see, our honored hostess!—
The love that follows us sometime is our trouble,
Which still we thank as love. Herein I teach you
How you shall bid God 'ild us for your pains
And thank us for your trouble.

**Lady Macbeth.**                    All our service,
15 In every point twice done and then done double,
Were poor and single business to contend
Against those honors deep and broad wherewith
Your Majesty loads our house. For those of old,
And the late dignities heaped up to them,
20 We rest your hermits.

**Duncan.**                    Where's the Thane of Cawdor?
We coursed him at the heels and had a purpose
To be his purveyor; but he rides well,
And his great love (sharp as his spur) hath helped him
To his home before us. Fair and noble hostess,
25 We are your guest tonight.

**Lady Macbeth.**                    Your servants ever
Have theirs, themselves, and what is theirs in compt
To make their audit at your Highness' pleasure,
Still to return your own.

**Duncan.**                    Give me your hand.

[*Taking her hand*]

Conduct me to mine host. We love him highly
30 And shall continue our graces towards him.
By your leave, hostess.

[*They exit.*]

**Scene 7** *A room in Macbeth's castle.*

[*Hautboys. Torches. Enter a* Sewer, *and divers* Servants *with dishes and service over the stage. Then enter* Macbeth.]

**1–10** If Duncan's murder would have no negative consequences and be successfully completed with his death (**surcease**), then Macbeth would risk eternal damnation. He knows, however, that terrible deeds (**bloody instructions**) often backfire.

**Macbeth.** If it were done when 'tis done, then 'twere well
It were done quickly. If th' assassination
Could trammel up the consequence and catch
With his surcease success, that but this blow
5 Might be the be-all and the end-all here,
But here, upon this bank and shoal of time,
We'd jump the life to come. But in these cases
We still have judgment here, that we but teach
Bloody instructions, which, being taught, return
10 To plague th' inventor. This even-handed justice
Commends th' ingredience of our poisoned chalice
To our own lips. He's here in double trust:
First, as I am his kinsman and his subject,
Strong both against the deed; then, as his host,
15 Who should against his murderer shut the door,
Not bear the knife myself. Besides, this Duncan
Hath borne his faculties so meek, hath been
So clear in his great office, that his virtues
Will plead like angels, trumpet-tongued, against
20 The deep damnation of his taking-off;
And pity, like a naked newborn babe
Striding the blast, or heaven's cherubin horsed
Upon the sightless couriers of the air,
Shall blow the horrid deed in every eye,
25 That tears shall drown the wind. I have no spur
To prick the sides of my intent, but only
Vaulting ambition, which o'erleaps itself
And falls on th' other—

[*Enter* Lady Macbeth.]

How now? What news?

**Lady Macbeth.** He has almost supped. Why have you left the
chamber?

30 **Macbeth.** Hath he asked for me?

**Lady Macbeth.**                      Know you not he has?

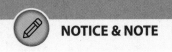
**32–35 I have . . . so soon:**
The praises that Macbeth
has received are, like new
clothes, to be worn, not
quickly thrown away.

**35–38** Lady Macbeth
sarcastically suggests that
Macbeth's ambition must
have been drunk, because it
now seems to have a hangover
(**to look so green and pale**).

**39–45** Lady Macbeth criticizes
Macbeth's weakened resolve
and compares him to a cat in
a proverb (**adage**) who
wouldn't catch fish because it
feared wet feet.

**TOUGH QUESTIONS**

**Notice & Note:** Mark the
question Lady Macbeth asks
in lines 47–48.

**Interpret:** Paraphrase Lady
Macbeth's question. What does
she really want to know, and
how should Macbeth answer?

**54 I have given suck:** I have
nursed a baby.

**60** When each string of a guitar
or lute is tightened to the peg
(**sticking place**), the instrument
is ready to be played.

**65–67** Lady Macbeth will get
the guards so drunk that their
reason will become like a still
(**limbeck**), producing confused
thoughts.

**Macbeth.** We will proceed no further in this business.
He hath honored me of late, and I have bought
Golden opinions from all sorts of people,
Which would be worn now in their newest gloss,
35  Not cast aside so soon.

**Lady Macbeth.**                         Was the hope drunk
Wherein you dressed yourself? Hath it slept since?
And wakes it now, to look so green and pale
At what it did so freely? From this time
Such I account thy love. Art thou afeard
40  To be the same in thine own act and valor
As thou art in desire? Wouldst thou have that
Which thou esteem'st the ornament of life
And live a coward in thine own esteem,
Letting "I dare not" wait upon "I would,"
45  Like the poor cat i' th' adage?

**Macbeth.**                         Prithee, peace.
I dare do all that may become a man.
Who dares do more is none.

**Lady Macbeth.**                    What beast was't, then,
That made you break this enterprise to me?
When you durst do it, then you were a man;
50  And to be more than what you were, you would
Be so much more the man. Nor time nor place
Did then adhere, and yet you would make both.
They have made themselves, and that their fitness now
Does unmake you. I have given suck, and know
55  How tender 'tis to love the babe that milks me.
I would, while it was smiling in my face,
Have plucked my nipple from his boneless gums
And dashed the brains out, had I so sworn as you
Have done to this.

**Macbeth.**              If we should fail—

**Lady Macbeth.**                              We fail?
60  But screw your courage to the sticking place
And we'll not fail. When Duncan is asleep
(Whereto the rather shall his day's hard journey
Soundly invite him), his two chamberlains
Will I with wine and wassail so convince
65  That memory, the warder of the brain,
Shall be a fume, and the receipt of reason
A limbeck only. When in swinish sleep
Their drenchèd natures lie as in a death,
What cannot you and I perform upon
70  Th' unguarded Duncan? What not put upon

His spongy officers, who shall bear the guilt
Of our great quell?

**Macbeth.**          Bring forth men-children only,
For thy undaunted mettle should compose
Nothing but males. Will it not be received,
75 When we have marked with blood those sleepy two
Of his own chamber and used their very daggers,
That they have done 't?

**Lady Macbeth.**          Who dares receive it other,
As we shall make our griefs and clamor roar
Upon his death?

**Macbeth.**          I am settled and bend up
80 Each corporal agent to this terrible feat.
Away, and mock the time with fairest show.
False face must hide what the false heart doth know.

[*They exit.*]

**NOTICE & NOTE**

72 **quell:** murder.

72–74 **Bring forth . . . males:**
Your bold spirit (**undaunted mettle**) is better suited to raising males than females.

79–82 Now that Macbeth has made up his mind, every part of his body (**each corporal agent**) is tightened like a bow. He and Lady Macbeth will deceive everyone (**mock the time**), hiding their evil plan with gracious faces.

## CHECK YOUR UNDERSTANDING

Answer these questions before moving on to the **Analyze the Text** section on the following page.

1  What good news occurs near the beginning of the play?

  **A** The King of Norway has been killed in battle.

  **B** Macbeth has been victorious against the King of Norway.

  **C** Macbeth has been named king.

  **D** The Thane of Cawdor has proven his loyalty.

2  What future do the Three Witches predict for Macbeth?

  **F** He will never be killed in battle.

  **G** He will be happier than Banquo in the future.

  **H** His children will become kings, though he will not.

  **J** He will become Thane of Cawdor and King of Scotland.

3  What does Lady Macbeth want Macbeth to do?

  **A** Kill King Duncan to become king

  **B** Return all their property to King Duncan

  **C** Ask King Duncan to make Macbeth heir to the throne

  **D** Order Banquo to kill King Duncan

## ANALYZE THE TEXT

Support your responses with evidence from the text. 📓 NOTEBOOK

1. **Analyze** What is the purpose of the first short scene? Explain.

2. **Draw Conclusions** A **paradox** is an apparent contradiction that reveals a truth. The witches end the first scene with a paradox: "Fair is foul, and foul is fair." Explain the ways in which this contradiction is shown to be true in Act 1.

3. **Analyze** How is Macbeth's conflict intensified by the events in Scene 4? What lines from his aside in Scene 4 (lines 48–53) develop the audience's understanding of this conflict?

4. **Infer** What does Lady Macbeth's response to the Witches' prophecy reveal about her character?

5. **Notice & Note** Review Act I to find images of darkness or night. How do these repeated references relate to plot events?

## CREATE AND DISCUSS

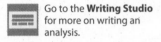

Go to the **Writing Studio** for more on writing an analysis.

**Writing Activity: Analysis** The characters of Macbeth and Lady Macbeth may have similar ambitions but they have different feelings and thoughts about their plans.

❏ With a small group, review their major speeches in Scene 7.

❏ Identify what lines 1–28 reveal about Macbeth as he lists the reasons they should not go ahead with the plan. What does he decide?

❏ Consider what is revealed about Lady Macbeth's character through her reaction to Macbeth's decision and her response in lines 47–59.

❏ Summarize their key differences in a paragraph. Share your analysis.

❏ Using your analysis of their differences, create a Venn diagram to compare and contrast Macbeth and Lady Macbeth. List what you know about their differences in the outside sections. Use the middle section to list how they compare. Cite scene and line references to support your conclusions. Discuss your ideas with your group.

**Macbeth**  **Both**  **Lady Macbeth**

## SETTING A PURPOSE

*As you read, look for details about how Macbeth conceals his plot. Think about the characters involved in and affected by the plot. Continue to fill in your character diagram to show the relationships between characters. Write down any questions you generate during reading.*

## ACT II

**Scene 1**  *The court of Macbeth's castle.*

[*Enter* Banquo, *and* Fleance *with a torch before him.*]

**Banquo.** How goes the night, boy?

**Fleance.** The moon is down. I have not heard the clock.

**Banquo.** And she goes down at twelve.

**Fleance.** I take 't, 'tis later, sir.

**Banquo.** Hold, take my sword. [*Giving his sword to* Fleance]

There's husbandry in heaven;
5 Their candles are all out. Take thee that too.
A heavy summons lies like lead upon me,
And yet I would not sleep. Merciful powers,
Restrain in me the cursèd thoughts that nature
Gives way to in repose.

[*Enter* Macbeth, *and a* Servant *with a torch.*]

Give me my sword.—Who's there?
10 **Macbeth.** A friend.

**Banquo.** What, sir, not yet at rest? The King's abed.
He hath been in unusual pleasure, and
Sent forth great largess to your offices.
This diamond he greets your wife withal,
15 By the name of most kind hostess, and shut up
In measureless content. [*He gives* Macbeth *a diamond.*]

**Macbeth.** Being unprepared,
Our will became the servant to defect,
Which else should free have wrought.

**Banquo.** All's well.
I dreamt last night of the three Weïrd Sisters.
20 To you they have showed some truth.

**Macbeth.** I think not of them.
Yet, when we can entreat an hour to serve,
We would spend it in some words upon that business,
If you would grant the time.

**4–5** The heavens show economy (**husbandry**) by keeping the lights (**candles**) out—it is a starless night.

**6 heavy summons:** desire for sleep.

**13 largess to your offices:** gifts to the servants' quarters.

**15 shut up:** went to bed.

**21 can entreat an hour:** both have the time.

**24–28** Macbeth asks Banquo for his support (**cleave to my consent**), promising honors in return. Banquo is willing to increase (**augment**) his honor provided he can keep a clear conscience and remain loyal to the king (**keep my bosom . . . clear**).

**Banquo.**                     At your kind'st leisure.

**Macbeth.** If you shall cleave to my consent, when 'tis,
25 It shall make honor for you.

**Banquo.**                     So I lose none
In seeking to augment it, but still keep
My bosom franchised and allegiance clear,
I shall be counseled.

**Macbeth.**           Good repose the while.

**Banquo.** Thanks, sir. The like to you.

[Banquo *and* Fleance *exit.*]

30 **Macbeth.** Go bid thy mistress, when my drink is ready,
She strike upon the bell. Get thee to bed.

[Servant *exits.*]

**32–42** Macbeth sees a dagger hanging in midair before him and questions whether it is real (**palpable**) or the illusion of a disturbed (**heat-oppressèd**) mind. The floating, imaginary dagger, which leads (**marshal'st**) him to Duncan's room, prompts him to draw his own dagger.

Is this a dagger which I see before me,
The handle toward my hand? Come, let me clutch thee.
I have thee not, and yet I see thee still.
35 Art thou not, fatal vision, sensible
To feeling as to sight? or art thou but
A dagger of the mind, a false creation
Proceeding from the heat-oppressèd brain?
I see thee yet, in form as palpable
40 As this which now I draw. [*He draws his dagger.*]
Thou marshal'st me the way that I was going,
And such an instrument I was to use.
Mine eyes are made the fools o' th' other senses
Or else worth all the rest. I see thee still,

**43–44** Either his eyes are mistaken (**fools**) or his other senses are.

**45** He sees drops of blood on the blade and handle.

45 And, on thy blade and dudgeon, gouts of blood,
Which was not so before. There's no such thing.
It is the bloody business which informs
Thus to mine eyes. Now o'er the one-half world
Nature seems dead, and wicked dreams abuse
50 The curtained sleep. Witchcraft celebrates
Pale Hecate's off 'rings, and withered murder,
Alarumed by his sentinel, the wolf,
Whose howl's his watch, thus with his stealthy pace,
With Tarquin's ravishing strides, towards his design
55 Moves like a ghost. Thou sure and firm-set earth,
Hear not my steps, which way they walk, for fear
Thy very stones prate of my whereabouts
And take the present horror from the time,
Which now suits with it. Whiles I threat, he lives.
60 Words to the heat of deeds too cold breath gives.

**ANALYZE DRAMA**
**Annotate:** Mark what Macbeth imagines seeing during this soliloquy.

**Analyze:** How does understanding Macbeth's thoughts at this point in the play help you understand the internal conflict he faces?

[*A bell rings.*]

I go, and it is done. The bell invites me.
Hear it not, Duncan, for it is a knell
That summons thee to heaven or to hell.

[*He exits.*]

**Scene 2** *Macbeth's castle.*

[*Enter* Lady Macbeth.]

**Lady Macbeth.** That which hath made them drunk hath made
    me bold.
What hath quenched them hath given me fire. Hark!—Peace.
It was the owl that shrieked, the fatal bellman,
Which gives the stern'st good-night. He is about it.
5 The doors are open, and the surfeited grooms
Do mock their charge with snores. I have drugged their possets,
That death and nature do contend about them
Whether they live or die.

**Macbeth** [*within*].       Who's there? what, ho!

**Lady Macbeth.** Alack, I am afraid they have awaked,
10 And 'tis not done. Th' attempt and not the deed
Confounds us. Hark!—I laid their daggers ready;
He could not miss 'em. Had he not resembled
My father as he slept, I had done 't.

[*Enter* Macbeth *with bloody daggers.*]

                  My husband?
**Macbeth.** I have done the deed. Didst thou not hear a noise?

15 **Lady Macbeth.** I heard the owl scream and the crickets cry.
Did not you speak?

**Macbeth.**        When?

**Lady Macbeth.**        Now.

**Macbeth.**          As I descended?

**Lady Macbeth.** Ay.

**Macbeth.**        Hark!—Who lies i' th' second chamber?

**Lady Macbeth.** Donalbain.

**Macbeth.**          This is a sorry sight.

**Lady Macbeth.** A foolish thought, to say a sorry sight.

20 **Macbeth.** There's one did laugh in 's sleep, and one cried "Murder!"
That they did wake each other. I stood and heard them.
But they did say their prayers and addressed them
Again to sleep.

---

**62 knell:** funeral bell.

**3 fatal bellman:** town crier.

**5 surfeited grooms:** drunken servants.

**6 possets:** drinks.

**11 confounds:** destroys. If Duncan survives, they will be killed (as his attempted murderers).

**ANALYZE DRAMA**
**Annotate:** Mark brackets around the beginnings and endings of lines 16, 17, and 18.

**Interpret:** Reread these lines to identify the iambic pentameter. What dramatic effect does Shakespeare achieve by breaking these lines between Lady Macbeth and Macbeth?

**25 As:** as if. He imagines that the sleepers could see him.

**AGAIN AND AGAIN**

**Notice & Note:** Mark the repeated word in lines 24–30 that Macbeth cannot say.

**Analyze:** How does his inability to say this word show a change in his character?

**34–38** Sleep eases worries (**knits up the raveled sleave of care**), relieves the aches of physical work (**sore labor's bath**), soothes the anxious (**hurt minds**), and nourishes like food.

**Lady Macbeth.** There are two lodged together.

**Macbeth.** One cried "God bless us" and "Amen" the other,
25 As they had seen me with these hangman's hands,
List'ning their fear. I could not say "Amen"
When they did say "God bless us."

**Lady Macbeth.** Consider it not so deeply.

**Macbeth.** But wherefore could not I pronounce "Amen"?
30 I had most need of blessing, and "Amen"
Stuck in my throat.

**Lady Macbeth.**      These deeds must not be thought
After these ways; so, it will make us mad.

**Macbeth.** Methought I heard a voice cry "Sleep no more!
Macbeth does murder sleep"—the innocent sleep,

King and Queen Macbeth, the Ice Globe Theatre in Jukkasjärvi, Sweden, 2004.

35 Sleep that knits up the raveled sleave of care,
The death of each day's life, sore labor's bath,
Balm of hurt minds, great nature's second course,
Chief nourisher in life's feast.

**Lady Macbeth.**               What do you mean?

**Macbeth.** Still it cried "Sleep no more!" to all the house.
40 "Glamis hath murdered sleep, and therefore Cawdor
Shall sleep no more. Macbeth shall sleep no more."

**Lady Macbeth.** Who was it that thus cried? Why, worthy thane,
You do unbend your noble strength to think
So brainsickly of things. Go get some water
45 And wash this filthy witness from your hand.—
Why did you bring these daggers from the place?
They must lie there. Go carry them and smear
The sleepy grooms with blood.

**Macbeth.**               I'll go no more.
I am afraid to think what I have done.
50 Look on 't again I dare not.

**Lady Macbeth.**          Infirm of purpose!
Give me the daggers. The sleeping and the dead
Are but as pictures. 'Tis the eye of childhood
That fears a painted devil. If he do bleed,
I'll gild the faces of the grooms withal,
55 For it must seem their guilt.

[*She exits with the daggers. Knock within.*]

**Macbeth.**              Whence is that knocking?
How is 't with me when every noise appalls me?
What hands are here? Ha, they pluck out mine eyes.
Will all great Neptune's ocean wash this blood
Clean from my hand? No, this my hand will rather
60 The multitudinous seas incarnadine,
Making the green one red.

[*Enter* Lady Macbeth.]

**Lady Macbeth.** My hands are of your color, but I shame
To wear a heart so white.               [*Knock*]

              I hear a knocking
At the south entry. Retire we to our chamber.
65 A little water clears us of this deed.
How easy is it, then! Your constancy
Hath left you unattended.              [*Knock*]

              Hark, more knocking.
Get on your nightgown, lest occasion call us
And show us to be watchers. Be not lost

**LANGUAGE CONVENTIONS**
**Annotate:** Mark the subject and verb in the first part of line 50.

**Analyze:** What is the effect of placing the verb first in this sentence?

**54–55** She'll cover (**gild**) the servants with blood, blaming them for the murder.

**59–61 this my hand . . . one red:** The blood on my hand will redden (**incarnadine**) the seas.

**66–67 Your constancy . . . unattended:** Your courage has left you.

**68–69 lest . . . watchers:** in case we are called for and found awake (**watchers**), which would look suspicious.

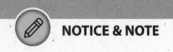
**71 To know ... myself:** To come to terms with what I have done, I must lose my conscience.

**2 old turning the key:** plenty of key turning. Hell's porter would be busy in such evil times.

**3 Beelzebub:** a devil.

**3–11** The porter pretends he is welcoming a farmer who killed himself after his schemes to get rich (**expectation of plenty**) failed, a double talker (**equivocator**) who perjured himself yet couldn't talk his way into heaven, and a tailor who cheated his customers by skimping on material (**stealing out of a French hose**).

**31–34** Alcohol is described as a wrestler thrown off (**cast**) by the porter, who thus paid him back (**requited him**) for disappointment in love. *Cast* also means "to vomit" and "to urinate."

70 So poorly in your thoughts.

**Macbeth.** To know my deed 'twere best not know myself.

[*Knock*]

Wake Duncan with thy knocking. I would thou couldst.

[*They exit.*]

**Scene 3** *Within Macbeth's castle, near the gate.*

[*Knocking within. Enter a* Porter.]

**Porter.** Here's a knocking indeed! If a man were porter of hell gate, he should have old turning the key. [*Knock*] Knock, knock, knock! Who's there, i' th' name of Beelzebub? Here's a farmer that hanged himself on th' expectation of plenty. Come in time! 5 Have napkins enough about you; here you'll sweat for 't. [*Knock*] Knock, knock! Who's there, in th' other devil's name? Faith, here's an equivocator that could swear in both the scales against either scale, who committed treason enough for God's sake yet could not equivocate to heaven. O, come in, equivocator. 10 [*Knock*] Knock, knock, knock! Who's there? Faith, here's an English tailor come hither for stealing out of a French hose. Come in, tailor. Here you may roast your goose. [*Knock*] Knock, knock! Never at quiet. —What are you? —But this place is too cold for hell. I'll devilporter it no further. I had thought to have 15 let in some of all professions that go the primrose way to th' everlasting bonfire. [*Knock*] Anon, anon! [*The* Porter *opens the door to* Macduff *and* Lennox.] I pray you, remember the porter.

**Macduff.** Was it so late, friend, ere you went to bed
That you do lie so late?

20 **Porter.** Faith, sir, we were carousing till the second cock, and drink, sir, is a great provoker of three things.

**Macduff.** What three things does drink especially provoke?

**Porter.** Marry, sir, nose-painting, sleep, and urine. Lechery, sir, it provokes and unprovokes. It provokes the desire, but it takes 25 away the performance. Therefore much drink may be said to be an equivocator with lechery. It makes him, and it mars him; it sets him on, and it takes him off; it persuades him and disheartens him; makes him stand to and not stand to; in conclusion, equivocates him in a sleep and, giving him the lie, 30 leaves him.

**Macduff.** I believe drink gave thee the lie last night.

**Porter.** That it did, sir, i' th' very throat on me; but I requited him for his lie, and, I think, being too strong for him, though he took up my legs sometime, yet I made a shift to cast him.

35 **Macduff.** Is thy master stirring?

[*Enter* Macbeth.]

Our knocking has awaked him. Here he comes.

[Porter *exits.*]

**Lennox.** Good morrow, noble sir.

**Macbeth.**                                    Good morrow, both.

**Macduff.** Is the King stirring, worthy thane?

**Macbeth.**                                    Not yet.

**Macduff.** He did command me to call timely on him.
40 I have almost slipped the hour.

**Macbeth.**                                    I'll bring you to him.

**Macduff.** I know this is a joyful trouble to you,
But yet 'tis one.

**Macbeth.** The labor we delight in physics pain.
This is the door.

**Macduff.**              I'll make so bold to call,
45 For 'tis my limited service. [Macduff *exits.*]

**Lennox.** Goes the King hence today?

**Macbeth.** He does. He did appoint so.

**Lennox.** The night has been unruly. Where we lay,
Our chimneys were blown down and, as they say,
50 Lamentings heard i' th' air, strange screams of death,
And prophesying, with accents terrible,
Of dire combustion and confused events
New hatched to th' woeful time. The obscure bird
Clamored the livelong night. Some say the earth
55 Was feverous and did shake.

**Macbeth.**                            'Twas a rough night.

**Lennox.** My young remembrance cannot parallel
A fellow to it.

[*Enter* Macduff.]

**Macduff.**       O horror, horror, horror!
Tongue nor heart cannot conceive nor name thee!

**Macbeth and Lennox.** What's the matter?

60 **Macduff.** Confusion now hath made his masterpiece.
Most sacrilegious murder hath broke ope
The Lord's anointed temple and stole thence
The life o' th' building.

**Macbeth.**                        What is 't you say? The life?

**39 timely:** early.

**40 slipped the hour:** missed the time.

**43 physics:** cures.

**45 limited service:** appointed duty.

**ANALYZE CHARACTER AND THEME**
**Annotate:** Mark descriptions in lines 48–55 of the turmoil that occurred overnight.

**Analyze:** How do these natural events reflect not only what has occurred inside the castle but what has occurred within Macbeth himself?

**60–63** Macduff mourns Duncan's death as the destruction (**confusion**) of order and as sacrilegious, violating all that is holy. In Shakespeare's time the king was believed to be God's sacred representative on earth.

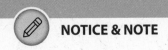
**Lennox.** Mean you his majesty?

65 **Macduff.** Approach the chamber and destroy your sight
With a new Gorgon. Do not bid me speak.
See and then speak yourselves.

[*Macbeth* and Lennox *exit.*]

                                                    Awake, awake!
Ring the alarum bell.—Murder and treason!
Banquo and Donalbain, Malcolm, awake!
70 Shake off this downy sleep, death's counterfeit,
And look on death itself. Up, up, and see
The great doom's image. Malcolm. Banquo.
As from your graves rise up and walk like sprites
To countenance this horror.—Ring the bell.

[*Bell rings.*]
[*Enter* Lady Macbeth.]

75 **Lady Macbeth.** What's the business,
That such a hideous trumpet calls to parley
The sleepers of the house? Speak, speak!

**Macduff.**                                         O gentle lady,
'Tis not for you to hear what I can speak.
The repetition in a woman's ear
80 Would murder as it fell.

[*Enter* Banquo.]

                                        O Banquo, Banquo,
Our royal master's murdered.

**Lady Macbeth.**                         Woe, alas!
What, in our house?

**Banquo.**                     Too cruel anywhere. —
Dear Duff, I prithee, contradict thyself
And say it is not so.

[*Enter* Macbeth, Lennox, *and* Ross.]

85 **Macbeth.** Had I but died an hour before this chance,
I had lived a blessèd time; for from this instant
There's nothing serious in mortality.
All is but toys. Renown and grace is dead.
The wine of life is drawn, and the mere lees
90 Is left this vault to brag of.

[*Enter* Malcolm *and* Donalbain.]

**Donalbain.** What is amiss?

**Macbeth.**                             You are, and do not know 't.
The spring, the head, the fountain of your blood
Is stopped; the very source of it is stopped.

**66 new Gorgon:** Macduff compares the shocking sight of the corpse to a Gorgon. In Greek mythology, anyone who saw a Gorgon turned to stone.

**70 counterfeit:** imitation.

**72 great doom's image:** a picture like the Last Judgment, the end of the world.

**73 sprites:** spirits. The spirits of the dead were supposed to rise on Judgment Day.

**76 trumpet calls to parley:** She compares the clanging bell to a trumpet used to call two sides of a battle to negotiation.

**86–90 for from . . . brag of:** From now on, nothing matters (**there's nothing serious**) in human life (**mortality**); even fame and grace have been made meaningless. The good wine of life has been removed (**drawn**), leaving only the dregs (**lees**).

**Macduff.** Your royal father's murdered.

**Malcolm.**                                O, by whom?

95 **Lennox.** Those of his chamber, as it seemed, had done 't.
Their hands and faces were all badged with blood.
So were their daggers, which unwiped we found
Upon their pillows. They stared and were distracted.
No man's life was to be trusted with them.

100 **Macbeth.** O, yet I do repent me of my fury,
That I did kill them.

**Macduff.**                  Wherefore did you so?

**Macbeth.** Who can be wise, amazed, temp'rate, and furious,
Loyal, and neutral, in a moment? No man.
Th' expedition of my violent love
105 Outrun the pauser, reason. Here lay Duncan,
His silver skin laced with his golden blood,
And his gashed stabs looked like a breach in nature
For ruin's wasteful entrance; there the murderers,
Steeped in the colors of their trade, their daggers
110 Unmannerly breeched with gore. Who could refrain
That had a heart to love, and in that heart
Courage to make 's love known?

**Lady Macbeth.**                        Help me hence, ho!

**Macduff.** Look to the lady.

**Malcolm** [*aside to* Donalbain]. Why do we hold our tongues,
That most may claim this argument for ours?

**Donalbain** [*aside to* Malcolm].
115 What should be spoken here, where our fate,
Hid in an auger hole, may rush and seize us?
Let's away. Our tears are not yet brewed.

**Malcolm** [*aside to* Donalbain].
Nor our strong sorrow upon the foot of motion.

**Banquo.** Look to the lady.

[Lady Macbeth *is assisted to leave.*]

120 And when we have our naked frailties hid,
That suffer in exposure, let us meet
And question this most bloody piece of work
To know it further. Fears and scruples shake us.
In the great hand of God I stand, and thence
125 Against the undivulged pretense I fight
Of treasonous malice.

**Macduff.**                  And so do I.

**96 badged:** marked.

**104–105** He claims his emotions overpowered his reason, which would have made him pause to think before he killed Duncan's servants.

**107 breach:** a military term to describe a break in defenses, such as a hole in a castle wall.

**112** Lady Macbeth faints.

**TOUGH QUESTIONS**

**Notice & Note:** Mark the questions Malcolm and Donalbain ask each other in lines 113–116.

**Interpret:** How do these questions reveal the complicated situation they are in?

**120–121** Banquo suggests that they all meet to discuss the murder after they have dressed (**our naked frailties hid**), since people are shivering in their nightclothes (**suffer in exposure**).

**123–126** Though shaken by fears and doubts (**scruples**), he will fight against the secret plans (**undivulged pretense**) of the traitor.

**All.**                                                 So all.

**Macbeth.** Let's briefly put on manly readiness
And meet i' th' hall together.

**All.**                                          Well contented.

[*All but* Malcolm *and* Donalbain *exit.*]

**Malcolm.** What will you do? Let's not consort with them.
130  To show an unfelt sorrow is an office
Which the false man does easy. I'll to England.

**Donalbain.** To Ireland I. Our separated fortune
Shall keep us both the safer. Where we are,
There's daggers in men's smiles. The near in blood,
135  The nearer bloody.

**129–131** Malcolm does not want to join (**consort with**) the others because one of them may have plotted the murder.

Teatro Regio Torino perform 'Verdi's Macbeth' at Festival Theatre, Edinburgh, Scotland, 2017.

**Malcolm.**         This murderous shaft that's shot
Hath not yet lighted, and our safest way
Is to avoid the aim. Therefore to horse,
And let us not be dainty of leave-taking
But shift away. There's warrant in that theft
140 Which steals itself when there's no mercy left.

[*They exit.*]

**Scene 4**  *Outside Macbeth's castle.*

[*Enter* Ross *with an* Old Man.]

**Old Man.** Threescore and ten I can remember well,
Within the volume of which time I have seen
Hours dreadful and things strange, but this sore night
Hath trifled former knowings.

**139–140 There's . . . left:**
There's good reason (**warrant**)
to steal away from a situation
that promises no mercy.

**1–4** Nothing the old man has
seen in 70 years (**threescore
and ten**) has been as strange
and terrible (**sore**) as this
night. It has made other times
seem trivial (**hath trifled**) by
comparison.

**Ross.**                                        Ha, good father,
5 Thou seest the heavens, as troubled with man's act,
Threaten his bloody stage. By th' clock 'tis day,
And yet dark night strangles the traveling lamp.
Is 't night's predominance or the day's shame
That darkness does the face of earth entomb
10 When living light should kiss it?

**Old Man.**                              'Tis unnatural,
Even like the deed that's done. On Tuesday last
A falcon, tow'ring in her pride of place,
Was by a mousing owl hawked at and killed.

**Ross.** And Duncan's horses (a thing most strange and certain),
15 Beauteous and swift, the minions of their race,
Turned wild in nature, broke their stalls, flung out,
Contending 'gainst obedience, as they would
Make war with mankind.

**Old Man.**                          'Tis said they eat each other.

**Ross.** They did so, to th' amazement of mine eyes
20 That looked upon 't.

[*Enter* Macduff.]

                                  Here comes the good Macduff.—
How goes the world, sir, now?

**Macduff.**                            Why, see you not?

**Ross.** Is 't known who did this more than bloody deed?

**Macduff.** Those that Macbeth hath slain.

**Ross.**                                    Alas, the day,
What good could they pretend?

**Macduff.**                          They were suborned.
25 Malcolm and Donalbain, the King's two sons,
Are stol'n away and fled, which puts upon them
Suspicion of the deed.

**Ross.**                      'Gainst nature still!
Thriftless ambition, that will ravin up
Thine own lives' means. Then 'tis most like
30 The sovereignty will fall upon Macbeth.

**Macduff.** He is already named and gone to Scone
To be invested.

**Ross.**            Where is Duncan's body?

**Macduff.** Carried to Colmekill,
The sacred storehouse of his predecessors
35 And guardian of their bones.

---

**6–10 By th' clock . . . kiss it:** Though daytime, an unnatural darkness blots out the sun (**strangles the traveling lamp**).

**12–13** The owl would never be expected to attack a high-flying (**tow'ring**) falcon, much less defeat one.

**15 minions:** best or favorites.

**17 Contending 'gainst obedience:** The well-trained horses rebelliously fought against all constraints.

**24 What . . . pretend:** Ross wonders what the servants could have hoped to achieve (**pretend**) by killing; **suborned:** hired or bribed.

**27–29** He is horrified by the thought that the sons could act contrary to nature (**'gainst nature still**) because of wasteful (**thriftless**) ambition and greedily destroy (**ravin up**) their father, the source of their own life (**thine own lives' means**).

**31–32** Macbeth went to the traditional site (**Scone**) where Scotland's kings were crowned.

**Ross.** Will you to Scone?

**Macduff.** No, cousin, I'll to Fife.

**Ross.** Well, I will thither.

**Macduff.** Well, may you see things well done there. Adieu,
Lest our old robes sit easier than our new.

**Ross.** Farewell, father.

40 **Old Man.** God's benison go with you and with those
That would make good of bad and friends of foes.

[*All exit.*]

**40–41** The old man gives his blessing (**benison**) to Macduff and all those who would bring peace to the troubled land.

## CHECK YOUR UNDERSTANDING

Answer these questions before moving on to the **Analyze the Text** section on the following page.

1   Why does Macbeth refuse to go back into the king's bedroom with the bloody knives?

   A   He is afraid that he has not killed the king and he might still live.

   B   He is so filled with guilt and remorse that he lacks the courage to return.

   C   He wants Lady Macbeth to do her share by taking the knives back.

   D   He thinks it will be harder for someone to catch him if he does not go back.

2   Which of the following is a central theme in Act II?

   F   The witches' prophecies will ultimately prove false.

   G   The knocking sounds are the ghost of the king coming back.

   H   Macbeth deserves the crown more than the king's sons do.

   J   The king's murder has upset the natural rule of order.

3   What happens to Malcolm and Donalbain at the end of Act II?

   A   They are found guilty of their father's murder.

   B   They prepare to assume the throne in Duncan's place.

   C   They flee because they fear that they, too, will be murdered.

   D   They accuse Macbeth of having committed Duncan's murder.

## ANALYZE THE TEXT

Support your responses with evidence from the text.  📓 NOTEBOOK

1. **Summarize** What are some examples of Macbeth's active imagination that add to his internal conflict?

2. **Analyze** What are some things the Porter says that provide comic relief? Why does Shakespeare include them in such a dramatic play?

3. **Infer** How is Macbeth's explanation of why he killed the king's servants an example of dramatic irony? Use text from Scene 3 lines 100–112 to support your answer.

4. **Cite Evidence** What does Shakespeare tell you about Lady Macbeth's and Macbeth's relationship in his description of the murder scene? Cite examples from Scene 2 to support your answer.

5. **Notice & Note** What is the effect of the repeated idea of sleep in Act II? How does this idea point toward a theme?

Go to the **Speaking and Listening Studio** for more on collaborative discussions.

## CREATE AND PRESENT

**Discuss** Why does Lady Macbeth faint? Is it a distraction, or is it real? Support your conclusion with evidence from the text.

❏ Jot down ideas about what Lady Macbeth does and says in Act II that might explain why she faints.

❏ Use cause-and-effect connecting words to link your ideas.

❏ In a small group, discuss these ideas and your interpretation of her action. Together, draw one or more conclusions about her motives.

❏ Summarize the group discussion and present your ideas to the class.

## SETTING A PURPOSE

*As you read Act III, refer to your character diagram and add any new information you learn about the characters and their relationships.*

### ACT III

**Scene 1**  *Macbeth's palace at Forres.*

[*Enter* Banquo.]

**Banquo.** Thou hast it now—King, Cawdor, Glamis, all
As the Weïrd Women promised, and I fear
Thou played'st most foully for 't. Yet it was said
It should not stand in thy posterity,
5 But that myself should be the root and father
Of many kings. If there come truth from them
(As upon thee, Macbeth, their speeches shine),
Why, by the verities on thee made good,
May they not be my oracles as well,
10 And set me up in hope? But hush, no more.

[*Sennet sounded. Enter* Macbeth *as King,* Lady Macbeth, Lennox,
Ross, Lords, *and* Attendants.]

**Macbeth.** Here's our chief guest.

**Lady Macbeth.**                    If he had been forgotten,
It had been as a gap in our great feast
And all-thing unbecoming.

**Macbeth.** Tonight we hold a solemn supper, sir,
15 And I'll request your presence.

**Banquo.**                    Let your Highness
Command upon me, to the which my duties
Are with a most indissoluble tie
Forever knit.

**Macbeth.**     Ride you this afternoon?

**Banquo.** Ay, my good lord.

20 **Macbeth.** We should have else desired your good advice
(Which still hath been both grave and prosperous)
In this day's council, but we'll take tomorrow.
Is 't far you ride?

**ANALYZE DRAMA**

**Annotate:** Mark what Banquo suspects in lines 1–10.

**Infer:** What does this soliloquy reveal about Banquo's internal conflict?

[Stage Direction] **Sennet sounded:** A trumpet is sounded.

**14–15** A king usually uses the royal pronoun *we.* Macbeth switches to the pronoun *I* with Banquo.

**15–18** Banquo says he is duty bound to serve the king.

**21 grave and prosperous:** thoughtful and profitable.

**25–27** If his horse goes no faster than usual, he'll be back an hour or two (**twain**) after dark.

**29 bloody cousins:** murderous relatives (Malcolm and Donalbain); **bestowed:** settled.

**32 strange invention:** lies; stories they have invented.

**33–34 when . . . jointly:** when matters of state will require the attention of us both.

**40 be master of his time:** do what he wants.

**43 while:** until.

**44–45 sirrah:** a term of address to an inferior; **Attend . . . pleasure:** Are they waiting for me?

**47–48 To be thus . . . safely thus:** To be king is worthless unless my position as king is safe.

**51 dauntless temper:** fearless temperament.

**55–56** Banquo's mere presence forces back (**rebukes**) Macbeth's ruling spirit (**genius**). In ancient Rome, Caesar, who became emperor, had the same effect on his rival, Mark Antony.

**Banquo.** As far, my lord, as will fill up the time

25 'Twixt this and supper. Go not my horse the better,

I must become a borrower of the night

For a dark hour or twain.

**Lady Macbeth.**                    Fail not our feast.

**Banquo.** My lord, I will not.

**Macbeth.** We hear our bloody cousins are bestowed

30 In England and in Ireland, not confessing

Their cruel parricide, filling their hearers

With strange invention. But of that tomorrow,

When therewithal we shall have cause of state

Craving us jointly. Hie you to horse. Adieu,

35 Till you return at night. Goes Fleance with you?

**Banquo.** Ay, my good lord. Our time does call upon 's.

**Macbeth.** I wish your horses swift and sure of foot,

And so I do commend you to their backs.

Farewell.

[Banquo *exits*.]

40 Let every man be master of his time

Till seven at night. To make society

The sweeter welcome, we will keep ourself

Till suppertime alone. While then, God be with you.

[Lords *and all but* Macbeth *and a* Servant *exit*.]

Sirrah, a word with you. Attend those men

45 Our pleasure?

**Servant.** They are, my lord, without the palace gate.

**Macbeth.** Bring them before us.

[Servant *exits*.]

                                   To be thus is nothing,

But to be safely thus. Our fears in Banquo

Stick deep, and in his royalty of nature

50 Reigns that which would be feared. 'Tis much he dares,

And to that dauntless temper of his mind

He hath a wisdom that doth guide his valor

To act in safety. There is none but he

Whose being I do fear; and under him

55 My genius is rebuked, as it is said

Mark Antony's was by Caesar. He chid the sisters

When first they put the name of king upon me

And bade them speak to him. Then, prophet-like,

They hailed him father to a line of kings.

60 Upon my head they placed a fruitless crown
    And put a barren scepter in my grip,
    Thence to be wrenched with an unlineal hand,
    No son of mine succeeding. If 't be so,
    For Banquo's issue have I filed my mind;
65 For them the gracious Duncan have I murdered,
    Put rancors in the vessel of my peace
    Only for them, and mine eternal jewel
    Given to the common enemy of man
    To make them kings, the seeds of Banquo kings.
70 Rather than so, come fate into the list,
    And champion me to th' utterance.—Who's there?

[*Enter* Servant *and two* Murderers.]

[*To the* Servant] Now go to the door, and stay there till we call.

[Servant *exits.*]

Was it not yesterday we spoke together?

**Murderers.** It was, so please your Highness.

**Macbeth.**                                         Well then, now
75 Have you considered of my speeches? Know
    That it was he, in the times past, which held you
    So under fortune, which you thought had been
    Our innocent self. This I made good to you
    In our last conference, passed in probation with you
80 How you were borne in hand, how crossed, the instruments,
    Who wrought with them, and all things else that might
    To half a soul and to a notion crazed
    Say "Thus did Banquo."

**First Murderer.**          You made it known to us.

**Macbeth.** I did so, and went further, which is now
85 Our point of second meeting. Do you find
    Your patience so predominant in your nature
    That you can let this go? Are you so gospeled
    To pray for this good man and for his issue,
    Whose heavy hand hath bowed you to the grave
90 And beggared yours forever?

**First Murderer.**                    We are men, my liege.

**Macbeth.** Ay, in the catalogue you go for men,
    As hounds and greyhounds, mongrels, spaniels, curs,
    Shoughs, water-rugs, and demi-wolves are clept
    All by the name of dogs. The valued file
95 Distinguishes the swift, the slow, the subtle,
    The housekeeper, the hunter, every one
    According to the gift which bounteous nature

**60–69** They gave me a childless (**fruitless, barren**) rule, which will be taken away by someone outside my family (**unlineal**). I have committed murder, poisoned (**filed**) my mind, and destroyed my soul (**eternal jewel**) only to benefit Banquo's heirs.

**ANALYZE CHARACTER AND THEME**
**Annotate:** Mark passages in lines 47–71 that reveal Macbeth's thoughts about what he has done and how he feels about Banquo.

**Infer:** What has Macbeth realized? How will he solve this problem?

**75–83** Macbeth supposedly proved (**passed in probation**) Banquo's deception (**how you were borne in hand**), methods, and allies. Even a half-wit (**half a soul**) or a crazed person would agree that Banquo caused their trouble.

**87–90** He asks whether they are so influenced by the gospel's message of forgiveness (**so gospeled**) that they will pray for Banquo and his children despite his harshness, which will leave their own families beggars.

**91–100** The true worth of a dog can be measured only by examining the record (**valued file**) of its special qualities (**particular addition**).

**103–107** Macbeth will give them a secret job (**business in your bosoms**) that will earn them his loyalty (**grapples you to the heart**) and love. Banquo's death will make this sick king healthy.

Hath in him closed; whereby he does receive
Particular addition, from the bill
100  That writes them all alike. And so of men.
Now, if you have a station in the file,
Not i' th' worst rank of manhood, say 't,
And I will put that business in your bosoms
Whose execution takes your enemy off,
105  Grapples you to the heart and love of us,
Who wear our health but sickly in his life,
Which in his death were perfect.

**Second Murderer.**                    I am one, my liege,
Whom the vile blows and buffets of the world
Hath so incensed that I am reckless what
110  I do to spite the world.

**111 tugged with:** knocked about by.

**First Murderer.**          And I another
So weary with disasters, tugged with fortune,
That I would set my life on any chance,
To mend it or be rid on 't.

**Macbeth.**                    Both of you
Know Banquo was your enemy.

**Murderers.**                              True, my lord.

**115–117** Banquo is near enough to draw blood, and like a menacing swordsman, his mere presence threatens (**thrusts against**) Macbeth's existence.

115  **Macbeth.** So is he mine, and in such bloody distance
That every minute of his being thrusts
Against my near'st of life. And though I could
With barefaced power sweep him from my sight
And bid my will avouch it, yet I must not,
120  For certain friends that are both his and mine,
Whose loves I may not drop, but wail his fall
Who I myself struck down. And thence it is
That I to your assistance do make love,
Masking the business from the common eye
125  For sundry weighty reasons.

**119 bid my will avouch it:** justify it as my will.

**Second Murderer.**              We shall, my lord,
Perform what you command us.

**First Murderer.**                    Though our lives—

**127 Your spirits shine through you:** Your courage is evident.

**Macbeth.** Your spirits shine through you. Within this hour at most
I will advise you where to plant yourselves,
Acquaint you with the perfect spy o' th' time,
130  The moment on 't, for 't must be done tonight
And something from the palace; always thought
That I require a clearness. And with him
(To leave no rubs nor botches in the work)
Fleance, his son, that keeps him company,
135  Whose absence is no less material to me

**131–132 something from... clearness:** The murder must be done away from the palace so that I remain blameless (**I require a clearness**).

**135 absence:** death.

Banquo and Fleance, The Conservatory of Theatre and Dance, Southeast Missouri State University, 2014.

Than is his father's, must embrace the fate
Of that dark hour. Resolve yourselves apart.
I'll come to you anon.

**Murderers.** We are resolved, my lord.

**Macbeth.** I'll call upon you straight. Abide within.

[*Murderers exit.*]

140 It is concluded. Banquo, thy soul's flight,
If it find heaven, must find it out tonight.

[*He exits.*]

**Scene 2** *Macbeth's palace at Forres.*

[*Enter* Lady Macbeth *and a* Servant.]

**Lady Macbeth.** Is Banquo gone from court?

**Servant.** Ay, madam, but returns again tonight.

**Lady Macbeth.** Say to the King I would attend his leisure
For a few words.

**Servant.** Madam, I will.

[*He exits.*]

**Lady Macbeth.** Naught's had, all's spent,
5 Where our desire is got without content.

**137 Resolve yourselves apart:** Decide in private.

**139 straight:** soon.

**4–7** Nothing (**naught**) has been gained; everything has been wasted (**spent**). It would be better to be dead like Duncan than to live in uncertain joy.

'Tis safer to be that which we destroy
Than by destruction dwell in doubtful joy.

[*Enter* Macbeth.]

How now, my lord? Why do you keep alone,
Of sorriest fancies your companions making,
10 Using those thoughts which should indeed have died
With them they think on? Things without all remedy
Should be without regard. What's done is done.

**Macbeth.** We have scorched the snake, not killed it.
She'll close and be herself whilst our poor malice
15 Remains in danger of her former tooth.
But let the frame of things disjoint, both the worlds suffer,
Ere we will eat our meal in fear, and sleep
In the affliction of these terrible dreams
That shake us nightly. Better be with the dead,
20 Whom we, to gain our peace, have sent to peace,
Than on the torture of the mind to lie
In restless ecstasy. Duncan is in his grave.
After life's fitful fever he sleeps well.
Treason has done his worst; nor steel nor poison,
25 Malice domestic, foreign levy, nothing
Can touch him further.

**Lady Macbeth.**          Come on, gentle my lord,
Sleek o'er your rugged looks. Be bright and jovial
Among your guests tonight.

**Macbeth.**                    So shall I, love,
And so I pray be you. Let your remembrance
30 Apply to Banquo; present him eminence
Both with eye and tongue: unsafe the while that we
Must lave our honors in these flattering streams
And make our faces vizards to our hearts,
Disguising what they are.

**Lady Macbeth.**          You must leave this.

35 **Macbeth.** O, full of scorpions is my mind, dear wife!
Thou know'st that Banquo and his Fleance lives.

**Lady Macbeth.** But in them Nature's copy's not eterne.

**Macbeth.** There's comfort yet; they are assailable.
Then be thou jocund. Ere the bat hath flown
40 His cloistered flight, ere to black Hecate's summons
The shard-borne beetle with his drowsy hums
Hath rung night's yawning peal, there shall be done
A deed of dreadful note.

**Lady Macbeth.**          What's to be done?

**16–22** He would rather have the world fall apart (**the frame of things disjoint**) than be afflicted with such fears and nightmares. Death is preferable to life on the torture rack of mental anguish (**restless ecstasy**).

**27 sleek:** smooth.

**30 present him eminence:** pay special attention to him.

**32 lave . . . streams:** wash (**lave**) our honor in streams of flattery—that is, falsify our feelings.

**33 vizards:** masks.

**37 in them . . . not eterne:** Nature did not give them immortality.

**39–43 jocund:** cheerful; merry; **Ere the bat . . . note:** Before nightfall, when the bats and beetles fly, something dreadful will happen.

**Macbeth.** Be innocent of the knowledge, dearest chuck,
45 Till thou applaud the deed.—Come, seeling night,
Scarf up the tender eye of pitiful day,
And with thy bloody and invisible hand
Cancel and tear to pieces that great bond
Which keeps me pale. Light thickens, and the crow
50 Makes wing to th' rooky wood.
Good things of day begin to droop and drowse,
Whiles night's black agents to their preys do rouse.—
Thou marvel'st at my words, but hold thee still.
Things bad begun make strong themselves by ill.
55 So prithee go with me.

[*They exit.*]

**Scene 3**  *A park near the palace.*

[*Enter three* Murderers.]

**First Murderer.** But who did bid thee join with us?

**Third Murderer.**                                        Macbeth.

**Second Murderer** [*to the* First Murderer].
He needs not our mistrust, since he delivers
Our offices and what we have to do
To the direction just.

**First Murderer.**         Then stand with us.—
5 The west yet glimmers with some streaks of day.
Now spurs the lated traveler apace
To gain the timely inn, and near approaches
The subject of our watch.

**Third Murderer.**          Hark, I hear horses.

**Banquo** [*within*]. Give us a light there, ho!

**Second Murderer.**                    Then 'tis he. The rest
10 That are within the note of expectation
Already are i' th' court.

**First Murderer.**          His horses go about.

**Third Murderer.** Almost a mile; but he does usually
(So all men do) from hence to th' palace gate
Make it their walk.

[*Enter* Banquo *and* Fleance, *with a torch.*]

**Second Murderer.** A light, a light!

**Third Murderer.**                  'Tis he.

15 **First Murderer.** Stand to 't.

**Banquo.** It will be rain tonight.

---

44 **chuck:** a term of affection.
45 **seeling:** blinding.

48 **great bond:** Banquo's life.

50 **rooky:** gloomy; also, filled with rooks, or crows.

54 Things brought about through evil need additional evil to make them strong.

2–5 **He needs . . . just:** Macbeth should not be distrustful, since he gave us the orders (**offices**) and we plan to follow his directions exactly.

6 **lated:** tardy; late.

9 **Give us a light:** Banquo, nearing the palace, calls for servants to bring a light.

9–11 **Then 'tis . . . court:** It must be Banquo, since all the other expected guests are already in the palace.

15 **Stand to 't:** Be prepared.

First Murderer.            Let it come down!

[*The three* Murderers *attack*.]

Banquo. O, treachery! Fly, good Fleance, fly, fly, fly!
Thou mayst revenge—O slave!

[*He dies.* Fleance *exits*.]

Third Murderer. Who did strike out the light?

First Murderer.                 Was 't not the way?

20 Third Murderer. There's but one down. The son is fled.

Second Murderer. We have lost best half of our affair.

First Murderer. Well, let's away and say how much is done.

[*They exit*.]

Scene 4  *The hall in the palace.*

[*Banquet prepared. Enter* Macbeth, Lady Macbeth, Ross, Lennox,
Lords, *and* Attendants.]

Macbeth. You know your own degrees; sit down. At first
And last, the hearty welcome.

[*They sit*.]

Lords.                 Thanks to your Majesty.

Macbeth. Ourself will mingle with society
And play the humble host.

5 Our hostess keeps her state, but in best time
We will require her welcome.

Lady Macbeth. Pronounce it for me, sir, to all our friends,
For my heart speaks they are welcome.

[*Enter First Murderer to the door*.]

Macbeth. See, they encounter thee with their hearts' thanks.
10 Both sides are even. Here I'll sit i' th' midst.
Be large in mirth. Anon we'll drink a measure
The table round. [*Approaching the* Murderer] There's blood upon
    thy face.

Murderer. 'Tis Banquo's then.

Macbeth. 'Tis better thee without than he within.
15 Is he dispatched?

Murderer. My lord, his throat is cut. That I did for him.

Macbeth. Thou art the best o' th' cutthroats,
Yet he's good that did the like for Fleance.
If thou didst it, thou art the nonpareil.

20 Murderer. Most royal sir, Fleance is 'scaped.

**18 Thou mayst revenge:** You might live to avenge my death.

**19 Was 't not the way:** Isn't that what we were supposed to do?

**1 your own degrees:** where your rank entitles you to sit.

**5 keeps her state:** sits on her throne rather than at the banquet table.

**11 measure:** toast. Macbeth keeps talking to his wife and guests as he casually edges toward the door to speak privately with the murderer.

**15 dispatched:** killed.

**19 nonpareil:** best.

**Macbeth** [*aside*]. Then comes my fit again. I had else been
  perfect,
Whole as the marble, founded as the rock,
As broad and general as the casing air.
But now I am cabined, cribbed, confined, bound in
25 To saucy doubts and fears.—But Banquo's safe?

**Murderer.** Ay, my good lord. Safe in a ditch he bides,
With twenty trenchèd gashes on his head,
The least a death to nature.

**Macbeth.**               Thanks for that.
There the grown serpent lies. The worm that's fled
30 Hath nature that in time will venom breed,
No teeth for th' present. Get thee gone. Tomorrow
We'll hear ourselves again.

[*Murderer exits.*]

**Lady Macbeth.**          My royal lord,
You do not give the cheer. The feast is sold
That is not often vouched, while 'tis a-making,
35 'Tis given with welcome. To feed were best at home;
From thence, the sauce to meat is ceremony;
Meeting were bare without it.

[*Enter the Ghost of* Banquo, *and sits in* Macbeth's *place.*]

**Macbeth** [*to* Lady Macbeth]. Sweet remembrancer!—
Now, good digestion wait on appetite
And health on both!

**Lennox.**          May't please your Highness sit.

40 **Macbeth.** Here had we now our country's honor roofed,
Were the graced person of our Banquo present,
Who may I rather challenge for unkindness
Than pity for mischance.

**Ross.**               His absence, sir,
Lays blame upon his promise. Please 't your Highness
45 To grace us with your royal company?

**Macbeth.** The table's full.

**Lennox.**               Here is a place reserved, sir.

**Macbeth.** Where?

**Lennox.** Here, my good lord. What is 't that moves your Highness?

**Macbeth.** Which of you have done this?

**Lords.**               What, my good lord?

50 **Macbeth** [*to the* Ghost]. Thou canst not say I did it. Never shake
Thy gory locks at me.

**23 casing:** surrounding.

**29 worm:** little serpent, that is, Fleance.

**31 no teeth for th' present:** too young to cause harm right now.

**32 hear ourselves:** talk together.
**32–37** Macbeth must not forget his duties as host. A feast will be no different from a meal that one pays for unless the host gives his guests courteous attention (**ceremony**), the best part of any meal.

**37 sweet remembrancer:** a term of affection for his wife, who has reminded him of his duty.

**40–43** The best people of Scotland would all be under Macbeth's roof if Banquo were present too. He hopes Banquo's absence is due to rudeness rather than to some accident (**mischance**).

**46** Macbeth notices Banquo's ghost sitting in the king's chair.

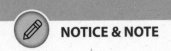

**Ross.** Gentlemen, rise. His Highness is not well.

**Lady Macbeth.** Sit, worthy friends. My lord is often thus
And hath been from his youth. Pray you, keep seat.
55 The fit is momentary; upon a thought
He will again be well. If much you note him
You shall offend him and extend his passion.
Feed and regard him not. [*Drawing* Macbeth *aside*] Are you a man?

**Macbeth.** Ay, and a bold one, that dare look on that
60 Which might appall the devil.

**60–68** She dismisses his
hallucination as utter nonsense
(**proper stuff**). His outbursts
(**flaws and starts**) are the
product of imaginary fears
(**impostors to true fear**)
and are unmanly, the kind
of behavior described in a
woman's story.

**Lady Macbeth.**                    O, proper stuff!
This is the very painting of your fear.
This is the air-drawn dagger which you said
Led you to Duncan. O, these flaws and starts,
Impostors to true fear, would well become
65 A woman's story at a winter's fire,
Authorized by her grandam. Shame itself!
Why do you make such faces? When all's done,
You look but on a stool.

**Macbeth.** Prithee see there. Behold, look! [*To the* Ghost] Lo, how
say you?
70 Why, what care I? If thou canst nod, speak too.—

**71–73** If burial vaults (**charnel
houses**) give back the dead,
then we may as well throw
our bodies to the birds (**kites**),
whose stomachs (**maws**)
will become our tombs
(**monuments**).

If charnel houses and our graves must send
Those that we bury back, our monuments
Shall be the maws of kites.

[Ghost *exits*.]

**Lady Macbeth.**                    What, quite unmanned in folly?

**Macbeth.** If I stand here, I saw him.

**Lady Macbeth.**                         Fie, for shame!

**75–78** Macbeth desperately
tries to justify his murder of
Banquo. Murder has been
common from ancient times
to the present, though laws
(**humane statute**) have tried
to rid civilized society (**gentle
weal**) of violence.

75 **Macbeth.** Blood hath been shed ere now, i' th' olden time,
Ere humane statute purged the gentle weal;
Ay, and since too, murders have been performed
Too terrible for the ear. The time has been
That, when the brains were out, the man would die,
80 And there an end. But now they rise again
With twenty mortal murders on their crowns
And push us from our stools. This is more strange
Than such a murder is.

**Lady Macbeth.**            My worthy lord,
Your noble friends do lack you.

**Macbeth.**                    I do forget.—

**85 muse:** wonder.

85 Do not muse at me, my most worthy friends.
I have a strange infirmity, which is nothing

Dmitry Belosselskiy and Zeljko
Lucic perform Guiseppe Verdi's
opera 'Macbeth', directed by
Peter Stein and conducted by
Ricardo Muti, Salzburg, 2011.

To those that know me. Come, love and health to all.
Then I'll sit down.—Give me some wine. Fill full.

[*Enter* Ghost.]

I drink to the general joy o' th' whole table
90 And to our dear friend Banquo, whom we miss.
Would he were here! To all and him we thirst,
And all to all.

**Lords.**　　　Our duties, and the pledge.

[*They raise their drinking cups.*]

**Macbeth** [*to the* Ghost]. Avaunt, and quit my sight! Let the earth
　　hide thee.
Thy bones are marrowless; thy blood is cold;
95 Thou hast no speculation in those eyes
Which thou dost glare with.

**Lady Macbeth.**　　　　Think of this, good peers,
But as a thing of custom. 'Tis no other;
Only it spoils the pleasure of the time.

**Macbeth** [*to the* Ghost]. What man dare, I dare.
100 Approach thou like the rugged Russian bear,
The armed rhinoceros, or th' Hyrcan tiger;
Take any shape but that, and my firm nerves
Shall never tremble. Or be alive again
And dare me to the desert with thy sword.
105 If trembling I inhabit then, protest me
The baby of a girl. Hence, horrible shadow!
Unreal mock'ry, hence!

[Ghost *exits*.]

　　　　　　　Why, so, being gone,
I am a man again.—Pray you sit still.

**Lady Macbeth.** You have displaced the mirth, broke the good
　　meeting

**ANALYZE DRAMA**

**Annotate:** Mark words that
reflect happiness and love in
lines 87–92.

**Analyze:** What is ironic about
these expressions, given what
Macbeth has done and what he
is seeing?

**93–96 avaunt:** go away.
Macbeth tells Banquo that he
is only a ghost, with unreal
bones, cold blood, and no
consciousness (**speculation**).

**99–104** Macbeth would be
willing to face Banquo in any
other form, even his living self.

**105–106 If trembling . . . girl:**
If I still tremble, call me a girl's
doll.

**110 admired:** astonishing.

**110–116** Macbeth is bewildered by his wife's calm, which makes him seem a stranger to himself (**strange even to the disposition that I owe**): she has all the courage, while he is white (**blanched**) with fear.

**119 Stand . . . going:** Don't worry about the proper formalities of leaving.

**122–126** Macbeth fears that Banquo's murder (**it**) will be revenged by his own murder. Stones, trees, or talking birds (**maggot pies and choughs and rooks**) may reveal the hidden knowledge (**augurs**) of his guilt.

**128–129 How say'st . . . bidding:** What do you think of Macduff's refusal to come?

**131–132** Macbeth has paid (**fee'd**) household servants to spy on every noble, including Macduff.

**133 betimes:** early.

**ANALYZE CHARACTER AND THEME**

**Annotate:** Reread lines 134–144 and mark words that indicate Macbeth has gone too far in his quest for power.

**Evaluate:** What theme is being developed in this scene?

**142–144** His vision of the ghost (**strange and self-abuse**) is only the result of a beginner's fear (**initiate fear**), to be cured with practice (**hard use**).

110   With most admired disorder.

**Macbeth.**                              Can such things be
And overcome us like a summer's cloud,
Without our special wonder? You make me strange
Even to the disposition that I owe,
When now I think you can behold such sights
115 And keep the natural ruby of your cheeks
When mine is blanched with fear.

**Ross.**                                    What sights, my lord?

**Lady Macbeth.** I pray you speak not. He grows worse and worse.
Question enrages him. At once, good night.
Stand not upon the order of your going,
120 But go at once.

**Lennox.**        Good night, and better health
Attend his Majesty.

**Lady Macbeth.**      A kind good night to all.

[Lords *and all but* Macbeth *and* Lady Macbeth *exit.*]

**Macbeth.** It will have blood, they say; blood will have blood.
Stones have been known to move, and trees to speak;
Augurs and understood relations have
125 By maggot pies and choughs and rooks brought forth
The secret'st man of blood.—What is the night?

**Lady Macbeth.** Almost at odds with morning, which is which.

**Macbeth.** How say'st thou that Macduff denies his person
At our great bidding?

**Lady Macbeth.**        Did you send to him, sir?

130 **Macbeth.** I hear it by the way; but I will send.
There's not a one of them but in his house
I keep a servant fee'd. I will tomorrow
(And betimes I will) to the Weïrd Sisters.
More shall they speak, for now I am bent to know
135 By the worst means the worst. For mine own good,
All causes shall give way. I am in blood
Stepped in so far that, should I wade no more,
Returning were as tedious as go o'er.
Strange things I have in head, that will to hand,
140 Which must be acted ere they may be scanned.

**Lady Macbeth.** You lack the season of all natures, sleep.

**Macbeth.** Come, we'll to sleep. My strange and self-abuse
Is the initiate fear that wants hard use.
We are yet but young in deed.

[*They exit.*]

**Scene 5** *A heath.*

[*Thunder. Enter the three* Witches, *meeting* Hecate.]

**First Witch.** Why, how now, Hecate? You look angerly.

**Hecate.** Have I not reason, beldams as you are,
Saucy and overbold, how did you dare
To trade and traffic with Macbeth
5 In riddles and affairs of death,
And I, the mistress of your charms,
The close contriver of all harms,
Was never called to bear my part
Or show the glory of our art?
10 And which is worse, all you have done
Hath been but for a wayward son,
Spiteful and wrathful, who, as others do,
Loves for his own ends, not for you.
But make amends now. Get you gone,
15 And at the pit of Acheron
Meet me i' th' morning. Thither he
Will come to know his destiny.
Your vessels and your spells provide,
Your charms and everything beside.
20 I am for th' air. This night I'll spend
Unto a dismal and a fatal end.
Great business must be wrought ere noon.
Upon the corner of the moon
There hangs a vap'rous drop profound.
25 I'll catch it ere it come to ground,
And that, distilled by magic sleights,
Shall raise such artificial sprites
As by the strength of their illusion
Shall draw him on to his confusion.
30 He shall spurn fate, scorn death, and bear
His hopes 'bove wisdom, grace, and fear.
And you all know, security
Is mortals' chiefest enemy.

[*Music and a song*]

Hark! I am called. My little spirit, see,
35 Sits in a foggy cloud and stays for me.

[Hecate *exits.*]

[*Sing within "Come away, come away," etc.*]

**First Witch.** Come, let's make haste. She'll soon be back again.

[*They exit.*]

**2 beldams:** hags.

**13 loves . . . you:** cares only about his own goals, not about you.

**15 Acheron:** a river in hell, according to Greek mythology.

**20–21 This . . . end:** Tonight I'm working for a disastrous (**dismal**) and fatal end for Macbeth.

**23–29** Hecate will obtain a magical drop from the moon, treat it with secret art, and so create spirits (**artificial sprites**) that will lead Macbeth to his destruction (**confusion**).

**34–35** Hecate has a demon helper (**my little spirit**), to which she is raised by pulley to "the heavens" of the stage.

**1–3** Lennox and the other lord have shared suspicions of Macbeth.

**6–7** Fleeing the scene of the crime must make Fleance guilty of his father's murder.

**8–10** Everyone agrees on the horror of Duncan's murder by his sons.

**12 pious:** holy.

**21 from broad words:** because of his frank talk.

**24 bestows himself:** is staying

**25** Macbeth keeps Malcolm from his rightful throne.

**27 Edward:** Edward the Confessor, king of England from 1042 to 1066, a man known for his virtue and religion.

**28–29 that . . . respect:** Despite his bad fortune, Malcolm is treated respectfully by Edward.

**29–37** Macduff wants the king to persuade the people of Northumberland and their earl, Siward, to join Malcolm's cause.

**Scene 6** *The palace at Forres.*

[*Enter* Lennox *and another* Lord.]

**Lennox.** My former speeches have but hit your thoughts,
Which can interpret farther. Only I say
Things have been strangely borne. The gracious Duncan
Was pitied of Macbeth; marry, he was dead.
5 And the right valiant Banquo walked too late,
Whom you may say, if 't please you, Fleance killed,
For Fleance fled. Men must not walk too late.
Who cannot want the thought how monstrous
It was for Malcolm and for Donalbain
10 To kill their gracious father? Damnèd fact,
How it did grieve Macbeth! Did he not straight
In pious rage the two delinquents tear
That were the slaves of drink and thralls of sleep?
Was not that nobly done? Ay, and wisely, too,
15 For 'twould have angered any heart alive
To hear the men deny 't. So that I say
He has borne all things well. And I do think
That had he Duncan's sons under his key
(As, an 't please heaven, he shall not) they should find
20 What 'twere to kill a father. So should Fleance.
But peace. For from broad words, and 'cause he failed
His presence at the tyrant's feast, I hear
Macduff lives in disgrace. Sir, can you tell
Where he bestows himself?

**Lord.**                    The son of Duncan
25 (From whom this tyrant holds the due of birth)
Lives in the English court and is received
Of the most pious Edward with such grace
That the malevolence of fortune nothing
Takes from his high respect. Thither Macduff
30 Is gone to pray the holy king upon his aid
To wake Northumberland and warlike Siward
That, by the help of these (with Him above
To ratify the work), we may again
Give to our tables meat, sleep to our nights,
35 Free from our feasts and banquets bloody knives,
Do faithful homage, and receive free honors,
All which we pine for now. And this report
Hath so exasperate the King that he
Prepares for some attempt of war.

**Lennox.**                    Sent he to Macduff?

40 **Lord.** He did, and with an absolute "Sir, not I,"
The cloudy messenger turns me his back
And hums, as who should say, "You'll rue the time
That clogs me with this answer."

    **Lennox.**                  And that well might
Advise him to a caution t' hold what distance
45 His wisdom can provide. Some holy angel
Fly to the court of England and unfold
His message ere he come, that a swift blessing
May soon return to this our suffering country
Under a hand accursed.

    **Lord.**               I'll send my prayers with him.

[*They exit.*]

**NOTICE & NOTE**

**40–43** The messenger, fearing Macbeth's anger, was unhappy (**cloudy**) with Macduff's refusal to cooperate. Because Macduff burdens (**clogs**) him with bad news, he will not hurry back.

## CHECK YOUR UNDERSTANDING

Answer these questions before moving on to the **Analyze the Text** section on the following page.

1  How does Macbeth attempt to solve a problem in Act III?

  **A** He tries to get past his guilt for Duncan's murder by admitting what he has done.

  **B** He attempts to have Banquo and Fleance killed to end a line of future kings.

  **C** He returns to visit the witches a second time because the prophecy is not working.

  **D** He resolves to have all of his opponents murdered because he feels insecure in his power.

2  How does Macbeth's guilt become apparent at the banquet?

  **F** Lady Macbeth must speak for him.

  **G** He feels ill and has to leave early.

  **H** He sees the ghost of Banquo.

  **J** He confesses his crimes to the gathering.

3  At the end of Act III, Macduff has traveled to England to —

  **A** hide in safety as he fears for his life

  **B** find Malcolm and return him to Scotland

  **C** pursue the men he believes murdered Duncan

  **D** ask the king for help in dealing with Macbeth

## ANALYZE THE TEXT

Support your responses with evidence from the text.  📓 NOTEBOOK

1. **Infer**  Reread lines 47–56 in Scene 1. Why does Macbeth fear Banquo and feel threatened by his "being"? What is suggested about Macbeth's character through his action of hiring murderers to carry out his plan?

2. **Analyze**  Review Scene 2. How has Duncan's murder affected the relationship between Macbeth and Lady Macbeth? Cite evidence from the text to support your ideas.

3. **Draw Conclusions**  What does Fleance's escape suggest about the witches' prophecy?

4. **Analyze**  What does Banquo's ghost in Scene 4 represent? Explain how the presence of the ghost affects Lady Macbeth's behavior even though she cannot see it.

5. **Compare**  Review lines 135–140 in Scene 4. What does Macbeth realize, and in what way does this speech reveal a change in Macbeth's attitude from how he has felt in the past about his deeds?

## CREATE AND DISCUSS

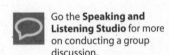

Go the **Speaking and Listening Studio** for more on conducting a group discussion.

**Share an Analysis**  How does dramatic irony intensify the impact of Act III?

❏ With a partner, identify the strongest instances of dramatic irony in Act III. Complete the chart below with details from those instances. Discuss how these instances affect the audience's understanding of Macbeth's character.

| LINES | WHAT CHARACTERS DO OR SAY | WHAT THE AUDIENCE KNOWS |
|---|---|---|
|  |  |  |
|  |  |  |
|  |  |  |

❏ Form a group with other students, and present your ideas about the impact of dramatic irony on the audience's understanding of Macbeth's character. Listen to their ideas, and arrive at a common analysis.

## SETTING A PURPOSE

*As you read, refer to your character diagram and add any new information you learn in Act IV about the characters and their relationships.*

## ACT IV

**Scene 1**  *A cave. In the middle, a boiling cauldron.*

[*Thunder. Enter the three* Witches.]

**First Witch.** Thrice the brinded cat hath mewed.

**Second Witch.** Thrice, and once the hedge-pig whined.

**Third Witch.** Harpier cries "'Tis time, 'tis time!"

**First Witch.** Round about the cauldron go;
5   In the poisoned entrails throw.
Toad, that under cold stone
Days and nights has thirty-one
Sweltered venom sleeping got,
Boil thou first i' th' charmed pot.

[*The* Witches *circle the cauldron.*]

10   **All.** Double, double toil and trouble;
Fire burn, and cauldron bubble.

**Second Witch.** Fillet of a fenny snake
In the cauldron boil and bake.
Eye of newt and toe of frog,
15   Wool of bat and tongue of dog,
Adder's fork and blindworm's sting,
Lizard's leg and howlet's wing,
For a charm of powerful trouble,
Like a hell-broth boil and bubble.

20   **All.** Double, double toil and trouble;
Fire burn, and cauldron bubble.

**Third Witch.** Scale of dragon, tooth of wolf,
Witch's mummy, maw and gulf
Of the ravined salt-sea shark,
25   Root of hemlock digged i' th' dark,
Liver of blaspheming Jew,
Gall of goat and slips of yew
Slivered in the moon's eclipse,
Nose of Turk and Tartar's lips,
30   Finger of birth-strangled babe

**1–3**  Magical signals and the call of the Third Witch's attending demon (**harpier**) tell the Witches to begin.

**4–34**  The Witches are stirring up a magical stew to bring trouble to humanity. Their recipe includes intestines (**entrails, chaudron**), a slice (**fillet**) of snake, eye of salamander (**newt**), snake tongue (**adder's fork**), a lizard (**blindworm**), a baby owl's (**howlet's**) wing, a shark's stomach and gullet (**maw and gulf**), the finger of a baby strangled by a prostitute (**drab**), and other gruesome ingredients. They stir their brew until it is thick and slimy (**slab**).

Ditch-delivered by a drab,
Make the gruel thick and slab.
Add thereto a tiger's chaudron
For th' ingredience of our cauldron.

35 **All.** Double, double toil and trouble;
Fire burn, and cauldron bubble.

**Second Witch.** Cool it with a baboon's blood.
Then the charm is firm and good.

[*Enter* Hecate *and the other three* Witches.]

**Hecate.** O, well done! I commend your pains,
40 And everyone shall share i' th' gains.
And now about the cauldron sing
Like elves and fairies in a ring,
Enchanting all that you put in.

[*Music and a song: "Black Spirits," etc.* Hecate *exits.*]

**Second Witch.** By the pricking of my thumbs,
45 Something wicked this way comes.
Open, locks,
Whoever knocks.

[*Enter* Macbeth.]

**Macbeth.** How now, you secret, black, and midnight hags?
What is 't you do?

**All.**                           A deed without a name.

50 **Macbeth.** I conjure you by that which you profess
(Howe'er you come to know it), answer me.
Though you untie the winds and let them fight
Against the churches, though the yeasty waves
Confound and swallow navigation up,
55 Though bladed corn be lodged and trees blown down,
Though castles topple on their warders' heads,
Though palaces and pyramids do slope
Their heads to their foundations, though the treasure
Of nature's germens tumble all together
60 Even till destruction sicken, answer me
To what I ask you.

**First Witch.**            Speak.

**Second Witch.**                 Demand.

**Third Witch.**                        We'll answer.

**First Witch.** Say if th' hadst rather hear it from our mouths
Or from our masters'.

**Macbeth.**            Call 'em. Let me see 'em.

**50–61** Macbeth calls upon (**conjure**) the Witches in the name of their dark magic (**that which you profess**). Though they unleash winds to topple churches and make foaming (**yeasty**) waves to destroy (**confound**) ships, though they flatten wheat (**corn**) fields, destroy buildings, and reduce nature's order to chaos by mixing all seeds (**germens**) together, he demands an answer to his question.

**63 masters:** the demons whom the Witches serve.

Universal Arts and Polish
Cultural Institute perform
*Macbeth* on stilts, Edinburgh
Fringe Festival 2007, Edinburgh,
Scotland.

**First Witch.** Pour in sow's blood that hath eaten
65 Her nine farrow; grease that's sweaten
From the murderers' gibbet throw
Into the flame.

**All.**                  Come high or low;
Thyself and office deftly show.

[*Thunder.* First Apparition, *an Armed Head.*]

**Macbeth.** Tell me, thou unknown power—

**First Witch.**                              He knows thy thought.
70 Hear his speech but say thou naught.

**First Apparition.** Macbeth! Macbeth! Macbeth! Beware Macduff!
Beware the Thane of Fife! Dismiss me. Enough.

[*He descends.*]

**Macbeth.** Whate'er thou art, for thy good caution, thanks.
Thou hast harped my fear aright. But one word more—

75 **First Witch.** He will not be commanded. Here's another
More potent than the first.

[*Thunder.* Second Apparition, *a Bloody Child.*]

**Second Apparition.** Macbeth! Macbeth! Macbeth!—

**Macbeth.** Had I three ears, I'd hear thee.

**Second Apparition.** Be bloody, bold, and resolute. Laugh to scorn
80 The power of man, for none of woman born
Shall harm Macbeth.

[*He descends.*]

**65–66 farrow:** newborn pigs;
**grease . . . gibbet:** grease from
a gallows where murderers
were hung.

[Stage Direction] Each of the
three apparitions holds a clue
to Macbeth's future.

**74 harped:** guessed.

**ANALYZE CHARACTER
AND THEME**
**Annotate:** Mark what is foretold
in lines 79–81.

**Predict:** Consider what you
know about the Witches. Can
Macbeth trust this prediction?
How might he act in response
to it?

**Macbeth.** Then live, Macduff; what need I fear of thee?
But yet I'll make assurance double sure
And take a bond of fate. Thou shalt not live,
85 That I may tell pale-hearted fear it lies,
And sleep in spite of thunder.

[*Thunder. Third Apparition, a Child Crowned, with a tree in his hand.*]

                                        What is this
That rises like the issue of a king
And wears upon his baby brow the round
And top of sovereignty?

**All.**                        Listen, but speak not to 't.

90 **Third Apparition.** Be lion-mettled, proud, and take no care
Who chafes, who frets, or where conspirers are.
Macbeth shall never vanquished be until
Great Birnam Wood to high Dunsinane Hill
Shall come against him.                    [*He descends.*]

**Macbeth.**                    That will never be.
95 Who can impress the forest, bid the tree
Unfix his earthbound root? Sweet bodements, good!
Rebellious dead, rise never till the wood
Of Birnam rise, and our high-placed Macbeth
Shall live the lease of nature, pay his breath
100 To time and mortal custom. Yet my heart
Throbs to know one thing. Tell me, if your art
Can tell so much: shall Banquo's issue ever
Reign in this kingdom?

**All.**                        Seek to know no more.

**Macbeth.** I will be satisfied. Deny me this,
105 And an eternal curse fall on you! Let me know!

                [*Cauldron sinks. Hautboys.*]
Why sinks that cauldron? And what noise is this?

**First Witch.** Show.

**Second Witch.** Show.

**Third Witch.** Show.

110 **All.** Show his eyes, and grieve his heart.
Come like shadows; so depart.

[*A show of eight kings, the eighth king with a glass in his hand, and* Banquo *last.*]

**Macbeth.** Thou art too like the spirit of Banquo. Down!
Thy crown does sear mine eyeballs. And thy hair,

---

**84** The murder of Macduff will give Macbeth a guarantee (**bond**) of his fate and put his fears to rest.

**87 issue:** child.
**88–89 the round and top:** the crown.

**90–94** The third apparition tells Macbeth to take courage. He cannot be defeated unless Birnam Wood travels the 12-mile distance to Dunsinane Hill, where his castle is located.

**95 impress:** force into service.
**96 bodements:** prophecies.
**97–100** Macbeth boasts that he will never again be troubled by ghosts (**rebellious dead**) and that he will live out his expected life span (**lease of nature**). He believes he will die (**pay his breath**) by natural causes (**mortal custom**).

[Stage Direction]
**A show . . . :** Macbeth next sees eight kings, the last carrying a mirror (**glass**). According to legend, Fleance escaped to England, where he founded the Stuart family, to which King James belonged.

Thou other gold-bound brow, is like the first.
115 A third is like the former.—Filthy hags,
Why do you show me this?—A fourth? Start, eyes!
What, will the line stretch out to th' crack of doom?
Another yet? A seventh? I'll see no more.
And yet the eighth appears who bears a glass
120 Which shows me many more, and some I see
That twofold balls and treble scepters carry.
Horrible sight! Now I see 'tis true,
For the blood-boltered Banquo smiles upon me
And points at them for his.

[*The* Apparitions *disappear.*]
What, is this so?

125 **First Witch.** Ay, sir, all this is so. But why
Stands Macbeth thus amazedly?
Come, sisters, cheer we up his sprites
And show the best of our delights.
I'll charm the air to give a sound
130 While you perform your antic round,
That this great king may kindly say
Our duties did his welcome pay.

[*Music. The* Witches *dance and vanish.*]

**Macbeth.** Where are they? Gone? Let this pernicious hour
Stand aye accursèd in the calendar!—
135 Come in, without there.

[*Enter* Lennox.]

**Lennox.** What's your Grace's will?

**Macbeth.** Saw you the Weïrd Sisters?

**Lennox.** No, my lord.

**Macbeth.** Came they not by you?

**Lennox.** No, indeed, my lord.

**Macbeth.** Infected be the air whereon they ride,
And damned all those that trust them! I did hear
140 The galloping of horse. Who was 't came by?

**Lennox.** 'Tis two or three, my lord, that bring you word
Macduff is fled to England.

**Macbeth.** Fled to England?

**Lennox.** Ay, my good lord.

**Macbeth** [*aside*]. Time, thou anticipat'st my dread exploits.
145 The flighty purpose never is o'ertook
Unless the deed go with it. From this moment

**112–124** All eight kings look like Banquo. The mirror shows a future with many more Banquo look-alikes as kings. The twofold balls and treble scepters foretell the union of Scotland and England in 1603, the year that James became king of both realms. Banquo, his hair matted (**boltered**) with blood, claims all the kings as his descendants.

**133 pernicious:** evil.
**134 aye:** always.
**135** After the Witches vanish, Macbeth hears noises outside the cave and calls out.

**144–156** Frustrated in his desire to kill Macduff, Macbeth blames his own hesitation, which gave his enemy time to flee. He concludes that one's plans (**flighty purpose**) are never achieved (**o'ertook**) unless carried out at once. From now on, Macbeth promises, he will act immediately on his impulses (**firstlings of my heart**) and complete (**crown**) his thoughts with acts. He will surprise Macduff's castle at Fife and kill his wife and children.

The very firstlings of my heart shall be
The firstlings of my hand. And even now,
To crown my thoughts with acts, be it thought and done:
150 The castle of Macduff I will surprise,
Seize upon Fife, give to th' edge o' th' sword
His wife, his babes, and all unfortunate souls
That trace him in his line. No boasting like a fool;
This deed I'll do before this purpose cool.
155 But no more sights!—Where are these gentlemen?
Come bring me where they are.

[*They exit.*]

**Scene 2** *Macduff's castle at Fife.*

[*Enter* Lady Macduff, *her* Son, *and* Ross.]

**Lady Macduff.** What had he done to make him fly the land?

**Ross.** You must have patience, madam.

**Lady Macduff.** He had none.
His flight was madness. When our actions do not,
Our fears do make us traitors.

**Ross.** You know not
5 Whether it was his wisdom or his fear.

**3–4** Macduff's wife is worried that others will think her husband a traitor because his fears made him flee the country (**our fears do make us traitors**), though he was guilty of no wrongdoing.

**Lady Macduff.** Wisdom? To leave his wife, to leave his babes,
His mansion and his titles in a place
From whence himself does fly? He loves us not;
He wants the natural touch; for the poor wren
10 (The most diminutive of birds) will fight,
Her young ones in her nest, against the owl.
All is the fear, and nothing is the love,
As little is the wisdom, where the flight
So runs against all reason.

**9 wants the natural touch:** lacks the instinct to protect his family.

**Ross.** My dearest coz,
15 I pray you school yourself. But for your husband,
He is noble, wise, judicious, and best knows
The fits o' th' season. I dare not speak much further;
But cruel are the times when we are traitors
And do not know ourselves; when we hold rumor
20 From what we fear, yet know not what we fear,
But float upon a wild and violent sea
Each way and move—I take my leave of you.
Shall not be long but I'll be here again.
Things at the worst will cease or else climb upward
25 To what they were before.—My pretty cousin,
Blessing upon you.

**14 coz:** cousin (a term used for any close relation).

**15 school:** control; **for:** as for.

**17 fits o' th' season:** disorders of the present time.

**18–22** Ross laments the cruelty of the times that made Macduff flee. Fears make people believe (**hold**) rumors, though they do not know what to fear and drift aimlessly like ships tossed by a tempest.

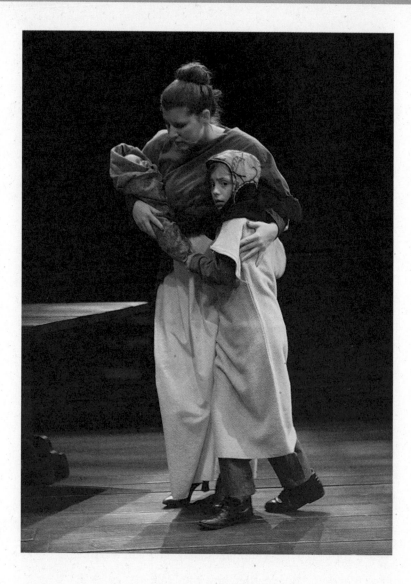

Lady Macduff and children, The Conservatory of Theatre and Dance, Southeast Missouri State University, 2014.

**Lady Macduff.** Fathered he is, and yet he's fatherless.

**Ross.** I am so much a fool, should I stay longer
It would be my disgrace and your discomfort.
30 I take my leave at once.         [Ross *exits.*]

**Lady Macduff.**       Sirrah, your father's dead.
And what will you do now? How will you live?

**Son.** As birds do, mother.

**Lady Macduff.**       What, with worms and flies?

**Son.** With what I get, I mean; and so do they.

**Lady Macduff.** Poor bird, thou'dst never fear the net nor lime,
35 The pitfall nor the gin.

**Son.** Why should I, mother? Poor birds they are not set for.
My father is not dead, for all your saying.

**Lady Macduff.** Yes, he is dead. How wilt thou do for a father?

**Son.** Nay, how will you do for a husband?

**28–30** Moved by pity for Macduff's family, Ross is near tears (**my disgrace**). He will leave before he embarrasses himself.

**32–35** The spirited son refuses to be defeated by their bleak situation. He will live as birds do, taking whatever comes his way. His mother responds in kind, calling attention to devices used to catch birds: nets, sticky birdlime (**lime**), snares (**pitfall**), and traps (**gin**).

**40–43** Lady Macduff and her son affectionately joke about her ability to find a new husband. She expresses admiration for his intelligence (**with wit enough**).

40 **Lady Macduff.** Why, I can buy me twenty at any market.

**Son.** Then you'll buy 'em to sell again.

**Lady Macduff.** Thou speak'st with all thy wit,
And yet, i' faith, with wit enough for thee.

**Son.** Was my father a traitor, mother?

45 **Lady Macduff.** Ay, that he was.

**Son.** What is a traitor?

**Lady Macduff.** Why, one that swears and lies.

**Son.** And be all traitors that do so?

**Lady Macduff.** Every one that does so is a traitor and must be
hanged.

50 **Son.** And must they all be hanged that swear and lie?

**Lady Macduff.** Every one.

**Son.** Who must hang them?

**Lady Macduff.** Why, the honest men.

**Son.** Then the liars and swearers are fools, for there are liars and
55 swearers enough to beat the honest men and hang up them.

**Lady Macduff.** Now God help thee, poor monkey! But how wilt
thou do for a father?

**Son.** If he were dead, you'd weep for him. If you would not, it
were a good sign that I should quickly have a new father.

60 **Lady Macduff.** Poor prattler, how thou talk'st!

[*Enter a* Messenger.]

**Messenger.** Bless you, fair dame. I am not to you known,
Though in your state of honor I am perfect.
I doubt some danger does approach you nearly.
If you will take a homely man's advice,
65 Be not found here. Hence with your little ones!
To fright you thus methinks I am too savage;
To do worse to you were fell cruelty,
Which is too nigh your person. Heaven preserve you!
I dare abide no longer.                    [Messenger *exits.*]

**Lady Macduff.**            Whither should I fly?
70 I have done no harm. But I remember now
I am in this earthly world, where to do harm
Is often laudable, to do good sometime
Accounted dangerous folly. Why then, alas,
Do I put up that womanly defense
75 To say I have done no harm?

**54–60** Her son points out that traitors outnumber honest men in this troubled time. The mother's terms of affection, **monkey** and **prattler** (childish talker), suggest that his playfulness has won her over.

**61–69** The messenger, who knows Lady Macduff is an honorable person (**in your state of honor I am perfect**), delivers a polite but desperate warning, urging her to flee immediately. While he apologizes for scaring her, he warns that she faces a deadly (**fell**) cruelty, one dangerously close (**too nigh**).

**TOUGH QUESTIONS**

**Notice & Note:** Mark the questions Lady Macduff asks herself in lines 69–75.

**Infer:** What do these questions reveal about Lady Macduff's view of the world? Can these questions be answered?

[*Enter* Murderers.]

What are these faces?

**Murderer.** Where is your husband?

**Lady Macduff.** I hope in no place so unsanctified
Where such as thou mayst find him.

**Murderer.**                         He's a traitor.

**Son.** Thou liest, thou shag-eared villain!

**Murderer.**                         What, you egg!

[*Stabbing him*]

80  Young fry of treachery!

**Son.**                 He has killed me, mother.
Run away, I pray you,

[Lady Macduff *exits, crying* "Murder!" *followed by the* Murderers
*bearing the* Son's *body.*]

**Scene 3**  *England. Before King Edward's palace.*

[*Enter* Malcolm *and* Macduff.]

**Malcolm.** Let us seek out some desolate shade and there
Weep our sad bosoms empty.

**Macduff.**                 Let us rather
Hold fast the mortal sword and, like good men,
Bestride our downfall'n birthdom. Each new morn
5  New widows howl, new orphans cry, new sorrows
Strike heaven on the face, that it resounds
As if it felt with Scotland, and yelled out
Like syllable of dolor.

**Malcolm.**             What I believe, I'll wail;
What know, believe; and what I can redress,
10  As I shall find the time to friend, I will.
What you have spoke, it may be so, perchance.
This tyrant, whose sole name blisters our tongues,
Was once thought honest. You have loved him well.
He hath not touched you yet. I am young, but something
15  You may deserve of him through me, and wisdom
To offer up a weak, poor, innocent lamb
T' appease an angry god.

**Macduff.** I am not treacherous.

**Malcolm.**                 But Macbeth is.
A good and virtuous nature may recoil

77  **unsanctified:** unholy.

79  **shag-eared:** longhaired.

80  **young fry:** small fish.

**1–8** Macduff advises that they grab a deadly (**mortal**) sword and defend their homeland (**birthdom**). The anguished cries of Macbeth's victims strike heaven and make the skies echo with cries of sorrow (**syllable of dolor**).

**8–15** Malcolm will strike back only if the time is right (**as I shall find the time to friend**). Macduff may be sincere, but he may be deceiving Malcolm to gain a reward from Macbeth (**something you may deserve of him through me**).

**18–24** Even a good person may fall (**recoil**) into wickedness because of a king's command (**imperial charge**). Suspicions cannot change (**transpose**) the nature (**that which you are**) of an innocent person. Virtue cannot be damaged even by those like Lucifer (**the brightest angel**), who can disguise themselves as virtuous (**wear the brows of grace**).

20 In an imperial charge. But I shall crave your pardon.
That which you are, my thoughts cannot transpose.
Angels are bright still, though the brightest fell.
Though all things foul would wear the brows of grace,
Yet grace must still look so.

**Macduff.**                    I have lost my hopes.

25 **Malcolm.** Perchance even there where I did find my doubts.
Why in that rawness left you wife and child,
Those precious motives, those strong knots of love,
Without leave-taking? I pray you,
Let not my jealousies be your dishonors,
30 But mine own safeties. You may be rightly just,
Whatever I shall think.

**Macduff.**                    Bleed, bleed, poor country!
Great tyranny, lay thou thy basis sure,
For goodness dare not check thee. Wear thou thy wrongs;
The title is affeered.—Fare thee well, lord.
35 I would not be the villain that thou think'st
For the whole space that's in the tyrant's grasp,
And the rich East to boot.

**Malcolm.**                    Be not offended.
I speak not as in absolute fear of you.
I think our country sinks beneath the yoke.
40 It weeps, it bleeds, and each new day a gash
Is added to her wounds. I think withal
There would be hands uplifted in my right;
And here from gracious England have I offer
Of goodly thousands. But, for all this,
45 When I shall tread upon the tyrant's head
Or wear it on my sword, yet my poor country
Shall have more vices than it had before,
More suffer, and more sundry ways than ever,
By him that shall succeed.

**Macduff.**                    What should he be?

50 **Malcolm.** It is myself I mean, in whom I know
All the particulars of vice so grafted
That, when they shall be opened, black Macbeth
Will seem as pure as snow, and the poor state
Esteem him as a lamb, being compared
55 With my confineless harms.

**Macduff.**                    Not in the legions
Of horrid hell can come a devil more damned
In evils to top Macbeth.

**26 rawness:** vulnerability.

**29 jealousies:** suspicions.

**34 affeered:** confirmed.

**46–49 yet my . . . succeed:**
To test Macduff's honor and
loyalty, Malcolm begins a
lengthy description of his own
fictitious vices.

**50–55** Malcolm says that his
own vices are so plentiful and
deeply planted (**grafted**) that
Macbeth will seem innocent by
comparison.

**Malcolm.**                         I grant him bloody,
Luxurious, avaricious, false, deceitful,
Sudden, malicious, smacking of every sin
60 That has a name. But there's no bottom, none,
In my voluptuousness. Your wives, your daughters,
Your matrons, and your maids could not fill up
The cistern of my lust, and my desire
All continent impediments would o'erbear
65 That did oppose my will. Better Macbeth
Than such an one to reign.

**Macduff.**                         Boundless intemperance
In nature is a tyranny. It hath been
Th' untimely emptying of the happy throne
And fall of many kings. But fear not yet
70 To take upon you what is yours. You may
Convey your pleasures in a spacious plenty
And yet seem cold—the time you may so hoodwink.
We have willing dames enough. There cannot be
That vulture in you to devour so many
75 As will to greatness dedicate themselves,
Finding it so inclined.

**Malcolm.**                         With this there grows
In my most ill-composed affection such
A stanchless avarice that, were I king,
I should cut off the nobles for their lands,
80 Desire his jewels, and this other's house;
And my more-having would be as a sauce
To make me hunger more, that I should forge
Quarrels unjust against the good and loyal,
Destroying them for wealth.

**Macduff.**                         This avarice
85 Sticks deeper, grows with more pernicious root
Than summer-seeming lust, and it hath been
The sword of our slain kings. Yet do not fear.
Scotland hath foisons to fill up your will
Of your mere own. All these are portable,
90 With other graces weighed.

**Malcolm.** But I have none. The king-becoming graces,
As justice, verity, temp'rance, stableness,
Bounty, perseverance, mercy, lowliness,
Devotion, patience, courage, fortitude,
95 I have no relish of them but abound
In the division of each several crime,
Acting it many ways. Nay, had I power, I should
Pour the sweet milk of concord into hell,

**58 luxurious:** lustful.

**61 voluptuousness:** lust.

**63 cistern:** large storage tank.

**63–65** His lust is so great that it would overpower (**o'erbear**) all restraining obstacles (**continent impediments**).

**66–76** Macduff describes uncontrolled desire (**boundless intemperance**) as a tyrant of human nature that has caused the early (**untimely**) downfall of many kings.

**76–78** Malcolm adds insatiable greed (**stanchless avarice**) to the list of evils in his disposition (**affection**).

**84–90** Macduff recognizes that greed is a deeper-rooted problem than lust, which passes as quickly as the summer (**summer-seeming**). But the king's property alone (**of your mere own**) offers plenty (**foisons**) to satisfy his desire. Malcolm's vices can be tolerated (**are portable**).

**91–95** Malcolm lists the kingly virtues he lacks: truthfulness (**verity**), consistency (**stableness**), generosity (**bounty**), humility (**lowliness**), and religious devotion.

Uproar the universal peace, confound
100 All unity on earth.

**Macduff.**                O Scotland, Scotland!

**Malcolm.** If such a one be fit to govern, speak.
I am as I have spoken.

**Macduff.**                Fit to govern?
No, not to live.—O nation miserable,
With an untitled tyrant bloody-sceptered,
105 When shalt thou see thy wholesome days again,
Since that the truest issue of thy throne
By his own interdiction stands accursed
And does blaspheme his breed?—Thy royal father
Was a most sainted king. The queen that bore thee,
110 Oft'ner upon her knees than on her feet,
Died every day she lived. Fare thee well.
These evils thou repeat'st upon thyself
Have banished me from Scotland.—O my breast,
Thy hope ends here!

**102–114** Macduff can see no relief for Scotland's suffering under a tyrant who has no right to the throne (**untitled**). The rightful heir (**truest issue**), Malcolm, bans himself from the throne (**by his own interdiction**) because of his evil. Malcolm's vices slander his parents (**blaspheme his breed**)—his saintly father and his mother who renounced the world (**died every day**) for her religion.

**Malcolm.** Macduff, this noble passion,
115 Child of integrity, hath from my soul
Wiped the black scruples, reconciled my thoughts
To thy good truth and honor. Devilish Macbeth
By many of these trains hath sought to win me
Into his power, and modest wisdom plucks me
120 From overcredulous haste. But God above
Deal between thee and me, for even now
I put myself to thy direction and
Unspeak mine own detraction, here abjure
The taints and blames I laid upon myself
125 For strangers to my nature. I am yet
Unknown to woman, never was forsworn,
Scarcely have coveted what was mine own,
At no time broke my faith, would not betray
The devil to his fellow, and delight
130 No less in truth than life. My first false speaking
Was this upon myself. What I am truly
Is thine and my poor country's to command—
Whither indeed, before thy here-approach,

**114–125** Macduff has finally convinced Malcolm of his honesty. Malcolm explains that his caution (**modest wisdom**) resulted from his fear of Macbeth's tricks. He takes back his accusations against himself (**unspeak mine own detraction**) and renounces (**abjure**) the evils he previously claimed.

**133–137** Malcolm already has an army, 10,000 troops belonging to old Siward, the earl of Northumberland. Now that Macduff is an ally, he hopes the battle's result will match the justice of their cause (**warranted quarrel**).

**141–159** Edward the Confessor, king of England, could reportedly heal the disease of scrofula (**the evil**) by his saintly touch. The doctor describes people who cannot be helped by medicine's best efforts (**the great assay of art**) waiting for the touch of the king's hand. Edward has cured many victims of this disease. Each time, he hangs a gold coin around their neck and offers prayers, a healing ritual that he will teach to his royal descendants (**succeeding royalty**).

**162–163 Good God . . . strangers:** May God remove Macbeth, who is the cause (**means**) of our being strangers.

Old Siward with ten thousand warlike men,
135 Already at a point, was setting forth.
Now we'll together, and the chance of goodness
Be like our warranted quarrel. Why are you silent?

**Macduff.** Such welcome and unwelcome things at once
'Tis hard to reconcile.

[*Enter a* Doctor.]

140 **Malcolm.** Well, more anon.—Comes the King forth, I pray you?

**Doctor.** Ay, sir. There are a crew of wretched souls
That stay his cure. Their malady convinces
The great assay of art, but at his touch
(Such sanctity hath heaven given his hand )
145 They presently amend.

**Malcolm.**                    I thank you, doctor.

[Doctor *exits.*]

**Macduff.** What's the disease he means?

**Malcolm.**                              'Tis called the evil:
A most miraculous work in this good king,
Which often since my here-remain in England
I have seen him do. How he solicits heaven
150 Himself best knows, but strangely visited people
All swoll'n and ulcerous, pitiful to the eye,
The mere despair of surgery, he cures,
Hanging a golden stamp about their necks
Put on with holy prayers; and, 'tis spoken,
155 To the succeeding royalty he leaves
The healing benediction. With this strange virtue,
He hath a heavenly gift of prophecy,
And sundry blessings hang about his throne
That speak him full of grace.

[*Enter* Ross.]

**Macduff.**                     See who comes here.

160 **Malcolm.** My countryman, but yet I know him not.

**Macduff.** My ever-gentle cousin, welcome hither.

**Malcolm.** I know him now.—Good God betimes remove
The means that makes us strangers!

**Ross.**                              Sir, amen.

**Macduff.** Stands Scotland where it did?

**Ross.**                                   Alas, poor country,
165 Almost afraid to know itself. It cannot

Be called our mother, but our grave, where nothing
But who knows nothing is once seen to smile;
Where sighs and groans and shrieks that rent the air
Are made, not marked; where violent sorrow seems
170 A modern ecstasy. The dead man's knell
Is there scarce asked for who, and good men's lives
Expire before the flowers in their caps,
Dying or ere they sicken.

**Macduff.** O relation too nice and yet too true!

175 **Malcolm.** What's the newest grief?

**Ross.** That of an hour's age doth hiss the speaker.
Each minute teems a new one.

**Macduff.**                           How does my wife?

**Ross.** Why, well.

**Macduff.**           And all my children?

**Ross.**                                    Well too.

**Macduff.** The tyrant has not battered at their peace?

180 **Ross.** No, they were well at peace when I did leave 'em.

**Macduff.** Be not a niggard of your speech. How goes 't?

**Ross.** When I came hither to transport the tidings
Which I have heavily borne, there ran a rumor
Of many worthy fellows that were out;
185 Which was to my belief witnessed the rather
For that I saw the tyrant's power afoot.
Now is the time of help. Your eye in Scotland
Would create soldiers, make our women fight
To doff their dire distresses.

**Malcolm.**                      Be 't their comfort
190 We are coming thither. Gracious England hath
Lent us good Siward and ten thousand men;
An older and a better soldier none
That Christendom gives out.

**Ross.**                           Would I could answer
This comfort with the like. But I have words
195 That would be howled out in the desert air,
Where hearing should not latch them.

**Macduff.**                               What concern they—
The general cause, or is it a fee-grief
Due to some single breast?

**Ross.**                          No mind that's honest

---

**174 relation too nice:** news that is too accurate.

**176–177** If the news is more than an hour old, listeners hiss at the speaker for being outdated; every minute gives birth to a new grief.

### ANALYZE DRAMA
**Annotate:** Mark lines that Ross speaks that relate to Macduff's family in lines 177–200.

**Analyze:** How does dramatic irony create tension in this scene?

**180 well at peace:** Ross knows about the murder of Macduff's wife and children, but the news is too terrible to report.

**182–189** Ross mentions the rumors of nobles who are rebelling (**out**) against Macbeth. Ross believes the rumors because he saw Macbeth's troops on the march (**tyrant's power afoot**). The presence (**eye**) of Malcolm and Macduff in Scotland would help raise soldiers and remove (**doff**) Macbeth's evil (**dire distresses**).

**195 would:** should.
**196 latch:** catch.

**197 fee-grief:** private sorrow.

**198–199 No mind ... woe:** Every honorable (**honest**) person shares in this sorrow.

But in it shares some woe, though the main part
200 Pertains to you alone.

    **Macduff.**               If it be mine,
Keep it not from me. Quickly let me have it.

    **Ross.** Let not your ears despise my tongue forever,
Which shall possess them with the heaviest sound
That ever yet they heard.

    **Macduff.**              Hum! I guess at it.

205 **Ross.** Your castle is surprised, your wife and babes
Savagely slaughtered. To relate the manner
Were on the quarry of these murdered deer
To add the death of you.

    **Malcolm.**         Merciful heaven!
What, man, ne'er pull your hat upon your brows.
210 Give sorrow words. The grief that does not speak
Whispers the o'erfraught heart and bids it break.

    **Macduff.** My children too?

    **Ross.** Wife, children, servants, all that could be found.

    **Macduff.** And I must be from thence? My wife killed too?

215 **Ross.** I have said.

    **Malcolm.** Be comforted.
Let's make us med'cines of our great revenge
To cure this deadly grief.

    **Macduff.** He has no children. All my pretty ones?
220 Did you say "all"? O hell-kite! All?
What, all my pretty chickens and their dam
At one fell swoop?

    **Malcolm.** Dispute it like a man.

    **Macduff.**                 I shall do so,
But I must also feel it as a man.
225 I cannot but remember such things were
That were most precious to me. Did heaven look on
And would not take their part? Sinful Macduff,
They were all struck for thee! Naught that I am,
Not for their own demerits, but for mine,
230 Fell slaughter on their souls. Heaven rest them now.

    **Malcolm.** Be this the whetstone of your sword. Let grief
Convert to anger. Blunt not the heart; enrage it.

    **Macduff.** O, I could play the woman with mine eyes
And braggart with my tongue! But, gentle heavens,

**206–208** Ross won't add to Macduff's sorrow by telling him how his family was killed. He compares Macduff's dear ones to the piled bodies of killed deer (**quarry**).

**210–211** **The grief . . . break:** Silence will only push an overburdened heart to the breaking point.

**219–222** **He has no children:** possibly a reference to Macbeth, who has no children to be killed for revenge. Macduff compares Macbeth to a bird of prey (**hell-kite**) who kills defenseless chickens and their mother.

**228 naught:** nothing.

**231 whetstone:** grindstone used for sharpening.

235 Cut short all intermission! Front to front
Bring thou this fiend of Scotland and myself.
Within my sword's length set him. If he scape,
Heaven forgive him too.

**Malcolm.**                   This tune goes manly.
Come, go we to the King. Our power is ready;
240 Our lack is nothing but our leave. Macbeth
Is ripe for shaking, and the powers above
Put on their instruments. Receive what cheer you may.
The night is long that never finds the day.

[*They exit.*]

**239–243** Our troops are ready to attack, needing only the king's permission (**our lack is nothing but our leave**). Like a ripe fruit, Macbeth is ready to fall, and heavenly powers are preparing to assist us.

## CHECK YOUR UNDERSTANDING

Answer these questions before moving on to the **Analyze the Text** section on the following page.

1  What does Macbeth learn from his visit to the Witches in Act IV?

   **A** That he can trust Macduff

   **B** How to conjure spirits for himself

   **C** That Banquo's line can no longer rule Scotland

   **D** That he will rule until the forest marches to his castle

2  Why does Macbeth decide to have Macduff's family killed?

   **F** He has resolved to act without hesitation and is angry at Macduff.

   **G** The Apparitions convince Macbeth that Macduff will kill him.

   **H** Macbeth hopes to make an example of Macduff to ensure others' loyalty.

   **J** Macduff has convinced everyone that Macbeth is unfit for the throne.

3  What advice does Malcolm give Macduff?

   **A** That he should be relieved that he was not at home when the murderers arrived

   **B** That he must admit defeat and never return to Scotland

   **C** To take all the time he needs to mourn his wife and children

   **D** To turn his strong emotions to the positive goal of eliminating Macbeth

## ANALYZE THE TEXT

Support your responses with evidence from the text.   NOTEBOOK

1. **Analyze**  How does Macbeth interpret the prophecies pronounced by the first three apparitions? Explain how knowledge of the witches' intent affects the audience's perception of these prophecies.

2. **Infer**  What is the purpose of the appearance and speech of the messenger in Scene 2? Who might have sent this messenger?

3. **Draw Conclusions**  Lady Macduff and Malcolm both question Macduff's motives for fleeing Scotland. Think about the crimes Macbeth has already committed. Why might the nature of these crimes have led Macduff to believe his family would be safe at his castle?

4. **Infer**  Why might Shakespeare have decided to show the murder of Lady Macduff's son on stage? Explain how watching this scene rather than hearing about the event occurring offstage might affect the audience's view of Macbeth.

5. **Notice & Note**  Consider Macduff's anguished question about his family in Scene 3: "Did heaven look on / And would not take their part?" How does the answer to this **Tough Question** point toward a possible theme of the play?

## CREATE AND DISCUSS

**Participate in a Debate**  Some directors omit much of the scene in which Malcolm tests Macduff. What would be lost or gained by omitting this part of the play?

❏ With a group, come to a consensus on the significance of that part of Scene 3. Create an outline that includes reasons and evidence to support your opinion.

| Opinion |
| --- |
| Reasons |
| Evidence |

❏ Present your argument in the form of a panel discussion or debate. Have other groups present their opposing arguments.

❏ Ask listening classmates to evaluate which argument is most compelling and why.

Go to the **Speaking and Listening Studio** for help with group discussions.

## SETTING A PURPOSE

*As you read, pay attention to how the prophecies pronounced by the apparitions are fulfilled. Think about the characters affected by the prophecies. Revisit your character diagram as needed to recall the relationships between characters.*

## ACT V

**Scene 1**  *Macbeth's castle at Dunsinane.*

[*Enter a* Doctor of Physic *and a* Waiting Gentlewoman.]

**Doctor.** I have two nights watched with you but can perceive no truth in your report. When was it she last walked?

**Gentlewoman.** Since his Majesty went into the field, I have seen her rise from her bed, throw her nightgown upon her,
5  unlock her closet, take forth paper, fold it, write upon' t, read it, afterwards seal it, and again return to bed; yet all this while in a most fast sleep.

**Doctor.** A great perturbation in nature, to receive at once the benefit of sleep and do the effects of watching. In this slumb'ry
10  agitation, besides her walking and other actual performances, what at any time have you heard her say?

**Gentlewoman.** That, sir, which I will not report after her.

**Doctor.** You may to me, and 'tis most meet you should.

**Gentlewoman.** Neither to you nor anyone, having no witness to
15  confirm my speech.

[*Enter* Lady Macbeth *with a taper.*]

Lo you, here she comes. This is her very guise and, upon my life, fast asleep. Observe her; stand close.

**Doctor.** How came she by that light?

**Gentlewoman.** Why, it stood by her. She has light by her
20  continually. 'Tis her command.

**Doctor.** You see her eyes are open.

**Gentlewoman.** Ay, but their sense are shut.

**Doctor.** What is it she does now? Look how she rubs her hands.

**Gentlewoman.** It is an accustomed action with her to seem thus
25  washing her hands. I have known her continue in this a quarter of an hour.

**Lady Macbeth.** Yet here's a spot.

**Doctor.** Hark, she speaks. I will set down what comes from her,

**3  went into the field:** went to battle.

**8–9  A great . . . of watching:** To behave as though awake (**watching**) while sleeping is a sign of a greatly troubled nature.

**13  meet:** appropriate.

**16  guise:** usual manner.
**17  stand close:** hide yourself.
**18  that light:** her candle.

## ANALYZE CHARACTER AND THEME
**Annotate:** Mark phrases in lines 23–37 that tell what Lady Macbeth is doing.

**Analyze:** What possible theme of the play might her actions support?

to satisfy my remembrance the more strongly.

30 **Lady Macbeth.** Out, damned spot, out, I say! One. Two. Why then, 'tis time to do 't. Hell is murky. Fie, my lord, fie, a soldier and afeard? What need we fear who knows it, when none can call our power to account? Yet who would have thought the old man to have had so much blood in him?

35 **Doctor.** Do you mark that?

**Lady Macbeth.** The Thane of Fife had a wife. Where is she now? What, will these hands ne'er be clean? No more o' that, my lord, no more o' that. You mar all with this starting.

**Doctor.** Go to, go to. You have known what you should not.

40 **Gentlewoman.** She has spoke what she should not, I am sure of that. Heaven knows what she has known.

**Lady Macbeth.** Here's the smell of the blood still. All the perfumes of Arabia will not sweeten this little hand. O, O, O!

**Doctor.** What a sigh is there! The heart is sorely charged.

45 **Gentlewoman.** I would not have such a heart in my bosom for the dignity of the whole body.

**Doctor.** Well, well, well.

**Gentlewoman.** Pray God it be, sir.

**Doctor.** This disease is beyond my practice. Yet I have known
50 those which have walked in their sleep, who have died holily in their beds.

**Lady Macbeth.** Wash your hands. Put on your nightgown. Look not so pale. I tell you yet again, Banquo's buried; he cannot come out on 's grave.

55 **Doctor.** Even so?

**Lady Macbeth.** To bed, to bed. There's knocking at the gate. Come, come, come, come. Give me your hand. What's done cannot be undone. To bed, to bed, to bed.

[Lady Macbeth *exits*.]

**Doctor.** Will she go now to bed?

60 **Gentlewoman.** Directly.

**Doctor.** Foul whisp'rings are abroad. Unnatural deeds
Do breed unnatural troubles. Infected minds
To their deaf pillows will discharge their secrets.
More needs she the divine than the physician.
65 God, God forgive us all. Look after her.
Remove from her the means of all annoyance
And still keep eyes upon her. So good night.

**36–38** Lady Macbeth shows guilt about Macduff's wife. Then she addresses her husband, as if he were having another ghostly fit (**starting**).

**44 sorely charged:** heavily burdened.
**45–46** The gentlewoman says that she would not want Lady Macbeth's heavy heart in exchange for being queen.

**49 practice:** skill.

**54 on 's:** of his.

**61 Foul whisp'rings are abroad:** Rumors of evil deeds are circulating.

**64** She needs a priest more than a doctor.

**66 annoyance:** injury. The doctor may be worried about the possibility of Lady Macbeth's committing suicide.

Russian soprano Anna Netrebko as Lady Macbeth in Verdi's 'Macbeth' at the Metropolitan Opera House, Lincoln Center, New York, 2014.

My mind she has mated, and amazed my sight.
I think but dare not speak.

**Gentlewoman.**              Good night, good doctor.

[*They exit.*]

68 **mated:** astonished.

**Scene 2** *The country near Dunsinane.*

[*Drum and Colors. Enter* Menteith, Caithness, Angus, Lennox, *and* Soldiers.]

**Menteith.** The English power is near, led on by Malcolm,
His uncle Siward, and the good Macduff.
Revenges burn in them, for their dear causes
Would to the bleeding and the grim alarm
5 Excite the mortified man.

3–5 **for their dear . . . man:** The cause of Malcolm and Macduff is so deeply felt that a dead (**mortified**) man would respond to their call to arms (**alarm**).

**Angus.**              Near Birnam Wood
Shall we well meet them. That way are they coming.

**Caithness.** Who knows if Donalbain be with his brother?

**Lennox.** For certain, sir, he is not. I have a file
Of all the gentry. There is Siward's son
10 And many unrough youths that even now
Protest their first of manhood.

10–11 **many . . . manhood:** many soldiers who are too young to grow beards (**unrough**).

**Menteith.**              What does the tyrant?

**Caithness.** Great Dunsinane he strongly fortifies.
Some say he's mad; others that lesser hate him
Do call it valiant fury. But for certain
15 He cannot buckle his distempered cause
Within the belt of rule.

15–16 Like a man so swollen with disease (**distempered**) that he cannot buckle his belt, Macbeth cannot control his evil actions.

**Angus.**              Now does he feel
His secret murders sticking on his hands.

**18** Every minute, revolts against Macbeth shame him for his treachery (**faith-breach**).

**22–25** Macbeth's nerves, troubled by guilt, (**pestered senses**) have made him jumpy.

**25–29** They give their loyalty to the only help (**med'cine**) for the sick country (**weal**). They are willing to sacrifice their last drop of blood to cleanse (**purge**) Scotland.

**29–31** Lennox compares Malcolm to a flower that needs the blood of patriots to water (**dew**) it and drown out weeds like Macbeth.

**1** Macbeth wants no more news of thanes who have gone to Malcolm's side.

**2–10** Macbeth will not be infected (**taint**) with fear, because the witches (**spirits**), who know all human events (**mortal consequences**), have convinced him that he is invincible. He mocks the self-indulgent English (**English epicures**), then swears that he will never lack confidence.

**11 loon:** stupid rascal.

**12 goose-look:** look of fear.

**14–17** Macbeth suggests that the servant cut his face so that blood will hide his cowardice. He repeatedly insults the servant, calling him a coward (**lily-livered**) and a clown (**patch**) and making fun of his white complexion (**linen cheeks, whey-face**).

Now minutely revolts upbraid his faith-breach.
Those he commands move only in command,
20 Nothing in love. Now does he feel his title
Hang loose about him, like a giant's robe
Upon a dwarfish thief.

**Menteith.**     Who, then, shall blame
His pestered senses to recoil and start
When all that is within him does condemn
25 Itself for being there?

**Caithness.**     Well, march we on
To give obedience where 'tis truly owed.
Meet we the med'cine of the sickly weal,
And with him pour we in our country's purge
Each drop of us.

**Lennox.**     Or so much as it needs
30 To dew the sovereign flower and drown the weeds.
Make we our march towards Birnam.

[*They exit marching.*]

**Scene 3** *Dunsinane. A room in the castle.*

[*Enter* Macbeth, *the* Doctor, *and* Attendants.]

**Macbeth.** Bring me no more reports. Let them fly all.
Till Birnam Wood remove to Dunsinane
I cannot taint with fear. What's the boy Malcolm?
Was he not born of woman? The spirits that know
5 All mortal consequences have pronounced me thus:
"Fear not, Macbeth. No man that's born of woman
Shall e'er have power upon thee." Then fly, false thanes,
And mingle with the English epicures.
The mind I sway by and the heart I bear
10 Shall never sag with doubt nor shake with fear.

[*Enter* Servant.]

The devil damn thee black, thou cream-faced loon!
Where got'st thou that goose-look?

**Servant.** There is ten thousand—

**Macbeth.**     Geese, villain?

**Servant.**     Soldiers, sir.

**Macbeth.** Go prick thy face and over-red thy fear,
15 Thou lily-livered boy. What soldiers, patch?
Death of thy soul! Those linen cheeks of thine
Are counselors to fear. What soldiers, whey-face?

**Servant.** The English force, so please you.

**Macbeth.** Take thy face hence.

[Servant *exits*.]

                            Seyton!—I am sick at heart

20 When I behold—Seyton, I say!—This push
Will cheer me ever or disseat me now.
I have lived long enough. My way of life
Is fall'n into the sere, the yellow leaf,
And that which should accompany old age,

25 As honor, love, obedience, troops of friends,
I must not look to have, but in their stead
Curses, not loud but deep, mouth-honor, breath
Which the poor heart would fain deny and dare not.—
Seyton!

[*Enter* Seyton.]

30 **Seyton.** What's your gracious pleasure?

**Macbeth.**                       What news more?

**Seyton.** All is confirmed, my lord, which was reported.

**Macbeth.** I'll fight till from my bones my flesh be hacked.
Give me my armor.

**Seyton.**            'Tis not needed yet.

**Macbeth.** I'll put it on.

35 Send out more horses. Skirr the country round.
Hang those that talk of fear. Give me mine armor.—
How does your patient, doctor?

**Doctor.**                  Not so sick, my lord,
As she is troubled with thick-coming fancies
That keep her from her rest.

**Macbeth.**                Cure her of that.

40 Canst thou not minister to a mind diseased,
Pluck from the memory a rooted sorrow,
Raze out the written troubles of the brain,
And with some sweet oblivious antidote
Cleanse the stuffed bosom of that perilous stuff

45 Which weighs upon the heart?

**Doctor.**                Therein the patient
Must minister to himself.

**Macbeth.** Throw physic to the dogs, I'll none of it.—
Come, put mine armor on. Give me my staff.

[Attendants *begin to arm him*.]

Seyton, send out.—Doctor, the thanes fly from me.—

**20–28 This push ... dare not:**
The upcoming battle will either
make Macbeth secure (**cheer
me ever**) or dethrone (**disseat**)
him. He bitterly compares his
life to a withered (**sere**) leaf.
He cannot look forward to old
age with friends and honor,
but only to curses and empty
flattery (**mouth-honor, breath**)
from those too timid (**the poor
heart**) to tell the truth.

**35 skirr:** scour

**47–54** Macbeth has lost his
faith in the ability of medicine
(**physic**) to help his wife. He
says that if the doctor could
diagnose Scotland's disease
(**cast ... land**) and cure it,
Macbeth would never stop
praising him.

50 Come, sir, dispatch.—If thou couldst, doctor, cast
   The water of my land, find her disease,
   And purge it to a sound and pristine health,
   I would applaud thee to the very echo
   That should applaud again.—Pull 't off, I say.—
55 What rhubarb, senna, or what purgative drug
   Would scour these English hence? Hear'st thou of them?

**Doctor.** Ay, my good lord. Your royal preparation
Makes us hear something.

**Macbeth.**                    Bring it after me.—
I will not be afraid of death and bane
60 Till Birnam Forest come to Dunsinane.

**Doctor.** [*aside*]. Were I from Dunsinane away and clear,
Profit again should hardly draw me here.

[*They exit.*]


**Scene 4** *The country near Birnam Wood.*

[*Drum and Colors. Enter* Malcolm, Siward, Macduff, Siward's
son, Menteith, Caithness, Angus, *and* Soldiers, *marching.*]

**Malcolm.** Cousins, I hope the days are near at hand
That chambers will be safe.

**Menteith.**                    We doubt it nothing.

**Siward.** What wood is this before us?

**Menteith.**                              The wood of Birnam.

**Malcolm.** Let every soldier hew him down a bough
5 And bear 't before him. Thereby shall we shadow
The numbers of our host and make discovery
Err in report of us.

**Soldiers.**           It shall be done.

**Siward.** We learn no other but the confident tyrant
Keeps still in Dunsinane and will endure
10 Our setting down before 't.

**Malcolm.**                    'Tis his main hope;
For, where there is advantage to be given,
Both more and less have given him the revolt,
And none serve with him but constrainèd things
Whose hearts are absent too.

**Macduff.**                    Let our just censures
15 Attend the true event, and put we on
Industrious soldiership.

**54 Pull 't off:** Macbeth is referring to a piece of armor.

**56 scour:** purge; **them:** the English.

**58–60** Macbeth leaves for battle, telling Seyton to bring the armor.

**ANALYZE DRAMA**
**Annotate:** Mark dialogue in lines 3–7 that reveals how Malcolm plans to attack Macbeth's castle.

**Infer:** How does this plan fulfill the prophecy Macbeth was given?

**10 setting down:** siege.

**10–14** Malcolm says that men of all ranks (**both more and less**) have abandoned Macbeth. Only weak men forced into service remain with him.

**14–16** Macduff warns against overconfidence and advises that they focus on fighting.

**Siward.**                    The time approaches
That will with due decision make us know
What we shall say we have and what we owe.
Thoughts speculative their unsure hopes relate,
20 But certain issue strokes must arbitrate;
Towards which, advance the war.

[*They exit marching.*]

**Scene 5** *Dunsinane. Within the castle.*

[*Enter* Macbeth, Seyton, *and* Soldiers, *with Drum and Colors.*]

**Macbeth.** Hang out our banners on the outward walls.
The cry is still "They come!" Our castle's strength
Will laugh a siege to scorn. Here let them lie
Till famine and the ague eat them up.
5 Were they not forced with those that should be ours,
We might have met them dareful, beard to beard,
And beat them backward home.

[*A cry within of women.*]

                    What is that noise?

**Seyton.** It is the cry of women, my good lord. [*He exits.*]

**Macbeth.** I have almost forgot the taste of fears.
10 The time has been my senses would have cooled
To hear a night-shriek, and my fell of hair
Would at a dismal treatise rouse and stir
As life were in 't. I have supped full with horrors.
Direness, familiar to my slaughterous thoughts,
15 Cannot once start me.

[*Enter* Seyton.]

                    Wherefore was that cry?

**Seyton.** The Queen, my lord, is dead.

**Macbeth.** She should have died hereafter.
There would have been a time for such a word.
Tomorrow and tomorrow and tomorrow
20 Creeps in this petty pace from day to day
To the last syllable of recorded time,
And all our yesterdays have lighted fools
The way to dusty death. Out, out, brief candle!
Life's but a walking shadow, a poor player
25 That struts and frets his hour upon the stage
And then is heard no more. It is a tale
Told by an idiot, full of sound and fury,
Signifying nothing.

**16–21** Siward says that the approaching battle will decide whether their claims will match what they actually possess (**owe**). Now, their hopes and expectations are guesswork (**thoughts speculative**); only fighting (**strokes**) can settle (**arbitrate**) the issue.

**4 ague:** fever.

**5–7** Macbeth complains that the attackers have been reinforced (**forced**) by deserters (**those that should be ours**), which has forced him to wait at Dunsinane instead of seeking victory on the battlefield.

**9–15** There was a time when a scream in the night would have frozen Macbeth in fear and a terrifying tale (**dismal treatise**) would have made the hair on his skin (**fell of hair**) stand on end. But since he has fed on horror (**direness**), it cannot stir (**start**) him anymore.

**17–18** Macbeth wishes that his wife had died later (**hereafter**), when he would have had time to mourn her.

▶ **AHA MOMENT**

**Notice & Note:** Mark words in lines 17–28 that reveal Macbeth's state of mind.

**Infer:** What has Lady Macbeth's death made Macbeth realize?

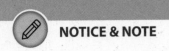
[*Enter a* Messenger.]

Thou com'st to use thy tongue: thy story quickly.

30 **Messenger.** Gracious my lord,
I should report that which I say I saw,
But know not how to do 't.

**Macbeth.**                              Well, say, sir.

**Messenger.** As I did stand my watch upon the hill,
I looked toward Birnam, and anon methought
35 The wood began to move.

**Macbeth.**                              Liar and slave!

**Messenger.** Let me endure your wrath, if 't be not so.
Within this three mile may you see it coming.
I say, a moving grove.

**Macbeth.**                    If thou speak'st false,
Upon the next tree shall thou hang alive
40 Till famine cling thee. If thy speech be sooth,
I care not if thou dost for me as much.—
I pull in resolution and begin
To doubt th' equivocation of the fiend,
That lies like truth. "Fear not till Birnam Wood
45 Do come to Dunsinane," and now a wood
Comes toward Dunsinane. —Arm, arm, and out!—
If this which he avouches does appear,
There is nor flying hence nor tarrying here.
I 'gin to be aweary of the sun
50 And wish th' estate o' th' world were now undone.—
Ring the alarum bell! —Blow wind, come wrack,
At least we'll die with harness on our back.

[*They exit.*]

**Scene 6** *Dunsinane. Before the castle.*

[*Drum and Colors. Enter* Malcolm, Siward, Macduff, *and their army, with boughs.*]

**Malcolm.** Now near enough. Your leafy screens throw down
And show like those you are. —You, worthy uncle,
Shall with my cousin, your right noble son,
Lead our first battle. Worthy Macduff and we
5 Shall take upon 's what else remains to do,
According to our order.

**Siward.**                              Fare you well.
Do we but find the tyrant's power tonight,
Let us be beaten if we cannot fight.

**38–52** The messenger's news has dampened Macbeth's determination (**resolution**); Macbeth begins to fear that the Witches have tricked him (**to doubt th' equivocation of the fiend**). His fear that the messenger tells the truth (**avouches**) makes him decide to confront the enemy instead of staying in his castle. Weary of life, he nevertheless decides to face death and ruin (**wrack**) with his armor (**harness**) on.

**1–6** Malcolm commands the troops to put down their branches (**leafy screens**) and gives the battle instructions.

**7 power:** forces.

**Macduff.** Make all our trumpets speak; give them all breath,
10 Those clamorous harbingers of blood and death.

[*They exit. Alarums continued.*]

**10 harbingers:** announcers.

**Scene 7** *Another part of the battlefield.*

[*Enter* Macbeth.]

**Macbeth.** They have tied me to a stake. I cannot fly,
But, bear-like, I must fight the course. What's he
That was not born of woman? Such a one
Am I to fear, or none.

[*Enter* Young Siward.]

5 **Young Siward.** What is thy name?

**Macbeth.**                              Thou'lt be afraid to hear it.

**Young Siward.** No, though thou call'st thyself a hotter name
Than any is in hell.

**Macbeth.**              My name's Macbeth.

**Young Siward.** The devil himself could not pronounce a title
More hateful to mine ear.

**1–4** Macbeth compares himself to a bear tied to a post (a reference to the sport of bearbaiting, in which a bear was tied to a stake and attacked by dogs).

Chinese bass Haojiang Tian performs Verdi's opera 'Macbeth' at the Hong Kong Cultural Centre, 2003.

**Macbeth.**                    No, nor more fearful.

10 **Young Siward.** Thou liest, abhorrèd tyrant. With my sword
I'll prove the lie thou speak'st.

[*They fight, and* Young Siward *is slain.*]

**Macbeth.**                    Thou wast born of woman.
But swords I smile at, weapons laugh to scorn,
Brandished by man that's of a woman born. [*He exits.*]
[*Alarums. Enter* Macduff.]

**Macduff.** That way the noise is. Tyrant, show thy face!
15 If thou beest slain, and with no stroke of mine,
My wife and children's ghosts will haunt me still.
I cannot strike at wretched kerns, whose arms
Are hired to bear their staves. Either thou, Macbeth,
Or else my sword with an unbattered edge
20 I sheathe again undeeded. There thou shouldst be;
By this great clatter, one of greatest note
Seems bruited. Let me find him, Fortune,
And more I beg not.

[*He exits. Alarums.*]

[*Enter* Malcolm *and* Siward.]

**Siward.** This way, my lord. The castle's gently rendered.
25 The tyrant's people on both sides do fight,
The noble thanes do bravely in the war,
The day almost itself professes yours,
And little is to do.

**Malcolm.**          We have met with foes
That strike beside us.

**Siward.**                Enter, sir, the castle.

[*He exits. Alarum.*]

**Scene 8** *Another part of the battlefield.*

[*Enter* Macbeth.]

**Macbeth.** Why should I play the Roman fool and die
On mine own sword? Whiles I see lives, the gashes
Do better upon them.

[*Enter* Macduff.]

**Macduff.**                Turn, hellhound, turn!

**Macbeth.** Of all men else I have avoided thee.
5 But get thee back. My soul is too much charged
With blood of thine already.

**14–20** Macduff hopes to find Macbeth before someone else has the chance to kill him. Macduff does not want to fight the miserable hired soldiers (**kerns**), who are armed only with spears (**staves**). If he can't fight Macbeth, Macduff will leave his sword unused (**undeeded**).

**22 bruited:** rumored or heard.

**24 gently rendered:** surrendered without a fight.

**27** You have almost won the day.

**28–29** During the battle many of Macbeth's men deserted to Malcolm's army.

**1–3** Macbeth refuses to commit suicide in the style of a defeated Roman general.

**4–6** Macbeth does not want to fight Macduff, having already killed so many members of Macduff's family.

**Macduff.**                              I have no words;
My voice is in my sword, thou bloodier villain
Than terms can give thee out.

[*Fight. Alarum.*]

**Macbeth.**                              Thou losest labor.
As easy mayst thou the intrenchant air
10 With thy keen sword impress as make me bleed.
Let fall thy blade on vulnerable crests;
I bear a charmèd life, which must not yield
To one of woman born.

**Macduff.**                              Despair thy charm,
And let the angel whom thou still hast served
15 Tell thee Macduff was from his mother's womb
Untimely ripped.

**Macbeth.** Accursèd be that tongue that tells me so,
For it hath cowed my better part of man!
And be these juggling fiends no more believed
20 That palter with us in a double sense,
That keep the word of promise to our ear
And break it to our hope. I'll not fight with thee.

**Macduff.** Then yield thee, coward,
And live to be the show and gaze o' th' time.
25 We'll have thee, as our rarer monsters are,
Painted upon a pole, and underwrit
"Here may you see the tyrant."

**Macbeth.**                              I will not yield
To kiss the ground before young Malcolm's feet
And to be baited with the rabble's curse.
30 Though Birnam Wood be come to Dunsinane
And thou opposed, being of no woman born,
Yet I will try the last. Before my body
I throw my warlike shield. Lay on, Macduff,
And damned be him that first cries "Hold! Enough!"

[*They exit fighting. Alarums.*]
[*They enter fighting, and* Macbeth *is slain.* Macduff *exits
carrying off* Macbeth's *body. Retreat and flourish. Enter, with
Drum and Colors,* Malcolm, Siward, Ross, Thanes, *and* Soldiers.]

35 **Malcolm.** I would the friends we miss were safe arrived.

**Siward.** Some must go off; and yet by these I see
So great a day as this is cheaply bought.

**Malcolm.** Macduff is missing, and your noble son.

**Ross.** Your son, my lord, has paid a soldier's debt.
40 He only lived but till he was a man,

**NOTICE & NOTE**

**8–13:** Macbeth says that Macduff is wasting his effort. Trying to wound Macbeth is as useless as trying to wound the invulnerable (**intrenchant**) air. Macduff should strike at the helmets (**crests**) of more vulnerable foes.

**15–16 Macduff . . . untimely ripped:** Macduff was a premature baby delivered by cesarean section, an operation that removes the child directly from the mother's womb.

**18 cowed:** made fearful.

**19–22** The cheating witches (**juggling fiends**) have tricked him (**palter with us**) with words that have double meanings.

**23–27** Macduff tells Macbeth to surrender and become a public spectacle (**the show and gaze o' th' time**), with his picture displayed (**painted upon a pole**) as if he were in a circus sideshow.

[Stage Direction] **Retreat . . . :** The first trumpet call (**retreat**) signals the battle's end. The next one (**flourish**) announces Malcolm's entrance.

**36–37** Though some must die (**go off**) in battle, Siward can see that their side does not have many casualties.

The which no sooner had his prowess confirmed
In the unshrinking station where he fought,
But like a man he died.

**Siward.**                    Then he is dead?

**Ross.** Ay, and brought off the field. Your cause of sorrow
45 Must not be measured by his worth, for then
It hath no end.

**Siward.**        Had he his hurts before?

**Ross.** Ay, on the front.

**Siward.**                    Why then, God's soldier be he!
Had I as many sons as I have hairs,
I would not wish them to a fairer death;
50 And so his knell is knolled.

**Malcolm.** He's worth more sorrow, and that I'll spend for him.

**Siward.** He's worth no more.
They say he parted well and paid his score,
And so, God be with him. Here comes newer comfort.

[*Enter* Macduff *with* Macbeth's *head.*]

55 **Macduff.** Hail, King! for so thou art. Behold where stands
Th' usurper's cursèd head. The time is free.
I see thee compassed with thy kingdom's pearl,
That speak my salutation in their minds,
Whose voices I desire aloud with mine.
60 Hail, King of Scotland!

**All.**                    Hail, King of Scotland!

[*Flourish.*]

**Malcolm.** We shall not spend a large expense of time
Before we reckon with your several loves
And make us even with you. My thanes and kinsmen,
Henceforth be earls, the first that ever Scotland
65 In such an honor named. What's more to do,
Which would be planted newly with the time,
As calling home our exiled friends abroad
That fled the snares of watchful tyranny,
Producing forth the cruel ministers
70 Of this dead butcher and his fiend-like queen
(Who, as 'tis thought, by self and violent hands,
Took off her life)—this, and what needful else

---

**46 hurts before:** wounds in the front of his body, which indicate he died facing his enemy.

**50 knell is knolled:** Young Siward's death bell has already rung.

[Stage Direction] Macduff is probably carrying Macbeth's head on a pole.

**56–57 The time . . . pearl:** Macduff declares that the age (**time**) is now freed from tyranny. He sees Malcolm surrounded by Scotland's noblest men (**thy kingdom's pearl**).

**61–76** Malcolm promises that he will quickly reward his nobles according to the devotion (**several loves**) they have shown. He gives the thanes new titles (**henceforth be earls**) and declares his intention, as a sign of the new age (**planted newly with the time**), to welcome back the exiles who fled Macbeth's tyranny and his cruel agents (**ministers**).

That calls upon us, by the grace of grace,
We will perform in measure, time, and place.
75 So thanks to all at once and to each one,
Whom we invite to see us crowned at Scone.

[*Flourish. All exit.*]

## CHECK YOUR UNDERSTANDING

Answer these questions before moving on to the **Analyze the Text** section on the following page.

**1** What happens to Lady Macbeth in Act V?

  **A** She briefly experiences horrible nightmares.

  **B** Overcome by guilt, she goes insane and dies.

  **C** Although she begins sleepwalking, she is happy.

  **D** She becomes fearful of germs and darkness.

**2** In scene 3, Macbeth complains that he can only look forward to —

  **F** a quiet death

  **G** having grandchildren

  **H** ruling Scotland

  **J** empty flattery

**3** How does Macbeth's rule end?

  **A** Overwhelming guilt and grief cause him to give up the throne.

  **B** He flees when he imagines that the forest is moving.

  **C** Macduff kills him on the battlefield to avenge his family.

  **D** His own soldiers turn on him and he is taken prisoner.

**RESPOND**

## ANALYZE THE TEXT

Support your responses with evidence from the text. ☷ NOTEBOOK

1. **Analyze** The Witches are sometimes seen as representing fate, or destiny. Do they merely reveal what will happen, or do they manipulate events? Explain your ideas.

2. **Cite Evidence** In what ways do Macbeth's strengths contribute to his downfall? Cite examples from the entire play to support your ideas.

3. **Interpret** In what ways are the Witches' prophecies revealed to be true in Act V?

4. **Evaluate** One scholar says that if we don't see ourselves in Macbeth, we misunderstand either the play or ourselves. In what way might this play be an allegory, or a lesson that we can apply to our own lives?

5. **Notice & Note** Explain how Lady Macbeth's actions in Act V, Scene 1, draw meaning from the repeated images of blood, darkness, and sleep that have run through the play. Does her deterioration redeem her character in the eyes of the audience? Why or why not?

## RESEARCH

**RESEARCH TIP**
Publishers of Shakespeare's plays often have additional information about each play on their websites. Some biography websites can also provide insight into Shakespeare's writings. Be sure to check the validity of the information and use websites that can be trusted.

When you finish reading a Shakespearian tragedy, sometimes you are left with more questions than answers. What do you wonder about after reading this play? Conduct research to explore the question of your choice about Macbeth. In the chart, record your question and the answers you find.

| QUESTION | POSSIBLE ANSWERS |
|---|---|
|  |  |

**Connect** In Scene 8, Macbeth says that it is impossible to kill him. He thinks this because the Witches told him that no man born of a woman can slay him. With a small group, discuss the ways in which people are misled by what other people tell them about dangers they may face.

## CREATE AND DISCUSS

**Document Information** Take a look back at your character diagram, and complete it using evidence from Act V.

- ❏ Add events from Act V, including the ultimate fate of the play's major characters.
- ❏ Review your previous entries in the diagram, revising as needed to enhance or confirm your understanding.
- ❏ Add visual cues such as drawings or symbols to sum up the roles or outcomes of characters as you choose.

**Discuss with a Small Group** Have a discussion about the drama's relationships and events based on the character diagram you created.

- ❏ In your group, share your completed character diagrams, noting evidence for your ideas as needed.
- ❏ Work together to create a timeline of key events. Reach a group consensus on the layout and content of your group's timeline.
- ❏ Share your group's timeline with the class, explaining your choices.

 Go to the **Speaking and Listening Studio** for help with having a group discussion.

## RESPOND TO THE ESSENTIAL QUESTION

 What are the sources of true power?

**Gather Information** Review your annotations and notes on *The Tragedy of Macbeth*. Then, add relevant information to your Response Log. As you determine which information to include, think about:

- the ways that power can corrupt people
- the ways in which power can be positive
- how people without power respond to those in power

At the end of the unit, use your notes to help you write a literary analysis.

**ACADEMIC VOCABULARY**

As you write and discuss what you learned from the play, be sure to use the Academic Vocabulary words. Check off each of the words that you use.

- ❏ **comprise**
- ❏ **incidence**
- ❏ **predominant**
- ❏ **priority**
- ❏ **ultimate**

## VOCABULARY STRATEGY:
### Archaic Language

**Archaic language** includes old words and phrases that are not commonly used in modern speech. Although Shakespeare's works brought to the English language a multitude of new words that people still use today, his poetic sentence structures are different from what we hear every day. In addition, many of the archaic words Shakespeare uses, such as *thee* and *hath,* fell out of fashion centuries ago, so their meanings are not always easy to understand.

To untangle a sentence, find the **subject** (who or what the sentence is about) and the **predicate** (what the subject is or does). Then you can separate out any other clauses in the sentence and consider the function of each one.

When you come across an unfamiliar word, use these strategies:

• Search the surrounding dialogue for helpful context clues.

• Try to break down the word into base or root words, suffixes, and prefixes and figure out the meaning from these parts.

• Use a dictionary to look up the definition of any unfamiliar words.

• Use the word in a sentence of your own to explore its meaning.

**Practice and Apply** Use the steps listed below to paraphrase what Macbeth asks of the Doctor in Act V, Scene 3:

> . . . If thou couldst, doctor, cast
> The water of my land, find her disease,
> And purge it to a sound and pristine health,
> I would applaud thee to the very echo
> That should applaud again. . . .

**1.** Mark archaic words and any other words with unclear meanings.

**2.** Reword as much of the speech as you can in today's English, maintaining a logical order of ideas. Leave a space in your rewording for any words whose meanings are still unclear.

**3.** In your reworded speech, bracket your best guesses from context at the meanings of the archaic words, or consult a dictionary.

## LANGUAGE CONVENTIONS:
### Inverted Sentence Structure

A key aspect of Shakespeare's style is his use of **inverted sentence structure.** In an inverted sentence, the normal word order is reversed. Some examples of inverted structure include:

• all or part of the predicate comes before the subject (*There go I.*)

• a subject comes between a helping verb and a main verb (*Had they known.*)

• a direct object precedes a verb (*Her triumph I celebrated.*)

• a prepositional phrase comes before the noun or verb it modifies (*Within the castle he waits.*)

Shakespeare includes many of these inverted sentence structures in his play. Read these lines from *The Tragedy of Macbeth*:

> **Come, go we to the King.** (Act IV, Scene 3, line 239)

> **The castle of Macduff I will surprise.** (Act IV, Scene 1, line 150)

Notice that in the first example the verb *go* precedes the subject *we*. In the second example, the direct object *the castle* and its modifier *of Macduff* appear before both the subject *I* and the verb phrase *will surprise*. Shakespeare could have written the lines this way:

> **Come, we go to the King.**

> **I will surprise the castle of Macduff.**

His use of inverted structures creates a poetic effect. Writers also use inverted sentence structures to add variety or to emphasize a word or an idea.

**Practice and Apply**  On your own, identify the part that is inverted in each sentence below. Rewrite each sentence without the inversion. Then, working with a partner, write five original sentences on topics of your choice that use the same inverted structures found in Shakespeare's sentences.

1. **O, full of scorpions is my mind, dear wife!** (Act III, Scene 2, line 35)

   _____

2. **I'll fight till from my bones my flesh be hacked.** (Act V, Scene 3, line 32)

   _____

3. **Retire we to our chamber.** (Act II, Scene 2, line 64)

   _____

4. **For them the gracious Duncan have I murdered.** (Act III, Scene 1, line 65)

   _____

5. **Then comes my fit again. (**Act III, Scene 4, line 21)

   _____

MEDIA

*from*
# MACBETH

Film by **Rupert Goold**

**? ESSENTIAL QUESTION:**

## What are the sources of true power?

## QUICK START

Have you ever watched a film adaptation of a classic play or story? Discuss your experiences with the class.

**GENRE ELEMENTS: FILM**

- intended to be viewed by a wide, public audience
- tells a story visually, using actors on sets or locations
- develops from screenplays with actors' lines and direction
- includes planned camera shots and angles to evoke a mood

## ANALYZE MEDIA REPRESENTATIONS

The Witches in *Macbeth* not only serve a crucial role in driving the plot, they also establish the tone of the entire play from their first appearance. Every director who stages the scene in which the Witches deliver their first prophecy to Macbeth brings a unique approach to it. This approach comprises a mix of Shakespeare's words, the mood the director wants to invoke, and the special effects that will create the strongest impact.

Consider what this production emphasizes in the scene as well as what it omits from the original play. Also consider how the director uses the medium of film in concert with Shakespeare's words. Note your responses in the chart.

| | |
|---|---|
| **SETTING / SETS** | How does the modern setting affect the tone and theme of the scene? |
| **FILM SHOTS AND ANGLES** | What is the effect of multiple cuts and shots from various angles? |
| **SPECIAL EFFECTS** | How does the director use special effects to capture the Witches' supernatural powers? |

## BACKGROUND

*In 2010, the BBC (British Broadcasting Corporation) broadcast a new version of Shakespeare's Scottish play starring Patrick Stewart in the title role. Director* **Rupert Goold** *(b. 1972) modernized the play's setting to place it in a twentieth-century military dictatorship while retaining Shakespeare's powerful language. Goold has directed numerous stage versions of Shakespeare's plays. This production won a Peabody Award and aired in the United States on PBS's Great Performances.*

## SETTING A PURPOSE

*As you view the film, consider how the modern setting creates a certain mood or tone. Write down any questions you have during viewing.* **NOTEBOOK**

To view the video, log in online and select **"from MACBETH"** from the unit menu.

As needed, pause the video to make notes about what impresses you or about ideas you might want to talk about later. Replay or rewind to clarify anything you do not understand.

## ANALYZE MEDIA

Support your responses with evidence from the text. 📝 NOTEBOOK

1. **Analyze** How do the choices made by director Rupert Goold help develop a particular tone? Cite specific images and staging to support your answer.

2. **Compare** Which passages of Shakespeare's original text are omitted from this production of the scene? Explain how leaving out these lines affects the pacing and theme of the scene.

3. **Evaluate** How do the actors' use of emphasis and expression add meaning to this scene and help clarify your understanding? Cite specific lines.

4. **Cite Evidence** How does the twentieth-century resetting of the play's action affect your understanding of the scene? Cite specific details about costumes, setting, and other modern aspects of the production to support your answer.

5. **Analyze** What special effects are used in this scene? How might these effects have been achieved in a stage production of Shakespeare's time?

## RESEARCH

Shakespeare's most well-known plays have been adapted for film and television many times. Research other film or television adaptations of *Macbeth,* and if possible, view a clip from one of the adaptations. How is the clip similar to the clip from Rupert Goold's version? How is it different? What atmosphere, or feeling, is conveyed in the clip? Record what you learn in the chart.

| *MACBETH* ADAPTATION: | | |
|---|---|---|
| **SIMILARITIES** | **DIFFERENCES** | **ATMOSPHERE/FEELING** |
|  |  |  |

**Connect** In film adaptations of plays, the camera shots and angles have a significant effect on the presentation of the story that a play in a theater cannot achieve. With a small group, discuss how the camera work of a film adaptation enhances or detracts from your enjoyment and understanding of the play.

## CREATE AND PRESENT

**Write an Analysis** Write a one-paragraph analysis of the clip you researched, using the information from your chart.

❏ Introduce the clip of the adaptation you found and cite its director, writer(s), and clip source.

❏ Explain the setting and how it affects the mood and tone of the film. Discuss the camera shots and angles and their effects as well.

❏ End your analysis with a critique of the clip. Is it a successful adaptation? Give details to support your ideas.

**Deliver an Argument** How effective was this modern resetting of *Macbeth* in expressing key themes of Shakespeare's play? Develop your thesis in a short speech, using domain-specific vocabulary.

❏ Review the clip from *Macbeth,* making notes about themes that emerge through the modern setting. Cite specific details from the film that support your ideas.

❏ Compare the themes you noted to major themes of the play.

❏ Draft a statement expressing your overall evaluation of the modern production's effectiveness.

❏ Present your evaluation in a short speech in which you support your claim with specific, relevant evidence from both the film and the play.

 Go to the **Writing Studio** for more on writing an analysis.

 Go to the **Speaking and Listening Studio** for help with delivering an argument.

## RESPOND TO THE ESSENTIAL QUESTION

**?** What are the sources of true power?

**Gather Information** Review your notes on the film clip from *Macbeth*. Then, add relevant information to your Response Log. As you determine what information to include, think about:

• themes of the play that are suggested in the film clip
• reasons for changing the setting of the play to a modern one
• the atmosphere and mood the setting evokes

At the end of the unit, use your notes to write a literary analysis.

**ACADEMIC VOCABULARY**
As you write and discuss what you learned from the film, be sure to use the Academic Vocabulary words. Check off each of the words that you use.

❏ **comprise**
❏ **incidence**
❏ **predominant**
❏ **priority**
❏ **ultimate**

# THE MACBETH MURDER MYSTERY

Short Story by **James Thurber**

**?** *ESSENTIAL QUESTION:*

What are the sources of true power?

## QUICK START

Have you ever read or watched a murder mystery? Were you able to guess who the murderer was before it was revealed at the end? With a partner, discuss the plot of the story and any clues that helped you to solve the crime.

## ANALYZE SATIRE

**Satire** is a literary work that ridicules a vice or folly found in society. Satirists use humor in their works to cause people to change how they think or what their priorities are. Satire can change society by forcing readers to see an idea, behavior, or custom in a critical light.

In "The Macbeth Murder Mystery," James Thurber draws upon Shakespeare's *Macbeth* to create a satire. Readers will be familiar with the references to *Macbeth*, but the unexpected way Thurber's characters transform the tragedy into a formulaic British murder mystery allows him to comment on how people approach literature. As you read, consider these questions:

- To which elements of Shakespeare's play does Thurber refer in his story?

- How are the play's elements transformed in the short story?

- What effect do these changes have on the characters? on the reader?

- What issue does Thurber ridicule in his story?

### GENRE ELEMENTS: SATIRE

- mocks common beliefs, social conventions, or institutions

- may be gentle and witty, slightly abrasive, or bitter and critical

- often uses humor, irony, and exaggeration to make a point

- written with the goal of improving society

## MAKE CONNECTIONS

The works of William Shakespeare have influenced many authors over the centuries. Shakespeare's plays contain insights on human nature that are timeless. For example, his tragedy *Macbeth* is known for themes of uncontrolled ambition, betrayal, and corrupting power, themes shared by many literary works. *Macbeth* is a serious drama. "The Macbeth Murder Mystery," however, is a humorous short story. James Thurber's short story relies upon his readers' knowledge of *Macbeth* to find humor in "rewriting" Shakespeare as if it were a British murder mystery. As you read, note the connections between elements of the three different genres.

| ELEMENT | SERIOUS DRAMA | BRITISH MURDER MYSTERY | HUMOROUS SHORT STORY / SATIRE |
|---|---|---|---|
| Setting | | | |
| Plot | | | |
| Characters | | | |
| Purpose / Theme | | | |

## CRITICAL VOCABULARY

**decisively    sacrilegious    secluded    contention    cryptically**

To see how many Critical Vocabulary words you already know, use them to complete the sentences.

1. The famous detective hid from the press at a _____ location.

2. A _____ act might offend members of certain religious groups.

3. Speaking _____ keeps others from knowing what you are saying.

4. The astronaut acted _____ and closed the hatch without hesitation.

5. It was the lawyer's _____ that the murderer knew the victim.

## LANGUAGE CONVENTIONS

**Pronoun-Antecedent Agreement**  A **pronoun** is a word used in place of a noun or another pronoun. The word to which the pronoun refers is its **antecedent**. Writers use pronouns to avoid repetition and for variety.  Here is an example of an antecedent and pronoun pair in the story you will read:

**"Tell me," I said. "Did you read (Macbeth)?" "I had to read it," she said.**

In this example, the noun "*Macbeth*" is the antecedent of the pronoun "it." As you read, determine the antecedent for each pronoun to help you understand the story's fast-paced dialogue.

---

ANNOTATION MODEL                                    NOTICE & NOTE

As you read, note how the author creates satire and makes connections. You can also mark evidence that supports your own ideas. Here are one reader's notes about connections in the story between Shakespeare and detective fiction:

"It was a stupid mistake to make," said the American woman I had met at my hotel in the English lake country, "but it was on the counter with the other Penguin books—the little sixpenny ones, you know, with the paper covers—and I supposed of course it was a detective story. All the others were detective stories. I'd read all the others, so I bought this one [without really looking at it carefully.] You can imagine how mad I was when I found out it was Shakespeare."

> connection between detective books and Shakespeare
>
> not very observant for someone who likes detective stories

## BACKGROUND

*English murder mysteries follow a predictable framework and typically contain these elements that help readers predict the conclusion: a dead body; an intelligent detective; an isolated setting; a group of suspects; clues, some of which are misleading; a surprise twist; a capture; and an explanation of how the crime was committed.*

**James Thurber** *(1894–1961) was an American humorist. His observational humor appeared in hundreds of essays, short stories, fables, and drawings and has been adapted for stage, film, and television. The Thurber Prize for American Humor was created in his honor. More information is available at www.ThurberHouse.org.*

# THE MACBETH MURDER MYSTERY

### Short Story by James Thurber

## SETTING A PURPOSE

*As you read, compare what you know about the plot and characters of Macbeth with the American woman's retelling of the story. What basic facts does she get right?*

1 "It was a stupid mistake to make," said the American woman I had met at my hotel in the English lake country, "but it was on the counter with the other Penguin books—the little sixpenny[1] ones, you know, with the paper covers—and I supposed of course it was a detective story. All the others were detective stories. I'd read all the others, so I bought this one without really looking at it carefully. You can imagine how mad I was when I found out it was Shakespeare." I murmured something sympathetically. "I don't see why the Penguin-books people had to get out Shakespeare's plays in the same size and everything as the detective stories," went on my companion. "I think they have different-colored jackets," I said. "Well, I didn't

---

[1] **sixpenny:** a former British monetary unit that is equal to six pennies.

### Notice & Note

**You can use the side margins to notice and note signposts in the text.**

---

**ANALYZE SATIRE**
**Annotate:** Mark the reason for the American woman's anger in paragraph 1.

**Analyze:** Why is this reason humorous?

notice that," she said. "Anyway, I got real comfy in bed that night and all ready to read a good mystery story and here I had 'The Tragedy of Macbeth'—a book for high-school students. Like 'Ivanhoe.'" "Or 'Lorna Doone,'"[2] I said. "Exactly," said the American lady. "And I was just crazy for a good Agatha Christie, or something. Hercule Poirot[3] is my favorite detective." "Is he the rabbity one?" I asked. "Oh, no," said my crime-fiction expert. "He's the Belgian one. You're thinking of Mr. Pinkerton, the one that helps Inspector Bull.[4] He's good, too."

2      Over her second cup of tea my companion began to tell the plot of a detective story that had fooled her completely—it seems it was the old family doctor all the time. But I cut in on her. "Tell me," I said. "Did you read 'Macbeth'?" "I had to read it," she said. "There wasn't a scrap of anything else to read in the whole room." "Did you like it?" I asked. "No, I did not," she said, **decisively**. "In the first place, I don't think for a moment that Macbeth did it." I looked at her blankly. "Did what?" I asked. "I don't think for a moment that he killed the King," she said. "I don't think the Macbeth woman was mixed up in it, either. You suspect them the most, of course, but those are the ones that are never guilty—or shouldn't be, anyway." "I'm afraid," I began, "that I—" "But don't you see?" said the American lady. "It would spoil everything if you could figure out right away who did it. Shakespeare was too smart for that. I've read that people never have figured out 'Hamlet,' so it isn't likely Shakespeare would have made 'Macbeth' as simple as it seems." I thought this over while I filled my pipe. "Who do you suspect?" I asked, suddenly. "Macduff," she said, promptly. "Good God!" I whispered, softly.

3      "Oh, Macduff did it, all right," said the murder specialist. "Hercule Poirot would have got him easily." "How did you figure it out?" I demanded. "Well," she said, "I didn't right away. At first I suspected Banquo. And then, of course, he was the second person killed. That was good right in there, that part. The person you suspect of the first murder should always be the second victim." "Is that so?" I murmured. "Oh, yes," said my informant. "They have to keep surprising you. Well after the second murder I didn't know who the killer was for a while." "How about Malcolm and Donalbain, the King's sons?" I asked. "As I remember it, they fled right after the first murder. That looks suspicious." "Too suspicious," said the American lady. "Much too suspicious. When they flee, they're never guilty. You can count on that." "I believe," I said, "I'll have a brandy," and I

decisively
(dĭ-sī′sĭv-lē) *adv.* in a firm and resolute manner.

**MAKE CONNECTIONS**
**Annotate:** Mark details that reveal the American woman's critical perspective of Shakespeare in paragraph 2.

**Analyze:** What is funny about this description?

---

[2] **Ivanhoe ... Lorna Doone:** historical romance novels set in England and written in the 1800s by Sir Walter Scott and Richard Doddridge Blackmore, respectively.
[3] **Agatha Christie ... Hercule Poirot:** Agatha Christie is a British author of crime novels, short stories, and plays; Hercule Poirot is a Belgian detective character who appears in many of her works.
[4] **Mr. Pinkerton ... Inspector Bull:** series characters in American David Frome's (pseudonym for Zenith Jones Brown) mystery novels.

summoned the waiter. My companion leaned toward me, her eyes bright, her teacup quivering. "Do you know who discovered Duncan's body?" she demanded. I said I was sorry, but I had forgotten. "Macduff discovers it," she said, slipping into the historical present. "Then he comes running downstairs and shouts, 'Confusion has broke open the Lord's anointed temple' and '**Sacrilegious** murder has made his masterpiece' and on and on like that." The good lady tapped me on the knee. "All that stuff was rehearsed," she said. "You wouldn't say a lot of stuff like that, off-hand, would you—if you had found a body?" She fixed me with a glittering eye. "I—" I began. "You're right!" she said. "You wouldn't! Unless you had practiced it in advance. 'My God, there's a body in here!' is what an innocent man would say." She sat back with a confident glare.

4      I thought for a while. "But what do you make of the Third Murderer?" I asked. "You know, the Third Murderer has puzzled 'Macbeth' scholars for three hundred years." "That's because they never thought of Macduff," said the American lady. "It was Macduff, I'm certain. You couldn't have one of the victims murdered by two ordinary thugs—the murderer always has to be somebody important." "But what about the banquet scene?" I asked, after a moment. "How do you account for Macbeth's guilty actions there, when Banquo's ghost came in and sat in his chair?" The lady leaned forward and tapped me on the knee again. "There wasn't any ghost," she said. "A big, strong man like that doesn't go around seeing ghosts—especially in a brightly lighted banquet hall with dozens of people around. Macbeth was shielding somebody!" "Who was he shielding?" I asked. "Mrs. Macbeth, of course," she said. "He thought she did it and he was going to take the rap himself. The husband always does that when the wife is suspected." "But what," I demanded, "about the sleepwalking scene, then?" "The same thing, only the other way around," said my companion. "That time she was shielding him. She wasn't asleep at all. Do you remember where it says, 'Enter Lady Macbeth with a taper'?" "Yes," I said. "Well, people who walk in their sleep never carry lights!" said my fellow-traveler. "They have second sight. Did you ever hear of a sleepwalker carrying a light?" "No," I said, "I never did." "Well, then, she wasn't asleep. She was acting guilty to shield Macbeth." "I think," I said, "I'll have another brandy," and I called the waiter. When he brought it, I drank it rapidly and rose to go. "I believe," I said, "that you have got hold of something. Would you lend me that 'Macbeth'? I'd like to look it over tonight. I don't feel, somehow, as if I'd ever really read it." "I'll get it for you," she said. "But you'll find that I am right."

**sacrilegious**
(săk-rə-lĭj´əs) *adj.*
grossly irreverent toward what is sacred.

**LANGUAGE CONVENTIONS**
**Annotate:** Mark pronouns in the part of paragraph 4 from "Macbeth was shielding somebody!" through "They have second sight."

**Interpret:** What are the antecedents of these pronouns? Do some pronouns lack antecedents?

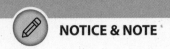
**secluded**
(sĭ-klōō´dĭd) *adj.*
hidden from view.

**ANALYZE SATIRE**

**Annotate:** Mark accusations the narrator makes in paragraph 5.

**Evaluate:** How have the roles of the narrator and the American woman reversed? What point does Thurber make with this reversal?

**contention**
(kən-tĕn´shən) *n.*
an assertion put forward in argument.

**cryptically**
(krĭp´tĭk-lē) *adv.*
in a secretive or mysterious manner.

5 I read the play over carefully that night, and the next morning, after breakfast, I sought out the American woman. She was on the putting green, and I came up behind her silently and took her arm. She gave an exclamation. "Could I see you alone?" I asked, in a low voice. She nodded cautiously and followed me to a **secluded** spot. "You've found out something?" she breathed. "I've found out," I said triumphantly, "the name of the murderer!" "You mean it wasn't Macduff?" she said. "Macduff is as innocent of those murders," I said, "as Macbeth and the Macbeth woman." I opened the copy of the play, which I had with me, and turned to Act II, Scene 2. "Here," I said, "you will see where Lady Macbeth says, 'I laid their daggers ready. He could not miss 'em. Had he not resembled my father as he slept, I had done it.' Do you see?" "No," said the American woman, bluntly, "I don't." "But it's simple!" I exclaimed. "I wonder I didn't see it years ago. The reason Duncan resembled Lady Macbeth's father as he slept is that it actually was her father!" "Good God!" breathed my companion, softly. "Lady Macbeth's father killed the King," I said, "and hearing someone coming, thrust the body under the bed and crawled into the bed himself." "But," said the lady, "you can't have a murderer who only appears in the story once. You can't have that." "I know that," I said, and I turned to Act II, Scene 4. "It says here, 'Enter Ross with an old Man.' Now, that old man is never identified and it is my **contention** that he was old Mr. Macbeth, whose ambition it was to make his daughter Queen. There you have your motive." "But even then," cried the American lady, "he's still a minor character!" "Not," I said, gleefully, "when you realize that he was also one of the weird sisters in disguise!" "You mean one of the three witches?" "Precisely," I said. "Listen to this speech of the old man's. 'On Tuesday last, a falcon towering in her pride of place, was by a mousing owl hawk'd at and kill'd.' Who does that sound like?" "It sounds like the way the three witches talk," said my companion, reluctantly. "Precisely!" I said again. "Well," said the American woman, "maybe you're right, but—" "I'm sure I am," I said. "And do you know what I'm going to do now?" "No," she said. "What?" "Buy a copy of 'Hamlet,'" I said, "and solve that!" My companion's eyes brightened. "Then," she said, "you don't think Hamlet did it?" "I am," I said, "absolutely positive he didn't." "But who," she demanded, "do you suspect?" I looked at her **cryptically.** "Everybody," I said, and disappeared into a small grove of trees as silently as I had come.

## CHECK YOUR UNDERSTANDING

Answer these questions before moving on to the **Analyze the Text** section on the following page.

**1** What problem does the American woman have at the beginning of the story?

**A** She has accidentally bought *Macbeth* but wants to read a mystery.

**B** She is having trouble solving the crimes committed in *Macbeth*.

**C** She is unable to convince the narrator that her theory is correct.

**D** She can't recall which detective is which from the books she has read.

**2** When the American woman reads *Macbeth,* she —

**F** enjoys it so much that she tries to convince strangers to read it

**G** sets it aside as soon as she can buy something different

**H** comes to a new appreciation of Shakespeare

**J** looks for clues that don't exist as if it's a mystery

**3** What point does Thurber make in this story?

**A** That Americans enjoy mysteries more than they enjoy Shakespeare

**B** That *Macbeth* is far more complicated than traditionally thought

**C** That people will stick with their views regardless of the facts

**D** That vacations are for relaxation, not for academic reading

## ANALYZE THE TEXT

Support your responses with evidence from the text. ☷ NOTEBOOK

1. **Analyze** Writers use satire to ridicule follies or foolish ideas commonly held in a society. What does Thurber ridicule in his satire? What point does he make regarding the expectations of reading different types of literature?

2. **Draw Conclusions** The American woman explains why some characters in the play are not guilty of murder. What reasons does she provide to prove that Malcolm, Donalbain, Macbeth, and Lady Macbeth are innocent? Does she have an understanding of Shakespeare's play? Explain your answer.

3. **Cause/Effect** At the end of paragraph 4, the narrator says of Shakespeare's play, "I don't feel, somehow, as if I'd ever really read it." Describe the American woman's critical perspective of *Macbeth* and why it makes the narrator feel this way.

4. **Connect** In the last paragraph, the narrator presents his solution to Macbeth's murder mystery. How does his version of Duncan's murder differ from Shakespeare's? Explain how the characters are recast and the events of the play are changed.

5. **Analyze** Thurber is known for his humor and wit. How does he convey humor in this story? Cite details from the text to support your response.

## RESEARCH

*Macbeth* has been performed countless times in many countries and languages around the world. Conduct research to find a review or analysis of any version of the play. Record main and supporting ideas as well as the reviewer's point of view or critical perspective in the chart.

### RESEARCH TIP

Sometimes opinions you uncover in your research may present opposing points of view. Both sides can support their opinions with evidence. Think critically about the evidence and the context of the evidence to understand which position is better supported. Also consider factors that lead two people to have opposing opinions about the same literary work or performance.

| VERSION / REVIEWER | MAIN IDEAS | SUPPORTING IDEAS | POINT OF VIEW |
|---|---|---|---|
| | | | |

**Connect** What review do you think the story's narrator would write of the version of *Macbeth* your source reviewed? What kind of review do you think the American woman would write?

## CREATE AND DISCUSS

**Write a Narrative** In this story, characters misinterpret a dramatic tragedy as a murder mystery. How does the understanding of literary genres shape the interpretation of a story? Can characteristics of one genre be applied to another for a different interpretation? Explore these ideas by transforming one type of story into another.

❏ With a partner, choose a familiar fable or fairy tale. Note the elements that make the story you chose a fable or fairy tale.

❏ Think about the conflict or characters in the story. In what different genre might the conflict or characters appear? List the elements of the new genre. Genres you might consider include romance, science fiction, mystery, and comedy.

❏ Rewrite your story so that it maintains the same events but contains the characteristics of the new genre. For example, a fairy tale can be rewritten as a science fiction story by eliminating the magical elements and by changing the setting.

❏ Exchange your story with another pair and try to identify the fairy tale or fable your classmates used as their source.

**Discuss Perspectives** In a small group, share your findings about the review or analysis of a version of *Macbeth* that you researched.

❏ Identify the version of the play that was reviewed and discuss the reviewer's opinion of the play.

❏ Draw conclusions about reviewers' opinions based on your discussion. For example, did reviewers prefer traditional versions of *Macbeth* or fresh takes on the story?

❏ Write a summary of your group discussion.

Go to the **Writing Studio** for more on writing a narrative.

 Go to the **Speaking and Listening Studio** for help with having a group discussion.

## RESPOND TO THE ESSENTIAL QUESTION

 What are the sources of true power?

**Gather Information** Review your annotations and notes on "The Macbeth Murder Mystery." Then, add relevant information to your Response Log. As you determine which information to include, think about:

- how Macbeth uses his power
- how interpretation and perspective can alter understanding
- how confidence can convince others that a baseless idea is a good idea

At the end of the unit, use your notes to help you write a literary analysis.

**ACADEMIC VOCABULARY**
As you write and discuss what you learned from the satire, be sure to use the Academic Vocabulary words. Check off each of the words that you use.

❏ **comprise**

❏ **incidence**

❏ **predominant**

❏ **priority**

❏ **ultimate**

## CRITICAL VOCABULARY

**Practice and Apply**  Explain which Critical Vocabulary word is most closely associated with each idea or situation.

**1.** Which word is associated with a disagreement? Why?

_____

**2.** Which word is associated with a mysterious note? Why?

_____

**3.** Which word is associated with a judge's ruling? Why?

_____

**4.** Which word is associated with an angry, irreverent comment? Why?

_____

**5.** Which word is associated with a secret hideout? Why?

_____

## VOCABULARY STRATEGY:
### Idioms

**Idioms** are expressions whose meanings differ from the literal meanings of their words. Often in satire, authors will use idioms because they are colorful or humorous. In "The Macbeth Murder Mystery," the characters' informal way of speaking and use of idioms contrast with the archaic lines from Shakespeare quoted in the story.

**Practice and Apply**  Read these idioms from the selection. Use context clues to define each phrase. Check your answers by substituting your definition in the idiom's place in the original sentence.

**1.** "I cut in on her" (paragraph 2)

_____

**2.** "mixed up in it" (paragraph 2)

_____

**3.** "fixed me" (paragraph 3)

_____

**4.** "take the rap" (paragraph 4)

_____

## LANGUAGE CONVENTIONS:
### Pronoun-Antecedent Agreement

A **pronoun** replaces a noun that has already been used (or sometimes another pronoun) to avoid repetition. The word the pronoun replaces is called its **antecedent.** Pronouns must agree with their antecedents in number. Here is an example from the story.

> "Hercule Poirot is my favorite detective." "Is he the rabbity one?" I asked.

The pronoun "he" is singular to match its antecedent, "Hercule Poirot." Use singular pronouns for singular antecedents. Use plural pronouns for plural antecedents.

| SINGULAR PRONOUNS | PLURAL PRONOUNS |
| --- | --- |
| I, me | we, us |
| you | you |
| he, she, it, him, her | they, them |

When you are reading a short story with dialogue, it is helpful to follow the pronouns and determine each pronoun's antecedent. A pronoun is vague when its antecedent is unclear.

In "The Macbeth Murder Mystery," the author presents conversations in which pronouns refer both to characters in the story and multiple characters in the play.

> "Do you remember where it says, 'Enter Lady Macbeth with a taper'?" "Yes," I said. "Well, people who walk in their sleep never carry lights!" said my fellow-traveler. "They have second sight. Did you ever hear of a sleepwalker carrying a light?" "No," I said, "I never did." "Well, then, she wasn't asleep."

The antecedent for "she" is found in the first sentence: "Lady Macbeth." However, if you are not following dialogue closely, you might think "she" refers to the American woman: "my fellow-traveler." The author intentionally uses vague pronouns to convey the idea of an intense and realistic face-to-face conversation.

**Practice and Apply**  Write a short paragraph reviewing "The Macbeth Murder Mystery" using pronouns and clear antecedents, checking to make sure they agree in number. Your paragraph should explain your opinion about the story with supporting evidence. When you have finished, share your paragraph with a partner. Have your partner identify the antecedent of each pronoun and note any vague pronouns for you to correct.

Go to the **Grammar Studio** for more on pronouns and antecedents.

GRAPHIC NOVEL

# *from*
# MANGA SHAKESPEARE: MACBETH

by **Robert Deas and Richard Appignanesi**

pages 503–517

### COMPARE ACROSS GENRES

The next two selections are different genres, or types of writing. One text, a book review, has been written in direct response to the other, a graphic novel. As you read, consider whether you agree with the opinions about the graphic novel that are expressed in the review.

**ESSENTIAL QUESTION:**

What are the sources of true power?

BOOK REVIEW

# SHAKESPEARE AND SAMURAI (AND ROBOT NINJAS?)

by **Caitlin Perry**

pages 518–519

## QUICK START

Think about a book, TV show, or movie you have read or watched recently. What did you think about it? Think about *why* you hold that opinion. Can you provide details that back up your opinion? Tell a partner what you thought of the work and give examples of details that helped you form that opinion.

## ANALYZE VISUAL ELEMENTS

A **graphic novel** is a book that tells a story through images and text that are laid out like a comic book. Pages of a graphic novel contain frames, which are boxes containing illustrations of events, actions, and reactions. Speech and thought bubbles often contain the characters' dialogue, and sometimes additional text on the edges of the frames provides narration. The visual elements of a graphic novel add depth, movement, drama, emotion, and meaning to the reader's experience. As you read the excerpt from *Manga Shakespeare: Macbeth*, use the chart below to record how different elements of graphic novels are reflected in the text.

### GENRE ELEMENTS: GRAPHIC NOVEL

- contains images, often accompanied by text, in individual frames or panels
- tells a narrative through images and text
- makes use of dialogue, characters' expressions, and onomatopoeia

| GRAPHIC NOVEL ELEMENT | HOW ELEMENT IS REFLECTED IN THE TEXT |
|---|---|
| Visual background details establish setting | |
| Characters' appearance, body language, and expressions reveal their traits | |
| Dialogue drives the action | |
| Styles of fonts reveal characters' intonation and expression | |

## ANALYZE EVIDENCE

In an opinion piece such as a book review, the author tells what he or she thinks about a work of art. To explain these opinions, the author gives reasons. A **reason** tells why an opinion or claim is valid. **Evidence** provides specific examples that illustrate a reason. For example, in a review of a production of *The Tragedy of Macbeth*, an author might express her opinion that a high school audience would enjoy the production. Her reason for the opinion might be, "*Macbeth* addresses the importance of balancing your ambitions and your morals, a theme young people can relate to."

As you read "Shakespeare and Samurai (and Robot Ninjas?)," look for the reasons and evidence the author provides to support her opinions.

### GENRE ELEMENTS: BOOK REVIEW

- provides a short summary of the work being reviewed
- includes the opinions of the reviewer, based on text evidence
- usually recommends or discourages the audience from reading or watching the work

## CRITICAL VOCABULARY

**sporadic**      **enraptured**      **daunting**

To preview Critical Vocabulary, use the words to complete the sentences.

1.  If the large project is too _____, break it up into smaller pieces.

2.  I enjoyed the concert. From the first chord, I was _____.

3.  I am only a(n) _____ spectator; I don't go to every game.

## LANGUAGE CONVENTIONS

**Parentheses** add or clarify information in a sentence. Usually, parentheses enclose information that is less important than the main part of a sentence. The text within parentheses is called a **parenthetical phrase** or **parenthetical expression**. Read the example below.

**My problem lay in the sudden use of the technology, from telescoping binoculars and very basic motorbikes, to holographic messages and (admittedly my favorite part of the book) teleporting robot ninjas.**

As you read the book review, notice how the reviewer uses parentheses to set apart less-important information within sentences.

## ANNOTATION MODEL

 **NOTICE & NOTE**

Look at the frame below from the graphic novel *Manga Shakespeare: Macbeth* and read the lines from the review. Notice how the reviewer uses evidence to support her opinion.

However, I found the artistry to be impressive, with randomly delightful tidbits of <u>hilarious facial expressions</u> (though not perhaps fitting with everyone's idea of the characters) and beautifully created weird sisters and spirit dragons.

## BACKGROUND

*Manga are Japanese comics that follow a style developed in the late 19th century. Characteristics of manga include expressive dialogue bubbles, lines that indicate movement and speed, and multiple flashbacks within the story. Today, manga has a growing global audience. Traditionally, manga comics are produced in black-and-white editions, and stories are often serialized, with new chapters published in separate editions. Genres are as varied as in other storytelling media, ranging from action and adventure to love stories to true historical events.*

### from MANGA SHAKESPEARE: MACBETH

**Graphic Novel by Robert Deas and Richard Appignanesi**

*The purpose of the Manga Shakespeare series is to bring Shakespeare's stories to a new audience by not only telling them through a different medium but also changing their context. With the help of Shakespeare scholars, a team of manga authors and artists have put new spins on classic stories. For example, The Tragedy of Romeo and Juliet moves to the streets of modern-day Tokyo, where Romeo is a rock star. And Macbeth combines a post-nuclear, futuristic setting with samurai—military leaders who rose to power in Japan between the twelfth and nineteenth centuries.*

*Canadian writer and editor **Richard Appignanesi** founded the Manga Shakespeare series with the hope that the adaptations would help educate readers about Shakespeare's stories. British artist **Robert Deas,** who has studied the manga style extensively, worked with Appignanesi to bring the Macbeth edition of the series to life.*

## PREPARE TO COMPARE

*As you read, notice which elements the graphic novelists used from Shakespeare's original play. Also notice where the authors had fun with new ideas. Ask yourself whether the manga version of the scene effectively conveys the events, ideas, and themes of Macbeth.*

---

**Notice & Note**

You can use the side margins to notice and note signposts in the text.

---

**ANALYZE VISUAL ELEMENTS**

**Annotate:** Take notes about how the first two pages of this excerpt are similar to the original *Macbeth* and how they are different.

**Analyze:** How do the images place Shakespeare's words in a different context?

## ANALYZE VISUAL ELEMENTS

**Annotate:** Write down details you notice about how the artist has chosen to portray Banquo.

**Analyze:** How do Banquo's appearance and facial expressions contribute to his characterization?

*from* Manga Shakespeare: Macbeth **507**

ANALYZE VISUAL
ELEMENTS

**Annotate:** Write notes about Macbeth's and Banquo's expressions and body language at the bottom of this page.

**Infer:** Why might the artist have chosen to draw the characters this way?

## ANALYZE VISUAL ELEMENTS

**Annotate:** Mark the speech bubble in the last frame of the page.

**Evaluate:** How would a playwright instruct an actor to deliver this line in the way that the manga artist depicts it visually?

*from* Manga Shakespeare: Macbeth   **509**

## ANALYZE VISUAL ELEMENTS

**Annotate:** Write brief descriptions of Macbeth's and Banquo's expressions here.

**Analyze:** How do these characters' facial expressions add meaning to their dialogue?

## ANALYZE VISUAL ELEMENTS

**Annotate:** Mark the illustration of Angus's memory.

**Analyze:** How does the illustration add to what Angus is saying about his memory?

## ANALYZE VISUAL ELEMENTS

**Annotate:** Mark details in the illustrations on this page and the previous one that give you a sense of setting.

**Evaluate:** How does the illustrator use different perspectives in the frames on these pages? What is the effect of the different perspectives?

*from* Manga Shakespeare: Macbeth   **517**

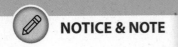
## BACKGROUND

*Author* **Caitlin Perry** *wrote this book review for publication on a blog. Perry herself writes fantasy and paranormal romance novels. She has published two books,* The Walker in the Dark *and* The Cursed Prophecy.

## PREPARE TO COMPARE

*As you read, prepare to defend or challenge the author's claims, marking relevant text evidence to support your ideas.*

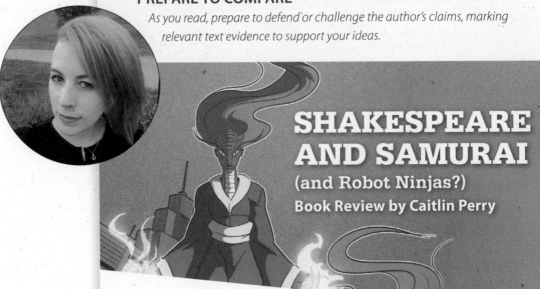

# SHAKESPEARE AND SAMURAI
## (and Robot Ninjas?)
**Book Review by Caitlin Perry**

### Notice & Note

You can use the side margins to notice and note signposts in the text.

### LANGUAGE CONVENTIONS

**Annotate:** Mark the parenthetical phrases in paragraph 2.

**Connect:** How does the information enclosed in parentheses add to the meaning and tone of the review?

1   I should start by saying that, while I don't dislike the "Scottish play", it is also not in my most beloved of Shakespeare's works. So when I give the Manga Shakespeare version of *Macbeth* a middling rating it is not a direct response to either the illustrations done by Robert Deas or the adaptation of the text as done by Richard Appignanesi. However, that is not to say that I was one hundred percent swayed by this adaptation either.

2   Initially I found the feudal-esque[1] Japanese samurai twist to be interesting (assuming you could ignore that it was intended to be a Scottish play, which I had no problem with). Jumping in head first, ready to see what delightful adaptations awaited me, I was met by a confusing but still interesting post-apocalyptic[2] world that combined feudal Japan with modern and futuristic technology alike, all in a world that had clearly been blown up quite a bit. My problem lay in the sudden use of the technology, from telescoping binoculars and very basic motorbikes, to holographic[3] messages and (admittedly my favorite part of the book) teleporting robot ninjas. However, as much as I loved some of these changes (mostly the ninjas), I became frustrated by how infrequently this technology was used, especially in a

---

[1] **feudal-esque** (fyo͞od-l-ĕsk´): resembling the feudal system, a social system involving nobility who held lands given by a monarch.

[2] **post-apocalyptic** (pōst-ə-pŏk-ə-lĭp´tĭk): referring to an era after the destruction of the world.

[3] **holographic** (hō-lə-grăf´ĭk): produced with three-dimensional images formed by light beams from a laser.

world that was both at war and had a murder to deal with. Obviously they couldn't have changed much of that without altering the whole story of *Macbeth*, but for that reason I feel like the story could have done without this **sporadic** technology. Perhaps sticking to a post-apocalyptic feudal Japan feel alone, with a heavier reliance on samurai history, would have been enough. That is, in truth, what I had been expecting when I'd picked it up, and I found the technology, while occasionally intriguing, to be quite jolting.

3    However, I found the artistry to be impressive, with randomly delightful tidbits of hilarious facial expressions (though not perhaps fitting with everyone's idea of the characters) and beautifully created weird sisters and spirit dragons. I also believe that this visual medium for Shakespeare would be a great way to get those less inclined toward literature to become interested in literature, and luckily the series offers a variety of the Bard's plays in various tellings based on Japanese history and culture. And despite not being overly **enraptured** with the work itself, I was impressed enough to want to read these other works, especially those that I hold higher in my personal esteem. Definitely worth a try for anyone with an interest in graphic novels as a genre, especially if they already have a love of Shakespeare's plays or would like to have but find the texts themselves **daunting**.

**sporadic**
(spə-răd´ĭk) *adj.* happening occasionally and at random.

**ANALYZE EVIDENCE**
**Annotate:** Mark evidence that the author gives in paragraph 3 to support her opinion about the book.

**Analyze:** What did Perry dislike about the book? How persuasive is the evidence she provides?

**enraptured**
(ĕn-răp´chərd) *adj.* filled with delight.

**daunting**
(dônt´ĭng) *adj.* seemingly impossible.

## CHECK YOUR UNDERSTANDING

Answer these questions before moving on to the **Analyze the Text** section.

**1** What is Perry's overall reaction to *Manga Shakespeare: Macbeth*?

**A** It's fantastic!

**B** It's OK.

**C** It's pretty bad.

**D** She didn't read it.

**2** What aspect of the graphic novel bothered Perry?

**F** The use of Shakespeare's language

**G** The feudal Japanese setting

**H** The sporadic use of technology

**J** The characters' expressions

**3** Which of these disclaimers does Perry give?

**A** She has never read manga.

**B** Her copy of the book was incomplete.

**C** She is mostly unfamiliar with samurai culture.

**D** *Macbeth* is not her favorite of Shakespeare's plays.

## ANALYZE THE TEXTS

Support your responses with evidence from the text. NOTEBOOK

1. **Analyze** How does the manga artist use the setting to establish a tone for the graphic novel?

2. **Analyze** The authors of the manga used much of Shakespeare's original language, but the play has been abridged, or shortened. How have the authors selected portions of the text to propel the story?

3. **Evaluate** In her review, Perry provides a disclaimer in the first sentence. How do you think this disclaimer should affect the way readers evaluate her opinion?

4. **Interpret** What is the effect of the parenthetical phrase in the title of the book review?

5. **Infer** In contrast to the first two paragraphs, what language does Perry use in the third paragraph to show that, despite her reservations, she recommends the book?

## RESEARCH

**RESEARCH TIP**

Samurai have appeared widely in pop-culture genres such as action movies. During your research on samurai, you might come across sources that have inaccurate information based on fictional representations of feudal Japan. Look for credible sources such as university or museum websites.

The authors of the graphic novel researched the role of samurai in feudal Japan, though they present elements of the culture with a twist. Since the samurai of the manga dwell in a post-apocalyptic world, they are similar to historical samurai in only some ways. Skim resources for characteristics of feudal Japan and complete the chart. Think about how well the manga fits the original story line of *The Tragedy of Macbeth*.

| FEUDAL JAPAN | |
|---|---|
| Time Period | |
| Social Hierarchy | |
| Clothing | |
| Role of Samurai | |

**Extend** Write a blog post that explains whether your evaluation of the graphic novel stayed the same as a result of your research or if you made adjustments when evidence warranted.

## CREATE AND DISCUSS

**Write a Comparison** Think about how the manga artist chose to portray the Witches of *The Tragedy of Macbeth*. Write a comparison about the effects of the Witches in the play and in the manga.

❏ Review Act I, Scene 3, of *Macbeth*. Think about the historical and cultural setting of the play: Scotland in medieval Europe. How do you visualize the Witches in this setting? How would you describe their effect on the scene and on the audience?

❏ Now, look back to see how the manga artist has drawn the Witches. What words would you use to describe them? How do they fit the setting of the manga? What effect do these images have on the reader?

❏ Write a paragraph comparing the two portrayals of the Witches. Then, using the play and the manga as evidence, write a paragraph generalizing how the historical and cultural setting of a work of fiction affects the text's plot, theme, and characters.

**Deliver a Pitch** *The Tragedy of Macbeth* has been adapted to many different media, such as movies and manga. What kind of media adaptation of the play would you like to see? Deliver a pitch—a persuasive presentation to someone who can fund a project.

❏ Look back at Perry's review and choose one of her points to incorporate into your idea. Then write a short pitch that persuades someone to fund your adaptation. Anticipate questions that the potential funders might ask you and prepare answers to those questions.

❏ Present your pitch to your group and answer their questions about your idea. After other group members deliver their pitches, ask them to clarify anything you don't understand about their ideas.

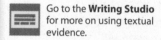 Go to the **Writing Studio** for more on using textual evidence.

 Go to the **Speaking and Listening Studio** for help with delivering a speech.

## RESPOND TO THE ESSENTIAL QUESTION

 What are the sources of true power?

**Gather Information** Review your annotations and notes on the excerpt from *Manga Shakespeare: Macbeth* and "Shakespeare and Samurai (and Robot Ninjas?)" and highlight those that help answer the Essential Question. Then, add relevant details to your Response Log.

At the end of the unit, you will use your notes to write a literary analysis.

**ACADEMIC VOCABULARY**
As you write and discuss what you learned from the graphic novel and the book review, be sure to use the Academic Vocabulary words. Check off each of the words that you use.

❏ comprise
❏ incidence
❏ predominant
❏ priority
❏ ultimate

**WORD BANK**
sporadic
enraptured
daunting

## CRITICAL VOCABULARY

**Practice and Apply**  Use your knowledge of the Critical Vocabulary words to respond to each question.

1. Name something that becomes a problem if you are **sporadic** about doing it. What might happen?

   _____

2. Describe a time when you were **enraptured** by a song, book, or other work of art. Why did you feel that way about it?

   _____

3. What advice would you give someone facing a **daunting** task?

   _____

Go to the **Vocabulary Studio** for more on word roots.

## VOCABULARY STRATEGY:
## Word Roots

A word's **etymology** is its origin and historical development. Many English words are derived from the Latin, Greek, and Anglo-Saxon (Old English) languages. For example, the Critical Vocabulary word *enraptured* contains the Latin root *rapt,* which means "carried away." You can see how this relates to the meaning of *enraptured,* as something that delights you and carries your mind away as you experience it. Understanding a word's etymology helps you grasp its meaning. In addition, knowing the meanings of roots will help you define other words with similar roots.

**Practice and Apply**  Follow these steps to complete the activity:

1. Use a dictionary to look up the etymology of each word in the chart, and write the meaning of its root or roots.

2. Identify two additional words that contain the same root.

3. Write three sentences for each root, one using the word that appears in the selection and two others using the additional words you identified.

| WORD | ROOT OR ROOTS |
|---|---|
| teleport: | *tele, port:* |
| graphic: | *graph:* |
| percent: | *cent:* |

## LANGUAGE CONVENTIONS
### Parentheses

Go to the **Grammar Studio** for more on parentheses.

**Parentheses** allow a writer to add or clarify information in a sentence. Usually, parentheses enclose nonessential information; if you remove the text within the parentheses, the sentence keeps its overall meaning.

Text enclosed by parentheses is called a **parenthetical phrase** or **parenthetical expression.** Parenthetical expressions can also be set apart with commas or dashes.

Think about the title of the review: "Shakespeare and Samurai (and Robot Ninjas?)." The parenthetical phrase isn't necessary to communicate the topic of the text. It adds a bit of humor, however, as it draws attention to something the reviewer found surprising.

Look at the following sentence from the book review:

**However, I found the artistry to be impressive, with randomly delightful tidbits of hilarious facial expressions (though not perhaps fitting with everyone's idea of the characters) and beautifully created weird sisters and spirit dragons.**

The author's main point would remain intact even if she removed the parenthetical phrase. But the parenthetical phrase gives additional information that she thinks might be useful to the reader.

**Practice and Apply**  Write a brief review stating your opinion of the excerpt you read from *Manga Shakespeare: Macbeth*. Include two parenthetical phrases in your review. Share your review with a partner and discuss what the parenthetical expressions add to your writing.

*from* **MANGA
SHAKESPEARE: MACBETH**
Graphic Novel by Robert Deas
and Richard Appignansi

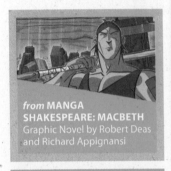

**SHAKESPEARE AND
SAMURAI
(AND ROBOT NINJAS?)**
Book Review by Caitlin Perry

# Collaborate & Compare

## COMPARE ACROSS GENRES

How would you defend or challenge Perry's overall opinion of the scene from *Manga Shakespeare: Macbeth*? Based on the excerpt that you read from the graphic novel, do you agree or disagree with her review? To better understand her analysis of the book, revisit the chart you used to record graphic novel elements while reading. Does Perry address any of these elements? If so, what is her assessment of how the authors of the manga handled them? Use a chart like the one below to describe Perry's analysis of the manga. Note that she may not have addressed all of these characteristics.

| GRAPHIC NOVEL ELEMENT | PERRY'S ASSESSMENT OF THE ELEMENT |
|---|---|
| Visual background details establish setting | |
| Characters' appearance, body language, and expressions reveal their traits | |
| Dialogue drives the action | |
| Font styles reflect characters' intonation and expression | |

## ANALYZE THE TEXTS

Discuss these questions in your group.

1. **Analyze** What evidence does Perry give for her positive feelings toward the excerpt from *Manga Shakespeare: Macbeth?* How does she present this evidence to portray it in a positive light?

2. **Evaluate** How would Perry have changed the graphic novel? Why do you think this change would change her opinion? What would you think of this change?

3. **Infer** What do you think Perry would say about the airplane in the first frame of the graphic novel?

4. **Connect** What does Perry think of similar work, in which a familiar text is explored in a different medium and context? What do you think are benefits of these kinds of works?

## COMPARE AND PRESENT

Now, you can deliver an argument agreeing or disagreeing with Perry's assessment of the manga version of *The Tragedy of Macbeth*.

1. **Plan Your Argument**  Review Perry's assessment of the book. Now, think about how you would respond to her opinion. Answer the following questions:

| | |
|---|---|
| What do I think of the change in setting? | |
| What details in the graphic novel do I find interesting? Which ones would I change? | |
| Do I think that a graphic novel is an effective medium for a Shakespeare play? | |
| Would I recommend this book to others? Why or why not? | |

Write your argument about whether or not you agree with Perry and why. You may find that you agree with some points but not others. Be sure to use evidence from both the graphic novel and the book review to support your argument.

2. **Present and Evaluate**  Present your argument to your class or a small group. Be sure to do the following:

   ❏ Speak clearly and make eye contact with your listeners.

   ❏ Provide relevant evidence from both sources. If possible, show or project specific frames from the graphic novel as you discuss them.

   ❏ As your group members present their arguments, briefly note what you think about their point of view, reasoning, rhetoric, and use of evidence from the texts. Also, write down words and phrases from their arguments that you found particularly persuasive.

   ❏ After everyone has had a turn, discuss as a group, pointing out elements in others' arguments that you found effective.

Go to the **Speaking and Listening Studio** for help with delivering an argument.

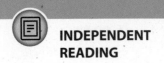

# Reader's Choice

**?  ESSENTIAL
QUESTION:**

What are the
sources of true
power?

**Setting a Purpose**   Select one or more of these options from your eBook to
continue your exploration of the Essential Question.

*   Read the descriptions to see which text grabs your interest.
*   Think about which genres you enjoy reading.

## Notice & Note

In this unit, you practiced noticing and noting these signposts: **Aha Moment,
Again and Again,** and **Tough Questions**. As you read independently, these
signposts and others will aid your understanding. Below are the anchor
questions to ask when you read literature and nonfiction.

| Reading Literature: Stories, Poems, and Plays | | |
|---|---|---|
| **Signpost** | **Anchor Question** | **Lesson** |
| **Contrasts and Contradictions** | Why did the character act that way? | p. 145 |
| **Aha Moment** | How might this change things? | p. 394 |
| **Tough Questions** | What does this make me wonder about? | p. 2 |
| **Words of the Wiser** | What's the lesson for the character? | p. 3 |
| **Again and Again** | Why might the author keep bringing this up? | p. 145 |
| **Memory Moment** | Why is this memory important? | p. 3 |

| Reading Nonfiction: Essays, Articles, and Arguments | | |
|---|---|---|
| **Signpost** | **Anchor Question** | **Lesson** |
| **Big Questions** | What surprised me? <br> What did the author think I already knew? <br> What challenged, changed, or confirmed what I already knew? | p. 220 <br> p. 319 <br> p. 74 |
| **Contrasts and Contradictions** | What is the difference, and why does it matter? | p. 318 |
| **Extreme or Absolute Language** | Why did the author use this language? | p. 221 |
| **Numbers and Stats** | Why did the author use these numbers or amounts? | p. 75 |
| **Quoted Words** | Why was this person quoted or cited, and what did this add? | p. 221 |
| **Word Gaps** | Do I know this word from someplace else? <br> Does it seem like technical talk for this topic? <br> Do clues in the sentence help me understand the word? | p. 75 |

You can preview these texts in Unit 6 of your eBook.

Then, check off the text or texts that you select to read on your own.

**HISTORY**

**from *Holinshed's Chronicles***
Raphael Holinshed

Was the historical Macbeth just as power-hungry as the character in Shakespeare's play?

**ARGUMENT**

**Why Read Shakespeare?**
Michael Mack

Hint: The answer isn't just because it's good for you. Find out how the Bard applies to today.

**POEM**

**Ozymandias**
Percy Bysshe Shelley

A renowned poet considers what the lasting legacy of a powerful leader might be.

**DRAMA**

***Julius Caesar*, Act III, Scene 2**
William Shakespeare

What kind of power did Caesar really want? And what kind of friend was Brutus, really? Mark Antony has his say.

**Collaborate and Share**   Discuss with a partner what you learned from at least one of your independent readings.

- Give a brief synopsis or summary of the text.
- Describe any signposts that you noticed in the text and explain what they revealed to you.
- Describe what you most enjoyed or found most challenging about the text. Give specific examples.
- Decide whether you would recommend the text to others. Why or why not?

Go to the **Reading Studio** for more resources on **Notice & Note**.

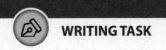
# Write a Literary Analysis

Go to the **Writing Studio** for help writing a literary analysis.

This unit focuses on human ambition and our eternal quest for power. What makes the character of Macbeth remarkable is that he's not a monster; he begins as someone we can empathize with, which makes his fall all the more shocking. Review the texts in this unit, including Shakespeare's *The Tragedy of Macbeth*. Then write a literary analysis that explains how one aspect of Macbeth's character represents a universal human trait. For an example of a well-written literary analysis you can use as a mentor text, look at the review "Shakespeare and Samurai (and Robot Ninjas?)."

As you write your analysis, you will want to look at the notes you made in your Response Log after reading the texts in this unit.

## Writing Prompt

**Read** the information in the box below.

> **Human ambition is timeless, and its fruits are fleeting.**

*This is the topic or context for your literary analysis.*

**Think** carefully about the following question.

> **What are the sources of true power?**

*This is the Essential Question for the unit. How would you answer this question, based on the texts in this unit?*

*To find a topic for your essay, think about an aspect of Macbeth's character that is a universal human trait.*

**Write** a literary analysis using multiple texts to explain how one aspect of Macbeth's character represents a universal human trait.

An effective literary analysis—

❑ includes a clear thesis about the universality of one of Macbeth's key personality traits

❑ engages readers with an interesting observation, quotation, or detail

❑ organizes central ideas in a logically structured body that clearly develops the thesis

*Review these points as you write and again when you finish. Make any needed changes.*

❑ uses precise word choice, domain-specific vocabulary, and logical transitions to clarify and connect ideas

❑ includes evidence from the texts to illustrate central ideas

❑ concludes by summing up central ideas in a way that follows logically from the body of the literary analysis

## 1 Plan

To begin planning your analysis, review *The Tragedy of Macbeth* and other texts in the unit. First, take notes on Macbeth's character traits. He is often used as an example of unbridled ambition, but that is only one of the aspects of his character that leads to his undoing. Look at the character of Macbeth from the perspective of psychological accuracy as well as from the perspective of effective drama. Then ask yourself, "Which of his traits are revealed in other texts in this unit and in people today?" Write a thesis statement that answers the question, "What trait of Macbeth's is a universal human trait?" Choose examples from two other texts and from life that provide strong support for your thesis.

Use the graphic organizer to write down important details, examples, and relevant quotations from all of your chosen sources that support your thesis.

| LITERARY ANALYSIS: MACBETH | | | |
|---|---|---|---|
| **Thesis:**<br>Macbeth's _____ is a universal human trait. | | | |
| **Supporting Details, Examples, and Quotations** | | | |
| **Text One:**<br>*Macbeth* | **Text Two:** | **Text Three:** | Life |
| | | | |

**Background Reading** Review the notes you have taken in your Response Log after reading the texts in this unit. These texts provide background reading that will help you think about what you want to say in your literary analysis.

Go to **Writing as a Process: Planning and Drafting** for help planning your literary analysis.

### Notice & Note

**From Reading to Writing**

As you plan your literary analysis, apply what you've learned about signposts to your own writing. Think about how you can incorporate **Contrasts and Contradictions** into your analysis.

Go to the **Reading Studio** for more resources on **Notice & Note**.

Use the notes from your Response Log as you plan your literary analysis.

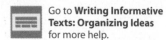
Go to **Writing Informative Texts: Organizing Ideas** for more help.

**Organize Your Ideas**  After you have examined your chosen texts, organize your ideas. Write a clear thesis statement about how a particular aspect of Macbeth's character represents a universal human trait. Search for an interesting quotation or detail to introduce your thesis statement.

❑ Decide which organizational pattern you will use to develop your essay. Present your key ideas and specific details, examples, and commentary in a logical order that flows smoothly from one thought to the next.

❑ Use your chosen organizational pattern to sort the evidence you have gathered. A hierarchy diagram like the one below can help you plan the body of your essay. Your diagram may need more ideas or evidence.

You might prefer to draft your essay online.

## ❷ Develop a Draft

Write a draft of your literary analysis, using information from your graphic organizer. Remember that a literary analysis requires formal language and a respectful tone. As you write, remember to analyze the text from the critical perspectives of both psychological accuracy and effective drama.

## Use the Mentor Text

▶ ### Author's Craft
A clear, effective thesis statement is crucial when you write a literary analysis. Imprecise wording in a thesis statement can confuse the reader. Look at this example of an effective thesis statement from Caitlin Perry's "Shakespeare and Samurai (and Robot Ninjas?)."

So when I give the Manga Shakespeare version of *Macbeth* a middling rating it is not a direct response to either the illustrations done by Robert Deas or the adaptation of the text as done by Richard Appignanesi. <u>However, that is not to say that I was one hundred percent swayed by this adaptation either.</u>

The author's thesis uses simple, clear language to state that she does not entirely like the Manga Shakespeare adaptation of Macbeth.

**Apply What You've Learned** State your thesis clearly, in one sentence, near the beginning of your literary analysis.

▶ ### Genre Characteristics
It is also important to be able to support your thesis statement with examples from the text you are analyzing. Here, Perry cites specific examples of what she did not think worked in Manga Shakespeare's *Macbeth*.

My problem lay in the sudden use of the technology, from telescoping binoculars and very basic motorbikes, to holographic messages and (admittedly my favorite part of the book) teleporting robot ninjas.

The examples provide clear, specific support for the author's thesis statement.

**Apply What You've Learned** Choose specific examples from the text or texts you're analyzing to support your thesis.

## ③ Revise

Go to **Writing Informative Texts: Precise Language and Vocabulary** for help revising your literary analysis.

**On Your Own**  After you write your draft, you will use the process of revision to turn that draft into a well-crafted literary analysis.

Introduce examples and quotations smoothly in your analysis. You might use a phrase such as "According to many experts…." Or you could use a dependent clause such as "As Gloria Perez points out…." The important thing is to use your own words as part of any sentence that includes an example or quotation from another text. The Revision Guide will help you focus on specific elements to make your writing stronger.

| REVISION GUIDE | | |
|---|---|---|
| **Ask Yourself** | **Tips** | **Revision Techniques** |
| 1. Does the introduction engage readers and state a clear thesis? | **Underline** the thesis statement and **mark** an engaging idea in the introduction. | **Add** a thesis statement and add an interesting example or detail from one of the texts you are analyzing. |
| 2. Are ideas organized logically and linked with transitions? | **Note** the idea explored in each paragraph. **Underline** transitional words and phrases. | **Reorder** evidence to center each paragraph around one idea. **Add** transitions to link ideas. |
| 3. Does text evidence support the ideas in each paragraph? | **Mark** text evidence in each paragraph. | **Add** evidence from more than one text to each paragraph. |
| 4. Are quotations smoothly integrated into the analysis? | **Mark** quotations that support ideas. **Underline** the introductory text for each quotation. | **Add** phrases or dependent clauses to introduce quotations. |
| 5. Does the conclusion effectively summarize ideas? | **Underline** the restated thesis or summary of ideas in the conclusion. | **Add** a restatement of the thesis or summary of the essay's ideas. |
| 6. Is the style appropriately formal, including domain-specific vocabulary? | **Note** slang or informal word choices. **Mark** terms specific to literary analysis. | **Replace** informal language. **Revise** to include literary, psychological, or academic language as appropriate. |

**ACADEMIC VOCABULARY**
As you conduct your peer review, try to use these words.

- ❏ **comprise**
- ❏ **incidence**
- ❏ **predominant**
- ❏ **priority**
- ❏ **ultimate**

**With a Partner**  After you have revised your analysis based on the Revision Guide, do a peer review by exchanging papers with a partner. Apply the guide to each other's essays. Explain how you think your partner could better accomplish his or her purpose in writing and share your specific suggestions for revision. Look for language that is too casual or conversational and for misspellings, either of which will make readers take the analysis less seriously.

##  Edit

After you have worked on the organization, development, and flow of ideas in your literary analysis, you can look carefully at the finer points of your draft. Edit for the proper use of standard English conventions and be sure to correct any misspellings or grammatical errors.

### Language Conventions

**Correct Spelling**  Take the time to check the spelling in your literary analysis, for two reasons:

> Go to **Spelling** in the **Grammar Studio** to learn more.

- **Misspellings** make your essays, articles, and reports more difficult to read. If you want a reader to pay attention to what you have to say, you should make it as easy as possible for them to read and understand your ideas.

- **Correct spelling** is an important part of meeting academic writing standards. Writing that does not meet academic standards will hurt your performance evaluations and prevent you from getting the credit you should have for otherwise good work.

Here are three types of spelling errors that you should avoid and that your computer's spell-check program will not catch for you.

| ERROR | EXAMPLE |
|---|---|
| Homophone Confusion | When the Witches make **there** first prediction, Macbeth does not know whether to believe them. <br><br> **Solution:** Replace *there* with *their*. |
| Easily Confused Words | Costume designers love designing the **Whiches'** costumes for Macbeth. <br><br> **Solution:** Replace *Whiches'* with *Witches'*. |
| Incorrectly Divided Compounds | The Witches' predictions are a remarkably effective use of **fore shadowing**. <br><br> **Solution:** Replace *fore shadowing* with *foreshadowing*. |

## ⑤ Publish

Finalize your literary analysis, and choose a way to share it with your audience. Consider these options:

- Present your literary analysis as a speech to the class.
- Post your literary analysis as a blog on a classroom or school website.

Use the scoring guide to evaluate your literary analysis.

## WRITING TASK SCORING GUIDE: LITERARY ANALYSIS

| | Organization/Progression | Development of Ideas | Use of Language and Conventions |
|---|---|---|---|
| **4** | • The organization is effective and appropriate to the purpose.<br>• All ideas are focused on the topic specified in the prompt.<br>• Transitions clearly show the relationship among ideas. | • The introduction catches the reader's attention and clearly states the thesis.<br>• The body of the analysis develops key ideas in a clear and logical way.<br>• The ideas are well supported by examples and details from literary texts and from life.<br>• The conclusion presents a thought-provoking statement about the topic. | • Language and word choice is purposeful and precise.<br>• The style is appropriately formal.<br>• Phrases and dependent clauses are used consistently to smoothly embed quotations in the text.<br>• Spelling, capitalization, and punctuation are correct.<br>• Grammar and usage are correct. |
| **3** | • The organization is, for the most part, effective and appropriate to the purpose.<br>• Most ideas are focused on the topic specified in the prompt.<br>• Transitions generally clarify the relationship among ideas. | • The introduction could be more engaging. The thesis is stated.<br>• The body of the essay develops key ideas in a fairly logical way.<br>• The ideas are supported by examples and details from the literary texts and from life.<br>• The conclusion presents a statement about the topic. | • Language is for the most part specific and clear.<br>• The style is mostly formal.<br>• Phrases and dependent clauses introduce most quotations.<br>• Some spelling, capitalization, and punctuation errors are present.<br>• Some grammar and usage errors occur. |
| **2** | • The organization is evident but is not always appropriate to the purpose.<br>• Only some ideas are focused on the topic specified in the prompt.<br>• More transitions are needed to show relationships among ideas. | • The introduction is not engaging. A vague thesis is stated.<br>• The analysis shares one or more key ideas but does not develop them in a logical way.<br>• Ideas are supported by few examples and details from the literary texts and/or from life.<br>• The conclusion merely restates the thesis. | • Language is somewhat vague and unclear.<br>• The style is often informal.<br>• Phrases and dependent clauses occasionally introduce quotations and examples.<br>• Several errors in spelling, capitalization, and punctuation occur.<br>• Grammar and usage are often incorrect, but the writer's ideas are still clear. |
| **1** | • The organization is not appropriate to the purpose.<br>• Ideas are not focused on the topic specified in the prompt.<br>• No transitions are used, making the essay difficult to understand. | • The introduction and thesis are missing or confusing.<br>• The analysis does not logically develop ideas that support the thesis statement.<br>• Ideas presented are not supported by evidence.<br>• The conclusion is missing or illogical. | • Language is vague and style is too informal.<br>• Quotations, if present, are not introduced.<br>• Many spelling, capitalization, and punctuation errors interfere with reading.<br>• Many grammatical and usage errors make it difficult to understand the writer's ideas. |

# Reflect on the Unit

In this writing task, you wrote about your own experience in the light of ideas and insights from the readings in this unit. Now is a good time to reflect on what you have learned.

## Reflect on the Essential Question

- What are the sources of true power? How has your answer to this question changed since you first considered it when you started this unit?

- What are some examples from the texts you've read that show the sources of true power?

## Reflect on Your Reading

- Which selections were the most interesting or surprising to you?

- From which selection did you learn the most about the nature of power and ambition?

## Reflect on the Writing Task

- What difficulties did you encounter while working on your literary analysis? How might you avoid them next time?

- What part of the literary analysis was the easiest and what part was the hardest to write? Why?

- What improvements did you make to your literary analysis as you were revising?

**UNIT 6 SELECTIONS**
- *The Tragedy of Macbeth*
- from *Macbeth* (film version)
- "The Macbeth Murder Mystery"
- from *Manga Shakespeare: Macbeth*
- "Shakespeare and Samurai (and Robot Ninjas?)"

# RESOURCES

| | |
|---|---|
| Response Logs | R1 |
| Using a Glossary | R7 |
| Pronunciation Key | R7 |
| Glossary of Academic Vocabulary | R8 |
| Glossary of Critical Vocabulary | R9 |
| Index of Skills | R12 |
| Index of Titles and Authors | R18 |
| Acknowledgments | R19 |

## HMH *INTO LITERATURE* STUDIOS

For more instruction and practice, visit the HMH *Into Literature* Studios.

 Reading Studio

 Writing Studio

 Speaking & Listening Studio

 Grammar Studio

 Vocabulary Studio

# UNIT 1
# RESPONSE LOG

Use this Response Log to record your ideas about how each of the texts in Unit 1 relates to or comments on the **Essential Question**.

**?** **Essential Question:**
How do we engage with others while staying true to ourselves?

| What, of This Goldfish, Would You Wish? | |
|---|---|
| By Any Other Name | |
| Without Title | |
| *from* Texas v. Johnson Majority Opinion | |
| American Flag Stands for Tolerance | |

# UNIT 2
# RESPONSE LOG

**?** **Essential Question:**
How does our point of view shape what we think we know?

| | |
|---|---|
| Coming to Our Senses | |
| The Night Face Up | |
| Mirror | |
| The World as 100 People | |
| A Contribution to Statistics | |

# UNIT 3
# RESPONSE LOG

Use this Response Log to record your ideas about how each of the texts in Unit 3 relates to or comments on the **Essential Question**.

**? Essential Question:**
What effect do we have on nature, and how does nature affect us?

| | |
|---|---|
| My Life as a Bat | |
| Joyas Voladoras | |
| Find Your Park | |
| The Seventh Man | |
| Carry | |

Use this Response Log to record your ideas about how each of the texts in Unit 4 relates to or comments on the **Essential Question**.

**?** **Essential Question:**
What do we need in order to feel free?

| | |
|---|---|
| Letter from Birmingham Jail | |
| Elsewhere | |
| The Hawk Can Soar | |
| The Briefcase | |
| *from* Letter to Viceroy, Lord Irwin | |
| *from* Gandhi: The Rise to Fame | |

# UNIT 5
# RESPONSE LOG

**?** **Essential Question:**
How do changes around us reveal who we are?

| | |
|---|---|
| *from* Total Eclipse | |
| *from* The Fever | |
| A Sound of Thunder | |
| 5 P.M., Tuesday, August 23, 2005 | |
| *from* Rivers and Tides | |
| Sonnets to Orpheus, Part Two, XII | |

# UNIT 6
# RESPONSE LOG

**?** **Essential Question:**
What are the sources of true power?

| | |
|---|---|
| The Tragedy of Macbeth | |
| *from* Macbeth (film version) | |
| The Macbeth Murder Mystery | |
| *from* Manga Shakespeare: Macbeth | |
| Shakespeare and Samurai (and Robot Ninjas?) | |

# Using a Glossary

A glossary is an alphabetical list of vocabulary words. Use a glossary just as you would a dictionary—to determine the meanings, parts of speech, pronunciation, and syllabification of words. (Some technical, foreign, and more obscure words in this book are defined for you in the footnotes that accompany many of the selections.)

Many words in the English language have more than one meaning. This glossary gives the meanings that apply to the words as they are used in the selections in this book.

The following abbreviations are used to identify parts of speech of words:

*adj.* adjective   *adv.* adverb   *n.* noun   *v.* verb

Each word's pronunciation is given in parentheses. A guide to the pronunciation symbols appears in the Pronunciation Key below. The stress marks in the Pronunciation Key are used to indicate the force given to each syllable in a word. They can also help you determine where words are divided into syllables.

For more information about the words in this glossary or for information about words not listed here, consult a dictionary.

# Pronunciation Key

| Symbol | Examples | Symbol | Examples | Symbol | Examples |
|--------|----------|--------|----------|--------|----------|
| ă | pat | m | mum | ûr | urge, term, firm, word, heard |
| ā | pay | n | no, sudden* (sud´n) | | |
| ä | father | ng | thing | v | valve |
| âr | care | ŏ | pot | w | with |
| b | bib | ō | toe | y | yes |
| ch | church | ô | caught, paw | z | zebra, xylem |
| d | deed, milled | oi | noise | zh | vision, pleasure, garage |
| ĕ | pet | o͝o | took | ə | about, item, edible, gallop, circus |
| ē | bee | o͞o | boot | | |
| f | fife, phase, rough | o͝or | lure | ər | butter |
| g | gag | ôr | core | | |
| h | hat | ou | out | | |
| hw | which | p | pop | **Sounds in Foreign Words** | |
| ĭ | pit | r | roar | KH | *German* ich, ach; *Scottish* loch |
| ī | pie, by | s | sauce | N | *French,* bon (bôn) |
| îr | pier | sh | ship, dish | œ | *French* feu, œuf; *German* schön |
| j | judge | t | tight, stopped | | |
| k | kick, cat, pique | th | thin | ü | *French* tu; *German* über |
| l | lid, needle* (nēd´l) | *th* | this | | |
| | | ŭ | cut | | |

*In English the consonants *l* and *n* often constitute complete syllables by themselves.

**Stress Marks**

The relative emphasis with which the syllables of a word or phrase are spoken, called stress, is indicated in three different ways. The strongest, or primary, stress is marked with a bold mark (´). An intermediate, or secondary, level of stress is marked with a similar but lighter mark (´). The weakest stress is unmarked. Words of one syllable show no stress mark.

# GLOSSARY OF
# ACADEMIC VOCABULARY

**abstract** (ăb-străkt´) *adj.* apart from physical existence; theoretical rather than concrete.

**advocate** (ăd´və-kāt) *v.* to argue for or plead in favor of.

**comprehensive** (kŏm-prĭ-hĕn´sĭv) *adj.* complete or of sufficient scope to include all aspects.

**comprise** (kəm-prīz´) *v.* to consist or be made up of.

**differentiate** (dĭf-ə-rĕn´shē-āt) *v.* to distinguish or demonstrate the individual qualities of.

**discrete** (dĭ-skrēt´) *adj.* made up of separate or distinct things or parts.

**discriminate** (dĭ-skrĭm´ə-nāt) *v.* to note clear differences; to separate into categories.

**diverse** (dĭ-vûrs´) *adj.* made up of elements that are different from each other.

**domain** (dō-mān´) *n.* a sphere of activity.

**enhance** (ĕn-hăns´) *v.* to make better, or add to the value or effectiveness.

**equivalent** (ĭ-kwĭv´ə-lənt) *adj.* equal to or similar.

**evoke** (ĭ-vōk´) *v.* to draw forth or produce.

**evolve** (ĭ-vŏlv´) *v.* to change or develop gradually over time.

**explicit** (ĭk-splĭs´ĭt) *adj.* clearly stated or expressed.

**facilitate** (fə-sĭl´ĭ-tāt) *v.* to make something easier.

**incentive** (ĭn-sĕn´tĭv) *n.* an inducement or motivation to do something.

**incidence** (ĭn´sĭ-dəns) *n.* the occurrence or frequency of something.

**incorporate** (ĭn-kôr´pə-rāt) *v.* to absorb or make part of a whole.

**infer** (ĭn-fûr´) *v.* to deduce from evidence or reason.

**inhibit** (ĭn-hĭb´ĭt) *v.* to hold back or prevent from acting.

**innovate** (ĭn´ə-vāt) *v.* to change or develop through new or original methods, processes, or ideas.

**intervene** (ĭn-tər-vēn´) *v.* to come between two things, persons, or events.

**mode** (mōd) *n.* a way or means for expressing or doing something.

**orient** (ôr´ē-ənt) *v.* to place or align in relation to something else.

**perspective** (pər-spĕk´tĭv) *n.* a viewpoint from a particular position; an outlook or standpoint.

**predominant** (prĭ-dŏm´ə-nənt) *adj.* having influence or importance.

**priority** (prī-ôr´ĭ-tē) *n.* something that is more important or considered more important than another thing.

**rational** (răsh´ə-nəl) *adj.* based on logic or sound reasoning.

**subordinate** (sə-bôr´dn-ĭt) *adj.* belonging to a lower class or rank.

**ultimate** (ŭl´tə-mĭt) *adj.* concluding a process or progression; final.

# GLOSSARY OF CRITICAL VOCABULARY

**acuity** (ə-kyōō´ĭ-tē) *n.* critical perceptiveness; awareness.

**anomalous** (ə-nŏm´ə-ləs) *adj.* unusual; different from the norm.

**atrophy** (ăt´rə-fē) *v.* to deteriorate due to disease, injury, or lack of use.

**beleaguered** (bĭ-lē´gərd) *adj.* troubled with many problems.

**beneficent** (bə-nĕf´ĭ-sənt) *adj.* beneficial; producing good.

**cognizant** (kŏg´nĭ-zənt) *adj.* aware or conscious of.

**complacency** (kəm-plā´sən-sē) *n.* contented self-satisfaction.

**compulsion** (kəm-pŭl´shən) *n.* forced obligation.

**consecrate** (kŏn´sĭ-krāt) *v.* to make or define as sacred.

**consensus** (kən-sĕn´səs) *n.* agreement.

**contemptuous** (kən-tĕmp´chōō-əs) *adj.* scornful.

**contention** (kən-tən´shən) *n.* an assertion put forward in argument.

**cryptically** (krĭp´tĭk-lē) *adv.* in a secretive or mysterious manner.

**daunting** (dônt´ing) *adj.* seemingly impossible.

**decisively** (dĭ-sī´sĭv-lē) *adv.* in a firm and resolute manner.

**delirium** (dĭ-lîr´ē-əm) *n.* a state of mental confusion.

**denizen** (dĕn´ĭ-zən) *n.* a resident.

**dogma** (dôg´mə) *n.* principles or beliefs that an authority insists are true.

**enraptured** (ĕn-răp´chərd) *adj.* filled with delight.

**entranced** (ĕn-trănsd´) *v.* filled with wonder and delight.

**equidistant** (ē-kwĭ-dĭs´tənt) *adj.* at equal distance from.

**expendable** (ĭk-spĕn´də-bəl) *adj.* worth sacrificing to gain an objective.

**felled** (fĕld) *v.* knocked down.

**flagrantly** (flā´grənt-lē) *adv.* in a blatantly or conspicuously offensive manner.

**flail** (flāl) *v.* to thrash or wave about wildly.

**fluent** (flōō´ənt) *adj.* able to express oneself clearly and easily.

**frail** (frāl) *adj.* physically weak.

**harrowed** (hăr´ōd) *adj.* greatly distressed.

**havoc** (hăv´ək) *n.* destructive disorder or chaos.

# GLOSSARY OF CRITICAL VOCABULARY

**hue** (hyōō) *n.* a color, shade, or tint.

**humility** (hyōō-mĭl´ĭ-tē) *n.* modesty; lack of superiority over others.

**icon** (ī´kŏn) *n.* symbol of deeply held values.

**implicit** (ĭm-plĭs´ĭt) *adj.* understood, but not expressed.

**incendiary** (ĭn-sĕn´dē-ĕr-ē) *adj.* intended to cause fire; flammable.

**iniquitous** (ĭ-nĭk´wĭ-təs) *adj.* wicked, evil.

**insidious** (ĭn-sĭd´ē-əs) *adj.* spreading harmfully in a subtle way.

**insular** (ĭn´sə-lər) *adj.* narrow-minded or detached from others.

**interlude** (ĭn´tər-lōōd) *n.* a time of rest between two tasks.

**intrinsic** (ĭn-trĭn´zĭk,-sĭk) *adj.* of or relating to the essential nature of a thing.

**inversion** (ĭn-vûr´zhən) *n.* reversal or upside-down placement.

**irrefutable** (ĭ-rĕf´yə-tə-bəl) *adj.* impossible to disprove; unquestionable.

**lucid** (lōō´sĭd) *adj.* thinking rationally and clearly.

**malevolence** (mə-lĕv´ə-ləns) *n.* the quality of having a harmful influence.

**manifest** (măn´ə-fĕst) *v.* to show or reveal.

**moratorium** (môr-ə-tôr´ē-əm) *n.* a temporary suspension or agreed-upon delay.

**mores** (môr´āz) *n.* established customs and conventions.

**occult** (ə-kŭlt´) *adj.* mysterious or hidden.

**paradox** (păr´ə-dŏks) *n.* something that has or seems to have contradictory qualities.

**peremptory** (pə-rĕmp´tə-rē) *adj.* imperative; required; not able to be denied.

**permeate** (pûr´mē-āt) *v.* to spread through an area.

**poignant** (poin´yənt) *adj.* emotionally moving or stimulating.

**precarious** (prĭ-kâr´ē-əs) *adj.* dangerously insecure.

**precipitate** (prĭ-sĭp´ĭ-tāt) *v.* to cause something to happen rapidly or unexpectedly.

**premonition** (prĕm-ə-nĭsh´ən) *n.* an unproven feeling that something specific will happen.

**propensity** (prə-pĕn´sĭ-tē) *n.* a tendency to behave in a certain way.

**provocation** (prŏv-ə-kā´shən) *n.* an action intended to elicit an angered response.

**reaffirmation** (rē-ăf-ər-mā´shən) *n.* the act of verifying or endorsing again.

**recede** (rĭ-sēd´) *v.* to move back or away from something.

**reconciliation** (rĕk-ən-sĭl-ē-ā´shən) *n.* the act of coming to an agreement.

**resilience** (rĭ-zĭl´yəns) *n.* ability to return to a normal state after a change or an injury.

**retaliate** (rĭ-tăl´ē-āt) *v.* to respond in kind to having been acted upon, often with harmful intent.

**sacrilegious** (săk-rə-lĭj´əs) *adj.* grossly irreverent toward what is sacred.

**sanctity** (săngk´tĭ-tē) *n.* sacredness or ultimate importance.

**saturate** (săch´ə-rāt) *v.* to soak with liquid to the point where nothing more can be absorbed.

**secluded** (sĭ-kloo´dĭd) *adj.* hidden from view.

**sedately** (sĭ-dāt´lē) *adv.* in a calm and dignified manner.

**sentiment** (sĕn´tə-mənt) *n.* the emotion behind something.

**sociable** (sō´shə-bəl) *adj.* able to enjoy the company of others.

**solace** (sŏl´ĭs) *n.* source of relief and comfort.

**sporadic** (spə-răd´ĭk) *adj.* happening occasionally and at random.

**stimuli** (stĭm´yə-lī) *n.* things that cause a response or reaction.

**subliminal** (sŭb-lĭm´ə-nəl) *adj.* below the level of awareness.

**subtle** (sŭt´l) *adj.* so slight as to be difficult to detect or describe.

**subtleties** (sŭt´l-tēz) *n.* fine details or nuances.

**taut** (tôt) *adj.* pulled tight; tense.

**tepid** (tĕp´id) *adj.* neither hot nor cold; lukewarm.

**transcend** (trăn-sĕnd´) *v.* to go beyond or rise above.

**translucent** (trăns-loo´sənt) *adj.* semitransparent; indistinct.

**transpire** (trăn-spīr´) *v.* to happen or occur.

**unadulterated** (ŭn-ə-dŭl´tə-rā-tĭd) *adj.* pure and untainted.

**undulate** (ŭn´jə-lāt) *v.* to move in waves.

**unpalatable** (ŭn-păl´ə-tə-bəl) *adj.* unpleasant or unacceptable.

**vestige** (vĕs´tĭj) *n.* a visible trace of something that once existed.

**virulence** (vîr´yə-ləns) *n.* the quality of aggressively causing disease.

**wane** (wān) *v.* to gradually decrease in size or intensity.

**wizened** (wĭz´ənd) *adj.* shrunken and wrinkled.

## A

Absolute Language. *See* Extreme or Absolute Language (Notice & Note)
Academic Vocabulary, 1, 73, 143, 219, 317, 393
accuracy, of sources, 38, 172, 328, 340
active voice, 286, 295
affixes, 342
Again and Again (Notice & Note), 96, 145, 152, 183, 288, 395, 406, 422
agreement
    pronoun-antecedent, 490, 499
    subject-verb, 334, 339, 343
Aha Moment (Notice & Note), 100, 354, 394, 408, 473
allusions, 266
    classical, 350
    historical, 326, 328, 350
    literary, 261
American Psychological Association (APA), 387
analysis, writing, 103, 155, 255, 293, 371, 418, 487
analyze, 14, 28, 38, 46, 56, 60, 102, 112, 126, 154, 166, 192, 202, 244, 254, 264, 280, 292, 360, 370, 378, 418, 432, 448, 466, 480, 496, 520, 524
accounts, 302
archetypes, 5, 11
argument, 228, 231, 238, 241, 242, 287
audience, 60
author's purpose, 19, 23, 27
character, 271, 275, 276, 277, 278
character and theme, 425, 467
development of ideas, 77, 80, 82, 84
diction and syntax, 259, 261, 262
drama, 413, 420, 443, 463
evidence, 519
figurative language, 108, 110
free verse, 198, 200
historical context, 19, 22, 25
language, 147, 150, 151
literary devices, 5, 8, 121, 124
literary nonfiction, 325
media, 172, 300, 486
media techniques and purposes, 170
motif, 251
motives, 116, 117
plot, 175, 178, 180, 190
plot structure, 91, 94, 95, 96, 98, 356
poetic structure, 252
purpose, 60
purpose and audience, 337

rhetoric, 51, 53, 288
satire, 491
setting, 33, 35, 356
speaker, 107, 109
structure, 122, 123, 147, 149, 153, 159, 162, 252
style, 159, 162, 327
symbols, 175, 181, 186, 187, 190, 197, 200
text structure, 260, 335
theme, 103, 175, 181, 186, 187, 190, 197, 200, 272
tone, 77, 79
visual elements, 505, 507, 511, 513
analytic writing, 103, 155, 255, 293, 371, 418, 487
Analyze the Text
    analyze, 14, 28, 38, 46, 56, 60, 102, 112, 126, 154, 166, 192, 202, 244, 254, 264, 280, 292, 360, 370, 378, 418, 432, 448, 466, 480, 496, 520, 524
    cause/effect, 496
    cite evidence, 28, 46, 264, 280, 292, 340, 370, 432, 480
    compare, 46, 60, 86, 102, 128, 154, 166, 204, 328, 378, 448
    connect, 46, 60, 204, 380, 496, 524
    contrast, 128, 380
    critique, 264, 328
    draw conclusions, 14, 112, 126, 244, 254, 280, 292, 360, 370, 418, 448, 466, 496
    evaluate, 14, 38, 56, 60, 86, 102, 126, 128, 154, 166, 192, 204, 254, 264, 292, 340, 480, 520, 524
    identify, 38, 86, 340, 378
    infer, 14, 28, 38, 46, 56, 102, 112, 126, 192, 264, 340, 360, 370, 378, 380, 418, 432, 448, 466, 520, 524
    interpret, 28, 38, 154, 166, 192, 202, 254, 280, 328, 370, 480, 520
    Notice & Note, 14, 56, 86, 102, 126, 154, 166, 192, 244, 292, 328, 340, 360, 418, 432, 466, 480
    summarize, 86, 202, 244, 280, 328, 378, 432
    synthesize, 112, 128, 360, 380
Anchor Questions (Notice & Note), 2, 3, 221, 318, 319, 394, 395
annotate, 41. *See also* Annotation Model
Annotation Model, 6, 20, 34, 42, 52, 78, 92, 108, 116, 122, 148, 160, 176, 198, 224, 250, 258, 270, 286, 322, 334, 346, 366, 400, 490, 502
antithesis, 51, 223, 230, 285, 288, 397
antonyms, 362

appeals, 51, 223, 285
archaic language, 482
archetypes, 5, 11
argumentative texts. *See* arguments
arguments,
    analyzing, 223, 285
    delivering, 313–314, 487, 525
    evaluating, 51
    writing, 306–312
asides, 396, 399
audience, 60, 313, 333
author's craft, 67, 135, 211, 309, 387, 531
author's purpose, 19, 23, 27, 333, 340

## B

bias, 46, 56, 244
Big Questions (Notice & Note), 74, 83, 220, 233, 319, 326, 336
blank verse, 396
book reviews, 501
brainstorming, 65, 129, 133
brochure, 341

## C

capitalization, 311
cause/effect, 351, 496
    transitions, 346, 351, 363, 432
central ideas, 77, 159, 166, 373
character, 11, 14, 102, 269, 271, 404, 480
character and theme, 399, 404, 425
character development, 269, 422, 448
character foils, 399
charts, 14, 28, 102, 112, 202, 250, 297
    podcast planning, 139
    in research, 244, 264, 280, 292, 300, 328, 340, 360, 480, 486, 496, 520
    for writing, 65, 133, 385
Check Your Understanding, 13, 27, 37, 45, 55, 85, 101, 111, 119, 125, 153, 165, 191, 201, 243, 253, 263, 279, 291, 327, 339, 359, 369, 377, 417, 431, 447, 465, 479, 495, 519
chronological order, 67, 192, 302
citations, of research sources, 102, 112, 254, 280, 387, 389
cite evidence, 28, 46, 172, 202, 264, 280, 292, 370, 432, 480, 486
claims, 41, 51, 195, 223, 285, 287
clauses
    adjective, 137
    adverb, 137
    dependent, 49, 92, 97, 137, 176, 181, 195
    independent, 49, 92, 97, 137, 176, 181, 195, 283

climax, 134, 147
Collaborate & Compare, 60, 128, 204, 302, 380, 524
Collaborate and Share, 207, 305
colons, 148, 157
   dashes instead of, 52
commas, 42, 45, 195
   dashes instead of, 52
   to set off phrases and clauses, 49
comma splice, 105, 137
commentary, 67, 302
compare, 46, 60, 86, 102, 109, 123, 128, 154, 166, 204, 299, 328, 347, 378, 448, 491
   accounts, 302
   across genres, 299, 372, 380, 500, 524
   arguments, 40, 60
   and debate, 303
   details, 114, 120
   media, 299, 486
   rhetoric, 288
   rhetorical devices, 230
   texts, 128, 204, 491, 503, 518
   themes, 174, 196, 199, 376, 380
comparisons, writing, 47, 329, 521
complex sentences, 92, 105, 137, 176, 195
concessions, 51, 223
conclusions,
   in an argument, 51, 223
   drawing. See draw conclusions
   in an essay, 77, 333
   in writing, 103, 155, 386
conflict, 15, 134, 418
conjunctions, 195
connect, 21, 46, 60, 204, 251, 380, 489, 496, 524
   in research, 86, 172, 264, 360, 480, 486, 496
connecting words, 67, 346, 363, 432
connotations, 58, 104, 168, 294, 365
consensus, 167, 193, 466, 481
context, historical, 19, 22, 28
context clues, 16, 151, 156, 246, 498
contrast, 35, 128, 154, 380
Contrasts and Contradictions (Notice & Note), 24, 125, 145, 151, 161, 179, 318, 325
conventions
   of genres, 396
   in speaking, 39
   standard English, 311
correspondence, 281
   friendly, 127, 245
   professional, 57, 173
counterarguments, 51, 56, 223, 285, 287, 308
counterclaims, 51, 287, 308, 313
craft, in writing, 67, 135, 211, 309, 387, 531
Create and Discuss
   analysis, 103, 255, 293
   comparison, 521

create a reflection, 379
   document information, 481
   free-verse poem, 203
   give instructions, 127
   letter, 127
   narrative, 39, 497
   opinions, 103
   participate in a debate, 466
   perspectives, 497
   pitch, 521
   poem, 29, 113
   present a narrative, 39
   share an analysis, 448
   share and discuss opinions, 379
   share information, 293
   vignette, 193
   web page, 265
   writing activity: analysis, 418
Create and Evaluate
   follow and give instructions, 341
   write a procedural brochure, 341
Create and Present, 432
   analysis, 155, 487
   argument, 487
   comparison, 47
   debate the issue, 57
   discussion, 301
   explanation, 87, 167
   fable, 15
   friendly letter, 245
   instructions, 173
   letter, 281
   letter to the editor, 57, 173
   literary analysis, 371
   multimedia presentation, 47
   multimodal presentation, 301
   panel discussion, 167
   poetry reading, 371
   presentation, 87
   research, 155, 245
   sales pitch, 361
   story, 361
   summary, 281
Create and Share
   plan your artwork, 205
   present, 205
   write statement, 205
create mental images, 366
credibility, 38, 56, 60, 202
critical perspective, 492, 496, 497, 530
Critical Vocabulary, 6, 16, 20, 30, 42, 48, 52, 58, 78, 88, 104, 148, 156, 160, 168, 176, 194, 224, 246, 258, 266, 270, 282, 286, 294, 322, 330, 334, 342, 346, 362, 490, 498, 502, 522
critique, 264, 328, 487
cultural context, 19, 204
cultural settings, 33, 91, 521
cultures, 38, 102, 520

**D**
dashes, 52, 55, 59
data, 116, 117, 126
debates, 57, 303, 466
deductive conclusions, 333
delivery, of presentations, 15, 39, 87, 216, 314
denotation, 104, 168, 294
dependent clause, 49, 137, 176, 195
derivation. See word origins
details, 159
   compare, 114, 120
develop a draft
   argument, 308
   explanatory essay, 210–211
   literary analysis, 530–531
   personal essays, 66–67
   research reports, 386–387
   short stories, 134–135
diagrams, 85, 115, 155, 402, 419, 433, 449, 467, 481, 530
dialogue, 399
diction, 159, 257
diction and syntax, 257, 259
dictionary, 156
discourse. See discuss; rhetoric
discuss, 29, 193, 203, 255, 265, 480, 481
discussion, rules for, 167, 203
documentation, of sources, 102, 112, 254, 328
drafting. See develop a draft
draw conclusions, 14, 112, 126, 129, 155, 244, 254, 280, 292, 335, 360, 370, 418, 432, 448, 466, 496
drawings, 86, 115, 177, 481

**E**
edit
   argument, 311
   explanatory essay, 213
   literary analysis, 533
   personal essays, 69
   research reports, 389
   short stories, 137
endnotes, 387, 389
essays. See writing activities
Essential Question, 4, 18, 32, 40, 50, 72, 76, 90, 106, 114, 120, 142, 146, 158, 170, 174, 196, 218, 222, 248, 256, 268, 284, 296, 316, 320, 332, 344, 364, 372, 392, 398, 484, 488, 500
   reflect on, 71, 141, 217, 315, 391, 535
   respond to, 1, 15, 29, 39, 47, 57, 73, 87, 103, 113, 127, 143, 155, 167, 173, 193, 203, 219, 245, 255, 265, 281, 293, 301, 317, 329, 341, 361, 371, 379, 393, 481, 487, 497, 521
etymology, 156, 522

evaluate, 14, 38, 56, 60, 86, 102, 126, 128, 154, 166, 192, 204, 254, 264, 292, 302, 480, 520, 524
arguments, 51, 54
evidence, 41, 44
media, 172, 300, 486
research methods, 166, 167
evidence, 51, 77, 171, 223, 285, 333, 335, 496, 501
in arguments, 285, 287, 292
citing, 14, 28, 38, 46, 56, 86, 102, 126, 154, 192, 202, 264, 280, 340, 370
evaluating, 41, 44
textual, 47, 57, 103, 155, 381, 386, 418, 448, 525, 531
exact rhyme, 249
explanations, writing, 87, 167
explanatory essay, 143, 159, 208–214
as multimedia presentation, 215–216
explicit meaning, of text, 41, 264
exposition, 147
expository essay. See explanatory essay; writing activities.
extended metaphor, 365
extend research, 14, 46, 154, 192, 244, 254, 280, 292, 300, 328, 340, 370, 520
Extreme or Absolute Language (Notice & Note), 221, 227, 319, 323
eye contact, 15, 87, 314
eye rhyme, 249

F
fables, 15, 497
fallacy, logical, 51, 56
falling action, 147
fiction, writing, 15, 39, 132–138, 361, 497
figurative language, 147, 194, 330, 365
metaphor, 108, 147
personification, 108
simile, 108, 147
flashback, 175
flash-forward, 14
footnotes, 387, 389
foreign words used in English, 30, 151
form, in poetry, 198
formal tone, 6, 530, 532
fragments, sentence, 105, 137, 258, 262, 267
frame story, 175
free verse, 29, 198, 203, 249
freewriting, 41, 133, 223
friendly letter, writing, 127, 245
function of literature, social, 254

G
generalizations, hasty, 385
genre characteristics, 67, 135, 211, 309, 354, 387, 489, 497, 531

Genre Elements
argument, 51, 223, 285
book reviews, 501
court opinion, 41
documentary film, 373
drama, 399
explanatory essay, 159
film, 484
graphic novels, 501
infographics, 115
informational text, 333
literary nonfiction, 321
lyric poetry, 33, 107, 365
memoir, 19, 257
poetry, 121, 197, 249
public service advertisements, 170
satire, 489
science essay, 77
science fiction, 345
short stories, 5, 91, 147, 175, 269
glossaries, using, 156, R7
graphic features. See graphics
graphic organizers, 134, 307, 529, 530. See also charts; Venn diagram
graphics
diagrams, 115
graphs, 115
infographics, 115
interpret, 115
photographs and drawings, 115
tables, 115

H
historical context, 19, 22, 25, 28
historical events, 292
historical settings, 33, 91, 521

I
iambic pentameter, 396, 421
ideas
central, 159
main, 159
organize, 134, 210, 308, 386, 530
synthesize, 129
identify, 38, 86
patterns, 340, 378
idioms, 121, 498
illustrating, 86, 115, 177, 481
implicit meaning, 34, 91, 112, 166
independent clauses, 49, 137, 176, 195
Independent Reading, 62–63, 130–131, 206–207, 304–305, 382–383, 526–527
inductive conclusions, 333
infer, 14, 28, 38, 46, 56, 91, 102, 112, 126, 192, 264, 345, 360, 370, 378, 380, 418, 432, 448, 466, 520, 524
media, 300
theme, 34
infographics, 115, 126

informal tone, 6, 10, 17, 532
information
conflicting, 244, 300
documenting, 481
gathering, 15, 29, 39, 47, 57, 87, 103, 113, 127, 129, 155, 167, 173, 193, 203, 245, 255, 265, 281, 293, 301, 329, 341, 361, 371, 379, 481, 487, 497, 521
informative essay. See explanatory essay
instructions
following, 61, 127, 341
giving, 61, 127, 173, 341
interpret, 28, 38, 154, 166, 202, 254, 280, 328, 370, 480, 520
accounts, 302
graphics, 115
media, 300
interpretive writing, 371
interviews, 298
inverted sentences, 400, 483
irony, 5, 77, 154, 396

J
journaling, 33, 133
juxtaposition, 298, 374, 378

K
key ideas, 79, 225. See also main ideas

L
language. See also Language Conventions; vocabulary; word choice
archaic, 482
loaded, 58
Language Conventions,
active and passive voice, 286, 295
colons, 148, 157
commas, 42, 49
complex sentences, 92, 105, 137, 176, 195
correct spelling, 533
dashes, 52, 59
inverted sentences, 400, 483
parallelism, 160, 169
parallel structure, 78, 89, 213
parentheses, 502, 523
parenthetical expression, 502, 523
parenthetical phrase, 502, 518, 520, 523
passive voice, 286, 295
pronoun-antecedent agreement, 490, 499
purposeful fragments, 258, 267
repetition and parallelism, 247
semicolons, 270, 283
sentence style, 322
sentence variety, 331
spelling, 533
subject-verb agreement, 334, 343
transitions, 346, 363
verb tense, 20, 69
Latin, words from, 48, 342, 522

letters
  writing, 127, 281
  writing friendly, 127, 245
  writing, letter to the editor, 57, 173
literary analysis, writing, 371, 528–534
literary devices
  idioms, 121
  parallelism, 121
  shifts, 121
literary elements. *See* archetypes; character
  development; conflict; theme
literary nonfiction, analyzing, 321
loaded language, 58
logical fallacies, 51, 56, 223
logical order, 530

## M

main ideas, 77, 80, 159
maps, 126
media, 172, 300, 486
media representations, 484
media techniques, 373
  analyze, 170, 300, 486
  interviews, 298
  juxtaposition, 298
  music and sound, 298
  narration, 298
  purposes, 170, 300
  voice-over, 298
Memory Moment (Notice & Note), 3, 11,
  144, 150
mental images, creating, 93, 177, 204, 366
mentor text, using for writing, 211, 309,
  387, 531
  author's craft, 67, 135
  genre characteristics, 67, 135
metacognitive skills. *See* monitor
  comprehension
metaphor, 108, 147, 365
  extended, 365
metrics, in poetry, 198, 396–397
misconceptions, 154, 244
Modern Language Association (MLA),
  254, 387
monitor comprehension, 259
  annotation, 41, 225
  freewriting, 41
  notetaking, 41, 225
mood, 257, 326, 373
motif, 5, 8, 14, 175, 250, 251
motivations, character, 269, 271, 281, 432
motives, 116, 170, 269, 297
multimedia presentations
  adapting explanatory essay as, 215–216
  creating, 47, 129
multimodal presentations, 301. *See also*
  multimedia presentations
music and sound, 298

## N

narration, in media, 298
narratives
  embedded, 211
  presenting, 39
  writing, 39, 497
narrator, 154, 192
nonverbal techniques
  eye contact, 15, 87, 314
  facial expression, 314
  gestures, 314
notetaking, 41, 43, 529
Notice & Note
  Again and Again, 96, 145, 152, 183, 288,
    395, 406, 422
  Aha Moment, 100, 354, 394, 408, 473
  Analyze the Text, 14, 28, 56, 86, 102, 126,
    154, 166, 244, 292, 328, 340, 360, 418,
    432, 466, 480
  Anchor Questions, 2, 3, 75, 144, 145, 221,
    318, 319, 394, 395
  Big Questions, 74, 83, 220, 233, 319, 326, 336
  Contrasts and Contradictions, 24, 125,
    145, 151, 161, 179, 318, 325
  Extreme or Absolute Language, 221, 227,
    319, 323
  Memory Moment, 3, 11, 144, 150
  Numbers & Stats, 75, 80
  Quoted Words, 225, 235, 242
  From Reading to Writing, 65, 133, 209,
    307, 385, 529
  Tough Questions, 2, 12, 395, 416, 427, 456
  Word Gaps, 54, 81
  Words of the Wiser, 3, 11
Numbers and Stats (Notice & Note), 75, 80

## O

omission, in research sources, 56, 244
opinions
  defend or challenge, 53
  share and discuss, 329, 379
oral instructions
  following, 61, 127, 341
  giving, 61, 127, 173, 341
organization, in writing, 66, 134, 386
organizational patterns, 210, 333, 340, 386, 530
outline, 210, 308

## P

pace, 91, 172
panel discussion, participating in, 167
paradox, 418
paragraphing, 293, 329, 521
parallel construction. *See* parallel structure
parallelism, 51, 121, 160, 164, 169, 223, 224,
  247, 285, 397
parallel plots, 91, 94, 95, 102
parallel structure, 78, 82, 89, 213, 309
paraphrase, 84, 123, 154, 397

parentheses, 502, 523
  dashes instead of, 52
parenthetical expression or phrase, 502,
  518, 520, 523
passive voice, 286, 295
past perfect tense, 69
past tense, 69
peer review, 68, 136, 212, 310, 387, 532
personal essays, writing, 64–70
personification, 108, 365
perspective, critical, 496, 497
persuasive techniques, 51, 58
persuasive writing. *See* arguments
photographs, 115
phrases
  commas to set off, 45, 49
  parenthetical, 502, 518, 520, 523
  prepositional, 49
plagiarism, 102, 387, 389
plan
  arguments, 307–308
  explanatory essay, 209–210
  literary analysis, 530–531
  personal essays, 65–66
  research reports, 385–386
  short stories, 133–134
plot, 91, 134, 345
plot and setting, 91, 345
plot structure, 91, 147, 175, 192
podcasts, creating, 139–140
poetic form, 198
poetic structure, 122, 123, 126, 198, 249
poetry reading, giving, 371
poetry, writing, 29, 113, 203
point of view
  author's, 19, 38
  speaker's, 314
position, in persuasive writing. *See* claims
Practice and Apply
  critical vocabulary, 6, 16, 48, 58, 88, 156,
    168, 194, 246, 282, 294, 330, 342, 362,
    498, 522
  language conventions, 17, 31, 49, 59, 89,
    105, 157, 169, 195, 247, 267, 283, 295,
    331, 343, 363, 483, 499, 523
  vocabulary strategy, 16, 30, 48, 58, 88,
    104, 156, 168, 194, 246, 266, 282, 294,
    330, 342, 362, 482, 498, 522
precedents, 41
predicate, 482
predict, 80, 96, 149, 154, 281, 354, 408, 451
premise. *See* claims
Prepare to Compare, 43, 53, 117, 123, 177,
  199, 287, 299, 375, 376, 503, 518
prepositional phrases, 49
presentations
  adapting argument for, 313
  giving, 87, 203, 381
  multimedia, 47, 129

multimodal, 301

nonverbal techniques, 15, 87, 314

research, 129, 155, 245, 293

verbal techniques, 140, 314

present tense, 69

primary sources, 292

print features, using, 341. *See also* text features

problems, solving, 61

procedural brochure, writing, 341

processes, complex, 61

pronoun-antecedent agreement, 490, 493, 499

public service advertisements, 170

publish

argument, 311

explanatory essay, 213

literary analysis, 533

personal essays, 69

research reports, 389

short stories, 137

punctuation

colons, 148, 157

commas, 42, 49

dashes, 52, 55, 59

parentheses, 503, 523

quotation marks, 112, 387

semicolons, 270, 273, 283

purpose

and audience, 60, 333

author's 19, 23, 27, 333, 340

for reading. *See* Setting a Purpose

and theme, 374, 376

for writing, 65, 133, 209, 307, 385, 529

## Q

questions

anchor, 2, 3, 221, 318, 319, 394, 395

big, 74, 83, 220, 233, 319, 326, 336

generating while reading, 7, 259, 271, 368

developing research, 126, 129, 280

rhetorical, 397

Quick Start, 5, 19, 33, 41, 51, 77, 91, 107, 121, 147, 159, 175, 197, 223, 249, 257, 269, 285, 297, 321, 333, 345, 365, 373, 399, 484, 489, 501

quotation marks, 112, 387

quotations, introducing, 387, 532

Quoted Words (Notice & Note), 221, 225, 235, 242

## R

rate, speaking, 140

Reader's Choice, 62, 130, 206, 304, 382, 526

reading

background, 65, 133, 209, 307, 529

independent, 62–63, 130–131, 206–207, 304–305, 382–383, 526–527

reflect on, 71, 141, 217, 315, 391, 535

reading strategies. *See* monitor comprehension

reasoning, faulty, 244, 385

reasons, 51, 223, 285, 287, 501

rebuttals, 51

reference sources, 88, 522

reflect, 61, 71, 341

reflections, create, 379

reflective writing, 64–70

Reflect on the Unit, 71, 141, 217, 315, 391, 535

register, 39, 388

repetition, 34, 46, 166, 224, 229, 247, 397

reports. *See* essays; research reports

research

bias of sources, 56

charts in, 244, 264, 280, 292, 300, 328, 340, 360, 480, 486, 496, 520

collaborative, 112

connect in, 264, 360, 480, 486, 496

credible sources in, 202, 244, 280

description in, 370

documenting sources, 280, 328

extend, 244, 254, 280, 292, 300, 328, 340, 370, 520

guidelines, ethical and legal, 102, 389, 486

online, 46, 56, 61, 192, 202, 254, 486

opinions in, 496

paraphrase, 154

primary sources, 292

process, 129, 166

research question, 126, 129, 264, 280, 480

search engines, 86

search terms, 14, 28, 192

secondary sources, 292

sources, 38, 102, 166, 340, 360, 520

synthesize, 14, 129

websites, 172, 254, 480

Research and Discuss

create a procedure, 61

give instructions, 61

research techniques, 61

Research and Present

develop a question, 129

gather information, 129

present to the class, 129

synthesize ideas, 129

research reports, writing, 317, 384–390

resolution, 147

resources

digital, 88, 342, 389

print, 88, 342, 389

Respond to the Essential Question, 1, 47, 73, 143, 219, 317, 393

gather information, 15, 29, 39, 47, 57, 87, 103, 113, 127, 155, 167, 173, 193, 203, 245, 255, 265, 281, 293, 301, 329, 341, 361, 371, 379, 481, 487, 497, 521

Response Logs, R1–R6

revise

argument, 310

explanatory essay, 212

literary analysis, 532

personal essays, 68

research reports, 388

short stories, 136

rhetoric, 51, 53, 223, 285, 288

rhetorical devices, 223, 226, 230, 233, 234

parallelism, 397

repetition, 397

rhetorical questions, 397

thesis, 397

rhetorical questions, 397

rhyme

end, 249

eye, 249

slant, 249

rising action, 147

roots, 48, 522

rules

for debates, 57, 303

for discussions, 167

run-on sentences, 105, 137

## S

sales pitch, delivering, 361

sarcasm, 5

satire, 489, 491, 494

secondary sources, 292

self-selected text, 63, 131, 207, 305, 383, 527

semicolons, 49, 270, 273, 283

sensory descriptions, 102, 135, 147

sentence fragments, 105, 137, 258, 262, 267

sentences

complex, 92, 105, 137, 176, 195

inverted, 400, 483

run-on, 105, 137

sentence variety, 181, 322, 326, 331

sequence of events, 351

setting, 33, 35, 345, 373, 375, 520

Setting a Purpose, 7, 21, 35, 79, 93, 109, 149, 161, 171, 206, 225, 251, 259, 271, 323, 335, 347, 368, 402, 419, 433, 449, 467, 485, 491

Shakespeare

language of, 396

reading, 397

Shakespearean tragedy, characteristics of, 396

shifts, 51, 121, 223, 285

short stories

adapting as a podcast, 139

writing, 15, 39, 132–138, 361, 497

simile, 108, 147

skim, 385

slant rhyme, 249

soliloquies, 396, 399, 420, 433

sound elements, 373

sources
  crediting, 102, 280, 389
  reliability, 38, 172, 340, 520
speaker, in poetry, 33, 107, 109, 113, 368
speaking activities
  debate, 57, 303, 466
  deliver an argument, 313, 314, 487, 525
  deliver a summary, 281
  discuss, 29, 61, 103, 113, 193, 203, 255, 265, 301, 329, 379, 432, 448, 481, 497
  give instructions, 127, 173, 341
  give a presentation, 87, 203, 381
  multimedia presentation, 47, 129, 215, 216
  multimodal presentation, 301
  panel discussion, 167
  persuasive pitch, 361, 521
  podcast, 139–140
  poetry reading, 371
  present a fable, 15
  present a narrative, 39
  present research, 129, 155, 245, 293
special effects, 373
spelling, correct, 533
stage directions, 397, 399, 411
standard English, 311
stanza, 122, 249
storytelling elements
  mood, 373
  sequence, 373
  setting, 373
structure
  analyze, 122, 123, 147, 149, 153, 159, 162
  climax, 134, 147
  evaluate, 14, 102, 192
  exposition, 147
  falling action, 147
  of poetry, 122, 123, 126, 198, 249
  resolution, 147
  rising action, 147
  of sentences, 137, 181, 321
style, 321
  analyze, 159, 162, 327
  formal, 17
  in writing, 161
subject of a sentence, 290, 423, 482, 483
subject-verb agreement, 334, 343
subordinate conjunctions, 195
summarize, 38, 47, 86, 202, 244, 280, 328, 378, 432
  media, 300
summary, deliver a, 281
suspense, 135
symbols, 8, 175, 181, 186, 187, 190, 197, 200
synonyms, 281, 362
syntax, 159, 198, 257
synthesize, 112, 128, 360, 380
  accounts, 302
  ideas, 129
  research, 14, 129

T
tables, 115
tense, verb, 20, 24, 31, 69
text features, 265
  headings, 147, 154
text structure, 257, 260, 333, 335
theme, 34, 36, 103, 175, 181, 186, 187, 190, 197, 200, 269, 272, 274, 278, 280, 399
thesaurus, 156, 362
thesis/thesis statement, 77, 80, 86, 309, 333, 386, 531
time lines, 31, 66, 293, 481
tone, 6, 17, 60, 86, 91, 147, 257, 321
  analyze, 77, 79, 370
  formal, 6, 17
  informal, 6, 10, 17
Tough Questions (Notice & Note), 2, 12, 395, 416, 427, 456
tragedy, 396
transitions, 67, 346, 351, 363

U
Unit, Reflect on the, 71, 141, 217, 315, 391, 535

V
validity, of sources, 56, 129, 202
Venn diagram, 155, 302, 370, 418
verbal techniques
  enunciation, 140, 314
  speaking rate, 140, 314
  voice modulation and pitch, 140, 314
  volume, 314
verb tense, 20, 24, 31, 69
verse dramas, 396
vignette, writing a, 193
visual elements, 373, 501, 505, 507, 508, 509, 511, 513, 517
vocabulary. See Academic Vocabulary; Critical Vocabulary; Vocabulary Strategy
Vocabulary Strategy
  affixes, 342
  allusions, 266
  antonyms, 363
  archaic language, 482
  connotations, 58, 104, 168, 294
  context clues, 16, 247
  denotations, 104, 168, 294
  denotations and connotations, 294
  discipline-specific terms, 282
  figurative language, 194, 330
  foreign words used in English, 30
  idioms, 498
  reference sources, 88, 156
  synonyms, 363
  word roots, 522
  words from Latin, 48

voice, 257, 388
  active, 286, 295
  passive, 286, 295
voice-over, 170, 298

W
web page, design a, 265
word choice, 292, 321, 328, 365, 368
Word Gaps (Notice & Note), 54, 75, 81
Word Networks, 1, 73, 143, 219, 317, 393
word origins, 48, 342
Words of the Wiser (Notice & Note), 3, 11
Write and Discuss, 1, 73, 143, 219, 317, 393
Write and Share
  share your opinion, 329
  write a comparison, 329
writing activities
  analysis, 103, 155, 255, 293, 418, 487
  argument, 285, 306–314
  comparison, 47, 329, 521
  explanation, 87, 167
  explanatory essay, 208–216
  fable, 15
  free-verse poem, 203
  letter, 57, 127, 173, 245, 281
  literary analysis, 371, 393, 528–534
  memoir, 257
  narrative, 39, 497
  personal essay, 64–70
  poem, 29, 113
  procedural brochure, 341
  reflection, 379
  research report, 317, 384–390
  short story, 73, 361
  vignette, 193
writing process, recursive steps
  develop a draft, 66, 134, 210, 308, 386, 530
  edit, 69, 137, 213, 311, 389, 533
  plan, 65–66, 133–134, 209–210, 307–308, 385–386, 529–530
  publish, 69, 137, 213, 311, 389, 533
  reflect, 71, 141, 217, 315, 391, 535
  revise, 68, 136, 212, 310, 388, 532
writing prompts
  argument, 306
  explanatory essay, 208
  literary analysis, 530
  personal essay, 64
  research report, 384
  short story, 132
writing task scoring guide
  argument, 312
  explanatory essay, 214
  literary analysis, 534
  personal essay, 70
  research report, 390
  short story, 138

# INDEX OF TITLES AND AUTHORS

## A

Allen, Ronald J., 50
*American Flag Stands for Tolerance,* 50
Appignanesi, Richard, 500
Atwood, Margaret, 146

## B

BBC, 296
Bradbury, Ray, 344
Brennan, William J., 40
*Briefcase, The,* 268
*By Any Other Name,* 18

## C

*Carry,* 196
*Coming to Our Senses,* 76
*Contribution to Statistics, A,* 120
Cortázar, Julio, 90

## D

Davenport, Randi, 256
Deas, Robert, 500
Dillard, Annie, 320
Doyle, Brian, 158

## E

*Elsewhere,* 248

## F

*Find Your Park,* 170
*5 P.M., Tuesday, August 23, 2005,* 364
*Fever, The* (excerpt), 332

## G

Gandhi, Mohandas K., 284
*Gandhi: The Rise to Fame* (excerpt), 296
Glancy, Diane, 32
Goold, Rupert, 484

## H

Hagley, Jack, 114
*Hawk Can Soar, The,* 256
Hogan, Linda, 196

## J

*Joyas Voladoras,* 158

## K

Keret, Etgar, 4
King, Martin Luther, Jr., 222

## L

*Letter from Birmingham Jail,* 222
*Letter to Viceroy, Lord Irwin,* (excerpt), 284

## M

*Macbeth* (excerpt), film version, 484
*Macbeth Murder Mystery, The,* 488
Makkai, Rebecca, 268
*Manga Shakespeare: Macbeth,* (excerpt), 500
*Mirror,* 106
Murakami, Haruki, 174
*My Life as a Bat,* 146

## N

National Park Service, 170
*Night Face Up, The,* 90

## P

Perry, Caitlin, 518
Plath, Sylvia, 106

## R

Rama Rau, Santha, 18
Riedelsheimer, Thomas, 372
Rilke, Rainer Maria, 376
*Rivers and Tides* (excerpt), 372

## S

*Seventh Man, The,* 174
Shah, Sonia, 332
*Shakespeare and Samurai (and Robot Ninjas?),* 518
Shakespeare, William, 398
Smith, Patricia, 364
*Sonnets to Orpheus, Part Two, XII,* 376
*Sound of Thunder, A,* 344
Szymborska, Wisława, 120

## T

*Texas v. Johnson Majority Opinion* (excerpt), 40
*Total Eclipse* (excerpt), 320
Thurber, James, 488
*Tragedy of Macbeth, The,* 398
Tyson, Neil deGrasse, 76

## W

Walcott, Derek, 248
*What, of This Goldfish, Would You Wish?,* 4
*Without Title,* 32
*World as 100 People, The,* 114

# ACKNOWLEDGMENTS

Excerpt from "American Flag Stands for Tolerance" by Ronald J. Allen from *Chicago Tribune*, June 30, 1989. Text copyright © 1989 by Ronald J. Allen. Reprinted by permission of Ronald J. Allen.

Excerpts from *The American Heritage Dictionary of The English Language, Fifth Edition*. Text copyright © 2016 by Houghton Mifflin Harcourt Publishing Company. Reprinted by permission of Houghton Mifflin Harcourt Publishing Company.

"The Briefcase" from *The New England Review*, Vol. 29, No. 2, 2008 and from *Music for Wartime: Stories* by Rebecca Makkai. Text copyright © 2008 and © 2015 by Rebecca Makkai Freeman. Reprinted by permission of Viking Books, an imprint of Penguin Publishing Group, a division of Penguin Random House LLC, Rebecca Makkai and Aragi, Inc. All rights reserved. Any third party use of this material, outside of this publication, is prohibited. Interested parties must apply directly to Penguin Random House LLC for permission.

"By Any Other Name" by Santha Rama Rau. Text copyright © 1951 by Santha Rama Rau. Originally published by *The New Yorker* on March 17, 1951. Reprinted by permission of the Estate of Santha Rama Rau, Sole Proprietor Jai Bowers.

"Carry" from *Dark. Sweet.: New and Selected Poems* by Linda Hogan. Text copyright © 1993 by Linda Hogan. Reprinted by permission of The Permissions Company on behalf of Coffee House Press, Minneapolis, Minnesota, www.coffeehousepress.org.

Excerpt from "Coming to Our Senses" by Neil deGrasse Tyson from *Natural History*, March 2001. Text copyright © 2001 by Natural History Magazine, Inc. Reprinted by permission of Natural History Magazine, Inc.

"A Contribution to Statistics" from *Poems, New and Collected: 1957–1997* by Wislawa Szymborska, English translation by Stanislaw Baranczak and Clara Cavanagh. Text copyright © 1998 by Harcourt, Inc. Reprinted by Houghton Mifflin Harcourt Publishing Company and Faber & Faber, Ltd.

"Elsewhere" from *The Arkansas Testament* by Derek Walcott. Text copyright © 1987 by Derek Walcott. CAUTION: Users are warned that this work is protected under copyright laws and downloading is strictly prohibited. The right to reproduce or transfer the work via any medium must be secured with Farrar, Straus and Giroux. Reprinted by permission of Farrar, Straus & Giroux and Faber & Faber, Ltd.

Excerpt from "Birth of a Killer" from *The Fever* by Sonia Shah. Text copyright © 2010 by Sonia Shah. CAUTION: Users are warned that this work is protected under copyright laws and downloading is strictly prohibited. The right to reproduce or transfer the work via any medium must be secured with Farrar, Straus and Giroux. Reprinted by permission of Farrar, Straus and Giroux and Charlotte Sheedy Literary Agency on behalf of Sonia Shah.

"5 p.m., Tuesday, August 23, 2005" from *Blood Dazzle* by Patricia Smith. Text copyright © 2008 by Patricia Smith. Reprinted by permission of The Permissions Company on behalf of Coffee House Press, www.coffeehousepress.com.

"The Hawk Can Soar" by Randi Davenport from *The New York Times*, April 5, 2017. Text copyright © 2017 by The New York Times. All rights reserved. Reprinted by permission of PARS International Corp. on behalf of The New York Times. Protected by the Copyright Laws of the United States. The printing, copying, redistribution, or retransmission of this Content without express written permission is prohibited. www.nytimes.com

"Joyas Voladores" from *Children and Other Wild Animals* by Brian Doyle. Text copyright © 2014 by Brian Doyle. Reprinted by permission of Oregon State University Press.

Excerpt from "Letter from Birmingham Jail" by Martin Luther King, Jr. Text copyright © 1963 by Martin Luther King, Jr. Text copyright renewed © 1991 by Coretta Scott King. Reprinted by permission of Writers House on behalf of the Heirs to the Estate of Martin Luther King, Jr.

"Letter to Viceroy, Lord Irwin" from *Famous Letters of Mahatma Gandhi* by Mohandas Gandhi and edited by R.L. Khipple. Text copyright © 1947 by Mohandas Gandhi. Reprinted by permission of Navajivan Trust.

"The Macbeth Murder Mystery" from *My World And Welcome To It* by James Thurber. Text copyright © 1942 by Rosemary A. Thurber. Reprinted by arrangement with Rosemary A. Thurber and The Barbara Hogenson Agency, Inc. All rights reserved.

Excerpt from *Manga Shakespeare: Macbeth* illustrated by Robert Deas. Illustration copyright © 2008 by SelfMadeHero, a division of Metro Media Ltd. Reprinted by permission of Express Permissions on behalf of Amulet Books, an imprint of Harry N. Abrams, Inc. New York www.abramsbooks.com and SelfMadeHero. All rights reserved.

"Mirror" from *The Collected Poems of Sylvia Plath* by Sylvia Plath, edited by Ted Hughes. Text copyright © 1960, 1965, 1971, 1981 by the Estate of Sylvia Plath. Reprinted by permission of HarperCollins Publishers and Faber & Faber, Ltd.

"My Life as a Bat" from *Good Bones and Simple Murders* by Margaret Atwood. Text copyright © 1983, 1992, 1994, by O.W. Toad Ltd. Any third party use of this material, outside of this publication, is prohibited. Interested parties must apply directly to Penguin Random House LLC for permission. Reprinted by permission of Nan A. Talese, an imprint of the Knopf Doubleday Publishing Group, a division of Penguin Random House LLC, McClelland & Stewart, a division of Penguin Random House Canada Limited, and Curtis Brown Group, Ltd on behalf of O.W. Toad. All rights reserved.

"The Night Face Up" from *End of the Game and Other Stories* by Julio Cortázar. Originally published in Spanish as "La noche boca arriba" from *Final del juego* by Julio Cortázar, translated by Paul Blackburn. Text copyright © 1956 by the Estate of Julio Cortázar. Translation copyright © 1967 by Random House LLC. Reprinted by permission of Pantheon Books, an imprint of the Knopf Doubleday Publishing Group, a division of Random House LLC and Agencia Literaria Carmen Balcells S.A. Any third party use of this material, outside of this publication, is prohibited. Interested parties must apply directly to Random House LLC for permission. All rights reserved.

# ACKNOWLEDGMENTS

Quote by Barbara Jordan from "All Together Now" from *Sesame Street Parents Magazine*, September 1994. Text copyright © 1994 by Barbara Jordan. Reprinted by permission of the Sesame Workshop. All Rights Reserved.

"The Seventh Man" from *Blind Willow Sleeping Woman* by Haruki Murakami. Text copyright © 2006 by Haruki Murakami. Reprinted by permission of ICM Partners.

"Shakespeare and Samurai (and Robot Ninjas?) - A Review of Manga Macbeth" by Caitlin Perry. Text copyright © 2013 by Caitlin Perry. Reprinted by permission of Caitlin Perry.

"Sonnets to Orpheus, Part Two, XII" from *In Praise of Mortality* by Rainer Maria Rilke, translated by Anita Barrows and Joanna Macy. Text copyright © 1996 by Anita Barrows and Joanna Macy. Reprinted by permission of the translators.

"A Sound of Thunder" by Ray Bradbury from *Collier's*, June 20, 1952. Text copyright © by the Crowell Collier Publishing Company, renewed © 1980 by Ray Bradbury. Reprinted by permission of Don Congdon Associates, Inc. Photocopying, printing and other reproduction rights are strictly reserved.

Excerpt from "Total Eclipse" from *Teaching a Stone to Talk: Expeditions and Encounters* by Annie Dillard. Text copyright © 1982 by Annie Dillard. Reprinted by permission of HarperCollins Publishers and Massie & McQuilkin as agents for the author.

"What, of This Goldfish, Would You Wish?" from *Suddenly, A Knock on the Door* by Etgar Keret, translated by Miriam Shlesinger, Sondra Silverston and Nathan Englander. Translation copyright © 2012 by Etgar Keret. CAUTION: Users are warned that this work is protected under copyright laws and downloading is strictly prohibited. The right to reproduce or transfer work via any medium must be secured with Farrar, Straus and Giroux. Reprinted by permission of Farrar, Straus and Giroux, Random House Australia Pty. Ltd, and the Random House Group Limited.

"Without Title" from *Iron Woman* by Diane Glancy. Text copyright © 1990 by Diane Glancy. Reprinted by permission of The Permissions Company on behalf of New Rivers Press.

"The World as 100 People" by Jack Hagley. Text copyright © 2014 by Jack Hagley. Reprinted by permission of Jack Hagley.